Oracle Exadata Recipes

A Problem-Solution Approach

John Clarke

apress®

Oracle Exadata Recipes

Copyright © 2013 by John Clarke

This work is subject to copyright. All rights are reserved by the Publisher, whether the whole or part of the material is concerned, specifically the rights of translation, reprinting, reuse of illustrations, recitation, broadcasting, reproduction on microfilms or in any other physical way, and transmission or information storage and retrieval, electronic adaptation, computer software, or by similar or dissimilar methodology now known or hereafter developed. Exempted from this legal reservation are brief excerpts in connection with reviews or scholarly analysis or material supplied specifically for the purpose of being entered and executed on a computer system, for exclusive use by the purchaser of the work. Duplication of this publication or parts thereof is permitted only under the provisions of the Copyright Law of the Publisher's location, in its current version, and permission for use must always be obtained from Springer. Permissions for use may be obtained through RightsLink at the Copyright Clearance Center. Violations are liable to prosecution under the respective Copyright Law.

ISBN-13 (pbk): 978-1-4302-4914-6

ISBN-13 (electronic): 978-1-4302-4915-3

Trademarked names, logos, and images may appear in this book. Rather than use a trademark symbol with every occurrence of a trademarked name, logo, or image, we use the names, logos, and images only in an editorial fashion and to the benefit of the trademark owner, with no intention of infringement of the trademark.

The use in this publication of trade names, trademarks, service marks, and similar terms, even if they are not identified as such, is not to be taken as an expression of opinion as to whether or not they are subject to proprietary rights.

While the advice and information in this book are believed to be true and accurate at the date of publication, neither the authors nor the editors nor the publisher can accept any legal responsibility for any errors or omissions that may be made. The publisher makes no warranty, express or implied, with respect to the material contained herein.

President and Publisher: Paul Manning
Lead Editor: Jonathan Gennick
Developmental Editor: Chris Nelson
Technical Reviewer: Arup Nanda
Editorial Board: Steve Anglin, Mark Beckner, Ewan Buckingham, Gary Cornell, Louise Corrigan, Morgan Ertel, Jonathan Gennick, Jonathan Hassell, Robert Hutchinson, Michelle Lowman, James Markham, Matthew Moodie, Jeff Olson, Jeffrey Pepper, Douglas Pundick, Ben Renow-Clarke, Dominic Shakeshaft, Gwenan Spearing, Matt Wade, Tom Welsh
Coordinating Editor: Anamika Panchoo
Copy Editor: Ann Dickson
Compositor: SPi Global
Indexer: SPi Global
Artist: SPi Global
Cover Designer: Anna Ishchenko

Distributed to the book trade worldwide by Springer Science+Business Media New York, 233 Spring Street, 6th Floor, New York, NY 10013. Phone 1-800-SPRINGER, fax (201) 348-4505, e-mail orders-ny@springer-sbm.com, or visit www.springeronline.com. Apress Media, LLC is a California LLC and the sole member (owner) is Springer Science+Business Media Finance Inc (SSBM Finance Inc). SSBM Finance Inc is a Delaware corporation.

For information on translations, please e-mail rights@apress.com, or visit www.apress.com.

Apress and friends of ED books may be purchased in bulk for academic, corporate, or promotional use. eBook versions and licenses are also available for most titles. For more information, reference our Special Bulk Sales–eBook Licensing web page at www.apress.com/bulk-sales.

Any source code or other supplementary materials referenced by the author in this text is available to readers at www.apress.com. For detailed information about how to locate your book's source code, go to www.apress.com/source-code/.

This book is dedicated to Anto.

Contents at a Glance

About the Author xxxiii

About the Technical Reviewer xxxv

Acknowledgments xxxvii

Introduction xxxix

■**Part 1: Exadata Architecture** 1

■Chapter 1: Exadata Hardware 3

■Chapter 2: Exadata Software 33

■Chapter 3: How Oracle Works on Exadata 53

■**Part 2: Preparing for Exadata** 75

■Chapter 4: Workload Qualification 77

■Chapter 5: Sizing Exadata 97

■Chapter 6: Preparing for Exadata 139

■**Part 3: Exadata Administration** 157

■Chapter 7: Administration and Diagnostics Utilities 159

■Chapter 8: Backup and Recovery 189

■Chapter 9: Storage Administration 239

■Chapter 10: Network Administration 297

■Chapter 11: Patching and Upgrades 331

■Chapter 12: Security 355

v

Part 4: Monitoring Exadata 369

Chapter 13: Monitoring Exadata Storage Cells 371

Chapter 14: Host and Database Performance Monitoring 411

Part 5: Exadata Software 445

Chapter 15: Smart Scan and Cell Offload 447

Chapter 16: Hybrid Columnar Compression 477

Chapter 17: I/O Resource Management and Instance Caging 505

Chapter 18: Smart Flash Cache and Smart Flash Logging 529

Chapter 19: Storage Indexes 553

Part 6: Post Implementation Tasks 577

Chapter 20: Post-Installation Monitoring Tasks 579

Chapter 21: Post-Install Database Tasks 599

Index 633

Contents

About the Author xxxiii

About the Technical Reviewer xxxv

Acknowledgments xxxvii

Introduction xxxix

■**Part 1: Exadata Architecture** 1

■**Chapter 1: Exadata Hardware** 3

    1-1. Identifying Exadata Database Machine Components 3

        Problem 3

        Solution 3

        How It Works 7

    1-2. Displaying Storage Server Architecture Details 10

        Problem 10

        Solution 10

        How It Works 12

    1-3. Displaying Compute Server Architecture Details 14

        Problem 14

        Solution 14

        How It Works 16

    1-4. Listing Disk Storage Details on the Exadata Storage Servers 17

        Problem 17

        Solution 17

        How It Works 21

1-5. Listing Disk Storage Details on the Compute Servers 23
Problem 23
Solution 23
How It Works 27

1-6. Listing Flash Storage on the Exadata Storage Servers 27
Problem 27
Solution 27
How It Works 29

1-7. Gathering Configuration Information for the InfiniBandSwitches 29
Problem 29
Solution 29
How It Works 32

Chapter 2: Exadata Software 33

2-1. Understanding the Role of Exadata Storage Server Software 33
Problem 33
Solution 33
How It Works 35

2-2. Validating Oracle 11gR2 Databases on Exadata 35
Problem 35
Solution 35
How It Works 38

2-3. Validating Oracle 11gR2 Grid Infrastructure on Exadata 38
Problem 38
Solution 38
How It Works 41

2-4. Locating the Oracle Cluster Registry and Voting Disks on Exadata 42
Problem 42
Solution 42
How It Works 43

2-5. Validating Oracle 11gR2 Real Application Clusters Installation and Database Storage on Exadata 44
Problem 44
Solution 44
How It Works 47

2-6. Validating Oracle 11gR2 Real Application Clusters Networking on Exadata 47
Problem 47
Solution 47
How It Works 52

Chapter 3: How Oracle Works on Exadata 53

3-1. Mapping Physical Disks, LUNs, and Cell Disks on the Storage Servers 53
Problem 53
Solution 53
How It Works 56

3-2. Mapping ASM Disks, Grid Disks, and Cell Disks 58
Problem 58
Solution 58
How It Works 60

3-3. Mapping Flash Disks to Smart Flash Storage 61
Problem 61
Solution 61
How It Works 62

3-4. Identifying Cell Server Software Processes 62
Problem 62
Solution 63
How It Works 63

3-5. Tracing Oracle I/O Requests on Exadata Compute Nodes 65
Problem 65
Solution 65
How It Works 65

3-6. Validating That Your Oracle RAC Interconnect Is Using InfiniBand 68
Problem 68
Solution 68
How It Works 70

3-7. Tracing cellsrv on the Storage Servers 71
Problem 71
Solution 71
How It Works 73

Part 2: Preparing for Exadata 75

Chapter 4: Workload Qualification 77

4-1. Quantifying I/O Characteristics of Your Current Database 77
Problem 77
Solution 77
How It Works 80

4-2. Conducting a Smart Scan Fit Analysis Using AWR 81
Problem 81
Solution 81
How It Works 85

4-3. Conducting a Smart Scan Fit Analysis Using Exadata Simulation 87
Problem 87
Solution 87
How It Works 91

4-4. Performing a Hybrid Columnar Compression Fit Assessment 93
Problem 93
Solution 93
How It Works 95

Chapter 5: Sizing Exadata 97

5-1. Determining CPU Requirements 98
Problem 98
Solution 98
How It Works 107

5-2. Determining IOPs Requirements 108
Problem 108
Solution 108
How It Works 112

5-3. Determining I/O Bandwidth Requirements 113
Problem 113
Solution 113
How It Works 118

5-4. Determining ASM Redundancy Requirements 119
Problem 119
Solution 119
How It Works 119

5-5. Forecasting Storage Capacity 122
Problem 122
Solution 122
How It Works 124

5-6. Planning for Database Growth 125
Problem 125
Solution 125
How It Works 133

5-7. Planning for Disaster Recovery 133
Problem 133
Solution 133
How It Works 133

5-8. Planning for Backups 134
Problem 134
Solution 134
How It Works 135

5-9. Determining Your Fast Recovery Area and RECO Disk Group Size Requirements 136
Problem 136
Solution 136
How It Works 138

Chapter 6: Preparing for Exadata 139

6-1. Planning and Understanding Exadata Networking 139
Problem 139
Solution 139
How It Works 141

6-2. Configuring DNS 143
Problem 143
Solution 143
How It Works 144

6-3. Running checkip.sh 144
Problem 144
Solution 144
How It Works 147

6-4. Customizing Your InfiniBand Network Configuration 147
Problem 147
Solution 147
How It Works 147

6-5. Determining Your DATA and RECO Storage Requirements 148
Problem 148
Solution 148
How It Works 149

6-6. Planning for ASM Disk Group Redundancy 149
Problem 149
Solution 149
How It Works 152

6-7. Planning Database and ASM Extent Sizes 152
Problem 152
Solution 152
How It Works 152

6-8. Completing the Pre-Delivery Survey 153
Problem 153
Solution 153
How It Works 154

6-9. Completing the Configuration Worksheet 154
Problem 154
Solution 154
How It Works 156

Part 3: Exadata Administration 157

Chapter 7: Administration and Diagnostics Utilities 159

7-1. Logging in to the Exadata Compute and Storage Cells Using SSH 159
Problem 159
Solution 159
How It Works 160

7-2. Configuring SSH Equivalency 161
Problem 161
Solution 161
How It Works 162

7-3. Locating Key Configuration Files and Directories on the Cell Servers 162
Problem 162
Solution 162
How It Works 163

7-4. Locating Key Configuration Files and Directories on the Compute Nodes 164
Problem 164
Solution 164
How It Works 164

7-5. Starting and Stopping Cell Server Processes 165
Problem 165
Solution 165
How It Works 166

7-6. Administering Storage Cells Using CellCLI 167
Problem 167
Solution 167
How It Works 168

7-7. Administering Storage Cells Using dcli 168
Problem 168
Solution 168
How It Works 170

7-8. Generating Diagnostics from the ILOM Interface 171
Problem 171
Solution 171
How It Works 173

7-9. Performing an Exadata Health Check Using exachk 173
Problem 173
Solution 173
How It Works 176

7-10. Collecting Compute and Cell Server Diagnostics Using the sundiag.sh Utility 176
Problem 176
Solution 176
How It Works 177

7-11. Collecting RAID Storage Information Using the MegaCLI utility 178
Problem 178
Solution 178
How It Works 179

7-12. Administering the Storage Cell Network Using ipconf 179
Problem 179
Solution 179
How It Works 180

7-13. Validating Your InfiniBand Switches with the CheckSWProfile.sh Utility 181
Problem 181
Solution 181
How It Works 182

7-14. Verifying Your InfiniBand Network Topology 182
Problem 182
Solution 182
How It Works 183

7-15. Diagnosing Your InfiniBand Network 183
Problem 183
Solution 183
How It Works 187

7-16. Connecting to Your Cisco Catalyst 4948 Switch and Changing Switch Configuration 187
Problem 187
Solution 187
How It Works 188

Chapter 8: Backup and Recovery 189

8-1. Backing Up the Storage Servers 189
Problem 189
Solution 189
How It Works 190

8-2. Displaying the Contents of Your CELLBOOT USB Flash Drive 191
Problem 191
Solution 191
How It Works 192

8-3. Creating a Cell Boot Image on an External USB Drive 192
Problem 192
Solution 193
How It Works 194

8-4. Backing Up Your Compute Nodes Using Your Enterprise Backup Software 195
Problem 195
Solution 195
How It Works 196

8-5. Backing Up the Compute Servers Using LVM Snapshots 196
Problem 196
Solution 197
How It Works 200

8-6. Backing Up Your Oracle Databases with RMAN 201
Problem 201
Solution 201
How It Works 201

8-7. Backing Up the InfiniBand Switches 202
Problem 202
Solution 203
How It Works 204

8-8. Recovering Storage Cells from Loss of a Single Disk 205
Problem 205
Solution 205
How It Works 208

8-9. Recovering Storage Cells from Loss of a System Volume Using CELLBOOT Rescue 210
Problem 210
Solution 210
How It Works 221

8-10. Recovering from a Failed Storage Server Patch 222
Problem 222
Solution 222
How It Works 223

8-11. Recovering Compute Server Using LVM Snapshots 223
Problem 223
Solution 223
How It Works 228

8-12. Reimaging a Compute Node 229
Problem 229
Solution 229
How It Works 231

8-13. Recovering Your InfiniBand Switch Configuration 232
Problem 232
Solution 232
How It Works 234

8-14. Recovering from Loss of Your Oracle Cluster Registry and Voting Disks 235
Problem 235
Solution 235
How It Works 237

■Chapter 9: Storage Administration 239

9-1. Building ASM Disk Groups on Exadata 239
Problem 239
Solution 239
How It Works 245

9-2. Properly Configuring ASM Disk Group Attributes on Exadata 246
Problem 246
Solution 246
How It Works 247

9-3. Identifying Unassigned Grid Disks 248
Problem 248
Solution 248
How It Works 248

9-4. Configuring ASM Redundancy on Exadata 248
Problem 248
Solution 248
How It Works 251

9-5. Displaying ASM Partner Disk Relationships on Exadata 253
Problem 253
Solution 253
How It Works 254

xvii

9-6. Measuring ASM Extent Balance on Exadata 254
Problem 254
Solution 254
How It Works 258

9-7. Rebuilding Cell Disks 258
Problem 258
Solution 258
How It Works 273

9-8. Creating Interleaved Cell Disks and Grid Disks 274
Problem 274
Solution 274
How It Works 280

9-9. Rebuilding Grid Disks 282
Problem 282
Solution 282
How It Works 284

9-10. Setting smart_scan_capable on ASM Disk Groups 286
Problem 286
Solution 286
How It Works 291

9-11. Creating Flash Grid Disks for Permanent Storage 292
Problem 292
Solution 292
How It Works 296

Chapter 10: Network Administration 297

10-1. Configuring the Management Network on the Compute Nodes 297
Problem 297
Solution 297
How It Works 299

10-2. Configuring the Client Access Network 299
Problem 299
Solution 299
How It Works 301

10-3. Configuring the Private Interconnect on the Compute Nodes 301
Problem 301
Solution 302
How It Works 303

10-4. Configuring the SCAN Listener 304
Problem 304
Solution 304
How It Works 305

10-5. Managing Grid Infrastructure Network Resources 306
Problem 306
Solution 306
How It Works 309

10-6. Configuring the Storage Server Ethernet Network 309
Problem 309
Solution 309
How It Works 311

10-7. Changing IP Addresses on Your Exadata Database Machine 312
Problem 312
Solution 312
How It Works 330

■Chapter 11: Patching and Upgrades 331
11-1. Understanding Exadata Patching Definitions, Alternatives, and Strategies 331
Problem 331
Solution 331
How It Works 333

11-2. Preparing to Apply Exadata Patches 333
Problem 333
Solution 333
How It Works 335

11-3. Patching Your Exadata Storage Servers 335
Problem 335
Solution 335
How It Works 341

11-4. Patching Your Exadata Compute Nodes and Databases 342
Problem 342
Solution 342
How It Works 349

11-5. Patching the InfiniBand Switches 349
Problem 349
Solution 349
How It Works 352

11-6. Patching Your Enterprise Manager Systems Management Software 352
Problem 352
Solution 352
How It Works 353

■Chapter 12: Security 355

12-1. Configuring Multiple Oracle Software Owners on Exadata Compute Nodes 355
Problem 355
Solution 355
How It Works 358

12-2. Installing Multiple Oracle Homes on Your Exadata Compute Nodes 359
Problem 359
Solution 359
How It Works 361

12-3. Configuring ASM-Scoped Security 362
Problem 362
Solution 362
How It Works 364

12-4. Configuring Database-Scoped Security 364
Problem 364
Solution 364
How It Works 367

■Part 4: Monitoring Exadata 369

■Chapter 13: Monitoring Exadata Storage Cells 371

13-1. Monitoring Storage Cell Alerts 371
Problem 371
Solution 371
How It Works 375

13-2. Monitoring Cells with Active Requests 376
Problem 376
Solution 376
How It Works 380

13-3. Monitoring Cells with Metrics 381
Problem 381
Solution 381
How It Works 386

13-4. Configuring Thresholds for Cell Metrics 389
Problem 389
Solution 389
How It Works 390

13-5. Using dcli with Special Characters 391
Problem 391
Solution 391
How It Works 393

xxi

13-6. Reporting and Summarizing metrichistory Using R 393
- Problem 393
- Solution 393
- How It Works 398

13-7. Reporting and Summarizing metrichistory Using Oracle and SQL 399
- Problem 399
- Solution 399
- How It Works 400

13-8. Detecting Cell Disk I/O Bottlenecks 400
- Problem 400
- Solution 400
- How It Works 402

13-9. Measuring Small I/O vs. Large I/O Requests 402
- Problem 402
- Solution 402
- How It Works 404

13-10. Detecting Grid Disk I/O Bottlenecks 404
- Problem 404
- Solution 404
- How It Works 405

13-11. Detecting Host Interconnect Bottlenecks 406
- Problem 406
- Solution 406
- How It Works 407

13-12. Measuring I/O Load and Waits per Database, Resource Consumer Group, and Resource Category 407
- Problem 407
- Solution 407
- How It Works 409

Chapter 14: Host and Database Performance Monitoring 411

14-1. Collecting Historical Compute Node and Storage Cell Host Performance Statistics........ 411
Problem 411
Solution 411
How It Works 413

14-2. Displaying Real-Time Compute Node and Storage Cell Performance Statistics 414
Problem 414
Solution 414
How It Works 417

14-3. Monitoring Exadata with Enterprise Manager 417
Problem 417
Solution 417
How It Works 421

14-4. Monitoring Performance with SQL Monitoring 421
Problem 421
Solution 421
How It Works 424

14-5. Monitoring Performance by Database Time 425
Problem 425
Solution 425
How It Works 431

14-6. Monitoring Smart Scans by Database Time and AAS 432
Problem 432
Solution 432
How It Works 434

14-7. Monitoring Exadata with Wait Events 435
Problem 435
Solution 435
How It Works 439

14-8. Monitoring Exadata with Statistics and Counters 440
Problem 440
Solution 440
How It Works 441

14-9. Measuring Cell I/O Statistics for a SQL Statement 442
Problem 442
Solution 442
How It Works 444

Part 5: Exadata Software 445

Chapter 15: Smart Scan and Cell Offload 447

15-1. Identifying Cell Offload in Execution Plans 447
Problem 447
Solution 447
How It Works 448

15-2. Controlling Cell Offload Behavior 450
Problem 450
Solution 450
How It Works 451

15-3. Measuring Smart Scan with Statistics 451
Problem 451
Solution 451
How It Works 455

15-4. Measuring Offload Statistics for Individual SQL Cursors 455
Problem 455
Solution 455
How It Works 457

15-5. Measuring Offload Efficiency 457
Problem 457
Solution 457
How It Works 460

15-6. Identifying Smart Scan from 10046 Trace Files 461
Problem 461
Solution 461
How It Works 462

15-7. Qualifying for Direct Path Reads 463
Problem 463
Solution 463
How It Works 468

15-8. Influencing Exadata's Decision to Use Smart Scans 469
Problem 469
Solution 469
How It Works 473

15-9. Identifying Partial Cell Offload 473
Problem 473
Solution 473
How It Works 474

15-10. Dealing with Fast Object Checkpoints 475
Problem 475
Solution 475
How It Works 475

Chapter 16: Hybrid Columnar Compression 477

16-1. Estimating Disk Space Savings for HCC 477
Problem 477
Solution 477
How It Works 479

16-2. Building HCC Tables and Partitions 479
Problem 479
Solution 479
How It Works 482

16-3. Contrasting Oracle Compression Types 482
Problem 482
Solution 482
How It Works 483

16-4. Determining the Compression Type of a Segment 487
Problem 487
Solution 487
How It Works 488

16-5. Measuring the Performance Impact of HCC for Queries 488
Problem 488
Solution 489
How It Works 491

16-6. Direct Path Inserts into HCC Segments 492
Problem 492
Solution 492
How It Works 493

16-7. Conventional Inserts to HCC Segments 493
Problem 493
Solution 494
How It Works 495

16-8. DML and HCC 495
Problem 495
Solution 495
How It Works 501

16-9. Decompression and the Performance Impact 502
Problem 502
Solution 502
How It Works 504

Chapter 17: I/O Resource Management and Instance Caging 505

17-1. Prioritizing I/O Utilization by Database 505
Problem 505
Solution 505
How It Works 507

17-2. Limiting I/O Utilization for Your Databases 507
Problem 507
Solution 507
How It Works 508

17-3. Managing Resources within a Database 508
Problem 508
Solution 508
How It Works 510

17-4. Prioritizing I/O Utilization by Category of Resource Consumers 511
Problem 511
Solution 511
How It Works 512

17-5. Prioritizing I/O Utilization by Categories of Resource Consumers and Databases 513
Problem 513
Solution 513
How It Works 514

17-6. Monitoring Performance When IORM Is Enabled 517
Problem 517
Solution 517
How It Works 520

17-7. Obtaining IORM Plan Information 521
Problem 521
Solution 521
How It Works 525

17-8. Controlling Smart Flash Cache and Smart Flash Logging with IORM 526
Problem 526
Solution 526
How It Works 526

17-9. Limiting CPU Resources with Instance Caging 527
Problem 527
Solution 527
How It Works 527

Chapter 18: Smart Flash Cache and Smart Flash Logging 529

18-1. Managing Smart Flash Cache and Smart Flash Logging 529
Problem 529
Solution 530
How It Works 531

18-2. Determining Which Database Objects Are Cached 532
Problem 532
Solution 532
How It Works 533

18-3. Determining What's Consuming Your Flash Cache Storage 534
Problem 534
Solution 534
How It Works 536

18-4. Determining What Happens When Querying Uncached Data 536
Problem 536
Solution 536
How It Works 540

18-5. Measuring Smart Flash Cache Performance 541
Problem 541
Solution 541
How It Works 546

18-6. Pinning Specific Objects in Smart Flash Cache 546
- Problem 546
- Solution 546
- How It Works 548

18-7. Quantifying Benefits of Smart Flash Logging 549
- Problem 549
- Solution 549
- How It Works 550

■Chapter 19: Storage Indexes 553

19-1. Measuring Performance Impact of Storage Indexes 553
- Problem 553
- Solution 553
- How It Works 555

19-2. Measuring Storage Index Performance with Not-So-Well-Ordered Data 557
- Problem 557
- Solution 557
- How It Works 559

19-3. Testing Storage Index Behavior with Different Query Predicate Conditions 559
- Problem 559
- Solution 560
- How It Works 564

19-4. Tracing Storage Index Behavior 564
- Problem 564
- Solution 565
- How It Works 568

19-5. Tracing Storage Indexes When More than Eight Columns Are Referenced 568
- Problem 568
- Solution 568
- How It Works 572

19-6. Tracing Storage Indexes when DML Is Issued against Tables 573
Problem 573
Solution 573
How It Works 574

19-7. Disabling Storage Indexes 575
Problem 575
Solution 575
How It Works 576

19-8. Troubleshooting Storage Indexes 576
Problem 576
Solution 576
How It Works 576

Part 6: Post Implementation Tasks 577

Chapter 20: Post-Installation Monitoring Tasks 579

20-1. Installing Enterprise Manager 12c Cloud Control Agents for Exadata 579
Problem 579
Solution 579
How It Works 591

20-2. Configuring Enterprise Manager 12c Cloud Control Plug-ins for Exadata 592
Problem 592
Solution 592
How It Works 592

20-3. Configuring Automated Service Requests 592
Problem 592
Solution 592
How It Works 597

Chapter 21: Post-Install Database Tasks 599

21-1. Creating a New Oracle RAC Database on Exadata 599
Problem 599
Solution 599
How It Works 601

21-2. Setting Up a DBFS File System on Exadata 601
Problem 601
Solution 601
How It Works 605

21-3. Configuring HugePages on Exadata 606
Problem 606
Solution 606
How It Works 609

21-4. Configuring Automatic Degree of Parallelism 610
Problem 610
Solution 610
How It Works 611

21-5. Setting I/O Calibration on Exadata 612
Problem 612
Solution 612
How It Works 614

21-6. Measuring Impact of Auto DOP and Parallel Statement Queuing 614
Problem 614
Solution 614
How It Works 619

21-7. Measuring Auto DOP and In-Memory Parallel Execution 620
Problem 620
Solution 621
How It Works 625

21-8. Gathering Optimizer Statistics on Exadata 625
Problem 625
Solution 626
How It Works 630

Index 633

xxxi

About the Author

John Clarke is a Senior Oracle Architect specializing in Oracle infrastructure, applications, and technologies. John has worked with Oracle as a database administrator, developer, Unix/Linux administrator, and storage administrator since 1992. During his career, he has focused on Oracle performance optimization, enterprise architecture design and implementation, high availability, and disaster recovery. He is also cofounder and managing partner of Centroid, an Oracle consulting firm headquartered in Troy, Michigan. John occasionally blogs at www.centroid.com and jccoracle.blogspot.com and enjoys speaking at Oracle conferences.

About the Technical Reviewer

Arup Nanda has been an Oracle DBA (and now a DMA) for the last 19 years, experienced in all aspects of Oracle Database from modeling to performance tuning and disaster recovery and everything in between. He has authored four books and 500 articles, and he has presented about 300 sessions all over the world. He is a frequent trainer and blogger (at arup.blogspot.com), and he works as the principal global database architect at a major New York area corporation. He is an Oracle ACE Director, a member of the Oak Table Network, and a member of the Board of Directors of the Exadata SIG of IOUG. He was the winner of DBA of the Year award in 2003 and the Enterprise Architect of the Year in 2012 from Oracle Corp. He lives in Danbury, Connecticut, with his family.

Acknowledgments

I want to first and foremost thank my son, Anto. Although just a kid, you handle the challenges of balancing work and life like an adult and, for this and much more, I couldn't be more fortunate. Anto, I love you and you are the reason I do all that I do.

To my parents, I'd like to say thank you for instilling the value of hard work and confidence in me and for accepting the too frequent one-word e-mail responses and terse telephone conversations. There's never enough time for the things that count, but you never make me feel guilty about it.

To my Centroid partners, I'd like to say thanks for agreeing to launch Centroid's Exadata initiative with me. Your willingness to take risks and invest outside of our comfort zone has provided opportunities that we can all benefit from.

To my Centroid coworkers, I'd like to give a special thank you for putting up with me during this endeavor. I've been more difficult than normal to work with and your patience and support is much appreciated. Those of you who've helped me the most know who you are.

Thanks to Jonathan Gennick for providing me with the opportunity to write this book. I look forward to working together on future projects. I also thank Arup Nanda for his valuable technical insights and Chris Nelson for his patience and useful feedback provided during the authoring of this book.

Finally, I'd like to thank everyone in the broader Oracle community who has inspired me to understand how Oracle works and, specifically, how Oracle works on Exadata. Over the years, your contributions and experiences have shaped me into the Oracle professional that I am. The names are too many to list, but know that if you've written an Oracle text, blogged about Exadata, posted to Oracle mailing lists, or presented Oracle performance optimization or Oracle Exadata topics, your signature is on every page of this book.

Introduction

The Oracle Exadata Database Machine is an engineered system designed to deliver extreme performance for all types of Oracle database workloads. Starting with the Exadata V2-2 platform and continuing with the Exadata X2-2, X2-8, X3-2, and X3-8 database machines, many companies have successfully implemented Exadata and realized these extreme performance gains. Exadata has been a game changer with respect to database performance, driving and enabling business transformation, increased profitability, unrivaled customer satisfaction, and improved availability and performance service levels.

Oracle's Exadata Database Machine is a pre-configured engineered system comprised of hardware and software, built to deliver extreme performance for Oracle 11gR2 database workloads. Exadata succeeds by offering an optimally balanced hardware infrastructure with fast components at each layer of the technology stack, as well as a unique set of Oracle software features designed to leverage the high-performing hardware infrastructure by reducing I/O demands.

As an engineered system, the Exadata Database Machine is designed to allow customers to realize extreme performance with zero application modification—if you have a database capable of running on Oracle 11gR2 and application supported with this database version, many of the features Exadata delivers are able to be capitalized on immediately, without extensive database and systems administrator modification. But, ultimately, Exadata provides the *platform* to enable extreme performance. As an Exadata administrator, you not only need to learn Exadata architecture and aspects of Exadata's unique software design, but you also need to *un-learn* some of your legacy Oracle infrastructure habits and thinking. Exadata not only changes the Oracle performance engineer's way of thinking, but it can also impose operations, administration, and organizational mindset changes.

Organizations with an existing Exadata platform are often faced with challenges or questions about how to maximize their investment in terms of performance, management, and administration. Organizations considering an Exadata investment need to understand not only whether Exadata will address performance, consolidation, and IT infrastructure roadmap goals, but also how the Exadata platform will change their day-to-day operational requirements to support Oracle on Exadata. *Oracle Exadata Recipes* will show you how to maintain and optimize your Exadata environment as well as how to ensure that Exadata is the right fit for your company.

Who This Book Is For

Oracle Exadata Recipes is for Oracle Database administrators, Unix/Linux administrators, storage administrators, backup administrators, network administrators, and Oracle developers who want to quickly learn to develop effective and proven solutions without reading through a lengthy manual scrubbing for techniques. A beginning Exadata administrator will find *Oracle Exadata Recipes* handy for learning a variety of different solutions for the platform, while advanced Exadata administrators will enjoy the ease of the problem-solution approach to quickly broaden their knowledge of the Exadata platform. Rather than burying you in architectural and design details, this book is for those who need to get work done using effective and proven solutions (and get home in time for dinner).

The Recipe Approach

Although plenty of Oracle Exadata and Oracle 11gR2 references are available today, this book takes a different approach. You'll find an example-based approach in which each chapter is built of sections containing solutions to specific, real-life Exadata problems. When faced with a problem, you can turn to the corresponding section and find a proven solution that you can reference and implement.

Each recipe contains a problem statement, a solution, and a detailed explanation of how the solution works. Some recipes provide a more detailed architectural discussion of how Exadata is designed and how the design differs from traditional, non-Exadata Oracle database infrastructures.

Oracle Exadata Recipes takes an example-based, problem-solution approach in showing how to size, install, configure, manage, monitor, and optimize Oracle database workloads with Oracle Exadata Database Machine. Whether you're an Oracle Database administrator, Unix/Linux administrator, storage administrator, network administrator, or Oracle developer, *Oracle Exadata Recipes* provides effective and proven solutions to accomplish a wide variety of tasks on the Exadata Database Machine.

How I Came to Write This Book

Professionally, I've always been the type to overdocument and take notes. When we embarked on our Exadata Center of Excellence Initiative in 2011, we made it a goal to dig as deeply as we could into the inner workings of the Exadata Database Machine and try our best to understand now just how the machine was built and how it worked, but also how the design differed from traditional Oracle database infrastructures. Through the summer of 2011, I put together dozens of white papers, delivered a number of Exadata webinars, and presented a variety of Exadata topics at various Oracle conferences.

In early 2012, Jonathan Gennick from Apress approached me about the idea of putting some of this content into something "more formal," and the idea of *Oracle Exadata Recipes* was born. We struggled a bit with the problem-solution approach to the book, mostly because unlike other Oracle development and administration topics, the design of the Exadata Database Machine is such that "problems," in the true sense of the word, are difficult to quantify with an engineered system. So, during the project, I had to constantly remind myself (and be reminded by the reviewers and editor) to pose the recipes as specific tasks and problems that an Exadata Database Machine administrator would likely need a solution to. To this end, the recipes in this book are focused on how to perform specific administration or monitoring and measurement techniques on Exadata. Hopefully, we've hit the target and you can benefit from the contents of *Oracle Exadata Recipes*.

How We Tested

The solutions in *Oracle Exadata Recipes* are built using Exadata X2-2 hardware and its associated Oracle software, including Oracle Database 11gR2, Oracle Grid Infrastructure 11gR2, Oracle Automated Storage Management (ASM), and Oracle Real Application Clusters (RAC). The solutions in this book contain many test cases and examples built with real databases installed on the Exadata Database Machine and, when necessary, we have provided scripts or code demonstrating how the test cases were constructed.

We used Centroid's Exadata X2-2 Quarter Rack for the recipes, test cases, and solutions in this book. When the project began, Oracle's Exadata X3-2 and X3-8 configurations had not yet been released, but in the appropriate sections of the book we have made references to Exadata X3 differences where we felt necessary.

Source Code

Source code is available for many of the examples in this book. All the numbered listings are included, and each one indicates the specific file name for that listing. You can download the source code from the book's catalog page on the Apress web site at `www.apress.com/9781430249146`.

PART 1

Exadata Architecture

Oracle's Exadata Database Machine is an engineered system comprised of high-performing, industry standard, optimally balanced hardware combined with unique Exadata software. Exadata's hardware infrastructure is designed for both performance and availability. Each Exadata Database Machine is configured with a compute grid, a storage grid, and a high-speed storage network. Oracle has designed the Exadata Database Machine to reduce performance bottlenecks; each component in the technology stack is fast, and each grid is well-balanced so that the storage grid can satisfy I/O requests evenly, the compute grid can adequately process high volumes of database transactions, and the network grid can adequately transfer data between the compute and storage servers.

Exadata's storage server software is responsible for satisfying database I/O requests and implementing unique performance features, including Smart Scan, Smart Flash Cache, Smart Flash Logging, Storage Indexes, I/O Resource Management, and Hybrid Columnar Compression.

The combination of fast, balanced, highly available hardware with unique Exadata software is what allows Exadata to deliver extreme performance. The chapters in this section are focused on providing a framework to understand and access configuration information for the various components that make up your Exadata Database Machine.

CHAPTER 1

Exadata Hardware

The Exadata Database Machine is a pre-configured, fault-tolerant, high-performing hardware platform built using industry-standard Oracle hardware. The Exadata hardware architecture consists primarily of a compute grid, a storage grid, and a network grid. Since 2010, the majority of Exadata customers deployed one of the four Exadata X2 models, which are comprised of Oracle Sun Fire X4170 M2 servers in the compute grid and Sun Fire X4270-M2 servers running on the storage grid. During Oracle Open World 2012, Oracle released the Exadata X3-2 and X3-8 In Memory Database Machines, which are built using Oracle X3-2 servers on the compute and storage grid. In both cases, Oracle runs Oracle Enterprise Linux or Solaris 11 Express on the compute grid and Oracle Linux combined with unique Exadata storage server software on the storage grid. The network grid is built with multiple high-speed, high-bandwidth InfiniBand switches.

In this chapter, you will learn about the hardware that comprises the Oracle Exadata Database Machine, how to locate the hardware components with Oracle's Exadata rack, and how the servers, storage, and network infrastructure is configured.

■ **Note** Oracle Exadata X3-2, introduced at Oracle Open World 2012, contains Oracle X3-2 servers on the compute node and Oracle X3-2 servers on the storage servers. The examples in this chapter will be performed on an Oracle Exadata X2-2 Quarter Rack, but, when applicable, we will provide X3-2 and X3-8 configuration details.

1-1. Identifying Exadata Database Machine Components
Problem
You are considering an Exadata investment or have just received shipment of your Oracle Exadata Database Machine and have worked with Oracle, your Oracle Partner, the Oracle hardware field service engineer, and Oracle Advanced Consulting Services to install and configure the Exadata Database Machine, and now you would like to better understand the Exadata hardware components. You're an Oracle database administrator, Unix/Linux administrator, network engineer, or perhaps a combination of all of the theseand, before beginning to deploy databases on Exadata, you wish to become comfortable with the various hardware components that comprise the database machine.

Solution
Oracle's Exadata Database Machine consists primarily of a storage grid, compute grid, and network grid. Each grid, or hardware layer, is built with multiple high-performing, industry-standard Oracle servers to provide hardware and system fault tolerance. Exadata comes in four versions—the Exadata X2-2 Database Machine, the Exadata X2-8 Database Machine, the Exadata X3-2 Database Machine, and the Exadata X3-8 Database Machine.

For the storage grid, the Exadata Storage Server hardware configuration for both the X2-2 and X2-8 models is identical:

- Sun Fire X4270 M2 server model
- Two socket, six-core Intel Xeon L5640 processors running at 2.26 GHz
- 24 GB memory
- Four Sun Flash Accelerator F20 PCIe Flash Cards, providing 384 GB of PCI Flash for Smart Flash Cache and Smart Flash Logging
- Twelve 600 GB High Performance (HP) SAS disks or twelve 3 TB High Capacity (HC) SAS disks connected to a storage controller with a 512 MB battery-backed cache
- Two 40 GbpsInfiniBand ports
- Embedded GbE Ethernet port dedicated for Integrated Lights Out Management (ILOM)

The Exadata Database Machine X2-2 compute grid configuration, per server, consists of the following:

- Sun Fire X4170 M2 server model
- Two six-core Intel Xeon X5675 processors running at 3.06 GHz
- 96 GB memory
- Four 300 GB, 10k RPM SAS disks
- Two 40 GbpsInfiniBand ports
- Two 10 GbE Ethernet ports
- Four 1 GbE Ethernet ports
- Embedded 1GbE ILOM port

For the Exadata Database Machine X2-8, the compute gridincludes the following:

- Oracle Sun Server X2-8 (formerly Sun Fire X4800 M2)
- Eight 10-core E7-8800 processors running at 2.4GHz
- 2 TB memory
- Eight 300 GB, 10k RPM SAS disks
- Eight 40 GbpsInfiniBand ports
- Eight 10 GbE Ethernet ports
- Eight 1 GbE Ethernet ports
- Embedded 1GbE ILOM port

On the X3-2 and X3-8 storage grid, the Exadata Storage Server hardware configuration is also identical:

- Oracle X3-2 server model
- Two socket, six-core Intel Xeon E5-2600 processors running at 2.9 GHz
- 64 GB memory
- FourPCIe Flash Cards, providing 1.6 TB GB of PCI Flash for Smart Flash Cache and Smart Flash Logging per storage cell

- Twelve 600 GB High Performance (HP) SAS disks or twelve 3 TB High Capacity (HC) SAS disks connected to a storage controller with a 512 MB battery-backed cache
- Two 40 GbpsInfiniBand ports
- Embedded GbE Ethernet port dedicated for Integrated Lights Out Management (ILOM)
- On the X3-2 Eighth Rack, only two PCI flash cards are enabled and 6 disks per storage cell are enabled

The Exadata Database Machine X3-2 compute grid configuration, per server, consists of the following:

- Oracle X3-2 server model
- Two eight-core Intel Xeon E5-2690 processors running at 2.9 GHz
- 128 GB memory
- Four 300 GB, 10k RPM SAS disks
- Two 40 GbpsInfiniBand ports
- Two 10 GbE Ethernet ports
- Four 1 GbE Ethernet ports
- Embedded 1GbE ILOM port

For the Exadata Database Machine X3-8, the compute grid includes the following:

- Eight 10-core E7-8870 processors running at 2.4GHz
- 2 TB memory
- Eight 300 GB, 10k RPM SAS disks
- Eight 40 GbpsInfiniBand ports
- Eight 10 GbE Ethernet ports
- Eight 1 GbE Ethernet ports
- Embedded 1GbE ILOM port

Exadata X2-2 comes in Full Rack, Half Rack, and Quarter Rack configurations, while the Exadata X2-8 is only offered in Full Rack. The X3-2 comes in a Full Rack, Half Rack, Quarter Rack, and Eighth Rack. The difference between the Full Rack, Half Rack, and Quarter Rack configuration is with the number of nodes in each of the three hardware grids. The X3-2 Eighth Rack has the same number of physical servers in the compute and storage grid but with processors disabled on the compute nodes and both PCI cards and disks disabled on the storage servers. Table 1-1 lists the X2-2, X2-8, X3-2, and X3-8 hardware configuration options and configuration details.

Table 1-1. Exadata X2 and X3 hardware configuration options, compute grid

	X2-2 QuarterRack	X2-2 Half Rack	X2-2 Full Rack	X2-8 Full Rack	X3-2 Eighth Rack	X3-2 QuarterRack	X3-2 Half Rack	X3-2 Full Rack	X3-8 Full Rack
Number of Compute Grid Servers	2	4	8	2	2	2	4	8	2
Total Compute Server Processor Cores	24	48	96	160	16	32	64	128	160
Total Compute Server Memory	196 GB	384 GB	768 GB	4 TB	256 GB	256 GB	512 GB	1024 GB	4 TB
Number of Storage Servers	3	7	14	14	3	3	7	14	14
Total Number of HP and HC SAS Disks in Storage Grid	36	84	168	168	18	36	84	168	168
Storage Server Raw Capacity, High Performance Disks	21.6 TB	50.4 TB	100.8 TB	100.8 TB	10.3 TB	21.6 TB	50.4 TB	100.8 TB	100.8 TB
Storage Server Raw Capacity, High Capacity Disks	108 TB	252 TB	504 TB	504 TB	54 TB	108 TB	252 Tb	504 TB	504 TB
Number of Sun QDR InfiniBand Switches	2	3	3	3	2	2	3	3	3

The Exadata network grid is comprised of multiple Sun QDR InfiniBand switches, which are used for the storage network as well as the Oracle Real Application Clusters (RAC) interconnect. The Exadata Quarter Rack ships with two InfiniBand leaf switches and the Half Rack and Full Rack configurations have two leaf switches and an additional InfiniBand spine switch, used to expand and connect Exadata racks. The compute and storage servers are configured with dual-port InfiniBand ports and connect to each of the two leaf switches.

In addition to the hardware in the storage grid, compute grid, and network grid, Exadata also comes with additional factory-installed and Oracle ACS configured components to facilitate network communications, administration, and management. Specifically, Exadata ships with an integrated KVM switch to provide administrative access to the compute and storage servers, a 48-port embedded Cisco Catalyst 4948 switch to provide data center network uplink capability for various interfaces, and two power distributions units (PDUs) integrated in the Oracle Exadata rack.

How It Works

The Oracle Exadata Database Machine is one of Oracle's Engineered Systems, and Oracle's overarching goal with the Exadata Database Machine is to deliver extreme performance for all database workloads. Software is the most significant factor to meet this end, which I'll present in various recipes throughout this book, but the balanced, high-performing, pre-configured hardware components that make up the Exadata Database Machine play a significant role in its ability to achieve performance and availability goals.

When you open the cabinet doors on your Exadata, you'll find the same layout from one Exadata to the next—ExadataStorage Servers at the bottom and top sections of the rack, compute servers in the middle, InfiniBand switches and the Cisco Catalyst 4948 switch and KVM switch placed between the compute servers. Oracle places the first of each component, relative to the model, at the lowest slot in the rack. Every Oracle Exadata X2-2, X2-8, X3-2, and X3-8 Database Machine is built identically from the factory; the rack layout and component placement within the rack is physically identical from one machine to the next:

- On Half Rack and Full Rack models, the InfiniBand spine switch is in position U1.
- Storage servers are 2U Sun Fire X4270 M2 or X3-2 servers places in positions U2 through U14, with the first storage server in U2/U3.
- For the Quarter Rack, the two 1U compute servers reside in positions U16 and U17. In the Half Rack and Full Rack configurations, two additional 1U compute servers reside in positions U18 and U19.
- In the Full Rack, positions U16 through U19 contain the first Oracle X2-8 compute server.
- The first InfiniBand leaf switch is placed in U20 for all X2-2, X2-8, X3-2, and X3-8 models.
- The Cisco Catalyst Ethernet switch is in position U21.
- The KVM switch is a 2U component residing in slots U22 and U23.
- U24 houses the second InfiniBand leaf switch for all Exadata models.
- For the X2-2 and X3-2 Full Rack, four 1U compute servers are installed in slots U25 through U28 and, in the X2-8 and X3-8 Full Rack, a single X2-8 4U server is installed.
- The seven additional 2U storage servers for the X2-2, X2-8, X3-2, and X3-8 Full Rack models are installed in positions U29 through U42.

Figure 1-1 displays an Exadata X2-2 Full Rack.

CHAPTER 1 ■ EXADATA HARDWARE

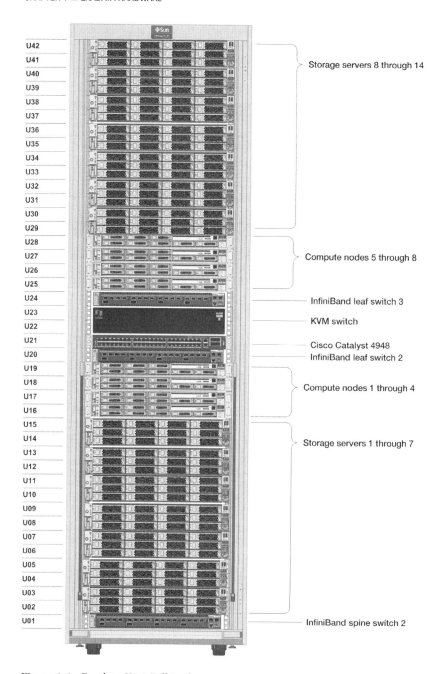

Figure 1-1. *Exadata X2-2 Full Rack*

The compute and storage servers in an Exadata Database Machine are typically connected to the Exadata InfiniBand switches, embedded Cisco switch, and data center networks in the same manner across Exadata customers. Figure 1-2 displays a typical Oracle Exadata network configuration for a single compute server and single storage server.

CHAPTER 1 ■ EXADATA HARDWARE

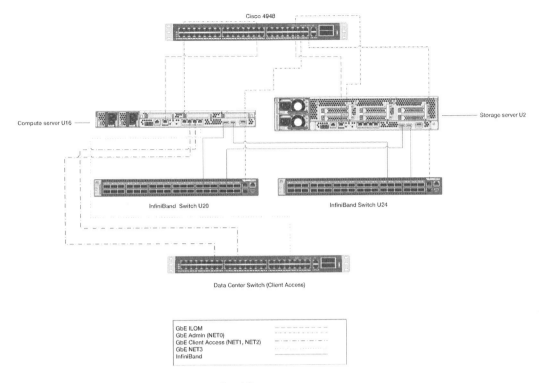

***Figure 1-2.** Typical Exadata X2-2 network cabling*

In the sample diagram, the following features are notable:

- InfiniBand ports for both the compute server and storage server are connected to each of the InfiniBand leaf switches; the spine switch is only used to connect the leaf switches or other Exadata racks.

- The ILOM port, marked "NET-MGMT" on the servers, is connected to the embedded Cisco switch.

- The NET0 management interface on both the compute server and storage server is connected to the Cisco switch. The Cisco switch uplinks to the data center network (not shown in Figure *1-3*) to provide access to the administrative interfaces.

- The NET1 and NET2 interfaces on the compute servers are connected to the client data center network and serve as the "Client Access Network." Typically, these are bonded to form a NET1-2 interface, which servers as the public network and VIP interface for the Oracle cluster.

- The Exadata Storage Servers have no direct connectivity to the client access network; they are accessed for administrative purposes via the administrative interface via the embedded Cisco switch.

Additional information about Exadata networking is discussed in Chapter 10.

1-2. Displaying Storage Server Architecture Details

Problem

As an Exadata administrator, you wish to better understand the overall hardware configuration, storage configuration, network configuration, and operating environment of the Exadata X2-2 or X2-8 Database Machine Storage Servers.

Solution

The X2-2 ExadataStorage Servers are Oracle Sun Fire X4270 M2 servers. The X3-2 and X3-8 models use Oracle X3-2 servers. Depending on the architecture details you're interested in, various commands are available to display configuration information. In this recipe, you will learn how to do the following:

- Validate your Oracle Linux operating system version
- Query system information using `dmidecode`
- Display the current server image version and image history
- Check your network configuration

> **Note** In this recipe we will be showing command output from an Exadata X2-2 Quarter Rack.

Begin by logging in to an ExadataStorage Server as rootand checking your operating system release. As you can see below, the Exadata Storage servers run Oracle Enterprise Linux 5.5:

```
Macintosh-7:~ jclarke$ ssh root@cm01cel01
root@cm01cel01's password:
Last login: Tue Jul 24 00:30:28 2012 from 172.16.150.10
[root@cm01cel01 ~]# cat /etc./enterprise-release
Enterprise Linux Enterprise Linux Server release 5.5 (Carthage)
[root@cm01cel01 ~]#
```

The kernel version for Exadata X2-2 and X2-8 models as of Exadata Bundle Patch 14 for Oracle Enterprise Linux is 64-bit `2.6.18-238.12.2.0.2.el5` and can be found using the uname -a command:

```
[root@cm01cel01 ~]# uname -a
Linux cm01cel01.centroid.com 2.6.18-238.12.2.0.2.el5 #1 SMP Tue Jun 28 05:21:19 EDT 2011 x86_64 x86_64 x86_64 GNU/Linux
[root@cm01cel01 ~]#
```

You can use `dmidecode` to obtain the server model and serial number:

```
[root@cm01cel01 ~]# dmidecode -s system-product-name
SUN FIRE X4270 M2 SERVER
[root@cm01cel01 ~]# dmidecode -s system-serial-number
1104FMM0MG
[root@cm01cel01 ~]#
```

The operating system and Exadata server software binaries are installed, patched, and maintained as images; when you install or patch an Exadata cell, a new image is installed. You can query your current active image by running the imageinfo command:

```
[root@cm01cel01 ~]# imageinfo

Kernel version: 2.6.18-238.12.2.0.2.el5 #1 SMP Tue Jun 28 05:21:19 EDT 2011 x86_64
Cell version: OSS_11.2.2.4.2_LINUX.X64_111221
Cell rpm version: cell-11.2.2.4.2_LINUX.X64_111221-1

Active image version: 11.2.2.4.2.111221
Active image activated: 2012-02-11 22:25:25-0500
Active image status: success
Active system partition on device: /dev/md6
Active software partition on device: /dev/md8

In partition rollback: Impossible

Cell boot usb partition: /dev/sdm1
Cell boot usb version: 11.2.2.4.2.111221

Inactive image version: 11.2.2.4.0.110929
Inactive image activated: 2011-10-31 23:08:44-0400
Inactive image status: success
Inactive system partition on device: /dev/md5
Inactive software partition on device: /dev/md7

Boot area has rollback archive for the version: 11.2.2.4.0.110929
Rollback to the inactive partitions: Possible
[root@cm01cel01 ~]#
```

From this output, you can see that our storage cell is running image version 11.2.2.4.2.111221, which contains cell version OSS_11.2.2.4.2_LINUX.X64_111221, kernel version 2.6.18-238.12.2.0.2.el5, with the active system partition on device /dev/md6 and the software partition on /dev/md8.

■ **Note** We will cover additional Exadata Storage Server details in Recipe 1-4.

You can also list all images that have at one point been installed on the Exadata cell by executing imagehistory:

```
[root@cm01cel01 ~]# imagehistory
Version                        : 11.2.2.2.0.101206.2
Image activation date          : 2011-02-21 11:20:38 -0800
Imaging mode                   : fresh
Imaging status                 : success

Version                        : 11.2.2.2.2.110311
Image activation date          : 2011-05-04 12:31:56 -0400
Imaging mode                   : out of partition upgrade
Imaging status                 : success
```

```
Version                          : 11.2.2.3.2.110520
Image activation date            : 2011-06-24 23:49:39 -0400
Imaging mode                     : out of partition upgrade
Imaging status                   : success

Version                          : 11.2.2.3.5.110815
Image activation date            : 2011-08-29 12:16:47 -0400
Imaging mode                     : out of partition upgrade
Imaging status                   : success

Version                          : 11.2.2.4.0.110929
Image activation date            : 2011-10-31 23:08:44 -0400
Imaging mode                     : out of partition upgrade
Imaging status                   : success

Version                          : 11.2.2.4.2.111221
Image activation date            : 2012-02-11 22:25:25 -0500
Imaging mode                     : out of partition upgrade
Imaging status                   : success

[root@cm01cel01 ~]#
```

From this output, you can see that this storage cell has had six different images installed on it over its lifetime, and if you examine the image version details, you can see when you patched or upgraded and the version you upgraded to.

The ExadataStorage Servers are accessible via SSH over a 1 GbEEthernet port and connected via dual InfiniBand ports to two InfiniBand switches located in the Exadata rack.

> **Note** For additional networking details of the ExadataStorage Servers, refer to Chapter 10.

How It Works

ExadataStorage Servers are self-contained storage platforms that house disk storage for an Exadata Database Machine and run Oracle's Cell Services (cellsrv) software. A single storage server is also commonly referred to as a *cell*, and we'll use the term *storage server* and *cell* interchangeably throughout this book.

The Exadata storage cell is the building block for the Exadata Storage Grid. In an Exadata Database Machine, more cells not only equates to increased physical capacity, but also higher levels of I/O bandwidth and IOPs (I/Os per second). Each storage cell contains 12 physical SAS disks; depending on your business requirements, these can be either 600 GB, 15,000 RPM High Performance SAS disks capable of delivering up to 1.8 GB per second of raw data bandwidth per cell, or 3 TB 7,200 RPM High Capacity SAS disks capable of delivering up to 1.3 GB per second of raw data bandwidth. Table 1-2 provides performance capabilities for High Performance and High Capacity disks for each Exadata Database Machine model.

Table 1-2. Exadata Storage Grid performance capabilities

	X2-2 Quarter Rack	X2-2 Half Rack	X2-2 Full Rack	X2-8 Full Rack	X3-2 Eighth Rack	X3-2 Quarter Rack	X3-2 Half Rack	X3-2 Full Rack	X3-8 Full Rack
Number of Storage Servers	3	7	14	14	3	3	7	14	14
SAS Disks/Cell	12	12	12	12	6	12	12	12	12
PCI Flash Cards/Cell	4	4	4	4	2	4	4	4	4
Raw Data Bandwidth, 600 GB HP disks	4.8 GBPS	11.2 GBPS	22.4 GBPS	22.4 GBPS	2.7 GBPS	5.4 GBPS	12.5 GBPS	25 GBPS	25 GBPS
Raw Data Bandwidth, 3 TB HP disks	3.9 GBPS	9.1 GBPS	18.2 GBPS	18.2 GBPS	2 GBPS	4.0 GBPS	9 GBPS	18 GBPS	18 GBPS
Disk IOPs, 600 GB HP disks	10.8k	25.2k	50.4k	50.4k	5.4k	10.8k	25.2k	50.4k	50.4k
Disk IOPs, 3 TB HC disks	6k	14k	28k	28k	3k	6k	14k	28k	28k
Flash IOPs, Read	375k	750k	1,500k	1,500k	187k	375k	750k	1,500k	1,500k

CHAPTER 1 ■ EXADATA HARDWARE

Databases in an Exadata Database Machine are typically deployed so that the database files are evenly distributed across all storage cells in the machine as well as all physical disks in an individual cell. Oracle uses Oracle Automated Storage Management (ASM) in combination with logical storage entities called *cell disks* and grid disks to achieve this balance.

■ **Note** To learn more about cell disks and grid disks, refer to Recipes 3-1 and 3-2.

To summarize, the ExadataStorage Server is quite simply an Oracle Sun Fire X4270 M2 server running Oracle Linux and Oracle's Exadata Storage Server software. Minus the storage server software component of Exadata (which is difficult to ignore since it's the primary differentiator with the machine), understanding the configuration and administration topics of an ExadataStorage Server is similar to any server running Linux. What makes Exadata unique is truly the storage server software combined with the manner in which Oracle has standardized its configuration to best utilize its resources and be positively exploited by the cellsrv software. The operating system, image, disk configuration, and network configuration in an ExadataStorage Server is the trademark of Oracle's entire Engineered Systems portfolio and as such, once you understand how the pieces fit together on one ExadataStorage Server, you can be confident that as an administrator you'll be comfortable with any storage cell.

1-3. Displaying Compute Server Architecture Details
Problem
As an Exadata DMA, you wish to better understand the overall hardware configuration, storage configuration, network configuration, and operating environment of the Exadata X2-2, X2-8, X3-2, or X3-8 Database Machine compute servers.

Solution
The ExadataX2-2 compute servers are Oracle Sun Fire X4170 M2 servers and the Exadata X3-2 compute nodes are built on Oracle X3-2 servers. Depending on the architecture details you're interested in, various commands are available to display configuration information. In this recipe, we will show you how to do the following:

- Validate your Oracle Linux operating system version
- Query system information using `dmidecode`
- Display the current server image version and image history
- Check your network configuration

■ **Note** In this recipe we will be showing command output from an Exadata X2-2 Quarter Rack.

Begin by logging in to an Exadata compute server as root and checking your operating system release:

```
Macintosh-7:~ jclarke$ ssh root@cm01dbm01
root@cm01dbm01's password:
Last login: Fri Jul 20 16:53:19 2012 from 172.16.150.10
[root@cm01dbm01 ~]# cat /etc./enterprise-release
Enterprise Linux Enterprise Linux Server release 5.5 (Carthage)
[root@cm01dbm01 ~]#
```

The Exadata compute servers run either Oracle Linux or Solaris 11 Express. In this example and all examples throughout this book, we're running Oracle Enterprise Linux 5.5:

The kernel version for Exadata X2-2 and X2-8 models as of Exadata Bundle Patch 14 for Oracle Enterprise Linux is 64-bit 2.6.18-238.12.2.0.2.el5 and can be found using the uname -a command:

```
[root@cm01dbm01 ~]# uname -a
Linux cm01dbm01.centroid.com 2.6.18-238.12.2.0.2.el5 #1 SMP Tue Jun 28 05:21:19 EDT 2011 x86_64
x86_64 x86_64 GNU/Linux
[root@cm01dbm01 ~]#
```

You can use dmidecode to obtain our server model and serial number:

```
[root@cm01dbm01 ~]# dmidecode -s system-product-name
SUN FIRE X4170 M2 SERVER
[root@cm01dbm01 ~]# dmidecode -s system-serial-number
1105FMM025
[root@cm01dbm01 ~]#
```

The function of the compute servers in an Oracle Exadata Database Machine is to run Oracle 11gR2 database instances. On the compute servers, one Oracle 11gR2 Grid Infrastructure software home is installed, which runs Oracle 11gR2 clusterware and an Oracle ASM instance. Additionally, one or more Oracle 11gR2 RDBMS homes are installed, which run the Oracle database instances. Installation or patching of these Oracle software homes is typically performed using the traditional Oracle OPatch utilities. Periodically, however, Oracle releases patches that require operating system updates to the Exadata compute node servers. In this event, Oracle maintains these as images. You can query your current active image by running the imageinfo command:

```
[root@cm01dbm01 ~]# imageinfo

Kernel version: 2.6.18-238.12.2.0.2.el5 #1 SMP Tue Jun 28 05:21:19 EDT 2011 x86_64
Image version: 11.2.2.4.2.111221
Image activated: 2012-02-11 23:46:46-0500
Image status: success
System partition on device: /dev/mapper/VGExaDb-LVDbSys1

[root@cm01dbm01 ~]#
```

We can see that our compute server is running image version 11.2.2.4.2.111221, which contains kernel version 2.6.18-238.12.2.0.2.el5. The active system partition is installed on /dev/mapper/VGExaDb-LVDbSys1.

> **Note** To learn more about compute server storage, refer to Recipe 1-5.

You can also list all images that have at one point been installed on the Exadata cell by executing imagehistory:

```
[root@cm01dbm01 ~]# imagehistory
Version                      : 11.2.2.2.0.101206.2
Image activation date        : 2011-02-21 11:07:02 -0800
Imaging mode                 : fresh
Imaging status               : success
```

```
Version                         : 11.2.2.2.2.110311
Image activation date           : 2011-05-04 12:41:40 -0400
Imaging mode                    : patch
Imaging status                  : success

Version                         : 11.2.2.3.2.110520
Image activation date           : 2011-06-25 15:21:42 -0400
Imaging mode                    : patch
Imaging status                  : success

Version                         : 11.2.2.3.5.110815
Image activation date           : 2011-08-29 19:06:38 -0400
Imaging mode                    : patch
Imaging status                  : success

Version                         : 11.2.2.4.2.111221
Image activation date           : 2012-02-11 23:46:46 -0500
Imaging mode                    : patch
Imaging status                  : success

[root@cm01dbm01 ~]#
```

Exadata compute servers have three required and one optional network:

- The NET0/Admin network allows for SSH connectivity to the server. It uses the eth0 interface, which is connected to the embedded Cisco switch.

- The NET1, NET2, NET1-2/Client Access provides access to the Oracle RAC VIP address and SCAN addresses. It uses interfaces eth1 and eth2, which are typically bonded. These interfaces are connected to your data center network.

- The IB network connects two ports on the compute servers to both of the InfiniBand leaf switches in the rack. All storage server communication and Oracle RAC interconnect traffic uses this network.

- An optional "additional" network, NET3, which is built on eth3, is also provided. This is often used for backups and/or other external traffic.

Note For additional networking details of the Exadata compute servers, refer to Chapter 10.

How It Works

Exadata compute servers are designed to run Oracle 11gR2 databases. Oracle 11gR2 Grid Infrastructure and RDBMS software is installed on these servers, and aside from the InfiniBand-aware communications protocols that enable the compute servers to send and receive I/O requests to and from the storage cells, the architecture and operating environment of the compute servers is similar to non-Exadata Linux environments running Oracle 11gR2. The collection of compute servers in an Exadata Database Machine makes up the compute grid.

All database storage on Exadata is done with Oracle ASM. Companies typically run Oracle Real Application Clusters (RAC) on Exadata to achieve high availability and maximize the aggregate processor and memory across the compute grid.

1-4. Listing Disk Storage Details on the Exadata Storage Servers

Problem

As an Exadata administrator, DBA, or storage administrator, you wish to better understand how storage is allocated, presented, and used in the Exadata storage cell.

Solution

In this recipe, we will show you how to do the following:

- Query your physical disk information using `lscssi`
- Use the `MegaCli64` utility to display your LSI MegaRAID device information
- List your physical disk information using Exadata's CellCLI interface
- Understand the `mdadm` software RAID configuration on the storage cells
- List your physical disk partitions using `fdisk-l`

From any of the Exadata storage servers, run an `lsscsi -v` command to list the physical devices:

```
[root@cm01cel01 ~]# lsscsi -v
[0:2:0:0]    disk    LSI      MR9261-8i    2.12  /dev/sda
  dir: /sys/bus/scsi/devices/0:2:0:0  [/sys/devices/pci0000:00/0000:00:05.0/0000:13:00.0/host0/
target0:2:0/0:2:0:0]
[0:2:1:0]    disk    LSI      MR9261-8i    2.12  /dev/sdb
  dir: /sys/bus/scsi/devices/0:2:1:0  [/sys/devices/pci0000:00/0000:00:05.0/0000:13:00.0/host0/
target0:2:1/0:2:1:0]
[0:2:2:0]    disk    LSI      MR9261-8i    2.12  /dev/sdc
  dir: /sys/bus/scsi/devices/0:2:2:0  [/sys/devices/pci0000:00/0000:00:05.0/0000:13:00.0/host0/
target0:2:2/0:2:2:0]
... output omitted
[8:0:0:0]    disk    ATA      MARVELL SD88SA02 D20Y  /dev/sdn
  dir: /sys/bus/scsi/devices/8:0:0:0  [/sys/devices/pci0000:00/0000:00:07.0/0000:19:00.0/
0000:1a:02.0/0000:1b:00.0/host8/port-8:0/end_device-8:0/target8:0:0/8:0:0:0]
[8:0:1:0]    disk    ATA      MARVELL SD88SA02 D20Y  /dev/sdo ...
```

The output shows both the physical SAS drives as well as flash devices—you can tell the difference based on the vendor and model columns. The lines showing LSI indicate our 12 SAS devices and you can see the physical device names in the last column of the output (i.e., /dev/sdk).

The physical drives are controlled via the LSI MegaRaid controller and you can use `MegaCli64` to display more information about these disks:

```
[root@cm01cel01 ~]# /opt/MegaRAID/MegaCli/MegaCli64 -ShowSummary -aALL

System
        OS Name (IP Address)      : Not Recognized
        OS Version                : Not Recognized
        Driver Version            : Not Recognized
        CLI Version               : 8.00.23
```

```
Hardware
      Controller
            ProductName       : LSI MegaRAID SAS 9261-8i(Bus 0, Dev 0)
            SAS Address       : 500605b002f4aac0
            FW Package Version: 12.12.0-0048
            Status            : Optimal
      BBU
            BBU Type          : Unknown
            Status            : Healthy
      Enclosure
            Product Id        : HYDE12
            Type              : SES
            Status            : OK

            Product Id        : SGPIO
            Type              : SGPIO
            Status            : OK

      PD
            Connector         : Port 0 - 3<Internal><Encl Pos 0 >: Slot 11
            Vendor Id         : SEAGATE
            Product Id        : ST360057SSUN600G
            State             : Online
            Disk Type         : SAS,Hard Disk Device
            Capacity          : 557.861 GB
            Power State       : Active

... Connectors omitted for brevity

Storage

      Virtual Drives
            Virtual drive     : Target Id 0 ,VD name
            Size              : 557.861 GB
            State             : Optimal
            RAID Level        : 0

            Virtual drive     : Target Id 1 ,VD name
            Size              : 557.861 GB
            State             : Optimal
            RAID Level        : 0

... Virtual drives omitted for brevity

Exit Code: 0x00
[root@cm01cel01 ~]#
```

CHAPTER 1 ■ EXADATA HARDWARE

You'll notice that we've got twelve 557.861 GB disks in this storage server. Based on the disk sizes, we know that this storage server has High Performance disk drives. Using CellCLI, we can confirm this and note the corresponding sizes:

```
[root@cm01cel01 ~]# cellcli
CellCLI: Release 11.2.2.4.2 - Production on Wed Jul 25 13:07:24 EDT 2012

Copyright (c) 2007, 2011, Oracle.  All rights reserved.
Cell Efficiency Ratio: 234

CellCLI> list physicaldisk where disktype=HardDisk attributes name,physicalSize
        20:0    558.9109999993816G
        20:1    558.9109999993816G
... Disks 20:2 through 20:10 omitted for brevity
        20:11   558.9109999993816G

CellCLI>
```

Each Exadata Storage Server has twelve physical SAS disks and four 96 GB PCIe Sun Flash Accelerator flash cards, each partitioned into four 24 GB partitions. From an operating system point of view, however, you can only see a small subset of this physical storage:

```
[root@cm01cel01 ~]# df -h
Filesystem            Size  Used Avail Use% Mounted on
/dev/md6              9.9G  3.5G  5.9G  38% /
tmpfs                  12G     0   12G   0% /dev/shm
/dev/md8              2.0G  651M  1.3G  35% /opt/oracle
/dev/md4              116M   60M   50M  55% /boot
/dev/md11             2.3G  204M  2.0G  10% /var/log/oracle
[root@cm01cel01 ~]#
```

In recipe 1-1, we introduced the imageinfo command, which lists our Exadata cell system image version. If you run imageinfo and search for lines containing the word "partition", you can see which device your system and software partitions are installed:

```
[root@cm01cel01 ~]# imageinfo | grep partition

Active system partition on device: /dev/md6
Active software partition on device: /dev/md8
Inactive system partition on device: /dev/md5
Inactive software partition on device: /dev/md7

[root@cm01cel01 ~]#
```

This storage, as well as the other mount points presented on your storage servers, is physically stored in two of the twelve physical SAS disks and is referred to as the *System Area* and the volumes are referred to as *System Volumes*.

Based on the /dev/md*Filesystem names, we know we've got software RAID in play for these devices and that this RAID was created using mdadm. Let's query our mdadm configuration on /dev/md6 (the output is similar for /dev/md5, /dev/md8, and /dev/md11):

```
[root@cm01cel01 ~]# mdadm -Q -D /dev/md6
/dev/md6:
        Version : 0.90
  Creation Time : Mon Feb 21 13:06:27 2011
     Raid Level : raid1
     Array Size : 10482304 (10.00 GiB 10.73 GB)
  Used Dev Size : 10482304 (10.00 GiB 10.73 GB)
   Raid Devices : 2
  Total Devices : 2
Preferred Minor : 6
    Persistence : Superblock is persistent

    Update Time : Sun Mar 25 20:50:28 2012
          State : active
 Active Devices : 2
Working Devices : 2
 Failed Devices : 0
  Spare Devices : 0

           UUID : 2ea655b5:89c5cafc:b8bacc8c:27078485
         Events : 0.49

    Number   Major   Minor   RaidDevice State
       0       8        6        0      active sync   /dev/sda6
       1       8       22        1      active sync   /dev/sdb6
[root@cm01cel01 ~]#
```

From this output, we can see that the /dev/sda and /dev/sdb physical devices are software mirrored via mdadm. If you do anfdisk -l on these devices, you will see the following:

```
[root@cm01cel01 ~]# fdisk -l /dev/sda

Disk /dev/sda: 598.9 GB, 598999040000 bytes
255 heads, 63 sectors/track, 72824 cylinders
Units = cylinders of 16065 * 512 = 8225280 bytes

   Device Boot      Start         End      Blocks   Id  System
/dev/sda1   *           1          15      120456   fd  Linux raid autodetect
/dev/sda2              16          16        8032+  83  Linux
/dev/sda3              17       69039   554427247+  83  Linux
/dev/sda4           69040       72824    30403012+   f  W95 Ext'd (LBA)
/dev/sda5           69040       70344    10482381   fd  Linux raid autodetect
/dev/sda6           70345       71649    10482381   fd  Linux raid autodetect
/dev/sda7           71650       71910     2096451   fd  Linux raid autodetect
/dev/sda8           71911       72171     2096451   fd  Linux raid autodetect
/dev/sda9           72172       72432     2096451   fd  Linux raid autodetect
/dev/sda10          72433       72521      714861   fd  Linux raid autodetect
```

```
/dev/sda11              72522       72824     2433816  fd  Linux raid autodetect
[root@cm01cel01 ~]# fdisk -l /dev/sdb

Disk /dev/sdb: 598.9 GB, 598999040000 bytes
255 heads, 63 sectors/track, 72824 cylinders
Units = cylinders of 16065 * 512 = 8225280 bytes

   Device Boot      Start         End      Blocks   Id  System
/dev/sdb1   *           1          15      120456   fd  Linux raid autodetect
/dev/sdb2              16          16        8032+  83  Linux
/dev/sdb3              17       69039   554427247+  83  Linux
/dev/sdb4           69040       72824    30403012+   f  W95 Ext'd (LBA)
/dev/sdb5           69040       70344    10482381   fd  Linux raid autodetect
/dev/sdb6           70345       71649    10482381   fd  Linux raid autodetect
/dev/sdb7           71650       71910     2096451   fd  Linux raid autodetect
/dev/sdb8           71911       72171     2096451   fd  Linux raid autodetect
/dev/sdb9           72172       72432     2096451   fd  Linux raid autodetect
/dev/sdb10          72433       72521      714861   fd  Linux raid autodetect
/dev/sdb11          72522       72824     2433816   fd  Linux raid autodetect
[root@cm01cel01 ~]#
```

This gives us the following information:

- /dev/sda[6,8,4,11] and /dev/sdb[6,8,4,11] are partitioned to contain OS storage, mirrored via software RAID via mdadm.

- /dev/sda3 and /dev/sdb3 don't have partitions usable for Linux file systems on them; they are used for database storage.

What about the disk storage that Exadata uses for database storage? These disk partitions are mapped to the Exadata logical unit, or LUN. Let's show an fdisk output of one of these devices, though, and see what it looks like:

```
[root@cm01cel01 ~]# fdisk -l /dev/sdc

Disk /dev/sdc: 598.9 GB, 598999040000 bytes
255 heads, 63 sectors/track, 72824 cylinders
Units = cylinders of 16065 * 512 = 8225280 bytes

Disk /dev/sdc doesn't contain a valid partition table
[root@cm01cel01 ~]#
```

We can see that there is not a valid partition table on the /dev/sdc. This device represents the Exadata Storage Server LUN.

> **Note** To learn more about Exadata storage entity mapping, please see Recipe 3-1.

How It Works

Each Exadata Storage Server is comprised of 12 physical SAS disks. These disks are primarily used for database storage, but Oracle uses a small 29 GB chunk of storage on the first two physical disks to house the Oracle Linux operating system, Exadata Storage Server software, the /boot file system, as well as /var/log/oracle, which contains Cell Services and log and diagnostics files. Oracle calls this 29 GB slice of storage the *System Area*.

All of the storage entities in the System Area are mirrored via software RAID using Linux software RAID. For example, the Cell Services operating system, cellsrv, is mounted on /opt/oracle on the storage cell. This device is comprised of physical partitions /dev/sda8 and /dev/sdb8:

```
[root@cm01cel01 oracle]# mdadm -Q -D /dev/md8
/dev/md8:
        Version : 0.90
  Creation Time : Mon Feb 21 13:06:29 2011
     Raid Level : raid1
     Array Size : 2096384 (2047.59 MiB 2146.70 MB)
  Used Dev Size : 2096384 (2047.59 MiB 2146.70 MB)
   Raid Devices : 2
  Total Devices : 2
Preferred Minor : 8
    Persistence : Superblock is persistent

    Update Time : Wed Jul 25 13:33:11 2012
          State : clean
 Active Devices : 2
Working Devices : 2
 Failed Devices : 0
  Spare Devices : 0

           UUID : 4c4b589f:a2e42e48:8847db6b:832284bd
         Events : 0.110

    Number   Major   Minor   RaidDevice State
       0       8        8        0      active sync   /dev/sda8
       1       8       24        1      active sync   /dev/sdb8
[root@cm01cel01 oracle]#
```

Since the System Area is built on the first two physical disks and only uses a small portion of the total physical size of the disk, Oracle leaves a large section of the disk unformatted from the host operating system's perspective. This resides on /dev/sda3 and /dev/sdb3 and is mapped to an Exadata LUN, available to be used for an Exadata cell disk.

```
[root@cm01cel01 oracle]# fdisk -l /dev/sda

Disk /dev/sda: 598.9 GB, 598999040000 bytes
255 heads, 63 sectors/track, 72824 cylinders
Units = cylinders of 16065 * 512 = 8225280 bytes

   Device Boot      Start         End      Blocks   Id  System
/dev/sda1   *           1          15      120456   fd  Linux raid autodetect
/dev/sda2              16          16        8032+  83  Linux
/dev/sda3              17       69039   554427247+  83  Linux
/dev/sda4           69040       72824    30403012+   f  W95 Ext'd (LBA)
/dev/sda5           69040       70344    10482381   fd  Linux raid autodetect
/dev/sda6           70345       71649    10482381   fd  Linux raid autodetect
/dev/sda7           71650       71910     2096451   fd  Linux raid autodetect
/dev/sda8           71911       72171     2096451   fd  Linux raid autodetect
/dev/sda9           72172       72432     2096451   fd  Linux raid autodetect
```

```
/dev/sda10          72433       72521      714861   fd  Linux raid autodetect
/dev/sda11          72522       72824     2433816   fd  Linux raid autodetect
[root@cm01cel01 oracle]#
```

> **Note** On the Exadata X3-2 Eighth Rack, only six SAS disks are enabled per storage cell.

1-5. Listing Disk Storage Details on the Compute Servers
Problem
As an Exadata administrator, DBA, or storage administrator, you wish to better understand how storage is allocated, presented, and used in the Exadata compute server.

Solution
In this recipe, we will show you how to do the following:

- Report your file system details using `df`
- List your disk partition information using `fdisk`
- Query your SCSI disk device information using `lsscsi`
- Use the `MegaCli64` utility to display your LSI MegaRAID device information
- List your physical volume, volume group, and logical volume information using `pvdisplay`, `vgdisplay`, and `lvdisplay`

Each Exadata compute server in the X2-2 and X3-2 models has four 300GB disks, which are partitioned and formatted to present a root file system and a single /u01 mount point. The Oracle Grid Infrastructure and 11gR2 Oracle RDBMS binaries are installed on the /u01 mount point. Referring to the `imageinfo` output, the root file system is installed on /dev/mapper/VGExaDb-LVDbSys1:

```
[root@cm01dbm01 ~]# df -h
Filesystem                      Size  Used Avail Use% Mounted on
/dev/mapper/VGExaDb-LVDbSys1    30G    22G  6.5G  78% /
/dev/sda1                       124M   48M   70M  41% /boot
/dev/mapper/VGExaDb-LVDbOra1    99G    52G   42G  56% /u01
tmpfs                           81G   4.0M   81G   1% /dev/shm
[root@cm01dbm01 ~]#
```

You can see a 30 GB root file system, a small boot file system, and a 100 GB /u01 mount point. Now let's look at an `fdisk` output:

```
[root@cm01dbm01 ~]# fdisk -l

Disk /dev/sda: 598.8 GB, 598879502336 bytes
255 heads, 63 sectors/track, 72809 cylinders
Units = cylinders of 16065 * 512 = 8225280 bytes
```

```
   Device Boot      Start         End      Blocks   Id  System
/dev/sda1   *           1          16      128488+  83  Linux
/dev/sda2              17       72809   584709772+  8e  Linux LVM
[root@cm01dbm01 ~]#
```

We see a 600 GB drive partitioned into /dev/sda1 and /dev/sda2 partitions. We know that /dev/sda1 is mounted to /boot from the df listing, so we also know that the / and /u01file systems are built on logical volumes. An lsscsi –v output clues us in that the disks are controlled via an LSI MegaRAID controller:

```
[root@cm01dbm01 ~]# lsscsi -v
[0:2:0:0]    disk    LSI      MR9261-8i        2.12  /dev/sda
  dir: /sys/bus/scsi/devices/0:2:0:0  [/sys/devices/pci0000:00/0000:00:03.0/0000:0d:00.0/host0/target0:2:0/0:2:0:0]
[root@cm01dbm01 ~]#
```

Using MegaCli64 we can display the physical hardware:

```
[root@cm01dbm01 ~]# /opt/MegaRAID/MegaCli/MegaCli64 -ShowSummary -aALL

System
        OS Name (IP Address)      : Not Recognized
        OS Version                : Not Recognized
        Driver Version            : Not Recognized
        CLI Version               : 8.00.23

Hardware
        Controller
                ProductName       : LSI MegaRAID SAS 9261-8i(Bus 0, Dev 0)
                SAS Address       : 500605b002f054d0
                FW Package Version: 12.12.0-0048
                Status            : Optimal
        BBU
                BBU Type          : Unknown
                Status            : Healthy
        Enclosure
                Product Id        : SGPIO
                Type              : SGPIO
                Status            : OK

        PD
                Connector         : Port 0 - 3<Internal>: Slot 3
                Vendor Id         : SEAGATE
                Product Id        : ST930003SSUN300G
                State             : Global HotSpare
                Disk Type         : SAS,Hard Disk Device
                Capacity          : 278.875 GB
                Power State       : Spun down

                Connector         : Port 0 - 3<Internal>: Slot 2
                Vendor Id         : SEAGATE
                Product Id        : ST930003SSUN300G
                State             : Online
```

```
            Disk Type              : SAS,Hard Disk Device
            Capacity               : 278.875 GB
            Power State            : Active

            Connector              : Port 0 - 3<Internal>: Slot 1
            Vendor Id              : SEAGATE
            Product Id             : ST930003SSUN300G
            State                  : Online
            Disk Type              : SAS,Hard Disk Device
            Capacity               : 278.875 GB
            Power State            : Active

            Connector              : Port 0 - 3<Internal>: Slot 0
            Vendor Id              : SEAGATE
            Product Id             : ST930003SSUN300G
            State                  : Online
            Disk Type              : SAS,Hard Disk Device
            Capacity               : 278.875 GB
            Power State            : Active

Storage

        Virtual Drives
            Virtual drive          : Target Id 0 ,VD name DBSYS
            Size                   : 557.75 GB
            State                  : Optimal
            RAID Level             : 5

Exit Code: 0x00
[root@cm01dbm01 ~]#
```

Based on this, we have four 300 GB drives—one hot spare and three active drives in slots 0, 1, and 2. The virtual drive created with the internal RAID controller matches up in size with the `fdisk` listing. Since our `df` listing indicates we're using logical volume management, we can do a `pvdisplay` to show our volume group name:

```
[root@cm01dbm01 ~]# pvdisplay
  --- Physical volume ---
  PV Name               /dev/sda2
  VG Name               VGExaDb
  PV Size               557.62 GB / not usable 1.64 MB
  Allocatable           yes
  PE Size (KByte)       4096
  Total PE              142751
  Free PE               103327
  Allocated PE          39424
  PV UUID               xKSxo7-k8Hb-HM52-iGoD-tMKC-Vhxl-OQuNFG
```

Note that the physical volume size equals the virtual drive size from the `MegaCli64` output. There's a single volume group created on /dev/sda2 called VGExaDB:

```
[root@cm01dbm01 ~]# vgdisplay | egrep '(VG Name|Alloc PE|Free PE)'
  VG Name               VGExaDb
  Alloc PE / Size       39424 / 154.00 GB
  Free  PE / Size       103327 / 403.62 GB
[root@cm01dbm01 ~]#
```

As you can see, there is approximately 400 GB of free space on the volume group. An `lvdisplay` shows the swap partition, LVDbSys1, and LVDbOra1, mounted to / and /u01, respectively:

```
[root@cm01dbm01 ~]# lvdisplay
  --- Logical volume ---
  LV Name                /dev/VGExaDb/LVDbSys1
  VG Name                VGExaDb
  LV UUID                wsj1Dc-MXvd-6haj-vCbO-I8dY-dlt9-18kCwu
  LV Write Access        read/write
  LV Status              available
  # open                 1
  LV Size                30.00 GB
  Current LE             7680
  Segments               1
  Allocation             inherit
  Read ahead sectors     auto
  - currently set to     256
  Block device           253:0

  --- Logical volume ---
  LV Name                /dev/VGExaDb/LVDbSwap1
  VG Name                VGExaDb
  LV UUID                iH64Ie-LJSq-hchp-h1sg-OPww-pTx5-jQpj6T
  LV Write Access        read/write
  LV Status              available
  # open                 1
  LV Size                24.00 GB
  Current LE             6144
  Segments               1
  Allocation             inherit
  Read ahead sectors     auto
  - currently set to     256
  Block device           253:1

  --- Logical volume ---
  LV Name                /dev/VGExaDb/LVDbOra1
  VG Name                VGExaDb
  LV UUID                CnRtDt-h6T3-iMFO-EZl6-OOHP-D6de-xZms6O
  LV Write Access        read/write
  LV Status              available
  # open                 1
  LV Size                100.00 GB
  Current LE             25600
```

```
Segments                1
Allocation              inherit
Read ahead sectors      auto
- currently set to      256
Block device            253:2
```

These logical volumes are mapped to /dev/mapper devices:

```
[root@cm01dbm01 ~]#  ls -ltar /dev/VGExaDb/LVDb*
lrwxrwxrwx 1 root root 28 Feb 20 21:59 /dev/VGExaDb/LVDbSys1 -> /dev/mapper/VGExaDb-LVDbSys1
lrwxrwxrwx 1 root root 29 Feb 20 21:59 /dev/VGExaDb/LVDbSwap1 -> /dev/mapper/VGExaDb-LVDbSwap1
lrwxrwxrwx 1 root root 28 Feb 20 21:59 /dev/VGExaDb/LVDbOra1 -> /dev/mapper/VGExaDb-LVDbOra1
[root@cm01dbm01 ~]#
```

How It Works

Each Exadata compute node in the Exadata X2-2 and X3-2 models contains four 300 GB SAS drives controlled with an LSI MegaRAID controller. Host operating system file systems are mounted from Linux logical volumes, which are built using volume groups that are based on the physical devices.

For the root and /u01 file systems, Oracle elected to employ the Linux kernel device mapper to map physical block devices to logical device names, which enables flexibility with logical volume management. Oracle does not, by default, use all of the physical space available; the volume groups have excess capacity, allowing an Exadata administrator to expand the size of /u01 if necessary, create LVM snapshots for backup and recovery purposes, and so forth.

1-6. Listing Flash Storage on the Exadata Storage Servers
Problem

As an Exadata administrator, you wish to better understand how flash storage is configured and presented on an ExadataStorage Server.

Solution

In this recipe, we will show you how to do the following:

- Query your SCSI flash device information using `lsscsi`
- List your PCI flash module configuration using `flash_dom`
- List your flash disk partition information using `fdisk`

From the storage server host's point of view, you can see your flash devices using `lsscsi`:

```
[root@cm01cel01 ~]# lsscsi -v|grep MARVELL
[8:0:0:0]    disk    ATA      MARVELL SD88SA02 D20Y   /dev/sdn
[8:0:1:0]    disk    ATA      MARVELL SD88SA02 D20Y   /dev/sdo
… Flash disks omitted for brevity
[11:0:3:0]   disk    ATA      MARVELL SD88SA02 D20Y   /dev/sdac
[root@cm01cel01 ~]#
```

CHAPTER 1 ■ EXADATA HARDWARE

The flash devices are split into groups of four, 8:,9:, 10:, and 11:; this is because each of the four flash cards have four FMods. Thus, every ExadataStorage Server will have (4 x 4) = 16 flash devices. You can also use flash_dom -l to display details for the PCI flash devices:

```
[root@cm01cel01 ~]# flash_dom -l
Aura Firmware Update Utility, Version 1.2.7
Copyright (c) 2009 Sun Microsystems, Inc. All rights reserved..
U.S. Government Rights - Commercial Software. Government users are subject
to the Sun Microsystems, Inc. standard license agreement and
applicable provisions of the FAR and its supplements.
Use is subject to license terms.
This distribution may include materials developed by third parties.
Sun, Sun Microsystems, the Sun logo, Sun StorageTek and ZFS are trademarks
or registered trademarks of Sun Microsystems, Inc. or its subsidiaries,
in the U.S. and other countries.

 HBA# Port Name         Chip Vendor/Type/Rev    MPT Rev  Firmware Rev  IOC    WWID
 Serial Number

 1.  /proc/mpt/ioc0     LSI Logic SAS1068E B3    105      011b5c00      0      5080020000f21140
 0111AP0-1051AU00C4

        Current active firmware version is 011b5c00 (1.27.92)
        Firmware image's version is MPTFW-01.27.92.00-IT
        x86 BIOS image's version is MPTBIOS-6.26.00.00 (2008.10.14)
        FCode image's version is MPT SAS FCode Version 1.00.49 (2007.09.21)

        D#  B   T  Type       Vendor    Product             Rev    Operating System Device Name
        1.  0   0  Disk       ATA       MARVELL SD88SA02    D20Y   /dev/sdn         [8:0:0:0]
        2.  0   1  Disk       ATA       MARVELL SD88SA02    D20Y   /dev/sdo         [8:0:1:0]
        3.  0   2  Disk       ATA       MARVELL SD88SA02    D20Y   /dev/sdp         [8:0:2:0]
        4.  0   3  Disk       ATA       MARVELL SD88SA02    D20Y   /dev/sdq         [8:0:3:0]

... Flash cards 2-4 omitted for brevity

[root@cm01cel01 ~]#
```

From CellCLI we can see how these flash devices are mapped to usable Exadata Flash entities:

```
CellCLI> list physicaldisk where disktype='FlashDisk' attributes name,disktype,physicalSize,
slotNumber
        FLASH_1_0      FlashDisk      22.8880615234375G      "PCI Slot: 1; FDOM: 0"
        FLASH_1_1      FlashDisk      22.8880615234375G      "PCI Slot: 1; FDOM: 1"
        FLASH_1_2      FlashDisk      22.8880615234375G      "PCI Slot: 1; FDOM: 2"
        FLASH_1_3      FlashDisk      22.8880615234375G      "PCI Slot: 1; FDOM: 3"
        FLASH_2_0      FlashDisk      22.8880615234375G      "PCI Slot: 2; FDOM: 0"
... Flash cards 2_1, 2_2, and 2_3 omitted
        FLASH_4_0      FlashDisk      22.8880615234375G      "PCI Slot: 4; FDOM: 0"
... Flash cards 4_1, 4_2, and 4_3 omitted
```

```
        FLASH_5_0         FlashDisk        22.8880615234375G        "PCI Slot: 5; FDOM: 0"
... Flash cards 5_1, 5_2, and 5_3 omitted

CellCLI>
```

Again, we can see the flash devices grouped in sets of four on PCI slots 1, 2, 4, and 5, with each device per PCI slot residing in FDOM 0, 1, 2, or 3. An fdisk output for one of the devices shows a 24.5 GB slice of storage. If we multiple this 24 GB by 16, we arrive at our total flash capacity of each storage cell at 384 GB:

```
[root@cm01cel01 ~]# fdisk -l /dev/sdz

Disk /dev/sdz: 24.5 GB, 24575868928 bytes
255 heads, 63 sectors/track, 2987 cylinders
Units = cylinders of 16065 * 512 = 8225280 bytes

Disk /dev/sdz doesn't contain a valid partition table
[root@cm01cel01 ~]#
```

How It Works

Exadata flash storage is provided by Sun Flash Accelerator F20 PCI flash cards. In the Exadata X2 models, there are four 96 GB PCI flash cards per storage cell, and on the X3-2 and X3-2 models, there are four 384 GB PCI flash cards per storage cell.

Each PCI flash card has a device partitioned per FDom, yielding 16 flash devices. These flash devices are manifested as ExadataStorage Server flash disks and used for Smart Flash Cache and Smart Flash Logging.

1-7. Gathering Configuration Information for the InfiniBandSwitches

Problem

As an Exadata administrator, you wish to better understand the configuration of your InfiniBand switches.

Solution

The quickest way to get a feel for how your InfiniBand switches are configured is to log in to the Web ILOM (Integrated Lights Out Management) interface. Figure 1-3 shows the InfiniBand firmware version details from the ILOM web interface:.

CHAPTER 1 ■ EXADATA HARDWARE

Figure 1-3. *InfiniBand firmware version from ILOM web interface*

Figure 1-4 displays the InfiniBand management network configuration.

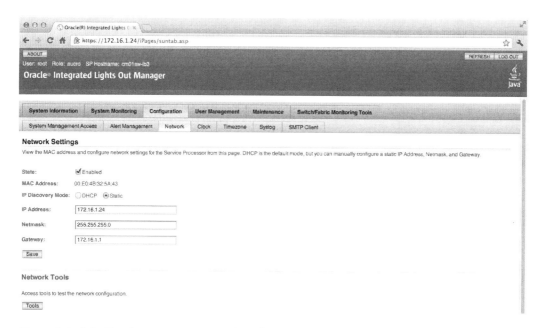

Figure 1-4. *InfiniBand management network configuration from ILOM web interface*

Now, log directly in to one of our InfiniBand switches as root and check your operating system version and release:

```
Macintosh-7:~ jclarke$ ssh root@cm01sw-ib2
root@cm01sw-ib2's password:
Last login: Sun Jul 22 02:34:23 2012 from 172.16.150.11
[root@cm01sw-ib2 ~]#uname -a
```

CHAPTER 1 ■ EXADATA HARDWARE

```
Linux cm01sw-ib2 2.6.27.13-nm2 #1 SMP Thu Feb 5 20:25:23 CET 2009 i686 i686 i386 GNU/Linux
[root@cm01sw-ib2 ~]# cat /etc./redhat-release
CentOS release 5.2 (Final)
[root@cm01sw-ib2 ~]#
```

The InfiniBand switches are running a 32-bit CentOS Linux operating system. The storage details can be displayed using df and fdisk commands, and show a small 471 MB root file system build on two internal disk drives.

```
[root@cm01sw-ib2 ~]# df -h
Filesystem            Size  Used Avail Use% Mounted on
/dev/hda2             471M  251M  197M  56% /
tmpfs                 250M   16K  250M   1% /dev/shm
tmpfs                 250M  228K  249M   1% /tmp
[root@cm01sw-ib2 ~]# fdisk -l

Disk /dev/hda: 512 MB, 512483328 bytes
255 heads, 63 sectors/track, 62 cylinders
Units = cylinders of 16065 * 512 = 8225280 bytes

   Device Boot      Start         End      Blocks   Id  System
/dev/hda1   *           1           1        8001   83  Linux
/dev/hda2               2          62      489982+  83  Linux
[root@cm01sw-ib2 ~]#
```

You can list InfiniBand version details by running the version command from the shell prompt on the InfiniBand switch:

```
[root@cm01sw-ib2 ~]# version
SUN DCS 36p version: 1.3.3-2
Build time: Apr  4 2011 11:15:19
SP board info:
Manufacturing Date: 2010.08.21
Serial Number: "NCD4V1753"
Hardware Revision: 0x0005
Firmware Revision: 0x0000
BIOS version: SUN0R100
BIOS date: 06/22/2010
[root@cm01sw-ib2 ~]#
```

The InfiniBand switches use an OpenSMInfiniBand subnet manager to manage the switch configuration. Details of the OpenSM configuration are contained in the /etc./opensm/opensm.conf file:

```
[root@cm01sw-ib2 opensm]# head -10 /etc/opensm/opensm.conf
#
# DEVICE ATTRIBUTES OPTIONS
#
# The port GUID on which the OpenSM is running
guid 0x0000000000000000

# M_Key value sent to all ports qualifying all Set(PortInfo)
m_key 0x0000000000000000
[root@cm01sw-ib2 opensm]#
```

How It Works

The Exadata compute servers communicate with the storage servers in the storage grid over InfiniBand. Additionally, the Oracle 11gR2 RAC cluster interconnect runs on the same InfiniBand network and over the same InfiniBand switches.

There are typically very few administrative tasks required on the InfiniBand switches. Periodically, as you patch Exadata, you may encounter the tasks of upgrading firmware on the InfiniBand switches. This has the effect of updating the firmware version and potentially changing the OpenSM configuration.

Both the storage servers and compute servers are dual-port connected to each of two InfiniBand leaf switches in an Exadata rack. In both cases, a bonded InfiniBand interface is created and enabled on the server.

CHAPTER 2

Exadata Software

Exadata's fast, balanced hardware configuration provides an Oracle infrastructure capable of delivering high performance for Oracle databases, but the hardware is only part of the equation. To truly deliver extreme performance, Oracle has designed and deployed several key software solutions inside Exadata, each of whose primary goal is to either reduce the demand for I/O resources or boost the speed of I/O operations. Oracle's performance goal with Exadata was to eliminate I/O as the bottleneck for database operations. Oracle has been successful in meeting this goal by not only leveraging performance capabilities with Oracle 11gR2 database, grid infrastructure, and Oracle ASM, but also by developing InfiniBand-aware I/O communication protocols into the Oracle software stack that fundamentally changes how Oracle performs physical I/O. Each of these Exadata software features works without application code modification and, under the right conditions, each of these can be used to deliver extreme performance.

This chapter will be centered on how Oracle 11gR2 software, database, and Automatic Storage Management (ASM) operates on an Oracle Exadata Database Machine, specifically focused on providing the reader with a technical understanding of Oracle on Exadata. In addition, we will include an introductory recipe that provides a description of some of Exadata's unique software features. Since Oracle's unique storage server software features are the keys to delivering extreme performance on Exadata, they will be covered in greater detail in Chapters 15 through 19.

2-1. Understanding the Role of Exadata Storage Server Software

Problem

As an Exadata owner or administrator, you've been sold on the extreme performance features that Exadata offers and wish to understand a brief summary of how these features will impact your workload.

Solution

In this recipe, we will provide a brief summary of what each of the unique Exadata Storage Server software features is designed to accomplish and point out any administrator or workload characteristic impact. Table 2-1 summarizes these additional Exadata software features.

CHAPTER 2 ■ EXADATA SOFTWARE

Table 2-1. *Exadata Storage Server software at a glance*

Software Feature	What It Does	How It's Used	Workload Impact	Reference
Smart Scan	Offloads I/O operations to storage servers	Used automatically for qualified SQL statements	Can dramatically improve performance for full-scan operations	Chapter 15
Hybrid Columnar Compression	Compresses tables	As administrator creates HCC table	Saves disk space and potentially I/O	Chapter 16
Smart Flash Cache	Provides 384 GB of PCI flash per storage cell on X2 and 1.6 TB of PCI flash on the X3 to reduce I/O latency	Implemented automatically and intelligently; only "smart" enabled operations and blocks are cached	Can provide performance improvements for OLTP applications and other workloads	Chapter 18
Smart Flash Logging	Utilizes a small chunk of PCI flash to cushion redo log writes	Used automatically when redo log writes to disk cache are saturated	Provides PCI flash- write speeds in the event disk cache is saturated, reducing likelihood for LGWR to become bottleneck	Chapter 18
Storage Indexes	Enables I/O requests to bypass storage regions on the Exadata cell, allowing queries to run faster	Storage server maintains high- and low-column values for predicate conditions enabling I/Os to be skipped	Can provide dramatic performance gains if data is well-sorted with respect to predicate conditions	Chapter 19
I/O Resource Management	Provides mechanism to prioritize and meter I/O to Exadata disk resources by database, consumer group, or category	IORM plans defined by administrator according to performance SLAs per database, category, or consumer group	Can enable I/O performance investment protection in consolidated environment	Chapter 17

How It Works

The Oracle Exadata Database Machine is a combination of balanced, fast hardware and unique Exadata Storage Server software. Exadata is designed for extreme performance for all database workloads, and the Exadata storage software is what enables the machine to deliver to these goals.

While Exadata's hardware configuration is designed to fully and evenly utilize the assorted hardware components that comprise the machine, the goal of the software is to reduce the demand for I/O resources by eliminating unnecessary operations. Each of Exadata's software features satisfies this goal in its own way:

- Smart Scan reduces storage interconnect traffic by eliminating unneeded rows and columns, improving query response times while reducing total CPU and memory requirements on the database server.
- Hybrid Columnar Compression reduces disk space usage and typically yields faster query times as fewer blocks are required to satisfy the same operation.
- Smart Flash Cache reduces physical disk I/O by caching data in PCI flash, which offers lower I/O latency than physical disks.
- Smart Flash Logging reduces write I/O to physical disks when the disk DRAM cache is saturated, cushioning redo writes in PCI flash.
- Storage Indexes enable Exadata to skip regions of storage without needing to actually read from disk.
- I/O Resource Management prioritizes I/O requests to more important resources higher than less important resources, enabling the critical databases to operate within the parameters of performance SLAs.

2-2. Validating Oracle 11gR2 Databases on Exadata

Problem

With help from Oracle ACS or a partner, you have just installed and configured the Oracle Exadata Database Machine in your environment and wish to validate the health and configuration of the Oracle 11gR2 database(s) on your platform. Specifically, you wish to understand how the Oracle RDBMS software and database installation is similar to or different from a non-Exadata Oracle 11gR2 installation on Linux.

Solution

On the Exadata compute servers or database servers, Oracle 11gR2 is installed and the database instances on each node are 11gR2 database instances. In this recipe, we will provide a number of steps to confirm Oracle software version information and Exadata-specific database configurations.

Begin by logging in to SQL*Plus on one of your Exadata databases and checking your Oracle version:

```
[oracle@cm01dbm01 ~]$ sqlplus / as sysdba
SQL*Plus: Release 11.2.0.3.0 Production on Fri Jul 27 01:40:00 2012
Copyright (c) 1982, 2011, Oracle.  All rights reserved.

Connected to:
Oracle Database 11g Enterprise Edition Release 11.2.0.3.0 - 64bit Production
With the Partitioning, Real Application Clusters, Automatic Storage Management, OLAP,
Data Mining and Real Application Testing options
```

CHAPTER 2 ■ EXADATA SOFTWARE

```
SQL> select * from v$version;

BANNER
--------------------------------------------------------------------------------
Oracle Database 11g Enterprise Edition Release 11.2.0.3.0 - 64bit Production
PL/SQL Release 11.2.0.3.0 - Production
CORE    11.2.0.3.0       Production
TNS for Linux: Version 11.2.0.3.0 - Production
NLSRTL Version 11.2.0.3.0 - Production

SQL>
```

From this output, you can see that you are running Oracle Enterprise Edition, 64-bit 11.2.0.3.0. If you query DBA_REGISTRY, you will see the various components installed, along with their versions, in this database:

```
SQL> select comp_name,version,status from dba_registry
  2 /

COMP_NAME                            VERSION                         STATUS
------------------------------------ ------------------------------- ----------
Oracle Expression Filter             11.2.0.3.0                      VALID
Oracle Enterprise Manager            11.2.0.3.0                      VALID
Oracle XML Database                  11.2.0.3.0                      VALID
Oracle Workspace Manager             11.2.0.3.0                      VALID
Oracle Database Catalog Views        11.2.0.3.0                      VALID
Oracle Database Packages and Types   11.2.0.3.0                      VALID
Oracle Real Application Clusters     11.2.0.3.0                      VALID
JServer JAVA Virtual Machine         11.2.0.3.0                      VALID
Oracle XDK                           11.2.0.3.0                      VALID
Oracle Database Java Packages        11.2.0.3.0                      VALID

10 rows selected.

SQL>
```

On Exadata, databases are typically clustered across compute server nodes with Oracle Real Application Clusters. You can validate this by checking your cluster-related database initialization parameters:

```
SQL> show parameter cluster

NAME                          TYPE         VALUE
----------------------------- ------------ ------------
cluster_database              boolean      TRUE
cluster_database_instances    integer      2
cluster_interconnects         string       192.168.10.1
SQL>
```

The cluster_inerconnects parameter, in this case, shows the InfiniBand IP address associated with the bonded InfiniBand interface on the instance's compute server.

Oracle databases on Exadata utilize the 11gR2 Grid Infrastructure. To manage or configure cluster resources on Exadata, use srvctl. The database resource configuration and bounce the database is displayed:

```
[oracle@cm01dbm01 ~]$ srvctl config database -d dwprd
Database unique name: dwprd
Database name: dwprd
Oracle home: /u01/app/oracle/product/11.2.0.3/dbhome_1
Oracle user: oracle
Spfile: +DATA_CM01/dwprd/spfiledwprd.ora
Domain:
Start options: open
Stop options: immediate
Database role: PRIMARY
Management policy: AUTOMATIC
Server pools: dwprd
Database instances: dwprd1,dwprd2
Disk Groups: DATA_CM01,RECO_CM01
Mount point paths:
Services:
Type: RAC
Database is administrator managed
[oracle@cm01dbm01 ~]$ srvctl stop database -d dwprd
[oracle@cm01dbm01 ~]$ srvctl start database -d dwprd
[oracle@cm01dbm01 ~]$ srvctl status database -d dwprd
Instance dwprd1 is running on node cm01dbm01
Instance dwprd2 is running on node cm01dbm02
[oracle@cm01dbm01 ~]$
```

All database storage on Exadata resides in Oracle Automated Storage Management, or Oracle ASM. You can run the query in Listing 2-1 to list the data files for the tablespaces in an Exadata database:

Listing 2-1. lst02-01-dbfiles.sql

```
SQL> select 'Data Files' type,substr(name,1,instr(name,'/',1,2)-1) asm_dg,count(*) cnt
from v$datafile
group by substr(name,1,instr(name,'/',1,2)-1)
union
select 'Temp Files',substr(name,1,instr(name,'/',1,2)-1) asm_dg, count(*) cnt
from v$tempfile
group by substr(name,1,instr(name,'/',1,2)-1)
union
select 'Redo Member',substr(member,1,instr(member,'/',1,2)-1) asm_dg, count(*) cnt
from v$logfile
group by substr(member,1,instr(member,'/',1,2)-1)
/

File Type         ASM Disk Location      Number of Files
--------------    --------------------   ---------------
Data Files        +DATA_CM01/visx                    239
Redo Member       +RECO_CM01/visx                      6
Temp Files        +DATA_CM01/visx                      5
```

You can see that in this database, the data files are stored in both the +DATA_CM01 and +RECO_CM01 ASM disk groups.

How It Works

As this recipe has hopefully demonstrated, the Oracle database on Exadata is just like any other Oracle 11gR2 database running Oracle Enterprise Edition with Oracle RAC and Oracle ASM. A database administrator can create, delete, and manage databases just as he or she would on a non-Exadata platform.

2-3. Validating Oracle 11gR2 Grid Infrastructure on Exadata
Problem

You've just installed your Exadata Database Machine and wish to understand the Grid Infrastructure details. Specifically, you wish to contrast Oracle Grid Infrastructure on Exadata with a Grid Infrastructure installation on non-Exadata environments.

Solution

In this recipe, we will examine Oracle Cluster Ready Services (CRS) configuration on Exadata. On Exadata, as is the case in non-Exadata systems, Oracle CRS runs as part of the Oracle 11gR2 Grid Infrastructure software stack.

Begin by logging in to a compute node server as the Grid Infrastructure software owner, which in our case is grid:

```
Macintosh-7:~ jclarke$ ssh grid@cm01dbm01
grid@cm01dbm01's password:
Last login: Mon Feb 20 23:03:49 2012 from cm01dbm02
The Oracle base has been set to /u01/app/grid
[grid@cm01dbm01 ~]$
```

We typically encourage setting an environment variable to specify the Grid Infrastructure software home. In this display, we've specified this as CRS_HOME:

```
[grid@cm01dbm01 ~]$ echo $CRS_HOME
/u01/app/11.2.0/grid
[grid@cm01dbm01 ~]$ grep CRS_HOME ~/.bash_profile
export CRS_HOME=/u01/app/11.2.0/grid
export ORACLE_HOME=$CRS_HOME
[grid@cm01dbm01 ~]$ cat /etc./oratab|grep ASM
+ASM1:/u01/app/11.2.0.3/grid:N
[grid@cm01dbm01 ~]$
```

We are also displaying the contents of /etc/oratab for our local Oracle ASM instance, which on the first compute node server is +ASM1. Oracle Grid Infrastructure is a collection of software and utilities designed to manage grid resources, such as database instances, Oracle ASM instances, grid network resources, and so forth. In other words, Grid Infrastructure is responsible for managing Oracle cluster resources. On an Exadata Database Machine with four Oracle RAC databases spread across two compute node servers, we can display our cluster resources using crsctl:

```
[grid@cm01dbm01 ~]$ $CRS_HOME/bin/crsctl stat res -t
```

```
--------------------------------------------------------------------------------
NAME              TARGET   STATE        SERVER                    STATE_DETAILS
--------------------------------------------------------------------------------
Local Resources
--------------------------------------------------------------------------------
ora.DATA_CM01.dg
                  ONLINE   ONLINE       cm01dbm01
                  ONLINE   ONLINE       cm01dbm02
ora.DBFS_DG.dg
                  ONLINE   ONLINE       cm01dbm01
                  ONLINE   ONLINE       cm01dbm02
ora.LISTENER.lsnr
                  ONLINE   ONLINE       cm01dbm01
                  ONLINE   ONLINE       cm01dbm02
... Addtional cluster resources omitted
```

We have abbreviated the previous output for sake of brevity, but if we format the output of crsctl using the following program, we can get an easy-to-read listing of our cluster resources, as displayed in Listing 2-2.

Listing 2-2. lst02-02-crsstat.sh

```
[grid@cm01dbm01 ~]$ cat /tmp/crsstat
#!/usr/bin/ksh
ORA_CRS_HOME=/u01/app/11.2.0.3/grid
RSC_KEY=$1
QSTAT=-u
AWK=/bin/awk       # if not available use /usr/bin/awk

# Table header:echo ""
$AWK \
  'BEGIN {printf "%-45s %-10s %-18s\n", "HA Resource", "Target", "State";
          printf "%-45s %-10s %-18s\n", "-----------", "------", "-----";}'

# Table body:
$ORA_CRS_HOME/bin/crs_stat $QSTAT | $AWK \
'BEGIN { FS="="; state = 0; }
  $1~/NAME/ && $2~/'$RSC_KEY'/ {appname = $2; state=1};
  state == 0 {next;}
  $1~/TARGET/ && state == 1 {apptarget = $2; state=2;}
  $1~/STATE/ && state == 2 {appstate = $2; state=3;}
  state == 3 {printf "%-45s %-10s %-18s\n", appname, apptarget, appstate;
state=0;}'

[grid@cm01dbm01 ~]$ crsstat
HA Resource                                   Target      State
-----------                                   ------      -----
ora.DATA_CM01.dg                              ONLINE      ONLINE on cm01dbm01
ora.DBFS_DG.dg                                ONLINE      ONLINE on cm01dbm01
ora.LISTENER.lsnr                             ONLINE      ONLINE on cm01dbm01
ora.LISTENER_SCAN1.lsnr                       ONLINE      ONLINE on cm01dbm02
ora.LISTENER_SCAN2.lsnr                       ONLINE      ONLINE on cm01dbm01
... Additional output omitted
[grid@cm01dbm01 ~]$
```

As you can see, we have multiple cluster resources in our cluster, including four databases, ASM instances, networks, SCAN listeners, ASM disk groups, Oracle Notification Services, and so on.

Oracle Grid Infrastructure cluster resources can be stopped and started using $CRS_HOME/bin/crsctl, just as you would with a non-Exadata Grid Infrastructure environment. Stop your cluster by running these commands:

```
[root@cm01dbm01 ~]# /u01/app/11.2.0.3/grid/bin/crsctl stop cluster -f -all
CRS-2673: Attempting to stop 'ora.crsd' on 'cm01dbm01'
CRS-2790: Starting shutdown of Cluster Ready Services-managed resources on 'cm01dbm01'
CRS-2673: Attempting to stop 'ora.DBFS_DG.dg' on 'cm01dbm01'
CRS-2673: Attempting to stop 'ora.registry.acfs' on 'cm01dbm01'
CRS-2673: Attempting to stop 'ora.dwprod.db' on 'cm01dbm01'
CRS-2673: Attempting to stop 'ora.dwprd.db' on 'cm01dbm01'
CRS-2673: Attempting to stop 'ora.visx.db' on 'cm01dbm01'
... lines omitted for brevity
CRS-2677: Stop of 'ora.cssd' on 'cm01dbm01' succeeded
CRS-2673: Attempting to stop 'ora.diskmon' on 'cm01dbm01'
CRS-2677: Stop of 'ora.diskmon' on 'cm01dbm01' succeeded
CRS-4688: Oracle Clusterware is already stopped on server 'cm01dbm02'
[root@cm01dbm01 ~]#
```

Stopping the cluster shuts down the cluster resources that Grid Infrastructure manages. You can see what processes are still running following a cluster shutdown:

```
[root@cm01dbm01 ~]# ps -ef|grep grid
root       7104     1  0 14:09 ?        00:00:02 /u01/app/11.2.0.3/grid/bin/ohasd.bin reboot
grid       8235     1  0 14:09 ?        00:00:00 /u01/app/11.2.0.3/grid/bin/oraagent.bin
grid       8247     1  0 14:09 ?        00:00:00 /u01/app/11.2.0.3/grid/bin/mdnsd.bin
grid       8257     1  0 14:09 ?        00:00:00 /u01/app/11.2.0.3/grid/bin/gpnpd.bin
root       8345     1  0 14:09 ?        00:00:08 /u01/app/11.2.0.3/grid/bin/orarootagent.bin
grid       8346     1  0 14:09 ?        00:00:02 /u01/app/11.2.0.3/grid/bin/gipcd.bin
root       8359     1  0 14:09 ?        00:00:02 /u01/app/11.2.0.3/grid/bin/osysmond.bin
root       9251     1  0 14:10 ?        00:00:00 /u01/app/11.2.0.3/grid/bin/ologgerd -m cm01dbm02 -r
-d /u01/app/11.2.0.3/grid/crf/db/cm01dbm01
root      10186 28645  0 14:51 pts/0    00:00:00 grep grid
grid      15037     1  0 14:15 ?        00:00:00 /u01/app/11.2.0.3/grid/ccr/bin/nmz -cron -silent
[root@cm01dbm01 ~]#
```

To shut down all of the Grid Infrastructure cluster components, run crsctl stop crs:

```
[root@cm01dbm01 ~]# /u01/app/11.2.0.3/grid/bin/crsctl stop crs
CRS-2791: Starting shutdown of Oracle High Availability Services-managed resources on 'cm01dbm01'
CRS-2673: Attempting to stop 'ora.mdnsd' on 'cm01dbm01'
CRS-2673: Attempting to stop 'ora.drivers.acfs' on 'cm01dbm01'
CRS-2673: Attempting to stop 'ora.crf' on 'cm01dbm01'
CRS-2677: Stop of 'ora.drivers.acfs' on 'cm01dbm01' succeeded
CRS-2677: Stop of 'ora.mdnsd' on 'cm01dbm01' succeeded
CRS-2677: Stop of 'ora.crf' on 'cm01dbm01' succeeded
CRS-2673: Attempting to stop 'ora.gipcd' on 'cm01dbm01'
CRS-2677: Stop of 'ora.gipcd' on 'cm01dbm01' succeeded
CRS-2673: Attempting to stop 'ora.gpnpd' on 'cm01dbm01'
CRS-2677: Stop of 'ora.gpnpd' on 'cm01dbm01' succeeded
CRS-2793: Shutdown of Oracle High Availability Services-managed resources on 'cm01dbm01' has
```

```
completed
CRS-4133: Oracle High Availability Services has been stopped.
[root@cm01dbm01 ~]#
```

To start your cluster resources, run the command on each compute node:

```
[root@cm01dbm01 ~]# /u01/app/11.2.0.3/grid/bin/crsctl start crs
CRS-4123: Oracle High Availability Services has been started.
[root@cm01dbm01 ~]#
```

How It Works

Exadata compute server nodes run Oracle Enterprise Edition 11gR2 Grid Infrastructure to facilitate and manage databases and other resources or processes across the compute grid. From a technical perspective, the installation, configuration, and administration of Grid Infrastructure on Exadata is identical to Grid Infrastructure on non-Exadata systems. Generally speaking, most companies segregate ownership of processes and software by running the Grid Infrastructure components with a different Linux account than the account that owns the Oracle 11gR2 RDBMS software and database instances, but this is not required.

An administrator manages Grid Infrastructure components the same way he or she would on a non-Exadata 11gR2 Grid Infrastructure environment. This is a key benefit of Exadata from an operational labor standpoint; if you have Oracle administrators who understand and are trained on Oracle 11gR2, Grid Infrastructure, and Oracle Real Application Clusters, you should be well-prepared to confidently manage your Oracle Exadata compute infrastructure.

On Exadata, Oracle has elected to store the Oracle Cluster Registry (OCR) and voting disks on Oracle ASM disk groups, mapped to Exadata storage server grid disks. Most processes in Exadata's Oracle 11gR2 Grid infrastructure perform the same functions as non-Exadata 11gR2 installations, but one software component that plays a special role in Exadata environments is the diskmon process and associated processes:

```
[root@cm01dbm01 ~]# ps -ef|egrep '(diskmon|dsk)'
root       884 23558  0 11:09 pts/0    00:00:00 egrep (diskmon|dsk)
grid     20500     1  0 Jul27 ?        00:01:00 /u01/app/11.2.0.3/grid/bin/diskmon.bin -d -f
grid     21408     1  0 Jul27 ?        00:00:00 asm_dskm_+ASM1
oracle   22179     1  0 Jul27 ?        00:00:01 ora_dskm_visx1
oracle   22217     1  0 Jul27 ?        00:00:01 ora_dskm_dwprd1
oracle   31932     1  0 Jul28 ?        00:00:00 ora_dskm_visy1
[root@cm01dbm01 ~]#
```

diskmon itself runs on all Oracle 11gR2 installations, but it only serves a true purpose on Exadata. Its role is to monitor storage network and cell monitoring processes, validate that the storage cells are alive, handle storage failures and I/O fencing, monitor and control messages from database and ASM instances to storage cells, and send database resource management plans to storage servers. In addition to the master diskmon process, each database instance on the compute nodes run a single ora_dskm slave process as previously displayed.

Along with diskmon, two additional ASM processes perform a role on the Exadata compute servers: xdmg and xdwk:

- XDMG monitors configured Exadata storage cells for storage state changes and performs whatever events are required with ASM disks based on these state changes.

- XDWK is started whenever state changes take place, such as when ASM disk DROP, ADD, or ONLINE operations are performed. It runs asynchronously and shuts down automatically after a period of inactivity.

You can see the xdmg and xdwk processes running on an Exadata compute nodes during a time after a cell server's grid disks are inactivated and subsequently activated:

```
[grid@cm01dbm01 ~]$ ps -ef|grep -i xd|grep -v grep
grid     15387     1  0 11:28 ?        00:00:00 asm_xdwk_+ASM1
grid     21441     1  0 Jul27 ?        00:00:10 asm_xdmg_+ASM1
[grid@cm01dbm01 ~]$
```

2-4. Locating the Oracle Cluster Registry and Voting Disks on Exadata

Problem

You wish to determine the location and configuration of your Oracle Cluster Registry and voting disks on Oracle Exadata.

Solution

The Oracle 11gR2 Cluster Registry (OCR) and voting disks are stored on Oracle ASM disk groups on Exadata. In an Oracle 11gR2 Grid Infrastructure environment running Oracle Clusterware, regardless of whether you are on Exadata or not, the OCR location is specified in /etc/oracle/ocr.loc. Begin by logging in to a compute node and checking the contents of your ocr.loc file:

```
[root@cm01dbm01 ~]# locate ocr.loc
/etc/oracle/ocr.loc
 [root@cm01dbm01 ~]# cat  /etc/oracle/ocr.loc
ocrconfig_loc=+DBFS_DG
local_only=FALSE
[root@cm01dbm01 ~]#
```

As you can see, the OCR is contained in the DBFS_DG ASM disk group. Starting with Oracle 11gR2, you can store your OCR inside an ASM disk group, and on Exadata this is the default and preferred. You can run ocrcheck from the Grid Infrastructure Oracle software location to examine additional details about your OCR:

```
[root@cm01dbm01 ~]# /u01/app/11.2.0.3/grid/bin/ocrcheck
Status of Oracle Cluster Registry is as follows :
         Version                  :          3
         Total space (kbytes)     :     262120
         Used space (kbytes)      :       3500
         Available space (kbytes) :     258620
         ID                       : 1833511320
         Device/File Name         :    +DBFS_DG
                                    Device/File integrity check succeeded
                                    Device/File not configured
                                    Device/File not configured
                                    Device/File not configured
                                    Device/File not configured
         Cluster registry integrity check succeeded
         Logical corruption check succeeded
[root@cm01dbm01 ~]#
```

As with non-Exadata Grid Infrastructure installations, Oracle automatically makes a backup of the OCR every four hours, and you can find the backup location and backup details using ocrconfig -showbackup:

CHAPTER 2 ■ EXADATA SOFTWARE

```
[root@cm01dbm01 ~]# /u01/app/11.2.0.3/grid/bin/ocrconfig -showbackup
cm01dbm01     2012/07/27 12:59:47     /u01/app/11.2.0.3/grid/cdata/cm01-cluster/backup00.ocr
cm01dbm01     2012/07/27 08:59:47     /u01/app/11.2.0.3/grid/cdata/cm01-cluster/backup01.ocr
cm01dbm01     2012/07/27 04:59:46     /u01/app/11.2.0.3/grid/cdata/cm01-cluster/backup02.ocr
cm01dbm01     2012/07/26 04:59:45     /u01/app/11.2.0.3/grid/cdata/cm01-cluster/day.ocr
cm01dbm01     2012/07/13 20:59:24     /u01/app/11.2.0.3/grid/cdata/cm01-cluster/week.ocr
cm01dbm01     2011/05/03 16:11:19     /u01/app/11.2.0/grid/cdata/cm01-cluster/
backup_20110503_161119.ocr
[root@cm01dbm01 ~]#
```

On Exadata, the clusterware voting disks are also stored in an Oracle ASM disk group, as indicated:

```
[root@cm01dbm01 ~]# /u01/app/11.2.0.3/grid/bin/crsctl query css votedisk
##  STATE    File Universal Id                File Name                                          Disk group
--  -----    ----------------                 ---------                                          ----------
 1. ONLINE   948f35d3d9c44f94bfe7bb831758104a  (o/192.168.10.4/DBFS_DG_CD_06_cm01cel02)  [DBFS_DG]
 2. ONLINE   61fb620328a24f87bf8c4a0ac0275cd1  (o/192.168.10.5/DBFS_DG_CD_05_cm01cel03)  [DBFS_DG]
 3. ONLINE   0bfafeda13974f16bf4d90ef6317aa7f  (o/192.168.10.3/DBFS_DG_CD_05_cm01cel01)  [DBFS_DG]
Located 3 voting disk(s).
[root@cm01        dbm01 ~]
```

You can see that Exadata builds three copies of the voting disk, each stored in the DBFS_DG ASM disk group, with copies on each of your three Exadata Storage Servers.

■ **Note** On Exadata Half Rack and Full Rack models, Oracle will create three copies of the voting disk on the first three grid disks containing the DBFS_DG disk group and not containing the System Area.

How It Works

On Exadata, Oracle has elected to store the Oracle Cluster Registry (OCR) and voting disks on Oracle ASM disk groups, mapped to Exadata storage server grid disks. The OCR and voting disks are typically stored in the DBFS_DG ASM disk group and associated grid disks.

It is worth mentioning Oracle's rationale for placing the OCR and voting disks in the DBFS_DG ASM disk group. Based on our experience, which started with Oracle Exadata X2-2 models in late 2010, a default Exadata installation will create and configure storage server grid disks and associated ASM disk groups based on customer requirements. It will also create a set of grid disks prefixed with DBFS_DG, intended for use with Oracle DBFS ASM disk groups. Contrary to the other grid disks, which span all 12 cell disks on all storage server nodes, the DBFS_DG grid disks are only built on the 10 cell disks that do not contain the storage cell's System Area. This is Oracle's solution to addressing a potential "gap" of unusable capacity.

```
CellCLI> list griddisk where name like 'DBFS_DG_.*' attributes name,cellDisk,size
         DBFS_DG_CD_02_cm01cel01          CD_02_cm01cel01          29.125G
         DBFS_DG_CD_03_cm01cel01          CD_03_cm01cel01          29.125G
         DBFS_DG_CD_04_cm01cel01          CD_04_cm01cel01          29.125G
         DBFS_DG_CD_05_cm01cel01          CD_05_cm01cel01          29.125G
         DBFS_DG_CD_06_cm01cel01          CD_06_cm01cel01          29.125G
         DBFS_DG_CD_07_cm01cel01          CD_07_cm01cel01          29.125G
         DBFS_DG_CD_08_cm01cel01          CD_08_cm01cel01          29.125G
         DBFS_DG_CD_09_cm01cel01          CD_09_cm01cel01          29.125G
         DBFS_DG_CD_10_cm01cel01          CD_10_cm01cel01          29.125G
```

CHAPTER 2 ■ EXADATA SOFTWARE

```
          DBFS_DG_CD_11_cm01cel01        CD_11_cm01cel01         29.125G
CellCLI>
```

Note that cell disks 00 and 01 are missing from the above grid disk listing. Building `DBFS_DG` grid disks on the remaining cell disks is Oracle's way of attempting to maximize capacity utilization across physical disks in an Exadata storage cell, and it happens to also be a convenient, but not required, location for the OCR file and voting disks.

■ **Note**   To learn more about how storage entities are defined on Exadata Storage Servers, please refer to Recipes 1-4, 3-1, and 3-2.

2-5. Validating Oracle 11gR2 Real Application Clusters Installation and Database Storage on Exadata
Problem

As an Exadata Database Machine administrator, or DMA, you wish to validate the Oracle Real Application Clusters configuration on your Exadata compute servers.

Solution

This recipe will focus on validating your Oracle 11gR2 Real Application Clusters installation and database storage on Oracle Exadata. Specifically, you will complete the following steps:

1. Log in to an Exadata compute node.
2. Check the status of the cluster resources.
3. Ensure that none of your resources are OFFLINE.
4. Check your Oracle CRS version and confirm that it conforms with your current Exadata software versions.
5. Query configuration information about one of your databases running on the compute node.
6. List Oracle ASM storage configuration for one of your databases.

Begin by logging in to one of our compute servers and listing your Oracle Clusterware resources:

```
Macintosh-7:~ jclarke$ ssh root@cm01dbm01
root@cm01dbm01's password:
Last login: Fri Jul 27 14:32:42 2012 from 172.16.150.10
[root@cm01dbm01 ~]# /u01/app/11.2.0.3/grid/bin/crsctl stat res -t
--------------------------------------------------------------------------------
NAME           TARGET  STATE        SERVER                   STATE_DETAILS
--------------------------------------------------------------------------------
Local Resources
--------------------------------------------------------------------------------
ora.DATA_CM01.dg
```

```
                    ONLINE   ONLINE        cm01dbm01
                    ONLINE   ONLINE        cm01dbm02
ora.DBFS_DG.dg
                    ONLINE   ONLINE        cm01dbm01
                    ONLINE   ONLINE        cm01dbm02
ora.LISTENER.lsnr
                    ONLINE   ONLINE        cm01dbm01
                    ONLINE   ONLINE        cm01dbm02
ora.RECO_CM01.dg
                    ONLINE   ONLINE        cm01dbm01
                    ONLINE   ONLINE        cm01dbm02
... Additional CRS resources omitted
[root@cm01dbm01 ~]#
```

As you can see, we have several Oracle Clusterware resources running under Oracle Grid Infrastructure CRS services. Query your Oracle CRS version by running crsctl query crs activeversion:

```
[root@cm01dbm01 ~]# /u01/app/11.2.0.3/grid/bin/crsctl query crs activeversion
Oracle Clusterware active version on the cluster is [11.2.0.3.0]
[root@cm01dbm01 ~]#
```

From this listing, we know that on this Exadata compute server we're running Oracle Clusterware 11.2.0.3.0. From the crs_stat output, we see four database resources (one of which is shut down), ASM resources, and Grid Infrastructure network resources.

You can examine the resource configuration of one of your databases using srvctl:

```
[oracle@cm01dbm01 ~]$ srvctl config database -d visx
Database unique name: visx
Database name: visx
Oracle home: /u01/app/oracle/product/11.2.0.3/dbhome_1
Oracle user: oracle
Spfile: +DATA_CM01/visx/spfilevisx.ora
Domain:
Start options: open
Stop options: immediate
Database role: PRIMARY
Management policy: AUTOMATIC
Server pools: visx
Database instances: visx1,visx2
Disk Groups: DATA_CM01,RECO_CM01
Mount point paths:
Services:
Type: RAC
Database is administrator managed
[oracle@cm01dbm01 ~]$
```

Our VISX database consists of two instances, visx1 and visx2, configured with Oracle RAC. We can also see that this database uses the DATA_CM01 and RECO_CM01 ASM disk groups, the binary server parameter file (spfile) resides in the DATA_CM01 ASM disk group, as well as the instance's Oracle software home. Let's validate which server each instance runs on:

```
[oracle@cm01dbm01 ~]$ srvctl status database -d visx
```

```
Instance visx1 is running on node cm01dbm01
Instance visx2 is running on node cm01dbm02
[oracle@cm01dbm01 ~]$ nslookup cm01dbm01
sServer:            11.11.1.250
Address:            11.11.1.250#53

Name:     cm01dbm01.centroid.com
Address: 172.16.1.10

[oracle@cm01dbm01 ~]$ nslookup cm01dbm02
Server:             11.11.1.250
Address:            11.11.1.250#53

Name:     cm01dbm02.centroid.com
Address: 172.16.1.11

[oracle@cm01dbm01 ~]$
```

We know from Oracle documentation that database storage on Exadata is achieved solely using Oracle ASM, so let's take a look at some of our tablespace data file storage:

```
SYS @ visx1> select tablespace_name,file_name
from dba_data_files
where rownum < 6
/

TABLESPACE_NAME           FILE_NAME
-------------------       ------------------------------------------------------------
SYSTEM                    +DATA_CM01/visx/datafile/system.329.784250757
APPS_TS_TX_DATA           +DATA_CM01/visx/datafile/apps_ts_tx_data.321.784250567
APPS_TS_TX_IDX            +DATA_CM01/visx/datafile/apps_ts_tx_idx.378.784251053
UNDO_TBS                  +DATA_CM01/visx/datafile/undo_tbs.259.784250095
APPS_TS_NOLOGGING         +DATA_CM01/visx/datafile/apps_ts_nologging.415.784251657

5 rows selected.
```

Our tablespaces are stored in an ASM disk group called DATA_CM01. Let's examine the disks that make up this ASM disk group:

```
SYS @ visx1> select a.name,b.path,b.state,a.type,b.failgroup
    from v$asm_diskgroup a, v$asm_disk b
    where a.group_number=b.group_number
    and a.name='DATA_CM01'
    order by 2,1
 /

Disk Group   Disk                                      State       TYPE      Failgroup
----------   ---------------------------------------   ---------   ------    -----------
DATA_CM01    o/192.168.10.3/DATA_CD_00_cm01cel01       NORMAL      NORMAL    CM01CEL01
DATA_CM01    o/192.168.10.3/DATA_CD_01_cm01cel01       NORMAL      NORMAL    CM01CEL01
DATA_CM01    o/192.168.10.3/DATA_CD_02_cm01cel01       NORMAL      NORMAL    CM01CEL01
```

```
DATA_CM01        o/192.168.10.3/DATA_CD_03_cm01cel01    NORMAL    NORMAL    CM01CEL01
DATA_CM01        o/192.168.10.3/DATA_CD_04_cm01cel01    NORMAL    NORMAL    CM01CEL01
... ASM disks omitted for brevity

36 rows selected.
```

We can see that DATA_CM01 is built on Exadata grid disks spanning each of three storage servers in our Exadata Quarter Rack (InfiniBand IP addresses 192.168.10.3, 192.168.10.4, and 192.168.10.5). When building ASM disk groups, the candidate storage servers are provided by a list of IP addresses in cellip.ora:

```
[grid@cm01dbm01 ~]$ locate cellip.ora
/etc/oracle/cell/network-config/cellip.ora
/opt/oracle.SupportTools/onecommand/tmp/cellip.ora
[grid@cm01dbm01 ~]$ cat /etc/oracle/cell/network-config/cellip.ora
cell="192.168.10.3"
cell="192.168.10.4"
cell="192.168.10.5"
[grid@cm01dbm01 ~]$
```

■ **Note** For more information about how Oracle ASM disks map to Exadata grid disks, please see Recipe 3-2.

As discussed in Recipe 2-3, the diskmon process on the Exadata compute nodes also plays a role on Exadata environments. diskmon is responsible for handling storage network and cell monitoring processes and spawns slave processes to handle I/O-related cell events and message broadcasting.

How It Works

For those of you who are familiar with Oracle 11gR2 Real Application Cluster, you'll find that on Exadata the overall Oracle RAC software architecture is the same as in non-Exadata clusters. There are, however, a few configuration details unique to Exadata with respect to database storage. Specifically, database storage is achieved exclusively with Oracle ASM. The disks that comprise Exadata disk groups are addressable using InfiniBand-aware naming conventions.

2-6. Validating Oracle 11gR2 Real Application Clusters Networking on Exadata

Problem

As an Exadata Database Machine administrator, or DMA, you wish to validate the Oracle Real Application Clusters network installation on your Exadata compute servers.

Solution

Exadata compute servers have three, and optionally four, types of networks: the InfiniBand network, the administration network, the client access network, and an optional additional network. For the purposes of the Oracle

RAC discussion, the relevant networks are the InfiniBand network and the client access network. In this recipe, you will do the following:

1. Learn how to display your server network interface details.
2. Validate your Oracle CRS interconnect resources.
3. List Oracle RAC/Grid Infrastructure network information.
4. Validate your network routing tables.
5. Confirm the Oracle RDS network protocol is used for Oracle RAC interconnect traffic.
6. Query your SCAN and SCAN listener configuration.
7. List your database listener and Virtual IP configuration.
8. Check your cluster_interconnects and listener-related database instance initialization parameters.

On Exadata, the Oracle RAC private interconnect runs on the InfiniBand network, which is the same network that Exadata's storage network runs on. This InfiniBand private interconnect runs on a bonded InfiniBand interface: bondib0. To validate this, log in to your compute server as root and run ifconfig on the bonded InfiniBand interface:

```
[root@cm01dbm01 ~]# ifconfig bondib0
bondib0   Link encap:InfiniBand  HWaddr 80:00:00:48:FE:80:00:00:00:00:00:00:00:00:00:00:00:00:00:00
          inet addr:192.168.10.1  Bcast:192.168.11.255  Mask:255.255.252.0
... Additional interface details omitted
[root@cm01dbm01 ~]#
```

The Oracle RAC interconnect is deployed using Oracle's Cluster High Availability IP framework, or HAIP. We can find the details of the Cluster HAIP by querying the relevant cluster resource:

```
[root@cm01dbm01 ~]# /u01/app/11.2.0.3/grid/bin/crsctl stat res -init -w "TYPE = ora.haip.type"
NAME=ora.cluster_interconnect.haip
TYPE=ora.haip.type
TARGET=ONLINE
STATE=ONLINE on cm01dbm01
[root@cm01dbm01 ~]#
```

■ **Note** In the above crsctl query, the -init argument lists the core Oracle CRS processes, such as ora.crsd, ora.cssd, ora.cluster_interconnect.haip, and so forth. The -w argument provides a means to display only a specific section of the resource by name. In the previous example, we are displaying the Oracle CRS processes where TYPE = ora.haip.type.

Using oifcfg, you can find where Oracle places the InfiniBand network. You see that the cluster interconnect is on network 192.168.8.0, the bondib0 interface:

```
[root@cm01dbm01 ~]# /u01/app/11.2.0.3/grid/bin/oifcfg getif
bondib0   192.168.8.0  global  cluster_interconnect
bondeth0  172.16.1.0   global  public
[root@cm01dbm01 ~]#
```

You can also log in to either a database instance or ASM instance to validate the cluster_interconnects initialization parameter. Next, you see the 192.168.10.1 and 192.168.10.2 IP addresses, which in this case, correspond to both of the two compute nodes in our Exadata Quarter Rack:

```
[grid@cm01dbm01 ~]$ sqlplus / as sysasm
SQL*Plus: Release 11.2.0.3.0 Production on Fri Jul 27 17:54:42 2012
Copyright (c) 1982, 2011, Oracle.  All rights reserved.

Connected to:
Oracle Database 11g Enterprise Edition Release 11.2.0.3.0 - 64bit Production
With the Real Application Clusters and Automatic Storage Management options

SQL> select * from gv$cluster_interconnects;

INST_ID NAME         IP_ADDRESS       IS_  SOURCE
------- ------------ ---------------- ---- ------------------------------
      1 bondib0      192.168.10.1     NO   cluster_interconnects parameter
      2 bondib0      192.168.10.2     NO   cluster_interconnects parameter

SQL>
```

If you examine your routing tables on an Exadata compute node server, you will see the destinations on the 192.168.8.0 subnet route through the bondib0 interface:

```
[root@cm01dbm01 ~]# route -v
Kernel IP routing table
Destination     Gateway         Genmask          Flags Metric Ref    Use Iface
172.16.20.0     *               255.255.255.0    U     0      0        0 eth3
172.16.1.0      *               255.255.255.0    U     0      0        0 eth0
172.16.10.0     *               255.255.255.0    U     0      0        0 bondeth0
192.168.8.0     *               255.255.252.0    U     0      0        0 bondib0
169.254.0.0     *               255.255.0.0      U     0      0        0 bondib0
default         172.16.10.1     0.0.0.0          UG    0      0        0 bondeth0
[root@cm01dbm01 ~]#
```

As stated, the Oracle interconnect traffic is over the InfiniBand network. You can confirm this by running skgxpinfo from the 11gR2 Grid Infrastructure software directory:

```
[grid@cm01dbm01 ~]$ which skgxpinfo
/u01/app/11.2.0.3/grid/bin/skgxpinfo
[grid@cm01dbm01 ~]$ /u01/app/11.2.0.3/grid/bin/skgxpinfo -v
Oracle RDS/IP (generic)
[grid@cm01dbm01 ~]$
```

This shows that the communication protocol is using Oracle RDS/IP. RDS is the InfiniBand protocol. If you contrast with an 11gR2 environment not running on Exadata, you will see that the interconnect runs over UDP:

CHAPTER 2 ■ EXADATA SOFTWARE

```
[oracle@rac1 ~]$ skgxpinfo -v
Oracle UDP/IP (generic)
[oracle@rac1 ~]$
```

■ **Note** To learn more about Exadata networking topics and how Exadata differs from non-Exadata Oracle RAC deployments, please see Recipes 3-5 and the recipes in Chapter 10.

With Oracle RAC, the client access network is the network upon which listeners, VIPs, and SCAN listeners run. From our oifcfg getif output, we see this network is on the 172.16.1.0 network:

```
[grid@cm01dbm01 ~]$ oifcfg getif
bondib0  192.168.8.0  global  cluster_interconnect
bondeth0  172.16.1.0  global  public
[grid@cm01dbm01 ~]$
```

You can take a closer look at the configuration of our network resources by using srvctl. First, run a srvctl config network:

```
[root@cm01dbm01 ~]# /u01/app/11.2.0.3/grid/bin/srvctl config network
Network exists: 1/172.16.10.0/255.255.255.0/bondeth0, type static
[root@cm01dbm01 ~]#
```

This output shows that the client access network for our Oracle RAC network resources is on the 172.16.10.0 network. Now examine your SCAN (Single Client Access Network) configuration and SCAN listener configuration:

```
[root@cm01dbm01 ~]# /u01/app/11.2.0.3/grid/bin/srvctl config scan
SCAN name: cm01-scan, Network: 1/172.16.10.0/255.255.255.0/bondeth0
SCAN VIP name: scan1, IP: /cm01-scan/172.16.10.16
SCAN VIP name: scan2, IP: /cm01-scan/172.16.10.15
SCAN VIP name: scan3, IP: /cm01-scan/172.16.10.14
[root@cm01dbm01 ~]# /u01/app/11.2.0.3/grid/bin/srvctl config scan_listener
SCAN Listener LISTENER_SCAN1 exists. Port: TCP:1521
SCAN Listener LISTENER_SCAN2 exists. Port: TCP:1521
SCAN Listener LISTENER_SCAN3 exists. Port: TCP:1521
[root@cm01dbm01 ~]#
```

We can see that our SCAN is defined with DNS name cm01-scan, using IP addresses 172.16.10.14, 172.16.10.15, and 172.16.10.16. There are three SCAN listeners called LISTENER_SCAN[1-3] listening on port 1521. Knowing that 11gR2 Clusterware/RAC distributes SCAN listeners on available nodes in a cluster, we can determine which of our two compute node servers the SCAN listeners are running on. Note that one SCAN listener is running on cm01dbm02 and two are running on cm01dbm01:

```
[root@cm01dbm01 ~]# /u01/app/11.2.0.3/grid/bin/crsctl stat res -w "TYPE = ora.scan_listener.type"
NAME=ora.LISTENER_SCAN1.lsnr
TYPE=ora.scan_listener.type
TARGET=ONLINE
STATE=ONLINE on cm01dbm02

NAME=ora.LISTENER_SCAN2.lsnr
```

```
TYPE=ora.scan_listener.type
TARGET=ONLINE
STATE=ONLINE on cm01dbm01

NAME=ora.LISTENER_SCAN3.lsnr
TYPE=ora.scan_listener.type
TARGET=ONLINE
STATE=ONLINE on cm01dbm01

[root@cm01dbm01 ~]#
```

Our database listener, LISTENER, is running on port 1521 and managed by CRS as well. From the compute node where we're running two SCAN listeners and a database LISTENER, we see the following:

```
[grid@cm01dbm01 ~]$ srvctl config listener
Name: LISTENER
Network: 1, Owner: grid
Home: <CRS home>
End points: TCP:1521
[grid@cm01dbm01 ~]$ ps -ef|grep tnsl
grid     14924 14310  0 20:59 pts/0    00:00:00 grep tnsl
grid     21887     1  0 15:03 ?        00:00:00 /u01/app/11.2.0.3/grid/bin/tnslsnr
LISTENER_SCAN3 -inherit
grid     21892     1  0 15:03 ?        00:00:00 /u01/app/11.2.0.3/grid/bin/tnslsnr
LISTENER_SCAN2 -inherit
grid     21904     1  0 15:03 ?        00:00:00 /u01/app/11.2.0.3/grid/bin/tnslsnr
LISTENER -inherit
[grid@cm01dbm01 ~]$
```

In 11gR2, Oracle RAC Virtual IP Addresses, or VIPs, can be listed by running `srvctl config nodeapps`. In the following script, we see two VIPs—one on each compute server—on interfaces with the IP addresses 172.16.10.12 and 172.16.10.13, respectively:

```
[grid@cm01dbm01 ~]$ srvctl config nodeapps
Network exists: 1/172.16.10.0/255.255.255.0/bondeth0, type static
VIP exists: /cm0101-vip/172.16.10.12/172.16.10.0/255.255.255.0/bondeth0, hosting node cm01dbm01
VIP exists: /cm0102-vip/172.16.10.13/172.16.10.0/255.255.255.0/bondeth0, hosting node cm01dbm02
GSD exists
ONS exists: Local port 6100, remote port 6200, EM port 2016
[grid@cm01dbm01 ~]$
```

Finally, inside our databases on Exadata, we will have the `local_listener` and `remote_listener` initialization parameters defined with the VIP listener address and SCAN address, respectively:

```
SYS @ visx1> show parameter listener

NAME                           TYPE         VALUE
------------------------------ ------------ ------------------------------
listener_networks              string
local_listener                 string       (DESCRIPTION=(ADDRESS_LIST=(ADDRESS=
                                            (PROTOCOL=TCP)(HOST=172.16.10.12)
                                            (PORT=1521))))
remote_listener                string       cm01-scan:1521
SYS @ visx1>
```

How It Works

For those of you who are familiar with Oracle 11gR2 Real Application Cluster, you'll find that the networking architecture on Exadata is similar to non-Exadata Oracle 11gR2 RAC environments. There are, however, some key differences that are unique to Exadata. Specifically, database storage is exclusively achieved with Oracle ASM over the InfiniBand network to the storage cells and the Oracle RAC interconnect traffic utilizes the high-speed InfiniBand network over Oracle's RDS network protocol.

As mentioned above, assorted Oracle RDBMS and network binaries are linked to use the RDS protocol, and running skgxpinfo on Exadata demonstrates this.

When attempting to understand how Exadata is allowed to use an InfiniBand-aware (iDB/RDS) disk strings when creating ASM disk groups, this too is also quite simple. If Oracle can find a valid version of /etc/oracle/cell/network-config/cellip.ora, you will be able to create ASM disk groups using the 'o/<IP>/<Grid Disk>' disk string.

In the Solution section of this recipe, you may have noticed that the bonded InfiniBand interface, bondib0, uses the 192.168.8.0/22 network with hosts using 192.168.10.1 through 192.168.10.22 (for an Exadata Full Rack). Oracle uses this 255.255.252.0 subnet to allow multiple Exadata, Exalogic, or other InfiniBand-capable systems to use the same InfiniBand network. This interconnect InfiniBand traffic is non-routable.

Before closing out this recipe, let's turn our attention to the Oracle SCAN and VIP configuration. On Oracle 11gR2 systems (whether you're on Exadata or not), you typically have three SCAN listeners running on one or more nodes in your compute grid as well as a database listener listening on the VIP address on each node. As Oracle Exadata comes in the X2-2 Quarter Rack, X2-2 Half Rack, X2-2 Full Rack, X2-8 Full Rack, X3-2 Eighth Rack, X3-2 Quarter Rack, X3-2 Half Rack, X3-2 Full Rack, and X3-8 Full Rack models, you will find the following:

- X2-2, X3-2 Eighth Rack, and X3-2 Quarter Rack: Three SCAN listeners, two running one node and one running on the other node (if healthy) and a local listener running on the VIP address

- X2-2 and X3-2 Half Rack: Three SCAN listeners, one running on three of the four compute nodes, one compute node without a SCAN listener, and a local listener running on the VIP address

- X2-2 and X3-2 Full Rack: Three SCAN listeners, one running on three of the eight compute nodes, five compute nodes without a SCAN listener, and a local listener running on the VIP address

- X2-8 and X3-8 Full Rack: Three SCAN listeners, two running one node and one running on the other node (if healthy) and a local listener running on the VIP address

CHAPTER 3

How Oracle Works on Exadata

The unique Exadata software presented in Chapter 2 is what enables Exadata to deliver unparalleled database performance. This software's features are what sets Exadata apart from non-Exadata platforms; Oracle has released this software only on the Exadata Database Machine. Experienced Oracle database administrators, Unix/Linux administrators, and storage administrators may be familiar with how Oracle performs I/O. With Exadata, Oracle has designed a new I/O communications protocol, changing how I/O is translated from the database instance to the operating system on which Oracle runs, over the storage interconnect, and to the storage servers.

In this chapter, we will cover how Oracle runs on Exadata and contrast it to non-Exadata database tier platforms and storage solutions. Readers will walk away from the sections in this chapter with a solid understanding of "how Exadata is different," which will help when troubleshooting and will provide a solid base for the information presented in the upcoming chapters in this book.

3-1. Mapping Physical Disks, LUNs, and Cell Disks on the Storage Servers

Problem

As an Exadata DMA, you wish to map the physical disks in an Exadata Storage Server to Logical Units (LUNs) and map LUNs to Exadata cell disks in order to understand how Exadata's disks are presented as usable storage entities.

Solution

In this recipe, you will learn how to identify your physical disk attributes, map these physical disks to LUNs, and identify how the LUNs are used to create cell disks. Start by running the following `lsscsi` command:

```
[root@cm01cel01 ~]# lsscsi
[0:2:0:0]    disk    LSI      MR9261-8i           2.12  /dev/sda
[0:2:1:0]    disk    LSI      MR9261-8i           2.12  /dev/sdb
[0:2:2:0]    disk    LSI      MR9261-8i           2.12  /dev/sdc
... Remaining 9 SAS disks omitted
[1:0:0:0]    disk    Unigen   PSA4000             1100  /dev/sdm
[8:0:0:0]    disk    ATA      MARVELL SD88SA02    D20Y  /dev/sdn
[8:0:1:0]    disk    ATA      MARVELL SD88SA02    D20Y  /dev/sdo
[8:0:2:0]    disk    ATA      MARVELL SD88SA02    D20Y  /dev/sdp
... Remaining 13 Flash disks omitted
[root@cm01cel01 ~]#
```

We can see 12 physical disks, as indicated by the LSI in the third column, at slots 0:2:[0-11]:0. The sixth column displays the physical device, /dev/sda through /dev/sdl.

We know from Oracle documentation that the first two disks contain the System Area, so if you do an fdisk on one of these, you'll see which sections of this device are used for the System Area and which partitions are used for Exadata database storage:

```
[root@cm01cel01 ~]# fdisk -l /dev/sda

Disk /dev/sda: 598.9 GB, 598999040000 bytes
255 heads, 63 sectors/track, 72824 cylinders
Units = cylinders of 16065 * 512 = 8225280 bytes

   Device Boot      Start         End      Blocks   Id  System
/dev/sda1   *           1          15      120456   fd  Linux raid autodetect
/dev/sda2              16          16        8032+  83  Linux
/dev/sda3              17       69039   554427247+  83  Linux
/dev/sda4           69040       72824    30403012+   f  W95 Ext'd (LBA)
/dev/sda5           69040       70344    10482381   fd  Linux raid autodetect
/dev/sda6           70345       71649    10482381   fd  Linux raid autodetect
/dev/sda7           71650       71910     2096451   fd  Linux raid autodetect
/dev/sda8           71911       72171     2096451   fd  Linux raid autodetect
/dev/sda9           72172       72432     2096451   fd  Linux raid autodetect
/dev/sda10          72433       72521      714861   fd  Linux raid autodetect
/dev/sda11          72522       72824     2433816   fd  Linux raid autodetect
[root@cm01cel01 ~]#
```

This fdisk listing shows that /dev/sda3, a large partition starting at sector 17 and ending at sector 69039, is likely our non-System Area storage area for database storage. If you perform a similar fdisk -l on the third disk, /dev/sdc, you can see that there are no host-usable partitions:

```
[root@cm01cel01 ~]# fdisk -l /dev/sdc

Disk /dev/sdc: 598.9 GB, 598999040000 bytes
255 heads, 63 sectors/track, 72824 cylinders
Units = cylinders of 16065 * 512 = 8225280 bytes

Disk /dev/sdc doesn't contain a valid partition table
[root@cm01cel01 ~]#
```

The lowest level disk entity for Exadata Storage Server disks is the physical disk. Using CellCLI, you can query your physical disks and their attributes:

```
CellCLI> list physicaldisk attributes name,diskType,luns,physicalsize,slotNumber
         20:0              HardDisk      0_0     558.9109999993816G     0
         20:1              HardDisk      0_1     558.9109999993816G     1
         20:2              HardDisk      0_2     558.9109999993816G     2
... Additional hard disks omitted
```

```
        FLASH_1_0      FlashDisk      1_0    22.8880615234375G    "PCI Slot: 1; FDOM: 0"
        FLASH_1_1      FlashDisk      1_1    22.8880615234375G    "PCI Slot: 1; FDOM: 1"
        FLASH_1_2      FlashDisk      1_2    22.8880615234375G    "PCI Slot: 1; FDOM: 2"
... Additional flash disks omitted

CellCLI>
```

We can see physical disks of type HardDisk with names 20:0 through 20:11 and disks of type FlashDisk grouped in sections of four per PCI flash card. We also are displaying the LUNs attribute, which shows us the physical disk to LUN mapping. If you would like to see all details for a physical disk, you can issue a list physicaldisk detail cellcli command:

```
CellCLI> list physicaldisk where name=20:2 detail
        name:                   20:2
        deviceId:               17
        diskType:               HardDisk
        enclosureDeviceId:      20
        errMediaCount:          0
        errOtherCount:          0
        foreignState:           false
        luns:                   0_2
        makeModel:              "SEAGATE ST360057SSUN600G"
        physicalFirmware:       0805
        physicalInsertTime:     2011-02-21T13:23:43-05:00
        physicalInterface:      sas
        physicalSerial:         E1R743
        physicalSize:           558.9109999993816G
        slotNumber:             2
        status:                 normal
CellCLI>
```

Oracle builds Exadata LUNs on the usable portions of each physical disk. Using CellCLI, query the LUN details:

```
CellCLI> list lun attributes name, deviceName, isSystemLun, physicalDrives, lunSize
        0_0      /dev/sda      TRUE     20:0          557.861328125G
        0_1      /dev/sdb      TRUE     20:1          557.861328125G
        0_2      /dev/sdc      FALSE    20:2          557.861328125G
... Additional hard disks omitted
        1_0      /dev/sds      FALSE    FLASH_1_0     22.8880615234375G
        1_1      /dev/sdr      FALSE    FLASH_1_1     22.8880615234375G
        1_2      /dev/sdt      FALSE    FLASH_1_2     22.8880615234375G
... Additional flash disks omitted

CellCLI>
```

The output displays LUNs for both physical disks and flash disks, the physical device name, TRUE or FALSE for the isSystemLun attribute, and the LUN size. From the LUN level in the storage hierarchy, the device mapping simply shows which physical device a LUN is built on; the actual physical partition for the disks in the System Area is displayed at the cell disk level.

Exadata cell disks are built on LUNs. A `CellCLI` listing of cell disks is provided:

```
CellCLI> list celldisk attributes name,deviceName,devicePartition,interleaving,lun,size
CD_00_cm01cel01      /dev/sda      /dev/sda3     normal_redundancy    0_0    528.734375G
CD_01_cm01cel01      /dev/sdb      /dev/sdb3     normal_redundancy    0_1    528.734375G
CD_02_cm01cel01      /dev/sdc      /dev/sdc      normal_redundancy    0_2    557.859375G
... Additional cell disks omitted
FD_00_cm01cel01      /dev/sds      /dev/sds      none                 1_0    22.875G
FD_01_cm01cel01      /dev/sdr      /dev/sdr      none                 1_1    22.875G
FD_02_cm01cel01      /dev/sdt      /dev/sdt      none                 1_2    22.875G
... Additional flash cell disks omitted

CellCLI>
```

The CellCLI `list celldisk` output tells us the following:

- There is one cell disk per LUN.

- We're displaying cell disks for both hard disks and flash disks.

- The `devicePartition` for cell disks `CD_00_cm01cel01` and `CD_01_cm01cel01`, which reside on LUNs on the first two physical disks, map to the `/dev/sda3` and `/dev/sdb3` partitions. This is consistent with what we expected from previous `fdisk` listings.

- The size of all but the first two disks equals the size of the LUN. For the cell disk built on LUNs that contain a System Area, Exadata automatically carves the cell disk boundaries to reside outside the System Area partitions.

- Each of the cell disks built on hard disks is defined with a `normal_redundancy` interleaving attribute, in this case.

How It Works

The storage grid in the Exadata Database Machine is made up of multiple storage servers, or storage cells. Each storage cell has 12 physical SAS disks. On the first two physical disks, Oracle reserves a small chunk of storage for the System Area. The System Area is used for the Oracle Linux operating system, the Exadata Storage Server software, log and alert files, and a metadata repository. The System Area is small in size—roughly 30 GB. The remainder of the capacity for the first two disks and all of the other ten disks are dedicated to database storage. Figure 3-1 shows the storage mapping for a disk containing the System Area, and Figure 3-2 shows mapping details for a non-System Area device.

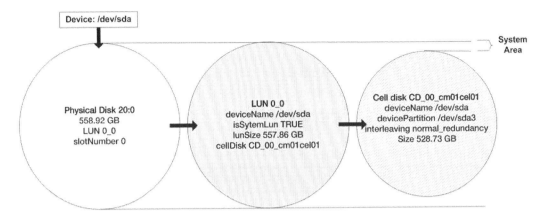

Figure 3-1. Storage entity mapping for disk containing System Area

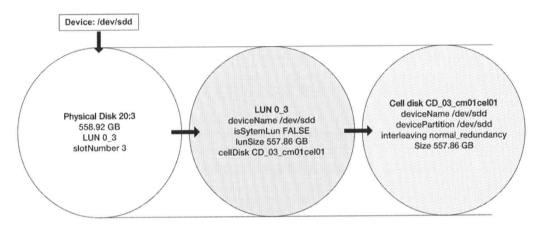

Figure 3-2. Storage entity mapping for disk not containing System Area

A LUN is automatically created on each physical disk and is mapped to the usable extents on the disk. An administrator cannot alter, create, or drop LUNs; they are wholly managed by the Exadata Storage Server software. The purpose of the LUN is to present capacity available to cell disks; on the first two disks, the LUN maps to the extents not used for the System Area, and on the remaining ten disks, the LUN represents the entire physical disk.

An Exadata cell disk is created on top of a LUN. The cell disk is another layer of logical abstraction from which grid disks can be created. An Exadata administrator can alter, create, or drop cell disks. A cell disk does not necessarily need to use all of the available storage that a LUN presents, but it most commonly does. A somewhat common scenario for cell disks may be for an administrator to define an interleaving attribute on the cell disk. When configured with interleaving, grid disks built on the cell disk have their extents "interleaved" across fixed extent boundaries on the physical disk, which has the impact of balancing extents for the grid disks evenly, starting with the outermost disk tracks.

The grid disk is the next logical storage entity inside Exadata storage cells. Grid disks are built on cell disks and are the storage entities on which Oracle ASM disk groups are built. Typically, grid disk planning and administration are done in tandem with ASM disk group planning.

Oracle ASM disk groups are built on collections of Exadata grid disks. ASM disk groups are used to store database files.

3-2. Mapping ASM Disks, Grid Disks, and Cell Disks

Problem

As an Exadata DMA, you wish to understand how your Oracle Automated Storage Management (ASM) disks are mapped to Exadata grid disks and how Exadata grid disks are built upon Exadata cell disks.

Solution

In this exercise, you will learn how to query your Oracle ASM disk group's disks and work your way down the technology stack from ASM disks to Exadata grid disks and finally to the Exadata cell disks. First, take a look at our ASM disk group and disk path configuration by logging in to one of your Exadata compute servers as the Grid Infrastructure owner, launching SQL*Plus, and executing the following script:

```
[grid@cm01dbm01 ~]$ sqlplus / as sysasm
SQL*Plus: Release 11.2.0.3.0 Production on Thu Jul 26 13:20:20 2012
Copyright (c) 1982, 2011, Oracle.  All rights reserved.

Connected to:
Oracle Database 11g Enterprise Edition Release 11.2.0.3.0 - 64bit Production
With the Real Application Clusters and Automatic Storage Management options

SQL> set lines 80
SQL> select name,type,total_mb,free_mb from v$asm_diskgroup;

NAME                           TYPE     TOTAL_MB    FREE_MB
------------------------------ ------ ---------- ----------
DATA_CM01                      NORMAL   10469376    2794528
DBFS_DG                        NORMAL     894720     892264
RECO_CM01                      NORMAL    2469888    2392080
SDATA_CM01                     NORMAL    5197824    1371036
SRECO_CM01                     NORMAL    1352448     957128

SQL>
```

In this script, we see five ASM disk groups available for database storage. Let's now examine the individual disks that make up one of these disk groups using the script in Listing 3-1:

Listing 3-1. lst03-01-asmdisks.sql

```
 SQL> select a.name,b.path,b.state,a.type,b.failgroup
    from v$asm_diskgroup a, v$asm_disk b
    where a.group_number=b.group_number
    and a.name='DATA_CM01'
    order by 2,1
/
```

```
Disk Group   Disk                                  State    TYPE     Failgroup
----------   ------------------------------------  -------  -------  ---------------
DATA_CM01    o/192.168.10.3/DATA_CD_00_cm01cel01   NORMAL   NORMAL   CM01CEL01
DATA_CM01    o/192.168.10.3/DATA_CD_01_cm01cel01   NORMAL   NORMAL   CM01CEL01
DATA_CM01    o/192.168.10.3/DATA_CD_02_cm01cel01   NORMAL   NORMAL   CM01CEL01
... ASM disks for CM01CEL01 omitted
DATA_CM01    o/192.168.10.4/DATA_CD_00_cm01cel02   NORMAL   NORMAL   CM01CEL02
DATA_CM01    o/192.168.10.4/DATA_CD_01_cm01cel02   NORMAL   NORMAL   CM01CEL02
DATA_CM01    o/192.168.10.4/DATA_CD_02_cm01cel02   NORMAL   NORMAL   CM01CEL02
... ASM disks for CM01CEL02 omitted
DATA_CM01    o/192.168.10.5/DATA_CD_00_cm01cel03   NORMAL   NORMAL   CM01CEL03
DATA_CM01    o/192.168.10.5/DATA_CD_01_cm01cel03   NORMAL   NORMAL   CM01CEL03
DATA_CM01    o/192.168.10.5/DATA_CD_02_cm01cel03   NORMAL   NORMAL   CM01CEL03
... ASM disks for CM01CEL03 omitted

36 rows selected.

SQL>
```

This output tells us that DATA_CM01 is built with 36 Exadata grid disks. And while this doesn't necessarily confirm that we're using an Exadata X2-2 Quarter Rack since an administrator can always build ASM disk groups on a list of any number of grid disks, in our case and in most customer scenarios, ASM disk groups are typically constructed using grid disks from each cell disk on every storage cell.

If you look at the second column in the previous output, you'll notice a disk path string convention of o/<IP address>/<grid disk name>. When building ASM disk groups on Exadata, this means the following:

- The leading o/ instructs Oracle ASM to search for disk paths using Exadata InfiniBand I/O protocol—from the compute node, you can find your available storage server IP addresses by looking in cellip.ora:

    ```
    [grid@cm01dbm01 ~]$ locate cellip.ora
    /etc/oracle/cell/network-config/cellip.ora
    /opt/oracle.SupportTools/onecommand/tmp/cellip.ora
    [grid@cm01dbm01 ~]$ cat /etc/oracle/cell/network-config/cellip.ora
    cell="192.168.10.3"
    cell="192.168.10.4"
    cell="192.168.10.5"
    [grid@cm01dbm01 ~]$
    ```

- The IP address in the second stanza of the disk string represents the InfiniBand IP address of the Exadata storage cell. We can see three IP addresses, 192.168.10.3, 192.168.10.4, and 192.168.10.5; each of these is the bonded InfiniBand address of an Exadata storage cell.

- The grid disk name in the third section of the ASM disk string represents the Exadata grid disk name.

When we created these ASM disk groups, we specified normal redundancy. With Exadata, external redundancy is not an option—you either need to use normal or high redundancy. With normal redundancy, each extent is mirrored to a different cell, and with high redundancy, they are mirrored via ASM to two additional cells. Specifically, extents are mirrored to partner disks in different failure groups.

On Exadata, grid disks are the logical storage entities on the storage cell upon which ASM disks can be discovered and ASM disk groups can be built. Let's look at some attributes of the grid disks that make up the DATA_CM01 ASM disk group from one of the Exadata storage cells, cm01cel01:

```
CellCLI> list griddisk where name like 'DATA_CD_.*' attributes name,asmDiskGroupName,asmDiskName,
cellDisk,size
 DATA_CD_00_cm01cel01      DATA_CM01      DATA_CD_00_CM01CEL01      CD_00_cm01cel01   284G
 DATA_CD_01_cm01cel01      DATA_CM01      DATA_CD_01_CM01CEL01      CD_01_cm01cel01   284G
 DATA_CD_02_cm01cel01      DATA_CM01      DATA_CD_02_CM01CEL01      CD_02_cm01cel01   284G
 DATA_CD_03_cm01cel01      DATA_CM01      DATA_CD_03_CM01CEL01      CD_03_cm01cel01   284G
... Additional grid disks omitted

CellCLI>
```

We can see that each grid disk belongs to the DATA_CM01 ASM disk group and that the ASM disk name is displayed in the third column. This disk path/string corresponds to V$ASM_DISK.PATH. Furthermore, we can see which cell disk each grid disk is part of and the grid disk size.

Each of the grid disks resides on an Exadata cell disk with a similarly named cell disk name, prefixed by DATA_. Again, this is a common but not required convention; when an administrator builds Exadata grid disks, he or she typically uses a prefix clause to seed a grid disk prefix and append the cell disk name.

The size of each grid disk is displayed in the sixth column. Note the uniform grid disk size. Uniform grid disk sizing is not required, but it is recommended to ensure database extents are evenly distributed across grid disks and, ultimately, ASM disk groups.

How It Works

Oracle uses ASM exclusively on Exadata for database storage. ASM disk groups consist of Exadata grid disks, and grid disks are built on Exadata cell disks. The general flow of creating Exadata database storage looks like the following:

- Install and validate the Exadata Database Machine.
- Create cell disks. This is typically done at the time of installation by Oracle ACS, but an administrator can reconfigure cell disks at a later time. Grid disk interleaving is done at the cell disk level.
- Build grid disks on Exadata cell disks. When building grid disks, pay special attention to the end goal, which is Oracle ASM storage. As an administrator, you want to ensure that grid disk sizes and placement is in alignment with business objectives.
- Create ASM disk groups with Exadata grid disks.

In short, grid disks are created on cell disks and represent the storage available for ASM disks. When you create ASM disk groups, the devices you use are grid disks, and grid disks are the disks exposed and available to Oracle ASM.

Exadata administrators are encouraged to strive for equally sized, well-balanced grid disk configurations. Doing so enables Exadata to maximize disk I/O bandwidth, I/Os per second, and ultimately ensure a well-balanced, high-performing storage platform on Exadata. Oracle truly makes this effort easy on Exadata—contrary to some other storage array vendors and the associated administrative processes, with Exadata the process of creating the most robust, balanced, and high-performing storage configuration is also the simplest and involves the least amount of keystrokes. After creating cell disks, the administrator would create grid disks with a unique grid disk prefix, starting with the "most important" storage so that the extents reside on the outermost disk tracks. In a single cellcli or dcli command, you can create grid disks that span every cell disk and every storage cell. Then, the administrator simply creates ASM disk groups using a wild-carded storage server InfiniBand IP address and wild-carded Exadata grid disks.

> **Note** Recipe 9-8 discusses the topic of interleaved grid disks, which is a feature created to enable the Exadata DMA to divide the cell disks into smaller sections of storage and spread the grid disks extents across a wider range of disk boundaries. Please refer to this recipe for additional information.

3-3. Mapping Flash Disks to Smart Flash Storage

Problem

As an Exadata DMA, you wish to map the physical PCI Flash disk storage to Exadata's Smart Flash Cache and Smart Flash Logging storage entities to better understand how the flash cards are used in the Exadata storage cells.

Solution

In Recipe 1-6, we presented information about how the storage server's PCI flash cards were partitioned and presented as flash storage in your Exadata Storage Servers. In this recipe, we will show you how to map this flash storage to Exadata's usable flash storage, which is used for Smart Flash Cache and Smart Flash Logging.

First, log in to an Exadata storage cell as root or celladmin, launch cellcli, and run the following commands:

```
CellCLI> list flashcache detail
         name:                   cm01cel01_FLASHCACHE
         cellDisk:               FD_06_cm01cel01,FD_01_cm01cel01,FD_08_cm01cel01,
FD_04_cm01cel01,FD_03_cm01cel01,FD_02_cm01cel01,FD_11_cm01cel01,FD_00_cm01cel01,FD_09_cm01cel01,
FD_12_cm01cel01,FD_07_cm01cel01,FD_13_cm01cel01,FD_15_cm01cel01,FD_05_cm01cel01,FD_14_cm01cel01,
FD_10_cm01cel01
         creationTime:           2012-05-26T21:48:38-04:00
         degradedCelldisks:
         effectiveCacheSize:     364.75G
         id:                     9b17f359-a600-4e86-be86-8c6ef0490f73
         size:                   364.75G
         status:                 normal

CellCLI> list flashlog detail
         name:                   cm01cel01_FLASHLOG
         cellDisk:               FD_13_cm01cel01,FD_08_cm01cel01,FD_06_cm01cel01,
FD_04_cm01cel01,FD_09_cm01cel01,FD_07_cm01cel01,FD_14_cm01cel01,FD_00_cm01cel01,FD_12_cm01cel01,
FD_02_cm01cel01,FD_11_cm01cel01,FD_05_cm01cel01,FD_03_cm01cel01,FD_15_cm01cel01,
FD_01_cm01cel01,FD_10_cm01cel01
         creationTime:           2012-05-26T21:58:42-04:00
         degradedCelldisks:
         effectiveSize:          512M
         efficiency:             100.0
         id:                     13a6c2d0-093a-41c1-a0ad-e8117071b771
         size:                   512M
         status:                 normal

CellCLI>
```

The output shows that each of the 16 flash modules is presented as a flash disk for both Smart Flash Cache and Smart Flash Logging.

From `CellCLI` we can see how these flash devices are mapped to usable Exadata Flash entities, as discussed in Recipe 1-6:

```
CellCLI> list physicaldisk where disktype='FlashDisk' attributes name,disktype,physicalSize,
slotNumber
        FLASH_1_0       FlashDisk       22.8880615234375G       "PCI Slot: 1; FDOM: 0"
        FLASH_1_1       FlashDisk       22.8880615234375G       "PCI Slot: 1; FDOM: 1"
        FLASH_1_2       FlashDisk       22.8880615234375G       "PCI Slot: 1; FDOM: 2"
        FLASH_1_3       FlashDisk       22.8880615234375G       "PCI Slot: 1; FDOM: 3"
        FLASH_2_0       FlashDisk       22.8880615234375G       "PCI Slot: 2; FDOM: 0"
... Flash cards 2_1, 2_2, and 2_3 omitted
        FLASH_4_0       FlashDisk       22.8880615234375G       "PCI Slot: 4; FDOM: 0"
... Flash cards 4_1, 4_2, and 4_3 omitted
        FLASH_5_0       FlashDisk       22.8880615234375G       "PCI Slot: 5; FDOM: 0"
... Flash cards 5_1, 5_2, and 5_3 omitted

CellCLI>
```

■ **Note** The above output is generated on an Exadata X2-2 Quarter Rack. On the X3-2 and X3-8 models, you will see larger amounts of PCI flash; each card is 384 GB in size as compared to 96 GB in size.

How It Works

Exadata Flash storage is provided by Sun Flash Accelerator F20 PCI flash cards. There are four 96 GB PCI flash cards per storage cell in the X2 models and four 384 GB cards on the X3 models. Each PCI flash card has a device partitioned per FDom, yielding 16 flash devices. These flash devices are manifested as Exadata Storage Server flash disks and used for Smart Flash Cache and Smart Flash Logging.

■ **Note** Recipes in Chapter 18 discuss various topics on Exadata's Smart Flash Cache and Smart Flash Logging features.

3-4. Identifying Cell Server Software Processes

Problem

You wish to identify the key operating system processes on the Exadata Storage Servers that run Exadata's unique storage server software and understand how the storage server's Cell Services processes are related and what function they perform.

Solution

In this recipe, we will show you how to identify the Exadata Cell Services operating system process. Start by logging in to a storage server and executing the ps -ef command:

```
[root@cm01cel01 ~]# ps -ef|grep oracle
root      4686  9108  0 Jul10 ?        00:00:04 
/opt/oracle/cell11.2.2.4.2_LINUX.X64_111221/cellsrv/bin/cellrsomt -ms 1 -cellsrv 1
root      4689  4686  2 Jul10 ?        13:54:03 
/opt/oracle/cell11.2.2.4.2_LINUX.X64_111221/cellsrv/bin/cellsrv 100 5000 9 5042
root      8220  6060  0 Jul30 ?        00:00:00 /bin/bash 
/opt/oracle.cellos/ExadataDiagCollector.sh
root      8224  6060  0 Jul30 ?        00:00:00 /bin/ksh ./oswsub.sh HighFreq 
/opt/oracle.oswatcher/osw/ExadataRdsInfo.sh
root      8249  8224  0 Jul30 ?        00:00:08 /bin/bash /
opt/oracle.oswatcher/osw/ExadataRdsInfo.sh HighFreq
root      9108     1  0 May25 ?        00:00:20 
/opt/oracle/cell11.2.2.4.2_LINUX.X64_111221/cellsrv/bin/cellrssrm -ms 1 -cellsrv 1
root      9114  9108  0 May25 ?        00:00:01 
/opt/oracle/cell11.2.2.4.2_LINUX.X64_111221/cellsrv/bin/cellrsbmt -ms 1 -cellsrv 1
root      9115  9108  0 May25 ?        00:00:00 
/opt/oracle/cell11.2.2.4.2_LINUX.X64_111221/cellsrv/bin/cellrsmmt -ms 1 -cellsrv 1
root      9116  9114  0 May25 ?        00:00:13 
/opt/oracle/cell11.2.2.4.2_LINUX.X64_111221/cellsrv/bin/cellrsbkm -rs_conf 
/opt/oracle/cell11.2.2.4.2_LINUX.X64_111221/cellsrv/deploy/config/cellinit.ora -ms_conf 
/opt/oracle/cell11.2.2.4.2_LINUX.X64_111221/cellsrv/deploy/config/cellrsms.state -cellsrv_conf 
/opt/oracle/cell11.2.2.4.2_LINUX.X64_111221/cellsrv/deploy/config/cellrsos.state -debug 0
root      9118  9115  2 May25 ?        1-16:01:41 /usr/java/jdk1.5.0_15/bin/java -Xms256m -
Xmx512m -Djava.library.path=/opt/oracle/cell11.2.2.4.2_LINUX.X64_111221/cellsrv/lib -
Ddisable.checkForUpdate=true -jar 
/opt/oracle/cell11.2.2.4.2_LINUX.X64_111221/oc4j/ms/j2ee/home/oc4j.jar -out 
/opt/oracle/cell11.2.2.4.2_LINUX.X64_111221/cellsrv/deploy/log/ms.lst -err 
/opt/oracle/cell11.2.2.4.2_LINUX.X64_111221/cellsrv/deploy/log/ms.err
root      9121  9116  0 May25 ?        00:00:01 
/opt/oracle/cell11.2.2.4.2_LINUX.X64_111221/cellsrv/bin/cellrssmt -rs_conf 
/opt/oracle/cell11.2.2.4.2_LINUX.X64_111221/cellsrv/deploy/config/cellinit.ora -ms_conf 
/opt/oracle/cell11.2.2.4.2_LINUX.X64_111221/cellsrv/deploy/config/cellrsms.state -cellsrv_conf 
/opt/oracle/cell11.2.2.4.2_LINUX.X64_111221/cellsrv/deploy/config/cellrsos.state -debug 0
root     27264 12322  0 01:16 pts/0    00:00:00 grep oracle
[root@cm01cel01 ~]#
```

How It Works

There are three main programs that run on the Exadata Storage Servers to facilitate cell operations:

- Cell Services, or cellsrv
- Management Server, or MS
- Restart Server, or RS

At system startup, Oracle runs /etc/init.d/cell.d. /etc/init.d/cell.d executes as the celladmin operating system account and runs "alter cell startup services rs" to start the Restart Server. After sleeping for a bit, the script runs "alter cell startup services all," which starts up remaining processes including cellsrv and MS. Logic exists within /etc/init.d/cell.d as well as /etc/init.d/precell to determine whether any failures or improper configurations exist. If so, Oracle will attempt to start from the last good status.

cellsrv is the primary process/software that runs on the storage servers. If you look at the process hierarchy (excluding OSWatcher processes) from the output listed in the Solution of this recipe, here's what it means:

- The cellrssrm process is the main Restart Server process. It launches three helper processes: cellrsomt, cellrsbmt, and cellrsmmt.

- The cellrsomt helper process is ultimately responsible for launching cellsrv.

- The cellrsbmt and cellrsmmt processes are additional helper processes responsible for launching cellrsbkm and the main Management Server Java process.

- cellrssmt is called by cellrsbkm, and its ultimate goal is to ensure cell configuration files are valid, consistent, and backed up.

- And of course, cellsrv is the main process that performs I/O on the Exadata cell.

cellsrv is a multithreaded process that essentially facilitates I/O requests from the compute nodes. It receives and unpacks iDB messages transmitted over the InfiniBand interconnect and examines metadata contained in the messages to determine the appropriate course of action. For example:

- If the request contains information that indicates a full scan via direct read, cellsrv can perform a Smart Scan.

- If the request is for a single-block read, cellsrv performs as a traditional block I/O server.

- If the request is tagged with data that falls within a bucket of conditions specified by an enabled I/O Resource Management plan, cellsrv will queue and prioritize I/O requests accordingly.

There are many other special activities that cellsrv performs and, in general, you can think of cellsrv as an intelligent set of I/O processes that execute different sections of Oracle code depending on data contained in the iDB messages. The iDB messages are essentially instructions that will result physical disk I/O, based on the data being requested and the metadata encapsulated in the iDB messages. In short, cellsrv is responsible for receiving I/O instructions and utilizing any and all unique Exadata software features along the way.

■ **Note** iDB = Intelligent Database Protocol, which is a network protocol designed by Oracle to facilitate InfiniBand aware I/O communication.

The Management Server, or MS, provides a Java interface to the CellCLI command line interface, as well as providing an interface for Enterprise Manager plugins. If MS is down, you won't be able to use cellcli.

The Restart Server, or RS, is a set of processes responsible for managing and restarting other processes.

In addition to the three main programs, Oracle runs OSWatcher on storage cells to collect performance metrics and publishes these to the OSWatcher archive directories.

Together, the three main storage cell programs are key components of the Exadata Storage Server software and overall functionality.

3-5. Tracing Oracle I/O Requests on Exadata Compute Nodes

Problem

You wish to confirm where physical database I/O is performed on Oracle Exadata. You've learned that the Exadata Storage Servers are responsible for handling physical I/O, and you wish to confirm via operating system tracing that this indeed is the case.

Solution

In this recipe, you will learn how to use strace to trace system calls from an Oracle instance process. Start by logging in to an Oracle Exadata compute server and trace system calls issued by the DBWR process for an instance. Find the process ID of a DBWR process and then use strace to examine the system calls it makes during a period of DBWR activity:

```
[root@cm01dbm01 ~]# ps -ef|grep visx|grep dbw
oracle    22251     1  0 Jul27 ?        00:00:03 ora_dbw0_visx1
oracle    22259     1  0 Jul27 ?        00:00:03 ora_dbw1_visx1
oracle    22261     1  0 Jul27 ?        00:00:02 ora_dbw2_visx1
[root@cm01dbm01 ~]# strace -c -p 22251
Process 22251 attached - interrupt to quit
Process 22251 detached
% time     seconds  usecs/call     calls    errors syscall
------ ----------- ----------- --------- --------- ----------------
   nan    0.000000           0         1           read
   nan    0.000000           0         1           open
   nan    0.000000           0         1           close
   nan    0.000000           0         1           poll
   nan    0.000000           0        14           sendmsg
   nan    0.000000           0        57         1 recvmsg
   nan    0.000000           0        28        14 setsockopt
   nan    0.000000           0         6           getrusage
   nan    0.000000           0        13           times
   nan    0.000000           0         4         3 semtimedop
------ ----------- ----------- --------- --------- ----------------
100.00    0.000000                   126        18 total
[root@cm01dbm01 ~]#
```

This shows us that the DBWR process used the sendmsg system call to package an I/O request, which ships the iDB message over the InfiniBand network in the case of Exadata, and a recvmsg call to receive the data from the storage servers.

How It Works

With Oracle Exadata, database I/O is handled exclusively by the cellsrv process/threads on the storage servers. The database tier nodes, operating with asynchronous I/O, bundle I/O requests into iDB messages and transmit these over the InfiniBand network grid to the Exadata Storage Servers. The storage servers perform the actual I/O and send data back to the compute nodes over InfiniBand. Compute servers ingest this data and process it according to the nature of the I/O request in an identical fashion to how physical I/O is consumed by the server process or database in non-Exadata systems. Figure 3-3 depicts this flow.

CHAPTER 3 ■ HOW ORACLE WORKS ON EXADATA

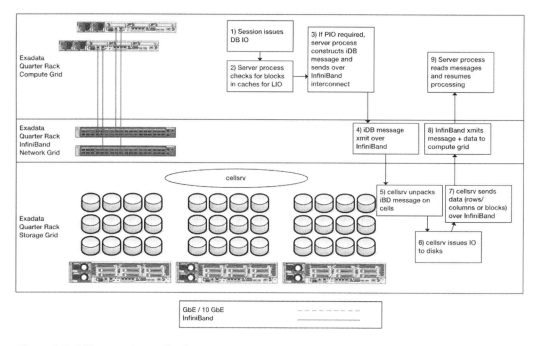

Figure 3-3. *I/O processing on Exadata*

Here's how it works:

- Oracle foreground or background processes issue database I/O calls, just as they do in non-Exadata environments.

- Oracle processes follow the same PARSE/EXEC/FETCH logic on Exadata as they do on non-Exadata. As blocks are requested, Oracle will check for copies of the blocks in both the local and all-remote database block buffer caches and perform a logical I/O or block-shipped logical I/O to satisfy the request. In other words, logical I/O on Exadata is the same as logical I/O on non-Exadata.

- If a physical I/O is required:

    1. On Exadata, the server process constructs an iDB message containing the list of extents to fetch. Additionally, various pieces of metadata are encapsulated in the messages that provide further details about the I/O request.

    2. On non-Exadata Oracle environments, the database server is responsible for issuing disk I/O calls.

- *iDB* = Intelligent Database Protocol. iDB is an InfiniBand-aware network protocol designed by Oracle, implemented on Reliable Datagram Sockets V3.

- iDB messages are transmitted over InfiniBand using sendmsg system calls. These messages are sent to *each* of the storage cells in the storage grid, independently.

- The messages are processed (in other words, received) by storage server cellsrv processes.

- cellsrv examines the contents and metadata inside the iDB message and makes I/O processing decisions based on the contents.

66

- cellsrv issues the physical I/O calls to the physical disks or flash disks.
- When I/O requests are fulfilled, cellsrv sends the requested data back over InfiniBand over the iDB protocol.
- The server process on the compute node receives these messages and processes the data just as if a local I/O had been submitted and data returned It will load the blocks, rows, or columns retrieved into the buffer cache or PGA, perform any sorting or row elimination options, and so forth.

There are a few items worth discussing on this topic of I/O on Exadata. First, cellsrv has the ability to act as both a traditional "block server" or as a row/column server. For traditional, non-offloadable single block reads, as are common with index lookups, cellsrv retrieves database blocks from disks and ships these blocks over the InfiniBand interconnect, at which point the server process will load these blocks in the SGA. If, however, the iDB message metadata indicates that a full scan operation is the selected mechanism to fetch I/O and if the server process has also determined that the I/O request is to be satisfied via direct path read (which indirectly provided part of the message's metadata), cellsrv can decide to issue a Smart Scan I/O request. After Smart Scan I/O requests are completed on the storage servers, the return iDB messages will contain rows and columns, not blocks.

Additionally, cellsrv is responsible for facilitating and implementing other pieces of unique storage server features, including I/O Resource Management, I/O queuing, Smart Flash Cache, and so forth. So, not only does cellsrv issue the physical I/O requests, but it is also responsible for triggering Exadata software features depending on the nature of the I/O requests and metadata associated with them.

The Exadata storage cells operate independently from each other. cellsrv on each storage server processes I/O requests via iDB message and independently transmits the return data/messages back to the compute grid. It is the responsibility of the compute server to sort, group, and process the results returned from each storage server.

The fundamental thing to understand with respect to I/O on Exadata is the concept of iDB message transmission. iDB messages are the engine for data transfer between the compute grid and storage grid, and the Oracle RDBMS and ASM instances are able to use iDB because they're linked with the libcell libraries. libcell provides code paths inside the Oracle kernel to specify whether the system is running on Exadata or not; if it is, the details in this recipe apply.

Contrasting the Approach for Non-Exadata Systems

In contrast, on non-Exadata systems, the operating system on which the database instance runs is responsible for issuing the I/O requests. In the following example, we will use truss on an IBM server with asynchronous I/O enabled, running Oracle 11gR2 on AIX 6.1, and trace a DBWR process:

```
$ truss -cf -p 5533870
Pstatus: process is not stopped
syscall               seconds      calls    errors
_thread_wait         1261.73          8
thread_post              .00          6
times                    .00          6
close                    .00          1
kread                    .00          1
kopen                    .00          1
listio64                 .00        132
aio_nwait_timeout64      .00        136
                        ----       ---      ---
sys totals:              .00        291        0
usr time:                            .00
elapsed:                             .00
oracle@aixserver:/home/oracle
$
```

The `listio64` system calls are a representation of AIX and Oracle determining which blocks to write to disk (and where), and the `aio_nwait_timeout64` are system calls representing the waits for asynchronous I/O to complete. From this `truss` listing, we can see that the database server is indeed initiating the physical I/O request. To compare with Figure 3-3, Figure 3-4 shows the I/O path for non-Exadata database servers.

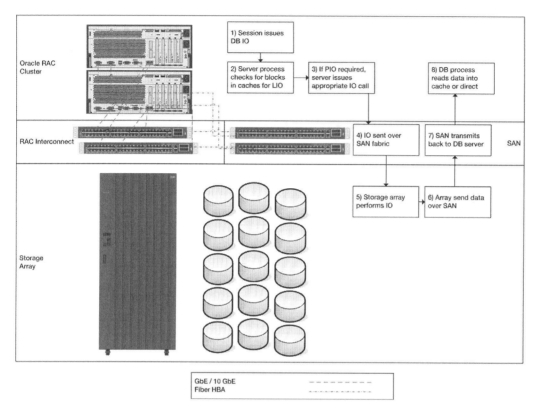

Figure 3-4. *Oracle I/O path example on non-Exadata systems*

3-6. Validating That Your Oracle RAC Interconnect Is Using InfiniBand
Problem
You know from Oracle documentation that the InfiniBand network serves as both the storage network and the Oracle RAC interconnect, but you wish to validate that the interconnect is indeed communicating over InfiniBand.

Solution
In this recipe, you will learn how to do the following:

1. Retrieve your cluster interconnect information
2. Validate the network interface that your cluster interconnect is deployed on
3. Ensure that the interface is an InfiniBand interface
4. Validate that you are running the RDS protocol on your cluster interconnect interface

First, log in to a compute node as the Grid Infrastructure software owner and validate your Oracle RAC interconnect details using oifcfg:

```
[grid@cm01dbm01 ~]$ oifcfg getif
bondib0   192.168.8.0  global  cluster_interconnect
bondeth0  172.16.1.0   global  public
[grid@cm01dbm01 ~]$
```

Next, check your routing tables to determine which interface this network resides on:

```
[root@cm01dbm01 ~]# route -v | grep 192.168
192.168.8.0     *               255.255.252.0   U     0      0        0 bondib0
[root@cm01dbm01 ~]#
```

We can see from this output that we are using the bondib0 interface. Use ifconfig to display details of this interface:

```
[root@cm01dbm01 ~]# ifconfig bondib0
bondib0   Link encap:InfiniBand  HWaddr 80:00:00:48:FE:80:00:00:00:00:00:00:00:00:00:00:00:00:00:00
          inet addr:192.168.10.1  Bcast:192.168.11.255  Mask:255.255.252.0
          inet6 addr: fe80::221:2800:1a1:25c5/64 Scope:Link
          UP BROADCAST RUNNING MASTER MULTICAST  MTU:65520  Metric:1
          RX packets:1970084 errors:0 dropped:0 overruns:0 frame:0
          TX packets:1923066 errors:0 dropped:69 overruns:0 carrier:0
          collisions:0 txqueuelen:0
          RX bytes:998645331 (952.3 MiB)  TX bytes:1168770033 (1.0 GiB)

[root@cm01dbm01 ~]#
```

The Link encap:InfiniBand text confirms we have an InfiniBand link on our private interconnect, but it doesn't show us whether we're running RDS over InfiniBand or possibly UDP. To determine this, use the skgxpinfo command:

```
[grid@cm01dbm01 ~]$ $ORACLE_HOME/bin/skgxpinfo -v
Oracle RDS/IP (generic)
[grid@cm01dbm01 ~]
```

For reference, on a traditional non-Exadata Oracle 11gR2 RAC Cluster, it would be common to see this command display udp:

```
[oracle@rac1 ~]$ $ORACLE_HOME/bin/skgxpinfo
udp
[oracle@rac1 ~]
```

On Exadata, you can also use ibdump to examine packets from your bonded InfiniBand interface to confirm the RAC interconnect traffic is using this network.

■ **Note** The traditional tcpdump command is not InfiniBand-aware and would tag its output as UDP packets.

Download ibdump from www.mellonix.com and install it on one of your compute servers and then run the ibdump command as root, ensuring to specify an -o option to save the output to a PCAP file:

```
[root@cm01dbm01 ~]# ibdump -o /tmp/ibdump.out
------------------------------------------------
IB device                      : "mlx4_0"
IB port                        : 1
Dump file                      : /tmp/ibdump.out
Sniffer WQEs (max burst size)  : 4096
------------------------------------------------
Initiating resources ...
searching for IB devices in host
Port active_mtu=2048
MR was registered with addr=0x1bcf7590, lkey=0x1000373a, rkey=0x1000373a, flags=0x1
QP was created, QP number=0x7c0056
Ready to capture (Press ^c to stop):
Captured:      2282 packets,  1505176 bytes
Interrupted (signal 2) - exiting ...
[root@cm01dbm01 ~]#
```

The ibdump command will run continuously until you interrupt with a CTRL-C. Once you stop your ibdump execution, transfer your PCAP output file to a workstation with WireShark installed. Open this PCAP file in WireShark to examine the InfiniBand traffic (see Figure 3-5).

Protocol	% Packets	Packets	% Bytes	Bytes	Mbit/s	End Packets	End Bytes	End Mbit/s
▽ Frame	100.00 %	1124	100.00 %	1048328	3.168	0	0	0.000
▽ Extensible Record Format	100.00 %	1124	100.00 %	1048328	3.168	0	0	0.000
▽ InfiniBand	100.00 %	1124	100.00 %	1048328	3.168	383	22698	0.069
▷ MDS Header	59.34 %	667	87.03 %	912358	2.757	0	0	0.000
▽ Internet Protocol Version 4	2.22 %	25	1.13 %	11870	0.036	0	0	0.000
▽ User Datagram Protocol	2.05 %	23	0.93 %	9726	0.029	0	0	0.000
Data	2.05 %	23	0.93 %	9726	0.029	23	9726	0.029
▽ Transmission Control Protocol	0.18 %	2	0.20 %	2144	0.006	1	70	0.000
Data	0.09 %	1	0.20 %	2074	0.006	1	2074	0.006
Data	4.36 %	49	9.67 %	101402	0.306	49	101402	0.306

Figure 3-5. WireShark display of InfiniBand traffic on a compute node

How It Works

Oracle elects to use the RDS protocol for the InfiniBand interconnect traffic based on the output of skgxpinfo. The $ORACLE_HOME/bin/skgxpinfo executable and other Oracle binaries are linked with the ipc_rds flag, which assumes that RDS modules are loaded in the kernel.

For the cluster interconnect to communicate via RDS over InfiniBand:

- InfiniBand/RDS drivers must be loaded into the kernel. On Exadata, this is always the case.

- Oracle binaries must be linked with ipc_rds. On Exadata, this will be true unless an Oracle DMA manually linked binaries without ipc_rds.

- The InfiniBand interfaces need to be properly configured and, on Exadata, bonded.

- The cluster interconnect needs to point to the bonded InfiniBand interface on the compute nodes. On Exadata, the Grid Infrastructure installation will properly set the cluster interconnect to the InfiniBand bonded interface.

3-7. Tracing cellsrv on the Storage Servers

Problem

You know from Oracle documentation or resources that cellsrv is responsible for performing I/O operations as well as delivering Exadata Storage Server software features, but in order to troubleshoot I/O performance issues and ensure that the Exadata cell servers are operating at their peak capacity, you wish to learn how to trace cellsrv on the Exadata storage cells.

Solution

First, log in to one of your Exadata Storage Servers as root and find the cellsrv Linux process. We'll search for "cellsrv 100," knowing that cellsrv is launched as a process with 100 threads:

```
[root@cm01cel01 ~]# ps -ef | grep "cellsrv 100"
root       570   569  0 Jul31 ?        00:03:59
/opt/oracle/cell11.2.2.4.2_LINUX.X64_111221/cellsrv/bin/cellsrv 100 5000 9 5042
root      2513  1641  0 02:21 pts/0    00:00:00 grep cellsrv 100
[root@cm01cel01 ~]#
```

In the output above, operating system process 570 represents the cellsrv process. Use strace -cf -p to summarize system calls for cellsrv and all its process threads:

```
[root@cm01cel01 ~]# strace -cf -p 570
Process 570 attached with 113 threads - interrupt to quit
Process 570 detached
<< lines omitted >>
Process 1253 detached

% time     seconds  usecs/call     calls    errors syscall
------ ----------- ----------- --------- --------- ----------------
 74.30  191.485468         830    230735     93329 futex
 13.19   33.993075        4162      8168           poll
 10.62   27.373752       16017      1709           nanosleep
  0.64    1.660603          18     89814           clock_gettime
  0.39    1.001690         135      7445           io_getevents
  0.36    0.931850          62     14984           io_submit
  0.16    0.421931       42193        10           restart_syscall
  0.15    0.391672          21     18420      4081 recvmsg
  0.12    0.306634          31     10006           sendmsg
 ... Additional output omitted
------ ----------- ----------- --------- --------- ----------------
100.00  257.723006                395386     97410 total
[root@cm01cel01 ~]#
```

To identify whether you have bottlenecks or performance issues, concentrate on overall time spent and time-per-call for the I/O-related system calls, `io_getevents` and `io_submit`. You would ideally strive for sub-5 millisecond service times or lower. Divide the `usecs/call` value for `io_getevents` and `io_submit` by 1,000 to determine if this is the case. In the previous example, a 135 usecs/call for `io_getevents` represents 0.135 ms.

- Here is some of the key information about the results: The `recvmsg` lines indicate iDB messages received over InfiniBand from the compute servers; these would have corresponding `sendmsg` calls from the database grid.

- The `sendmsg` lines represent iDB messages returned to the compute grid from the storage server, typically indicating the completion of an I/O.

- `io_getevents` and `io_submit` work in tandem to collect asynchronous I/O requests and perform the actual I/Os being requested.

In short, `cellsrv` on the storage servers are handling database I/O and communicating via messaging over the InfiniBand interconnect. In Recipe 3-5, we discussed the I/O path from the compute node servers; this recipe is a complement to Recipe 3-5.

If you look more closely into `sendmsg` and `recvmsg` system calls, you will be able to see the InfiniBand IP addresses of the two compute nodes. If you took the time to weed through the output, you would learn that the IP addresses for the `recvmsg` and `sendmsg` calls *only* come from and to the InfiniBand IP addresses of the compute servers:

```
[root@cm01cel01 ~]# grep recvmsg /tmp/cellsrv.trc |more
[pid  1185] recvmsg(127, <unfinished ...>
[pid  1185] <... recvmsg resumed> {msg_name(16)={sa_family=AF_INET, sin_port=htons(20938),
sin_addr=inet_addr("192.168.10.2")}, msg_iov(3)=
[{"\4\3\2\1\240\226\26\27\0\0\0\0OMRON\4\3\0\0\0\0\0\0\237>\343W\0\0\0\0"..., 76},
{"\1\0\0\0\215\330\201\242(\0\0\0\0\0\0\0\0\0\0\2\2\0\0\0\0\0\0", 28},
{"\4\3\2\1\31\0\0\0004\214\231\35\0\0\0\0\373\177\0\0\233\323\252\2\0\10\250\300\2\2\2"..., 576}],
msg_controllen=0, msg_
flags=0}, 0) = 144
[pid  1185] recvmsg(127, <unfinished ...>
[pid  1185] <... recvmsg resumed> {msg_name(16)={sa_family=AF_INET, sin_port=htons(28810),
sin_addr=inet_addr("192.168.10.1")}, msg_iov(3)=
[{"\4\3\2\1\234\226\26\27\0\0\0\0OMRON\4\3\0\0\0\0\0\0\350\217\225\30\0\0\0\0"..., 76},
{"\1\0\0\0\215x\240\376(\0\0\0\0\0\0\0\0\0\0\1\2\0\0\0\0\0\0", 28},
{"\4\3\2\1\31\0\0\0004\214\231\35\0\0\0\0\374\177\0\0tP8b\0\10\250\300\1\2\1\2"..., 576}],
msg_controllen=0, msg_flags=0}

root@cm01cel01 ~]# grep sendmsg /tmp/cellsrv.trc |more
[pid  1185] sendmsg(127, {msg_name(16)={sa_family=AF_INET, sin_port=htons(20938),
sin_addr=inet_addr("192.168.10.2")}, msg_iov(3)=[{"\4\3\2\1\2
5\360C\5\0\0\0OMRON\4\3\0\0\0\0\0\0004\214\231\35\0\0\0\0"..., 76},
{"\1\0\0\0\0\0\0,\0\0\0\0\0\0\0\0\0\0\0\0\0\0\0\0\0\0\0", 28}, {"\4\3\2\
1\24\0\0\0\237>\343W\0\0\0\0004\214\231\35\373\177\0\0\233\323\252\2\0\10\250\300"..., 44}],
msg_controllen=0, msg_flags=0}, 0 <unfinished ...>
[pid  1185] <... sendmsg resumed> )      = 148
[pid  1185] sendmsg(127, {msg_name(16)={sa_family=AF_INET, sin_port=htons(28810),
sin_addr=inet_addr("192.168.10.1")}, msg_iov(3)=[{"\4\3\2\1\2
```

```
5\360C\5\0\0\0\0MRON\4\3\0\0\0\0\0\0004\214\231\35\0\0\0\0"..., 76},
{"\1\0\0\0\0\0\0\0,\0\0\0\0\0\0\0\0\0\0\0\0\0\0\0\0\0\0\0", 28}, {"\4\3\2\
1\24\0\0\0\350\217\225\30\0\0\0\0004\214\231\35\374\177\0\0tP8b\0\10\250\300"..., 44}],
msg_controllen=0, msg_flags=0}, 0 <unfinished ...>
[pid  1185] <... sendmsg resumed> )      = 148
```

How It Works

On the Exadata Storage Servers, `cellsrv` performs I/O requests to SAS disks or PCI flash devices. Tracing `cellsrv` from a storage server shows these I/O calls as well as the interconnect messaging provided by the iDB and RDS over InfiniBand.

PART 2

Preparing for Exadata

With a solid understanding of the Oracle Exadata Database Machine hardware and software architecture and a firm grasp of your current database workload characteristics, you should be able to begin forming an opinion as to whether Exadata is the right fit for your database environment. The chapters in this section will help validate these opinions and provide a framework for developing an Exadata fit analysis.

If you've already made an Exadata investment and feel that you are not realizing the extreme performance benefits that Exadata has promised, this chapter can be used to validate your initial assumptions and, ideally, provide insight to serve as basis for improvement.

CHAPTER 4

Workload Qualification

Is Exadata the right database platform for every Oracle database, or does Exadata only make sense for certain kinds of Oracle databases? Does it shine with data warehouses but provide limited benefit for online transaction processing databases? Most importantly, is Oracle Exadata the right fit for *your* database workload?

The answers to these questions can be complex, as they entail measuring the benefits an Oracle Exadata Database Machine may deliver in your business against the financial investment it entails. An Exadata investment is typically a non-trivial expense in most companies, both from a hardware purchase and software licensing perspective. As such, properly qualifying your workload in preparation for Exadata is important.

Other vendors provide very fast and often cheaper per-component hardware solutions, but none of these can interject the Exadata software functionality into their solution. As explained in Chapters 2 and 3, Oracle performs I/O differently on Exadata under certain conditions, and this is what allows an Exadata solution to deliver extreme database performance. As such, database workload qualification for Oracle Exadata really boils down to a few questions:

- Will Exadata software features be utilized with my current workload?
- Will the performance gains offered by these software features provide enough business value to justify the cost?

Of course, the best way to answer these questions is to run your databases on Exadata, perform a formal load test, and collect performance benchmarks. This effort often requires considerable planning and investment, both on the part of your company, Oracle, and/or the Oracle Partner providing the machine. The recipes in this chapter should help you make intelligent decisions up front, using data you already have in your database environment to provide a reasonable level of confidence in what Exadata will do for you. If you are already an Exadata customer, the methods in this chapter can still be valuable in troubleshooting and future system considerations.

4-1. Quantifying I/O Characteristics of Your Current Database

Problem

You are considering Oracle Exadata and wish to have some guidelines in determining whether your current database workload will be well suited to take advantage of the Oracle Exadata Database Machine in order to achieve as-advertised levels of "extreme performance."

Solution

In this recipe, we will show you how to:

- Use an Oracle AWR report on your current database to identify your database's workload characteristics and assess whether it is likely to benefit from Exadata Smart Scan
- Use an Oracle AWR report to identify your SQL statements, performing physical reads to assess whether they are likely to benefit from Smart Scan

- Use an Oracle AWR report to capture the top segments that are accessed via physical reads to predict whether they will benefit from Smart Scan

- Assess whether your current workload will benefit from other Exadata Storage Server software features such as Hybrid Columnar Compression, Storage Indexes, I/O Resource Management, and so forth

The first task is to identify workload patterns that could qualify for Exadata Smart Scan. Smart Scan is arguably the *most* important software feature bundled in the Exadata Storage Server software and generally provides the most significant performance benefit. On Exadata, Smart Scans occur when Oracle's optimizer chooses a full table scan or fast full index scan and when the query is able to access the data using serial or parallel direct reads.

> **Note** Please see Recipe 15-10 for more information about Oracle's direct read algorithm.

A good place to start in assessing Smart Scan workload qualification is with the Automatic Workload Repository (AWR). In your current database, select a representative time interval and generate an AWR report. The first thing we recommend to look at is the Top 5 Timed Foreground Events section, depicted in Figure 4-1.

Top 5 Timed Foreground Events

Event	Waits	Time(s)	Avg wait (ms)	% DB time	Wait Class
DB CPU		3,930		64.93	
direct path read	348,106	1,104	3	18.24	User I/O
db file sequential read	78,321	363	5	6.00	User I/O
db file scattered read	12,153	131	11	2.17	User I/O
log file sync	10,426	27	3	0.44	Commit

Figure 4-1. Top 5 Timed Foreground Events from AWR report

We see database CPU consuming 64.93% of our overall time, which alone doesn't necessarily qualify this workload for Exadata, but we're also seeing direct path read and db file scattered read wait events. Both of these typically indicate we're doing full scanning of some sort, and potentially these could be offloaded and optimized with Exadata Smart Scan. Next, jump to the SQL Ordered by Physical Reads section to get a picture of which SQL statements are doing physical I/O. Figure 4-2 displays an example of this section from the AWR report generated previously.

SQL ordered by Physical Reads (UnOptimized)

- UnOptimized Read Reqs = Physical Read Reqs - Optimized Read Reqs
- %Opt - Optimized Reads as percentage of SQL Read Requests
- %Total - UnOptimized Read Reqs as a percentage of Total UnOptimized Read Reqs
- Total Physical Read Requests: 881,637
- Captured SQL account for 90.0% of Total
- Total UnOptimized Read Requests: 881,637
- Captured SQL account for 90.0% of Total
- Total Optimized Read Requests: 1
- Captured SQL account for 0.0% of Total

UnOptimized Read Reqs	Physical Read Reqs	Executions	UnOptimized Reqs per Exec	%Opt	%Total	SQL Id	SQL Module	SQL Text
554,690	554,690	127	4,367.64	0.00	62.92	c4g3860gd5adm	FNDWFBG	SELECT WN.NOTIFICATION_ID FROM...
550,910	550,910	72	7,651.53	0.00	62.49	d1swc9auhtxwd	FNDWFBG	BEGIN WF_ENGINE_BACKGROUNDCONC.
72,116	72,116	18	4,006.44	0.00	8.18	2vb1q3p3nhg11	XXPOIRTOJREXTPKG	SELECT TOTAL_RECS_CNT, SUCCESS...
60,379	60,379	3	20,126.33	0.00	6.85	0r1zf55mxauld	emagent_SQL_oracle_database	/* OracleOEM */ declare lv_sql...
60,374	60,374	11	5,488.55	0.00	6.85	99rkbtksr6rpp	emagent_SQL_oracle_database	select queue, consumer_name, a...
53,534	53,534	2	26,767.00	0.00	6.07	89dhu8bb05uvn	emagent_SQL_oracle_database	/* OracleOEM */ declare lv_sql...
53,480	53,480	10	5,348.00	0.00	6.07	24mtfafk3lws4	emagent_SQL_oracle_database	select queue, avg(sysdate-ENQ_...
49,102	49,102	13	3,777.08	0.00	5.57	10grkt4jry1xc	XXPOIRTOJREXTPKG	BEGIN xx_csd_ext_1_poreq_pkg.m...
28,768	28,768	4	7,192.00	0.00	3.26	1qfhrwxmh4u9s	emagent_SQL_oracle_apps_wfmlr	/* OracleOEM */ SELECT count(*...
26,144	26,144	6	4,357.33	0.00	2.97	1zy4b2kh397c7	JDBC Thin Client	BEGIN :1 := wf_rule.default_ru...
10,451	10,451	1	10,451.00	0.00	1.19	8pnxmbvdzn63s	SQL Developer	SELECT DISTINCT OA_NUMBER, NUL...

Figure 4-2. SQL ordered by Physical Reads

At this point, assuming the workload depicted in Figure 4-2 is representative of a typical load, you have some data points to help facilitate your Exadata fit assessment. But to make intelligent decisions about the data, you need to understand what business processes or functions these SQL statements are associated to, and more so, whether these are important to optimize. This is not a technical analysis. Rather, it's a business analysis supported by metrics and data.

Next, take a look at the Segments by Physical Reads section of your AWR report, as displayed in Figure 4-3.

Segments by Physical Reads

- Total Physical Reads: 12,657,062
- Captured Segments account for 90.0% of Total

Owner	Tablespace Name	Object Name	Subobject Name	Obj. Type	Physical Reads	%Total
APPLSYS	APPS_TS_TX_DATA	WF_COMMENTS		TABLE	8,814,619	69.64
ASO	APPS_TS_QUEUES	ASO_ORDER_FEEDBACK_T		TABLE	1,890,934	14.94
APPLSYS	APPS_TS_QUEUES	WF_NOTIFICATION_OUT		TABLE	458,068	3.62
APPLSYS	APPS_TS_TX_DATA	WF_ITEM_ACTIVITY_STATUSES		TABLE	168,452	1.33
APPLSYS	APPS_TS_TX_DATA	FND_CONCURRENT_REQUESTS		TABLE	24,428	0.19

Figure 4-3. *Segments by Physical Reads*

The information in Figure 4-3 requires an even deeper understanding of how physical I/O on these objects is related to overall performance for key business objectives.

The points we're attempting to illustrate are as follows:

- Use data from your existing database's workload repository to understand what your I/O workload profile is.

- Determine whether you have important business functions whose throughput or response time is limited by physical I/O.

- Furthermore, determine whether the queries accessing this data are performing full scans to retrieve the data.

- Do not rely on macroscopic, system-level statistics to drive your decision. Start by looking at the SQL statement level and ensure that you've got a collection of "important" SQL statements that is frequently performing full scans, is I/O-bound, and requires performance improvement to enable business success or reduce business risk.

What about Exadata's other software features? Table 4-1 provides brief explanations of how we recommend conducting an Exadata fit assessment based on your current database.

Table 4-1. *Exadata Storage Software workload fit assessment*

Software Feature	What to Look for in Current Database	Exadata Fit Assessment Comments
Hybrid Columnar Compression	Very large tables with static data that undergo near-zero DML	HCC is typically not an Exadata "driver," but in certain situations it can be depending on data volumes and DML patterns. If disk capacity is your #1 business problem, there are probably cheaper ways to solve it than with Exadata.

(*continued*)

Table 4-1. (*continued*)

Software Feature	What to Look for in Current Database	Exadata Fit Assessment Comments
Smart Flash Cache	Variable data access patterns on databases with active data sets larger than a very large buffer cache can support, combined with a requirement to avoid unnecessary disk I/O or desire to bypass SSD/PCI flooding by non-critical operations (such as backups)	Smart Flash Cache is a feature that can only help and never hurt, but many competitors offer SSD/Flash solutions at lower costs.
Smart Flash Logging	Very active bursts of redo log writer activity that physical disks and disk cache can't consistently handle	Smart Flash Logging is a recent Exadata enhancement that provides physical disk redo write relief in times of high LGWR activity; alone, probably not a driver for Exadata.
Storage Indexes	Frequent large sequential scans on well-ordered, un-indexed data. You can obtain this by examining data access patterns from AWR/ADDM and having a deep understanding of your data.	Storage indexes are another software feature that never hurts and always helps. Storage indexes are not a means to provide performance assurance. Storage index entities are transient in nature and outside control of administrator or developer and thus shouldn't be a driving factor for Exadata.
I/O Resource Management	You have a desire to consolidate your database platform and ensure I/O performance isolation between competing resources.	Depending on your budget, IORM could be a key Exadata enabler in your business. IORM provides more granular, Oracle-aware I/O prioritization and SLA isolation than other hardware vendors can offer.

How It Works

With Exadata's software functionality in the storage servers, combined with its balanced, high-performing hardware, Oracle has designed the platform to reduce or eliminate disk I/O as a bottleneck. As such, when performing a workload fit assessment for Exadata, you should focus on identifying areas where disk I/O latency and/or throughput is a bottleneck, and further understand whether Exadata's software functionality is well suited to address, reduce, or eliminate the bottleneck.

This recipe is clearly geared toward Exadata Smart Scan. Most companies that purchase or are evaluating Exadata do so for performance reasons. Smart Scan provides Exadata's most important performance-related advantage and the software that allows Exadata to be more than "just a bunch of fast hardware." Exadata's other software and hardware capabilities certainly provide advantages over many competing solutions or products, but in the real world these rarely provide the overall business value Smart Scan does.

One of the points in the Smart Scan examples above should help illustrate that the "Exadata fit discussion" is not necessarily a matter of "data warehouse vs. OLTP vs. mixed workload." These workload classifications have industry-defined definitions that are relatively well accepted, but in the real world the application and database design are the factors that truly identify your data access patterns. Your data access patterns are the key to unlock Exadata software features.

In contrast with most of the other recipes in this book, the main emphasis here isn't technical in nature, and it's really not even directly related to Oracle Exadata; it's about your guiding processes to provide the right technical solution to a business problem. You first need to understand where your business problem lies. Do you have application performance issues that are directly limiting your ability to generate revenue? Do you have performance problems that are negatively impacting end-user experience? What is the cost, in dollars, to the business, based on these problems? How much are you willing to spend to resolve these issues? With these questions answered, you can begin diving into the details of your current environment and outline where your performance bottlenecks reside. Work with application engineers, business analysts, or end users to map their performance issues to bottlenecks in the database. Once you've done this, classify these bottlenecks by via response time or throughput profiling and understand whether I/O is the main component of your performance profile. If so, identify whether this is occurring due to large full scan operations. At this point, with an understanding of how Oracle Exadata addresses I/O bottlenecks, you will be positioned to build the business case for an Exadata investment.

4-2. Conducting a Smart Scan Fit Analysis Using AWR

Problem

You are evaluating Oracle Exadata for your database platform in hopes of significantly improving performance and you want to assess your current database workload to predict whether existing queries will be offloaded and improved with Exadata Smart Scan.

Solution

In this recipe, we will be retrieving data from Oracle's Automatic Workload Repository (AWR) for full scan operations. Specifically, we will be looking for full table scans against heap tables that do not contain data types restricted by cell offload, tables, indexes, or table partitions that are full-scanned and eligible for direct reads, as well as queries performing full scans without using functions restricted by cell offload. In this recipe, we'll start with a few scripts and build on them to demonstrate the process required to yield a comprehensive analysis.

Start by examining DBA_HIST_SEG_STAT by running the script in Listing 4-1 below, assuming you are on Oracle 10g or higher:

Listing 4-1. lst04-01-segstat-scans.sql

```
SQL> select * from (
select tab.owner,tab.table_name,count(ss.table_scans_delta) cnt
from dba_tables tab, dba_hist_seg_stat ss, dba_objects obj
where ss.obj#=obj.object_id
and obj.object_type in ('TABLE','TABLE PARTITION','TABLE SUBPARTITION')
and tab.table_name=obj.object_name
group by tab.owner,tab.table_name
order by 3 desc)
where rownum < &&display_rows
/
Enter value for display_rows: 6
old  12: where rownum < &&display_rows
new  12: where rownum < 6

Owner           Table                           Table Scans
-----------     -----------------------------   ------------
ZX              ZX_DETAIL_TAX_LINES_GT                 5254
QP              QP_PREQ_LINES_TMP_T                    2836
APPS            CSP_SUP_DEM_PN_MV                      1888
APPLSYS         FND_CONCURRENT_REQUESTS                 859
APPLSYS         FND_CONCURRENT_PROCESSES                851

5 rows selected.
```

The output in Listing 4-1 shows that we have a number of tables that are full-scanned. Now, add criteria to only display tables that are full-scanned with a size greater than 2% the size of a specified buffer cache size, as provided in Listing 4-2:

Listing 4-2. lst04-02-segstat-scans-large.sql

```
SQL> select * from (
select tab.owner,tab.table_name,count(ss.table_scans_delta) cnt
from dba_tables tab, dba_hist_seg_stat ss, dba_objects obj
where ss.obj#=obj.object_id
and obj.object_type in ('TABLE','TABLE PARTITION','TABLE SUBPARTITION')
and tab.table_name=obj.object_name
and tab.blocks >=
   ( select .02 * ((&&cache_size_gb*1024*1024*1024)/&&db_blk_size) from dual )
     group by tab.owner,tab.table_name
order by 3 desc)
where rownum < &&display_rows
/
Enter value for cache_size_gb: 4
Enter value for db_blk_size: 8192
old   12:  select .02 * ((&&cache_size_gb*1024*1024*1024)/&&db_blk_size)
new   12:  select .02 * ((4*1024*1024*1024)/8192)
Enter value for display_rows: 6
old   17: where rownum < &&display_rows
new   17: where rownum < 6

Owner            Table                              Table Scans
-----------      --------------------------         ------------
APPLSYS          FND_CONCURRENT_REQUESTS                    859
APPLSYS          WF_ITEM_ATTRIBUTE_VALUES                   839
APPLSYS          WF_ITEM_ACTIVITY_STATUSES                  804
APPLSYS          WF_COMMENTS                                757
WSH              WSH_EXCEPTIONS                             745
5 rows selected.

SQL>
```

Expanding on this example, you can try different combinations of your target buffer cache size to see what the impact will be for potentially larger SGA sizes. Oracle Exadata X2-2 compute nodes have 96 GB of physical memory and with hugepages configured, you can have relatively large SGA sizes. Re-run the query with different values for &&cache_size_gb to compare the differences.

Let's expand our example in Listing 4-3 to only include full table scans on tables without BLOB, CLOB, BFILE, or LONG data types, as these data types are not Smart Scan eligible:

Listing 4-3. lst04-03-segstat-scans-large-supp.sql

```
SQL> select *
{ ... code from lst04-02-segstat-scans-large-supp.sql ... }
and not exists
( select 'x' from dba_tab_columns c
where tab.owner=c.owner
```

```
and tab.table_name=c.table_name
and c.data_type in ('BLOB','CLOB','BFILE','LONG')
)
{ ... code from lst04-02-segstat-scans-large-supp.sql ... }
/
Enter value for cache_size_gb: 10
Enter value for db_blk_size: 8192
old  12:   select .02 * ((&&cache_size_gb*1024*1024*1024)/&&db_blk_size)
new  12:   select .02 * ((10*1024*1024*1024)/8192)
Enter value for display_rows: 6
old  23: where rownum < &&display_rows
new  23: where rownum < 6

Owner           Table                               Table Scans
------------    ------------------------------      ------------
APPLSYS         FND_CONCURRENT_REQUESTS                      860
APPLSYS         WF_ITEM_ATTRIBUTE_VALUES                     840
APPLSYS         WF_ITEM_ACTIVITY_STATUSES                    805
APPLSYS         WF_COMMENTS                                  757
WSH             WSH_EXCEPTIONS                               746

5 rows selected.
```

Thus far, we've shown some interesting information that may be helpful in your Exadata Smart Scan analysis, but unless you're intimately familiar with your application code, a simple listing of table scans on a large table may not necessarily allow you to make intelligent decisions when planning for Exadata. So let's expand our analysis to examine data in Oracle's historical Active Session History view, DBA_HIST_ACTIVE_SESS_HISTORY. In the query in Listing 4-4, we will search for full scan SQL plan operations:

Listing 4-4. lst04-04-scans-ash.sql

```
SQL> select sql_id,sql_child_number,sql_plan_operation||' '||sql_plan_options sqlop,
owner||'.'||object_name seg,
sum(sql_secs_per_snap)/60 dbt from (
SELECT ash.snap_id,ash.sample_id,ash.sql_id, ash.sql_child_number,
ash.sql_plan_operation, ash.sql_plan_options, obj.owner, obj.object_name,
10*(count(sample_id) over (partition by ash.sql_id,ash.sql_child_number,ash.snap_id))
    sql_secs_per_snap
FROM dba_hist_active_sess_history ash,
dba_objects obj
WHERE ash.wait_class = 'User I/O'
AND  (   (    ash.sql_plan_operation = 'TABLE ACCESS' AND ash.sql_plan_options LIKE '%FULL%')
     OR  (    ash.sql_plan_operation = 'INDEX' AND ash.sql_plan_options LIKE '%FAST%FULL%'))
and obj.object_id=ash.current_obj#
and obj.owner not in ('SYS','SYSTEM')
and obj.object_type in ('TABLE','INDEX')
)
group by sql_id,sql_child_number,sql_plan_operation, sql_plan_options,owner, object_name
order by 5 desc
/
```

```
                                                              Time spent
SQL ID           Child#    Operation + Options    Segment                         (Secs)
--------------   ------    -------------------    ---------------------------     -----------
c4g3860gd5adm    1         TABLE ACCESS FULL      APPLSYS.WF_COMMENTS             1883794.33
c4g3860gd5adm    4         TABLE ACCESS FULL      APPLSYS.WF_COMMENTS              603418.17
6v2ckrt9j1j6g    0         INDEX FAST FULL SCAN   BOM.CST_ITEM_COST_DETAILS_N       50592.33
1qfhrwxmh4u9s    0         TABLE ACCESS FULL      APPLSYS.WF_NOTIFICATION_OUT       29762.67
... Additional SQL operations omitted for brevity
```

Now you can add in criteria to our SQL statement to limit the output to SQL operations doing full scans on segments that are large (in other words, those that will qualify for direct reads), as displayed in Listing 4-5:

Listing 4-5. lst04-05-scans-ash-large.sql

```
SQL> select
{ ... Code from lst04-04-scans-ash.sql ...}
and seg.blocks >
    (select .02 * ((&&target_cache_size_gb*1024*1024*1024)/&&target_db_blk_size) from dual))
group by sql_id,sql_child_number,sql_plan_operation, sql_plan_options,
owner, object_name,blocks
order by 6 desc
/
old   25:     select .02 * ((&&target_cache_size_gb*1024*1024*1024)/&&target_db_blk_size)
new   25:     select .02 * ((10*1024*1024*1024)/8192)

SQL ID           Child#    Operation + Options    Segment                         Blks      Time (Secs)
--------------   ------    -------------------    ---------------------------     -------   -----------
c4g3860gd5adm    1         TABLE ACCESS FULL      APPLSYS.WF_COMMENTS             70048     1883794.33
c4g3860gd5adm    4         TABLE ACCESS FULL      APPLSYS.WF_COMMENTS             70048      603418.17
1qfhrwxmh4u9s    0         TABLE ACCESS FULL      APPLSYS.WF_NOTIFICATION_OUT     15072       29762.67
26chjdn37vcb7    0         TABLE ACCESS FULL      CN.CN_NOTIFY_LOG_ALL             0688       18969.67
... Additional output omitted
```

In Listing 4-5, we've queried our ASH data to show SQL statements that included a full table scan or fast full index scan operations on segments larger than 2% the size of a 10 GB database buffer cache. What if we want to also examine SQL with filter predicates not eligible for Smart Scan? AWR tables do not publish the FILTER_PREDICATES and ACCESS_PREDICATES columns, unfortunately. But if your library cache happens to still have some of your "important" cursors in it, you can revise the previous query on DBA_HIST_SQL_PLAN to use V$SQL_PLAN as displayed in Listing 4-6:

Listing 4-6. lst04-06-scans-sqlplans-large-supp.sql

```
SQL> select s.sql_id,s.object_owner||'.'||s.object_name obj,
s.operation||' '||s.options op
from v$sql_plan s, dba_segments seg
where s.options like '%FULL%'
and   s.object_name=seg.segment_name
and   s.object_owner=seg.owner
and seg.blocks >
   ( select .02 * ((&&cache_size_gb*1024*1024*1024)/&&db_blk_size) from dual
)
and not exists
 ( select 'x'
```

```
    from v$sqlfn_metadata md
    where md.offloadable='NO'
    and nvl(instr(s.filter_predicates,md.name),0) > 0
 )
order by s.sql_id,s.position
/
Enter value for cache_size_gb: 10
Enter value for db_blk_size: 8192
old   10:   select .02 * ((&&cache_size_gb*1024*1024*1024)/&&db_blk_size)
new   10:   select .02 * ((10*1024*1024*1024)/8192)

SQL_ID           Object                                Operation
-------------    ----------------------------------    --------------------
01rfy6p73njyj    APPLSYS.FND_CONCURRENT_REQUESTS       TABLE ACCESS FULL
0w91uqngszqj8    VXTXJ.LINEITEM                        TABLE ACCESS FULL
0wshuscduszjs    INV.MTL_SYSTEM_ITEMS_TL               TABLE ACCESS FULL
0z6883trn65pq    AR.HZ_RELATIONSHIPS                   TABLE ACCESS FULL
                 AR.HZ_RELATIONSHIPS                   TABLE ACCESS FULL
                 AR.HZ_RELATIONSHIPS                   TABLE ACCESS FULL
                 AR.HZ_RELATIONSHIPS                   TABLE ACCESS FULL
```

How It Works

In order to qualify for Exadata Smart Scan, the following requirements must be met:

- A table or index must be full-scanned
- The segment must qualify for direct reads
- The SQL operations must not include filter operations ineligible for Smart Scan, as outlined in V$SQLFN_METADATA

Table scans occur for a SQL statement when no indexes exist on a table, when the indexes on the table are not suitable based on the query predicates in the SQL statement, when the optimizer determines it is more effective to read all of the table's blocks than it would be to read an available index, and so forth. In other words, Oracle's optimizer is responsible for choosing a full table scan operation based on the information it has about the base table and indexes, combined with the relative costs of performing indexed scans versus table scans.

If the data required for a SQL operation can be wholly met based on an existing index, and the cost of full scanning indexes root, branch, and leaf blocks is determined to be less expensive than other available operations, Oracle can choose to perform a fast full index scan. Fast full index scans qualify for Smart Scan on Exadata.

The V$SQLFN_METADATA view contains metadata about operators and built-in functions. The view contains an important column, OFFLOADABLE, which indicates whether the function or operator is eligible for cell offload and Smart Scan. This is important on Exadata and could have a large bearing on your ability to leverage Smart Scan. Some of the common operators that are eligible for cell offload are <, >, =, and so forth, as displayed:

```
SYS @ edw1> select name,offloadable from v$sqlfn_metadata
where offloadable='YES'
/
```

```
NAME                OFFLOADABLE
-----------         ---------------
>                   YES
<                   YES
>=                  YES
<=                  YES
=                   YES
TO_NUMBER           YES
TO_CHAR             YES
... Output omitted for brevity
```

Many operators and functions are not eligible for cell offload and Smart Scan, as shown in the following code. If your most I/O-intensive SQL statements in your current environment include operators or functions that are not offloadable, you will not fully get the benefit of Smart Scan:

```
SYS @ edw1> select name,offloadable from v$sqlfn_metadata
where offloadable='NO'
/

NAME                OFFLOADABLE
-----------         ---------------
OPTTIS              NO
AVG                 NO
SUM                 NO
COUNT               NO
MAX                 NO
... Output omitted for brevity
```

■ **Note** Please consult the Oracle Exadata documentation to learn more about Smart Scan enablers and disablers.

In this recipe we've provided several scripts that query data on the AWR views DBA_HIST_SEG_STAT and DBA_HIST_SQL_PLAN in order to arm you with the means to qualify your existing workload for Exadata Smart Scan. Much of the same information can be retrieved via Enterprise Manager, including Oracle's Exadata Simulator presented in Recipe 4-3.

As is the case in Recipe 4-1, the information you gather in assessing whether your current database workload is a good or poor fit for Exadata isn't really a matter of table names, table scan frequencies, and so forth. The data you collect in this recipe should be associated with business functions and business priorities in order to make sound judgments.

If, at the end of your AWR analysis, you can clearly communicate something akin to the following statements, you should be able to make a business case for Exadata:

- "25% of the queries that run against our production database perform full scans."

- "80% of these full scans occur on large tables; tables that, when full-scanned, are likely to be accessed via direct read."

- "Direct reads are a prerequisite for Exadata Smart Scan, and Smart Scan is the most important performance feature on Exadata."

- "Furthermore, in working with the application owners and key business stakeholders, more than half of these SQL statements are part of critical business thread."

- "In most of these critical business threads, we experience performance problems that impact revenue."
- "The cost to the business of not addressing the problems is $1,000,000 per month."

4-3. Conducting a Smart Scan Fit Analysis Using Exadata Simulation

Problem

You are running Oracle 11gR2 and wish to analyze your current Oracle database workload. You want to determine its workload fit using built-in Oracle 11gR2 utilities without manually mining Oracle AWR and Oracle ASH reports and data.

Solution

In this recipe, we will demonstrate the use of Oracle's SQL Performance Analyzer with Exadata Simulation to analyze your current database workload for Exadata.

The first thing you need to do is identify which time ranges and methods to use for your SQL Tuning Set. For example, if you wanted to use the last three days of AWR snapshots, you could do the following:

```
SQL> select min(snap_id),max(snap_id)
from dba_hist_snapshot
where begin_interval_time > sysdate-3
/

MIN(SNAP_ID) MAX(SNAP_ID)
------------ ------------
       22919        22966
```

Next, create a SQL Tuning and load your SQL Tuning Set with data from Oracle AWR, as displayed in Listing 4-7.

Listing 4-7. lst04-07-create-sqlset.sql

```
SQL> exec DBMS_SQLTUNE.CREATE_SQLSET('EXA_SIM_STS');

PL/SQL procedure successfully completed.

SQL>
SQL> declare
  baseline_ref_cursor DBMS_SQLTUNE.SQLSET_CURSOR;
begin
  open baseline_ref_cursor for
    select VALUE(p)
    from table(DBMS_SQLTUNE.SELECT_WORKLOAD_REPOSITORY(&&snap_low,&&snap_high,
        NULL,NULL,NULL,NULL,NULL,NULL,NULL,'ALL')) p;
  DBMS_SQLTUNE.LOAD_SQLSET('EXA_SIM_STS', baseline_ref_cursor);
end;
/
```

```
Enter value for snap_low: 22919
Enter value for snap_high: 22966

PL/SQL procedure successfully completed.

SQL>
```

For purposes of the example below, we've decided to build a SQL Tuning Set based on three minutes of activity from our cursor cache:

```
SQL> begin
        dbms_sqltune.create_sqlset(sqlset_name=>'EXA_SIM2',
            description=>'Exadata tcellsim test #2');
    end;
/

PL/SQL procedure successfully completed.

SQL>
SQL> begin
        dbms_sqltune.capture_cursor_cache_sqlset (
            sqlset_name     => 'EXA_SIM2',
            time_limit      => 180,
            repeat_interval => 10
        );
    end;
/

PL/SQL procedure successfully completed.

SQL>
```

■ **Note** We chose to create our SQL Tuning Set without using Enterprise Manager to show how easy this can be done outside of the browser interface, but you can also use Grid Control to accomplish the same task. The choice of whether to use Enterprise Manager versus Oracle's built-in PL/SQL package is generally a matter of personal preference. The use of Enterprise Manager assumes functional, current versions of the software, and since not all organizations upgrade or patch their Enterprise Manager Grid Control software to the most recent versions and may have Oracle 11gR2 databases monitored and managed by earlier versions of Grid Control, we elected to demonstrate using built-in Oracle PL/SQL packages in this recipe.

Once your SQL Tuning Set is created, change directories to $ORACLE_HOME/rdbms/admin, log in to SQL*Plus as SYSDBA, and run tcellsim.sql. This will use SQL Performance Analyzer to perform storage cell simulation.

■ **Note** This process will execute SQL Performance Analyzer tests against the SQL in your SQL Tuning Set and could introduce a non-trivial load on your test system, so plan accordingly if you wish to run this on a production environment.

Once your SQL Tuning Set is created, change directories to $ORACLE_HOME/rdbms/admin, log in to SQL*Plus, and launch tcellsim.sql. It will prompt you for your SQL Tuning Set name and owning schema:

```
$ cd $ORACLE_HOME/rdbms/admin
oracale@aixserver:/PROD/bin/db/tech_st/11.2.0/rdbms/admin
$ sqlplus / as sysdba

SQL*Plus: Release 11.2.0.2.0 Production on Tue Aug 7 09:09:08 2012

Copyright (c) 1982, 2010, Oracle.  All rights reserved.

Connected to:
Oracle Database 11g Enterprise Edition Release 11.2.0.2.0 - 64bit Production
With the Partitioning, Automatic Storage Management, OLAP, Data Mining
and Real Application Testing options

SQL> @tcellsim

10 Most active SQL tuning sets
~~~~~~~~~~~~~~~~~~~~~~~~~~~~~~~~~~~~~~~~~~~~~~~~~~~

NAME                      OWNER               SQL_COUNT    DESCP
------------------------  ------------------  -----------  ----------
EXA_SIM2                  SYS                        8587  Exadata tcellsim tes
EXA_SIM_STS               SYS                         819

Specify the name and owner of SQL tuning set to use
~~~~~~~~~~~~~~~~~~~~~~~~~~~~~~~~~~~~~~~~~~~~~~~~~~~
Enter value for sts_name: EXA_SIM2
Enter value for sts_owner: SYS

 >> SQL tuning set specified: EXA_SIM2 owned by SYS

Run Cell simulation
~~~~~~~~~~~~~~~~~~~~~~~~~~~~~~~~~~~~~~~~~~~~~~~~~~~
>> 1. create a spa analysis task to test cell simulation
~~~~~~~~~~~~~~~~~~~~~~~~~~~~~~~~~~~~~~~~~~~~~~~~~~~

 >> Name of SPA analysis task: TASK_29102

... tcellsim.sql output omitted for brevity

General Information
-------------------------------------------------------------------------------

 Task Information:                    Workload Information:
 ---------------------------------    ---------------------------------------
  Task Name      : TASK_29102          SQL Tuning Set Name         : EXA_SIM2
  Task Owner     : SYS                 SQL Tuning Set Owner        : SYS
  Description    :                     Total SQL Statement Count   : 8587
```

```
Execution Information:
-----------------------------------------------------------------------------------------------
  Execution Name         : EXEC_28484              Started              : 08/07/2012 10:49:59
  Execution Type         : COMPARE PERFORMANCE     Last Updated         : 08/07/2012 10:51:34
  Description            :                         Global Time Limit    : UNLIMITED
  Scope                  : COMPREHENSIVE           Per-SQL Time Limit   : UNUSED
  Status                 : COMPLETED               Number of Errors     : 18

  Number of Unsupported SQL   : 102

Analysis Information:
-----------------------------------------------------------------------------------------------
 Before Change Execution:                          After Change Execution:
 -----------------------------------------         ------------------------------------------
  Execution Name      : cell_simulation_DISABLED    Execution Name      : cell_simulation_ENABLED
  Execution Type      : TEST EXECUTE                Execution Type      : TEST EXECUTE
  Scope               : COMPREHENSIVE               Scope               : COMPREHENSIVE
  Status              : COMPLETED                   Status              : COMPLETED
  Started             : 08/07/2012 09:09:19         Started             : 08/07/2012 09:55:19
  Last Updated        : 08/07/2012 09:54:49         Last Updated        : 08/07/2012 10:49:24
  Global Time Limit   : UNLIMITED                   Global Time Limit   : UNLIMITED
  Per-SQL Time Limit  : UNUSED                      Per-SQL Time Limit  : UNUSED
  Number of Errors    : 18                          Number of Errors    : 17
 -----------------------------------------

 Comparison Metric: IO_INTERCONNECT_BYTES
 ------------------
 Workload Impact Threshold: 1%
 -------------------------
 SQL Impact Threshold: 1%
 --------------------
Report Summary
-----------------------------------------------------------------------------------------------
 Projected Workload Change Impact:
 -----------------------------------------
  Overall Impact         :  4.05%
  Improvement Impact     :  11.84%
  Regression Impact      :  -7.79%
 SQL Statement Count
 -----------------------------------------
  SQL Category   SQL Count  Plan Change Count
  Overall            8587                  0
  Improved              2                  0
  Regressed             1                  0
 Unchanged           8464                  0
  with Errors          18                  0
  Unsupported         102                  0
```

```
Top 10 SQL Sorted by Absolute Value of Change Impact on the Workload
---------------------------------------------------------------------------
|           |              | Impact on | Execution | Metric    | Metric   | Impact  |
| object_id | sql_id       | Workload  | Frequency | Before    | After    | on SQL  |
---------------------------------------------------------------------------
|     24835 | f4x52g9jsx0f |    -7.79% |     53953 |   3194880 |  3563520 | -11.54% |
|     23748 | c4g3860gd5adm|     7.58% |       492 |  39460864 |    98304 |  99.75% |
|     21978 | 8u5bcx7k90a60|     4.26% |       508 |  21422080 |     8192 |  99.96% |
|     18138 | 1qfhrwxmh4u9s|     -.13% |        40 | 928636928 |937123840 |   -.91% |
|     17861 | 19cz7fwyszdq4|     -.04% |        50 |  54280192 | 56573952 |  -4.23% |
|     22446 | 9qp9c0785fyxz|      .03% |       152 |    458752 |    24576 |  94.64% |
|     22561 | 9w340a4dj3bdb|     -.02% |        55 |   7618560 |  8486912 |  -11.4% |
|     21793 | 8fh50ckd20cu6|      .02% |     47368 |       910 |        0 |    100% |
---------------------------------------------------------------------------
Note: time statistics are displayed in microseconds
```

As you can see in this output, two of the top ten SQL statements sampled show a relatively significant performance savings based on the Exadata Simulation. The Exadata Simulation uses the IO_INTERCONNECT_BYTES metrics to form its comparison.

A logical next step may be to query the actual SQL text from any of the SQL statements in the report and perform additional analysis. For example, let's consider SQL_ID c4g3860gd5adm in the previous script:

```
SQL> select sql_text from v$sql
    where sql_id='c4g3860gd5adm'
/
SELECT WN.NOTIFICATION_ID FROM WF_NOTIFICATIONS WN, WF_COMMENTS WC WHERE EXISTS
( SELECT /*+ NO_UNNEST */ 'x' FROM WF_ITEM_ACTIVITY_STATUSES_H WIASH WHERE WIASH
.NOTIFICATION_ID= WN.NOTIFICATION_ID AND WIASH.ITEM_TYPE = WN.MESSAGE_TYPE AND W
IASH.ITEM_TYPE = :B3 AND WIASH.ITEM_KEY = :B2 AND WIASH.PROCESS_ACTIVITY = :B1 )
 AND WN.STATUS = 'CLOSED' AND WN.NOTIFICATION_ID = WC.NOTIFICATION_ID AND WC.TO_
ROLE = 'WF_SYSTEM' AND WC.ACTION_TYPE = 'RESPOND'

SQL>
```

This SQL statement reflects an Oracle Workflow query that runs as part of a Workflow Background Process, which we know based on our understanding of the application. The Exadata Simulator measured a 99.75% improvement for this SQL statement based on its simulation. With this information we can begin to communicate that at least part of the Workflow processing will benefit substantially with Exadata.

How It Works

Starting with Oracle database versions 11.1.0.7 and above, along with Oracle Enterprise Manager 10.2.0.5 with 11gR1/11gR2 database targets, Oracle provides an interesting feature called the Exadata Simulator. This capability can be launched from Enterprise Manager or $ORACLE_HOME/rdbms/admin/tcellsim.sql.

The Exadata Simulation utility uses SQL Performance Analyzer to compare before-and-after results based on SQL Tuning Sets. Specifically, it uses SQL Performance Analyzer to test Exadata cell storage in *simulation mode*.

It does this by accepting a SQL Tuning Set and launching SQL Performance Analyzer with cell_simulation_enabled= FALSE, then with cell_simulation_enabled = TRUE. At its completion, it compares the results of the SQL Performance Analyzer executions. Specifically:

1. An administrator creates a SQL Tuning Set.

2. An administrator runs the Exadata Simulator using either tcellsim.sql or Enterprise Manager.

3. SQL Performance Analyzer performs an initial analysis with Exadata cell simulation disabled:

```
dbms_sqlpa.execute_analysis_task(
    task_name => :aname,
    execution_type => 'execute',
    execution_name => 'cell_simulation_DISABLED',
    execution_params => dbms_advisor.arglist('cell_simulation_enabled',
    'FALSE'));
```

4. SQL Performance Analyzer then performs an analysis with cell simulation enabled:

```
dbms_sqlpa.execute_analysis_task(
    task_name => :aname,
    execution_type => 'execute',
    execution_name => 'cell_simulation_ENABLED,
    execution_params => dbms_advisor.arglist('cell_simulation_enabled',
    'TRUE'));
```

5. When complete, performance results between the two tests are compared using the IO_INTERCONNECT_BYTES metric:

```
dbms_sqlpa.execute_analysis_task(:aname, 'compare',
    execution_params => dbms_advisor.arglist('comparison_metric',
    'io_interconnect_bytes'));
```

6. Finally, the simulator displays output in a report:

```
select dbms_sqlpa.report_analysis_task(:aname, 'text', top_sql => 10) spa_summary
```

The Exadata Simulator is designed to analyze and capture the metrics from the most relevant Exadata Storage Server metric, IO_INTERCONNECT_BYTES, based on logic built within SQL Performance Analyzer to estimate the savings in I/O to be expected if/when the workload SQL statements run on an Exadata platform. The results give an indication of the extent of the benefit you could possibly expect to get from a database workload port to Exadata. One of the nice things about this simulation analysis is that it takes in to consideration your *current*, unmodified workload, without application design change or SQL refactoring.

■ **Note** The results from Exadata Simulation can provide a frame of reference for expected benefit on Exadata, but many other factors can also contribute to this analysis.

4-4. Performing a Hybrid Columnar Compression Fit Assessment

Problem
You wish to identify tables that may be suitable for Hybrid Columnar Compression on Exadata to understand the extent of the benefit you may receive from both a disk capacity and potentially a performance perspective.

Solution
In this recipe, we will provide some guidelines to identify tables that are potential candidates for Hybrid Columnar Compression on Exadata. Specifically, we will outline steps to measure your segment sizes and capture DML activity on your candidate tables.

The first step is to understand your data and decide "how large is too large?" Different companies have different tolerances for table or table partition sizes. In Listing 4-8, let's assume we want to find all of our segments consuming more than 2% of the total size of the database:

Listing 4-8. lst04-08-hcc-candidate.sql

```
SQL> select    owner,segment_name,
               segment_type,partition_name,bytes/1024/1024/1024 gb,
               round(100*(bytes/totbytes),2) pctofdb
from ( select owner,segment_name,segment_type,partition_name, bytes,(sum(bytes) over ())
    totbytes
         from dba_segments order by 4 asc)
where 100*(bytes/totbytes) > 2 --- where size > 2% the size of the database
order by 5 desc
/
```

Owner	Segment	SEGMENT_TYPE	Partition	Size (GB)	% DB Size
MYFACT	FACT_DETAIL	TABLE PARTITION	SYS_P488	206.35	7.19
MYDIM	ITEM_LOC_DIM	TABLE		185.69	6.47
MYDIM	ITEMS_DIM	TABLE		185.17	6.45
MYFACT	FACT_DETAIL	TABLE PARTITION	SYS_P469	154.30	5.38
MYFACT	FACT_DETAIL	TABLE PARTITION	SYS_P508	129.17	4.50
MYDIM	CIL_INDX_UKY_01	INDEX PARTITION	SYS_P41	92.99	3.24
MYFACT	FACT_DETAIL	TABLE PARTITION	SYS_P445	89.16	3.11

... Output omitted for brevity

With this information, you can correlate the tables in the list above with the associated DML by looking at the view DBA_HIST_SEG_STAT. DBA_HIST_SEG_STAT provides many segment-level statistics, including the number of physical writes and block changes. Listing 4-9 displays the DML activity for potential HCC candidates.

Listing 4-9. lst04-09-hcc-candidate-segstat.sql

```
SQL> select    seg.owner,seg.segment_name,
               seg.segment_type,seg.partition_name,seg.bytes/1024/1024/1024 gb,
               round(100*(seg.bytes/seg.totbytes),2) pctofdb,
               nvl(sum(segstat.pwrites),0) pwrites, nvl(sum(segstat.blkchanges),0)
                   blkchanges
```

```
from (
       select owner,segment_name,segment_type,partition_name,bytes,(sum(bytes) over ())
           totbytes
       from dba_segments order by 4 asc) seg,
       (
       select obj.owner,obj.object_name,obj.object_id, obj.data_object_id,
           sum(physical_writes_delta) pwrites,
              sum(db_block_changes_delta) blkchanges
       from dba_objects obj, dba_hist_seg_stat ss
       where obj.object_id=ss.obj#(+)
       and obj.data_object_id=ss.dataobj#(+)
       group by obj.owner,obj.object_name,obj.object_id,obj.data_object_id
       ) segstat
where 100*(seg.bytes/seg.totbytes) > 2  --- where size > 2% the size of the database
and seg.owner=segstat.owner
and seg.segment_name=segstat.object_name
group by seg.owner, seg.segment_name,seg.segment_type,seg.partition_name,seg.bytes,seg.totbytes
order by 5 desc
/
```

Owner	Segment	SEGMENT_TYPE	Partition	GB	%DB Size	Writes	Changes
MYFACT	FACT_DETAIL	TABLE PARTITION	SYS_P488	206.35	7.19	0	0
MYDIM	ITEM_LOC_DIM	TABLE		185.69	6.47	0	0
MYDIM	ITEMS_DIM	TABLE		185.17	6.45	2	16
MYFACT	FACT_DETAIL	TABLE PARTITION	SYS_P469	154.30	5.38	0	0
MYFACT	FACT_DETAIL	TABLE PARTITION	SYS_P508	129.17	4.50	0	0
MYDIM	CIL_INDX_UKY_01	INDEX PARTITION	SYS_P41	92.99	3.24	0	0
MYFACT	FACT_DETAIL	TABLE PARTITION	SYS_P445	89.16	3.11	0	0

... Output omitted

Based on this output, we can see that the only segment that has experienced any DML activity is the MYDIM.ITEMS_DIM table, which would indicate that this table may not be a good candidate for Hybrid Columnar Compression.

Let's run another scenario on a database that's experiencing more activity; in this example, we're looking at an Oracle E-Business Suite environment:

Owner	Segment	Type	(GB)	%DB	Writes	Blk Chg
AZ	AZ_REPORT	TABLE	25.67	10.34	0	0
XXTAMS	XX_EMF_DEBUG_TRACE	TABLE	21.40	8.61	2825341	22860608
APPLSYS	SYS_LOB0000135842C00015$$	LOBSEGMENT	16.60	6.68	312793	395504
APPLSYS	WF_ITEM_ATTRIBUTE_VALUES_PK	INDEX	10.95	4.41	3084226	84775376
XXTAMS	XX_EMF_DEBUG_TRACE_TEMP	TABLE	9.82	3.95	1464681	8213072
APPLSYS	WF_ITEM_ATTRIBUTE_VALUES	TABLE	6.52	2.63	1791574	205069728
CS	CS_INCIDENTS_AUDIT_B	TABLE	6.44	2.59	139510	1558560
AZ	AZ_DIFF_RESULTS	TABLE	5.53	2.23	0	0

This example shows that many of our larger tables experience relatively high DML activity and thus would not be candidates for Hybrid Columnar Compression.

This analysis alone, as you may expect, is truly just the beginning of what a Hybrid Columnar Compression fit assessment would entail. You may have cases in which only the most recent blocks in your table have DML activity against them and, in these cases, you could elect to partition the tables based on "activity dates," compress the older, dormant partitions with Hybrid Columnar Compression, leave the more active partitions uncompressed, and employ a partition maintenance strategy that strikes a balance between your capacity and performance goals.

How It Works

Performing an Exadata Hybrid Columnar Compression fit-analysis is primarily a matter of "knowing your database." Most seasoned Oracle database administrators have a relatively good grasp of what their largest tables are, how fast they're growing, how they're accessed, how data is loaded into them, and whether their current storage footprint is imposing challenges.

Analyzing your database for Hybrid Columnar Compression is in many regards similar to analyzing for OLTP or standard compression, with a few key differences. With Hybrid Columnar Compression:

- Data must be loaded via direct path read
- Compressed tables should expect very little DML

While convention `INSERT` or load operations will function without error on Hybrid Columnar Compressed tables, the result is that new blocks are created as OLTP-compressed. This by itself may not be a significant issue, but over time it could reduce your storage savings.

If you have a Hybrid Columnar Compressed table that experiences frequent `DELETE` and `UPDATE` DML operations, Oracle will perform a few activities that could negatively impact performance:

- Oracle will lock the *entire compression unit* during the operation, which could lead to significant concurrency issues. Since a compression unit is comprised of multiple blocks and each block will contain many rows, other sessions issuing DML may experience significant wait times.

- Oracle *migrates* the blocks to OLTP-compressed blocks (in other words, row migration). Depending on the number of blocks impacted by the `UPDATE` or `DELETE` operation, this can be extremely CPU-intensive. Additionally, subsequent I/O requests for rows in these updated blocks will require extra I/O as a result of the row migration.

This being said, if you have very large tables with static data or data that is periodically loaded via direct path loads, Hybrid Columnar Compression can provide significant disk space savings. As data is retrieved from these HCC tables, fewer blocks will need to be read, yielding less I/O and better performance. Additionally, if the data is accessed via cell offload functions such as Smart Scan the data is uncompressed on the storage tier, so the CPU penalty for decompression is serviced from the multiple storage cells, each with 12 processor cores.

As you analyze the tables in your database for Hybrid Columnar Compression, consider the data usage and access patterns of your data. A very large table that only has a small percentage of "recent" rows that undergo DML may be a candidate for the following strategy:

- Partition the table according to a meaningful column, such as a DATE data type
- Compress the older, static partitions using Hybrid Columnar Compression
- Leave the current partitions uncompressed to avoid the performance overhead associated with DML and Hybrid Columnar Compressed segments

CHAPTER 5

Sizing Exadata

Prior to making an Exadata investment and periodically after the investment, especially in cases where databases are consolidated on Exadata, it is vital to perform a proper capacity-planning exercise. In our opinion, capacity planning for Oracle databases and Oracle workloads should include the following analysis:

- Processor requirements planning
- Oracle database server memory and SGA planning
- Network planning
- Disk IOPs planning
- Disk data bandwidth
- Storage capacity planning
- Storage capacity organic growth planning
- Oracle ASM disk group redundancy planning
- Disaster recovery planning
- Backup planning
- Fast Recovery Area sizing and planning

The recipes in this chapter provide specific solutions that you can use as guidelines for each of the capacity-planning areas outlined above, with the exception of memory and network capacity planning.

■ **Note** Since Exadata comes in one of four configurations, it is our assumption that the aggregate compute and storage server memory configurations and InfiniBand network capabilities will meet most environment requirements.

Throughput this chapter, we will focus on using information for your current database's Automatic Workload Repository, or AWR, to conduct each capacity-planning exercise. If you are embarking on an Exadata fit analysis for pre-Oracle 10g databases or yet to be designed/deployed environments, different capacity-planning tasks will need to be performed.

Additionally, in each recipe we will operate under the assumption that SQL refactoring and application code redesign will *not* be in scope as part of the Exadata capacity-planning exercise. In other words, scripts in each recipe as well as content in each "How It Works" section will be geared toward driving a sizing effort based on no code or application design changes.

5-1. Determining CPU Requirements

Problem

You wish to determine whether an Exadata Database Machine will provide enough CPU processing horsepower to meet your database workload requirements.

Solution

To conduct an Exadata processor capacity-planning exercise, we recommend the following approach:

- Query raw CPU-related data from Oracle AWR, export to Excel, and optionally plot trends and/or identify outlier conditions.

- Query CPU utilization averages, maximums, and other statistical information to understand usage patterns.

- Add relevant processor numbers for all environments targeted for Exadata deployment.

- Determine Exadata and Exadata model specific fit based on measured CPU-related performance data from AWR.

First, log in to SQL*Plus in your current database and connect as a user who has access to Oracle's AWR views. Run the query in Listing 5-1, which displays CPU-related information from an Oracle 11gR2 database running on a non-Exadata platform. Subsequent code listings in this recipe will expand upon this script, adding logic to ultimately allow us to complete a CPU sizing analysis for Exadata.

Listing 5-1. lst05-01-awr-cpu.sql

```
SYS @ PROD> select  snaps.id, snaps.tm,snaps.dur,snaps.instances,
       osstat.num_cpus CPUs,
       osstat.num_cpus * dur * 60 cap,
       ((timemodel.dbt - lag(timemodel.dbt,1) over (order by snaps.id)))/1000000 dbt,
       ((timemodel.dbc - lag(timemodel.dbc,1) over (order by snaps.id)))/1000000 dbc,
       ((timemodel.bgc - lag(timemodel.bgc,1) over (order by snaps.id)))/1000000 bgc,
       ((timemodel.rmanc - lag(timemodel.rmanc,1) over (order by snaps.id)))/1000000 rmanc,
       (((timemodel.dbt - lag(timemodel.dbt,1) over (order by snaps.id)))/1000000)/dur/60 aas ,
       (((timemodel.dbc - lag(timemodel.dbc,1) over (order by snaps.id)))/1000000) +
         (((timemodel.bgc - lag(timemodel.bgc,1) over (order by snaps.id)))/1000000) totora ,
       osstat.load load           ,
       ((osstat.busy_time - lag(osstat.busy_time,1) over (order by snaps.id)))/100 totos,
          round(100*(((((timemodel.dbc - lag(timemodel.dbc,1) over (order by
          snaps.id)))/1000000) +
          (((timemodel.bgc - lag(timemodel.bgc,1) over (order by snaps.id)))/1000000)) /
             (osstat.num_cpus * 60 * dur)),2) oracpupct,          round(100*(((((timemodel.rmanc
              - lag(timemodel.rmanc,1) over (order by snaps.id)))/1000000) /
             (osstat.num_cpus * 60 * dur)),2) rmancpupct,
        round(100*(((((osstat.busy_time - lag(osstat.busy_time,1) over (order by snaps.id)))/100) /
             (osstat.num_cpus * 60 * dur)),3) oscpupct,
        round(100*(((((osstat.user_time - lag(osstat.user_time,1) over (order by snaps.id)))/100) /
             (osstat.num_cpus * 60 * dur)),3) usrcpupct,
        round(100*(((((osstat.sys_time - lag(osstat.sys_time,1) over (order by snaps.id)))/100) /
             (osstat.num_cpus * 60 * dur)),3) syscpupct,
```

```sql
            round(100*((((osstat.iowait_time - lag(osstat.iowait_time,1) over (order by
                snaps.id)))/100) /
                    (osstat.num_cpus * 60 * dur)),3) iowaitcpupct,
            sysstat.logons_curr ,
            ((sysstat.logons_cum - lag (sysstat.logons_cum,1) over (order by snaps.id)))/dur/60
                logons_cum,
            ((sysstat.execs - lag (sysstat.execs,1) over (order by snaps.id)))/dur/60 execs
from
( /* DBA_HIST_SNAPSHOT */
select distinct id,dbid,tm,instances,max(dur) over (partition by id) dur from (
select distinct s.snap_id id, s.dbid,
    to_char(s.end_interval_time,'DD-MON-RR HH24:MI') tm,
    count(s.instance_number) over (partition by snap_id) instances,
    1440*((cast(s.end_interval_time as date) - lag(cast(s.end_interval_time as date),1) over
        (order by s.snap_id))) dur
from    dba_hist_snapshot s,
    v$database d
where s.dbid=d.dbid)
) snaps,
( /* Data from DBA_HIST_OSSTAT */
  select *
        from
            (select snap_id,dbid,stat_name,value from
            dba_hist_osstat
        ) pivot
    (sum(value) for (stat_name)
        in ('NUM_CPUS' as num_cpus,'BUSY_TIME' as busy_time,
            'LOAD' as load,'USER_TIME' as user_time, 'SYS_TIME' as sys_time, 'IOWAIT_TIME' as
                iowait_time))
  ) osstat,
  ( /* DBA_HIST_TIME_MODEL */
   select * from
        (select snap_id,dbid,stat_name,value from
        dba_hist_sys_time_model
    ) pivot
    (sum(value) for (stat_name)
        in ('DB time' as dbt, 'DB CPU' as dbc, 'background cpu time' as bgc,
            'RMAN cpu time (backup/restore)' as rmanc))
  ) timemodel,
  ( /* DBA_HIST_SYSSTAT */
    select * from
        (select snap_id, dbid, stat_name, value from
        dba_hist_sysstat
    ) pivot
    (sum(value) for (stat_name) in
        ('logons current' as logons_curr, 'logons cumulative' as logons_cum, 'execute count' as
            execs))
  ) sysstat
where dur > 0
and snaps.id=osstat.snap_id
and snaps.dbid=osstat.dbid
```

CHAPTER 5 ■ SIZING EXADATA

```
and snaps.id=timemodel.snap_id
and snaps.dbid=timemodel.dbid
and snaps.id=sysstat.snap_id
and snaps.dbid=sysstat.dbid
order by id asc
/
... Output omitted for brevity
```

This report will contain a number of columns including AWR snapshot information, database and CPU time information for both foreground, background, and RMAN sessions, Average Active Sessions information, a number of CPU load and utilization metrics for various Oracle session types, I/O utilization metrics, as well as other related workload metrics. Due to the number of columns in the report output, we generally open the report in Excel for readability; Figure 5-1 depicts the output from the above script in Excel.

Snap ID	Time	Snap Dur	Instances	CPUs	Tot CPU (s) Avail	DB Time (s)	DB CPU (s)	BG CPU (s)	RMAN CPU (s)	AAS	Total Oracle CPU	Tot OS Load	Tot OS CPU (s)	Oracle CPU	RMAN CPU%	OS CPU %	Usr CPU %	Sys CPU %	IO Wait CPU %	Logons curr	Logons/s
22006	6/24/12 2:00	60.67	1	12	43680	24394.34	4466	351.11	0	6.7	4817.1	4.3	8842.6	11	0	20.24	15.34	4.91	9.13	262	
22007	6/24/12 3:00	59.57	1	12	42888	8332.99	2009.85	207.35	0	2.3	2217.2	3.2	3236	5.2	0	7.55	5.81	1.73	2.15	262	
22008	6/24/12 4:00	60.62	1	12	43644	4860.73	2001.06	211.17	0	1.3	2212.2	4.3	3300.9	5.1	0	7.56	5.75	1.81	0.37	287	
22009	6/24/12 5:00	59.58	1	12	42900	8882.49	4777.56	213.33	0	2.5	4990.9	2.6	6322.6	11.6	0	14.74	12.9	1.84	2.1	297	
22010	6/24/12 6:00	59.57	1	12	42888	7009.52	3507.7	213.2	0	2	3720.9	3.3	4906	8.7	0	11.44	9.62	1.82	1.08	293	
22011	6/24/12 7:00	60.58	1	12	43620	8325.79	5134.91	215.52	0	2.3	5350.4	3	6615.8	12.3	0	15.17	13.35	1.82	1.82	303	
22012	6/24/12 8:00	59.62	1	12	42924	5363.28	3407.86	213.44	0	1.5	3621.3	1.3	4766.1	8.4	0	11.1	9.25	1.86	1.18	326	
22013	6/24/12 9:00	60.6	1	12	43632	3456.33	1963.75	256.66	37.11	1	2220.4	3.7	3044	5.1	0.1	6.98	5.72	1.26	0.75	295	
22014	6/24/12 10:00	59.65	1	12	42948	6261.05	2492.71	790	581.33	1.7	3282.7	2.6	4734.9	7.6	1.4	11.03	8.91	2.12	6.54	297	
22015	6/24/12 11:00	59.58	1	12	42900	4639.75	2412.54	252.01	36.46	1.3	2604.6	1.6	3904	6.2	0.1	9.1	6.93	2.17	1.71	307	
22016	6/24/12 12:00	60.68	1	12	43692	6319.09	2525.06	423.13	207.06	1.7	2948.2	3.7	4273.5	6.8	0.5	9.78	7.81	1.97	6.59	313	

Figure 5-1. *Database CPU statistics from AWR*

Again, your goal is to size your workload for Exadata, so the important columns/metrics you need are the Oracle-related CPU statistics. Legacy environment and server processor utilization numbers are certainly interesting but could also include processor time from non-Oracle related components and thus add an amount of "background noise" to our analysis. So, the important columns and metrics to examine from the Figure 5-1 are the following:

- Snapshot duration: This is the duration, in minutes, between AWR snapshots. It provides a time element by which to divide our counter-based AWR metrics, yielding utilization-per-second numbers.

- Number of CPUs: This reflects the number of processor cores in your existing database-tier environment and is required to scope processing metrics by processor core.

- Total Oracle CPU seconds: This is all of the Oracle-related CPU time during the snapshot interval.

- Oracle CPU %: This is the total time, from `DBA_HIST_SYS_TIME_MODEL`, for `DB CPU` and `background cpu time` metrics divided by the sampling interval, in seconds, multiplied by the processor count.

- Average Active Sessions, or AAS: This is the average number of active sessions over the snap of the AWR snapshot range. Active sessions are defined as either actively assigned to a processor and consuming CPU time or actively waiting on resources, such as I/O.

With this information, you can graph the data from the spreadsheet to display our Oracle-related CPU statistics. Please refer to Figure 5-2.

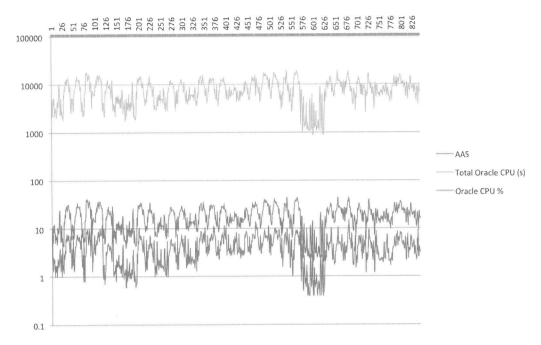

Figure 5-2. Oracle CPU seconds, Oracle CPU utilization, and Average Active Sessions from Oracle AWR

Based on the data collected so far, you can begin predicting your CPU requirements by examining two important pieces of information: Average Active Sessions and Oracle CPU utilization multiplied by the processor core count. The Average Active Sessions metric is worth discussing in more detail.

Average Active Sessions, or AAS, is a measure of "DB time" over a time interval. DB time includes time spent by sessions actively engaged on a processor (for example, performing logical I/O, parsing, and so on) as well as sessions currently in a wait status for any number of Oracle wait events. For example, sessions performing physical I/O will have their time-in-wait (perhaps with the DB file scattered read wait event) tracked in the DB time time-model metric. With these types of sessions, it is important to have processor cycles available at the time the wait events complete; otherwise, you will experience CPU queuing, an indication that you may have insufficient CPU bandwidth to meet your workload. For I/O-bound workloads, it is common to see AAS numbers greater than Oracle CPU utilization numbers, as AAS metrics include time-in-wait.

For purposes of CPU planning using the method of extrapolation from Oracle AWR data, you can derive your target number of CPU processor cores by evaluating the *greater* of AAS and Oracle CPU utilization.

Run the following script in Listing 5-2 to estimate your target processor requirements:

Listing 5-2. lst05-02-awr-cpu-corecnt.sql

```
SYS @ PROD> select  snaps.id, snaps.tm,snaps.dur,
         osstat.num_cpus CPUs,
         ((((timemodel.dbt -lag(timemodel.dbt,1) over (order by snaps.id)))/1000000)/dur/60
             aas ,
         round(100*(((((timemodel.dbc - lag(timemodel.dbc,1) over (order by
             snaps.id)))/1000000) +
            (((timemodel.bgc - lag(timemodel.bgc,1) over (order by snaps.id)))/1000000)) /
                (osstat.num_cpus * 60 * dur)),2) oracpupct,
         greatest(((((timemodel.dbt - lag(timemodel.dbt,1) over (order by
             snaps.id)))/1000000)/dur/60,
```

```
            osstat.num_cpus * ((((((timemodel.dbc - lag(timemodel.dbc,1) over (order by
                snaps.id)))/1000000) +
               (((timemodel.bgc - lag(timemodel.bgc,1) over (order by snaps.id)))/1000000)) /
                (osstat.num_cpus * 60 * dur)))) cpuneed
    from
    ( /* DBA_HIST_SNAPSHOT */
    select distinct id,dbid,tm,instances,max(dur) over (partition by id) dur from (
    select distinct s.snap_id id, s.dbid,
        to_char(s.end_interval_time,'DD-MON-RR HH24:MI') tm,
        count(s.instance_number) over (partition by snap_id) instances,
        1440*((cast(s.end_interval_time as date)
                - lag(cast(s.end_interval_time as date),1) over (order by s.snap_id))) dur
    from    dba_hist_snapshot s,v$database d
    where s.dbid=d.dbid)
    ) snaps,
    ( /* Data from DBA_HIST_OSSTAT */
     select *
            from
            (select snap_id,dbid,stat_name,value from
            dba_hist_osstat
     ) pivot
     (sum(value) for (stat_name)
            in ('NUM_CPUS' as num_cpus,'BUSY_TIME' as busy_time,'LOAD' as load,'USER_TIME' as
                user_time,
                'SYS_TIME' as sys_time, 'IOWAIT_TIME' as iowait_time))
     ) osstat,
    ( /* DBA_HIST_TIME_MODEL */
        select * from
            (select snap_id,dbid,stat_name,value from
             dba_hist_sys_time_model
        ) pivot
        (sum(value) for (stat_name)
            in ('DB time' as dbt, 'DB CPU' as dbc, 'background cpu time' as bgc,
'RMAN cpu time (backup/restore)' as rmanc))
        ) timemodel
    where dur > 0
    and snaps.id=osstat.snap_id
    and snaps.dbid=osstat.dbid
    and snaps.id=timemodel.snap_id
    and snaps.dbid=timemodel.dbid
    order by id asc
/
```

SnapID	Start Time	Mins	CPUs	AAS	CPU%	CPUs Required
22006	24-JUN-12 02:00	60.67	12	6.70	11.0	6.70
22007	24-JUN-12 03:00	59.57	12	2.33	5.2	2.33
22008	24-JUN-12 04:00	60.62	12	1.34	5.1	1.34

... Additional output omitted

The right-most column in the output displays the number of processors required to support our workload.

With an Exadata capacity-planning exercise, however, you will also have a large number of processors on the Exadata Storage Servers. Thus, it is important to differentiate between *processor requirements for I/O* and *processor requirements for non-I/O* wait-related database operations. You can calculate this by subtracting DB CPU time from AAS to arrive at I/O-related CPU numbers. For this type of analysis, we recommend adding a margin of error for the DB CPU time metrics, assuming that I/O requests will be satisfied faster with Exadata and potentially place greater CPU demands on the database tier nodes. In the query below we will assume the following:

- I/O-related CPU demand = (Average Active Sessions) − ((DB CPU + background CPU))
- No I/O-related CPU demand = (DB CPU + background CPU) + (50% * I/O-related CPU)

Next, run the script in Listing 5-3 to account for I/O versus non-I/O processor requirements:

Listing 5-3. lst05-03-awr-cpu-corecnt-ioadj.sql

```
SYS @ PROD> select id,tm,dur,CPUs,
            aas, oracpupct,
            (case
               when (greatest(0,aas - (oracpupct * CPUs))) > 0 then
                   ((oracpupct * CPUs) + (.5 * (aas - (oracpupct * CPUs))))
               else (oracpupct * CPUs)
            end) OraCPU,
            greatest(0,aas - (oracpupct * CPUs)) OraIOCPU,
            (( oracpupct * CPUs) + greatest(0,aas - (oracpupct * CPUs))) OraCPUTot
    from (
{ ... Code from LIsting 5-2 ...}
)
/

 Snap|Snap             |Duration|Current|       |   Ora|Non-IO |     IO|Total CPU
   ID|Start            |    Mins|   CPUs|    AAS|  CPU%|CPU Req|CPU Req|      Req
------|-----------------|--------|-------|-------|------|-------|-------|---------
 22006|24-JUN-12 02:00|   60.67|     12|   6.70|   0.1|   4.01|   5.38|     6.70
 22007|24-JUN-12 03:00|   59.57|     12|   2.33|   0.1|   1.48|   1.71|     2.33
 22008|24-JUN-12 04:00|   60.62|     12|   1.34|   0.1|   0.97|   0.73|     1.34
 22009|24-JUN-12 05:00|   59.58|     12|   2.48|   0.1|   1.94|   1.09|     2.48
... output omitted
```

Now, calculate the average, maximum, and standard deviations for the CPU numbers in Listing 5-3, as in Listing 5-4:

Listing 5-4. lst05-04-awr-cpu-corecnt-sum.sql

```
SYS @ PROD> select avg(OraCPU) AvgOraCPU, max(OraCPU) MaxOraCPU, stddev(OraCPU) StdOraCPU,
avg(OraIOCPU) AvgOraIOCPU, max(OraIOCPU) MaxOraIOCPU, stddev(OraIOCPU) StdOraIOCPU,
avg(OraCPUTot) AvgOraCPUTot, max(OraCPUTot) MaxOraCPUTot, stddev(OraCPUTot) StdOraCPUTot
from ({... Code from Listing 5-3 ...})
/

Avg NonIO| Max Non IO|StdDev Non IO|  Avg IO| Max IO| StdDev IO| Avg Total| Max Total|    StdDev
 CPU Req|    CPU Req|      CPU Req| CPU Req|CPU Req|   CPU Req|   CPU Req|   CPU Req| Total Req
---------|-----------|-------------|--------|-------|----------|----------|----------|----------
    3.22|      10.38|         1.75|    1.99|  14.47|      1.78|      4.21|     17.52|      2.56
```

Based on these numbers, for this single database we can assume that we need the following:

- 10.38 CPUs on the compute grid
- 14.47 CPUs for the storage grid
- 17.52 CPUs in total. Note that this number is smaller than the sum of compute grid and storage grid estimates; this is due to a bit of estimation for compute node (that is, DB_CPU) metrics.

> **Note** For this analysis, we propose using the maximum values to account for resource consumptions spikes.

Next, you should expand your analysis to account for additional environments, an estimated percentage of resource consumption expected across these databases, as well as add a "margin of error." Use the following SQL*Plus script to perform this task, with the following input variable descriptions:

- &num_addtl_dbs = Number of additional, potentially non-production databases that we will plan on consolidating on the same Exadata Database Machine.
- &pct_resource_load = Estimated fraction of CPU consumption that each additional environment will consume with respect to the database analyzed. For this, "1" = equal CPU weight compared to the database you're running the analysis on, ".1" = 10% the CPU load of your database, and so on.
- &margin_err = Factor of safety. For this, "1" = no margin of error, "2" = multiply our measured numbers by two, and so on.

In Listing 5-5, we will assume that we will have five additional databases, each with 25% the CPU load of our original database, and add a 20% margin of error for our CPU calculations.

> **Note** Of course, it's always more accurate to measure true CPU requirements for each database targeted for the Exadata migration but in many cases, non-production databases may have a variable workload and usage pattern.

Listing 5-5. lst05-05-awr-cpu-corecnt-sum-extr.sql

```
SYS @ PROD> select  avg(OraCPU) AvgOraCPU, max(OraCPU) MaxOraCPU, stddev(OraCPU) StdOraCPU,
avg(OraIOCPU) AvgOraIOCPU, max(OraIOCPU) MaxOraIOCPU, stddev(OraIOCPU) StdOraIOCPU,
avg(OraCPUTot) AvgOraCPUTot, max(OraCPUTot) MaxOraCPUTot, stddev(OraCPUTot) StdOraCPUTot
from (
select
(aas + (&&num_addtl_dbs * &&pct_resource_load * &&margin_err * aas )) aas,
(oracpupct+ (&&num_addtl_dbs * &&pct_resource_load * &&margin_err * oracpupct)) oracpupct,
(OraCPU + (&&num_addtl_dbs * &&pct_resource_load * &&margin_err * OraCPU)) OraCPU,
(OraIOCPU + (&&num_addtl_dbs * &&pct_resource_load * &&margin_err * OraIOCPU)) OraIOCPU,
(OraCPUTot + (&&num_addtl_dbs * &&pct_resource_load * &&margin_err * OraCPUTot)) OraCPUTot
from ( {... code from Listing 5-4 ...} )
... output omitted
 75  order by id asc
 76  ) where OraCPUTot < 100
```

```
 77  )
 78  /
Enter value for num_addtl_dbs: 5
Enter value for pct_resource_load: .25
Enter value for margin_err: 1.2

Avg NonIO| Max Non IO|StdDev Non IO|  Avg IO| Max IO| StdDev IO| Avg Total| Max Total|    StdDev
  CPU Req|    CPU Req|      CPU Req| CPU Req|CPU Req|    CPU Req|   CPU Req|   CPU Req| Total Req
---------|-----------|--------------|--------|-------|-----------|----------|----------|----------
     8.05|      25.95|          4.38|    4.97|  36.19|       4.44|     10.53|     43.79|      6.39
```

Based on the numbers above, for our consolidated workload, our CPU requirements are as follows:

- 26 CPUs on the compute grid
- 37 CPUs for the storage grid
- 44 CPUs in total

Finally, map these CPU requirements to the various Exadata configurations. In the next script, we will input the same parameters as in the previous script and additionally introduce a "core multiplier" parameter:

- &core_multiplier = Relative processor speed weight of your current database-tier environment as compared to Exadata compute and storage server CPUs. For this parameter, enter ".5" if your current CPUs have the speed of those on Exadata, ".75" if they're three-fourths as capable, "1" if they're the same, "2" if they're twice as fast, and so forth.

■ **Note** We recommend reading about Exadata CPU details in Recipe 1-1 of this book and comparing it with your current environment. In this text, we will not attempt to enable our scripts to automatically calculate the multiplier based on CPU clock speeds, manufacturers, and so on, but a good resource for comparison is http://tcp.org.

Using the same values for target number of instances (5), a relative percent CPU load for the remaining databases of 0.25, a margin of error of 1.2, and a 0.5 CPU core multiplier (indicating your current CPUs are half as capable as Exadata processors), the script in Listing 5-6 reports our required target Exadata environment.

■ **Note** In the script in Listing 5-6, we will also make an assumption that we want to keep our CPU utilization below 65% across compute nodes. This is Oracle's Real World Performance Group recommendation and for the purposes of this example, provides an extra level of comfort over our already-provided margin of error.

Listing 5-6. lst05-06-awr-cpu-corecnt-forexa.sql

```
SYS @ PROD> SELECT MAX(OraCPU) MaxOraCPU,
  MAX(OraIOCPU) MaxOraIOCPU,
  (
  CASE
    WHEN MAX(OraCPU) < (.65*48)
    THEN 'Quarter Rack'
```

```
      WHEN MAX(OraCPU) BETWEEN (.65*48) AND (.65*96)
      THEN 'Half Rack'
      WHEN MAX(OraCPU) BETWEEN (.65*96) AND (.65*192)
      THEN 'Full Rack'
      ELSE 'Full Rack +'
   END) exa_for_compute,
   (
   CASE
      WHEN MAX(OraIOCPU) < 72
      THEN 'Quarter Rack'
      WHEN MAX(OraIOCPU) BETWEEN 72 AND 168
      THEN 'Half Rack'
      WHEN MAX(OraIOCPU) BETWEEN 168 AND 336
      THEN 'Full Rack'
      ELSE 'Full Rack +'
   END) exa_for_storage
FROM
   (SELECT (OraCPU         + (
      &&num_addtl_dbs       *
      &&pct_resource_load  *
      &&margin_err          * OraCPU))  *
      &&core_multiplier OraCPU,
      (OraIOCPU            + (
      &&num_addtl_dbs       *
      &&pct_resource_load  *
      &&margin_err          * OraIOCPU)) *
      &&core_multiplier OraIOCPU
   FROM
      ( { ... code from Listing 5-3 ...}
      ORDER BY id ASC
      )
   WHERE OraCPUtot < 100
/
Enter value for num_addtl_dbs: 5
Enter value for pct_resource_load: .25
Enter value for margin_err: 1.2
Enter value for core_multiplier: .5

 Max Non-IO|  Max IO| Exadata Recommendation | Exadata Recommendation
    CPU Req| CPU Req| Compute Grid           | Storage Grid
-----------|--------|------------------------|-------------------------
      12.98|   18.09| Quarter Rack           | Quarter Rack
```

Based on our existing CPU workload and overall sizing and processor comparison numbers entered, the workload above will fit within an Exadata X2-2 Quarter Rack.

■ **Note** Please see Recipe 1-1 for Exadata Database Machine configuration details.

How It Works

Processor capacity planning for Exadata is primarily a matter of understanding your current CPU demands. Using data from Oracle AWR is a good way to forecast Exadata CPU requirements and Exadata configuration details. Using scripts to extract data from AWR is a relatively straightforward method to accurately size your database workloads for Exadata. As you can probably gather, the approach in this recipe is not limited to Exadata CPU capacity planning; with slight adjustments to the last script in the solution of this recipe, you can follow this approach to conduct CPU capacity-planning analysis for any Oracle target platform.

The code listings in this recipe select data from Oracle AWR views DBA_HIST_SNAPSHOT, DBA_HIST_OSSTAT, DBA_HIST_TIME_MODEL, and DBA_HIST_SYSSTAT. We used DBA_HIST_SNAPSHOT to provide detailed listing of the snapshot ID, snapshot begin interval time and end interval time. Using Oracle's LAG analytic function, we calculated the minutes between intervals and used this to calculate rate-based metrics.

DBA_HIST_OSSTAT was used to retrieve the per snapshot aggregate processor core/thread count as well as host-based processor utilization metrics. These host-based utilization metrics are likely not relevant for purposes of conducting an Exadata processor sizing assessment, as they could include non-Oracle components of CPU load and additional Oracle environment's load, and they are also dependent somewhat on the operating system and hardware that the database runs on.

DBA_HIST_TIME_MODEL can be used to measure and forecast Oracle-related CPU load. In the examples in this recipe, we used the LAG analytic function to calculate differences between snapshot intervals for DB time, DB CPU, background cpu time, and RMAN cpu time statistics.

DBA_HIST_SYSSTAT was used to query logons per second and executions per second. This information is not necessarily required when performing processor capacity planning, but it is often nice to see alongside Oracle CPU usage statistics to correlate metrics to workload.

We've attempted to make the approach relatively scientific, but there are certainly conditions under which a bit of educated guesswork may be required. Table 5-1 provides some recommendations to help refine your assumptions and confidently perform your processor capacity-planning efforts.

Table 5-1. Refining our CPU planning assumptions

Risk or Assumption	Recommendation and Comments
Uncertain how many additional databases will be consolidated to Exadata	Strive to consolidate what makes sense from a storage capacity standpoint (see Recipe 5-5) and eliminate candidate databases when capacity becomes a limiter as a first-pass. CPU bandwidth is rarely a limiting factor when consolidating on Exadata; typically, disk capacity is the most important factor that determines how many databases can fit on your database machine.
	Work with your management team to understand consolidation goals for Exadata.
Uncertain how to establish a resource load percentage for non-production databases	Run the scripts in this recipe on all of your databases to arrive at a representative number or run each step manually.
Unsure how to establish a "margin of error" for calculations	Be safe but not overly conservative. This is typically a judgment call by the administrator. Overestimating your margin of error could be the difference between a Quarter Rack and a Half Rack or a Half Rack and a Full Rack, which equates to a significant amount of money.
Historical AWR metrics not representative of expected usage patterns	Use the margin of error conditions to amplify your CPU requirements numbers. For example, if your business is planning a business acquisition or new application functionality rollout, use this information to your advantage.
Unsure how to measure the core multiplier	Refer to the TPC website (http://tpc.org) to find processor comparisons.

5-2. Determining IOPs Requirements

Problem

You wish to determine whether an Exadata Database Machine will provide enough I/Os per second, or IOPs, to meet your database workload requirements.

Solution

To conduct an Exadata IOPs capacity-planning exercise, we recommend the following approach:

- Query raw IOPs-related data from Oracle AWR, export to Excel, and optionally plot trends and/or identify outlier conditions.
- Query IOPs averages, maximums, and other statistical information to understand usage patterns.
- Add IOPs numbers for additional Oracle databases targeted to be deployed on Exadata.
- Determine Exadata and Exadata model specific fit based on measured IOPs data from AWR.

The script in Listing 5-7 displays your disk IOPs numbers for read requests, write requests, and redo log writes. Log in to SQL*Plus on your current database and run this script to collect IOPs-related information from your Oracle AWR repository.

Listing 5-7. lst05-07-awr-iops.sql

```
SYS @ PROD> SELECT snaps.id,
  snaps.tm,
  snaps.dur,
  snaps.instances,
  ((sysstat.IOPsr      - lag (sysstat.IOPsr,1) over (order by snaps.id)))/dur/60 IOPsr,
  ((sysstat.IOPsw      - lag (sysstat.IOPsw,1) over (order by snaps.id)))/dur/60 IOPsw,
  ((sysstat.IOPsredo   - lag (sysstat.IOPsredo,1) over (order by snaps.id)))/dur/60 IOPsredo,
  (((sysstat.IOPsr     - lag (sysstat.IOPsr,1) over (order by snaps.id)))/dur/60) +
     (((sysstat.IOPsw - lag (sysstat.IOPsw,1) over (order by snaps.id)))/dur/60) +
     (((sysstat.IOPsredo - lag (sysstat.IOPsredo,1) over (order by snaps.id)))/dur/60) Totiops,
  sysstat.logons_curr ,
  ((sysstat.logons_cum - lag (sysstat.logons_cum,1) over (order by snaps.id)))/dur/60
     logons_cum,
  ((sysstat.execs      - lag (sysstat.execs,1) over (order by snaps.id)))/dur/60 execs
FROM
  (
  /* DBA_HIST_SNAPSHOT */
  SELECT DISTINCT id,
    dbid,
    tm,
    instances,
    MAX(dur) over (partition BY id) dur
  FROM
    ( SELECT DISTINCT s.snap_id id,
      s.dbid,
```

```
      TO_CHAR(s.end_interval_time,'DD-MON-RR HH24:MI') tm,
      COUNT(s.instance_number) over (partition BY snap_id) instances,
      1440*((CAST(s.end_interval_time AS DATE) - lag(CAST(s.end_interval_time AS DATE),1) over
          (order by s.snap_id))) dur
    FROM dba_hist_snapshot s,
      v$database d
    WHERE s.dbid=d.dbid
    )
  ) snaps,
  (
  /* DBA_HIST_SYSSTAT */
  SELECT *
  FROM
    (SELECT snap_id, dbid, stat_name, value FROM dba_hist_sysstat
    ) pivot (SUM(value) FOR (stat_name) IN ('logons current' AS logons_curr, 'logons cumulative'
        AS logons_cum, 'execute count' AS execs, 'physical read IO requests' AS IOPsr,
        'physical write IO requests' AS IOPsw, 'redo writes' AS IOPsredo))
  ) sysstat
WHERE dur       > 0
AND snaps.id    =sysstat.snap_id
AND snaps.dbid=sysstat.dbid
ORDER BY id ASC
/

  Snap| Snap             | Duration|  RAC|   IOPs|   IOPs|  IOPs|    IOPs| Logons| Logons|   Execs
    ID| Start            |    Mins|Nodes|  Reads|  Write|  Redo|   Total|Current|Per Sec| Per Sec
------|------------------|---------|-----|-------|-------|------|--------|-------|-------|--------
 22006|24-JUN-12 02:00|    60.67|    1| 880.43| 850.46|  7.01| 1737.90|  262.0|    0.5|   432.1
 22007|24-JUN-12 03:00|    59.57|    1| 750.65|  36.06|  5.46|  792.17|  262.0|    0.5|   410.0
 22008|24-JUN-12 04:00|    60.62|    1| 499.39|   5.92|  5.45|  510.76|  287.0|    0.6|   453.7
... Additional snapshot information omitted
```

The output from this script could be lengthy, so we recommend pulling the data into Excel and charting your IOPs numbers. Figure 5-3 displays an example of IOPs metrics from AWR.

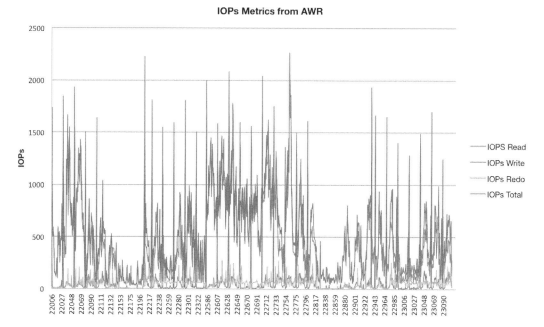

Figure 5-3. Database IOPs statistics from Oracle AWR

With this information, summarize your IOPs metrics using the code in Listing 5-8:

Listing 5-8. lst05-08-awr-iops-sum.sql

```
SYS @ PROD> select
        avg(IOPsr) AvgIOPsr, max(IOPsr) MaxIOPsr,
        avg(IOPsw) AvgIOPsw, max(IOPsw) MaxIOPsw,
        avg(IOPsr) AvgIOPsredo, max(IOPsredo) MaxIOPsredo,
        avg(Totiops) AvgTotiops, max(Totiops) MaxTotiops
from { ... code from Listing 5-7 ...}
```

Avg IOPs Reads	Max IOPs Reads	Avg IOPs Write	Max IOPs Write	Avg IOPs Redo	Max IOPs Redo	Avg IOPs Total	Max IOPs Total
432.06	2026.94	63.58	1003.31	432.06	291.94	547.46	2262.43

This output shows that our workload requires an I/O subsystem capable of handling 2262.43 IOPs. Now, introduce additional logic into the script to extrapolate these IOPs numbers and account for additional databases, an estimated percentage of IOPs demand expected across these databases, as well as add a margin of error. In the next script:

- &num_addtl_dbs = Number of additional, potentially non-production databases that we will plan on consolidating on the same Exadata Database Machine.
- &pct_resource_load = Estimated fraction of IOPs demand that each additional environment will consume with respect to the database analyzed. For this, "1" = equal IOPS demand compared to the database you're running the analysis on, ".1" = 10% the IOPS demand of your database, and so forth.
- &margin_err = Factor of safety. For this, "1" = no margin of error, "2" = multiply our measured IOPs numbers by two, and so on.

In the example in Listing 5-9, we will assume that we will have four additional databases, each with 10% the IOPs demand of our original database, and add a 30% margin of error for our IOPs calculations:

Listing 5-9. lst05-09-awr-iops-sum-extr.sql

```
SYS @ PROD> select
        avg(IOPsr) AvgIOPsr, max(IOPsr) MaxIOPsr,
        avg(IOPsw) AvgIOPsw, max(IOPsw) MaxIOPsw,
        avg(IOPsr) AvgIOPsredo, max(IOPsredo) MaxIOPsredo,
        avg(Totiops) AvgTotiops, max(Totiops) MaxTotiops
from (
select
        (IOPsr + (&&num_addtl_dbs * &&pct_resource_load * &&margin_err * IOPsr)) IOPsr,
        (IOPsw + (&&num_addtl_dbs * &&pct_resource_load * &&margin_err * IOPsw)) IOPsw,
        (IOPsredo + (&&num_addtl_dbs * &&pct_resource_load * &&margin_err * IOPsredo)) IOPsredo,
        (Totiops+ (&&num_addtl_dbs * &&pct_resource_load * &&margin_err * Totiops)) Totiops from (
{ ... Code from Listing 5-7 ... }
)
/
Enter value for num_addtl_dbs: 4
Enter value for pct_resource_load: .1
Enter value for margin_err: 1.3


 Avg IOPs|  Max IOPs| Avg IOPs|  Max IOPs| Avg IOPs|  Max IOPs| Avg IOPs|  Max IOPs
    Reads|     Reads|    Write|     Write|     Redo|      Redo|    Total|     Total
---------|----------|---------|----------|---------|----------|---------|----------
   656.73|   3080.95|    96.64|   1525.04|   656.73|    443.75|   832.14|   3438.89
```

With estimated forecasts for additional environments and their relative IOPs weight, our adjusted IOPs demand is now 3438.89.

Finally, take the information collected thus far and map these requirements to disk IOPs capabilities on Exadata. The following script evaluates IOPs data from AWR and compares with Exadata IOPs capabilities for both High Performance and High Capacity SAS disks, taking into consideration whether you will use Oracle ASM normal or high redundancy (see Recipe 5-4 for additional details). In Listing 5-10, two additional input parameters are provided:

- &asm_redundancy_data is used to multiply the calculated write IOPs by either two or three, depending on whether normal or high redundancy is used for database files
- &asm_redundancy_reco is used to multiply the calculated redo IOPs by either two or three, depending on whether normal or high redundancy is used for redo log files

Note Please refer to Recipe 1-1 to learn more about Exadata IOPs capabilities.

Listing 5-10. lst05-10-awr-iops-forexa.sql

```
SYS @ PROD> select
        max(IOPsr) MaxIOPsr,
        max(IOPsw) MaxIOPsw,
```

```
            max(IOPsredo) MaxIOPsredo,
            max(Totiops) MaxTotiops,
            (case
              when max(Totiops) < 10000 then 'Quarter Rack'
              when max(Totiops) between 10000 and 25200 then 'Half Rack'
              when max(Totiops) between 25200 and 50400 then 'Full Rack'
              when max(Totiops) > 50400 then 'Full Rack+'
            end) exa_hp,
            (case
              when max(Totiops) < 6000 then 'Quarter Rack'
              when max(Totiops) between 6000 and 14000 then 'Half Rack'
              when max(Totiops) between 14000 and 28000 then 'Full Rack'
              when max(Totiops) > 28000 then 'Full Rack+'
            end) exa_hc
from (
{ ... Code from Listing 5-9 ... })
/
Enter value for num_addtl_dbs: 4
Enter value for pct_resource_load: .1
Enter value for margin_err: 1.3
Enter value for asm_redundancy_data: normal
Enter value for asm_redundancy_reco: high


 Max IOPs|  Max IOPs|  Max IOPs|  Max IOPs| Exadata Recommendation | Exadata Recommendation
    Reads|     Write|      Redo|     Total| HP Disks               | HC Disks
---------|----------|----------|----------|------------------------|--------------------------
  3080.95|   3050.07|   1331.26|   4956.76| Quarter Rack           | Quarter Rack
```

How It Works

Disk IOPs planning for Exadata is primarily a matter of understanding your current IOPs demands. Using data from Oracle AWR is a good way to forecast Exadata IOPs requirements and Exadata configuration details. Using scripts to extract data from AWR is a relatively straightforward method to accurately size your database IOPS workloads for Exadata. The approach in this recipe is not limited to Exadata IOPs capacity planning; with slight adjustments to the script in Listing 5-10, you can follow this approach to conduct a IOPs planning analysis for any target platform.

In Recipe 1-1, we provided Oracle-published disk IOPs capabilities for each of the available configuration models. Oracle states that each SAS disk in each cell is capable of delivering approximately 267 IOPs for High Performance disks and 166 IOPs for High Capacity SAS disks. Using these numbers with your current workloads, you can determine whether Exadata will provide the necessary disk IOPs to meet your performance demands, and if so, which Exadata configuration is best suited for your environment.

The code listings in this recipe select data from Oracle AWR views DBA_HIST_SNAPSHOT and DBA_HIST_SYSSTAT. We used DBA_HIST_SNAPSHOT to provide detailed listing of the snapshot ID, snapshot begin interval time and end interval time. Using Oracle's LAG analytic function, we calculated the minutes between intervals and used this to calculate rate-based metrics.

DBA_HIST_SYSSTAT contains the information needed for IOPs demand capacity planning. In this recipe, we ran queries based on three system statistics: physical read IO requests, physical write IO requests, and redo writes. The physical read IO requests and physical write IO requests are both incremented at each read or write call, whether the reads are buffered reads or direct reads. As such, they serve as a good measure of I/O demand. When divided by the number of seconds between AWR samples, we arrived at our IOPs numbers for both reads and writes.

The `redo writes` statistic is slightly different. This statistic is incremented each time LGWR successfully flushes the contents of the log buffer to disk. Contrary to the `physical read IO requests` and `physical write IO requests` statistics, `redo writes` is a reflection of "completed I/O," not I/O demand. However, for purposes of conducting a IOPs analysis, it is often acceptable to treat this statistic the same as the read and write request statistics.

Physical write and redo write IOPs numbers as measured from Oracle system statistics (V$SYSSTAT or DBA_HIST_SYSSTAT) are reflections of Oracle's write calls but do not account for the fact that extents will be mirrored with either ASM normal or high redundancy. When sizing for Exadata, you need to multiply the system statistics by either two for normal redundancy or three for high redundancy disk group configurations.

Since many of statistics are counter-based metrics that continuously increment over time, you need to subtract the previous snapshot's value from the current snapshot's value and divide by the number of seconds between snapshots to calculate your I/O bandwidth rates. In this recipe, we used Oracle's LAG function to achieve this. We also used 11g PIVOT method to dynamically build a list of aliased columns for each of the metrics we wanted to capture. We like this approach because it reduces the number of lines of code and reduces self-joining potentially large AWR tables.

■ **Caution** If your current databases are experiencing significant redo log write wait activity, the redo write statistic may not be an entirely accurate picture of redo writing IOPs demand. If you experience significant wait time for `log file sync` waits it can be an indication of an I/O issue or configuration issue on your current environment. Exadata can help address this with its disk cache on the storage servers and Smart Flash Logging. To learn more about these features, please see Recipe 18-9.

While the methods presented in this recipe should help you to properly size your environment for Exadata, other factors also play a significant role. CPU processor capacity planning, I/O bandwidth capacity planning, and certainly storage capacity planning are other important tasks. Please read the other recipes in this chapter to learn more about these capacity-planning activities.

5-3. Determining I/O Bandwidth Requirements
Problem
You wish to determine whether an Exadata Database Machine will provide enough I/O bandwidth, or data transfer capacity, to meet your database workload requirements. Furthermore, you wish to decide which Exadata configuration will meet your needs based on information gleaned from AWR data.

Solution
To conduct an Exadata I/O bandwidth capacity-planning exercise, we recommend the following approach:

- Query raw I/O bandwidth information from Oracle AWR, export to Excel, and optionally plot trends and/or identify outlier conditions.
- Determine I/O bandwidth averages, maximums, and other statistical information to understand usage patterns.
- Add I/O bandwidth numbers for additional Oracle databases targeted to be deployed on Exadata.
- Determine Exadata and Exadata model specific fit based on measured I/O bandwidth from AWR.

Chapter 5 ■ Sizing Exadata

The following code displays your disk I/O bandwidth numbers for read requests, write requests, and redo log writes. Log in to SQL*Plus from your current database and run the script in Listing 5-11 to collect I/O bandwidth information from your Oracle AWR repository:

Listing 5-11. lst05-11-awr-iobw.sql

```
SYS @ PROD> select  snaps.id, snaps.tm,snaps.dur,snaps.instances,
         ((  (bs.db_block_size * (sysstat.IOmbpsr - lag (sysstat.IOmbpsr,1) over (order by
             snaps.id)))/1024/1024))/dur/60   IOmbpsr,
         ((  (bs.db_block_size * (sysstat.IOmbpsw - lag (sysstat.IOmbpsw,1) over (order by
             snaps.id)))/1024/1024))/dur/60   IOmbpsw,
         ((  ((sysstat.IOmbpsredo - lag (sysstat.IOmbpsredo,1) over (order by
             snaps.id)))/1024/1024))/dur/60   IOmbpsredo,
         (((  (bs.db_block_size * (sysstat.IOmbpsr - lag (sysstat.IOmbpsr,1) over (order by
             snaps.id)))/1024/1024))/dur/60) +
          (((  (bs.db_block_size * (sysstat.IOmbpsw - lag (sysstat.IOmbpsw,1) over (order by
             snaps.id)))/1024/1024))/dur/60) +
          (((  ((sysstat.IOmbpsredo - lag (sysstat.IOmbpsredo,1) over (order by
             snaps.id)))/1024/1024))/dur/60)  Totmbps,
         sysstat.logons_curr ,
         ((sysstat.logons_cum - lag (sysstat.logons_cum,1) over (order by snaps.id)))/dur/60
             logons_cum,
         ((sysstat.execs - lag (sysstat.execs,1) over (order by snaps.id)))/dur/60 execs
  from
( /* DBA_HIST_SNAPSHOT */
select distinct id,dbid,tm,instances,max(dur) over (partition by id) dur from (
select distinct s.snap_id id, s.dbid,
   to_char(s.end_interval_time,'DD-MON-RR HH24:MI') tm,
   count(s.instance_number) over (partition by snap_id) instances,
   1440*((cast(s.end_interval_time as date) - lag(cast(s.end_interval_time as date),1) over
       (order by s.snap_id))) dur
from    dba_hist_snapshot s,
   v$database d
where s.dbid=d.dbid)
) snaps,
 ( /* DBA_HIST_SYSSTAT */
   select * from
       (select snap_id, dbid, stat_name, value from
       dba_hist_sysstat
   ) pivot
   (sum(value) for (stat_name) in
       ('logons current' as logons_curr, 'logons cumulative' as logons_cum, 'execute count' as
             execs,
        'physical reads' as IOmbpsr, 'physical writes' as IOmbpsw,
        'redo size' as IOmbpsredo))
 ) sysstat,
 ( /* V$PARAMETER */
   select value as db_block_size
   from v$parameter where name='db_block_size'
 ) bs
```

```
where dur > 0
and snaps.id=sysstat.snap_id
and snaps.dbid=sysstat.dbid
order by id asc
/

 Snap| Snap             | Duration|  RAC |  MBPS |  MBPS|  MBPS|   MBPS| Logons | Logons |  Execs
   ID| Start            |    Mins | Nodes|  Reads|  Write|  Redo|  Total|Current | Per Sec| Per Sec
------|-----------------|---------|------|-------|------|------|-------|--------|--------|--------
 22006|24-JUN-12 02:00  |   60.67 |    1 |  19.87|  8.60|  3.10|  31.57|  262.0 |    0.5 |   432.1
 22007|24-JUN-12 03:00  |   59.57 |    1 |  78.72|  0.44|  0.11|  79.27|  262.0 |    0.5 |   410.0
 22008|24-JUN-12 04:00  |   60.62 |    1 |  61.05|  0.09|  0.06|  61.20|  287.0 |    0.6 |   453.7
... output omitted
```

As the output from the script can be lengthy, we recommend pulling the data into Excel and charting your I/O bandwidth numbers. Figures 5-4 displays examples of I/O bandwidth metrics from AWR.

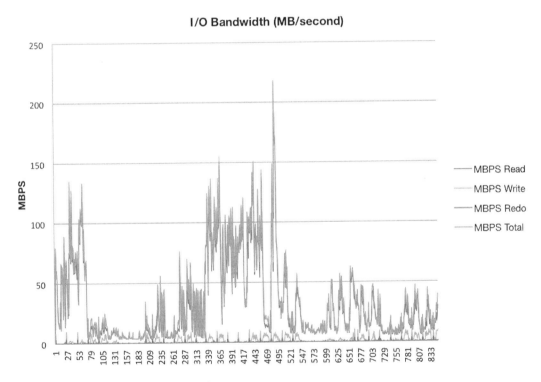

Figure 5-4. *I/O bandwidth from Oracle AWR*

Now, summarize your I/O bandwidth data from AWR using the script in Listing 5-12:

Listing 5-12. lst05-12-awr-iobw-sum.sql

```
SYS @ PROD> select avg(IOmbpsr) AvgIOmbpsr, max(IOmbpsr) MaxIOmbpsr,
       avg(IOmbpsw) AvgIOmbpsw, max(IOmbpsw) MaxIOmbpsw,
       avg(IOmbpsredo) AvgIOmbpsredo, max(IOmbpsredo) MaxIOmbpsredo,
```

```
        avg(Totmbps) AvgTotmbps, max(Totmbps) MaxTotmbps
      from ( { ... Code from Listing 5-11 ... })
/
Avg MBPS|Max MBPS|Avg MBPS|Max MBPS|Avg MBPS|Max MBPS|Avg MBPS| Max MBPS
   Reads|   Reads|   Write|   Write|    Redo|    Redo|   Total|    Total
--------|--------|--------|--------|--------|--------|--------|----------
   32.47|  209.66|    1.89|   11.68|    0.33|    3.63|   34.69|    218.18
```

Based on the numbers above you can see that the maximum I/O bandwidth in MB/second from the AWR sample set is approximately 218 MB/second.

Next, introduce logic into your script to extrapolate your I/O demand numbers to account for additional databases, an estimated percentage of I/O bandwidth demand expected across these databases, as well as add a "margin of error." In the next script:

- &num_addtl_dbs = Number of additional, potentially non-production databases that we will plan on consolidating on the same Exadata Database Machine.

- &pct_resource_load = Estimated fraction of I/O bandwidth demand that each additional environment will consume with respect to the database analyzed. For this, "1" = equal IOPS demand compared to the database you're running the analysis on, ".1" = 10% the IOPS demand of your database, and so forth.

- &margin_err = Factor of safety. For this, "1" = no margin of error, "2" = multiply our measured IOPs numbers by two, and so on.

In the example in Listing 5-13, we will assume five additional databases, each with a 1:2 ratio of I/O demand compared to our current database (1:2 = 50% = pct_resource_load=.5), and a 25% margin of error:

Listing 5-13. lst05-13-awr-iobw-sum-extr.sql

```
SYS @ PROD> select  avg(IOmbpsr) AvgIOmbpsr, max(IOmbpsr) MaxIOMbpsr,
        avg(IOmbpsw) AvgIOmbpsw, max(IOmbpsw) MaxIOMbpsw,
        avg(IOmbpsredo) AvgIOMbpsredo, max(IOmbpsredo) MaxIOMbpsredo,
        avg(Totmbps) AvgTotmbps, max(Totmbps) MaxTotmbps
     from (
  select (IOmbpsr + (&&num_addtl_dbs * &&pct_resource_load * &&margin_err * IOmbpsr)) IOmbpsr,
         (IOmbpsw + (&&num_addtl_dbs * &&pct_resource_load * &&margin_err * IOmbpsw)) IOmbpsw,
         (IOmbpsredo + (&&num_addtl_dbs * &&pct_resource_load * &&margin_err * IOmbpsredo))
             IOmbpsredo,
         (Totmbps+ (&&num_addtl_dbs * &&pct_resource_load * &&margin_err * Totmbps)) Totmbps
             from (
{ ... Code from Listing 5-11 ...}
/
Enter value for num_addtl_dbs: 5
Enter value for pct_resource_load: .5
Enter value for margin_err: 1.25


Avg MBPS|  Max MBPS|  Avg MBPS|  Max MBPS|  Avg MBPS|  Max MBPS|  Avg MBPS|  Max MBPS
   Reads|     Reads|     Write|     Write|      Redo|      Redo|     Total|     Total
--------|----------|----------|----------|----------|----------|----------|----------
  133.95|    864.85|      7.78|     48.19|      1.37|     14.99|    143.10|    900.00
```

With these revised, extrapolated numbers, our I/O bandwidth demand maximum values are now approximately 900 MB/second.

CHAPTER 5 ■ SIZING EXADATA

Finally, take the information collected thus far and map these requirements to disk I/O bandwidth capabilities on Exadata. The script in Listing 5-14 compares our I/O bandwidth demand from AWR with Exadata I/O bandwidth capabilities for both High Performance and High Capacity SAS disks, taking into consideration whether you will use Oracle ASM normal or high redundancy (see Recipe 5-4 for additional details). In Listing 4-14, two additional input parameters are provided:

- &asm_redundancy_data is used to multiply the calculated write IOPs by either two or three, depending on whether normal or high redundancy is used for database files

- &asm_redundancy_reco is used to multiply the calculated redo IOPs by either two or three, depending on whether normal or high redundancy is used for redo log files

■ **Note** Please refer to Recipe 1-1 to learn more about Exadata I/O bandwidth capabilities.

Listing 5-14. lst05-14-awr-iobw-forexa.sql

```
SYS @ PROD> select
        max(IOPsr) MaxIOPsr,
        max(IOPsw) MaxIOPsw,
        max(IOPsredo) MaxIOPsredo,
        max(Totiops) MaxTotiops,
        (case
         when max(Totiops) < 10000 then 'Quarter Rack'
         when max(Totiops) between 10000 and 25200 then 'Half Rack'
         when max(Totiops) between 25200 and 50400 then 'Full Rack'
         when max(Totiops) > 50400 then 'Full Rack+'
        end) exa_hp,
        (case
         when max(Totiops) < 6000 then 'Quarter Rack'
         when max(Totiops) between 6000 and 14000 then 'Half Rack'
         when max(Totiops) between 14000 and 28000 then 'Full Rack'
         when max(Totiops) > 28000 then 'Full Rack+'
        end) exa_hc
from (
select
        (IOPsr + (&&num_addtl_dbs * &&pct_resource_load * &&margin_err * IOPsr)) IOPsr,
        (IOPsw + (&&num_addtl_dbs * &&pct_resource_load * &&margin_err * IOPsw)) IOPsw,
        (IOPsredo + (&&num_addtl_dbs * &&pct_resource_load * &&margin_err * IOPsredo)) IOPsredo,
        (Totiops+ (&&num_addtl_dbs * &&pct_resource_load * &&margin_err * Totiops)) Totiops from (
{ ... Code from Listing 5-11 ... }
)
/
Enter value for num_addtl_dbs: 5
Enter value for pct_resource_load: .5
Enter value for margin_err: 1.25
Enter value for asm_redundancy_data: normal
Enter value for asm_redundancy_reco: high
```

```
  Max MBPS|  Max MBPS|  Max MBPS|  Max MBPS| Exadata Recommendation | Exadata Recommendation
      Reads|      Write|      Redo|      Total| HP Disks               | HC Disks
----------|----------|----------|----------|------------------------|------------------------
     864.85|      96.38|       4.96|     936.59| Quarter Rack           | Quarter Rack
```

From this output, we can determine that an Exadata Quarter Rack will meet these specific database's I/O bandwidth requirements.

■ **Note** The script in Listing 5-14 does not account for storage capabilities of the X3-2 Eighth Rack.

How It Works

I/O bandwidth planning for Exadata is primarily a matter of understanding your current I/O bandwidth demands. Using data from Oracle AWR is a good way to forecast Exadata I/O bandwidth requirements and Exadata configuration details. Using scripts to extract data from AWR is a relatively straightforward method to accurately size your database I/O bandwidth on Exadata. The approach in this recipe is not limited to Exadata I/O capacity planning; with slight adjustments to the script in Listing 5-14, you can follow this approach to conduct an I/O bandwidth planning analysis for any target platform.

In Recipe 1-1, we provided Oracle-published disk I/O bandwidth capabilities for each of the available configuration models. Using these numbers with your current workloads, you can determine whether Exadata will provide the necessary disk I/O bandwidth to meet your performance demands, and if so, which Exadata configuration is best suited for your environment.

If you use the methods in this recipe, you will very likely arrive at overly conservative I/O bandwidth numbers for Exadata. The Exadata Storage Servers are equipped with PCI Flash and Smart Flash Cache functionality, which can greatly increase your overall bandwidth capabilities. Additionally, software features such as Smart Scan, Hybrid Columnar Compression, and storage indexes can potentially greatly reduce the volume of data transmitted over your storage interconnect, reducing your bandwidth requirements. In other words, if your system is servicing 1 GB/second of I/O from your current storage array now, it very well may not need to do this much work on Exadata. This being said, we recommend taking the first pass at your I/O bandwidth capacity-planning assessment without taking into consideration all of Exadata's hardware and software features.

■ **Note** If your I/O bandwidth assessment shows that your environments do not comfortably fit into the capabilities of Exadata, explore whether you can and will exploit features such as Smart Scan and HCC. Please refer to Chapters 15 through 19 to learn more.

The code listings in this recipe select data from Oracle AWR views DBA_HIST_SNAPSHOT and DBA_HIST_SYSSTAT. We used DBA_HIST_SNAPSHOT to provide detailed listing of the snapshot ID, snapshot begin interval time and end interval time. Using Oracle's LAG analytic function, we calculated the minutes between intervals and used this to calculate rate-based metrics.

DBA_HIST_SYSSTAT contains the information needed to conduct an I/O bandwidth capacity-planning exercise. In this recipe, we ran queries based on three system statistics: physical reads, physical writes, and redo size. The physical reads statistic is incremented as disk read I/O operations complete, whether satisfied via buffered reads of direct path read mechanism. Since non-Exadata environments always perform I/O in units of a database block, each read metric equates to one block size worth of data, so multiply your physical reads values by our database block size and convert to whichever rate metric you wish to report on. In this recipe, we reported on megabytes per second, or MB/second, so we divided our I/O metrics by (1024 * 1204).

The `physical write` statistics are handled the same was as `physical reads`, but the redo size metric is handled a bit differently. Oracle's redo size metric represents the volume of redo generated, in bytes, so we simply divided these values by (1024 * 1024) to arrive at our redo I/O bandwidth in units of MB/second.

Since these statistics are counter-based metrics that continuously increment over time, you need to subtract the previous snapshot's value from the current snapshot's value and divide by the number of seconds between snapshots to calculate your I/O bandwidth rates. In this recipe, we used Oracle's LAG function to achieve this. We also used 11g PIVOT method to dynamically build a list of aliased columns for each of the metrics we wanted to capture. We like this approach because it reduces the number of lines of code and reduces self-joining, potentially large AWR tables.

Additionally, similar to logic presented in Recipe 5-3, you need to adjust your write-related I/O bandwidth numbers to account for either ASM normal or high redundancy. For example, write operations with normal redundancy will write to both primary and mirrored extents, so a single physical write as measured from database-level system statistics will translate to two physical writes inside the storage. When conducting I/O bandwidth capacity planning for ASM, these additional mirrored writes will need to be considered and weighed against the capabilities of the storage infrastructure.

5-4. Determining ASM Redundancy Requirements

Problem

You need to decide what type of Oracle ASM redundancy to configure for your ASM disk groups on Exadata.

Solution

Determining your ASM disk group redundancy configuration is a matter of understanding data protection levels offered with normal or high ASM redundancy, forecasting your usable disk space needs for the databases you will place on Exadata, and the economics involved with under-protecting or over-protecting your disk storage.

> **Note** For additional details on Oracle ASM redundancy on Exadata, please see Recipes 6-5 and 9-4.

With Oracle ASM normal redundancy, assuming you've spread your underlying Exadata grid disks evenly across cell disks and storage cell, your databases can survive the failure or planned outage of an entire cell disk without causing an availability outage. With ASM high redundancy, you can survive two simultaneous storage cell outages without impacting data availability.

The decision to choose normal or high redundancy, or even no redundancy, is a matter of balancing your organization's tolerance for risk and the economics of reduced storage capacity. For example, some companies select a high redundancy ASM disk group configuration to protect against media failure that may occur during Exadata Storage Server patching; when patching, it is usually necessary to take a storage server and all its disks offline. With normal redundancy configurations, doing so will leave you vulnerable in the event another storage server or set of disks fails while patching.

How It Works

Normal redundancy mirrors primary ASM extents on disks in a different storage cell, where high redundancy establishes two primary extent mirrors on different storage cells. In each case, this reduces your total usable storage capacity or database storage. With a normal redundancy configuration, you lose half of our raw capacity and with high redundancy you lose two-thirds of your usable capacity. Table 5-2 provides a summary of total usable capacity based on your Oracle ASM disk group redundancy configuration.

Table 5-2. *ASM redundancy and data storage usable capacity*

	X3-2 Eighth Rack	X2-2 and X3-2 Quarter Rack	X2-2 and X3-2 Half Rack	X2-2, X3-2, X2-8, and X3-8 Full Rack
Usable Capacity, High Performance Disks, **Normal Redundancy**	5.15 TB	10.3 TB	25.2 TB	50.4 TB
Usable Capacity, High Performance Disks, **High Redundancy**	3.6 TB	7.2 TB	16.8 TB	33.6 TB
Usable Capacity, High Capacity Disks, **Normal Redundancy**	27 TB	54 TB	126 TB	252 TB
Usable Capacity, High Capacity Disks, **Normal Redundancy**	18 TB	36 TB	84 TB	168 TB

■ **Note** The usable capacity numbers in Table 5-2 do not account for Fast Recovery Area storage versus "normal" database storage, nor do they account for a normally small DBFS disk group. Typically, if you elect to configure an FRA and back up internally to Exadata, Oracle will allocate 60% of your usable capacity for the RECO grid disks. This will reduce your usable capacity for database files storage to roughly 40% of the numbers displayed in Table 5-2. For example, for a Full Rack configured with High Performance disks and normal ASM redundancy, your available capacity for non-recovery structures (that is, database files) is reduced to approximately 20 TB. Please see Recipes 5-5, 5-8, and 5-9 to learn more about this topic.

On Exadata, the Oracle ASM *external* redundancy is not supported. On non-Exadata storage environments, many clients elect external redundancy and rely on host-based or array-based RAID to provide data protection. With Exadata the storage servers do not provide RAID protection; data is protected solely with Oracle ASM redundancy. You can elect to configure ASM disk groups with no redundancy, but this is not recommended for obvious reasons.

Let's discuss disk drive failure probabilities. Referencing studies conducted by Paris/Long in www.ssrc.ucsc.edu/Papers/paris-storagess06.pdf, we can consider two types of failure probabilities:

- Independent disk drive failures
- Correlated drive failures based on a global defect with a collection of drives. In this case, we may expected an "accelerated" failure rate, such as that caused by defects from the same batch of disk drives, escalated temperatures in the drive enclosure or data center, and so forth.

For this discussion, we will define a few probability definitions:

- `P(surv)` = The probability of survival in the event of single drive failure. In other words, the probability of *not* losing access to data
- n = The number of disks that comprise a failure set. With Oracle ASM on systems with "many disks," you will have eight (8) partner disks for each mirror, whether the disk group is configured with normal or high redundancy—the difference between the two is the number of mirrors, not the number of partner disks.
- λ = Rate of failure of a disk drive. This is the inverse of the drive's published Mean Time Between Failure (MTBF).
- `Trepair` = Time to repair a failed drive

Our formulas for measuring probability of survival, which is a measure of risk of data loss, can be expressed as the following:

- ASM Normal Redundancy: `P(surv) = exp(-n*λ*Trepair)`
- ASM High Redundancy: `P(surv) = (1+n*λ*Trepair) * exp(-n*λ*Trepair)`

If we consider independent disk drive failures and use a 1,000,000-hour failure rate and a 24-hour time to repair a failed disk, our probability of survival with ASM normal redundancy is the following:

```
P(surv) = exp(-n*λ*Trepair)
        = exp(-8 * (1/1000000) * 24)
        = 99.98%
```

With ASM high redundancy, our survival probability:

```
P(surv) = (1+nλTrepair) * exp(-nλTrepair)
        = (1+8*(1/1000000)*24) ( exp(-8 * (1/1000000) * 24)
        = 99.99%
```

If you now consider a potential accelerated failure rate for disk drives, which often is a more realistic scenario considering environmental reasons for failure, let's see what our probabilities of survival look like when our MTBF is once per month. In the example below, considering a failure rate of once per month:

With ASM normal redundancy:

```
P(surv) = exp(-n*λ*Trepair)
        = exp(-8 * (1/720) * 24)
        = 76.59%
```

With ASM high redundancy:

```
P(surv) = (1+n*λ*Trepair) * exp(-n*λ*Trepair)
        = (1+8*(1/720)*24) ( exp(-8 * (1/720) * 24)
        = 97.01%
```

As you can see, accelerate failure rates yield much lower survival probabilities than independent failure rates. Furthermore, ASM disk groups configured with high redundancy offer much better protection in an accelerated failure rate scenario as compared to normal redundancy ASM disk groups.

CHAPTER 5 ■ SIZING EXADATA

In summary, deciding your ASM disk group redundancy configuration is a matter of asking these questions:

- How much usable storage do you need for your databases?
- How risk-averse is your organization to loss of data availability in the event of multiple storage cell failures or simultaneous maintenance operations?
- How much are you willing to spend to limit this risk? If ASM high redundancy pushes you from, say, a Half Rack to a Full Rack configuration, does the risk justify the cost?

5-5. Forecasting Storage Capacity

Problem

You wish to determine whether your current databases will fit, from a disk space standpoint, on an Oracle Exadata Database Machine. Furthermore, you want to forecast which Exadata configuration is best suited for your environment based on your disk storage needs.

Solution

In this recipe, you will learn how to calculate the size of your current database and measure the amount of space required to store your archived redo logs in order to properly size your environment for Exadata.

First, determine the size of each of your database's database files by logging in to SQL*Plus in your current environment and running the script in Listing 5-15:

Listing 5-15. lst05-15-db-size.sql

```
SQL> select 'Data Files' type, sum(bytes)/1024/1024/1024 szgb,count(*) cnt
from     v$datafile group by substr(name,1,instr(name,'/',1,2)-1)
union
select 'Temp Files', sum(bytes)/1024/1024/1024 szgb,count(*) cnt
from v$tempfile group by substr(name,1,instr(name,'/',1,2)-1)
union
select 'Redo Member',sum(l.bytes)/1024/1024/1024 szgb,count(*) cnt
from v$logfile lf, v$log l
where l.group#=lf.group# group by substr(member,1,instr(member,'/',1,2)-1)
/

File Type     Size (GB)   Number of files
-----------   ---------   ---------------
Data Files     2950.68          36
Redo Membe       32.00           8
Temp Files       72.00           4
```

The output above shows that for this database, we require approximately 3 TB of usable storage. Run the same query for each database you plan on deploying to Exadata.

Next, calculate the disk space requirements for our archived redo logs. The script in Listing 5-16 below accepts an input parameter &days_to_keep, which defines the number of days of archived redo to maintain on disk. This value should be governed by your organization's backup and recovery strategy.

Listing 5-16. lst05-16-archive-size.sql

```
SYS @ PROD> select avg(gbpd) AvgGBpd, max(gbpd) MaxGBpd,
         avg(gbpd) * &&num_days AvgReq,
         max(gbpd) * &&num_days MaxReq
   from (
          select   al.dt, (al.blks * kc.blksize)/1024/1024/1024 gbpd
          from
                (select trunc(completion_time) dt, sum(blocks) blks
                 from v$archived_log
                 group by trunc(completion_time)) al,
                (select max(lebsz) blksize
                  from x$kccle) kc
   )
/
Enter value for num_days: 3
old     2:         avg(gbpd) * &&num_days AvgReq,
new     2:         avg(gbpd) * 3 AvgReq,
old     3:         max(gbpd) * &&num_days MaxReq
new     3:         max(gbpd) * 3 MaxReq

Avg GB per Day      Max GB per Day       GB Req Avg       GB Req Max
-----------------   -----------------   ---------------   ---------------
           6.11                123.16             18.34            369.48

1 row selected.
```

The output above shows that for this particular database, we need about 125 GB to store one day's worth of archived redo on disk and approximately 370 GB to store three days on disk. Add the values for all of your databases running in `ARCHIVELOG` mode to arrive at a total disk space requirement for Exadata. Typically, customers store archived redo logs in a Fast Recovery Area ASM disk group. For details on this topic, please refer to Recipe 5-9.

Next, you should attempt to determine your current growth rates for your databases. We will cover this topic in Recipe 5-6.

■ **Note** Please reference Recipe 5-6 to learn how to estimate your database growth rates using Oracle AWR data.

Hybrid Columnar Compression can offer a tremendous amount of disk space savings on Exadata. If you know which tables, and their sizes, will be converted to Hybrid Columnar Compressed tables as part of the Exadata migration, reduce your database size estimates by the appropriate sizing factor. We will not attempt to provide insight on how to predict this in this recipe as mileage with Hybrid Columnar Compression will vary from organization to organization and is predicated on how many and which tables are "fits" for HCC.

■ **Note** Recipe 4-4 provides some insight on how to assess your workload and database for Hybrid Columnar Compression.

The next decision to make is whether to use normal or high ASM disk group redundancy. This is usually a non-technical business decision based on risk tolerance and economics. From a storage capacity-planning perspective, this can play a large role in determining whether you decide on a Quarter Rack, Half Rack, or Full Rack, and even on your choice between High Performance and High Capacity disks.

> **Note** For more information on ASM disk group redundancy, please refer to Recipe 5-4.

Finally, understand how much physical capacity and usable capacity exists for each Exadata configuration. This information, combined with the other recipes in this chapter, should ultimately drive your Exadata configuration alternative selection.

- Whether you will elect ASM normal redundancy or high redundancy as your ASM disk group protection strategy
- The usable storage capacity of each Exadata X2-2, X2-8, X3-2, and X3-8 configuration when configured with either or both normal redundancy or high redundancy ASM disk groups

How It Works

To determine your disk storage needs for Exadata, you need to consider the following:

- The size of all data files, temp files, redo logs, and control files for all databases you're planning on deploying on Exadata
- For each database targeted to run in `ARCHIVELOG` mode, the volume of archived redo logs you generate within the time period in which you desire to have on-disk copies
- Forecasted organic growth estimates for each database
- Optionally, an assessment of which tables may be candidates for Hybrid Columnar Compression and for these, which compression flavor you will select
- Whether you will select ASM normal redundancy or high redundancy as your ASM disk group protection strategy
- The usable storage capacity of each Exadata X2-2, X2-8, X3-2, and X3-8 configuration when configured with either or both normal redundancy or high redundancy ASM disk groups

> **Note** Consult Oracle documentation of Table 5-2 in Recipe 5-4 to understand the physical storage capacity for each Exadata configuration.

With your storage requirements calculated from scripts in this recipe along with performance-based requirements, you can properly size and scope your Exadata configuration. One topic worth reiterating is that the Oracle Exadata Database Machine is an engineered system that is delivered in one of three different storage configurations, each with either 600 GB high performance or 3 TB high capacity SAS disks. So, you've only got six different options for raw disk capacity. As an administrator, you have influence over your usable capacity based on your choice of ASM redundancy and how large to size your FRA storage. Additionally, in 2012, Oracle began shipping and supporting Storage Expansion Racks, which are essentially sets of storage servers, to handle the demand for more storage capacity. If your performance requirements fit nicely in a smaller Exadata configuration but usable storage requirements push you beyond this configuration, Expansion Racks provide a lower-cost alternative. As this sometimes can upset the hardware balance between the compute, storage, and network grids, use caution when going down the Storage Server Expansion Rack route.

5-6. Planning for Database Growth

Problem

You wish to measure your storage consumption growth rates to properly size your databases for Oracle Exadata.

Solution

If you're running your current environments Oracle 10g or 11g, use Oracle AWR data to calculate your growth rates. In this recipe, we will show you how to calculate your current database's growth rate on a per-tablespace basis, how to summarize these growth rates, and how to forecast your capacity requirements based on these growth rates. Additionally, you will learn how to map these storage requirements to the appropriate Exadata configuration.

The script in Listing 5-17 can be used to calculate your database growth on a per-tablespace basis. Log in to SQL*Plus in your current database, connect as a database user with access to the AWR views, and run the following script:

Listing 5-17. lst05-17-db-growth.sql

```
SYS @ PROD> break on report
SYS @ PROD> compute sum of initalloc initused curralloc currused alloc_gbpd used_gbpd on report
SYS @ PROD> set echo on
SYS @ PROD> SELECT tbs tbs, ROUND (init_alloc_gb, 2) initalloc,
       ROUND (init_used_gb, 2) initused, ROUND (curr_alloc_gb, 2) curralloc,
       ROUND (curr_used_gb, 2) currused,
       ROUND (100 * (curr_used_gb / curr_alloc_gb), 2) PCTUSED,
       ROUND (alloc_gbperday, 2) alloc_gbpd,
       ROUND (used_gbperday, 2) used_gbpd
  FROM (SELECT tsmin.tsname tbs, tsmin.tablespace_size init_alloc_gb,
               tsmin.tablespace_usedsize init_used_gb,
               tsmax.tablespace_size curr_alloc_gb,
               tsmax.tablespace_usedsize curr_used_gb,
                 (tsmax.tablespace_size - tsmin.tablespace_size) / (tsmax.snaptime -
                    tsmin.snaptime) alloc_gbperday,
                 (tsmax.tablespace_usedsize - tsmin.tablespace_usedsize)
               / (tsmax.snaptime - tsmin.snaptime) used_gbperday
          FROM (SELECT *
                  FROM (SELECT TRUNC (s.begin_interval_time) snaptime,
                               t.tsname, (ts.BLOCKSIZE * u.tablespace_size) / 1024 / 1024 / 1024
                                  tablespace_size,
                                 (ts.BLOCKSIZE * u.tablespace_usedsize) / 1024 / 1024 / 1024
                                    tablespace_usedsize,
                               (RANK () OVER (PARTITION BY t.tsname ORDER BY s.snap_id ASC)
                               ) latest,
                               s.end_interval_time endtime
```

```
                    FROM dba_hist_snapshot s, v$instance i, v$database
                        d,dba_hist_tablespace_stat t,
                          dba_hist_tbspc_space_usage u,SYS.ts$ ts
                    WHERE s.snap_id = t.snap_id
                      AND s.dbid=d.dbid
                      AND s.dbid=t.dbid
                      AND s.dbid=u.dbid
                      AND i.instance_number = s.instance_number
                      AND s.instance_number = t.instance_number
                      AND ts.ts# = t.ts#
                      AND t.snap_id = u.snap_id
                      AND t.ts# = u.tablespace_id)
              WHERE latest = 1) tsmin,
            (SELECT *
              FROM (SELECT TRUNC (s.begin_interval_time) snaptime,
                          t.tsname,
                            (ts.BLOCKSIZE * u.tablespace_size) / 1024 / 1024 / 1024
                              tablespace_size,
                            (ts.BLOCKSIZE * u.tablespace_usedsize) / 1024 / 1024 / 1024
                              tablespace_usedsize,
                          (RANK () OVER (PARTITION BY t.tsname ORDER BY s.snap_id DESC)
                          ) latest,
                          s.end_interval_time endtime
                      FROM dba_hist_snapshot s,v$instance i,v$database
                          d,dba_hist_tablespace_stat t,
                          dba_hist_tbspc_space_usage u,SYS.ts$ ts
                    WHERE s.snap_id = t.snap_id
                      AND s.dbid=d.dbid
                      AND s.dbid=t.dbid
                      AND s.dbid=u.dbid
                      AND i.instance_number = s.instance_number
                      AND s.instance_number = t.instance_number
                      AND t.snap_id = u.snap_id
                      AND ts.ts# = t.ts#
                      AND t.ts# = u.tablespace_id)
              WHERE latest = 1) tsmax
  WHERE tsmin.tsname = tsmax.tsname and tsmax.snaptime > tsmin.snaptime)
/
                     Start         Start         Curr          Curr         Alloc Growth   Used       Growth
Tablespace           Alloc (GB)    Used (GB)    Alloc (GB)    Used (GB)    % Use          GB/day     GB/day
---------------      ----------    ----------    ----------    ---------    ------------   --------   ------
AMAPS_DATA                 1.95         0.00          1.95         0.00            .05        .00        .00
APPS_TS_ARCHIVE            0.73         0.51          0.73         0.52          70.62        .00        .00
APPS_TS_INTERFACE          6.61         5.53          6.61         5.67          85.83        .00        .00
APPS_TS_MEDIA              2.72         2.57          3.78         3.57          94.37        .02        .02
... output omitted for brevity
---------------      ----------    ----------    ----------    ---------    ------------   --------   -----
sum                      257.77       177.61        303.84       209.90                      .95        .66
```

CHAPTER 5 ■ SIZING EXADATA

For the database above, we are experiencing an *allocated* daily growth rate of 0.95 GB per day and a *used* growth rate of 0.66 GB/day, between the oldest and most recent AWR snapshot time range. Unless you're concerned about per-tablespace growth, you can summarize your growth using the script in Listing 5-18:

Listing 5-18. lst05-18-db-growth-sum.sql

```
SYS @ PROD> SELECT
       ROUND (sum(curr_alloc_gb), 2) curralloc,
       ROUND (sum(curr_used_gb), 2) currused,
       ROUND (100 * (sum(curr_used_gb) / sum(curr_alloc_gb)), 2) PCTUSED,
       ROUND (sum(alloc_gbperday), 2) alloc_gbpd,
       ROUND (sum(used_gbperday), 2) used_gbpd
  FROM (SELECT tsmin.tsname tbs, tsmin.tablespace_size init_alloc_gb,
               tsmin.tablespace_usedsize init_used_gb,
               tsmax.tablespace_size curr_alloc_gb,
               tsmax.tablespace_usedsize curr_used_gb,
                 (tsmax.tablespace_size - tsmin.tablespace_size) / (tsmax.snaptime -
                   tsmin.snaptime) alloc_gbperday,
                 (tsmax.tablespace_usedsize - tsmin.tablespace_usedsize)
               / (tsmax.snaptime - tsmin.snaptime) used_gbperday
          FROM (SELECT *
                  FROM (SELECT TRUNC (s.begin_interval_time) snaptime,
                               t.tsname, (ts.BLOCKSIZE * u.tablespace_size) / 1024 / 1024 / 1024
                                  tablespace_size,
                                 (ts.BLOCKSIZE * u.tablespace_usedsize) / 1024 / 1024 / 1024
                                   tablespace_usedsize,
                               (RANK () OVER (PARTITION BY t.tsname ORDER BY s.snap_id ASC)
                               ) latest,
                               s.end_interval_time endtime
                          FROM dba_hist_snapshot s,v$instance i,v$database d,
                               dba_hist_tablespace_stat t,dba_hist_tbspc_space_usage u,SYS.ts$
                                 ts
                         WHERE s.snap_id = t.snap_id
                           AND s.dbid=d.dbid and s.dbid=t.dbid and s.dbid=u.dbid
                           AND i.instance_number = s.instance_number
                           AND s.instance_number = t.instance_number
                           AND ts.ts# = t.ts#
                           AND t.snap_id = u.snap_id
                           AND t.ts# = u.tablespace_id)
                 WHERE latest = 1) tsmin,
               (SELECT *
                  FROM (SELECT TRUNC (s.begin_interval_time) snaptime,
                               t.tsname,
                                 (ts.BLOCKSIZE * u.tablespace_size) / 1024 / 1024/  1024
                                   tablespace_size,
                                 (ts.BLOCKSIZE * u.tablespace_usedsize) / 1024 / 1024 / 1024
                                   tablespace_usedsize,
                               (RANK () OVER (PARTITION BY t.tsname ORDER BY s.snap_id DESC)
                               ) latest,
                               s.end_interval_time endtime
```

```
                      FROM dba_hist_snapshot s,v$instance i, v$database d,
                           dba_hist_tablespace_stat t,dba_hist_tbspc_space_usage u,SYS.ts$
                               ts
                      WHERE s.snap_id = t.snap_id
                        AND s.dbid=d.dbid and s.dbid=t.dbid and s.dbid=u.dbid
                        AND i.instance_number = s.instance_number
                        AND s.instance_number = t.instance_number
                        AND t.snap_id = u.snap_id
                        AND ts.ts# = t.ts#
                        AND t.ts# = u.tablespace_id)
                 WHERE latest = 1) tsmax
  WHERE tsmin.tsname = tsmax.tsname and tsmax.snaptime > tsmin.snaptime)
/
     Curr           Curr                        Alloc Growth     Used Growth
 Alloc (GB)      Used (GB)      % Used          GB/day           GB/day
------------    ----------    ----------    --------------    -------------
     303.84        209.92         69.09               .96              .67
```

Now you can forecast how large you expect your database to be based on the current growth rates. Typically, organizations will forecast capacity based on long term budgetary milestones and with an Exadata deployment on the horizon, the example below in Listing 5-19 displays a 1-year, 2-year, 3-year, and 5-year capacity plan:

Listing 5-19. lst05-19-db-growth-horizon.sql

```
SYS @ PROD> SELECT
       ROUND (sum(curr_alloc_gb), 2) curralloc,
       greatest(sum(alloc_gbperday),sum(used_gbperday)) grate,
       (sum(curr_alloc_gb) +
              365*(greatest(sum(alloc_gbperday),sum(used_gbperday))))
                     -(sum(curr_alloc_gb)-sum(curr_used_gb)) year1,
       (sum(curr_alloc_gb) +
              2*365*(greatest(sum(alloc_gbperday),sum(used_gbperday))))
                     -(sum(curr_alloc_gb)-sum(curr_used_gb)) year2,
       (sum(curr_alloc_gb) +
              3*365*(greatest(sum(alloc_gbperday),sum(used_gbperday))))
                     -(sum(curr_alloc_gb)-sum(curr_used_gb)) year3,
       (sum(curr_alloc_gb) +
              5*365*(greatest(sum(alloc_gbperday),sum(used_gbperday))))
                     -(sum(curr_alloc_gb)-sum(curr_used_gb)) year5
  FROM (SELECT tsmin.tsname tbs, tsmin.tablespace_size init_alloc_gb,
               tsmin.tablespace_usedsize init_used_gb,
               tsmax.tablespace_size curr_alloc_gb,
               tsmax.tablespace_usedsize curr_used_gb,
                 (tsmax.tablespace_size - tsmin.tablespace_size) / (tsmax.snaptime -
                    tsmin.snaptime) alloc_gbperday,
                 (tsmax.tablespace_usedsize - tsmin.tablespace_usedsize)
               / (tsmax.snaptime - tsmin.snaptime) used_gbperday
        FROM    (SELECT *
                 FROM (SELECT TRUNC (s.begin_interval_time) snaptime,
                              t.tsname, (ts.BLOCKSIZE * u.tablespace_size) / 1024 / 1024 / 1024
                              tablespace_size,
```

```
                            (ts.BLOCKSIZE * u.tablespace_usedsize) / 1024 / 1024 / 1024
                                tablespace_usedsize,
                            (RANK () OVER (PARTITION BY t.tsname ORDER BY s.snap_id ASC)
                            ) latest,
                            s.end_interval_time endtime
                       FROM dba_hist_snapshot s,
                            v$instance i, v$database d,
                            dba_hist_tablespace_stat t,
                            dba_hist_tbspc_space_usage u,
                            SYS.ts$ ts
                      WHERE s.snap_id = t.snap_id
                        AND s.dbid=d.dbid and s.dbid=t.dbid and s.dbid=u.dbid
                        AND i.instance_number = s.instance_number
                        AND s.instance_number = t.instance_number
                        AND ts.ts# = t.ts#
                        AND t.snap_id = u.snap_id
                        AND t.ts# = u.tablespace_id)
                WHERE latest = 1) tsmin,
               (SELECT *
                  FROM (SELECT TRUNC (s.begin_interval_time) snaptime,
                            t.tsname,
                              (ts.BLOCKSIZE * u.tablespace_size) / 1024 / 1024/   1024
                                tablespace_size,
                            (ts.BLOCKSIZE * u.tablespace_usedsize) / 1024 / 1024 / 1024
                                tablespace_usedsize,
                            (RANK () OVER (PARTITION BY t.tsname ORDER BY s.snap_id DESC)
                            ) latest,
                            s.end_interval_time endtime
                       FROM dba_hist_snapshot s,
                            v$instance i, v$database d,
                            dba_hist_tablespace_stat t,
                            dba_hist_tbspc_space_usage u,
                            SYS.ts$ ts
                      WHERE s.snap_id = t.snap_id
                        AND s.dbid=d.dbid and s.dbid=t.dbid and s.dbid=u.dbid
                        AND i.instance_number = s.instance_number
                        AND s.instance_number = t.instance_number
                        AND t.snap_id = u.snap_id
                        AND ts.ts# = t.ts#
                        AND t.ts# = u.tablespace_id)
                 WHERE latest = 1) tsmax
 WHERE tsmin.tsname = tsmax.tsname and tsmax.snaptime > tsmin.snaptime)
/

Curr          Growth Rate   1-year       2-year       3-year       5-year
Alloc (GB)    GB/day        Size (GB)    Size (GB)    Size (GB)    Size (GB)
-----------   -----------   ----------   ----------   ----------   ----------
    303.84           .96       561.34       911.73      1262.11      1962.88
```

Finally, you can add additional logic into the script to determine which Exadata configuration you need to target based on your growth rate, number of similarly sized databases (think in terms of production clones), percentage of primary database size that each clone consumes, whether you're targeting High Performance or High Capacity disk drives, the percentage of space reserved for "data" vs. your Fast Recovery Area, and whether you're electing ASM normal redundancy or ASM high redundancy.

■ **Note** Please see Recipes 5-4 and 6-6 to learn more about ASM redundancy and Recipe 5-9 to understand techniques for measuring your Fast Recovery Area.

In the script in Listing 5-20 below:

- &num_dbs = Number of additional databases that are copies or clones of the database you're running the query against.

- &pct_db_size = Percentage of size for each additional database with respect to the database you're running the query against. For example, "1" means that each additional database will be the same size, ".25" means each additional database is one-fourth the size, and so forth.

- &hp_or_hc = Whether you're using High Performance or High Capacity Disk drives. For this parameter, enter either "HC" or "HP." If the string is unmatched, the query assumes High Performance disks.

- &pct_for_data = Percentage of disk space reserved for database files, excluding FRA requirements. For example, if you wish to size your FRA to 50% available storage, enter .5. If you need a 25% reservation for the FRA, enter .75.

- &asm_redundancy = Normal or high ASM redundancy. If string is unmatched, the query will assume NORMAL redundancy.

For the execution of this script in our environment, we will assume five additional databases, each equally sized to the current database, and use of ASM normal redundancy with High Performance drives. We will further assume we will reserve half of our Exadata storage capacity for our FRA.

■ **Note** As executed, the script below assumes a five-year capacity plan. You can adjust the script for a one-year, two-year, or three-year forecast by changing the "year5" references in the top section of the code.

Listing 5-20. lst05-20-db-growth-forexa.sql

```
SYS @ PROD> select curralloc,grate,year5,
    decode(upper('&&hp_or_hc'),'HP','High Performance','HC','High Capacity','High Performance')
drivetype,
    decode(upper('&&asm_redundancy'),'NORMAL','Normal','HIGH','High','Normal') asmredund,
    case
        when upper('&&hp_or_hc') = 'HP' then
            case
                when upper('&&asm_redundancy') = 'NORMAL' then
                    case
                        when year5 < (10547*&&pct_for_data) then 'Quarter Rack'
```

```
                    when year5 between (10547*&&pct_for_data) and (25804*&&pct_for_data)
                        then 'Half Rack'
                    when year5 between (25804*&&pct_for_data) and (51609*&&pct_for_data)
                        then 'Full Rack'
                    when year5 > (51609*&&pct_for_data) then 'Full Rack+'
              end
          when upper('&&asm_redundancy') = 'HIGH'     then
            case
                    when year5 < (7372*&&pct_for_data) then 'Quarter Rack'
                    when year5 between (7372*&&pct_for_data) and (17203*&&pct_for_data)
                        then 'Half Rack'
                    when year5 between (17203*&&pct_for_data) and (34406*&&pct_for_data)
                        then 'Full Rack'
                    when year5 > (34406*&&pct_for_data) then 'Full Rack+'
            end
          else
            case
                    when year5 < (10547*&&pct_for_data) then 'Quarter Rack'
                    when year5 between (10547*&&pct_for_data) and (25804*&&pct_for_data)
                        then 'Half Rack'
                    when year5 between (25804*&&pct_for_data) and (51609*&&pct_for_data)
                        then 'Full Rack'
                    when year5 > (51609*&&pct_for_data) then 'Full Rack+'
              end
      end
  when upper('&&hp_or_hc') = 'HC' then
    case
          when upper('&&asm_redundancy') = 'NORMAL' then
            case
                    when year5 < (55296*&&pct_for_data) then 'Quarter Rack'
                    when year5 between (55296*&&pct_for_data) and (129024*&&pct_for_data)
                        then 'Half Rack'
                    when year5 between (129024*&&pct_for_data) and (258048*&&pct_for_data)
                        then 'Full Rack'
                    when year5 > (258048*&&pct_for_data) then 'Full Rack+'
              end
          when upper('&&asm_redundancy') = 'HIGH'    then
            case
                    when year5 < (36864*&&pct_for_data) then 'Quarter Rack'
                    when year5 between (36864*&&pct_for_data) and (86016*&&pct_for_data)
                        then 'Half Rack'
                    when year5 between (86016*&&pct_for_data) and (172032*&&pct_for_data)
                        then 'Full Rack'
                    when year5 > (172032*&&pct_for_data) then 'Full Rack+'
                    when year5 > (172032*&&pct_for_data) then 'Full Rack+'
              end
          else
            case
                    when year5 < (55296*&&pct_for_data) then 'Quarter Rack'
                    when year5 between (55296*&&pct_for_data) and (129024*&&pct_for_data)
                        then 'Half Rack'
```

```
                              when year5 between (129024*&&pct_for_data) and (258048*&&pct_for_data)
                                  then 'Full Rack'
                              when year5 > (258048*&&pct_for_data) then 'Full Rack+'
                          end
               end
           else
               case
                   when upper('&&asm_redundancy') = 'NORMAL' then
                       case
                              when year5 < (10547*&&pct_for_data) then 'Quarter Rack'
                              when year5 between (10547*&&pct_for_data) and (25804*&&pct_for_data)
                                  then 'Half Rack'
                              when year5 between (25804*&&pct_for_data) and (51609*&&pct_for_data)
                                  then 'Full Rack'
                              when year5 > (51609*&&pct_for_data) then 'Full Rack+'
                          end
                   when upper('&&asm_redundancy') = 'HIGH'    then
                       case
                              when year5 < (7372*&&pct_for_data) then 'Quarter Rack'
                              when year5 between (7372*&&pct_for_data) and (17203*&&pct_for_data)
                                  then 'Half Rack'
                              when year5 between (17203*&&pct_for_data) and (34406*&&pct_for_data)
                                  then 'Full Rack'
                              when year5 > (34406*&&pct_for_data) then 'Full Rack+'
                          end
                   else
                       case
                              when year5 < (10547*&&pct_for_data) then 'Quarter Rack'
                              when year5 between (10547*&&pct_for_data) and (25804*&&pct_for_data)
                                  then 'Half Rack'
                              when year5 between (25804*&&pct_for_data) and (51609*&&pct_for_data)
                                  then 'Full Rack'
                              when year5 > (51609*&&pct_for_data) then 'Full Rack+'
                          end
               end
       end exa_model
from (
select curralloc, grate ,
       year1+(&&num_dbs * &&pct_db_size * year1) year1,
       year2+(&&num_dbs * &&pct_db_size * year2) year2,
       year3+(&&num_dbs * &&pct_db_size * year3) year3,
       year5+(&&num_dbs * &&pct_db_size * year5) year5
from ( { ... Code from Listing 5-19 ... }
))
/
Enter value for hp_or_hc: HP
Enter value for asm_redundancy: NORMAL
Enter value for pct_for_data: .5
Enter value for num_dbs: 5
Enter value for pct_db_size: 1
```

```
Curr            Growth Rate    5-year         ASM                               Exadata Config
Alloc (GB)      GB/day         Size (GB)      Drive Type        Redundancy      Recommendation
----------      -----------    ---------      -----------------  ----------     ----------------
    303.84             .96      11778.08      High Performance  Normal          Half Rack
```

Based on our current growth rates and estimated five-year size of our database, combined with the aforementioned inputs, we can assume that an Exadata Half Rack with ASM normal redundancy and High Performance disks can support our capacity requirements.

How It Works

Similar to information in Recipe 5-5, analyzing your disk storage needs for Exadata is a matter of capturing your current database size, calculating growth rates, multiplying or adding based on the number of databases planned to be deployed on Exadata, deciding on an ASM redundancy strategy, deciding between High Performance or High Capacity disk drives, and finally understanding Exadata storage capacities. With the exception of FRA sizing, which is covered in Recipe 5-9, you can gather all of this information based on your current database footprint using data from Oracle AWR, assuming that the current growth rates are representative of your forecasted growth rates.

Using SQL scripts like the ones contained in this recipe is a good way to conduct this type of capacity-planning exercise. There may, of course, be unknown variables that contribute to your capacity-planning efforts. You can account for these by adjusting some of your input criteria in the final SQL script in this recipe.

5-7. Planning for Disaster Recovery

Problem

You are planning on deploying Oracle Exadata and wish to make intelligent decisions about your database disaster recovery strategy.

Solution

If your organization has business requirements for disaster recovery for your Oracle database residing on Oracle Exadata, Oracle Data Guard is Oracle's recommended solution. Oracle's Maximum Availability Architecture (MAA) paper can be downloaded at
www.oracle.com/technetwork/database/features/availability/exadata-maa-131903.pdf.

Oracle Data Guard on Exadata functions identically to 11gR2 Data Guard on non-Exadata databases. Your standby database can be either a physical standby or a logical standby and can also use Advanced Data Guard features. Additionally, your standby does not have to reside on an Oracle Exadata database machine, although some software features would be limited in the event of a disaster and Data Guard switchover.

How It Works

The Oracle Exadata Database Machine does not support array replication or any other means of maintaining duplicate copies of data outside of Oracle-provided technologies and solutions. Data Guard is typically the disaster recovery solution of choice, but other Oracle products such as Oracle Golden Gate could also be used to meet your needs.

There are a few topics worth mentioning when discussing disaster recovery in the context of Oracle databases residing on Exadata. First, if you choose to deploy your standby environment on a different architecture (in other words, not Oracle Exadata), Oracle storage server software features will not function on the standby environment. Clearly, if you're relying on these software features to meet performance SLAs, you will be at risk of reduced performance in the event of a failure.

Hybrid Columnar Compression is not supported on a non-Exadata standby environment; the reason we mention this specifically is not just to discuss a potential performance impact in the event of a failover, but more so to mention the potentially significant storage impact. Tables that are compressed with Hybrid Columnar Compression are decompressed in flight to a non-Exadata standby, imposing both a performance impact and potentially significant disk capacity impact.

From a planning and economics perspective, the decision to deploy a disaster recovery environment on Exadata is, for many customers, a non-trivial budgetary line item. As such, like all disaster recovery planning, it is important to build and communicate the business justification for a standby Exadata environment and be prepared to present cost benefit analysis. One strategy that often helps customers justify a multisite Exadata deployment is to run non-production databases at the disaster recovery site on the DR Exadata Database Machine.

5-8. Planning for Backups
Problem

You're running your Oracle databases on Exadata and are looking for options to back up your environments.

Solution

The backup and recovery topic for Oracle database environments, in general, is relatively broad. With Oracle Exadata environment, the topic is no less complex; to provide continuity and protect your data, you need to back it up. With Oracle Exadata environments, this means backing up your database files and software on both the compute, storage, and network grids.

We're going to keep this recipe relatively short and not dive into installation or configuration details with either Oracle backup solutions or other vendor products solutions. In short, these are the elements you need to be concerned with:

- Back up your operating system binaries, Oracle software homes, and Oracle files on the compute nodes just as you would on a non-Exadata environment. In other words, if you use a vendor backup solution or software that requires backup agents to be installed on your compute nodes, ensure that your vendor backup agents are supported by Exadata compute node operating systems.

- You can also back up your compute server binaries by using LVM snapshots. Recipe 14-5 provides an example of this method.

- Your Exadata Storage Servers do not need to be backed up; Exadata automatically backs these up using a self-maintained internal USB drive.

- Back up your InfiniBand switch configuration using Backup/Restore functionality in the InfiniBand ILOM web interface.

- Backup your Oracle databases using Oracle RMAN, optionally storing copies in your Fast Recovery Area inside your ASM "RECO" disk group.

- You can optimize your backups by backing up over your InfiniBand network:
    - Install InfiniBand drivers on backup media servers, or
    - Back up to Oracle ZFS storage appliance share over InfiniBand.

From a planning perspective, the most important of the above considerations is usually the topic of your database backups, since the strategy you deploy could have impacts beyond data recovery and availability. For example, if you choose to reserve enough capacity in your Fast Recovery Area for one day's worth of activity and an

RMAN level 0 backup, the disk space required for this will impact your overall usable capacity. Also, your decision about how much archived redo to maintain on disk (in other words, inside an ASM group) as well as your frequency of performing RMAN backups also has an effect on your usable capacity.

Another factor for many organizations is backup and recovery performance. Backups to ASM disk groups containing a Fast Recovery Area are cell offloadable operations and can be very fast, but backups to external storage devices (disk, tape, virtual tape, and so forth) typically incur more overhead. You can address this overhead by using your high-speed, high-bandwidth InfiniBand network, a dedicated 10 GbE network, and using other Oracle RMAN performance optimization techniques.

How It Works

Backing up your Oracle environments on Exadata is not much different than non-Exadata backups, but here are some things to think about:

- Since your database storage will always be with Oracle ASM, you need to use RMAN to back up your database files.

- When you fill out your Exadata DB Machine Configuration worksheet (please refer to Recipes 8-1, 9-2, and/or 9-3), you will be asked whether to back up to external media or internal to Exadata. If you select external, the configuration process will establish at 80:20 split between DATA and RECO, leaving 20% of the usable capacity for archive logs and other archived redo logs, one plex of your online redo log groups, and flashback logs. I you choose "internal to the database machine," the configuration process will allocate at 40:60 split between DATA and RECO storage, with 60% accounting for the aforementioned recovery structures/files plus RMAN backups.

- Your decision on whether to employ Flashback features, perform RMAN backups to your FRA, and how long to retain recovery data (archive logs, and so forth) on disk can have a profound impact on usable storage capacities. With non-Exadata storage arrays, there tends to be a lower incremental cost to scale capacity for these types of purposes; on Exadata, if your recovery policies alone push you from a Quarter Rack to a Half Rack, the cost of this jump is generally considered nontrivial. You should be aware of this when designing your backup and recovery strategy.

- Databases residing on Exadata tend to be "large." When planning for large database backups, ensure your network bandwidth is capable of supporting your backup operations. Since Exadata is an engineered system with reserved and preconfigured network interfaces, you won't have as much flexibility to add network cards or drastically change network configurations as you may in non-Exadata systems. Oracle provides for an "additional network" (NET3) to address this and you can use 10 GbE NICs.

- When possible, leverage your InfiniBand network to facilitate faster backup and restore times. An Oracle-centric architecture we've been successful with for both Exadata and Exalogic backup solutions is comprised of leveraging the InfiniBand network as the backup network and backing up to Oracle ZFS Storage Appliance shares over InfiniBand.

Oracle has written a backup and recovery best practices paper called *Backup and Recovery Performance and Best Practices for Exadata Cell and Oracle Exadata Database Machine*, which you can download from www.oracle.com/technetwork/database/features/availability/maa-tech-wp-sundbm-backup-11202-183503.pdf. We strongly recommend reading this paper.

5-9. Determining Your Fast Recovery Area and RECO Disk Group Size Requirements

Problem

You wish to properly estimate the size of your Fast Recovery Area (FRA) for your Oracle 11gR2 databases, or perhaps more specifically the selection you choose for "Backup method" in your Exadata configuration worksheet.

Solution

In this recipe, you will learn how to size your Fast Recovery and RECO disk storage on Exadata. Your first choice is to determine whether you will be storing RMAN backups inside your Fast Recovery Area. Doing so will allow for the fastest recovery duration, at the expense of reduced usable disk capacity for your data files inside your storage grid. If you choose to store RMAN backups inside your FRA/RECO disk group, you should select "Backups internal to Oracle Exadata Database Machine" as your backup method in your configuration spreadsheet. Doing so will allocate 60% of your usable capacity for the RECO disk groups.

This choice is customizable; if, for example, you're moving one production database and multiple nonproduction databases to Exadata that each run in NOARCHIVELOG mode, you can size your RECO disk group smaller than 60% of usable capacity. We recommend sizing this portion to be 100% the size of each database running in ARCHIVELOG mode that you wish to store RMAN backups inside your FRA.

Other database entities that you need to account for include archived red logs, flashback logs, online redo log files, and control files. Your control files will be small in size, so we will ignore this in the calculations below. This leaves you with the task of calculating the size required for archived redo logs, flash back logs, and redo log files. The following script can be used to display, for a single database, the estimated size required for your FRA and RECO structures. The script prompts for the following information and returns a percentage required; this percentage should be used to decide what your ratio should be between DATA and RECO storage:

- &backups_to_exa: Enter "Y" or "N" to decide between backing up your database to Exadata vs. backing up externally.

- &num_days: Enter an integer representing the number of days you wish to retain archived logs on disk. This is decided in accordance with your organization's database backup and recovery strategy.

- &use_flashlog: Enter "Y" or "N" to indicate whether you plan to use flashback logging. If you choose "Y," the script will use the volume of archive log generation to represent the rate of change (that is, DML volume) per interval.

Log in to your current database as SYSDBA and execute the script in Listing 5-21:

Listing 5-21. lst05-21-db-reco-fra.sql

```
SYS @ PROD> select dbgb, redogb, ArchMaxReq,
       rmangb,flgb,
       100*((dbgb+redogb)/(dbgb+redogb+ArchMaxReq+rmangb+flgb)) pct_for_data,
       100*((ArchMaxReq+redogb+rmangb+flgb)/(dbgb+redogb+ArchMaxReq+rmangb+flgb)) pct_for_reco
from
 ( select       db.dbgb, redo.redogb,
       (arch.gbpd * &&num_days) ArchMaxReq,
       (case
          when upper('&&backups_to_exa') like 'Y%' then (db.dbgb + arch.gbpd)
          else 0
        end) rmangb,
```

```
            (case
              when upper('&&use_flashlog') like 'Y%' then (arch.gbpd)
              else 0
            end) flgb
from (
      select
                  max((al.blks * kc.blksize)/1024/1024/1024) gbpd
            from
                  (select
                      trunc(completion_time) dt,
                      sum(blocks) blks
                    from v$archived_log
                    group by trunc(completion_time)) al,
                  (select
                      max(lebsz) blksize
                    from x$kccle) kc
      ) arch,
      (
        select sum(bytes)/1024/1024/1024 dbgb
        from v$datafile
      ) db,
      (
        select sum(bytes)/1024/1024/1024 redogb
        from v$log
      ) redo
)
/
Enter value for num_days: 3
old    7:         (arch.gbpd * &&num_days) ArchMaxReq,
new    7:         (arch.gbpd * 3) ArchMaxReq,
Enter value for backups_to_exa: Y
old    9:           when upper('&&backups_to_exa') like 'Y%' then (db.dbgb + arch.gbpd)
new    9:           when upper('Y') like 'Y%' then (db.dbgb + arch.gbpd)
Enter value for use_flashlog: Y
old   13:           when upper('&&use_flashlog') like 'Y%' then (arch.gbpd)
new   13:           when upper('Y') like 'Y%' then (arch.gbpd)

DB           OnlineLog    ArchLog      RMAN         FlashLog
Req.(GB)     Req.(GB)     Req.(GB)     Req.(GB)     Req.(GB))    % for Data   % for Reco/FRA
---------    ---------    ---------    ---------    ---------    ----------   --------------
   291.74         3.95       369.48       414.90       123.16         24.57            75.75
```

In the example above, we've chosen to perform RMAN backups to Exadata, store three days' worth of archived redo logs on disk, and use Flashback features and retain one day of change on disk. Based on this database's change rates, we arrive at a 25:75 split between storage requirements for database files and recovery-related files.

■ **Note** The logic presented in this recipe only considers a single database targeted for migration or deployment to Exadata. You will need to follow a similar approach to properly size your consolidated database footprint. Also, the script calculates its percentages based on *current* database size and *current* rates of archived redo generation.

CHAPTER 5 ■ SIZING EXADATA

How It Works

Sizing your RECO disk groups and Fast Recovery Area is a matter of deciding whether or not you want to use Exadata storage for your RMAN backups, implement Flashback features, and then computing the size of your database in relation to the rate of change.

The script provided in the solution of this recipe does make some conservative assumptions. First, we've assumed that the disk space required for RMAN backups is the same as the size of your database. Typically this is not the case—with block change tracking enabled, as is typically recommended, Oracle will only back up changed blocks, which will lead to a much smaller RMAN backup storage requirement.

We also used the "worst case" rates for archive log generation based on selecting the maximum number of bytes generated in any day since history was stored in V$ARCHIVED_LOG. This may or may not be a good assumption. For example, your database may have had a day in recent history in which a large data load job was executed with LOGGING enabled for DML operations. This would skew the projections on the high side. You can counter this by changing the MAX to AVG in the archive log section of the script provided in the solution of this recipe.

In short, forecasting and sizing your FRA and RECO disk storage can be as straightforward as understanding what types of files are stored inside these entities and calculating storage requirements based on current and historical data stored in your current database's data dictionary.

CHAPTER 6

Preparing for Exadata

Before you receive your Exadata Database Machine, several important tasks are required to ensure a successful installation.

Prior to delivery, Oracle or your Oracle Partner will send you a configuration worksheet. This worksheet is your chance to fill in configuration details for your database machine, specific to your usage requirements and planning efforts followed in Chapter 5. Specifically, your desired network and storage configuration details are entered in the configuration worksheet and in order to enter accurate information, you should be familiar with Exadata networking requirements and conduct network-related, pre-installation tasks.

Additionally, the configuration worksheet also presents an opportunity to configure your Exadata storage based on your business requirements. As an engineered system, each Exadata Storage Server has a fixed number of physical disks, each with a fixed size. Depending on your Exadata configuration, this means you will either have 36, 84, or 168 SAS disks of either the 600 GB High Performance variety or the 3 TB High Capacity flavor. This storage grid is dedicated to storing your Oracle database files and because both the total storage capacity and performance capabilities will be fixed, it is important to properly plan how you will store your databases on Exadata.

Finally, prior to delivery, Oracle coordinates a site preparation checklist to help ensure a successful delivery and installation. It is important to complete the pre-delivery survey accurately to ensure that your machine can be powered on and connected to your data center network.

This chapter will guide you through the important network, storage, and site planning tasks required for installing Exadata in your environment.

6-1. Planning and Understanding Exadata Networking

Problem

You've recently purchased an Exadata Database Machine and wish to plan for your Exadata network.

Solution

Exadata network planning involves understanding and planning the following networks:

- The InfiniBand network
- The administration network, also known as the management network
- The client access network
- The optional additional network

The InfiniBand network is used as the Exadata storage network and Oracle RAC interconnect. This network typically requires no planning, as Oracle will configure each InfiniBand interface and its bonding configuration identically on all Exadata deployments. The exception from this is if you have a requirement to perform cross-rack communication over InfniBand; for example, if you have multiple Exadata or Exalogic racks that need to be uniquely addressed from an InfiniBand-aware backup media server.

The administration management network is used to provide SSH access to the compute servers, storage servers, and InfiniBand servers. The NET0 and ILOM interfaces on the compute, storage, and InfiniBand switches are connected to the embedded Cisco Catalyst 4948 switch, which is then uplinked to your data center network. To prepare for your administration network, you need to enter the following information in your database machine configuration worksheet:

- The starting IP address for the administration network. The network must be distinct from all other networks in the Exadata Database Machine. An example of this starting IP address could be 172.16.1.10.

- The network subnet mask, such as 255.255.255.0.

- The gateway IP address, for example, 172.16.1.1.

Note The database machine configuration worksheet is supplied by Oracle prior to the machine arriving onsite and is used by Oracle ACS to install and configure Exadata. Please see Recipe 6-9 for additional details.

During the Exadata installation process, each NET0 and ILOM network is configured based on the values in the configuration worksheet. Specifically, the Exadata installation process uses a utility called ipconf, which sets values in the cell.conf configuration file. This file is read during the Exadata storage cell or compute node process to set values in the /etc/sysconfig/network-scripts/ifcfg-eth0 configuration file, which in turn configures your eth0 network.

Planning for your client access network is similar to planning your administration network on the compute servers. You'll need to enter the following information in your configuration worksheet:

- Whether or not to use channel bonding. YES means to bond the NET1 and NET2 interfaces on the compute server, NO indicates to not use bonding. Oracle recommends using channel bonding for availability reasons.

- Starting IP address = the starting IP address to use for your client access network. This needs to be on a distinct network from all others inside your database machine—for example, 172.16.10.10.

- Subnet mask, for example, 255.255.255.0.

- Gateway IP address, for example, 172.16.10.1.

The client access network is configured during the Exadata installation process in a similar manner to the administration network, as discussed above. If you decide to bond your client access network interfaces, they will be configured with the bondeth0 interface and after a successful installation, you can examine the /etc/sysconfig/network-scripts/ifcfg-bondeth0 and /etc/oracle/cell/network-config/cellip.ora files for configuration details.

The compute server additional network (NET3) is an optional network designed to provide network connectivity for the NET3 interface. This network should be separate from your administration and client access networks and involves specifying a starting IP address, subnet mask, and gateway IP address. The NET3 network is also configured during the installation process in the same way the administration and client access networks are configured.

In addition to these networks, your Power Distribution Units (PDUs) and `ILOM` interfaces will need to be provided IP addresses and connected to either your data center network or internal Cisco Catalyst switch.

At a high level, your database machine configuration worksheet will also require you to enter "general" network configuration details. These configuration details are used across compute servers, storage servers, and InfiniBand switches in your Exadata deployment:

- Domain name
- IP address of DNS server(s)
- IP address of NTP server(s)

How It Works

Exadata Database Machines consist of a compute grid, storage grid, and network grid. Each grid is comprised of multiple physical servers, each with multiple network interfaces designed to carry different types of network traffic. Oracle names these networks as follows:

- `NET0` = Exadata's administration management network, which provides for SSH connectivity to components in the various servers in the database machine including compute servers, storage servers, and InfiniBand servers.

- `NET1, NET2, NET1-2` = Exadata's client access networks, as defined on the compute servers. These networks provide Oracle Grid Infrastructure network-related connectivity, including Virtual IP addresses (VIPs), database listener addresses, and SCAN listener addresses.

- `NET3` = Exadata's "additional network," an optional network designed to provide additional network connectivity to the compute servers. Organizations often choose to use this network as their backup network to separate backup network traffic from the client access or administration network.

- `IB` = InfiniBand network, a network designed to facilitate communication between the compute servers and storage servers as well as the Oracle RAC interconnect.

When planning your Exadata network configuration, there are a few key considerations. First, you need to understand the purpose of each of the networks, determine your network IP address ranges, subnet masks, and gateway IP addresses. Isolation of these networks is important; you should not define Exadata networks on an existing data center network—although this type of configuration can be made to work, it can lead to routing issues (outside the rack) under some circumstances.

Name resolution and DNS configuration is also very important and Recipe 6-2 provides information about DNS configuration with Exadata.

An example of an Exadata network planning exercise follows.

General Information

- Oracle Exadata Database Machine Name: `cm01`
- Type of system: Quarter Rack, Half Rack, or Full Rack
- Domain name: `company.com`
- IP addresses of DNS servers: `11.11.1.250, 11.11.1.251`
- IP addresses of NTP server: `108.61.73.243` (`pool.ntp.org`)

Management Network

- Starting IP address: 172.16.1.10
- Subnet mask: 255.255.248.0
- Gateway: 172.16.1.1
- Total IP addresses: 16 for a Quarter Rack, 29 for a Half Rack, and 51 for a Full Rack
- Connectivity information
  - The internal Cisco switch has one uplink to the data center network.
  - The KVM and each PDU has one connection to the data center network.

Client Access Network

- Starting IP address: 172.16.10.10
- Subnet mask: 255.255.248.0
- Gateway: 172.16.10.1
- Total IP addresses: 7 for a Quarter Rack, 11 for a Half Rack, and 19 for a Full Rack
- Connectivity information: Each client access network interface is connected to your data center network.

InfiniBand Network

- Network: 192.168.10.0/8
- Total IP addresses: 5 for a Quarter Rack, 11 for a Half Rack, and 22 for a Full Rack

Figure 6-1 provides an Exadata network topology for a single compute server and storage server.

CHAPTER 6 ■ PREPARING FOR EXADATA

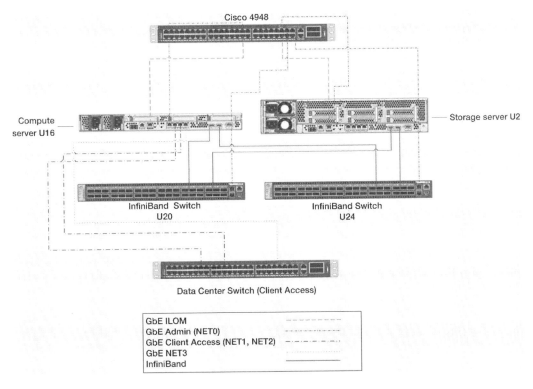

Figure 6-1. *Exadata network topology*

6-2. Configuring DNS

Problem

You wish to configure your DNS servers to support an Exadata installation.

Solution

DNS configuration is a prerequisite to a successful Exadata Database Machine installation. As outlined in Recipe 6-1, your Exadata configuration will have multiple IP addresses and use your entered database machine name to identify hostnames for each server and component inside your Exadata.

After completing your configuration worksheet, Oracle or your Oracle Partner will send you a script called checkip.sh and an associated dbm.dat file. The purpose of checkip.sh, as outlined in Recipe 6-3, is to validate your DNS and network configuration for all Exadata network components as specified in your configuration worksheet.

For checkip.sh to succeed and to ensure a smooth Exadata installation, use the values you supplied in your configuration spreadsheet and enter the following fully qualified hostnames in your DNS servers:

- SCAN names and addresses
- Compute server names and addresses
- Cell server names and IP addresses
- VIP names and IP addresses

143

- ILOM names and IP addresses
- InfiniBand switch names and IP addresses

When entering DNS entries for Exadata, be sure to create both forward and reverse lookup entries. checkip.sh requires that this be performed, as do the Exadata installation and validation processes. Depending on your DNS software or solution, the steps necessary to create your DNS entries will vary, but you need to have entries for each of your nodes in both a Forward Lookup Zone and Reverse Lookup Zone.

How It Works

When you fill out your database machine configuration worksheet, Oracle will use this information to build its configuration files and use these files to configure the various network components. In order for the installation process to succeed, most of the IP addresses and corresponding hostnames must be entered in DNS. Once the database machine is configured, both forward and reverse lookup must succeed for all of the required names and IP addresses; during the installation itself, forward and reverse lookups should resolve names to the proper IP addresses but be unable to ping any of the interfaces.

■ **Note** If an IP address provided in the configuration worksheet is pingable at the time of installation, it means that an existing interface exists with this IP address on your network and the installation will fail.

6-3. Running checkip.sh
Problem

You are planning on installing your Exadata Database Machine and are ready to run checkip.sh, as directed by Oracle, and wish to understand what tasks checkip.sh performs and how it works.

Solution

Oracle's checkip.sh script is designed to validate the networking details provided to Oracle in your configuration worksheet to ensure that the Exadata installation succeeds. In this recipe, we will demonstrate how to run checkip.sh and explain how it works.

First, enter your Exadata hostnames and IP addresses in DNS, as discussed in Recipe 6-2.

Next, we recommend viewing the contents of the dbm.dat file and ensuring that each entry exists in your DNS server. The dbm.dat file is delivered by Oracle with the checkip.sh script, and checkip.sh reads values from dbm.dat in order to conduct its network validation. As such, the hostname and IP address information in dbm.dat represents the complete list of entries required in DNS.

■ **Note** checkip.sh does not alter or configure your network; it simply validates your network entries in DNS. If checkip.sh fails forward or reverse resolution for any of your nodes, you can resolve your DNS entry and run checkip.sh again.

After you have entered your Exadata network names and IP addresses in your DNS server, simply run checkip.sh from a location on your network that has connectivity to each network in your planned Exadata environment. As stated, the checkip.sh script will read your dbm.dat file, as built by Oracle based on your database machine configuration worksheet. checkip.sh logs its output to a file called dbm.out in the directory in which you ran checkip.sh. Following is a sample, abbreviated output of a successful checkip.sh execution prior to an Exadata Quarter Rack installation. In this output, we will number each line and explain what each section means after the output:

```
1.  Running in mode pre_applyconfig
2.  Using name server 11.11.1.250 found in dbm.dat for all DNS lookups
3.  Processing section DOMAIN
4.  centroid.com
5.  Processing section NAME
6.  GOOD : 11.11.1.250 responds to resolve request for cm01db01.centroid.com
7.  Processing section NTP
8.  GOOD : pool.ntp.org responds to time server query (/usr/sbin/ntpdate -q)
9.  Processing section GATEWAY
10. GOOD : 172.16.1.1 pings successfully
11. GOOD : 172.16.10.1 pings successfully
12. GOOD : 172.16.100.1 pings successfully
13. Processing section SCAN
14. GOOD : cm01-scan.centroid.com resolves to 3 IP addresses
15. GOOD : cm01-scan.centroid.com forward resolves to 172.16.10.14
16. GOOD : 172.16.10.14 reverse resolves to cm01-scan.centroid.com.
17. GOOD : 172.16.10.14 does not ping
18. ... output omitted
19. Processing section COMPUTE
20. GOOD : cm01dbm01.centroid.com forward resolves to 172.16.1.10
21. GOOD : 172.16.1.10 reverse resolves to cm01db01.centroid.com.
22. GOOD : 172.16.1.10 does not ping
23. GOOD : cm01dbm02.centroid.com forward resolves to 172.16.1.11
24. GOOD : 172.16.1.11 reverse resolves to cm01db02.centroid.com.
25. GOOD : 172.16.1.11 does not ping
26. GOOD : cm0101.centroid.com forward resolves to 172.16.10.10
27. GOOD : 172.16.10.10 reverse resolves to cm0101.centroid.com.
28. GOOD : 172.16.10.10 does not ping
29. GOOD : cm0102.centroid.com forward resolves to 172.16.10.11
30. GOOD : 172.16.10.11 reverse resolves to cm0102.centroid.com.
31. GOOD : 172.16.10.11 does not ping
32. Processing section CELL
33. GOOD : cm01cel01.centroid.com forward resolves to 172.16.1.12
34. GOOD : 172.16.1.12 reverse resolves to cm01cel01.centroid.com.
35. GOOD : 172.16.1.12 does not ping
36. ... output omitted
37. Processing section ILOM
38. GOOD : cm01db01-ilom.centroid.com forward resolves to 172.16.1.15
39. GOOD : 172.16.1.15 reverse resolves to cm01dbm01-ilom.centroid.com.
40. GOOD : 172.16.1.15 does not ping
41. ... output omitted
42. Processing section SWITCH
43. GOOD : cm01sw-kvm.centroid.com forward resolves to 172.16.1.20
44. GOOD : 172.16.1.20 reverse resolves to cm01sw-kvm.centroid.com.
45. GOOD : 172.16.1.20 does not ping
```

```
46. GOOD : cm01sw-ip.centroid.com forward resolves to 172.16.1.21
47. GOOD : 172.16.1.21 reverse resolves to cm01sw-ip.centroid.com.
48. GOOD : 172.16.1.21 does not ping
49. GOOD : cm01sw-ib2.centroid.com forward resolves to 172.16.1.23
50. GOOD : 172.16.1.23 reverse resolves to cm01sw-ib2.centroid.com.
51. GOOD : 172.16.1.23 does not ping
52. GOOD : cm01sw-ib3.centroid.com forward resolves to 172.16.1.24
53. GOOD : 172.16.1.24 reverse resolves to cm01sw-ib3.centroid.com.
54. GOOD : 172.16.1.24 does not ping
55. GOOD : cm01-pdua.centroid.com forward resolves to 172.16.1.25
56. GOOD : 172.16.1.25 reverse resolves to cm01-pdua.centroid.com.
57. GOOD : 172.16.1.25 does not ping
58. GOOD : cm01-pdub.centroid.com forward resolves to 172.16.1.26
59. GOOD : 172.16.1.26 reverse resolves to cm01-pdub.centroid.com.
60. GOOD : 172.16.1.26 does not ping
61. Processing section VIP
62. GOOD : cm0101-vip.centroid.com forward resolves to 172.16.10.12
63. GOOD : 172.16.10.12 reverse resolves to cm0101-vip.centroid.com.
64. GOOD : 172.16.10.12 does not ping
65. GOOD : cm0102-vip.centroid.com forward resolves to 172.16.10.13
66. GOOD : 172.16.10.13 reverse resolves to cm0102-vip.centroid.com.
67. GOOD : 172.16.10.13 does not ping
68. .... output omitted
```

Here's how to interpret the previous output:

- Lines 3 through 5 list the validation of your DNS server address and DNS domain name.

- Lines 7 and 8 validate your NTP server settings.

- Lines 9 through 12 report the validation of your administration, client access, and additional network gateways. This section assumes that these gateway IP addresses are available on your network and typically represent networks you have already established in your data center.

- Lines 13 through 17 represent the SCAN IP addresses. Each Exadata installation requires three SCAN IP addresses, each must be resolvable via forward and reverse lookup, and in pre-installation mode, none of these IP addresses should be pingable as this would indicate that you either have other servers or devices using this IP address or that you have already installed and configured your machine.

- Lines 19 through 31 represent the checkip.sh validation for your compute nodes. Similar to the SCAN addresses, each address must be resolvable in DNS and not pingable.

- Lines 32 through 35 represent the validation of one of your storage cells. Again, these addresses should be forward and reverse resolvable but not pingable.

- Lines 37 through 40 list the output for your ILOM network addresses and have the same resolution and ping requirements as the other networks.

- Lines 42 through 60 represent the network validation for the KVM switch, embedded Cisco switch, the InfiniBand switches, and PDUs. Each of these IP addresses should be resolvable in DNS but not pingable.

- Lines 61 through 67 represent your the Oracle VIP addresses, each of which should be forward and reverse resolvable but not pingable in pre-installation mode.

After your installation is complete, you can run `checkip.sh` with the `-m post_deploy112` argument to validate your configuration.

How It Works

The `checkip.sh` script verifies network configuration for Exadata Database Machine pre-installation, during installation, and post-installation. The following conditions are verified by `checkip.sh`:

- IP addresses that should be pingable are reachable.
- IP addresses that should not be pingable are not reachable.
- Hostnames that are expected to be registered in DNS are both forward and reverse resolvable using the first name server in the `dbm.dat` file.

After running `checkip.sh`, any success or failure messages are logged to `dbm.out`. Prior to scheduling Oracle ACS to perform your Exadata installation, you will need a clean run of `checkip.sh`. The reason this is so important is because Exadata's onecommand process, discussed in Chapter 6, automates the installation of your Exadata Database Machine and expects that your network's IP addresses and names match the configuration information provided to Oracle and used during the installation. Failure to assign or resolve IP addresses and hostnames during the installation will cause implementation delays and rework.

6-4. Customizing Your InfiniBand Network Configuration

Problem

You wish to change the default InfiniBand network configuration to support InfiniBand addressing flexibility across multiple Exadata Database Machines. For example, if you wish to perform Exadata or Exalogic backups on your InfiniBand network with IB-aware backup media servers, it may be important to have nonstandard and different InfiniBand network configurations for multiple machines.

Solution

As each organization's nonstandard InfiniBand network configuration requirements may be different, it is important to discuss your site's requirements with Oracle or your Oracle Partner prior to installing and configuring InfiniBand networking on your Exadata Database Machine. By default, the InfiniBand network addresses on each Exadata Database Machine will be configured the same; in other words, 192.168.10.1 will be the InfiniBand IP address on your first database server, 192.168.10.2 will be configured on your second database server, and so forth. These are set when `/opt/oracle.SupportTools/firstconf/applyconfig.sh` is run, which reads the `/opt/oracle.SupportTools/onecommand/preconf.csv` file. To change these default InfiniBand IP addresses, you'll need to work with Oracle to modify the standard templates (`preconf.csv`) used by Exadata's onecommand installation process so that the proper IP addresses will be configured.

How It Works

Each Exadata Database Machine of each configuration (Quarter Rack, Half Rack, or Full Rack) will have identical InfiniBand IP addresses unless you specifically change these when building your configuration. The `applyconfig.sh` script, which is executed as part of your Exadata installation process, will set these IP addresses based on settings established in a `preconf.csv` file. To deviate from these default settings, you need to ensure that your `preconf.csv` file contains the desired information.

> **Note** If you need to modify the default InfiniBand network addresses for your Exadata Database Machine, inform your Oracle sales representative ahead of time to ensure that Oracle ACS arrives at your site prepared to perform a nonstandard installation.

6-5. Determining Your DATA and RECO Storage Requirements

Problem

You are filling out your database machine configuration worksheet prior to your Exadata Database Machine being delivered and you need to decide how to configure storage for the DATA and RECO ASM disk groups.

Solution

In the *General Configuration* section of the Database Machine configuration worksheet, as discussed in Recipe 6-9, there is a section named *Backup Method*. The valid choices include *Backups Internal to Oracle Exadata Database Machine* and *Backups External to Exadata Database Machine*. When selecting to back up internal to the database machine, the installation will build Exadata Storage Server grid disks and ASM disk groups under the assumption that you will store your archived redo logs, Fast Recovery Area logs, and an RMAN level 0 backup inside an ASM RECO* ASM disk group, and will allocate 60% of the available space to this set of RECO grid disks and 40% to DATA disks. If you choose to back up external to the database machine, the installation will allocate 80% of available storage to data and 20% for recovery structures.

It is important to evaluate your overall backup strategy along with your usable storage capacity requirements when deciding how to size your DATA and RECO storage. Several considerations should be evaluated prior to completing your configuration worksheet:

- Your desired ASM disk group redundancy, as discussed in detail in Recipes 5-4 and 6-6

- Your current and projected usable storage capacity requirements, as presented in Recipes 5-5 and 5-6

- Your database backup requirements and strategy, as presented in Recipe 5-8

- Calculations to estimate your Fast Recovery Area and RECO ASM disk group sizing, as presented in Recipe 5-9

> **Note** During the installation process, Oracle ACS will configure your cell disk, grid disk, and ASM disk group storage as you've specified in the configuration worksheet and will also build an Oracle RAC database on your compute nodes. Don't worry if you're unsure of your final storage configuration; many organizations will drop and delete Oracle ACS-installed databases and storage configurations, and if you're comfortable with storage administration topics on Exadata, you can recreate your storage at a later date. It becomes more difficult to change your configuration once you have production databases installed and operational on your Exadata, but this too can be adjusted with proper planning.

How It Works

Sizing your DATA and RECO storage configuration and requirements is primarily a planning exercise. Each Exadata Database Machine of the same configuration is going to have the same number of physical disk drives in the storage cells. You will have 36 disks to work with on a Quarter Rack, 84 on a Half Rack, and 168 on a Full Rack. These can either be 600 GB High Performance or 3 TB High Capacity disks, and your disk type selection will dictate your overall *raw* storage capacity.

Configuring disk groups with ASM normal redundancy will leave you with half of your raw capacity for usable database storage, and high redundancy will cut your usable capacity to a third of your raw capacity. Assuming that you only store recovery structures in your RECO disk groups, the capacity available for database file storage will be further reduced.

Table 6-1 provides a summary of Exadata usable disk capacity with both ASM normal and high redundancy as well as with a 60:40 split between RECO and DATA, as is the default when you elect to perform backups internal to Exadata.

Table 6-1. Exadata usable storage capacity

	X2-2 Quarter Rack	X2-2 Half Rack	X2-2/X2-8 Full Rack
Storage Server Usable Capacity, *High Performance* Disks, **Normal Redundancy**	10.3 TB Usable 4.12 TB for Data	25.2 TB 10.08 TB for Data	50.4 TB 20.16 TB for Data
Storage Server Usable Capacity, *High Performance* Disks, **High Redundancy**	7.2 TB 2.88 TB for Data	16.8 TB 6.72 TB for Data	33.6 TB 13.44 TB for Data
Storage Server Usable Capacity, *High Capacity* Disks, **Normal Redundancy**	54 TB 21.6 TB for Data	126 TB 50.4 TB for Data	252 TB 100.8 TB for Data
Storage Server Usable Capacity, *High Capacity* Disks, **High Redundancy**	36 TB 14.4 TB for Data	84 TB 33.6 TB for Data	168 TB 67.2 TB for Data

6-6. Planning for ASM Disk Group Redundancy
Problem

You've decided your Oracle ASM disk group redundancy configuration using methods presented in Recipe 5-4 and you wish to calculate your overall usable capacity for both DATA and RECO data files.

Solution

The shell script in Listing 6-1 can be used to show your overall usable capacity per database storage type. It will prompt for your Exadata model configuration, desired ASM disk group redundancy, and the percentage to allocate for RECO disk storage.

Listing 6-1. lst06-01-storageplan.sh

```sh
#!/bin/sh
# Name:         lst06-01-storageplan.sh
# Purpose:      Calculates usable storage based on input criteria
# Usage:        ./lst06-01-storageplan.sh

# raw storage variables
export q_raw_hp=21.6;   export q_raw_hp_dbfs=$(echo "$q_raw_hp * .05"| bc)
export h_raw_hp=50.4;   export h_raw_hp_dbfs=$(echo "$h_raw_hp * .05"| bc)
export f_raw_hp=100.8;  export f_raw_hp_dbfs=$(echo "$f_raw_hp * .05"| bc)
export q_raw_hc=108;    export q_raw_hc_dbfs=$(echo "$q_raw_hc * .01"| bc)
export h_raw_hc=252;    export h_raw_hc_dbfs=$(echo "$h_raw_hc * .01"| bc)
export f_raw_hc=504;    export f_raw_hc_dbfs=$(echo "$f_raw_hc * .01"| bc)

failme() {
  echo "Invalid choice" && exit 1
}

choose_config() {
echo "Choose Exadata Configuration"
echo "1. Quarter Rack High Performance"
echo "2. Quarter Rack High Capacity"
echo "3. Half Rack High Performance"
echo "4. Half Rack High Capacity"
echo "5. Full Rack High Performance"
echo "6. Full Rack High Capacity"
read config
case $config in
1) export raw_sz=$q_raw_hp;export raw_sz_dbfs=$q_raw_hp_dbfs;;
2) export raw_sz=$q_raw_hc;export raw_sz_dbfs=$h_raw_hp_dbfs;;
3) export raw_sz=$h_raw_hp;export raw_sz_dbfs=$f_raw_hp_dbfs;;
4) export raw_sz=$h_raw_hc;export raw_sz_dbfs=$q_raw_hc_dbfs;;
5) export raw_sz=$f_raw_hp;export raw_sz_dbfs=$h_raw_hc_dbfs;;
6) export raw_sz=$f_raw_hc;export raw_sz_dbfs=$f_raw_hc_dbfs;;
*) failme
esac
}

choose_reco_pct() {
 echo "Enter % allocation for RECO storage (i.e., 40 = 40%): \c"
 read recopct
 recopct=`echo "scale=4; $recopct/100"| bc`
 datapct=$(echo "1 - $recopct"| bc)
 export reco_raw_sz=$(echo "($raw_sz - $raw_sz_dbfs) * $recopct"| bc)
 export data_raw_sz=$(echo "($raw_sz - $raw_sz_dbfs)  * $datapct"| bc)
}

choose_asm() {
echo "Choose ASM Configuration"
echo "1. Data: Normal, Reco: Normal"
echo "2. Data: Normal, Reco: High"
```

```
echo "3. Data: High,    Reco: High"
echo "4. Data: High,    Reco: Normal"
read asmpick
case $asmpick in
1) dc='echo "scale=2; $data_raw_sz/2"| bc'
   rc='echo "scale=2; $reco_raw_sz/2"| bc'
   dbc='echo "scale=2; $raw_sz_dbfs/2"| bc' ;;
2) dc='echo "scale=2; $data_raw_sz/2"| bc'
   rc='echo "scale=2; $reco_raw_sz/3"| bc'
   dbc='echo "scale=2; $raw_sz_dbfs/3"| bc';;
3) dc='echo "scale=2; $data_raw_sz/3"| bc'
   rc='echo "scale=2; $reco_raw_sz/3"| bc'
   dbc='echo "scale=2; $raw_sz_dbfs/3"| bc';;
4) dc='echo "scale=2; $data_raw_sz/3"| bc'
   rc='echo "scale=2; $reco_raw_sz/2"| bc'
   dbc='echo "scale=2; $raw_sz_dbfs/3"| bc';;
*) failme
esac
}

choose_config
choose_reco_pct
choose_asm

echo "Exadata Storage Sizing Details"
echo "=============================="
echo "Initial raw capacity is $raw_sz TB"
echo "Final DATA usable capacity is $dc TB"
echo "Final RECO usable capacity is $rc TB"
echo "Final DBFS_DG usable capacity is $dbc TB"
```

If you run the script, the output will look like this:

```
Macintosh-7:source jclarke$ ./ lst06-01-storageplan.sh
Choose Exadata Configuration
1. Quarter Rack High Performance
2. Quarter Rack High Capacity
3. Half Rack High Performance
4. Half Rack High Capacity
5. Full Rack High Performance
6. Full Rack High Capacity
4
Enter % allocation for RECO storage (i.e., 40 = 40%): 20
Choose ASM Configuration
1. Data: Normal, Reco: Normal
2. Data: Normal, Reco: High
3. Data: High,    Reco: High
4. Data: High,    Reco: Normal
3
Exadata Storage Sizing Details
==============================
```

```
Initial raw capacity is 252 TB
Final DATA usable capacity is 66.91 TB
Final RECO usable capacity is 16.72 TB
Final DBFS_DG usable capacity is .36 TB
Macintosh-7:source jclarke$
```

How It Works

Each storage server in an Exadata Database Machine has 12 physical disks of either the 600 GB High Performance or the 3 TB High Capacity flavor. Based on your drive type and whether you've purchased a Quarter Rack, Half Rack, or Full Rack, you will have a specific and fixed raw capacity for your database storage. The choice of ASM redundancy, combined with the percentage allocation you decide for DATA and RECO database storage, will determine your usable ASM disk group capacity.

6-7. Planning Database and ASM Extent Sizes
Problem

You're migrating databases to Exadata or installing new databases on Oracle Exadata and wish to configure your database and Oracle ASM extent sizes for optimal performance.

Solution

You should create your ASM disk groups with a 4 MB allocation unit size for all ASM disk groups, per Oracle recommendations. This recommendation is based on the physical mechanics of the storage cell SAS disks and the 1 MB I/O block size that Cell Services software operates with.

■ **Note** Recipe 9-2 discusses ASM disk group attributes on Exadata. Please refer to allocation unit size settings and other disk group attributes in this recipe.

For your databases, Oracle recommends establishing large, (8 MB or greater) extent size for your large extents and a minimum 1 MB extent size for smaller extents, if possible. The 8 MB extent size complements a 4 MB ASM allocation unit size, reduces the proliferation of small extents in your database, which ultimately can help with capacity management and performance, as well as minimizes the potential for suboptimal reads. Using a minimum of 1 MB extent sizes aligns with the nature of how Exadata Storage Servers store data in 1 MB storage regions and issue I/Os in 1 MB chunks.

You should use locally managed tablespaces and, generally speaking, auto-allocate extents in the tablespace definitions or provide same-sized uniform extent sizes. With auto-allocation in place for your tablespaces and a minimum extent size of 1 MB, you will ensure that your I/O request will be aligned with the storage infrastructure's capabilities, which will help you avoid performing too many I/O requests or too few.

How It Works

There are a couple of key concepts to understand about how Oracle ASM allocates extents and how physical I/O is performed inside the Exadata Storage Servers. First, with ASM (on Exadata or not), a segment's extents are striped across disks in an ASM disk group in units of the allocation unit size, or AU size. For example, if you specify a

4 MB AU size, the first 4 MB of data for a newly created segment will be placed on the first disk in the disk group, the second 4 MB will be stored on the second disk, the third 4 MB on the third disk, and so forth. In other words, the ASM AU size can be viewed as the stripe size.

When physical I/O is performed on the Exadata storage cells, `cellsrv` reads and writes in units of a *storage region*. These storage regions are 1 MB in size, and you can confirm this by tracing the `cellsrv` process or running the following `MegaCli64` command:

```
[root@cm01cel01 ~]# /opt/MegaRAID/MegaCli/MegaCli64 -LDInfo -Lall –aALL | grep Stripe
Stripe Size         : 1.0 MB
```

Knowing that I/O is conducted in units of the 1 MB storage region implies that I/O for database extents with smaller sizes will still perform 1 MB reads and writes regardless of a potentially smaller extent size. Thus, unless you can guarantee that nearly all your I/O will be buffered I/O satisfied via database buffer cache logical reads, there is no benefit in configuring smaller extent sizes and, in fact, it could be detrimental from a performance perspective.

6-8. Completing the Pre-Delivery Survey

Problem

You're the proud owner of a brand new Exadata Database Machine and would like some guidance filling out Exadata's pre-delivery survey. Specifically, you would like to know which parts of the pre-delivery survey are the most important to enter correctly to ensure a smooth, delay-free installation.

Solution

After you place your Exadata Database Machine order, Oracle or your Oracle Partner will send a pre-delivery survey that you must fill out. The pre-delivery spreadsheet is a simple Excel spreadsheet containing a number of delivery logistics questions.

Filling out the pre-delivery survey should be relatively straightforward. In our experience, the most important consideration is to ensure you enter information accurately in the power-related sections. This governs which power distribution units are shipped with your Exadata rack. If you happen to provide the incorrect power specifications, it can lead to delays and either a potentially costly data center power circuit change or complicated PDU change order process. The Exadata PDUs are available in single-phase low voltage, single-phase high voltage, three-phase low voltage, and three-phase high voltage. You should select the power option that matches the power circuit capabilities in your data center. Additionally, an important point to consider is the location of your power plugs (above rack or under the floor).

In addition to the power specifications, there are a few other aspects of the pre-delivery survey to take note of. Look closely at the physical dimensions in the Exadata pre-delivery survey under the *Internal Delivery Questions* section and validate that you have enough floor space to support your new Exadata rack.

In addition to validating the weight requirements and physical dimensions of your doors, elevators, and hallways, pay special attention to the floor footprint requirements (23.6" x 47.2"). Data centers may have unique floor tile arrangements and structures so it is important to have precise tile measurements to ensure the Exadata rack will fit nicely on your data center floor.

One data center detail not covered in the pre-delivery survey is the topic of interconnected Exadata machines. The InfiniBand switch cables are 50' in length, so your racks should be less than 50', plus any additional distance required to accommodate any top-rack or below-rack cabling distances. You can, at additional cost, elect to purchase 100' InfiniBand cables, but this can be expensive.

CHAPTER 6 ■ PREPARING FOR EXADATA

■ **Note** The InfiniBand cable lengths do not just apply to interconnected Exadata racks. If you plan on connecting any of Oracle's InfiniBand-capable systems, such as Exalogic, ZFS Storage Appliances, and so forth, you should take these restrictions into account.

How It Works

Again, completing your pre-delivery survey should be the easiest thing you'll have to do as part of an Exadata Database Machine order and deployment. You need to ensure power specifications are correct and the internal and site delivery information is accurate.

If you happen to specify the wrong power requirements, you won't be able to power your Exadata rack on. Without being able to power the rack and its components on, you will not be able to install and configure your machine. To correct this, you will either have to install proper power circuits in your data center or request a re-shipment of either the correct PDUs or a rack replacement. In both cases, this will lead to delays and potentially additional cost.

Internal and site delivery sections of the pre-delivery survey include information such as business hours, data center security requirements, loading dock information, delivery truck restrictions, and so forth. Providing incorrect information in these sections is not necessarily catastrophic, as an Oracle field engineer will conduct an on-site pre-delivery survey to validate this information.

Each of the Exadata Database Machine configurations (Quarter Rack, Half Rack, and Full Rack) is shipped in a standard 42U Oracle rack. Both the rack and packaging material dimensions are the same regardless of the configuration you've purchased. Each configuration has different weights based on the components installed inside the rack. These dimensions and weights are contained in the pre-delivery survey.

6-9. Completing the Configuration Worksheet
Problem

You are tasked with filling in Oracle's Exadata Database Machine configuration worksheet and need to understand what the various fields mean and why they are important.

Solution

The configuration worksheet has four sections that require customer input:

- Default Oracle Environment Settings
- General Configuration Worksheet
- Network Configuration Worksheet
- Cell Alert Delivery Configuration Worksheet

The *Default Oracle Environment Settings* section is intended to specify the Oracle software owners and groups on the compute nodes, default password(s), Oracle base and home directories, database name, character set, and block size, as well as the ASM disk group prefix for database storage, and the starting IP address for the InfiniBand network (typically `192.168.10.1`), and so forth. In other words, this section allows the customer to configure their Oracle operating environment on the compute nodes.

On Exadata, Oracle allows for *Standard OS Authentication* or *Role Separated Authentication*, and subsections under the *Default Oracle Environment Setting* section of the configuration worksheet for both of these. Your choice here will dictate the Oracle RDBMS and Grid Infrastructure software owner, group membership, and permissions. Think carefully about your long-term security requirements when filling out this section—if you foresee a need to segregate administrative responsibility between your Grid Infrastructure (including Oracle ASM instances) and your databases, you should choose *Role Separated Authentication*. Doing so will create a separate Linux account to own the Grid Infrastructure binaries than the RDBMS software.

Typically, we recommended the following on all Exadata deployments with respect to the *Default Oracle Environment Settings* section of the configuration worksheet:

- Choose Role Separated Authentication and use a software owner called `grid` for the Grid Infrastructure.

- For the RDBMS software owner, choose either the `oracle` account or provide a different account name based on your database administration segregation policies. Some sites use the `oracle` account for an Enterprise Manager Grid Control agent installation and different account names for each Oracle database you plan on installing; if unsure, choose `oracle`.

- For the initial installation, we recommend using the default paths for each of the software components. For example, your RDBMS base directory would be `/u01/app/oracle` and your Grid Infrastructure would be `/u01/app/grid`.

For the fields in the *General Configuration Worksheet* section of the configuration worksheet, Table 6-2 provides some general considerations and comments.

Table 6-2. General configuration guidelines

	Considerations and Comments
Oracle Exadata Database Machine name	Ensure you enter the name you plan to use. This has networking impact, DNS impact for SCAN addresses, and hostnames. This is difficult to change after installation and should be accurate.
Type of system	Choose Eighth Rack, Quarter Rack, Half Rack, or Full Rack.
Disk type	Choose High Performance or High Capacity.
Country	Enter your country.
Time zone name	Enter your time zone; for example, America/Detroit. This can be changed post-install, but it is a manual process.
Workload type	Choose either OLTP or DW.
Backup Method	Choose either Internal to Exadata or External to Exadata. Please see storage sizing recipes in Chapter 5.

Under the *Network Configuration Worksheet* section in the configuration worksheet, there are a number of sub-sections, each to supply network information for each type of network within the Exadata Database Machine. Recipe 6-1 provides detail for this section of the configuration worksheet.

Finally, the *Cell Alert Delivery Configuration Worksheet* allows you to provide SMTP details to allow for e-mail communication of various cell alerts and failures. This section does not need to be completed prior to installation; you can easily change or add this after the machine is configured.

How It Works

The configuration worksheet is typically an editable Adobe Acrobat document that allows you to enter customer-specific configuration values in a number of fields. Additionally, the configuration worksheet provides a narrative presenting the overall configuration process.

Each section inside the configuration worksheet is important, but some sections are worth special attention based on their overall configuration impact. Every configuration choice and decision is modifiable, but some require considerable planning and effort to change post-installation, as well as potentially introducing outages. Below is a list of what we consider to be the most important configuration attributes to get right the first time:

- The choice of *Role Separated Authentication* vs. *Standard OS Authentication*. If you do not supply the proper Grid Infrastructure software owner at installation time, you'll need to re-install Grid Infrastructure to remain supported, which will introduce downtime.

- The database machine name. This will set hostnames, and changing hostnames can be difficult post installation.

- IP address ranges and all network information. While less difficult than changing hostnames, changing IP address information post-installation is not trivial.

The choice of whether to back up your Exadata databases internal to Exadata or external to Exadata has a bearing on how large Oracle ACS configures the RECO grid disks and associated ASM disk groups, as discussed in Recipe 6-5. You can rebuild your Exadata storage entities after the initial installation using recipes in Chapter 9 so it is not absolutely vital that this configuration is the way you want it, but if you are planning on adjusting this, it is best to do so before any important databases are migrated to Exadata to avoid downtime.

PART 3

Exadata Administration

Now that you're the proud owner of an Exadata Database Machine, how do you manage it? With Exadata, the job role of the database machine administrator (DMA) was born. Since Exadata is constructed and, more specifically, *managed* as a complete, engineered system, the DMA's responsibilities span not only traditional Oracle DBA functions but also delve into network administration, storage administration, Linux administration, and all other architecture design components that comprise the Exadata Database Machine.

To successfully manage and administer your Exadata Database Machine, a firm understanding of Oracle 11gR2, Oracle Real Application Clusters, Oracle Automated Storage Management, Unix/Linux administration, and network administration is a must.

While Oracle's *Exadata Owner's Guide* provides the definitive source of information for administering Exadata, the chapters in this section cover an assortment of Exadata administration tasks in detail and outline specific examples for a variety of administration, diagnostics, backup, recovery, patching, and security topics. Hopefully, after reading the chapters in this section, you will be able to confidently navigate the administration landscape of your Exadata Database Machine.

CHAPTER 7

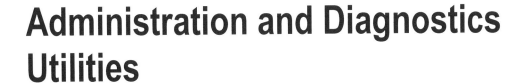

Administration and Diagnostics Utilities

Exadata provides several interfaces and utilities to help access, monitor, and generate diagnostics for Exadata hardware components. In this chapter, we will present and provide usage details for many of the more common administration tasks and utilities than an Exadata Database Machine administrator (DMA) will perform.

Note My Oracle Support document 1274324.1 provides updated information on the topic of Exadata X2-2 and X2-8 diagnostics and troubleshooting best practices.

7-1. Logging in to the Exadata Compute and Storage Cells Using SSH

Problem

You wish to log in to your Exadata Storage and Compute Servers as root, the Oracle software owner, or the Grid Infrastructure owner.

Solution

Each Exadata compute and storage node is accessible using Secure Shell (SSH) via the administration (management) interface. You will have registered your server names in DNS by the management network interface, as is presented in Recipe 6-2. From a shell or DOS prompt, ping your servers by their hostname and you will see the management interface:

```
Macintosh-7:~ jclarke$ ping cm01dbm01
PING cm01dbm01.centroid.com (172.16.1.10): 56 data bytes
64 bytes from 172.16.1.10: icmp_seq=0 ttl=61 time=129.812 ms
64 bytes from 172.16.1.10: icmp_seq=1 ttl=61 time=127.084 ms
^C
--- cm01dbm01.centroid.com ping statistics ---
2 packets transmitted, 2 packets received, 0.0% packet loss
round-trip min/avg/max/stddev = 127.084/128.448/129.812/1.364 ms
Macintosh-7:~ jclarke$ ping cm01cel01
```

159

```
PING cm01cel01.centroid.com (172.16.1.12): 56 data bytes
64 bytes from 172.16.1.12: icmp_seq=0 ttl=61 time=126.853 ms
64 bytes from 172.16.1.12: icmp_seq=1 ttl=61 time=136.280 ms
^C
--- cm01cel01.centroid.com ping statistics ---
3 packets transmitted, 3 packets received, 0.0% packet loss
round-trip min/avg/max/stddev = 126.853/130.822/136.280/3.990 ms
Macintosh-7:~ jclarke$
```

Using nslookup, you should also be able to validate the fully qualified domain name:

```
Macintosh-7:~ jclarke$ nslookup 172.16.1.12
Server:         11.11.1.250
Address:        11.11.1.250#53
12.1.16.172.in-addr.arpa        name = cm01cel01.
12.1.16.172.in-addr.arpa        name = cm01cel01.centroid.com.
Macintosh-7:~ jclarke$
```

With the terminal emulator of your choice, simply establish an SSH connection to the server that you wish to log on to. In the example below, we're using ssh from a Mac OSX shell prompt:

```
Macintosh-7:~ jclarke$ ssh root@cm01dbm01
root@cm01dbm01's password:
Last login: Mon Aug 27 00:15:42 2012 from cm01dbm02
[root@cm01dbm01 ~]#
```

Note You can use any terminal emulator or shell that supports SSH to log in to the Exadata Compute and Storage Node.

Once logged in, you can manage and administer your system.

Note In addition to gaining shell access via SSH to manage your Exadata servers, you can also access them from the Integrated Lights Out Management (ILOM) console or KVM console. You can find information about these administrative interfaces in your Exadata Owner's Guide.

How It Works

Each Exadata Compute and Storage Node is configured to run OpenSSH, which you can validate using the service sshd status command as root:

```
[root@cm01dbm01 ~]# service sshd status
openssh-daemon (pid  7030) is running...
[root@cm01dbm01 ~]#
```

CHAPTER 7 ■ ADMINISTRATION AND DIAGNOSTICS UTILITIES

The sshd daemon on each node uses the /etc./ssh/sshd_config configuration file. In your configuration file, barring any site-specific customizations, you will find the following sshd listen addresses, which specify that SSH will accept incoming connections on the management network and InfiniBand network:

```
#### Generated by Exadata by ipconf. BEGIN. DO NOT MODIFY ####
ListenAddress 172.16.1.10
ListenAddress 192.168.10.1
```

Also by default, UsePAM and PasswordAuthenticaton are set to yes and root logins via SSH are available. If these do not meet your site's security requirements, you can modify these (as well as other sshd defaults), but be aware that with UsePAM set to no you will be unable to modify your user limits and may run into issues starting cluster resources as a result.

7-2. Configuring SSH Equivalency

Problem

You wish to establish SSH user equivalency between your Exadata Compute and Storage Servers.

Solution

In the example below, we'll set up SSH equivalency from the oracle account on one of our compute nodes to the three Exadata Storage Servers in an Exadata Quarter Rack. First, run the following dcli commands to connect to a storage server and run a cellcli command. The dcli utility will prompt for passwords if the SSH key has not been pushed to the cell:

```
[oracle@cm01dbm01 ~]$ dcli -c cm01cel01 cellcli -e list cell
celladmin@cm01cel01's password:
cm01cel01: cm01cel01         online
[oracle@cm01dbm01 ~]$


[oracle@cm01dbm01 ~]$ dcli -c cm01cel01 -l root cellcli -e list cell
root@cm01cel01's password:
cm01cel01: cm01cel01         online
[oracle@cm01dbm01 ~]$
```

■ **Note** If you do not supply the –l option to dcli, dcli will log in as the celladmin operating system account.

Now let's push SSH keys to the storage cells:

```
[oracle@cm01dbm01 ~]$ dcli -g ./cell_group -k
celladmin@cm01cel02's password:
celladmin@cm01cel01's password:
celladmin@cm01cel03's password:
cm01cel01: ssh key added
cm01cel02: ssh key added
cm01cel03: ssh key added
[oracle@cm01dbm01 ~]$ dcli -g ./cell_group cellcli -e list cell
```

161

```
cm01cel01: cm01cel01      online
cm01cel02: cm01cel02      online
cm01cel03: cm01cel03      online
[oracle@cm01dbm01 ~]$
```

The cellcli command issues above and lack of the password prompt confirmed that our SSH keys have been stored on the storage cells.

How It Works

The dcli utility, stored in /usr/local/bin/dcli, is a Python script designed to run commands on remote servers and is typically used in an Exadata environment to run cellcli commands. When you issue a dcli -k command, it will append the SSH keys from the originating host and account's ~/.ssh/id_dsa.pub key file to destination server(s)/account's ~/.ssh/authorized_keys file. In the example above, we ran dcli -k as the oracle account and without a -l option. This pushed the /home/oracle/.ssh/id_dsa.pub contents to /home/celladmin/.ssh/authorized_keys on each server listed in the cell_group file.

7-3. Locating Key Configuration Files and Directories on the Cell Servers

Problem

You wish to identify some of the key configuration files and directories on your Exadata storage cells in order to confidently manage and administer your storage servers.

Solution

As an Exadata Database Machine administrator, or DMA, it is important to understand where the key software components reside within each Exadata storage cell. Table 7-1 outlines some of the key software component directories, files, executables, and purpose.

Table 7-1. Key software locations and executables, Exadata Storage Server

Directory/Executable/File	Purpose
/opt/oracle	Top level directory containing Oracle storage server software
/opt/oracle.cellos	Directory containing Exadata cell software and utilities
/opt/oracle.cellos/cell.conf	Cell configuration file
/opt/oracle.cellos/CheckHWnFWProfile	Utility to validate hardware profile
/opt/oracle.cellos/ExadataDiagCollector.sh	Utility to collect cell diagnostics data, valuable for SRs
/opt/oracle.cellos/functions_cellos	Contains various Cell OS function calls
/opt/oracle.cellos/imageinfo	Shows current image information
/opt/oracle.cellos/imagehistory	Shows image history
/opt/oracle.cellos/ipconf[.pl]	Displays or configures cell network environment

(*continued*)

Table 7-1. (*continued*)

Directory/Executable/File	Purpose
/opt/oracle.cellos/iso	Contains kernel ISO images
/opt/oracle.cellos/make_cellboot_usb.sh	Creates a USB rescue image
/opt/oracle.cellos/MegaCli64	MegaCLI—also in /opt/MegaRAID/MegaCli
/opt/oracle.cellos/patch	Directory for staged patches
/opt/oracle.cellos/restore_cellboot.sh	Restores from USB rescue image
/opt/oracle.cellos/validations_cell	Directory containing output from cell server validations
/opt/oracle.cellos/vldconfig	Configures cell validation
/opt/oracle.cellos/vldrun	Runs cell validation scripts and logs to /opt/oracle.cellos/validations_cellw
/opt/oracle/cell	Symlink to /opt/oracle.cell[VERSION]
/opt/oracle/cell[VERSION]	Directory containing current cell software. For example, /opt/oracle/cell11.2.2.4.2_LINUX.X64_111221
/opt/oracle/cell[VERSION]/cellsrv	Directory containing cellsrv software
/opt/oracle/cell[VERSION]/cellsrv/deploy/config	Configuration deployment files for active cell image
/opt/oracle/cell[VERSION]/cellsrv/deploy/config/cellinit.ora	Cell initialization parameter file
/var/log/oracle	Directory containing cell server log files, alerts, and trace files
/var/log/oracle/cellos	Directory containing log and trace files for Cell Services utilities, validation framework, and cell server startup/shutdown events
/var/log/oracle/diag/asm	Directory containing log and trace files for cell storage-related events in your cell

How It Works

Each Exadata storage cell is installed with its Cell Services software, configuration files, diagnostics utilities, and log/trace file directories in the same locations. At a high level:

- Cell Services software and diagnostics utilities are installed in /opt/oracle.cellos;
- Cell Services configuration files are located in /opt/oracle/cell[VERSION], where VERSION is the current image version of your cell;
- Cell server log files, trace files, and alerts are stored in assorted directories under /var/log/oracle.

7-4. Locating Key Configuration Files and Directories on the Compute Nodes

Problem

You wish to identify some of the key configuration files and directories on your Exadata Compute Nodes in order to confidently manage and administer your Exadata database servers.

Solution

On each compute server in an Exadata Database Machine, Oracle installs software, binaries, or configuration files in a few key locations. Table 7-2 provides some of these important files or directories.

Table 7-2. Key software locations and executables, Exadata Compute Server

Directory/Executable/File	Purpose
/u01	Default directory housing GI and RDBMS Oracle binaries
/opt/oracle.cellos	Contains all cell OS configuration files, image executables, and so forth
/opt/oracle.SupportTools	Contains support and configuration files
/opt/oracle.SupportTools/onecommand	Directory containing OneCommand files, used for install/config
/opt/oracle.SupportTools/onecommand/firstconf	Directory containing files to perform initial installation
/etc./oracle/cell/network-config	Contains files that enable compute servers to communicate with storage servers
/etc./oracle/cell/network-config/cellinit.ora	Contains IB IP subnet for storage cells
/etc./oracle/cell/network-config/cellip.ora	Contains IB IP addresses for each storage cell
$ORACLE_HOME	RDBMS Oracle Home
$GI_ORACLE_HOME	Grid Infrastructure Oracle Home—not typically specified as $GI_ORACLE_HOME but usually /u01/app/11.2.0.X/grid
/opt/oracle.oswatcher	Directory containing OSWatcher utilities and output
/etc./rc.d/rc.Oracle.Exadata	Run control/init scripts for Exadata

How It Works

Exadata Compute Nodes are installed with key configuration and software files in the same locations from one Exadata Compute Node to the next, as listed in Table 7-2. The only variation that you may see, as an Exadata DMA, is a different location for your Oracle RDBMS and Grid Infrastructure software binaries in the event you elect to customize your software deployment or install multiple Oracle Homes for security reasons, as presented in Recipes 12-1 and 12-2.

7-5. Starting and Stopping Cell Server Processes

Problem

You wish to stop or start storage server cell server processes.

Solution

Exadata's Cell Services processes are started automatically at system startup and stopped automatically when the server is shut down, but as an Oracle DMA there are situations in which you may need to stop and start Cell Services processes manually. In this recipe, we will show you how to stop and start Cell Services software on an Exadata Storage Server using both the `service celld` command and the `cellcli` command.

> **Note** Before testing these commands, be aware of active grid disks with ASM disk groups mounted to them. Stopping Cell Services will dismount ASM disks as the grid disks are taken offline and after the ASM disk group attribute `disk_repair_time` is exceeded, disks will be dropped.

1. To stop all Cell Services software on a storage server, log in as root or celladmin and run the following command:

   ```
   [root@cm01cel01 ~]# service celld stop

   Stopping the RS, CELLSRV, and MS services...
   The SHUTDOWN of services was successful.
   [root@cm01cel01 ~]#
   ```

2. After doing this, you can examine your ASM instance's alert log and see that our ASM instance is offlining the disks in the storage cell we stopped. Don't worry though—when we start up services on the storage cell, ASM will automatically correct itself:

```
NOTE: cache closing disk 31 of grp 1: (not open) DATA_CD_01_CM01CEL01
NOTE: cache closing disk 32 of grp 1: (not open) DATA_CD_11_CM01CEL01
NOTE: cache closing disk 33 of grp 1: (not open) DATA_CD_05_CM01CEL01
NOTE: cache closing disk 34 of grp 1: (not open) DATA_CD_08_CM01CEL01
NOTE: cache closing disk 35 of grp 1: (not open) DATA_CD_02_CM01CEL01
NOTE: PST update grp = 1 completed successfully
NOTE: Attempting voting file refresh on diskgroup DBFS_DG
NOTE: Voting file relocation is required in diskgroup DBFS_DG
NOTE: Attempting voting file relocation on diskgroup DBFS_DG
Tue Jul 31 02:03:25 2012
WARNING: Disk 24 (DATA_CD_10_CM01CEL01) in group 1 will be dropped in: (12960) secs on ASM inst 1
WARNING: Disk 25 (DATA_CD_07_CM01CEL01) in group 1 will be dropped in: (12960) secs on ASM inst 1
```

3. Now, start your Cell Services using the Linux service command:

```
[root@cm01cel01 ~]# service celld start

Starting the RS, CELLSRV, and MS services...
Getting the state of RS services...
 running
Starting CELLSRV services...
The STARTUP of CELLSRV services was successful.
Starting MS services...
The STARTUP of MS services was successful.
[root@cm01cel01 ~]#
```

4. Once you are comfortable with the service celld start and stop commands, you can also manage Cell Services software using CellCLI's alter cell command. Assuming your services are running, log in to your compute node as root or celladmin and run the cellcli command:

```
[root@cm01cel01 ~]# cellcli -e alter cell shutdown services all

Stopping the RS, CELLSRV, and MS services...
The SHUTDOWN of services was successful.
[root@cm01cel01 ~]#
```

5. Start your Cell Services software by running the cellcli command:

```
[root@cm01cel01 ~]# cellcli -e alter cell startup services all

Starting the RS, CELLSRV, and MS services...
CELL-01510: Cannot start a new Restart Server (RS) at port number: 9903. An instance of RS might be already running.
Getting the state of RS services...
 running
Starting CELLSRV services...
The STARTUP of CELLSRV services was successful.
Starting MS services...
The STARTUP of MS services was successful.
[root@cm01cel01 ~]#
```

■ **Note** Note If you stop your Cell Services with `cellcli -e alter cell shutdown services all`, Exadata's Restart Server (RS) process will automatically start. Running `cellcli -e alter cell startup services all` will generate a CELL-01510 error indicating that the RS process is already running. In contrast, when you run `service celld stop`, the Restart Server will not restart and all services will be down.

How It Works

The /etc/init.d/celld process is called at system boot to start your Exadata Cell Services software, but an Exadata DMA can also manage Cell Services software by running either `service celld` or CellCLI's `alter cell` commands.

The commands inside /etc./init.d/celld actually perform cellcli -e alter cell commands to stop and start the RS, MS, and cellsrv processes; both approaches will yield the same result.

You can also manage individual processes (RS, MS, or cellsrv) manually using CellCLI alter cell commands. For example, to restart the cellsrv software, you could run the following command:

```
[root@cm01cel01 ~]# cellcli -e alter cell restart services cellsrv

Restarting CELLSRV services...
The RESTART of CELLSRV services was successful.
[root@cm01cel01 ~]#
```

Rebooting a healthy storage server will nearly always leave you in a good state in terms of overall cell health and functionality since the overall storage server processes are automatically started from system initialization scripts. During patching and upgrades, which are presented in Recipe 11-1, Oracle's patching software will commonly stop, start, or restart Cell Services software components.

7-6. Administering Storage Cells Using CellCLI
Problem
You wish to list, modify, create, drop, or manage objects and attributes for your Exadata storage cells.

Solution
Oracle's storage cell command line interface is called CellCLI. CellCLI is invoked by running the cellcli command when logged in to a storage server.

Log in to your desired storage cell as root, celladmin, or cellmonitor and issue the cellcli command:

```
[celladmin@cm01cel01 ~]$ cellcli
CellCLI: Release 11.2.2.4.2 - Production on Tue Aug 28 00:41:00 EDT 2012

Copyright (c) 2007, 2011, Oracle.  All rights reserved.
Cell Efficiency Ratio: 666

CellCLI> help

 HELP [topic]
   Available Topics:
        ALTER
        ALTER ALERTHISTORY
        ALTER CELL
... CellCLI output omitted for brevity
        LIST GRIDDISK
        LIST IBPORT
        LIST IORMPLAN
... CellCLI output omitted for brevity

CellCLI>
```

How It Works

Oracle's CellCLI interface is a Java-based framework delivered by the storage cell's management server process (MS) that provides administrative capabilities to your storage server entities. In short, if you wish to configure, change, create, drop, or alter your storage server configuration, CellCLI is the interface to do so.

Within CellCLI, you can perform the following types of actions, each of which you can learn more about using the CellCLI HELP command as displayed in the solution of this recipe:

- ALTER alert history, cell attributes, cell disks, grid disks, InfiniBand ports, IORM plans, LUNs, physical disks, quarantines, and thresholds

- ASSIGN ASM-scope or database-scoped security keys

- CALIBRATE your cell using Oracle's adaptation of the Orion calibration toolkit

- CREATE and DROP cells, cell disks, flashcache, flashlog, grid disks, security keys, quarantines, thresholds, alerts

- DESCRIBE object types

- EXPORT and IMPORT cell disks

- LIST attributes of your storage cell, cell disks, grid disks, flashcache, flashlog, InfiniBand port, IORM plans, keys, LUNs, physical disks, quarantines, and thresholds

- LIST reporting metrics for active requests, alerts and alert definition, current metrics, and historical metrics

The CellCLI utility is used extensively in recipes throughout this book, and if you're reading the chapters in the book sequentially, you have already undoubtedly launched `cellcli` on your Exadata storage cells. Chapter 13 as well as all the chapters in Part V of this book will provide detail on many aspects of real-world usage of CellCLI.

7-7. Administering Storage Cells Using dcli

Problem

You wish to monitor or administer multiple Exadata Storage Servers simultaneously on your Exadata environment without having to log in to each storage cell individually.

Solution

The `dcli` utility can be used to run remote commands on one, multiple, or all storage or compute nodes that a server can communicate with. In Exadata environments, it is common to use `dcli` to manage or monitor multiple storage servers simultaneously.

■ **Note** In this recipe, we will focus on using `dcli` from the oracle account on an Exadata Compute Server, but you could perform the same steps under any operating system account on either the compute or storage nodes, if desired.

The first task you should perform to be successful with `dcli` is to establish trust between your hosts. In other words, configure your environment to enable automatic authentication as `dcli` executes remote commands. This is accomplished by distributing SSH keys between hosts using the `dcli -k` command.

Note Please refer to Recipe 7-2 for details on how to distribute SSH keys to bypass password entry with dcli.

Once this is done, log in to a compute node as the oracle operating system account and run the dcli -h command to display the usage guidelines:

```
[oracle@cm01dbm01 ~]$ dcli -h
... Output omitted
Examples:
 dcli -g mycells -k
 dcli -c stsd2s2,stsd2s3 vmstat
 dcli -g mycells cellcli -e alter iormplan active
 dcli -g mycells -x reConfig.scl

usage: dcli [options] [command]
... Output omitted
[oracle@cm01dbm01 ~]$
```

This output displays a number of options and associated command syntax, but the most common usage for dcli with respect to storage server management is to run cellcli commands on the storage cells. Run the following command to list your storage cell details on your first storage cell:

```
[oracle@cm01dbm01 ~]$ dcli -c cm01cel01 cellcli -e list cell detail
cm01cel01: name:                cm01cel01
cm01cel01: bbuTempThreshold:    45
cm01cel01: bbuChargeThreshold:  800
cm01cel01: bmcType:             IPMI
cm01cel01: cellVersion:         OSS_11.2.2.4.2_LINUX.X64_111221
cm01cel01: cpuCount:            24
cm01cel01: diagHistoryDays:     7
cm01cel01: events:
cm01cel01: fanCount:            12/12
... Output omitted
```

The -c option is followed by a storage server name, which is cm01cel01 in the example above. You can also run this same command for multiple servers by delineating your storage cells with a comma:

```
[oracle@cm01dbm01 ~]$ dcli -c cm01cel01,cm01cel02 cellcli -e list cell
cm01cel01: cm01cel01    online
cm01cel02: cm01cel02    online
[oracle@cm01dbm01 ~]$
```

The power of dcli comes when you wish to run a cellcli command on all of your storage servers. To enable this, first create a text file containing the names of all your storage cells, each on its own line. In the example below, we've created a file called cell_group that contains the names of each of our storage cells in our Quarter Rack:

```
[oracle@cm01dbm01 ~]$ cat cell_group
cm01cel01
cm01cel02
cm01cel03
[oracle@cm01dbm01 ~]$
```

When this is complete, launch `dcli` with the –g option to run the same command on each server in your cell_group text file:

```
[oracle@cm01dbm01 ~]$ dcli -g ./cell_group cellcli -e list cell
cm01cel01: cm01cel01     online
cm01cel02: cm01cel02     online
cm01cel03: cm01cel03     online
[oracle@cm01dbm01 ~]$
```

How It Works

Each Exadata Compute and Storage Server Node ships with a Python utility developed under Oracle's Open Source software initiative called `dcli`. `dcli` stands for "Distributed Command Line Interface"; Oracle created the utility as a method to manage multiple servers from a single command.

The `dcli` Python script is installed in /usr/local/bin on each compute and storage node in your Exadata Database Machine, which implies that you can run `dcli` commands from each node.

Typically, Exadata DMAs will create text files containing the names of the storage servers and compute servers in their environment. In fact, you will also find multiple files staged in /opt/oracle.SupportTools/onecommand that Oracle uses during the Exadata installation to perform various installation and configuration tasks:

```
[root@cm01dbm01 ~]# ls /opt/oracle.SupportTools/onecommand/*group
/opt/oracle.SupportTools/onecommand/all_group
        /opt/oracle.SupportTools/onecommand/cell_ib_group
/opt/oracle.SupportTools/onecommand/all_ib_group
        /opt/oracle.SupportTools/onecommand/dbs_group
/opt/oracle.SupportTools/onecommand/all_nodelist_group
        /opt/oracle.SupportTools/onecommand/dbs_ib_group
/opt/oracle.SupportTools/onecommand/cell_group
        /opt/oracle.SupportTools/onecommand/priv_ib_group
[root@cm01dbm01 ~]# cat /opt/oracle.SupportTools/onecommand/cell_group
cm01cel01
cm01cel02
cm01cel03
[root@cm01dbm01 ~]
```

While the most common usage for `dcli` is to run CellCLI commands, you can also use `dcli` for running just about any Linux script. For example, the command below reports disk space utilization for the root file system on each storage cell in your Exadata environment:

```
[oracle@cm01dbm01 ~]$ dcli -g ./cell_group df -h /
cm01cel01: Filesystem          Size  Used Avail Use% Mounted on
cm01cel01: /dev/md6            9.9G  3.6G  5.9G  38% /
cm01cel02: Filesystem          Size  Used Avail Use% Mounted on
cm01cel02: /dev/md6            9.9G  3.6G  5.9G  38% /
cm01cel03: Filesystem          Size  Used Avail Use% Mounted on
cm01cel03: /dev/md6            9.9G  3.6G  5.9G  38% /
[oracle@cm01dbm01 ~]$
```

Some Exadata administration tasks are made significantly easier and arguably less error-prone when using `dcli`. For example, when configuring storage entities such as cell disks and grid disks, implementing I/O Resource

Management Plans, and so forth, using `dcli` to run identical `cellcli` commands on each storage server not only reduces manual effort and keystrokes, but also ensures consistent configuration across nodes. Recipes in Chapters 13 will make this point more clear.

7-8. Generating Diagnostics from the ILOM Interface

Problem

You are troubleshooting an issue or working with Oracle Support on a Service Request and need to generate a diagnostics snapshot.

Solution

There are two methods available to generate a Data Collection Snapshot, which is the official name for Oracle's ILOM 3.0.X Service Snapshot utility: with the `ILOB` web interface and the `ILOM` command line interface. To generate a data collection snapshot using the web interface, start a browser, connect to the server's `ILOM` interface, and navigate to the Maintenance-Snapshot tab as depicted in Figure 7-1.

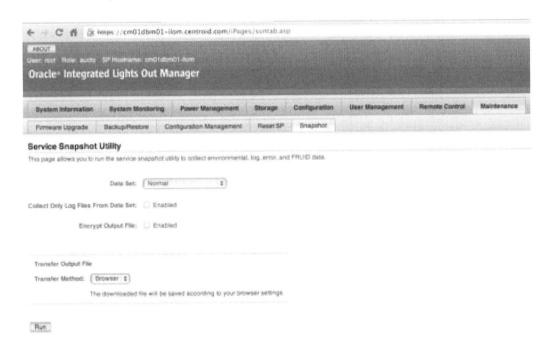

Figure 7-1. *ILOM web interface service snapshot utility*

Next, select the Transfer Method from the bottom drop-down box. Your choices will be Browser, SFTP, or FTP as displayed in Figure 7-2. We typically recommend selecting the Browser method.

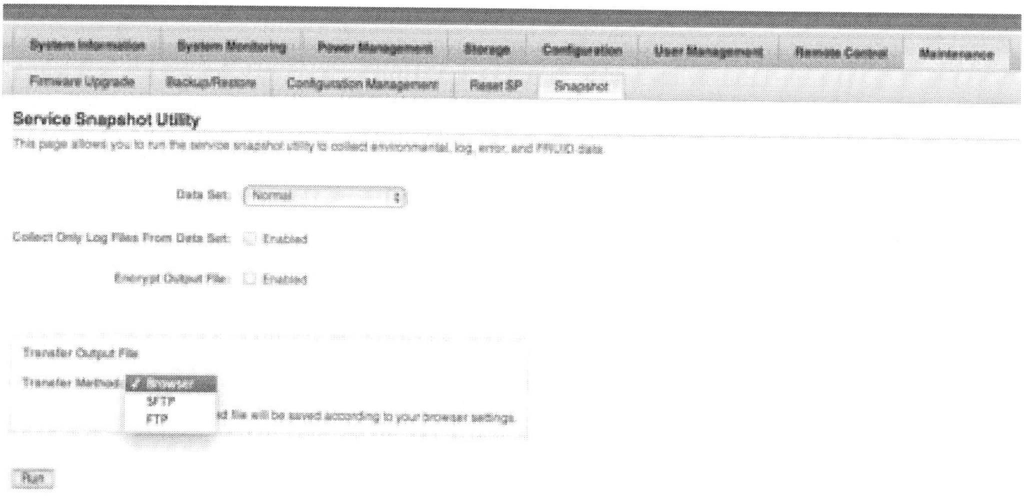

Figure 7-2. Service snapshot transfer method

Once you've selected the transfer method, the service snapshot utilities will run and transfer via HTTPS to your local machine, at which point you can upload to Oracle Support.

To use the ILOM command line interface to generate your snapshot, establish an SSH connection to the ILOM interface:

```
Macintosh-7:~ jclarke$ ssh root@cm01dbm01-ilom
Password:
Oracle(R) Integrated Lights Out Manager
Version 3.0.16.10 r65138
Copyright (c) 2011, Oracle and/or its affiliates. All rights reserved.
->
```

■ **Note** For your compute and storage servers, the ILOM hostname will be named servername-ilom, where "servername" is the name of your server.

Next, optionally set your snapshot dataset mode to either normal (default), full, FRUID, or custom. Unless specifically requested by Oracle Support, using the default normal should be sufficient.

```
-> set /SP/diag/snapshot dataset=normal
Set 'dataset' to 'normal'
->
```

■ **Note** To learn more about the dataset options, please consult your Oracle documentation or refer to http://docs.oracle.com/cd/E19464-01/820-6850-11/ILOM30.html#50602037_68461.

Then, generate your snapshot providing a URI to upload the snapshot information to. In the example below, we're selecting an Oracle ZFS Storage Appliance share with ftp services enabled on it:

```
-> set /SP/diag/snapshot dump_uri=ftp://11.11.1.170/export/esx_hosts/
Enter remote user password:
<< output omitted >>
```

How It Works

On Oracle's Integrated Lights Out Management software built on each Exadata Compute, Storage, and InfiniBand node, ILOM software provides the ability to generate and bundle snapshot diagnostics information. The service snapshot diagnostics utilities collect log files and run various commands, assimilate the output, and transfer to a data collection location as specified by the administrator.

An Exadata DMA would typically only need to run these utilities under the guidance of Oracle Support. In general, this is a required step when filing a hardware-related Oracle Service Request.

7-9. Performing an Exadata Health Check Using exachk
Problem

You want to conduct a comprehensive Exadata health check on your Exadata Database Machine to validate your hardware, firmware, and configuration.

Solution

Oracle's exachk utility is designed to perform a comprehensive health check of your Exadata Database Machine. In recent versions of Exadata, exachk is located under /opt/oracle.SupportTools on your first compute node.

> ■ **Note** Oracle ACS typically runs the exachk utility as a post-installation step to validate the Exadata installation. Historically, this functionality was provided with the HealthCheck utility, located in /opt/oracle.SupportTools/onecommand/HealthCheck. HealthCheck has been phased out and replaced with exachk.

If you do not have the exachk utility installed on a compute node, you can download the exachk from My Oracle Support document 1070954.1. After downloading the latest version of exachk, transfer the zip file to one of your compute node servers and unzip it.

After unzipping, you can determine the version of exachk by running exachk -v:

```
[root@cm01dbm01 stg]# ./exachk -v
EXACHK  VERSION: 2.1.6_20120817
[root@cm01dbm01 stg]#
```

The readme.txt file contains information about how to use exachk; in the example below, we'll launch it with the -a option, which will perform all Exadata checks. You need to be logged in as the oracle (RBDMS) software owner to run exachk:

```
[oracle@cm01dbm01 stg]$ ./exachk -a

CRS stack is running and CRS_HOME is not set. Do you want to set CRS_HOME to /u01/app/11.2.0.3/
grid?[y/n][y]y

Checking ssh user equivalency settings on all nodes in cluster

Node cm01dbm02 is configured for ssh user equivalency for oracle user

Searching for running databases . . . . .

. . . . .
List of running databases registered in OCR
1. dwprd
2. visx
3. visy
4. All of above
5. None of above

Select databases from list for checking best practices. For multiple databases, select 4 for All or
comma separated number like 1,2 etc. [1-5][4].
... Output omitted
```

When launched, exachk will supply several self-explanatory prompts, including prompts for the root password on the storage servers, compute servers, InfiniBand switches, and so forth. When exachk is running, you'll see output from the script that resembles the following output:

```
... Output omitted
Collecting - Verify Hardware and Firmware on Database and Storage Servers (CheckHWnFWProfile)
[Database Server]
Collecting - Verify InfiniBand Address Resolution Protocol (ARP) Configuration on Database Servers
Collecting - Verify InfiniBand Fabric Topology (verify-topology)
Collecting - Verify InfiniBand subnet manager is running on an InfiniBand switch
Collecting - Verify Master (Rack) Serial Number is Set [Database Server]
Collecting - Verify RAID Controller Battery Condition [Database Server]
Collecting - Verify RAID Controller Battery Temperature [Database Server]
Collecting - Verify database server disk controllers use writeback cache
Collecting - root time zone check

Preparing to run root privileged commands on STORAGE SERVER cm01cel01

root@192.168.10.3's password:
Collecting - Ambient Temperature on storage server
Collecting - Exadata software version on storage server
Collecting - Exadata software version on storage ...
<< output truncated>>
```

After exachk completes, unzip the output files and open the exachk HTML file in a web browser. Figure 7-3 shows the header page of the exachk summary screen for exachk version 2.1.6.

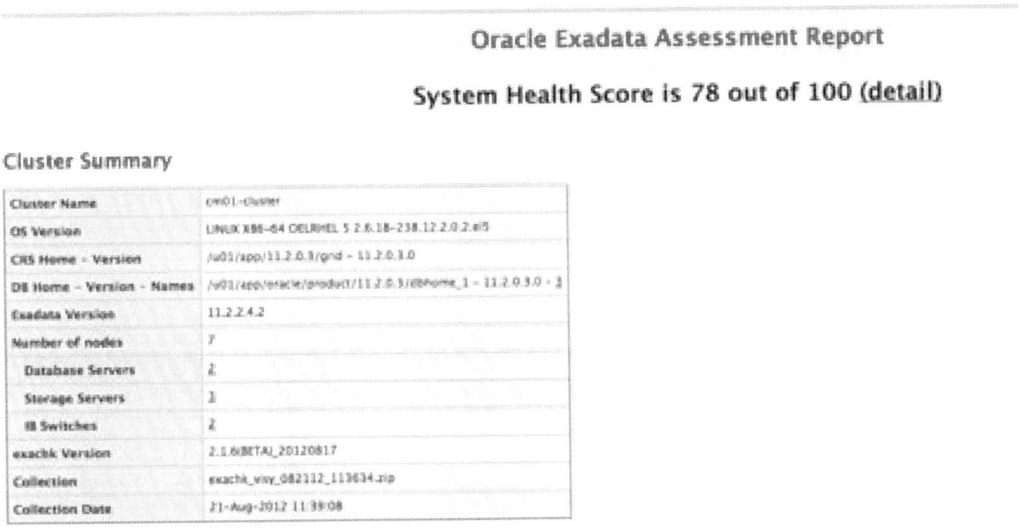

Figure 7-3. exachk cluster summary

The exachk summary report is broken down into four main sections: *Findings Needing Attention, Findings Passed, MAA Scorecard,* and *Systemwide firmware and software versions*. You can navigate to each of these sections in the summary report to gather more information about each one. For example, Figure 7-4 displays a screen shot of Findings Needing Attention for the database server:

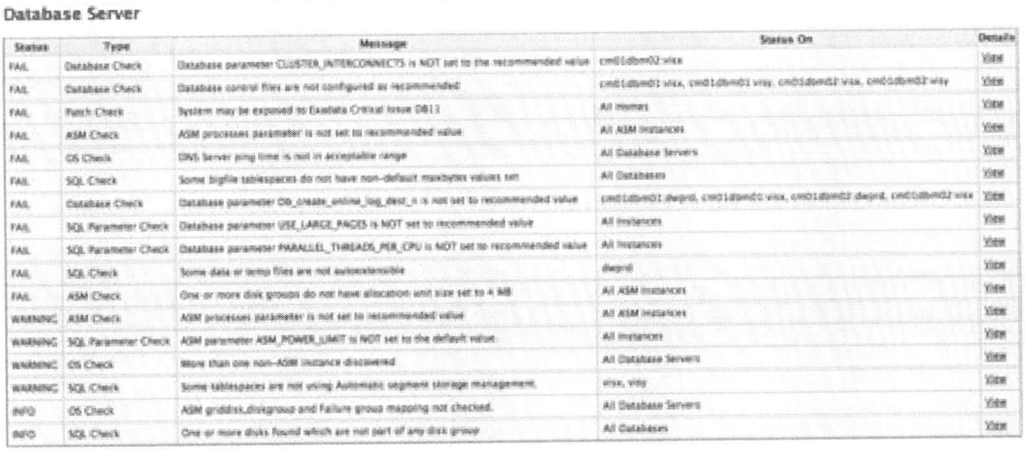

Figure 7-4. Findings needing attention for database server, exachk

How It Works

Oracle replaced its HealthCheck utility with exachk in late 2011 and recommends that Exadata DMAs use exachk to validate their Exadata environment. Typically an Exadata DMA will run exachk prior to and after Exadata system maintenance, including patching, upgrades, and so forth.

exachk is designed to collect software, hardware, firmware, and configuration data for Exadata. When exachk runs, it will log in to each of the compute server, storage server, and InfiniBand switches in your database machine and perform a series of system configuration and health checks.

Each test that exachk performs generates output files and messages indicating whether the test passed or failed. When complete, exachk zips the output files together and builds an HTML report that a DMA can use to view the output of the test.

7-10. Collecting Compute and Cell Server Diagnostics Using the sundiag.sh Utility

Problem

You wish to collect generic server and storage diagnostics on a single Exadata compute server or storage server using Oracle's sundiag.sh tool.

Solution

On each Exadata compute and storage cell nodes, Oracle delivers a utility called sundiag.sh. The sundiag.sh script is installed in /opt/oracle.SupportTools. Log in to one of your servers as root and run /opt/oracle.SupportTools/sundiag.sh:

```
[root@cm01cel01 ~]# /opt/oracle.SupportTools/sundiag.sh
Disk /dev/sdc doesn't contain a valid partition table
Disk /dev/sdd doesn't contain a valid partition table
... Output omitted for brevity

Success in AdpEventLog

Exit Code: 0x00
sundiag_2012_08_28_12_45/
sundiag_2012_08_28_12_45/cm01cel01_celldisk-detail_2012_08_28_12_45.out
<< lines omitted for brevity
sundiag_2012_08_28_12_45/cm01cel01_fdisk-l_2012_08_28_12_45.out
================================================================================
Done the report files are in bzip2 compressed /tmp/sundiag_2012_08_28_12_45.tar.bz2
================================================================================
[root@cm01cel01 ~]#
```

When complete, the output of the sundiag.sh utility will be stored in /tmp with a date-stamped BZ2-compressed file. Typically, you would upload this file to Oracle Support.

■ **Note** In the previous example, we ran sundiag.sh on one of our storage servers. As such, we received a number of messages concerning disks with no valid partition table; this is normal for storage servers.

How It Works

Oracle's sundiag.sh utility is used to generate server diagnostics and is installed in /opt/oracle.SupportTools on every Exadata Compute Server and Storage Server. When logging Oracle Service Requests, it is common for Oracle Support to request the output of the sundiag.sh utility so it is important to know where the utility it is, how to run it, and understand what it does.

On both compute servers and storage cells, sundiag.sh generates the following output:

- The output of the dmesg command, which contains kernel-level diagnostics from the kernel ring buffer
- The output of fdisk -l, which contains a list of all disk partitions
- The output of lspci, which contains a list of all PCI buses on the system
- The output of lsscsi, which contains a list of all SCSI drives on the system
- Various outputs of MegaCli64, which provides MegaRAID controller diagnostics
- The output from ipmitool sel elist, which queries the ILOM interface for assorted sensor readings for all IPMI enabled devices
- A copy of /var/log/messages
- A file called MegaSAS.log, which provides information about your SAS disks

In addition, when launched from an Exadata Storage Server, sundiag.sh also collected the following information:

- The output of cellcli list cell detail
- The output of cellcli list celldisk detail
- The output of cellcli list lun detail
- The output of cellcli list physicaldisk detail
- The output of all physical disks not in a normal state
- The output of cellcli list griddisk detail
- The output of cellcli list flashcache detail
- The output of cellcli list alerthistory
- A copy of your storage cell alert.log, ms-odl.log, and ms-odl.trc files
- Information about your PCI flash modules, or FDOMs, by using the /usr/bin/flash_dom -l command
- The output of /opt/oracle/cell/cellsrv/deploy/scripts/unix/hwadapter/diskadp/scripts_aura.sh, which provides details about your disk adapters
- Additional information about your disk devices from the /opt/oracle/cell/cellsrv/deploy/scripts/unix/hwadapter/diskadp/get_disk_devices.pl script

In short, sundiag.sh generates a comprehensive set of diagnostics output, tailored to whether you run it from a compute node or storage server.

7-11. Collecting RAID Storage Information Using the MegaCLI utility

Problem

You wish to generate diagnostics or configuration information about your MegaRAID-controlled disk devices on an Exadata Storage Server or Compute Server.

Solution

Log in to an Exadata Compute or Storage Server as root; in the following example, we're connecting a storage server. Check the version of the MegaCli64 utility:

```
[root@cm01cel01 ~]# ls /opt/MegaRAID/MegaCli/MegaCli64
/opt/MegaRAID/MegaCli/MegaCli64
[root@cm01cel01 ~]# /opt/MegaRAID/MegaCli/MegaCli64 -v
      MegaCLI SAS RAID Management Tool  Ver 8.00.23 May 17, 2010
   (c)Copyright 2010, LSI Corporation, All Rights Reserved.
Exit Code: 0x00
[root@cm01cel01 ~]#
```

MegaCLI can provide a wealth of information about your storage devices. In Table 7-3, we provide the commands required to generate some of the more common inquiry tasks you may perform with MegaCLI.

Table 7-3. Common MegaCLI commands

Command	Description
# /opt/MegaRAID/MegaCli/MegaCli64 -AdpAllInfo –aALL	Lists detailed disk adapter information for all adapters
# /opt/MegaRAID/MegaCli/MegaCli64 -PDList –aALL	Lists detailed physical disk information for all disks
# /opt/MegaRAID/MegaCli/MegaCli64 -AdpEventLog -GetEvents -f [output file] -aALL	Displays disk adapter events
/opt/MegaRAID/MegaCli/MegaCli64 -fwtermlog -dsply –aALL	Displays firmware information for your system's storage devices
# /opt/MegaRAID/MegaCli/MegaCli64 -cfgdsply –aALL	Lists disk configuration information for all of your devices
# /opt/MegaRAID/MegaCli/MegaCli64 -adpbbucmd -aALL	Displays information about the status of your battery-backed disk cache (BBU)
# /opt/MegaRAID/MegaCli/MegaCli64 -LdPdInfo -aALL	Provides detailed information about your virtual disks
# /opt/MegaRAID/MegaCli/MegaCli64 -PDList -aALL	Lists physical disk and adapter information
# /opt/MegaRAID/MegaCli/MegaCli64 -LDInfo -LALL –aALL	Displays virtual drive information
# /opt/MegaRAID/MegaCli/MegaCli64 -ShowSummary -aALL	Displays summary information for your LSI MegaRAID devices

How It Works

The physical SAS disks in both the storage servers and compute servers are managed with an LSI MegaRAID SAS controller and can be managed and queried using the 64-bit MegaCLI RAID management tool, /opt/MegaRAID/MegaCli/MegaCli64.

MegaCLI is used by various support tools, such as sundiag.sh, and also used or requested when troubleshooting, patching, or working with Oracle Support. MegaCLI also provides a valuable mechanism to understand your Exadata storage devices; understanding the various command-line options to MegaCli64 is often important for an Oracle Exadata DMA.

7-12. Administering the Storage Cell Network Using ipconf

Problem

You wish to view your storage cells network configuration and optionally use ipconf to modify your storage server or compute server's network configuration.

Solution

Oracle's ipconf utility is used on Exadata servers to configure server network interfaces. It is invoked during system startup and is invoked from the /opt/oracle.cellos/cellFirstboot.sh script.

ipconf will set network information based on information in your cell.conf file. The default cell.conf file is located in /opt/oracle.cellos/cell.conf:

```
[root@cm01cel01 ~]# more /opt/oracle.cellos/cell.conf
$VAR1 = {
        'Internal' => {
                      'Interface infiniband prefix' => 'ib',
                      'Interface ethernet prefix' => 'eth'
                    },
        'Hostname' => 'cm01cel01.centroid.com',
        'Timezone' => 'America/Detroit',
        'Ntp drift' => '/var/lib/ntp/drift',
        'Interfaces' => [
                        {
                          'Hostname' => 'cm01cel01-priv.centroid.com',
                          'IP address' => '192.168.10.3',
                          'Net type' => 'Private',
                          'Netmask' => '255.255.252.0',
                          'Slaves' => [
                                      'ib0',
                                      'ib1'
                                    ],
                          'State' => 1,
                          'Name' => 'bondib0'
                        },
... Additional information omitted
```

You can validate a cell.conf network configuration file by running the `ipconf -verify` command as displayed:

```
[root@cm01cel01 ~]# /opt/oracle.cellos/ipconf -verify \
> -conf /opt/oracle.cellos/cell.conf
Verifying of Exadata configuration file /opt/oracle.cellos/cell.conf
Done. Configuration file /opt/oracle.cellos/cell.conf passed all verification checks
[root@cm01cel01 ~]#
```

In general, an Oracle Exadata DMA would not manually invoke `ipconf` unless changing the server's networking information.

> **Note** Recipes 10-6 and 10-7 provide detailed information about how to change Exadata server network information and includes multiple references to `ipconf`.

How It Works

The `ipconf` utility is installed in /opt/oracle.cellos on both the Exadata Storage Servers and Compute Nodes and is symbolically linked to /usr/local/bin/ipconf. As mentioned previously, `ipconf` is called at system startup time to set and validate your Exadata server network information. Specifically:

- At run level 3, the /etc./init.d/precell script is launched (/etc./rc3.d/S08precell).
- /etc./init.d/precell calls /opt/oracle.cellos/cellFirstboot.sh.
- /opt/oracle.cellos/cellFirstboot.sh checks for the existence of /opt/oracle.cellos/cell.conf. If it does not exist, the network configuration will call /opt/oracle.cellos/ipconf, which in turn calls /opt/oracle.cellos/ipconf.pl. The ipconf.pl Perl script will supply a configuration menu from which you can set your network settings.
- If /opt/oracle.cellos/cell.conf does exist, /opt/oracle.cellos/ipconf.pl will read /opt/oracle.cellos/cell.conf, configure the network per directives in cell.conf, and handle a number of other network tasks.

If, after your Exadata installation you wish to change network information, including IP addresses, DNS servers, NTP servers, and so on, you would move a copy of your cell.conf file to a new location, validate it using the `ipconf -verify` command, and then deploy using the command below:

```
# /opt/oracle.cellos/ipconf -force -newconf /tmp/new.cell.conf -reboot
```

In general, `ipconf` would be required only if changing network information.

> **Note** Please see Recipe 10-7 to learn how to change Exadata network information in a supported manner.

7-13. Validating Your InfiniBand Switches with the CheckSWProfile.sh Utility

Problem

You wish to validate your InfiniBand switch software and firmware versions.

Solution

Use the CheckSWProfile.sh utility, which is designed to check your InfiniBand switch software and firmware versions. Log in to one of your compute or storage servers as root and run the command below:

```
[root@cm01dbm01 ~]# /opt/oracle.SupportTools/CheckSWProfile.sh -I cm01sw-ib2,cm01sw-ib3
Checking if switch cm01sw-ib2 is pingable...
Checking if switch cm01sw-ib3 is pingable...
Use the default password for all switches? (y/n) [n]: n
Use same password for all switches? (y/n) [n]: y
Enter admin or root password for All_Switches:
Confirm password:
[INFO] SUCCESS Switch cm01sw-ib2 has correct software and firmware version:
        SWVer: 1.3.3-2
[INFO] SUCCESS Switch cm01sw-ib2 has correct opensm configuration:
        controlled_handover=TRUE polling_retry_number=5 routing_engine=ftree
            sminfo_polling_timeout=1000 sm_priority=5

[INFO] SUCCESS Switch cm01sw-ib3 has correct software and firmware version:
        SWVer: 1.3.3-2
[INFO] SUCCESS Switch cm01sw-ib3 has correct opensm configuration:
        controlled_handover=TRUE polling_retry_number=5 routing_engine=ftree
            sminfo_polling_timeout=1000 sm_priority=5

[INFO] SUCCESS All switches have correct software and firmware version:
        SWVer: 1.3.3-2
[INFO] SUCCESS All switches have correct opensm configuration:
        controlled_handover=TRUE polling_retry_number=5 routing_engine=ftree
            sminfo_polling_timeout=1000 sm_priority=5 for non spine and 8 for spine switch5
[root@cm01dbm01 ~]#
```

From the above display:

- Both of our Exadata InfiniBand leaf switches are supplied in a comma-separated list following the –I argument.
- In our machine, we've changed the default admin and root password on our InfiniBand switches, so we chose to enter them when prompted.
- CheckSWProfile.sh reported the correct software, firmware, and OpenSM configuration.

How It Works

The CheckSWProfile.sh script is supplied on each Exadata Compute and Storage Server and can be found in /opt/oracle.SupportTools/CheckSWProfile.sh. CheckSWProfile.sh processes the list of InfiniBand switch names and passwords provided, logs in to each switch, and runs a series of InfiniBand commands such as version show, module-firmware, and also copies the contents of /etc./opensm/opensm.conf to temporary files in /tmp. CheckSWProfile.sh also conducts an RPM search on each switch to confirm software versions. When complete, the utility will parse the temporary output files and display its status to the calling window.

The CheckSWProfile.sh utility is typically executed as a pre-patch or post-patch procedure but can be executed at any time.

7-14. Verifying Your InfiniBand Network Topology
Problem

You wish to report your Exadata InfiniBand network topology.

Solution

With Exadata, Oracle supplies a script called /opt/oracle.SupportTools/ibdiagtools/verify-topology, which is used to do just what its name implies, validate your InfiniBand network layout. To execute this utility, log in to a compute server or storage cell as root, change directories to /opt/oracle.SupportTools, and execute the command below:

```
[root@cm01dbm01 ~]# cd /opt/oracle.SupportTools/ibdiagtools/
[root@cm01dbm01 ibdiagtools]# ./verify-topology

        [ DB Machine Infiniband Cabling Topology Verification Tool ]
            [Version IBD VER 2.c 11.2.2.4.2   111221]
Leaf switch found: cm01sw-ib2 (21284697f9a0a0)
Leaf switch found: cm01sw-ib3 (2128469c6da0a0)

Found 2 leaf, 0 spine, 0 top spine switches

Check if all hosts have 2 CAs to different switches...............[SUCCESS]
... Output omitted
Spine switch check: Are any Exadata nodes connected ..............[SUCCESS]
Spine switch check: Any inter spine switch links..................[SUCCESS]
Spine switch check: Any inter top-spine switch links..............[SUCCESS]
Spine switch check: Correct number of spine-leaf links............[SUCCESS]
Leaf switch check: Inter-leaf link check..........................[SUCCESS]
Leaf switch check: Correct number of leaf-spine links.............[SUCCESS]
[root@cm01dbm01 ibdiagtools]#
```

■ **Note** You must execute the verify-topology command from the /opt/oracle.SupportTools/ibdiagtools directory because the script attempts to read the VERSION_FILE file from the current working directory. Not doing so will yield a head: cannot open 'VERSION_FILE' for reading: No such file or directory error message.

How It Works

The /opt/oracle.SupportTools/ibdiagtools/verify-topology utility is used to validate the InfiniBand cabling within your Exadata Database Machine. It uses ibnetdiscover, ibhosts, and ibswitches commands, located in /usr/sbin, to conduct its tests.

7-15. Diagnosing Your InfiniBand Network

Problem

You wish to conduct a health check on your Exadata InfiniBand network to validate that the components are functioning as expected.

Solution

Exadata provides several commands and utilities to validate the health of your Exadata InfiniBand network and network switches, many of which can be executed from your compute servers or storage servers. With any of these commands and utilities, you want to look for errors or warnings and resolve as appropriate.

1. First, log in to a compute server as root and run /usr/bin/ibdiagnet to determine if any bad links, GUIDs, or illegal PM counters exist:

```
[root@cm01dbm01 ibdiagtools]# ibdiagnet
Loading IBDIAGNET from: /usr/lib64/ibdiagnet1.2
-W- Topology file is not specified.
    Reports regarding cluster links will use direct routes.
Loading IBDM from: /usr/lib64/ibdm1.2
-W- A few ports of local device are up.
    Since port-num was not specified (-p option), port 1 of device 1 will be
    used as the local port.
-I- Discovering ... 7 nodes (2 Switches & 5 CA-s) discovered.
-I---------------------------------------------------
-I- Bad Guids/LIDs Info
-I---------------------------------------------------
-I- No bad Guids were found
-I---------------------------------------------------
-I- Links With Logical State = INIT
-I---------------------------------------------------
-I- No bad Links (with logical state = INIT) were found
-I---------------------------------------------------
-I- PM Counters Info
-I---------------------------------------------------
-I- No illegal PM counters values were found
-I---------------------------------------------------
-I- Fabric Partitions Report (see ibdiagnet.pkey for a full hosts list)
-I---------------------------------------------------
-I-    PKey:0x7fff Hosts:10 full:10 partial:0
-I---------------------------------------------------
-I- IPoIB Subnets Check
-I---------------------------------------------------
-I- Subnet: IPv4 PKey:0x7fff QKey:0x00000b1b MTU:2048Byte rate:10Gbps SL:0x00
```

```
            -W- Suboptimal rate for group. Lowest member rate:40Gbps > group-rate:10Gbps
            -I---------------------------------------------------
            -I- Bad Links Info
            -I- No bad link were found
            -I---------------------------------------------------
            ----------------------------------------------------------------
            -I- Stages Status Report:
               STAGE                                       Errors    Warnings
               Bad GUIDs/LIDs Check                           0          0
               Link State Active Check                        0          0
               Performance Counters Report                    0          0
               Partitions Check                               0          0
               IPoIB Subnets Check                            0          1
            Please see /tmp/ibdiagnet.log for complete log
            ----------------------------------------------------------------
            -I- Done. Run time was 1 seconds.
            [root@cm01dbm01 ibdiagtools]#
```

2. Run /usr/sbin/ibqueryerrors.pl to check whether any errors are returned. In the example below, we can see a small number of relay errors for each of our switches:

```
[root@cm01dbm01 ibdiagtools]# ibqueryerrors.pl
Errors for 0x2128469c6da0a0 "SUN DCS 36P QDR cm01sw-ib3"
   GUID 0x2128469c6da0a0 port 7: [RcvSwRelayErrors == 1] [XmtDiscards == 4]
[XmtWait == 2534716]
   GUID 0x2128469c6da0a0 port 10: [XmtWait == 5716382]
   GUID 0x2128469c6da0a0 port 13: [XmtWait == 10210]
   GUID 0x2128469c6da0a0 port 14: [XmtWait == 7434]
   GUID 0x2128469c6da0a0 port 17: [XmtWait == 5748]
Errors for 0x21284697f9a0a0 "SUN DCS 36P QDR cm01sw-ib2"
   GUID 0x21284697f9a0a0 port 1: [RcvSwRelayErrors == 48] [XmtWait == 16528234]
   GUID 0x21284697f9a0a0 port 2: [RcvSwRelayErrors == 48] [XmtWait == 16088954]
   GUID 0x21284697f9a0a0 port 4: [RcvSwRelayErrors == 48] [XmtWait == 16789105]
   GUID 0x21284697f9a0a0 port 7: [XmtDiscards == 2] [XmtWait == 1273404511]
   GUID 0x21284697f9a0a0 port 10: [RcvSwRelayErrors == 83] [XmtDiscards == 1]
[XmtWait == 1331113845]
   GUID 0x21284697f9a0a0 port 15: [XmtWait == 2388489]
   GUID 0x21284697f9a0a0 port 16: [XmtWait == 5043445]
[root@cm01dbm01 ibdiagtools]#
```

3. To check your InfiniBand network performance, run the /opt/oracle.SupportTools/ibdiagtools/infinicheck command. For this test, you will need SSH keys to be distributed to the nodes in your Exadata cluster; if not already performed as the root user, issue the following command:

```
[root@cm01dbm01 ibdiagtools]# ssh-keygen -t dsa
Generating public/private dsa key pair.
Enter file in which to save the key (/root/.ssh/id_dsa):
Enter passphrase (empty for no passphrase):
Enter same passphrase again:
Your identification has been saved in /root/.ssh/id_dsa.
Your public key has been saved in /root/.ssh/id_dsa.pub.
```

```
The key fingerprint is:
7f:9e:54:6d:31:39:20:87:09:c7:a9:c7:e0:ac:26:15 root@cm01dbm01.centroid.com
[root@cm01dbm01 ibdiagtools]#
```

4. Next, run infinicheck with the -s option to push the SSH keys to each host, by its InfiniBand IP address, as listed in the nodes.lst file:

```
[root@cm01dbm01 ibdiagtools]# ./infinicheck -g ./nodes.lst -u root -s

                INFINICHECK
        [Network Connectivity, Configuration and Performance]
        [Version IBD VER 2.c  11.2.2.4.2   111221]
The authenticity of host '192.168.10.3 (192.168.10.3)' can't be established.
RSA key fingerprint is ad:6e:df:9c:05:2c:32:d7:c3:62:31:03:ad:ca:60:74.
Are you sure you want to continue connecting (yes/no)? yes

 Verifying User Equivalance of user=root to all hosts.
 (If it isn't setup correctly, an authentication prompt will appear to push keys to all
 the nodes)

<< lines omitted for brevity >>

Checking if Host cm01dbm02 knows about Host cm01dbm02:
Adding to known hosts public key:
[root@cm01dbm01 ibdiagtools]#
```

■ **Note** The infinicheck utility will perform its tests using the InfiniBand network, so previous SSH keys exchanges between hosts with dcli -k will be of no value.

5. Now you can run the infinicheck utility. Make sure you are in the /opt/oracle.SupportTools/ibdiagtools directory and run the command below.

■ **Note** Running infinicheck will conduct performance tests that will saturate your InfiniBand network. As such, the test should be scheduled during a maintenance window or quiet time.

```
[root@cm01dbm01 ibdiagtools]# ./infinicheck -g ./nodes.lst -u root

                INFINICHECK
        [Network Connectivity, Configuration and Performance]
        [Version IBD VER 2.c  11.2.2.4.2   111221]

Verifying User Equivalance of user=root to all hosts.
(If it isn't setup correctly, an authentication prompt will appear to push keys to all the nodes)

Verifying User Equivalance of user=root to all cells.
(If it isn't setup correctly, an authentication prompt will appear to push keys to all the nodes)
```

```
                    ####  CONNECTIVITY TESTS   ####
                  [COMPUTE NODES -> STORAGE CELLS]
                         (30 seconds approx.)
[ WARNING  ] on cm01cel01... Cant open /etc./oracle/cell/network-config/cellinit.ora
[ WARNING  ] on cm01cel01... No cellip.ora found at /etc./oracle/cell/network-config!
[ WARNING  ] on cm01cel02... Cant open /etc./oracle/cell/network-config/cellinit.ora
[ WARNING  ] on cm01cel02... No cellip.ora found at /etc./oracle/cell/network-config!
[ WARNING  ] on cm01cel03... Cant open /etc./oracle/cell/network-config/cellinit.ora
[ WARNING  ] on cm01cel03... No cellip.ora found at /etc./oracle/cell/network-config!

        Verifying Subnet Masks on all nodes
[SUCCESS] ........ Subnet Masks is same across the network
        Prechecking for uniformity of rds-tools on all nodes
[SUCCESS].... rds-tools version is the same across the cluster
        Checking for bad links in the fabric
[SUCCESS].......... No bad fabric links found
                  [COMPUTE NODES -> COMPUTE NODES]
                         (30 seconds approx.)

.. Additional output omitted for brevity
```

6. When finished, check for errors or warnings in the output generated to your console window.
7. Finally, you can check your interfaces on the InfiniBand switches for error, packet drops, and overall configuration by logging in to an InfiniBand switch as root and executing the following ip command:

```
Macintosh-7:~ jclarke$ ssh root@cm01sw-ib2
root@cm01sw-ib2's password:
Last login: Tue Aug 28 15:22:08 2012 from cm01dbm01
[root@cm01sw-ib2 ~]# ip -s link show
1: lo: <LOOPBACK,UP,LOWER_UP> mtu 16436 qdisc noqueue
    link/loopback 00:00:00:00:00:00 brd 00:00:00:00:00:00
    RX: bytes  packets  errors  dropped overrun mcast
    829497365  572499012 0      0       0       0
    TX: bytes  packets  errors  dropped carrier collsns
    829497365  572499012 0      0       0       0
2: dummy0: <BROADCAST,NOARP> mtu 1500 qdisc noop
    link/ether e2:27:90:40:b0:fc brd ff:ff:ff:ff:ff:ff
    RX: bytes  packets  errors  dropped overrun mcast
    0          0        0       0       0       0
    TX: bytes  packets  errors  dropped carrier collsns
    0          0        0       0       0       0
3: eth0: <BROADCAST,MULTICAST,UP,LOWER_UP> mtu 1500 qdisc pfifo_fast qlen 1000
    link/ether 00:e0:4b:32:67:a7 brd ff:ff:ff:ff:ff:ff
    RX: bytes  packets  errors  dropped overrun mcast
    146453473  1074611  2       0       0       4
    TX: bytes  packets  errors  dropped carrier collsns
    195273463  1084941  0       0       0       0
4: ib0: <BROADCAST,MULTICAST> mtu 4092 qdisc noop qlen 256
    link/infiniband 00:00:00:02:00:00:00:00:00:00:00:00:00:21:28:46:97:f9:a0:a0 brd 00:ff
 :ff:ff:ff:12:40:1b:ff:ff:00:00:00:00:00:00:ff:ff:ff:ff
```

```
        RX: bytes    packets   errors    dropped  overrun  mcast
        0            0         0         0        0        0
        TX: bytes    packets   errors    dropped  carrier  collsns
        0            0         0         0        0        0
[root@cm01sw-ib2 ~]#
```

How It Works

Oracle provides several utilities and commands to validate your InfiniBand network on Exadata. Table 7-4 summarizes these utilities.

Table 7-4. InfiniBand diagnostics utilities and scripts

Utility	Usage	Description
ibdiagnet	From compute or storage server, run `# /usr/bin/ibdiagnet`	Validates InfiniBand link status, performance counters report, and other information
ibqueryerrors.pl	From compute or storage server, run `#/usr/sbin/ibqueryerrors.pl`	Reports InfiniBand network transmission errors
infinicheck	From the compute or storage server, change directories to /opt/oracle.SupportTools/ibdiagtools and run `# ./infinicheck -g [text file listing nodes] -u root`	Conducts a series of InfiniBand network performance tests
ip	From an InfiniBand switch, run `# ip -s link show`	Displays the InfiniBand link statuses

7-16. Connecting to Your Cisco Catalyst 4948 Switch and Changing Switch Configuration

Problem

You wish to connect to your embedded Cisco Catalyst 4948 switch inside your Exadata rack to perform configuration changes.

Solution

First, connect a serial cable from the Cisco switch console to a laptop using the RJ45 to DB9 serial cable included with your Exadata package. Once you've got a serial connection, connect at 9600 baud, 8 bits, no parity, 1 stop bit, and no handshake.

Once connected, change to enable mode using the following command:

```
Switch> enable
Switch#
```

Enter configuration mode by entering the `configure terminal` command:

```
Switch # configure terminal
Enter configuration commands, one per line.End with CTRL/Z.
Swich(config)#
```

If you wish, for example, to change your Name Server IP address, enter the following:

```
Switch(config)# ip name-server 11.11.1.252
```

To save changes, enter end and save changes by typing write memory:

```
Switch(config)# end
*Aug 27 18:01:26.155:%SYS-5-CONFIG_I:Configured from console by console
Switch # write memory
Building configuration ...
```

How It Works

The embedded Cisco switch inside the Exadata rack can be connected to via the Cisco RJ45 to DB9 serial cable included with your Exadata parts shipment. The switch has a very minimal configuration at time of installation and should typically not require modifications unless you have changed network information inside your database machine. You can use the Cisco's `Command Line Interface` to change configuration information once connected.

CHAPTER 8

Backup and Recovery

As an Exadata Database Machine administrator (DMA), it is important to be able to back up your databases and software and, ultimately, be able to recover failed components in the event of failure. Since the Exadata Database Machine consists of multiple servers of different types as well as Oracle databases, a strong, tested, backup strategy is vital to administering Exadata.

Fortunately for the Exadata DMA, Oracle does a nice job of making your backup and recovery tasks manageable. Backup, restore, and recovery operations on your compute nodes and Oracle databases will likely be similar to your processes on non-Exadata Oracle environments. The storage cells are pre-configured with their own backup and validation framework. Additionally, most of the common backup and recovery tasks are outlined nicely in the *Exadata Owner's Manual*.

In this chapter, we will present assorted Oracle Exadata backup and recovery strategies, techniques, processes, and supporting information that will enable the DMA to successfully develop a backup strategy and confidently perform recovery operations.

8-1. Backing Up the Storage Servers
Problem
You wish to back up your Exadata Storage Servers and validate your backups.

Solution
Oracle automatically performs backups of the operating system and cell software on each Exadata Storage Server. The contents of the system volumes are automatically backed up and require no Oracle DMA intervention or operational processes.

Oracle assumes responsibility for backing up the critical files of the storage cells to an internal USB drive called the CELLBOOT USB Flash Drive. You can validate the contents of your /opt/oracle.cellos/iso and CELLBOOT USB Flash Drive as detailed below:

```
[root@cm01cel01 iso]# ls /opt/oracle.cellos/iso
lboot.cat     image.id                              initrd.img      lastGoodConfig  trans.tbl
boot.msg      imgboot.lst                           isolinux.bin    memtest         vmlinuz
cellbits      initrd-2.6.18-238.12.2.0.2.el5.img    isolinux.cfg    splash.lss      vmlinuz-2.6.18-
238.12.2.0.2.el5
[root@cm01cel01 iso]#

[root@cm01cel01 iso]# ls /mnt/usb
boot.cat      image.id                                              isolinux.bin    lost+found      vmlinuz-2.6.18-
194.3.1.0.2.el5
```

```
boot.msg          imgboot.lst                       isolinux.cfg    memtest      vmlinuz-2.6.18-
238.12.2.0.2.el5
cellbits          initrd-2.6.18-194.3.1.0.2.el5.img  kernel.ver     splash.lss
grub              initrd-2.6.18-238.12.2.0.2.el5.img lastGoodConfig trans.tbl
I_am_CELLBOOT_usb initrd.img                         log                         vmlinuz
[root@cm01cel01 iso]#
```

> **Note** Please see Recipe 8-2 to learn how to mount your CELLBOOT USB Flash Drive.

Oracle does *not* support the installation of any software, of any type, on the Exadata storage cells. This restriction includes third-party backup client or agent software, so even if you wanted to bypass Oracle's automatic storage cell backup process, you would not be supported if you installed backup software on the storage cells.

How It Works

Each Exadata Storage Server has 12 disk drives, and on these disks Oracle places the operating system and storage cell software mirrored partitions on the first two drives. This section of storage is called the System Area, and the Linux partitions created in the area are commonly referred to as the system volumes.

> **Note** Recipes 1-2, 1-4, and 3-1 discuss the cell server disk storage in detail. Please refer to these recipes to gain a better understanding of how Oracle uses the System Area and how the disks in the storage servers are partitioned and used.

One of the interesting design elements on the Exadata storage servers is that Oracle automatically creates backups of the operating system and Cell Services software; as an Oracle DMA, you are not required to back up your storage server operating system or storage cell software.

Oracle maintains copies of the latest cell boot images and Cell Server software in /opt/oracle.cellos/iso/lastGoodConfig. Additionally, Oracle maintains two sets of system volume partitions, Active and Inactive. These partitions are used to allow for Oracle to perform both In-Partition and Out-of-Partition patches and upgrades; patches are typically performed to the Inactive partitions first with Out-of-Partition upgrades and, if successful, these partitions are marked Active. With this combination of automated backups, Oracle ensures that bootable, valid copies of your system volumes and configuration files will nearly always be available.

> **Note** For a more comprehensive discussion about storage server patches, please see Recipe 11-2.

The bulk of the physical storage on the disks inside the storage server is used for Oracle database storage. As this capacity is presented to the compute servers as grid disks and these grid disks comprise Oracle ASM disk group disks, the Exadata DMA needs to use Oracle Recovery Manager (RMAN) to back up the databases that reside on Exadata.

> ■ **Note** Please see Recipe 8-6 for a high-level overview of using Oracle RMAN to back up databases with Oracle ASM storage.

You can elect to back up your storage cell image to an external USB drive for an extra level of backup redundancy. Recipe 8-3 provides instructions to accomplish this task.

8-2. Displaying the Contents of Your CELLBOOT USB Flash Drive

Problem

You wish to validate the contents of your CELLBOOT USB Flash Drive to ensure that your storage server is being backed up.

Solution

In this recipe, we will show you how to identify your CELLBOOT USB Flash Drive partition, mount the CELLBOOT USB drive, and display its contents.

> ■ **Note** The CELLBOOT USB Flash Drive is installed on every Exadata Storage Server and is used to store a bootable backup image of your storage cell, complete with your latest valid configurations.

1. Log in to one of your storage servers as root and run fdisk -l to find your internal USB drive partition. At the time of this writing, the size of the internal USB drive is 4009 MB.

   ```
   [root@cm01cel01 ~]# fdisk -l 2>/dev/null

   ... output omitted
   Disk /dev/sdm: 4009 MB, 4009754624 bytes
   126 heads, 22 sectors/track, 2825 cylinders
   Units = cylinders of 2772 * 512 = 1419264 bytes

      Device Boot      Start         End      Blocks   Id  System
   /dev/sdm1               1        2824     3914053   83  Linux
   [root@cm01cel01 ~]#
   ```

2. Create or validate a directory to mount the /dev/sdm1 partition to. Typically, this would be /mnt/usb, but for purposes of validating the contents of the CELLBOOT USB Flash Drive, you can mount this to a directory of your choice. The output below shows we have a /mnt/usb directory, which is currently not mounted.

   ```
   [root@cm01cel01 ~]# ls /mnt
   dev  imaging  usb  usb.image.info  usb.make.cellboot  usb.saved.cellos
   [root@cm01cel01 ~]# mount
   /dev/md6 on / type ext3 (rw,usrquota,grpquota)
   ```

```
proc on /proc type proc (rw)
sysfs on /sys type sysfs (rw)
devpts on /dev/pts type devpts (rw,gid=5,mode=620)
tmpfs on /dev/shm type tmpfs (rw)
/dev/md8 on /opt/oracle type ext3 (rw,nodev)
/dev/md4 on /boot type ext3 (rw,nodev)
/dev/md11 on /var/log/oracle type ext3 (rw,nodev)
none on /proc/sys/fs/binfmt_misc type binfmt_misc (rw)
[root@cm01cel01 ~]#
```

Note Oracle uses the /mnt/usb directory to perform its automatic CELLBOOT USB Flash Drive backups.

3. Now, mount your USB drive and validate:

```
[root@cm01cel01 ~]# mount /dev/sdm1 /mnt/usb
[root@cm01cel01 ~]# df -k /mnt/usb
Filesystem           1K-blocks      Used Available Use% Mounted on
/dev/sdm1              3852548   1079708   2577140  30% /mnt/usb
[root@cm01cel01 ~]#
```

4. You can check the contents of the CELLBOOT USB Flash Drive as listed below.

```
[root@cm01cel01 ~]# ls /mnt/usb
boot.cat            image.id                          isolinux.bin    lost+found    vmlinuz-2.6.18-
194.3.1.0.2.el5
boot.msg            imgboot.lst                       isolinux.cfg    memtest       vmlinuz-2.6.18-
238.12.2.0.2.el5
cellbits            initrd-2.6.18-194.3.1.0.2.el5.img kernel.ver      splash.lss
grub                initrd-2.6.18-238.12.2.0.2.el5.img lastGoodConfig trans.tbl
I_am_CELLBOOT_usb   initrd.img                        log                           vmlinuz
[root@cm01cel01 ~]#
```

How It Works

Oracle automatically backs up your system volumes on the internal CELLBOOT USB Flash Drive, as discussed in Recipe 8-1. This drive is typically built on partition /dev/sdm1, which can be mounted to /mnt/usb or a mount directory of your choosing.

Oracle will boot to this CELLBOOT USB Flash Drive in the event of loss or corruption of the system volume partitions.

8-3. Creating a Cell Boot Image on an External USB Drive
Problem

You wish to create an external bootable recovery image in addition to the internal CELLBOOT USB Flash Drive for backup redundancy purposes.

Solution

Oracle provides a utility to create a bootable rescue image for your storage cells using an external USB drive. In this recipe, we will provide instructions to create your external USB bootable recovery image.

1. First, locate or purchase an unformatted USB drive and put it into either of the empty USB slots in the front of your storage server. The front panel in your Exadata storage cell has two USB slots; make sure you only have one external device plugged in.

2. The device should appear as /dev/sdad; log in as root and run the following fdisk command to validate this:

```
[root@cm01cel01 ~]# fdisk -l /dev/sdad
... output omitted
Disk /dev/sdad: 32.35 GB, 34735548006 bytes
63 heads, 32 sectors/track, 30848 cylinders
... output omitted
Disk /dev/sdac doesn't contain a valid partition table

[root@cm01cel01 ~]#
```

3. Create a partition on your USB drive, create an EXT3 file system on your partition, and label your volume:

```
[root@cm01cel01 ~]# fdisk   /dev/sdad
... output omitted for brevity
Command (m for help): p
Command (m for help): n
Command action
   e   extended
   p   primary partition (1-4)
p
Partition number (1-4): 1
First cylinder (1-30848, default 1):
Using default value 1
Last cylinder or +size or +sizeM or +sizeK (1-30848, default 30848):
Using default value 30848

Command (m for help): w
The partition table has been altered!

Calling ioctl() to re-read partition table.
Syncing disks.
Command (m for help): q

[root@cm01cel01 ~]# mkfs.ext3 /dev/sdad1
... output omitted for brevity

[root@cm01cel01 ~]# e2label /dev/sdad1 CELLBOOTEXTERNAL
... output omitted for brevity
```

■ **Note** The *Exadata Owner's Manual* does not reference creating a partition on the external USB drive and, in fact, it should create one for you if not already done. In our experience, however, we have needed to create a partition, format it, and label it in order for the make_cellboot_usb command to succeed. Additionally, if the USB drive you have inserted is larger than 4 GB, you will need to increase the setting of USB_SIZE_POTENTIAL_MAX inside the /opt/oracle.cellos/image_functions file.

4. Create a CELLBOOT image on the external USB drive. Once your external USB drive is formatted and labeled, run the following command:

   ```
   [root@cm01cel01 ~]# /opt/oracle.SupportTools/make_cellboot_usb \
   -verbose -force
   ```

   The make_cellboot_usb drive will create a boot image for your storage cell, identical to that contained on the internal CELLBOOT USB drive.

5. When finished, unmount your USB drive, remove it from your storage cell, and keep it in a safe place.

■ **Note** To learn about the internal CELLBOOT USB drive, please refer to Recipe 8-2.

How It Works

The /opt/oracle.SupportTools/make_cellboot_usb script is use to create a CELLBOOT USB image on an external USB drive. With this bootable USB image, you will be able to boot and recover your storage cell if necessary.

The make_cellboot_usb script performs similar tasks to those performed as part of the standard Exadata storage cell process to back up your image to the internal CELLBOOT USB drive, as discussed in Recipe 8-3.

When make_cellboot_usb runs, it first will identify candidate USB devices to write the boot image to. Below is an example of the first portion of the output from running the command:

```
[WARNING] More than one USB devices suitable for use as Oracle Exadata Cell start up boot device.
Candidate for the Oracle Exadata Cell start up boot device       : /dev/sdad
Partition on candidate device                                    : /dev/sdad1
The current product verison                                      : 11.2.2.4.2.111221
Label of the current Oracle Exadata Cell start up boot device    : CELLBOOTEXTERNAL
Product version not found in /mnt/usb.make.cellboot/image.id
Unable to get image version of cellboot usb from /mnt/usb.make.cellboot/mage.id
The current CELLBOOT USB product version
[DEBUG] set_cell_boot_usb: cell usb                              : /dev/sdad
[DEBUG] set_cell_boot_usb: mnt sys                               : /
[DEBUG] set_cell_boot_usb: preserve                              : preserve
[DEBUG] set_cell_boot_usb: mnt usb                               : /tmp/usb.make.cellboot
[DEBUG] set_cell_boot_usb: lock                                  : /tmp/usb.make.cellboot.lock
[DEBUG] set_cell_boot_usb: serial console                        :
[DEBUG] set_cell_boot_usb: kernel mode                           : kernel
[DEBUG] set_cell_boot_usb: mnt iso save                          :
```

```
Create CELLBOOT USB on device /dev/sdad
... output omitted for brevity
```

Next, the process will format the USB device:

```
The number of cylinders on this disk is set to 30848.
... output omitted for brevity
Command (m for help): Command action
   e   extended
   p   primary partition (1-4)
Partition number (1-4): First cylinder (1-30848, default 1): Last cylinder or +size or +sizeM
or +sizeK (1-3048, default 30848):
Command (m for help): The partition table has been altered!

Calling ioctl() to r-read partition table.
Syncing disks.
mke2fs 1.39 (29-May-2006)
Filesystem label=
OS type: Linux
Block sie=4096 (log=2)
Fragment size=4096(log=2)
3948544 inodes, 7896828 blocks
394841 blocks (5.00%) reserved for the super user
```

After the USB device is formatted and mounted, make_cell_usb will begin copying your configuration to the external USB drive. Excerpts from the output will appear similar to the following code:

```
Copying ./vmlinuz to /mnt/usb.make.cellboot/. ...
Copying ./lastGoodConfig/passwd.tbz to /mnt/usb.make.cellboot/./lastGoodConfig ...
Copying ./lastGoodConfig/etc/ntp/step-tickers to /mnt/usb.make.cellboot/./lastGoodConfig/etc/ntp ...
Copying ./lastGoodConfig/etc/ntp/keys to /mnt/usb.make.cellboot/./lastGoodConfig/etc/ntp ...
... output omitted for brevity
Copying ./lastGoodConfig/etc/sysconfig/network-scripts/ifcfg-ib1 to
/mnt/usb.make.cellboot/./lastGoodConfig/etc/sysconfig/network-scripts
... output omitted for brevity
```

8-4. Backing Up Your Compute Nodes Using Your Enterprise Backup Software

Problem

You wish to use your current enterprise backup software to back up files on your Exadata Compute Nodes.

Solution

In this recipe, we will discuss some high-level topics concerning backing up the Oracle software on the Exadata Compute Nodes using your organization's current backup software.

The first task you should perform is to determine how your data will physically be copied from the compute servers to your backup media. In other words, how the data will move from disks on the compute nodes to tape, virtual tape, external disk, or the backup media used in your environment. Typically, companies define pools of storage, use backup media servers to communicate with agent software on the servers, and use backup mechanisms to copy data over a supported transport medium to the storage pools.

On the Exadata Compute Nodes, you have the choice of using Ethernet or InfiniBand as your transport protocol, so your backup media servers must be able to communicate with the compute nodes over Ethernet or InfiniBand network protocols.

Once you've designed your backup strategy, install your third party or Oracle Secure Backup agent software on your compute nodes, configure the software according to vendor documentation, and design and execute your backups according to your organization's policies.

■ **Note** Backup network planning and design are outside the scope of this recipe as most organizations have unique network topologies and enterprise backup policies or designs. Additonally, third-party vendor backup agent installation and configuration steps are outside the scope of this recipe.

How It Works

Oracle allows for the installation of third-party backup software and agents on the Exadata Compute Servers, such as IBM Tivoli, Symantec NetBackup, EMC Networker, Oracle Secure Backup, or any backup agent certified on your compute node operating system.

Below are some items to consider when designing your third-party backup solution for your Exadata Compute Nodes:

- An Exadata DMA can leverage existing corporate backup software and infrastructure to backup software on the Exadata Compute Nodes.

- The compute nodes do *not* have fiber HBA cards, nor do they have physical capacity to install them, so your backups will need to be done over either 1 GbE, 10 GbE (if you have ordered 10gbE cards for your machine), or InfiniBand.

- Some organizations use Exadata's NET3 *Additional Network* as the backup network; if this is your choice, ensure that the NET3 configuration meets your backup network configuration requirements in terms of network bandwidth and redundancy.

- Customers are increasingly adopting backup strategies that use the high-speed, high-bandwidth InfiniBand network to minimize backup times and optimize the overall backup strategy. If this is the policy you adopt, ensure your backup media servers are capable of communicating over the InfiniBand network.

- If you wish to back up multiple Exadata Database Machines using the same InfiniBand network, you may have to take care to use distinct ranges of InfiniBand IP addresses when configuring your switches so as to avoid IP address conflicts.

8-5. Backing Up the Compute Servers Using LVM Snapshots
Problem

You wish to use available capacity in your compute node's local SAS disks and logical volume management features to perform backups of your compute node software.

Solution

In this recipe, you will learn how to do the following:

- Display available space in your current compute node volume groups
- Create an additional logical volume to store your backups
- Create a file system on your backup logical volume and mount the file system
- Mount the file system
- Create LVM snapshots on your / and /u01 file systems
- Mount your snapshot volumes
- Back up the contents of the snapshot file systems to your backup volume
- Unmount and remove your snapshot file systems

Begin by logging in to the compute node server that you wish to back up as root and perform the following steps:

1. Run vgdisplay to display your free storage capacity:

   ```
   [root@cm01dbm01 ~]# vgdisplay | egrep '(VGExaDb|Alloc PE|Free PE)'
     VG Name               VGExaDb
     Alloc PE / Size       39424 / 154.00 GB
     Free  PE / Size       103327 / 403.62 GB
   [root@cm01dbm01 ~]#
   ```

   Unless you have previously extended VGExaDb, you should see about 400 GB of free space for the volume group.

■ **Note** The /u01 file system on the Exadata Compute Nodes is created on a 100 GB logical volume. The underlying volume group for this logical volume is used for both the /u01 and root file system, as well as a swap partition, and is 600 GB in size. This means that you will typically have a large amount of unallocated disk storage to use for either extending the default volumes or creating new logical volumes.

---

2. Since we want to back up our root and /u01 file systems, which currently use 154 GB of space from the VGExaDb volume group, we will create a new logical volume in this volume group. In this example, we're calling this backup:

   ```
   [root@cm01dbm01 ~]# lvcreate -L 154G -n /dev/VGExaDb/backup
     Logical volume "backup" created
   [root@cm01dbm01 ~]#
   ```

3. When your backup volume group is created, format it using mkfs.ext3 using a 4 KB block size with the following command:

   ```
   [root@cm01dbm01 ~]# mkfs.ext3 -m 0 -b 4096 /dev/VGExaDb/backup
   mke2fs 1.39 (29-May-2006)
   Filesystem label=
   ```

```
        OS type: Linux
        Block size=4096 (log=2)
        Fragment size=4096 (log=2)
        20185088 inodes, 40370176 blocks
        0 blocks (0.00%) reserved for the super user
        First data block=0
        Maximum filesystem blocks=4294967296
        1232 block groups
        32768 blocks per group, 32768 fragments per group
        16384 inodes per group
        Superblock backups stored on blocks:
                32768, 98304, 163840, 229376, 294912, 819200, 884736, 1605632, 2654208,
                4096000, 7962624, 11239424, 20480000, 23887872

        Writing inode tables: done
        Creating journal (32768 blocks): done
        Writing superblocks and filesystem accounting information: done

        This filesystem will be automatically checked every 25 mounts or
        180 days, whichever comes first.  Use tune2fs -c or -i to override.
        [root@cm01dbm01 ~]#
```

4. After your file system is built on your backup logical volume, create a directory to mount it to, mount the file system, and validate its capacity:

```
[root@cm01dbm01 ~]# mkdir -p /mnt/backup
[root@cm01dbm01 ~]# mount /dev/VGExaDb/backup /mnt/backup
[root@cm01dbm01 ~]# df -h
Filesystem                     Size   Used  Avail  Use%  Mounted on
/dev/mapper/VGExaDb-LVDbSys1    30G    23G   5.1G   82%  /
/dev/sda1                      124M    48M    70M   41%  /boot
/dev/mapper/VGExaDb-LVDbOra1    99G    59G    36G   63%  /u01
tmpfs                           81G     0    81G    0%  /dev/shm
/dev/mapper/VGExaDb-backup     152G   188M   152G    1%  /mnt/backup
[root@cm01dbm01 ~]#
```

5. To prepare for your LVM snapshots, query your current logical volume names and note the logical volumes used for your / and /u01 file systems. In the following output, these are /dev/VGExaDb/LVDbSys1 and /dev/VGExaDb/LVDbOra1, respectively:

```
[root@cm01dbm01 ~]# lvdisplay | grep "LV Name"
  LV Name                /dev/VGExaDb/LVDbSys1
  LV Name                /dev/VGExaDb/LVDbSwap1
  LV Name                /dev/VGExaDb/LVDbOra1
  LV Name                /dev/VGExaDb/backup
[root@cm01dbm01 ~]#
```

6. Now, create LVM snapshots on the /dev/VGExaDb/LVDbSys1 and /dev/VGExaDb/LVDbOra1 volumes using `lvcreate` and the -s option, a size of 1 GB and 5 GB, respectively, and name the root_snap and u01_snap:

```
[root@cm01dbm01 ~]# lvcreate -L1G -s -n root_snap /dev/VGExaDb/LVDbSys1
  Logical volume "root_snap" created
[root@cm01dbm01 ~]# lvcreate -L5G -s -n u01_snap /dev/VGExaDb/LVDbOra1
  Logical volume "u01_snap" created
[root@cm01dbm01 ~]#
```

7. You can confirm your snapshot volume devices have been created by listing the contents in /dev/VGExaDb:

```
[root@cm01dbm01 ~]# ls /dev/VGExaDb/*snap*
/dev/VGExaDb/root_snap /dev/VGExaDb/u01_snap
[root@cm01dbm01 ~]#
```

8. Mount your LVM snapshot volume. Create directories to mount first, and then use mount to mount the snapshot volumes:

```
[root@cm01dbm01 mnt]# mkdir -p /mnt/snap/root
[root@cm01dbm01 mnt]# mkdir -p /mnt/snap/u01
[root@cm01dbm01 mnt]# mount /dev/VGExaDb/root_snap /mnt/snap/root/
[root@cm01dbm01 mnt]# mount /dev/VGExaDb/u01_snap /mnt/snap/u01
[root@cm01dbm01 mnt]# df -h
Filesystem                         Size  Used  Avail  Use%  Mounted on
/dev/mapper/VGExaDb-LVDbSys1        30G   23G   5.1G   82%  /
/dev/sda1                          124M   48M    70M   41%  /boot
/dev/mapper/VGExaDb-LVDbOra1        99G   59G    36G   63%  /u01
tmpfs                               81G     0    81G    0%  /dev/shm
/dev/mapper/VGExaDb-backup         152G  188M   152G    1%  /mnt/backup
/dev/mapper/VGExaDb-root_snap       30G   23G   5.1G   82%  /mnt/snap/root
/dev/mapper/VGExaDb-u01_snap        99G   59G    36G   63%  /mnt/snap/u01
[root@cm01dbm01 mnt]#
```

Notice that the available and used capacity is the same for each set of snapshot volumes with respect to their source volumes.

9. Back up your file systems from the LVM snapshot.

10. Now, you can back up the contents of your system using the point-in-time snapshots of your / and /u01 volumes. You can use whichever backup mechanism you want to back these files up; in this recipe, we created a backup logical volume and /mnt/backup file system for these purposes. In the following code, we will use tar to create our backups from the snapshot volumes:

```
[root@cm01dbm01 snap]# cd /mnt/snap
[root@cm01dbm01 snap]# tar -pjcvf /mnt/backup/cm01dbm01.t.bz2 \
> * /boot --exclude /mnt/backup/cm01dbm01.t.bz2 \
> > /tmp/cm01dbm01.stdout 2>/tmp/cm01dm01.stderr
```

The preceding `tar` command will create a BZ2 compressed `tar` backup of the contents of the snapshot directories, excluding backing up the backup file, and redirecting `stdout` and `stderr` to log files in `/tmp`. If you `tail` your `/tmp/cm01dbm01.stdout` file, it looks like the following output:

```
[root@cm01dbm01 tmp]# tail -f cm01dbm01.stdout
root/opt/oracle.cellos/iso/cellbits/
root/opt/oracle.cellos/iso/cellbits/exaos.tbz
root/opt/oracle.cellos/iso/cellbits/dbboot.tbz
root/opt/oracle.cellos/iso/cellbits/dbfw.tbz
root/opt/oracle.cellos/iso/cellbits/diag.iso
root/opt/oracle.cellos/iso/cellbits/kernel.tbz
```

11. When your backups are complete, unmount the snapshot file systems and destroy your snapshot volumes:

```
[root@cm01dbm01 ~]# umount /mnt/snap/root
[root@cm01dbm01 ~]# umount /mnt/snap/u01
[root@cm01dbm01 ~]# rm -rf /mnt/snap
[root@cm01dbm01 ~]# lvremove /dev/VGExaDb/root_snap
Do you really want to remove active logical volume root_snap? [y/n]: y
  Logical volume "root_snap" successfully removed
[root@cm01dbm01 ~]# lvremove /dev/VGExaDb/u01_snap
Do you really want to remove active logical volume u01_snap? [y/n]: y
  Logical volume "u01_snap" successfully removed
[root@cm01dbm01 ~]#
```

How It Works

Use of LVM snapshots is an excellent means of providing a point-in-time copy of your file systems for backup purposes. LVM snapshots provide a nearly instantaneous snapshot of your data; from the operating system's perspective, the file systems on LVM snapshot logical volumes will contain the contents of the source volumes but for the duration of the snapshot's existence as of the time the snapshot was established.

When using `lvcreate` to build your snapshots, the `-s` and the `-L` options are important. The `-s` option is used to define the snapshot name; you will need this to locate the device to mount. The `-L` option specifies the size of the snapshot volume. To properly size your snapshot volumes, estimate the expected data volume change for the source volume plus the snapshot volume over the intended lifetime of your snapshot. For example, if it takes an hour to back up the contents of the /u01 file system, you should estimate how much change, in GB, will occur in the source volume over the span of an hour and use this as your `-L` argument. Undersizing snapshot volumes will cause Linux to unmount your snapshots, which could be disruptive if it occurs during an active backup. You can determine how much space is being used in your snapshots with `lvdisplay`. The following output shows that the /dev/VGExaDb/u01_snap is currently using 4.45% of its allocated 5 GB:

```
[root@cm01dbm01 backup]# lvdisplay /dev/VGExaDb/u01_snap | egrep '(COW-table size|Allocated)'
  COW-table size         5.00 GB
  Allocated to snapshot  4.45%
[root@cm01dbm01 backup]#
```

■ **Note** On Exadata Compute Nodes, it is not common for high rates of change on your active / and /u01 file systems. Typically, trace files, audit files, and other log files are your most actively created or changed files. Knowing this, your snapshot volumes probably do not need to be sized very large; in this recipe, we sized the `root_snap` volume at 1 GB and the `u01_snap volume` at 5 GB.

In the example in this recipe, as stated in the Solution section, we created an additional physical volume called backup and mounted this to /mnt/backup. This task by itself was not directly related to LVM snapshots; we simply created this volume to back up the contents of our active file systems to.

■ **Note** Please see Recipe 8-11 to learn how to restore your compute nodes from LVM snapshot backups.

8-6. Backing Up Your Oracle Databases with RMAN

Problem

You want to back up your Oracle databases running on Exadata.

Solution

Oracle databases on Exadata use Oracle Automatic Storage Management (ASM). Oracle Recovery Manager, or RMAN, is the only supported means to create restorable backup copies of ASM data files and, as such, RMAN must be part of your backup strategy on Exadata if you plan on backing up your database.

How It Works

On Oracle Exadata, if you wish to back up your Oracle databases, you must use Oracle RMAN because the database files will reside on Oracle ASM storage. Using RMAN with Oracle backups is a lengthy topic and deserves a complete text in and of itself. As such, this recipe only scratches the surface of Oracle RMAN's functionality and usage. To learn more about Oracle RMAN, please consult the product documentation at http://docs.oracle.com/cd/E11882_01/backup.112/e10642/toc.htm.

Optimizing your Oracle RMAN backups starts by understanding the physical capabilities of your Exadata Compute Nodes, storage cells, and network components. When backing up internal to Exadata using your Fast Recovery Area, Oracle has benchmarked up to 3 TB/hour for an Eighth Rack, 5 TB/hour for a Quarter Rack, 8-9 TB/hour for a Half Rack, and between 17 and 18 TB/hour for an Exadata Full Rack using full RMAN image copies. Incremental backups, in each case, will achieve even faster results depending on your workload.

Following are a series of recommendations based on our experience in the field on a number of RMAN backup topics for Exadata:

- If you can justify the disk space requirement, perform RMAN backups to Exadata using the Fast Recovery Area (FRA). This will provide the highest performance, lead to the highest performing recovery times, and provide the greatest amount of flexibility in your recovery scenarios.

- When backing up to the FRA, perform an RMAN Level 0 backup once per week and incremental backups on the other six days.

- Back up your archived redo logs to the FRA as frequently as your recovery time objective (RTO) dictates.

- Connect to your target database in RMAN using a service name to distribute RMAN channels across your Oracle RAC instances.

- Use between two and eight channels per instance by setting your `DEVICE TYPE DISK PARALLELISM` configuration.

- Implement Block Change Tracking in your database to reduce backup times and backup storage requirements.

- If you have read only tablespaces or a large amount of dormant data, configure backup optimization by issuing `CONFIGURE BACKUP OPTIMIZATION ON` in RMAN.

- If you are backing up external to your Exadata storage (that is, outside the FRA to an external device), choose your network wisely. You can use your 1 GbE NET3 networks for smaller databases, 10 GbE NET3 interfaces for larger databases, or your InfiniBand fabric to get the highest performance over the network.

- When using Oracle Secure Backup or third-party backup solutions, configure your backup media servers to maximum your network bandwidth; for example, when possible, use InfiniBand or 10 GbE on the media servers for large backups.

- When backing up to tape, allocate as many SBT channels in RMAN as tape drives. The goal is to work in parallel.

When performing RMAN backups to tape or network-attached storage external to Exadata, the network, media servers, or backup pools are much more likely to present the limiting factor to your database backup times. Optimizing these types of configurations is most often a matter of allocating sufficient channels, both inside RMAN and from a physical perspective, such as networks, tape drives, and so forth. Oracle provides a number of solutions and products to provide an integrated, high-performing Oracle database backup solution for Exadata including Oracle Secure Backup, the ZFS Storage Appliance, and other backup solutions capable of using 10 GbE or InfiniBand networks.

Note Oracle has published several Maximum Availability Architecture white papers on the topic of RMAN backups and Oracle Exadata. We recommend downloading and reading *Backup and Recovery Performance and Best Practices for Exadata Cell and Oracle Exadata Database Machine* at `http://www.oracle.com/technetwork/database/features/availability/maa-tech-wp-sundbm-backup-11202-183503.pdf` and *Oracle Exadata Database Machine—Backup & Recovery Sizing: Tape Backups* at `http://www.oracle.com/technetwork/database/availability/maa-exadata-backup-methodology-495297.pdf`.

8-7. Backing Up the InfiniBand Switches
Problem

You wish to back up your InfiniBand switch image and key configuration files.

Solution

Backing up your InfiniBand switches is accomplished by using the Web ILOM interface to back up your InfiniBand configuration and, additionally, periodically backing up your OpenSM configuration file.

1. First, log in to the InfiniBand ILOM web interface.
2. Click on the *Maintenance* tab.
3. Click the *Backup/Restore* tab.
4. Select *Backup* for the *Operation* and any of the desired methods for the *Transfer Method*.

    We typically choose to back up using the Browser method, but if you have a backup device or network file system that supports any of the protocols listed in the Transfer Method drop-down list, this may be appropriate. Figure 8-1 displays the InfiniBand ILOM Configuration Backup/Restore screen:

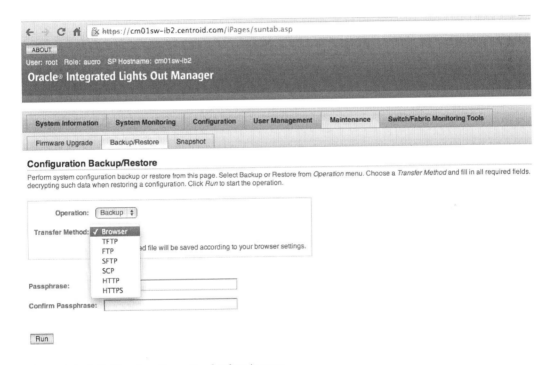

Figure 8-1. InfiniBand configuration backup/restore

5. After selecting your transfer method, simply click the Run button. If you wish to secure the transmission of the backup, enter a passphrase in the appropriate text boxes. If you select not to enter a passphrase, the web interface will issue a warning message, as depicted in Figure 8-2.

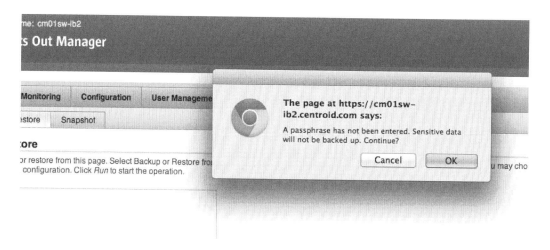

Figure 8-2. *InfiniBand configuration backup/restore passphrase warning*

6. When the backup is complete, a `config_backup.xml` file will be downloaded to your browser or file transfer location. Once your configuration is downloaded, you can back it up using the backup method or software of your choice.

In addition to backing up your InfiniBand switch configuration via the `ILOM`, you should also plan on periodically backing up your OpenSM configuration file, `/etc/opensm/opensm.conf`. OpenSM is InfiniBand's subnet manager software.

■ **Note** Oracle does not provide tools or an interface to back up your OpenSM configuration file; you will need to transfer the file externally and back it up according to your backup policies.

How It Works

The InfiniBand switches in an Exadata Database Machine are highly capable but minimally complex from an administration standpoint. As such, the files and software running on the InfiniBand switches do not change very often. However, as an Exadata DMA, you should still perform backups of your configuration and `opensm.conf` file for the following reasons:

- If you experience a hardware failure and require a replacement InfiniBand switch, restoring from the `config_backup.xml` will restore your settings to an operational state.

- InfiniBand switch patches can update firmware and the switch configuration. On the rare occasion that these patches introduce errors, you will need to have backups in order to restore from a failure.

- Patches could also introduce changes to your subnet manager configuration in `/etc/opensm/opensm.conf`.

> **Note** In Recipe 8-13, we discuss InfiniBand recovery topics using the backup method presented in this recipe.

Since the backup methods for the InfiniBand switches are relatively straightforward and the recovery is equally simplistic, we generally recommend implementing operational procedures to save your `opensm.conf` and `config_backup.xml` files into a version control repository of your choice.

8-8. Recovering Storage Cells from Loss of a Single Disk

Problem

You have had a disk drive failure in your Exadata cell server and wish to recover from the failure.

Solution

In this recipe, we will discuss how to do the following:

- Identify a failed disk drive in an Exadata Storage Server
- Use CellCLI commands to display its status
- Determine how Oracle ASM handles a failed disk
- Perform the process to replace the disk drive and return operations to normal.

We recommend proactively monitoring your Exadata Database Machine with Enterprise Manager, Automated Service Requests, and/or via Oracle's Platinum Support Services to ensure that hardware faults will be captured and appropriate communications issued.

Assuming you are working with Oracle Support on an automatically or manually created Service Request, it is common for Oracle to request output of the `sundiag.sh` script in order to properly assess the situation. Recipe 7-10 discusses the steps required to run the `sundiag.sh` utility. It is important that you provide Oracle with the requested information in order to schedule an Oracle hardware engineer to replace the failed disk drive.

> **Note** If you have configured Automated Service Requests, per Recipe 20-3, an Oracle Service Request will be automatically created for hardware faults such as a failed disk drive. Additionally, with the latest Exadata plug-ins installed and Enterprise Manager agents configured on your database machine components, Enterprise Manager can also notify you when you have hardware errors.

Regardless of your Service Request status, there are a number of tasks you can perform to better understand the scope of your failure. Start by checking the status of your failed disk drive using the CellCLI `list physicaldisk` command. Log in to the Exadata storage cell as `root` or `celladmin` on the server that has the failed drive, launch `cellcli`, and execute the following query:

```
[root@cm01cel01 ~]# cellcli -e list physicaldisk where diskType=HardDisk | grep -iv normal
cm01cel01: 20:5 E1QZ42 critical
[root@cm01cel01 ~]#
```

In the output above, we can see that disk 20:5 has a status of critical, indicating it is in a failed state. Next, query the LUN information using the CellCLI list lun command to obtain information about the cell disk on this physical disk:

```
CellCLI> list lun where physicalDrives=20:5 attributes name,cellDisk,status
         0_5       CD_05_cm01cel01         critical

CellCLI>
```

Using the output above, query your cell disk status using the following command:

```
CellCLI> list celldisk where name=CD_05_cm01cel01 detail
         name:              CD_05_cm01cel01
         comment:
         creationTime:      2011-08-27T01:20:08-04:00
         deviceName:        /dev/sdf
         devicePartition:   /dev/sdf
         diskType:          HardDisk
         errorCount:        0
         freeSpace:         0
         id:                ae5252be-05cf-412d-a761-560670d135d2
         interleaving:      normal_redundancy
         lun:               0_5
         raidLevel:         0
         size:              557.859375G
         status:            not present

CellCLI>
```

In the output above, we see that our storage cell is not sensing the existence of a cell disk on this LUN, which is an indication we've received a physical disk error. In the How It Works section of this recipe, we will discuss additional status values that Oracle uses to signify faults on Exadata Storage Server disks. Next, check your grid disk statuses on this cell disk:

```
CellCLI> list griddisk where cellDisk=CD_05_cm01cel01 attributes name,status
         DATA_CD_05_cm01cel01           not present
         DBFS_DG_CD_05_cm01cel01        not present
         RECO_CD_05_cm01cel01           not present
         SDATA_CD_05_cm01cel01          not present
         SRECO_CD_05_cm01cel01          not present

CellCLI>
```

Next, check your ASM instance's alert log on the compute node by logging in to the Exadata Compute Server as the Grid Infrastructure owner, changing directories to the trace file directory under the diagnostics destination, and searching for references to your failed disks. The alert log entries of relevance in the case above look like the following:

```
WARNING: Disk 35 (RECO_CD_05_CM01CEL01) in group 3 mode 0x7f is now being offlined
WARNING: Disk 35 (RECO_CD_05_CM01CEL01) in group 3 in mode 0x7f is now being taken
offline on ASM inst 1
NOTE: initiating PST update: grp = 3, dsk = 35/0xec5ff760, mode = 0x6a, op = 4
```

```
GMON updating disk modes for group 3 at 14 for pid 30, osid 8507
NOTE: PST update grp = 3 completed successfully
NOTE: initiating PST update: grp = 3, dsk = 35/0xec5ff760, mode = 0x7e, op = 4
GMON updating disk modes for group 3 at 15 for pid 30, osid 8507
NOTE: cache closing disk 35 of grp 3: RECO_CD_05_CM01CEL01
NOTE: PST update grp = 3 completed successfully
NOTE: process _user8507_+asm1 (8507) initiating offline of disk 33.3965712156
(DATA_CD_05_CM01CEL01) with mask 0x7e in group 1
NOTE: checking PST: grp = 1
GMON checking disk modes for group 1 at 16 for pid 30, osid 8507
NOTE: checking PST for grp 1 done.
WARNING: Disk 33 (DATA_CD_05_CM01CEL01) in group 1 mode 0x7f is now being offlined
WARNING: Disk 33 (DATA_CD_05_CM01CEL01) in group 1 in mode 0x7f is now being taken offline on
ASM inst 1
... output omitted for brevity
WARNING: Disk 33 (DATA_CD_05_CM01CEL01) in group 1 will be dropped in: (12960) secs on ASM inst 1
WARNING: Disk 35 (RECO_CD_05_CM01CEL01) in group 3 will be dropped in: (12960) secs on ASM inst 1
```

As you can see, your Oracle ASM instance will automatically offline the failed disks from the appropriate ASM disk group.

Now it's time to replace your failed disk drive. If you have a spare drive in your Exadata spares kit, you can use this as your replacement and replenish your spare via your Service Request. If you require an Oracle Support hardware engineer to bring a new disk drive to your data center because you do not have an available spare, you must wait for the drive to arrive.

■ **Note** We recommend using one of your spares to replace failed disks once Oracle Support confirms that the disk drive is indeed in a failed state. It is worth mentioning, however, that some types of drive failures are transient in nature and can be resolved simply by reseating the disk drive. You can do this by simply pressing the release button on the failed drive, removing it, and inserting it back into its slot. In some cases, this will correct transient errors; if it does, the server will automatically sense the correction and set the status back to `normal`.

When you have a replacement drive in hand, simply remove the failed disk drive by depressing the release button and insert the replacement drive. You should be able to identify the failed drive based on a blinking amber LED on the left side of the disk drive; if you do not see a blinking light, log in as root to the storage server and run the following MegaCli64 command to turn the service LED on:

```
[root@cm01cel01 ~]# /opt/MegaRAID/MegaCli/MegaCli64 -pdlocate -physdrv \[20:5\] -a0
Adapter: 0: Device at EnclId-20 SlotId-5 -- PD Locate Start Command was successfully sent to
Firmware
Exit Code: 0x00
[root@cm01cel01 ~]#
```

Note that you can turn off the service light by using the following command:

```
[root@cm01cel01 ~]# /opt/MegaRAID/MegaCli/MegaCli64 -pdlocate -stop -physdrv \[20:5\] -a0
Adapter: 0: Device at EnclId-20 SlotId-5 -- PD Locate Stop Command was successfully sent to
Firmware
Exit Code: 0x00
[root@cm01cel01 ~]#
```

Once the replacement disk has been seated in the proper slot, Oracle will automatically set the physical disk status to normal and the LUN status to normal:

```
CellCLI> list physicaldisk where name=20:5 attributes name,status
        20:5        normal

CellCLI> list lun where physicaldrives=20:5 attributes name,cellDisk,status
        0_5         CD_05_cm01cel01         normal

CellCLI> list celldisk where name=CD_05_cm01cel01 attributes name,status
        CD_05_cm01cel01         normal

CellCLI> list griddisk where celldisk=CD_05_cm01cel01 attributes
name,asmDiskGroupName,asmDiskName,status
        DATA_CD_05_cm01cel01        DATA_CM01        DATA_CD_05_CM01CEL01        active
        DBFS_DG_CD_05_cm01cel01     DBFS_DG          DBFS_DG_CD_05_CM01CEL01     active
        RECO_CD_05_cm01cel01        RECO_CM01        RECO_CD_05_CM01CEL01        active
        SDATA_CD_05_cm01cel01       SDATA_CM01       SDATA_CD_05_CM01CEL01       active

CellCLI>
```

The Oracle ASM disks will be automatically onlined once the grid disks report an active status. After ASM resynchronizes the disks, run the SQL*Plus script in Listing 8-1 to check your ASM disk status.

Listing 8-1. lst08-01-asm-disk-status.sql

```
SQL> select a.name,b.path,b.state,b.mode_status,b.failgroup
from v$asm_diskgroup a, v$asm_disk b
where a.group_number=b.group_number
and b.failgroup='CM01CEL01'
and b.path like '%CD_05_cm01cel01%'
order by 2,1
/

Disk Group   Disk                                      State     Disk Status    Failgroup
----------   ---------------------------------------   -------   ------------   ----------
DATA_CM01    o/192.168.10.3/DATA_CD_05_cm01cel01       NORMAL    ONLINE         CM01CEL01
DBFS_DG      o/192.168.10.3/DBFS_DG_CD_05_cm01cel01    NORMAL    ONLINE         CM01CEL01
RECO_CM01    o/192.168.10.3/RECO_CD_05_cm01cel01       NORMAL    ONLINE         CM01CEL01
SDATA_CM01   o/192.168.10.3/SDATA_CD_05_cm01cel01      NORMAL    ONLINE         CM01CEL01

SQL>
```

How It Works

Hard disk failures are one of the most common types of hardware outages in most compute systems, and on Exadata this is no exception. Our experience with Exadata is that, not unlike other manufacturers, disk drive failure is often most common in the early stages after an Exadata deployment.

When a disk drive in the Exadata Storage Server experiences an unrecoverable, non-transient hardware fault, the physical disk and LUN is marked with a status of critical and the cell disks and underlying grid disks are marked with a status of not present. However, a physical drive failure is not the only kind of error condition that an Exadata Storage Server disk can have. In addition to a physical failure, Oracle also can raise Predictive Failure and Poor

Performance disk statuses by way of its built-in monitoring. Exadata Storage Servers monitor disk drives and collect information such as temperate, read/write errors, speed, and performance.

If a disk shows a predictive failure condition, it means that the server has experienced one or more read/write error conditions, temperature threshold conditions, and so forth; this indicates that a disk failure could be imminent. In this case, you should replace your disk using the same procedures outlined in the Solution of this recipe.

When a disk reports a poor performance condition, it should also be replaced using the steps provided in this recipe. Each Exadata cell disk should exhibit the same performance characteristics and if one is performing poorly based on performance metrics collected by the storage server, it could impact you database performance adversely.

In the case of a physical disk failure, Oracle automatically changes the physicaldisk and lun statuses change from normal to critical. It then drops the celldisk and each griddisk on the celldisk. When the grid disk or disks are dropped, ASM will drop its corresponding grid disks using the FORCE option as displayed from the ASM instance's alert log:

```
SQL> /* Exadata Auto Mgmt: Proactive DROP ASM Disk */
alter diskgroup RECO_CM01 drop
  disk RECO_CD_05_CM01CEL01 force

NOTE: GroupBlock outside rolling migration privileged region
NOTE: requesting all-instance membership refresh for group=3
Tue Jul 05 21:48:13 2011
NOTE: Attempting voting file refresh on diskgroup DBFS_DG
GMON updating for reconfiguration, group 3 at 28 for pid 35, osid 12377
NOTE: group 3 PST updated.
NOTE: membership refresh pending for group 3/0x833f0667 (RECO_CM01)
WARNING: Disk 35 (_DROPPED_0035_RECO_CM01) in group 3 will be dropped in: (12960) secs on ASM inst 1
GMON querying group 3 at 29 for pid 19, osid 11535
SUCCESS: refreshed membership for 3/0x833f0667 (RECO_CM01)
SUCCESS: /* Exadata Auto Mgmt: Proactive DROP ASM Disk */
alter diskgroup RECO_CM01 drop
  disk RECO_CD_05_CM01CEL01 force
```

When a physical disk enters a predictive failure state, the physicaldisk and lun statuses change from normal to predictive failure. After this, the celldisk and each griddisk on the celldisk are dropped. When this happens, the ASM disks are dropped without the FORCE option.

When the failed disk is replaced, the following things occur:

- The firmware on the new disk is updated to reflect the same firmware version as the other disks in the cell.
- The cell disk is recreated to match the disk it replaced.
- The replacement celldisk is brought online and its status is set to normal.
- Each griddisk on the celldisk is onlined and has its status marked active.
- The grid disks will automatically be added to Oracle ASM, resynchronized, and brought online in its ASM disk group.

If you look in your ASM instance's alert log after replacing a failed disk, you will see messages similar to the following ones. These are examples of Exadata's automatic disk management capability:

```
SQL> /* Exadata Auto Mgmt: ADD ASM Disk in given FAILGROUP */
alter diskgroup DATA_CM01 add
  failgroup CM01CEL01
  disk 'o/192.168.10.3/DATA_CD_05_cm01cel01'
```

```
name DATA_CD_05_CM01CEL01
rebalance nowait
NOTE: Assigning number (1,33) to disk (o/192.168.10.3/DATA_CD_05_cm01cel01)
NOTE: requesting all-instance membership refresh for group=1
NOTE: initializing header on grp 1 disk DATA_CD_05_CM01CEL01
NOTE: requesting all-instance disk validation for group=1
```

If you manually inactivate grid disks, the ASM disks will be automatically offlined by ASM and you will have up to the amount of time specified by the disk group attribute disk_repair_time to resolve the situation without incurring an ASM disk group rebalance operation. Each ASM disk group has a disk_repair_time attribute, which defaults to 3.6 hours. This represents how long the Exadata DMA has to replace an inactivated grid disk before the ASM disk is dropped from the disk group. If the threshold is crossed and the disk is dropped from the ASM disk group, ASM will need to perform a disk group rebalance operation prior to bringing the disk online. In either case, the intervention required by the Exadata DMA is typically minimal due to Exadata's automatic disk management modules.

Note If you experience a simultaneous loss of both disk drives in slots 0 and 1, your situation is a bit more complicated since these disks are where your system area and system volume reside. Please see Recipe 8-9 for details on how to recover from this scenario.

How do you protect yourself against disk drive failure? You can't protect yourself entirely from a hard drive crashing; after all, a disk drive is a piece of mechanics and electronics that will at some point fail. However, you can (and should) protect against loss of data or loss of access to your data by implementing ASM normal or high redundancy. With ASM redundancy on Exadata, you can afford to lose an entire storage server and all its disks (or any number of disks in a storage cell) and still maintain access to your data.

Oracle does make life easier for you on Exadata by constantly monitoring your disks and reporting failure conditions to its alert repository and, alternatively, by sending SNMP traps to monitoring software. To provide the best level of monitoring coverage, you should configure Automated Service Requests, monitor your systems using Enterprise Manager, or make it an operational practice to check your Exadata storage cell alerts.

8-9. Recovering Storage Cells from Loss of a System Volume Using CELLBOOT Rescue

Problem

You have either corrupted your system volume images or suffered from simultaneous loss of the first two disk drives in your Exadata storage cell, and you wish to use the internal CELLBOOT USB drive to recover from failure.

Solution

In this section, we will outline the steps necessary to invoke the storage cell rescue procedure to restore your system volume. At a high level, these are the steps you should take:

- Understand the scope of the failure
- Contact Oracle Support and open a Service Request
- Boot your system from the internal CELLBOOT USB image

- Recover your storage cell using the cell rescue procedure
- Perform post-recovery steps and validation

> **Note** To learn more about the internal CELLBOOT USB drive, please see Recipe 8-1.

The first step to take is to understand the scope of your failure. In other words, confirm whether you have hardware failure and if so, whether you have a multiple disk failure impacting both disks that comprise your system area. If your outage is deemed unrecoverable using single disk drive replacement, it's time to initiate the storage cell rescue procedure.

> **Note** If you have only lost a single disk containing your system volumes, use the recovery steps provided in Recipe 8-8. We don't advise performing a storage cell rescue from the CELLBOOT USB drive unless you need to or wish to test the procedure in non-production environment.

If your outage is deemed unrecoverable using single disk drive replacement, it's time to initiate the storage cell rescue procedure.

1. Before starting the rescue, we recommend contracting Oracle Support to open a Service Request.
2. To start the procedure, log in to your ILOM web console and reboot your storage cell.

> **Note** We recommend using the ILOM console as opposed to the KVM console during this process. When logged in to the KVM console, you may experience "green-out" periods in which you lose visibility to the console. Since some of the steps in the storage cell recovery process require you to press keys within a fixed time interval, you may lose the ability to act promptly and this can delay your rescue process.

3. As soon as you see the Oracle Exadata splash screen, press any key on the keyboard. You will need to do this quickly as the screen only displays for five seconds. Figure 8-3 shows what this splash screen looks like.

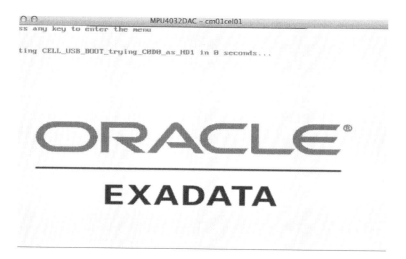

Figure 8-3. Storage cell splash screen

4. In the displayed list of boot options, scroll down to the bottom option, CELL_USB_BOOT_CELLBOOT_usb_in_rescue_mode, and select this option, as shown in Figure 8-4.

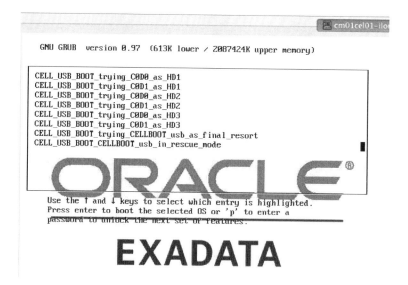

Figure 8-4. Selecting the CELL_USB_BOOT_CELLBOOT_usb_in_rescue_mode

5. After the node has booted, select your rescue option. You will be provided two choices, as listed in Figure 8-5.

```
Copyright (c) 1999-2010 Intel Corporation.
Image id in memory: 1324538570
Waiting for USB devices to be ready...may take few minutes
kjournald starting.  Commit interval 5 seconds
EXT3 FS on sdm1, internal journal
EXT3-fs: mounted filesystem with ordered data mode.
last console command line option: tty1
Reset LVM support for the cell node
[INFO] /dev/md6 is a candidate for the root filesystem
[INFO] /dev/md5 is a candidate for the inactive root filesystem
[INFO] /dev/md8 is a candidate for the cell software partition
[INFO] /dev/md7 is a candidate for the inactive cell software partition
Installation media has version 11.2.2.4.2.111221
kjournald starting.  Commit interval 5 seconds
EXT3 FS on md6, internal journal
EXT3-fs: mounted filesystem with ordered data mode.
The current installation has version 11.2.2.4.2.111221

[INFO] Installation already exists.

Choose from following by typing letter in '()':
  (e)nter interactive diagnostics shell. Must use credentials from Oracle
      support to login (reboot or power cycle to exit the shell),
  (r)einstall or try to recover damaged system,
Select: r_
```

Figure 8-5. Select cell rescue option

There are two choices, entering a diagnostics shell or reinstalling and recovering a damaged system. Assuming you have to recover a damaged system, enter r at the Select prompt to continue. With this option, the rescue procedure will destroy and recreate all of your partitions and then restore the system volumes using the data backed up to the CELLBOOT USB image.

6. At the next prompt, shown in Figure 8-6, enter y to continue.

CHAPTER 8 ■ BACKUP AND RECOVERY

```
Waiting for USB devices to be ready...may take few minutes
kjournald starting.  Commit interval 5 seconds
EXT3 FS on sdm1, internal journal
EXT3-fs: mounted filesystem with ordered data mode.
last console command line option: tty1
Reset LVM support for the cell node
[INFO] /dev/md6 is a candidate for the root filesystem
[INFO] /dev/md5 is a candidate for the inactive root filesystem
[INFO] /dev/md8 is a candidate for the cell software partition
[INFO] /dev/md7 is a candidate for the inactive cell software partition
Installation media has version 11.2.2.4.2.111221
kjournald starting.  Commit interval 5 seconds
EXT3 FS on md6, internal journal
EXT3-fs: mounted filesystem with ordered data mode.
The current installation has version 11.2.2.4.2.111221

[INFO] Installation already exists.

Choose from following by typing letter in '()':
  (e)nter interactive diagnostics shell. Must use credentials from Oracle
      support to login (reboot or power cycle to exit the shell),
  (r)einstall or try to recover damaged system,
Select: r
Reinstall or try to recover damaged system
Continue (y/n) [n]: y_
```

Figure 8-6. Choosing to reinstall or recover from a damaged system

7. The rescue process will prompt you for your root rescue password next. This is *not* the server's root password; the root rescue password is typically sos1exadata. If this password does not work, contact Oracle Support.

8. When asked to erase all data partitions and data disks, choose to *not* erase your partitions, if possible; this will allow all of your cell disks to be importable after the process completes.

■ **Note**   There may be situations in which you are required to erase your partitions, but in the example in this recipe, we will elect not to. If you do choose to erase partitions and data disks, you will need to recreate your cell disks and underlying grid disks as part of the post-rescue process outlined below.

At this point, the first phase or the CELLBOOT rescue process begins. You will see it partition your volumes and restore the cell server software and image information from your CELLBOOT USB drive. The process will take a few minutes to complete and, while waiting, you will see output like that shown in Figures 8-7 and 8-8.

```
mke2fs 1.39 (29-May-2006)
Filesystem label=
OS type: Linux
Block size=1024 (log=0)
Fragment size=1024 (log=0)
1008 inodes, 8032 blocks
401 blocks (4.99%) reserved for the super user
First data block=1
1 block group
8192 blocks per group, 8192 fragments per group
1008 inodes per group

Writing inode tables: done
Writing superblocks and filesystem accounting information: done

This filesystem will be automatically checked every 38 mounts or
180 days, whichever comes first.  Use tune2fs -c or -i to override.
tune2fs 1.39 (29-May-2006)
Setting maximal mount count to -1
Setting interval between checks to 0 seconds
EXT4-fs (sda2): mounted filesystem without journal

Partitioning /dev/sdb
Partitioning /dev/sdb using parted. Disk label: msdos
```

Figure 8-7. Cell rescue partitioning

```
Copying /mnt/iso/initrd.img to /mnt/imaging/sys/opt/oracle.cellos/iso ...
Verifying MD5 checksum for /mnt/imaging/sys/opt/oracle.cellos/iso/initrd.img ...
Copying /mnt/iso/isolinux.bin to /mnt/imaging/sys/opt/oracle.cellos/iso ...
Verifying MD5 checksum for /mnt/imaging/sys/opt/oracle.cellos/iso/isolinux.bin .
..
Copying /mnt/iso/isolinux.cfg to /mnt/imaging/sys/opt/oracle.cellos/iso ...
Verifying MD5 checksum for /mnt/imaging/sys/opt/oracle.cellos/iso/isolinux.cfg .
..
Copying /mnt/iso/memtest to /mnt/imaging/sys/opt/oracle.cellos/iso ...
Verifying MD5 checksum for /mnt/imaging/sys/opt/oracle.cellos/iso/memtest ...
Copying /mnt/iso/splash.lss to /mnt/imaging/sys/opt/oracle.cellos/iso ...
Verifying MD5 checksum for /mnt/imaging/sys/opt/oracle.cellos/iso/splash.lss ...
Copying /mnt/iso/trans.tbl to /mnt/imaging/sys/opt/oracle.cellos/iso ...
Verifying MD5 checksum for /mnt/imaging/sys/opt/oracle.cellos/iso/trans.tbl ...
Copying /mnt/iso/vmlinuz to /mnt/imaging/sys/opt/oracle.cellos/iso ...
Verifying MD5 checksum for /mnt/imaging/sys/opt/oracle.cellos/iso/vmlinuz ...
[INFO] Kernel 2.6.18-238.12.2.0.2.el5 is in use
Copying /mnt/iso/lastGoodConfig/cell.conf to /mnt/imaging/sys/.cell.conf ...
Copying /mnt/iso/cellbits/exaos.tbz to /mnt/imaging/sys/opt/oracle.cellos/iso/ce
llbits ...
Verifying MD5 checksum for /mnt/imaging/sys/opt/oracle.cellos/iso/cellbits/exaos
.tbz ...
Running "tar -x -j -p -C /mnt/imaging/sys -f /mnt/imaging/sys/opt/oracle.cellos/
iso/cellbits/exaos.tbz" ...
```

Figure 8-8. Restoring from CELLBOOT USB drive to temporary system volumes

9. When the first phase of the storage cell rescue procedure is complete, log in to your rescue shell as root and use the root rescue password, typically `sos1exadata`. The login prompt will show the `localhost login` text, as displayed in Figure 8-9.

```
 disk 1, wo:0, o:1, dev:sdb1
md: md1: resync done.
md: resync of RAID array md6
md: delaying resync of md5 until md6 has finished (they share one or more physic
al units)
RAID1 conf printout:
 --- wd:2 rd:2
 disk 0, wo:0, o:1, dev:sda10
 disk 1, wo:0, o:1, dev:sdb10
md: minimum _guaranteed_  speed: 1000 KB/sec/disk.
md: using maximum available idle IO bandwidth (but not more than 200000 KB/sec)
for resync.
md: using 128k window, over a total of 10490304 blocks.

Login timed out after 60 seconds.
localhost login: root
Password:
======================= NOTE ==================================
=                                                              =
= ---- YOU ARE IN RESCUE MODE AFTER FIRST PHASE OF RESCUE ---- =
= Imaging pre-boot phase finished with success.                =
= Execute reboot to continue installation.                     =
=                                                              =
================================================================
-sh-3.1# _
```

Figure 8-9. *Rescue mode shell login*

10. At the shell prompt, issue the reboot command to reboot your storage cell. As the system is rebooting and before the Oracle Exadata splash screen is displayed, press the F8 key to access the boot device selection window, as displayed in Figure 8-10. Select the RAID controller as your boot device. This will cause the system to boot from your hard disks instead of the CELLBOOT USB drive or any other bootable device.

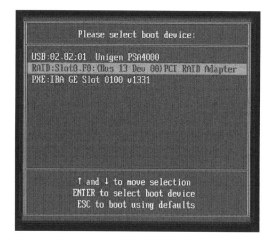

Figure 8-10. *Boot device selection*

As the storage cell boots, the rescue procedure will restore the remaining software from the CELLBOOT USB drive and bring your storage cell to a semi-operational status. One thing you will notice is that during this phase of the procedure, Oracle will run its cell validation code in reimage_boot mode, as displayed in Figure 8-11.

```
Starting atd:                                                    [  OK  ]
Logging started to /var/log/cellos/validations.log
Command line is /opt/oracle.cellos/validations/bin/vldrun.pl -mode reimage_boot
-force -quiet -all
INIT: version 2.86 reloading
type=1108 audit(1346779467.097:3): user pid=6633 uid=0 auid=4294967295 msg='op=a
dding user acct="nscd" exe="/usr/sbin/useradd" (hostname=?, addr=?, terminal=? r
es=failed)'
```

Figure 8-11. Running cell validation in reimage_boot mode

11. When the reimage process is complete, the cell should reboot. Your storage cell may power off during this phase of the rescue process; don't panic, simply log in to your ILOM console and power the cell on, as displayed in Figure 8-12.

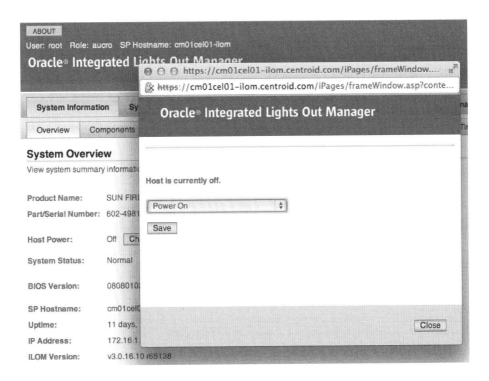

Figure 8-12. Powering on your storage cell from the ILOM web interface

As the storage cell is started, it will perform a number of processes to return the cell to an operational state. You will notice that on its first pass, your CELLSRV software will not start, as shown in Figure 8-13. This is normal at this state of the rescue process.

```
           inflating: /tmp/oc4jpatch/8513914/etc/config/inventory
           inflating: /tmp/oc4jpatch/8513914/etc/config/actions
            creating: /tmp/oc4jpatch/8513914/etc/xml/
           inflating: /tmp/oc4jpatch/8513914/etc/xml/GenericActions.xml
           inflating: /tmp/oc4jpatch/8513914/etc/xml/ShiphomeDirectoryStructure.xml
           inflating: /tmp/oc4jpatch/8513914/README.txt
          apply -jdk /usr/java/jdk1.5.0_15/ -oh /opt/oracle/cell11.2.2.4.2_LINUX.X64_1112
         21/oc4j/ms -silent /tmp/oc4jpatch/85139140
         0

         Starting the RS, CELLSRV, and MS services...
         CELL-01510: Cannot start a new Restart Server (RS) at port number: 9903. An inst
         ance of RS might be already running.
         Getting the state of RS services...
          running
         Starting CELLSRV services...
         The STARTUP of  CELLSRV services was not successful. Error: Start Failed
         Starting MS services...
         The STARTUP of MS services was successful.
                                                                                [  OK  ]
         Logging started to /var/log/cellos/validations.log
         Command line is /opt/oracle.cellos/validations/bin/vldrun.pl -mode first_boot -f
         orce -quiet -all
         Run validation beginfirstboot - PASSED
         Run validation ipmisettings -
```

Figure 8-13. CELLSRV unsuccessful after reboot from rescued cell

12. After a few minutes, you will see that the storage cell will be recreated and validated in first_boot mode. When a login screen appears, log in to your storage server using its normal credentials.

13. When the storage cell rescue procedure is complete, you must perform a few tasks. One of the first things we recommend is to validate the cell image and compare with another healthy cell in your storage grid using the imageinfo command:

```
[root@cm01cel01 ~]# imageinfo
Kernel version: 2.6.18-238.12.2.0.2.el5 #1 SMP Tue Jun 28 05:21:19 EDT 2011 x86_64
Cell version: OSS_11.2.2.4.2_LINUX.X64_111221
Cell rpm version: cell-11.2.2.4.2_LINUX.X64_111221-1
Active image version: 11.2.2.4.2.111221
Active image activated: 2012-09-04 13:46:01 -0400
Active image status: success
Active system partition on device: /dev/md5
Active software partition on device: /dev/md7
In partition rollback: Impossible
Cell boot usb partition: /dev/sdm1
Cell boot usb version: 11.2.2.4.2.111221
Inactive image version: undefined
Rollback to the inactive partitions: Impossible
[root@cm01cel01 ~]#
```

14. Next, check the status of your cell disks. The following output shows that they each have a status of importForceRequired. Your cell disks will have this status if you completed your storage cell rescue procedure and did *not* choose to repartition your devices, as we have done in this example:

```
[root@cm01cel01 ~]# cellcli -e list celldisk
        CD_00_cm01cel01         importForceRequired
        CD_01_cm01cel01         importForceRequired
        CD_02_cm01cel01         importForceRequired
        CD_03_cm01cel01         importForceRequired
... output omitted for brevity
        FD_00_cm01cel01         importForceRequired
        FD_01_cm01cel01         importForceRequired
        FD_02_cm01cel01         importForceRequired
... output omitted for brevity
[root@cm01cel01 ~]#
```

15. When your cell disks show a status of importForceRequired after a cell rescue procedure, import your cell disks using the CellCLI import celldisk all force command:

```
CellCLI> import celldisk all force
CellDisk CD_00_cm01cel01 successfully imported
CellDisk CD_01_cm01cel01 successfully imported
CellDisk CD_02_cm01cel01 successfully imported
... output omitted for brevity

CellCLI> list celldisk
        CD_00_cm01cel01         normal
        CD_01_cm01cel01         normal
        CD_02_cm01cel01         normal
... output omitted for brevity
CellCLI>
```

The import celldisk all force command will also import and activate all of your grid disks:

```
CellCLI> list griddisk
        DATA_CD_00_cm01cel01         active
        DATA_CD_01_cm01cel01         active
        DATA_CD_02_cm01cel01         active
... output omitted for brevity

CellCLI>
```

16. Next, you must online your grid disks for each ASM disk group. The output in Listing 8-2 shows your disk group status prior to onlining the disks, the commands to online your disks, and the status after onlining. Note that in the first output, the disk path is missing from the display; this is because it is not onlined to the disk group yet.

Listing 8-2. lst08-02-failgroup-status.sql

```
SQL> select a.name,b.path,b.state,b.mode_status,b.failgroup
    from v$asm_diskgroup a, v$asm_disk b
    where a.group_number=b.group_number
```

```
            and b.failgroup='CM01CEL01'
        order by 2,1
/

Disk Group      Disk              State       Disk Status     Failgroup
----------      ----------        ----------  -----------     --------------------
DATA_CM01                         NORMAL      ONLINE          CM01CEL01
DATA_CM01                         NORMAL      ONLINE          CM01CEL01
DATA_CM01                         NORMAL      ONLINE          CM01CEL01
... output omitted for brevity

46 rows selected.

SQL> alter diskgroup data_cm01 online disks in failgroup cm01cel01;

Diskgroup altered.

... Repeat for your remaining ASM disk groups

SQL> select a.name,b.path,b.state,b.mode_status,b.failgroup
    from v$asm_diskgroup a, v$asm_disk b
    where a.group_number=b.group_number
    and b.failgroup='CM01CEL01'
    order by 2,1
/

Disk Group   Disk                                      State       Disk Status    Failgroup
----------   ------------------------------------      ----------  -----------    ----------
DATA_CM01    o/192.168.10.3/DATA_CD_00_cm01cel01       NORMAL      ONLINE         CM01CEL01
DATA_CM01    o/192.168.10.3/DATA_CD_01_cm01cel01       NORMAL      ONLINE         CM01CEL01
DATA_CM01    o/192.168.10.3/DATA_CD_02_cm01cel01       NORMAL      ONLINE         CM01CEL01
... output omitted for brevity

46 rows selected.

SQL>
```

17. When your ASM disk groups and disks are online and healthy, create your cell's flash cache:

```
CellCLI> create flashcache all
Flash cache cm01cel01_FLASHCACHE successfully created
CellCLI>
```

18. Next, configure your cell's custom SNMP, SMTP, alert settings, threshold settings, and so forth using the `alter cell`, `alter threshold`, and other similar commands as these cell configurations will not be carried forward during a storage cell rescue procedure. Unless you have documented these configurations, a good way to restore them to their previous settings is to compare to another cell in your storage grid. Use the `cellcli list cell detail` CellCLI command to compare your settings.

19. Finally, you may want to clear your alert history on the cell. It is common to see a handful of cell alerts after performing the storage cell rescue process:

```
CellCLI> list alerthistory
     1       2012-09-04T13:43:31-04:00       critical       "RS-7445 [Required IP
             parameters missing] [Check cellinit.ora] [] [] [] [] [] [] [] [] [] []"
     2_1     2012-09-04T13:45:10-04:00       critical       "InfiniBand Port HCA-1:2 is
             showing non-zero error counts."
     2_2     2012-09-04T13:45:10-04:00       clear          "InfiniBand Port HCA-1:2 status
             is OK."

CellCLI> drop alerthistory all
Alert 1 successfully dropped
Alert 2_1 successfully dropped
Alert 2_2 successfully dropped

CellCLI> list alerthistory

CellCLI>
```

After your rescue process completes and your storage cell is recovered to its pre-failure state, you will notice that your cell does not have its Inactive partitions defined:

```
[root@cm01cel01 ~]# imageinfo | grep device
Active system partition on device: /dev/md5
Active software partition on device: /dev/md7
[root@cm01cel01 ~]#
```

This is because after a storage cell rescue process, you will not restore your inactive partitions. Don't worry though, the next time you apply a patch, Exadata will automatically create these.

How It Works

There are a few scenarios in which you may need or want to invoke the CELLBOOT rescue procedure:

- Corruption of the storage server's boot partition
- A logical error introduced by an Exadata DMA, such as accidentally deleting cell software, binaries, or configuration files
- Patch or upgrade failure
- Simultaneous loss of each of the first two disk drives in your storage server

The Exadata Storage Server rescue procedure will restore your boot image, system volumes, and cell software from the internal (or external) CELLBOOT USB drive, which is automatically created and maintained by Exadata and outlined in Recipe 8-1. When you boot using the USB rescue option, you will be directed through a series of screens that will facilitate a storage cell recovery and rescue. After completion, several steps are required to restore your overall configuration to its pre-failure state.

Since Exadata mirrors the contents of your system volume data across partitions of the two disks in slots 0 and 1, loss of your system volume should be a very rare occurrence. In our experience, it is more likely to experience a bug that corrupts your boot volume or, even more common, a human error that introduces logical corruption.

If you find yourself in a storage cell rescue procedure situation, we recommend engaging Oracle Support and working with Support not only to ensure that the steps you take are supported, but to guide you through the potentially daunting rescue procedure. The rescue procedure itself is relatively straightforward and robust, but care must me taken to ensure that your recovery experience is positive. Following is a list of recommendations to ensure you will be able to confidently navigate through a cell rescue using your CELLBOOT USB image:

- Periodically mount your CELLBOOT USB drive and confirm its contents, per Recipe 8-2. If your server is experiencing issues backing up the boot image and system volumes to your CELLBOOT USB drive, you will likely become aware of this during reboots or patching, but it helps to know that your CELLBOOT USB drive contains the data it should.

- Make it a practice to create an additional cell boot image on an external USB drive, as discussed in Recipe 8-3. The storage cell rescue procedure will clearly not work as planned if your internal CELLBOOT USB drive is damaged.

- When performing your cell rescue procedure, read the prompts carefully and understand your data loss risk. The storage cell rescue procedure will not destroy the contents of the data disks or data partitions on the system area disks unless you explicitly tell it to do so during the rescue.

- Configure your ASM storage with normal or high redundancy and create your ASM disk groups with grid disks spanning storage cell disks. In other words, follow Exadata best practices; not doing so could lead to data loss during a system volume rescue and mandate restore and recovery of your data from tape or external RMAN backups.

- Document your cell and grid disk configuration to reduce errors when rebuilding your grid disks.

- Document any custom cell attributes, including SNMP configuration, SMTP details, alert, and threshold information.

- Use the ILOM console to perform your storage cell rescue procedure.

8-10. Recovering from a Failed Storage Server Patch
Problem

You have experienced a failure applying a storage server patch and wish to recover its state to an operable status.

Solution

To recover from a failed storage server patch, the Exadata DMA should simply rely on Exadata's patching process and validation utilities to perform the rollback and recovery. It is very rare that the Exadata DMA will need to perform any specific steps as part of a failed patch application and, if required, it is generally best to contact Oracle Support to guide you through the process.

■ **Note** To learn more about the Exadata storage cell patching process, please refer to Recipes 11-2 and 11-3.

How It Works

When patching Exadata storage cells, the patch process uses the active and inactive partitions to provide rollback and recovery in the event of a patch failure. To see your active and inactive partitions, run the following imageinfo command:

```
[root@cm01cel02 ~]# imageinfo | grep device
Active system partition on device: /dev/md6
Active software partition on device: /dev/md8
Inactive system partition on device: /dev/md5
Inactive software partition on device: /dev/md7
[root@cm01cel02 ~]#
```

In this listing, we see that for this storage cell, our active partitions reside on /dev/md6 and /dev/md8 and the inactive partitions on /dev/md5 and /dev/md7.

Exadata storage cell patches can be either Out-of-Partition or In-Partition patches. With Out-of-Partition patches, the inactive partitions are activated and patched first. When complete, Oracle's validation framework is executed at reboot and the previously inactive partitions are switched to the active partitions. The previously active partitions are marked inactive and synchronized with the newly activated partitions.

If during system startup or cell service startup Oracle's validation framework detects an error or failure condition, the patched partitions are rolled back and the system boots from the un-patched active partitions.

We will cover more details on the Exadata storage cell patching process in Recipes 11-2 and 11-3.

8-11. Recovering Compute Server Using LVM Snapshots

Problem

You wish to recover files or software on your compute nodes using backups taken with LVM snapshots.

Solution

In this recipe, we will assume you have backed up your compute nodes using LVM snapshots as presented in Recipe 8-5 and walk you through the steps to restore components of your volumes using these LVM snapshot backups. The steps provided in this recipe will include the following:

- Performing a few pre-recovery checks on your compute node
- Staging your backup image to an NFS mount directory accessible from the failed compute node on your network
- Attaching the diagnostics ISO file to your CD-ROM drive via the ILOM
- Booting your failed compute node from the diagnostics ISO image
- Performing your restore from the backup image stored on the NFS mount
- Detaching the diagnostics ISO and rebooting the system
- Validating your restore and starting your databases

Start by validating your image information on your server by running the `imageinfo` command:

```
[root@cm01dbm02 ~]# imageinfo
Kernel version: 2.6.18-238.12.2.0.2.el5 #1 SMP Tue Jun 28 05:21:19 EDT 2011 x86_64
Image version: 11.2.2.4.2.111221
Image activated: 2012-02-11 23:26:55 -0500
Image status: success
System partition on device: /dev/mapper/VGExaDb-LVDbSys1
[root@cm01dbm02 ~]#
```

■ **Note** In this example, the compute node we are restoring is currently available and not in a failed state. In real-world scenarios in which you need to perform LVM snapshot-based recoveries, it may be likely you will not have access to the compute node due to failure.

If you have any applications or software currently running and have access to your compute server, you should shut them down prior to continuing with the next steps.

1. Ensure that your backup is located on an NFS share that the compute node can access. In the case of the following example, our backup image is located on an NFS share called 172.16.1.200:/exadump/cm01dbm02_bkp/ cm01dbm02.t.bz2:

    ```
    [root@cm01dbm02 ~]# ls -l /dump/cm01dbm02_bkp/
    total 24157948
    -rw-r--r-- 1 root root 24737733538 Jan 20  1993 cm01dbm02.t.bz2
    [root@cm01dbm02 ~]# df -h /dump
    Filesystem                      Size  Used Avail Use% Mounted on
    172.16.1.200:/exadump            14T  6.8T  6.8T  50% /dump
    [root@cm01dbm02 ~]#
    ```

2. Now, you need to attach your diagnostics image to the ILOM. Transfer /opt/oracle.SupportTools/diagnostics.iso from any of your other compute nodes to your workstation:

    ```
    Macintosh-7:jclarke$ scp root@cm01dbm01:/opt/oracle.SupportTools/diagnostics.iso.
    root@cm01dbm01's password:
    diagnostics.iso       100%   31MB 923.5KB/s   00:34
    Macintosh-7:ch14 jclarke$
    ```

3. Enable redirection in the ILOM web console by logging in to the ILOM web console of the compute node that you wish to restore and navigating to *Remote Control – Redirection*, as depicted in Figure 8-14.

CHAPTER 8 ■ BACKUP AND RECOVERY

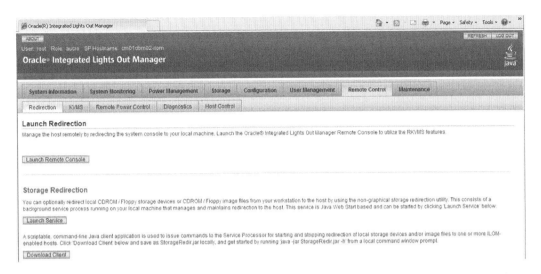

Figure 8-14. *ILOM web console redirection*

4. Click the *Launch Remote Console* button, and after your console is displayed select *Devices-CD ROM Image* from the drop-down menu.

5. Then select the `diagnostics.iso` image that you transferred to your workstation, as shown in Figure 8-15.

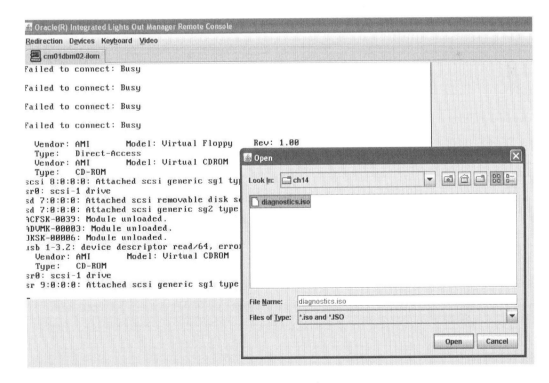

Figure 8-15. *Attaching ISO image to CD-ROM ILOM console*

225

6. Next, go to *Remote Control-Host Control* from the ILOM web interface, select *CDROM* as the boot device, and save your changes. Please see Figure 8-16.

Figure 8-16. Changing boot device to CDROM

7. After saving your changes, you are ready to reboot your system. While logged in as root to the ILOM console, type shutdown -r -y now to reboot your compute node. As the system is starting, you should see the splash screen in Figure 8-17. This may take a few minutes to complete.

Figure 8-17. Diagnostics boot splash screen

8. When your server boots from the diagnostics.iso ISO image, it will begin a recovery process and prompt you to respond to several questions:

   a. Select r to restore your system from an NFS based backup archive and then y to confirm your selection

   b. Enter the path to your NFS backup file using the format `<IP>:/<share>/<backup file>`

   c. Choose y to use an LVM based scheme

   d. Enter your management network interface, eth0, for the Ethernet interface

   e. Enter your management network IP address

   f. Enter the subnet mask and default gateway

   Figure 8-18 displays an example of responses to the recovery process questions.

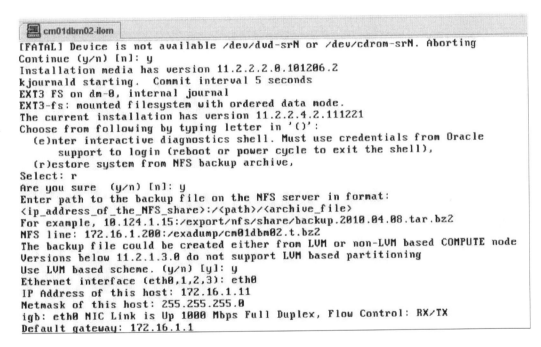

Figure 8-18. Compute node recovery from LVM-based snapshots

9. After responding to the prompts, the recovery process will begin. It will take a bit of time depending on your network bandwidth between the compute node and your NFS share as well as the performance capabilities of your backup location. When complete, log in as root with the recovery password, sos1exadata.

10. From the ILOM console, detach your CDROM Image and change your boot device to the default, as displayed in Figure 8-19.

Figure 8-19. *Changing boot device back to the default*

11. When complete, issue the reboot command from the ILOM console. After your compute node starts, log in as root and validate your image by running the imagehistory command. Note the `restore from nfs backup` text in the last stanza.

```
[root@cm01dbm02 ~]# imagehistory
Version                          : 11.2.2.2.0.101206.2
Image activation date            : 2011-02-21 11:16:12 -0800
Imaging mode                     : fresh
Imaging status                   : success

... output omitted for brevitty

Version                          : 11.2.2.4.2.111221
Image activation date            : 2012-02-11 23:26:55 -0500
Imaging mode                     : patch
Imaging status                   : success

Version                          : 11.2.2.4.2.111221
Image activation date            : 2012-09-06 14:19:55 -0500
Imaging mode                     : restore from nfs backup
Imaging status                   : success

[root@cm01dbm02 ~]#
```

12. Finally, validate and/or start your cluster resources and databases.

How It Works

Recovering your compute nodes from LVM-based snapshots is a good way to restore your system to a working state, assuming that you have employed LVM snapshot backups using steps outlined in Recipe 8-6. This type of compute node recovery is enabled via a special recovery process built into the bootable diagnostics.iso image, installed on each compute node in the /opt/oracle.SupportTools directory. /opt/oracle.SupportTools/diagnostics.iso is symbolically linked to /opt/oracle.cellos/iso/cellbits/diagnostics.iso.

> **Note** Exadata Storage Servers also have a `diagnostics.iso` file in the same location, but you cannot use this ISO to perform LVM-based snapshot recovery of compute nodes.

To perform this type of recovery on your compute nodes, you must perform the following tasks:

- Transfer the `diagnostics.iso` file to a location on your local workstation or NFS share.
- Set the CDROM image to this `diagnostics.iso` file via the ILOM.
- Change your server's boot order to boot from CDROM. This will cause the server to boot from a virtual CDROM drive containing the diagnostics ISO image.
- Respond to the recovery process prompts as outlined in the Solution of this recipe.
- Disconnect your CDROM image and restore the boot settings of your node to the defaults.
- Reboot your compute node and validate the recovery.

While conducting recovery, the diagnostics process will extract the contents of your backup image, restore to the proper locations on your server, and configure the server to look as it did at the time the LVM-snapshot-based backups were taken.

8-12. Reimaging a Compute Node

Problem

Your compute node server has become corrupt and you wish to reimage it from the default configuration and patch or upgrade to the latest software image applied prior to the corruption.

Solution

In this recipe, we will outline the steps required to reimage a compute node that has been become corrupt.

> **Note** Reimaging an Exadata Compute Server is a complex process and should not be undertaken without the guidance of Oracle Support. It is usually preferable to restore your compute nodes from backups as your first option, assuming you have valid backups. Please refer to Recipes 8-5, 8-6, 8-12, or consult your Enterprise software recovery manuals to restore your compute nodes using other means if you have valid backups.

1. The first step you must perform is to remove your node from the RAC cluster. Refer to the *Exadata Owner's Manual* or Oracle documentation for details.
2. Next, log a Service Request with Oracle Support to obtain a `computeImageMaker` file. The `computeImageMaker` file is release-specific and should look like this:

```
[root@cm01dbm01 stg]# ls -l computeImageMaker_11.2.3.1.0_LINUX.X64_120304-1.x86_64.tar.zip
-rwxrwxrwx  1 root  root   310607872 May  31 21:51 computeImageMaker_11.2.3.1.0_LINUX.X64_120304-1.x86_64.tar.zip
[root@cm01dbm01 stg]#
```

You can also download the computeImageMaker zip file from edelivery.oracle.com, but as your image needs to identically match your current version, we recommend obtaining your file from Oracle Support.

3. After obtaining the computeImageMaker zip file from Oracle Support, stage it on one of your surviving compute nodes and unzip the contents.

4. Insert a blank USB drive into the server on the functional compute node on which you staged the zip file above. Once the USB drive is plugged in, change directories to the dl360 directory where the computeImageMaker zip file was unzipped and untarred:

```
[root@cm01dbm01 dl360]# ls
boot  doc  grub  initrd  makeImageMedia.sh  README_FOR_FACTORY.txt  tmp
[root@cm01dbm01 dl360]#
```

5. Create your bootable image media by running the makeImageMedia.sh command:

```
[root@cm01dbm01 dl360]# ./makeImageMedia.sh -dualboot no
```

6. When complete your external USB drive will contain a bootable, factory-default image that you can use to restore your failed server to its factory defaults. Eject the USB drive from your healthy server and optionally delete your dl360 directory and computeImageMaker zip file.

7. Insert the USB drive into the compute node that you wish to reimage. Log in to the ILOM console and power the server off. Then power it back on and perform the following tasks:

    a. Press F2 when the BIOS screen is displayed to enter into the BIOS setup.

    b. Press F8 to select a one-time boot order, and select your USB flash drive as the first boot sequence.

    c. Allow the system to boot.

    d. When prompted, remove the USB drive and press Enter to power the server down.

    At this point, the server will be restored to its Exadata factory defaults. It will have lost all of its configuration details, including the IP addresses for all networks, DNS server information, NTP server information, the hostname, the subnet mask, and the default gateway.

8. Next, power on the server. This will automatically launch the Exadata configuration routine and take you into a menu to configure your network information and other details. After entering the appropriate values, allow the server to reboot and, once it is back up, validate your network configuration.

9. Now, you need to validate several configuration files that are customized as part of a normal Exadata installation. Specifically, you will have to validate and configure the following:

    - /etc/security/limits.conf
    - /etc/hosts, /etc/oracle/cell/network-config/cellinit.ora
    - /etc/oracle/cell/network-config/cellip.ora
    - /etc/modprobe.conf

Edit these files and set to the appropriate values for your environment; we recommend referencing a healthy compute node and making the necessary adjustments. When finished, reboot your system and again validate the configuration.

10. The next phase of the process involves preparing the node to be added to your cluster. You must manually perform the following tasks:

    a. Replicate Linux groups and user accounts from a healthy compute node

    b. Create directories under the /u01 mount point to store your Oracle 11gR2 RDBMS software and Oracle 11gR2 Grid Infrastructure software and configure permissions

    c. Setup SSH between hosts and distribute SSH keys for dcli to function

11. After these tasks are complete, run imageinfo -ver to validate your image and compare against another compute node in your machine:

```
[root@cm01dbm01 ~]# imageinfo -ver
11.2.2.4.2.111221
[root@cm01dbm01 ~]#
```

12. If the versions are different, you will need to patch your machine to the same version using methods presented in Recipe 11-3.

13. After you have patched your node to the same image version, run cluvfy with the following syntax to ensure your server is ready for an Oracle cluster installation. The command will compare your current, reimaged server with a healthy server in your cluster:

```
[root@cm01dbm01 ~]# cluvfy stage -post hwos -n cm01dbm01,cm01dbm02 -verbose
```

14. Next, verify the peer compatibility between your nodes. In the following example, cm01dbm01 is the reimaged server and cm01dbm02 is a healthy server:

```
[root@cm01dbm01 ~]# cluvfy comp peer -refnode cm01dbm02 -n cm01dbm01 -orainv \
> oinstall -osdba dba   | grep -B 3 -A 2 mismatched
```

15. After resolving issues, you can begin adding your reimaged server back into the cluster using addNode.sh from a functional node:

```
[root@cm01dbm02 bin]# ./addNode.sh -silent "CLUSTER_NEW_NODES=cm01dbm01" \
> "CLUSTER_NEW_VIRTUAL_HOSTNAMES=cm01dbm01-vip"
```

Follow a similar process to clone your database home from a healthy server to the compute server, as outlined in the *Exadata Owner's Manual*.

How It Works

At a high level, reimaging a compute node server entails booting from an external USB drive that contains a factory boot image and using Exadata's boot process to configure your network information and install an Exadata image onto your compute node. After a successful compute node reinstall, several manual steps must be performed by the Exadata DMA to bring the compute node to an operational state.

Some of the post-reimage steps are specific to Oracle Exadata, whereas others could be more accurately classified as being related to adding a database server than to an Oracle RAC cluster. These steps are documented very well in the *Exadata Owner's Manual*. Preparation, experience, and confidence in a few key areas should be met in order to successfully reimage an Exadata Compute Node. Specifically:

- You should carefully read the steps in the Exadata owner's guide prior to beginning.

- You should know how to remove a node from an Oracle RAC cluster.

- You should know what your IP addresses are for each network on your node, the hostname, DNS information, NTP information, subnet mask, and default gateway information. After installing the factory image on a compute node, you will be required to enter this information. You can use a working compute, your own documentation, your configuration worksheet, or DNS entries as a reference.

- You should know how to update several key configuration files, such as /etc/security/limits.conf, /etc/hosts, and so on. Refer to a working compute node as a reference.

- You should know how to perform common Linux administration tasks such as creating Linux groups and users, creating directories and setting file permissions, and so forth.

- You should know how to apply patches to an Exadata Compute Node.

- You should be familiar with Oracle's Cluster Verification Utility.

- You should be comfortable running addNode.sh to add Grid Infrastructure and RDBMS Oracle software to a new node.

8-13. Recovering Your InfiniBand Switch Configuration
Problem
You have a corrupt InfiniBand switch image or your InfiniBand switch has failed, and you wish to restore your InfiniBand switch and its configuration.

Solution
In this recipe, we will discuss the steps required to restore your InfiniBand switch from configuration backups and OpenSM configuration file backups.

■ **Note** The steps in this recipe assume you have backed up your switch configuration using the steps outlined in Recipe 8-7. If you have not performed backups of your switch configuration, please contact Oracle Support.

First, after replacing your switch or after a corruption has been detected, log in to your InfiniBand switch ILOM interface. If you have replaced your switch, the default admin password will be set to its default password, ilom-admin.

Once logged in, navigate to the *Maintenance - Backup/Restore*, select *Restore* from the top drop-down list, and choose an appropriate *Transfer Method*. In the example in Figure 8-20, we are displaying a Browser-based restore; if this option is selected, you will need to click on the *Select File-Choose* button and locate your config_backup.xml file.

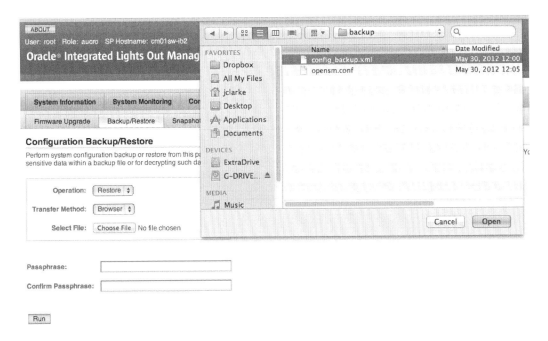

Figure 8-20. Restore config_backup.xml for InfiniBand switch

After selecting your configuration file to restore, click the Run button. You will be presented a dialog box indicating that the process may take a few minutes to complete, as shown in Figure 8-21. Click OK to resume.

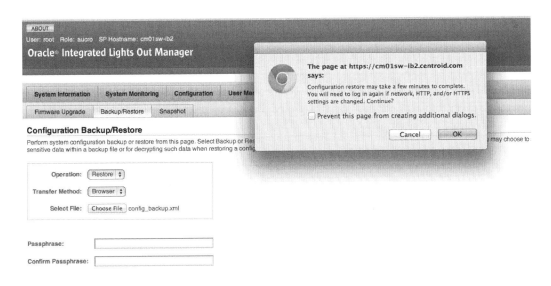

Figure 8-21. Restore InfiniBand dialog window

When finished, you can log on to your switch as root and run the following find command to determine which configuration files have been restored:

```
[root@cm01sw-ib2 conf]# find /conf -type f -mtime -1
/conf/cliconfig.xml~
/conf/smtp.conf
/conf/cliconfig.xml
/conf/user_attr
/conf/syslog.conf
/conf/alertrule.xml
/conf/cfgdb/servicetag.xml
/conf/cfgdb/servicetag.xml~
/conf/snmpd.conf
/conf/timezone
/conf/snmpd.local.conf
[root@cm01sw-ib2 conf]#
```

To restore your OpenSM configuration file, transfer your backup opensm.conf file via SCP from your backup location to /etc/opensm/opensm.conf and run the following service command to restart OpenSM:

```
[root@cm01sw-ib2 init.d]# service opensmd restart
smconfigtest:ERR_trap: /etc/opensm/opensm.conf file has log_max_size out of range: 8, should not be greater than 4
Stopping IB Subnet Manager..                [  OK  ]
Starting IB Subnet Manager.                 [  OK  ]
[root@cm01sw-ib2 init.d]#
```

How It Works

Restoring an Exadata InfiniBand switch configuration is a straightforward process, assuming you have created backups of your switch configuration and OpenSM configuration file as provided in Recipe 8-7.

When you restore your InfiniBand switch configuration, you most likely will not be required to restart any processes or reboot your switch, but you should make it a practice to validate your switch version prior to and after restoring your config_backup.xml file:

```
[root@cm01sw-ib2 ~]# version
SUN DCS 36p version: 1.3.3-2
Build time: Apr  4 2011 11:15:19
SP board info:
Manufacturing Date: 2010.08.21
Serial Number: "NCD4V1753"
Hardware Revision: 0x0005
Firmware Revision: 0x0000
BIOS version: SUN0R100
BIOS date: 06/22/2010
[root@cm01sw-ib2 ~]#
```

After restoring the opensm.conf file, you will need to restart OpenSM.

> **Note** The steps in this recipe assume you are using InfiniBand firmware version 1.1.3-2 or later. To restore your switch configuration from previous firmware versions, please consult your Exadata owner's manual.

8-14. Recovering from Loss of Your Oracle Cluster Registry and Voting Disks

Problem

You have lost your Oracle Cluster Registry on your compute nodes and need to restore your environment to enable ClusterWare resources to start.

Solution

In this recipe, we will demonstrate how to recover from loss of your Oracle Cluster Registry, or OCR, and your Oracle RAC voting disks.

Recovering Your OCR

There are some rare occurrences in which restoring your OCR may be necessary; the most common of which is if you wish to restore your cluster resource definitions to previous values, but you could find yourself in a situation in which you've lost the Exadata grid disks on which the mirrored versions of the OCR reside.

> **Note** Oracle protects and mirrors your OCR inside an Oracle ASM disk group. While it is possible to lose a mirror of your OCR, it is highly unlikely that events such as disk failure would leave your OCR unprotected. It is perhaps more common for human error to lead to this event.

The first step you should perform is to log in to your compute node as root and determine the location of your Oracle Cluster Registry by looking at /etc/oracle/ocr.loc:

```
[root@cm01dbm01 ~]# cat /etc/oracle/ocr.loc
ocrconfig_loc=+DBFS_DG
local_only=FALSE
[root@cm01dbm01 ~]#
```

The above information tells you that for this Exadata installation, clusterware is expecting the OCR to be located in an ASM disk group called DBFS_DG, which is common on recent versions of Exadata.

> **Note** If you have physically lost the ASM disk group on which your OCR resided, CRS will fail to start. You should disable automatic restart of Oracle High Availability Services by performing a crsctl disable crs as root, rebooting your nodes, and then running crsctl start crs -excl on one of your nodes. This will start enough CRS services to perform the remainder of the tasks in this recipe.

Next, list your OCR backups:

```
[root@cm01dbm01 ~]# /u01/app/11.2.0.3/grid/bin/ocrconfig -showbackup
cm01dbm01     2012/09/07 09:28:52     /u01/app/11.2.0.3/grid/cdata/cm01-cluster/backup00.ocr
cm01dbm01     2012/09/07 05:28:52     /u01/app/11.2.0.3/grid/cdata/cm01-cluster/backup01.ocr
cm01dbm01     2012/09/07 01:28:51     /u01/app/11.2.0.3/grid/cdata/cm01-cluster/backup02.ocr
cm01dbm01     2012/09/06 09:28:50     /u01/app/11.2.0.3/grid/cdata/cm01-cluster/day.ocr
cm01dbm01     2012/08/31 01:28:40     /u01/app/11.2.0.3/grid/cdata/cm01-cluster/week.ocr
cm01dbm01     2011/05/03 16:11:19     /u01/app/11.2.0/grid/cdata/cm01-
cluster/backup_20110503_161119.ocr
[root@cm01dbm01 ~]#
```

As you can see, Oracle maintains five backups of OCR file backups on local file systems by default. This is not specific to Oracle Exadata; this is true with Oracle 11gR2 Grid Infrastructure.

At this point, since your cluster expects the OCR to reside in the DBFS_DG ASM disk group, you must have this disk group created and mounted prior to restoring your OCR file. If you have lost or dropped your DBFS_DG ASM disk group, you must create it first while connected as SYSASM to an ASM instance. This implies that you have a collection of DBFS_DG grid disks created on your storage cells. If you do need to recreate your DBFS_DG ASM disk group, log in to a compute node as the Grid Infrastructure owner, connect to your ASM instance as SYSASM, and create your disk group using a command similar to one in Listing 8-3.

Listing 8-3. lst08-03-create-diskgroup.sql

```sql
SQL> create diskgroup DBFS_DG
    normal redundancy
    disk 'o/*/DBFS_DG*'
    attribute 'compatible.rdbms' = '11.2.0.3.0',
              'compatible.asm' = '11.2.0.3.0',
              'cell.smart_scan_capable' = 'TRUE',
              'au_size' = '4M';

Diskgroup created.

SQL>
```

> **Note** When starting your ASM instance, if your DBFS_DG did not already exist, you may receive ORA-15032, ORA-15017, and ORA-15063 errors. You can proceed to create the ASM disk group using the previous command.

Once your ASM disk group is created, you can restore your OCR using the following command while logged in as root to a compute node:

```
[root@cm01dbm01 ~]# /u01/app/11.2.0.3/grid/bin/ocrconfig -restore \
    /u01/app/11.2.0.3/grid/cdata/cm01-cluster/backup00.ocr
[root@cm01dbm01 ~]#
```

In situations when you have also lost your voting disks, you need to restore your OCR first and then your voting disks. Please refer to recipe 8-14 for details on how to restore your voting disks.

When complete, enable your Oracle High Availability Services for automatic restart and reboot your compute nodes.

```
[root@cm01dbm01 ~]# dcli -g ./dbs_group -l root /u01/app/11.2.0.3/grid/bin/crsctl enable crs
cm01dbm01: CRS-4622: Oracle High Availability Services autostart is enabled.
cm01dbm02: CRS-4622: Oracle High Availability Services autostart is enabled.
[root@cm01dbm01 ~]# shutdown -r 0
... output omitted
```

Once your compute nodes are back up, validate your OCR by running the following command as root or the Grid Infrastructure software owner:

```
[root@cm01dbm01 ~]# /u01/app/11.2.0.3/grid/bin/ocrcheck
Status of Oracle Cluster Registry is as follows :
         Version                  :          3
         Total space (kbytes)     :     262120
         Used space (kbytes)      :       3464
         Available space (kbytes) :     258656
         ID                       : 1833511320
         Device/File Name         :    +DBFS_DG
                                    Device/File integrity check succeeded
                                    Device/File not configured
                                    Device/File not configured
                                    Device/File not configured
                                    Device/File not configured
         Cluster registry integrity check succeeded
         Logical corruption check succeeded
[root@cm01dbm01 ~]#
```

Finally, run `crsctl stat resource` to ensure that your cluster resources are started.

Restoring Your Voting DIsks

First, you must start CRS on your Exadata Compute Nodes. If all three copies of your voting disks are lost, you will have issues starting each piece of your Oracle RAC infrastructure, but you should be able to query your OCR location using the $GI_HOME/bin/ocrcheck command as listed in the previous section.

Assuming that your OCR is healthy, use the following command to restore your voting disks while logged in as root to a compute server:

```
[root@cm01dbm01 ~]# /u01/app/11.2.0.3/grid/bin/crsctl replace votedisk +DBFG_DG
Sucessful addition of voting disk 36c247152bc4f48bf7bc76b101623a8.
Sucessful addition of voting disk a8d245a33c6d4ff9bf76b53f9a6c3cce.
Sucessful addition of voting disk 3d6011e464284f20bf1869c45d45358e
CRS-4266: Voting file(s) successfully replaced
[root@cm01dbm01 ~]#
```

After successful voting disk restore, restart CRS on each node in your cluster.

How It Works

Oracle allows you to restore your Oracle Cluster Registry using the `ocrconfig -restore` command. This command accepts a backup OCR file as its argument, which you can choose by running `ocrconfig -showbackup` and selecting the appropriate backup copy that resides on your compute node file system.

When you execute the `ocrconfig -restore` command, Oracle will copy the backup OCR file and place it into the location specified in `/etc/oracle/ocr.loc`. On Exadata, this will refer to an ASM disk group location, typically DBFS_DG.

Without your Oracle Cluster Registry available, your Oracle RAC cluster will not be able to cleanly start any of its resources, including listeners, networks, ASM instances, and databases. Oracle protects against loss of your OCR by mirroring its contents using ASM redundancy in an ASM disk group built on Exadata grid disks.

With Oracle 11gR2 on Exadata, Oracle can reconstruct and restore each of three copies of your voting disks from your Oracle Cluster Registry. By default, the `crsctl replace votedisk` command will create three copies of your voting disk inside the ASM disk group specified.

It is worth mentioning that restoring your OCR and voting disks on Exadata is no different from restoring it on non-Exadata Oracle RAC environments. Exadata's standards are to place the OCR in the `DBFS_DG` ASM disk group and, as such, this disk group must exist and be mounted in order to restore your OCR.

CHAPTER 9

Storage Administration

Understanding Exadata Storage Server architecture is one of the more important tasks for an Exadata administrator, and an end-to-end knowledge of how storage "works" on Exadata is of critical importance. Chapters 1, 2, and 3 provided the foundation for the Exadata Storage Grid, and in this chapter, we'll cover some of the common administration tasks as they relate to Exadata storage.

9-1. Building ASM Disk Groups on Exadata

Problem

You need to create one or more Oracle ASM disk groups on Exadata for Oracle database storage. In your non-Exadata environments, you typically work with your storage administrator to identify candidate ASM disks or storage array LUNs, but on Exadata, you're not sure where to find available storage or how to make free storage available for ASM disk groups.

Solution

In this recipe, we will demonstrate how to identify Exadata grid disks using CellCLI commands and create Oracle ASM disk groups on your Exadata grid disks.

Begin by using Exadata storage server `cellcli` commands to list existing grid disks and their sizes and pay special attention to the disk prefix. I'll only display the first two lines:

```
[oracle@cm01dbm01 ~]$ dcli -g ./cell_group cellcli -e list griddisk attributes name,size
cm01cel01: DATA_CD_00_cm01cel01        284G
cm01cel01: DATA_CD_01_cm01cel01        284G
... Additional grid disk details omitted for brevity
```

The goal is to determine if you have available capacity on your Exadata cell disks to create new grid disks—at this point, we may not want to actually do this depending on whether we already have ASM disk groups built on all of our grid disks across all cells. Run another `cellcli` command and sort the output to show the unique grid disk sizes:

```
[oracle@cm01dbm01 ~]$ dcli -g ./cell_group cellcli -e list griddisk attributes name,size \
> | awk '{print $1, $3}'|sort -u
cm01cel01: 141G
cm01cel01: 284G
cm01cel01: 29.125G
cm01cel01: 36.6875G
cm01cel01: 67G
cm01cel02: 141G
```

```
cm01cel02: 284G
cm01cel02: 29.125G
cm01cel02: 36.6875G
cm01cel02: 67G
cm01cel03: 141G
cm01cel03: 284G
cm01cel03: 29.125G
cm01cel03: 36.6875G
cm01cel03: 67G
[oracle@cm01dbm01 ~]$
```

From this output, we see a repeating pattern of grid disk sizes across all cell disks and all storage servers.

> **Note** This is often the expected configuration when grid disk management best practices are followed.

If you total the size for each grid disk, you arrive at a total size of 557.8395 GB. Now, validate the size of each cell disk to determine whether you have capacity to add grid disks:

```
[oracle@cm01dbm01 ~]$ dcli -g ./cell_group cellcli -e list celldisk where disktype=hardDisk
attributes name,size \
> | awk '{print $3}'|sort -u
528.734375G
557.859375G
[oracle@cm01dbm01 ~]$
```

As expected, in this output, we have two different cell disk sizes—one of the two cell disks that reside on physical disks where the System Area resides and ten with the larger size. Based on this and our grid disk sizes, we can see that in this case we do *not* have physical capacity to add additional Exadata grid disks. To ensure that you're actually using all the grid disks on your system, log in to one of your ASM instances and run the query in Listing 9-1.

Listing 9-1. lst09-01-asm-disk-details.sql

```
SQL> col name format a12 head 'Disk Group'
SQL> col total_mb format 999999999 head 'Total MB|Raw'
SQL> col free_mb format 999999999 head 'Free MB|Raw'
SQL> col avail_mb format 999999999 head 'Total MB|Usable'
SQL> col usable_mb format 999999999 head 'Free MB|Usable'
SQL> col cdisks format 99999 head 'Cell|Disksl'
SQL> select a.name,a.total_mb,a.free_mb,a.type,
    decode(a.type,'NORMAL',a.total_mb/2,'HIGH',a.total_mb/3) avail_mb,
    decode(a.type,'NORMAL',a.free_mb/2,'HIGH',a.free_mb/3) usable_mb,
    count(b.path) cdisks
    from v$asm_diskgroup a, v$asm_disk b
    where a.group_number=b.group_number
    group by a.name,a.total_mb,a.free_mb,a.type,
    decode(a.type,'NORMAL',a.total_mb/2,'HIGH',a.total_mb/3) ,
    decode(a.type,'NORMAL',a.free_mb/2,'HIGH',a.free_mb/3)
  order by 2,1
/
```

```
Disk         Total MB     Free MB                   Total MB     Free MB     # Cell
Group        (Raw)        (Raw)        Redundancy   (Usable)     (Usable)    Disks
----------   ----------   ----------   -----------  ----------   ---------   --------
DBFS_DG          894720       892264   NORMAL           447360      446132         30
SRECO_CM01      1352448       957128   NORMAL           676224      478564         36
RECO_CM01       2469888      2423820   NORMAL          1234944     1211910         36
SDATA_CM01      5197824      1371036   NORMAL          2598912      685518         36
DATA_CM01      10469376      2794528   NORMAL          5234688     1397264         36

SQL>
```

This query shows that the SRECO_CM01, RECO_CM01, SDATA_CM01, and DATA_CM01 are each using 36 grid disks with 12 physical disks per storage cell. This, in combination with our `cellcli` lists previously, confirms that our existing ASM disk groups already consume all of the available grid disks. To confirm, you can query the individual disk paths for one or more of your ASM disk groups. In Listing 9-2, the grid disks that make up the DATA_CM01 disk group are listed.

Listing 9-2. lst09-02-asm-disks.sql

```
SQL> select a.name,b.path
    from v$asm_diskgroup a, v$asm_disk b
    where a.group_number=b.group_number
    and a.name='DATA_CM01'
    order by 2,1
/

Disk Group      Disk
----------      ------------------------------------------
DATA_CM01       o/192.168.10.3/DATA_CD_00_cm01cel01
DATA_CM01       o/192.168.10.3/DATA_CD_01_cm01cel01
... lines omitted for brevity
DATA_CM01       o/192.168.10.5/DATA_CD_10_cm01cel03
DATA_CM01       o/192.168.10.5/DATA_CD_11_cm01cel03
... lines omitted for brevity
36 rows selected.

SQL>
```

Another way to validate this grid disk to ASM disk group mapping is to query the asmDiskGroupName and asmDiskName attributes of the griddisk object in `cellcli`. Following is an abbreviated output:

```
[root@cm01cel01 ~]# cellcli -e list griddisk attributes name,asmDiskGroupName,asmDiskname
        DATA_CD_00_cm01cel01        DATA_CM01       DATA_CD_00_CM01CEL01
        DATA_CD_01_cm01cel01        DATA_CM01       DATA_CD_01_CM01CEL01
        DATA_CD_02_cm01cel01        DATA_CM01       DATA_CD_02_CM01CEL01
        DATA_CD_03_cm01cel01        DATA_CM01       DATA_CD_03_CM01CEL01
        DATA_CD_04_cm01cel01        DATA_CM01       DATA_CD_04_CM01CEL01
        DATA_CD_05_cm01cel01        DATA_CM01       DATA_CD_05_CM01CEL01
        DATA_CD_06_cm01cel01        DATA_CM01       DATA_CD_06_CM01CEL01
        DATA_CD_07_cm01cel01        DATA_CM01       DATA_CD_07_CM01CEL01
        DATA_CD_08_cm01cel01        DATA_CM01       DATA_CD_08_CM01CEL01
        DATA_CD_09_cm01cel01        DATA_CM01       DATA_CD_09_CM01CEL01
        DATA_CD_10_cm01cel01        DATA_CM01       DATA_CD_10_CM01CEL01
        DATA_CD_11_cm01cel01        DATA_CM01       DATA_CD_11_CM01CEL01
```

CHAPTER 9 ■ STORAGE ADMINISTRATION

At this point in the example, we're a bit out of luck—to create new ASM disk groups, you need available, unallocated Exadata grid disks. If you attempt to create an ASM disk group, it will fail with the message shown in Listing 9-3.

Listing 9-3. lst09-03-create_diskgroup.sql

```
SQL> create diskgroup MY_DG
    normal redundancy
    disk 'o/*/DATA*'
    attribute 'compatible.rdbms' = '11.2.0.3',
              'compatible.asm' = '11.2.0.3.0',
              'cell.smart_scan_capable' = 'TRUE',
              'au_size' = '4M';
create diskgroup MY_DG
*
ERROR at line 1:
ORA-15018: diskgroup cannot be created
ORA-15029: disk 'o/192.168.10.5/DATA_CD_11_cm01cel03' is already mounted by
this instance

SQL>
```

■ **Caution** With Exadata, grid disks and ASM disk groups are intimately related; when planning your overall storage design, these two entities should be planned in parallel. Not doing so may lead to situations where you exhaust available cell disk capacity, preventing additional grid disks and ASM disk groups from being created. This could impose a non-trivial impact if you have live databases on your Exadata Database Machine or if you have security requirements that mandate creating additional grid disks. To understand ASM-scoped and database-scoped security steps, please see Recipes 12-3 and 12-4.

To continue with this recipe, we're going to drop some ASM disk groups and the underlying grid disks so we can provide a working example. Assuming we've already dropped a handful of ASM disk groups and have also dropped the associated grid disks, let's resume by creating a new collection of grid disks:

```
[oracle@cm01dbm01 ~]$ dcli -g ./cell_group cellcli -e \
> create griddisk all harddisk prefix=SDATA, size=141G
cm01cel01: GridDisk SDATA_CD_00_cm01cel01 successfully created
cm01cel01: GridDisk SDATA_CD_01_cm01cel01 successfully created
... lines omitted for brevity
cm01cel02: GridDisk SDATA_CD_00_cm01cel02 successfully created
cm01cel02: GridDisk SDATA_CD_01_cm01cel02 successfully created
... lines omitted for brevity
cm01cel03: GridDisk SDATA_CD_00_cm01cel03 successfully created
cm01cel03: GridDisk SDATA_CD_01_cm01cel03 successfully created
... lines omitted for brevity
 [oracle@cm01dbm01 ~]$
```

After you've created or validated grid disks, you can create an ASM disk group:

```
SQL> select instance_name from v$instance;

INSTANCE_NAME
----------------
+ASM1
```

1. SQL> create diskgroup SDATA_CM01
2. normal redundancy
3. disk 'o/*/SDATA*'
4. attribute 'compatible.rdbms' = '11.2.0.3',
5.   'compatible.asm' = '11.2.0.3.0',
6.   'cell.smart_scan_capable' = 'TRUE',
7.   'au_size' = '4M';

```
Diskgroup created.

SQL>
```

Following is an explanation of what each line means:

- In line 1, we're simply creating the disk group with a name SDATA_CM01.
- In line 2, we're specifying ASM normal redundancy. With Exadata, there are two options—normal redundancy and high redundancy. Normal redundancy, in this case, means that Oracle will create a two-way mirror, mirroring primary extents to disks on one of the other storage servers.

Note Please see Recipe 9-4 for additional details about ASM redundancy options and implications on Exadata.

- Line 3 specifies the ASM disk string. There are three sections, divided by a /:
  - o indicates to search for disks over the Exadata storage network.
  - * tells the ASM instance to build the ASM disk group across all storage cells, listed by InfiniBand IP address in /etc/oracle/cell/network-config/cellip.ora.
  - SDATA* instructs the ASM instance to use grid disks prefixed with SDATA.
- Lines 4 through 7 specify ASM disk group attributes. If your RDBMS and Grid Infrastructure environments are running Oracle 11.2.0.3, the compatible settings in your ASM disk group should match your software versions. cell_smart_scan_capable=TRUE is the default on Exadata. Using an au_size of 4 MB is strongly recommended on Exadata based on the physical characteristics of the physical SAS disks and the I/O size used with the Exadata storage cells.

The net result of the CREATE DISKGROUP command above is to create an ASM disk group using all grid disks with prefix SDATA, spread across all storage cells listed in your cellip.ora file. Let's take a look at the grid disk details in Listing 9-4.

CHAPTER 9 ■ STORAGE ADMINISTRATION

Listing 9-4. lst09-04-asm-disks.sql

```
SQL> select a.name,b.path
    from v$asm_diskgroup a, v$asm_disk b
    where a.group_number=b.group_number
    and a.name='SDATA_CM01'
    order by 2,1
 /

Disk Group       Disk
----------       ------------------------------------------
SDATA_CM01       o/192.168.10.3/SDATA_CD_00_cm01cel01
SDATA_CM01       o/192.168.10.3/SDATA_CD_01_cm01cel01
... lines omitted for brevity
SDATA_CM01       o/192.168.10.4/SDATA_CD_00_cm01cel02
SDATA_CM01       o/192.168.10.4/SDATA_CD_01_cm01cel02
... lines omitted for brevity
SDATA_CM01       o/192.168.10.5/SDATA_CD_00_cm01cel03
SDATA_CM01       o/192.168.10.5/SDATA_CD_01_cm01cel03
... lines omitted for brevity
36 rows selected.

SQL>
```

From `cellcli` you can also determine which ASM disk group and ASM disk name is associated with your grid disks:

```
CellCLI> list griddisk where name like 'SDATA_.*' attributes name,asmDiskGroupName,asmDiskName
        SDATA_CD_00_cm01cel01     SDATA_CM01     SDATA_CD_00_CM01CEL01
        SDATA_CD_01_cm01cel01     SDATA_CM01     SDATA_CD_01_CM01CEL01
        ... Grid disks omitted for brevity
        SDATA_CD_11_cm01cel01     SDATA_CM01     SDATA_CD_11_CM01CEL01
CellCLI>
```

While this example represents a typical Exadata disk group configuration in which disk groups contain disks spread evenly across all storage servers, this practice is not *required*. You could build ASM disk groups on a subset of a storage server's grid disks or even a subset of grid disks within your storage grid, using a script similar to that in Listing 9-5.

Listing 9-5. lst09-05-create_diskgroup.sql

```
SQL> create diskgroup SDATA_CM01
    normal redundancy
    failgroup cm01cel01
    disk     'o/192.168.10.3/SDATA_CD_00_cm01cel01,
              o/192.168.10.3/SDATA_CD_01_cm01cel01'
    failgroup cm01ce0l2
    disk     'o/192.168.10.4/SDATA_CD_00_cm01cel02,
              o/192.168.10.4/SDATA_CD_01_cm01cel02'
    attribute 'compatible.rdbms' = '11.2.0.3',
              'compatible.asm' = '11.2.0.3.0',
```

```
            'cell.smart_scan_capable' = 'TRUE',
            'au_size' = '4M';
```

```
Diskgroup created.

SQL>
```

In this example, we're creating a four-disk ASM disk group using two grid disks from two of our storage cells. Note that in this case, we need to specify a failure group and the overall syntax and planning becomes a bit more complicated as compared to cases in which wild-carded cell server IP addresses and grid disks prefixes are provided in the CREATE DISKGROUP statement.

How It Works

The task of creating Oracle ASM disk groups entails not only using the CREATE DISKGROUP statement, but also understanding the relationship between ASM disk groups and Exadata grid disks. To learn more about the overall storage entity relationships on Exadata, please see Recipes 3-1 and 3-2.

In order to create ASM disk groups, you need available, unassigned Exadata grid disks.

> **Note** Please see Recipe 9-3 to learn how to find Exadata grid disks that are not assigned to an ASM disk group.

Once you identify candidate grid disks, use the CREATE DISKGROUP command to create your ASM disk groups. Here are some of the more important considerations to think about when creating ASM disk groups on Exadata:

- Simplicity is best on Exadata. Using wild-carded CREATE DISKGROUP syntax not only offers the most terse command syntax, but also ensures your ASM disk groups are spread evenly across your Exadata Storage Server disks.

- Oracle automatically assigns the proper failure groups, depending on your redundancy level, when you create ASM disk groups spanning all storage cells and grid disks.

- When capacity planning, take your redundancy specification into consideration. Normal redundancy will have the effect of reducing your usable storage to half the raw capacity, and high redundancy will shrink it to a third of your raw disk capacity.

- Take the time to plan grid disk prefix names and overall grid disk configuration in the context of your desired ASM disk group design.

- Make sure to set the appropriate compatible.asm and compatible.rdbms attributes when creating ASM disk groups.

- Whenever possible, use a 4 MB extent size when creating disk groups on ASM storage.

One of the nice things about ASM storage on Exadata is that the planning aspect is relatively straightforward and automatically handles some of the more complex aspects of ASM storage planning. As an Exadata administrator, you simply need to size your grid disks appropriately (ensuring to spread evenly across storage server), give them a meaningful prefix, and then build ASM disk groups on a wild-carded set of Exadata grid disks.

9-2. Properly Configuring ASM Disk Group Attributes on Exadata
Problem
You wish to properly configure your ASM disk group attributes when creating disk groups for Exadata.

Solution
There are a number of ASM disk group attributes that you can set when creating your disk groups, but the following are the most important:

- au_size: Set this to 4 MB.
- compatible.asm: Set this to the software version of your Grid Infrastructure home.
- compatible.rdms: Set this to the software version of your RDBMS home.
- cell.smart_scan_capable: Set this to TRUE. If this attribute is set to FALSE, Smart Scan will be disabled to segments that reside in the disk group.
- disk_repair_time: Leave this defaulted to 3.6 hours unless you're performing maintenance on a call and know that your outage window will be greater than 3.6 hours.

For example:

```
SQL> create diskgroup SDATA_CM01
    normal redundancy
    disk 'o/*/SDATA*'
    attribute 'compatible.rdbms' = '11.2.0.3.0',
              'compatible.asm' = '11.2.0.3.0',
              'cell.smart_scan_capable' = 'TRUE',
              'au_size' = '4M';

SQL> Disk group created
```

You can also alter an ASM disk group's attribute using the ALTER DISKGROUP command. For example, to change an ASM disk group's disk_repair_time attribute, issue the following SQL statement:

```
SQL> alter diskgroup RECO_CM01
set attribute 'disk_repair_time'='7.2h'
/
Diskgroup altered.
SQL>
```

■ **Note** When altering ASM disk group attributes, some attributes will not take effect retroactively. For example, if you modify the au_size of an ASM disk group, the new allocation unit size will only impact the behavior for new extents; old extents will continue to be stored according to their old au_size.

How It Works

Specifying your ASM disk group attributes on Exadata is similar to non-Exadata Oracle ASM attributes, but on Exadata there are a few attributes that bear special consideration.

The au_size attribute determines your ASM allocation unit size, which is essentially the ASM stripe size, and governs how much data is written to one disk in an ASM disk group before continuing to the next disk. In Oracle 11gR2, Oracle defaults this AU_SIZE to 1 MB, but on Exadata, 4 MB is preferred and optimal for performance. When Oracle allocates extents, it does so in units of this AU size. If we consider an example when 64 MB of extents are required to be allocated for, say, an INSERT statement, it means 16 AUs will have data "copied to them" in 4 MB increments. If the storage characteristics of the segment/tablespace are such that the extent sizes are less than 4 MB, then (4 MB / extent size) worth of contiguous data is written to an ASM disk prior to moving to the next disk. If the extent size of the table is larger than 4 MB, then extents will span AUs. So, let's consider an example when the AU size is 4 MB and a tablespace's storage characteristics are such that the uniform extent length is 64 KB and 64 MB of data is being inserted:

- As data is being inserted, the first 64 KB goes into "AU #1", which happens to be on disk o/192.168.10.3/DATA_CD_00_cm01cel01
- Since 64K < AU_SIZE, up to 64 extents are written to o/192.168.10.3/DATA_CD_00_cm01cel01 (4MB / 64 KB = 64 extents)
- When the 65th extent is required to be allocated, Oracle will, say, jump to o/192.168.10.5/DATA_CD_00_cm01cel03 and write extents 65-128
- The next set of 64 extents will be written to, say, o/192.168.10.4/DATA_CD_00_cm01cel02
- This pattern continues until all 1000 64k extents are allocated

In this example, we randomly decided which physical disks to write extents to. In reality, ASM will balance this over time and ensure an even distribution of extents among all data files. Please see Recipe 9-6 to learn how to measure this.

Both the compatible.rdbms and compatible.asm attributes should be set to the version of the software you're running in the RDBMS Oracle Home and Grid Infrastructure Oracle Home.

■ **Note** In cases where your Grid Infrastructure software is patched to a higher level than your RDBMS binaries, it is possible to have a lower compatible.rdbms version. However, if you're patching your Exadata Database Machine on a regular basis, these will very likely be set to the same version and values.

The cell.smart_scan_capable attribute should be set to TRUE if you wish to utilize Smart Scan for your ASM disk group. There may be cases where you do not, but typically you should rely on your workload to dictate this and not override Exadata's most powerful feature with an ASM disk group configuration.

Oracle ASM will drop grid disks from an ASM disk group if they remain offline greater than the value specified by the disk_repair_time disk group attribute. With Exadata, this attribute specifies how long to wait before offlining disks based on the cell disk being offline, not the actual grid disk—this behavior is slightly different on Exadata as compared to non-Exadata ASM storage environments. When a physical disk goes offline due to disk failure, Exadata will automatically and immediately drop grid disks from ASM disk groups based on its *Pro-Active Disk Quarantine* functionality. However, if the entire cell goes offline, as is the case during cell server patching, ASM will wait for the value specified by the disk_repair_time attribute before dropping grid disks.

9-3. Identifying Unassigned Grid Disks

Problem

You are preparing to create Oracle ASM disk groups and need to identify unassigned Exadata grid disks to use as your disk group disks.

Solution

Log in to an Exadata Storage Server as `root` or `celladmin` and run the following `cellcli` command:

```
[root@cm01cel01 ~]# cellcli -e list griddisk attributes name,asmDiskGroupName,asmDiskname where asmDiskGroupName=\'\'
        SDATA_CD_00_cm01cel01
        SDATA_CD_01_cm01cel01
        ... Output omitted for brevity
[root@cm01cel01 ~]#
```

You can also use `dcli` to query unassigned grid disks across all of your storage cells:

```
[oracle@cm01dbm01 iorm]$ dcli -g ./cell_group "cellcli -e list \
> griddisk attributes name,asmDiskGroupName,asmDiskname where asmDiskGroupName=\'\'"
cm01cel01: SRECO_CD_00_cm01cel01
cm01cel01: SRECO_CD_01_cm01cel01
cm01cel01: SRECO_CD_02_cm01cel01
cm01cel01: SRECO_CD_03_cm01cel01
... Additional grid disks omitted for brevity
```

How It Works

When Oracle ASM disk groups are created on Exadata grid disks, the `asmDiskGroupName` attribute is populated on the grid disk object with the ASM disk group name. Grid disks that are not assigned to an ASM disk group have a null `asmDiskGroupName` attribute, which you can query using `cellcli` by escaping two single quotes with a backslash.

9-4. Configuring ASM Redundancy on Exadata

Problem

You wish to configure redundancy on your Oracle ASM disk groups to protect against disk drive failures in the Exadata Storage Servers.

Solution

In this recipe, we will demonstrate two examples—one showing how to create ASM disk groups with normal redundancy and one with high redundancy. Normal redundancy means two-way extent mirroring and high redundancy equates to three-way extent mirroring. With Exadata, disk protection is handled exclusively with Oracle ASM mirroring, or Oracle ASM redundancy. External redundancy on Exadata is not allowed.

Normal Redundancy

Listing 9-6 demonstrates what it looks like to create an ASM disk group with normal redundancy.

Listing 9-6. lst09-06-create-diskgroup.sql

```
SQL> create diskgroup SDATA_CM01
    normal redundancy
    disk 'o/*/SDATA*'
    attribute 'compatible.rdbms' = '11.2.0.3',
              'compatible.asm' = '11.2.0.3.0',
              'cell.smart_scan_capable' = 'TRUE',
              'au_size' = '4M';

Diskgroup created.

SQL>
```

If we take a look at the raw and usable capacity numbers from V$ASM_DISKGROUP, we can see that the usable capacity is half the raw capacity of the disk group (see Listing 9-7).

Listing 9-7. lst09-07-asm-normalredundancy.sql

```
SQL> col name format a12 head 'Disk Group'
SQL> col total_mb format 999999999 head 'Total MB|Raw'
SQL> col free_mb format 999999999 head 'Free MB|Raw'
SQL> col avail_mb format 999999999 head 'Total MB|Usable'
SQL> col usable_mb format 999999999 head 'Free MB|Usable'
SQL> col cdisks format 99999 head 'Cell|Disks'
SQL> select a.name,a.total_mb,a.free_mb,a.type,
    decode(a.type,'NORMAL',a.total_mb/2,'HIGH',a.total_mb/3) avail_mb,
    decode(a.type,'NORMAL',a.free_mb/2,'HIGH',a.free_mb/3) usable_mb,
    count(b.path) cdisks
    from v$asm_diskgroup a, v$asm_disk b
    where a.group_number=b.group_number
    and a.name='SDATA_CM01'
    group by a.name,a.total_mb,a.free_mb,a.type,
    decode(a.type,'NORMAL',a.total_mb/2,'HIGH',a.total_mb/3) ,
    decode(a.type,'NORMAL',a.free_mb/2,'HIGH',a.free_mb/3)
    order by 2,1
 /
```

Disk Group	Total MB (Raw)	Free MB (Raw)	Redundancy	Total MB (Usable)	Free MB (Usable)	# Cell Disks
SDATA_CM01	5197824	5197320	NORMAL	2598912	2598660	36

```
SQL>
```

You can see the disks that make up our newly creating disk group by running the script in Listing 9-8.

Listing 9-8. lst09-08-asm-disks.sql

```
SQL> select a.name,b.path,b.state,a.type,b.failgroup
    from v$asm_diskgroup a, v$asm_disk b
    where a.group_number=b.group_number
    and a.name='SDATA_CM01'
    order by 2,1
  /

Disk Group   Disk                                      State     Redundancy   Failgroup
----------   ---------------------------------------   -------   ----------   ---------
SDATA_CM01   o/192.168.10.3/SDATA_CD_00_cm01cel01      NORMAL    NORMAL       CM01CEL01
SDATA_CM01   o/192.168.10.3/SDATA_CD_01_cm01cel01      NORMAL    NORMAL       CM01CEL01
... lines omitted for brevity

36 rows selected.

SQL>
```

High Redundancy

Let's now try to create an ASM disk group with high redundancy on our Quarter Rack:

```
SQL> create diskgroup SDATA_CM01
    high redundancy
    disk 'o/*/SDATA*'
    attribute 'compatible.rdbms' = '11.2.0.3',
              'compatible.asm' = '11.2.0.3.0',
              'cell.smart_scan_capable' = 'TRUE',
              'au_size' = '4M';
create diskgroup SDATA_CM01
*
ERROR at line 1:
ORA-15018: diskgroup cannot be created
ORA-15067: command or option incompatible with diskgroup redundancy

SQL>
```

As you can see, the CREATE DISKGROUP command failed. On an Exadata Quarter Rack, Oracle only supports normal redundancy because there are only three failure groups, one for each cell. While this certainly seems like it should be enough failure groups to support three extent mirrors, the challenges comes with Oracle's requirement on OCR and voting disks. With high redundancy ASM disk groups, Oracle requires five failure groups. Since Oracle cannot guarantee that you won't place your OCR/voting disks on this ASM disk group, it simply prevents you from creating it. This being said, the syntax above for creating a high redundancy ASM disk group is valid for the Half Rack and Full Rack configurations.

How It Works

Mirroring protects data by storing copies of data across different disks, providing access to user data in the event of a disk failure. When you create an ASM disk group, you specify a level of redundancy—this redundancy level dictates how many copies of data are maintained:

- Normal redundancy = two-way mirror
- High redundancy = three-way mirror
- External redundancy = no ASM mirroring; ASM uses mirroring functionality in the storage array/subsystem, if available, to provide protection

With Exadata, Oracle protects and mirrors storage *exclusively* with ASM normal or high redundancy; there is no external redundancy alternative on Exadata.

> **Note** You can elect to configure ASM disk groups with no mirroring (that is, no redundancy), even on Exadata, but this practice is not recommended. Disk drives are one of the hardware components that are typically most prone to failure.

The redundancy level controls how many disk failures are tolerated without ASM un-mounting the disk group or losing data.

When ASM allocates an extent for a mirrored file, it allocates a *primary* copy and one or two *mirror* copies. Oracle places the mirror copy on a disk that's part of a different *failure group*. Failure groups are where mirror copies are stored. If you lost disks in either the primary location or failure group(s) (but not both or all), Oracle would continue to operate normally on the surviving copy.

ASM doesn't mirror physical disks or LUNs like traditional RAID—it mirrors database *extents*. This is a very important design aspect of ASM—with normal or high redundancy, extents are mirrored on sectors from disks on one or more failure groups. These failure groups consist of disks different from the primary extents.

On Oracle Exadata, Oracle always places mirrored extents on grid disks located in a different storage server. This provides the flexibility that if you lost an entire storage server, you would still have access to either the primary or mirrored extents.

> **Note** This also means that you can reboot a storage cell, patch it, or otherwise take disks offline in a storage cell without impacting storage availability.

When ASM disk group redundancy is normal or high, database extents in a file for the disk group are mirrored to a failure group. As such, failure groups are defined at the ASM disk group level. Again, normal redundancy means two copies of an extent are created, one for the primary extent and one in a failure group. Loss of either disk, but not both, will provide uninterrupted availability. For high redundancy, three copies (one primary and two failure group copies) are created. In this configuration, Oracle can tolerate two failed disks across multiple failure groups.

Each disk in a disk group can belong to one and only one failure group. Failure groups should all be the same size, or availability is impacted. With normal redundancy, at least two failure groups are required; for high redundancy, three failure groups are required. On Exadata, Oracle ASM creates a set of failure groups for each cell.

One thing that's interesting about Oracle ASM is that if insufficient disks are available to satisfy mirroring based on a redundancy level, Oracle will do as much as it can to mirror and then subsequently allocate remaining mirrors when sufficient disks are available.

Let's walk through how Oracle allocates an extent with normal redundancy ASM disk groups:

- First, the primary extent is allocated on a primary disk (in the disk group).
- Next, ASM creates the second extent/copy on a different failure group from the primary copy.
- Each copy is on a disk in a different failure group, so loss of all disks in a failure group does not result in data loss.

A failure group is simply a subset of disks within a disk group. Failure groups always exist, whether they're manually created or not.

On Exadata, a failure group is created on each storage server. In the following examples, we're using an Exadata Quarter Rack, with three storage servers as indicated by the three InfiniBand IP addresses in the disk strings, each with 12 physical disks:

```
SQL> select a.name,b.path,b.state,a.type,b.failgroup
    from v$asm_diskgroup a, v$asm_disk b
    where a.group_number=b.group_number
    and a.name like '%DATA%'
    order by 2,1
  /
```

Disk Group	Disk	State	Type	Failgroup
DATA_CM01	o/192.168.10.3/DATA_CD_00_cm01cel01	NORMAL	NORMAL	CM01CEL01
DATA_CM01	o/192.168.10.3/DATA_CD_01_cm01cel01	NORMAL	NORMAL	CM01CEL01
DATA_CM01	o/192.168.10.3/DATA_CD_02_cm01cel01	NORMAL	NORMAL	CM01CEL01

... lines omitted for brevity

36 rows selected.

SQL>

The ASM disk string is of the form o/<InfiniBand IP of the storage cell>/<Grid Disk name>. As you can see, 36 disks comprise the DATA_CM01 ASM disk group, and each disk has its own failure group assigned. You can also see that the redundancy type is normal, which means we've got two-way mirroring in place.

The failure group is assigned at the disk level. Extents are allocated and "striped" in chunks defined by the ASM allocation unit size, or au_size, as discussed in the How It Works section of Recipe 9-2. If, for example, you are formatting 64 MB worth of extents and a uniform extent size of 64 KB, Oracle allocates extents in the following manner:

- The primary extents for the first 64 KB extents are written to o/192.168.10.3/DATA_CD_00_cm01cel01
- Since the failure group for this disk is CM01CEL01, Oracle will choose a different failure group for the mirrored extents—in this case, it'll take a disk from either CM01CEL02 or CM01CEL03
- The next set of primary extents are written to o/192.168.10.5/DATA_CD_00_cm01cel03
- The mirrored extents for this next round are distributed to CM01CEL01 or CM01CEL02 disks
- The next primary set of 64 extents will be written to o/192.168.10.4/DATA_CD_00_cm01cel02
- The mirrored extents for these will distributed between CM01CEL01 and CM01CEL03

If you expand this example and consider high redundancy ASM disk groups, then steps in the second, fourth, and sixth bullets will write mirrored extents to disks in *both* the remaining failure groups.

One fact to note, as mentioned in the solution of this recipe, is that high redundancy is not supported on an Exadata Quarter Rack.

In summary, Oracle ASM on Exadata mirrors storage similarly to how extents are mirrored on non-Exadata systems. The primary differences are that external redundancy is not an option and that Exadata automatically places mirrored extents on different storage servers. Since external redundancy is not an option with Exadata, be sure to take into consideration your desired protection level when conducting Exadata storage capacity planning.

9-5. Displaying ASM Partner Disk Relationships on Exadata

Problem

As an Exadata administrator, you wish to understand or confirm where ASM disk group mirror extents reside in order to validate that your database storage platform is offering a suitable level of disk protection.

Solution

In an Oracle ASM instance, X$KFDPARTNER provides information on the ASM disk group partner relationship. Log in to your Oracle ASM instance and connect as SYSASM, and then issue the query in Listing 9-9 to demonstrate this relationship.

■ **Note** In the following query, we're restricting our output to examine the ASM partner disk relationships to the third cell disk on each of our three storage cells and the DATA_CM01 ASM disk group.

Listing 9-9. lst09-09-asm-partnerdisk.sql

```
SQL> SELECT dg.name,
    d.disk_number "Disk#",
    d.path disk_path,
    p.number_kfdpartner ,
    pd.path partner_path
    FROM x$kfdpartner p,
    v$asm_disk d,
    v$asm_disk pd,
    v$asm_diskgroup dg
    WHERE p.disk=d.disk_number
    and p.grp=d.group_number
    and p.number_kfdpartner = pd.disk_number
    and p.grp=pd.group_number
    and d.group_number=dg.group_number
    and dg.name='DATA_CM01'
    and d.path like '%DATA_CD_03%'
    ORDER BY 1, 2, 3;
```

Disk Group	Primary Disk	Primary Path	Partner Disk	Partner Path
DATA_CM01	3	o/192.168.10.5/DATA_CD_03_cm01cel03	29	o/192.168.10.3/DATA_CD_03_cm01cel01
DATA_CM01	3		15	o/192.168.10.4/DATA_CD_06_cm01cel02
DATA_CM01	3		19	o/192.168.10.4/DATA_CD_04_cm01cel02

```
DATA_CM01      3                           22 o/192.168.10.4/DATA_CD_08_cm01cel02
DATA_CM01      3                           23 o/192.168.10.4/DATA_CD_03_cm01cel02
DATA_CM01      3                           26 o/192.168.10.3/DATA_CD_04_cm01cel01
DATA_CM01      3                           32 o/192.168.10.3/DATA_CD_11_cm01cel01
DATA_CM01      3                           34 o/192.168.10.3/DATA_CD_08_cm01cel01
... Additional disks omitted

24 rows selected.

SQL>
```

This output is telling us the following:

- Each disk has eight partner disks
- The partner disks for each of the disks are unique and balanced across the remaining two failure groups but *not* located inside the same failure group. To illustrate this, consider primary disk number 3, o/192.168.10.5/DATA_CD_03_cm01cel03. This resides on cell server 192.168.10.5 and its partner disks are split evenly between 192.168.10.3 and 192.168.10.4

How It Works

With Oracle ASM normal redundancy or high redundancy, Oracle mirrors extents in an ASM disk group to one or more partner disks. When mirroring extents, ASM uses a design concept called Disk Partnership. Each disk in a normal or high redundancy disk group has one or more partners, used to mirror extents from the primary disk. If you lose a primary disk, as well as the partner disk where extents are mirrored, you'll experience loss of access to data.

Oracle ASM tracks partner disk relationships for every disk in a disk group inside the Partnership Status Table, or PST. Oracle reserves AU #1 on every ASM disk for the PST. So the PST specifies the list of partner disks for each disk.

Oracle Exadata environments have a minimum of 36 physical disks in a Quarter Rack and since this qualifies as an environment with "a lot of disks," ASM will maintain eight partner disks for each primary disk in the PST. This means that for every primary extent allocated, Oracle will select from any one of the partner disks to write the mirrored extents. For ASM disk groups configured with normal redundancy, Oracle will create the mirror extent on one of the eight partner disks. With high redundancy, two mirror extents will be created on different partner disks.

It's worth stating again—ASM mirrors extents to partner disks on a *different* failure group. On Exadata, there is one failure group per storage cell.

9-6. Measuring ASM Extent Balance on Exadata
Problem

To ensure that I/O requests are optimally balanced and serviced across Exadata Storage Server disks, you wish to show the distribution of ASM extents across these Exadata disks in your Exadata environment.

Solution

In this recipe, we will provide several SQL scripts that will enable you to measure your database extent balance across Oracle ASM grid disks. On Exadata and on all Oracle ASM environments, a well-balanced distribution of extents is important for both performance and capacity management reasons.

Measuring Your ASM Extent Balance

Log in to SQL*Plus to an Oracle ASM instance and connect as SYSASM. Then, run the query in Listing 9-10 to determine your extent balance across your Exadata grid disks.

Listing 9-10. lst09-10-asm-extentbalance.sql

```
SQL> select distinct name,
    maxtpd, mintpd, maxfpd, minfpd,
    round(100*((maxtpd-mintpd)/maxfpd),2) var1,
    round(100*((maxfpd-minfpd)/maxfpd),2) var2
    from (
    select dg.name,
    dg.total_mb tpdg,
    dg.free_mb fpdg,
    d.total_mb tpd,
    d.free_mb fpd,
    max(d.total_mb) over (partition by dg.name) maxtpd,
    min(d.total_mb) over (partition by dg.name) mintpd,
    max(d.free_mb) over (partition by dg.name) maxfpd,
    min(d.free_mb) over (partition by dg.name) minfpd
    from v$asm_diskgroup dg, v$asm_disk d
    where dg.group_number=d.group_number)
 /

Disk        Max disk    Min disk    Max free    Min free    Disk size   Extent imbalance
Group       size (MB)   size (MB)   size (MB)   size (MB)   variance    variance
---------   ---------   ---------   ---------   ---------   ---------   ----------------
DATA_CM01      290816      290816       78336       76924         .00               1.80
DBFS_DG         29824       29824       29800       29424         .00               1.26
RECO_CM01       68608       68608       67436       67228         .00                .31
SDATA_CM01     144384      144384      144376      144360         .00                .01

SQL>
```

This query is telling us the following:

- We have four ASM disk groups.

- The maximum and minimum disk sizes are the same for all disk groups. This is telling us that each of the grid disks in each disk group is the same size, which is an optimal configuration for both Exadata and non-Exadata systems.

- The maximum free space and minimum free space for each ASM disk group are outlined in columns 4 and 5. As extents are allocated in an ASM disk group, Oracle will attempt to evenly create extents across the disks that comprise the disk group. Note the small delta between the disk with the most and least amount of free space.

- The disk size variance column shows the variance in grid disk sizes for each ASM disk group. In our case, there is no variance as our underlying grid disks are the same size.

- The extent imbalance variance column represents the difference between the disk group disk with the greatest and least amount of free space. Ideally, we would see numbers close to 0%. This would indicate that Oracle ASM is balancing extents as it should (evenly) across disks in an ASM disk group.

Let's manually rebalance our DATA_CM01 disk group and see if we can get the 1.8% number closer to zero. After rebalancing the disk group, the script in Listing 9-11 will display the extent imbalance variance.

```sql
SQL> alter diskgroup data_cm01 rebalance power 11;

Diskgroup altered.

SQL>
```

Listing 9-11. lst09-11-asm-extentbal-variance.sql

```sql
SQL> select distinct name,
    round(100*((maxfpd-minfpd)/maxfpd),2) var2
    from (
    select dg.name,
    dg.total_mb tpdg,
    dg.free_mb fpdg,
    d.total_mb tpd,
    d.free_mb fpd,
    max(d.total_mb) over (partition by dg.name) maxtpd,
    min(d.total_mb) over (partition by dg.name) mintpd,
    max(d.free_mb) over (partition by dg.name) maxfpd,
    min(d.free_mb) over (partition by dg.name) minfpd
    from v$asm_diskgroup dg, v$asm_disk d
    where dg.group_number=d.group_number
    and dg.name='DATA_CM01')
/

                    Extent imbalance
Disk Group             variance
----------          --------------------
DATA_CM01                .89

SQL>
```

As we can see, rebalancing the ASM disk group yielded a lower variance in free space.

Measuring Your ASM Partner Disk Balance

Now, measure the ASM partner disk balance using the script in Listing 9-12. Ideally, you would have a near perfect balance of ASM partner disk counts and partner disk sizes to the primary disks that make up an ASM disk group.

Listing 9-12. lst09-12-asm-partnerdisk-balance.sql

```sql
SQL> select
        g.name "Diskgroup",
        max(p.cnt)-min(p.cnt)
        "PImbalance",
        100*(max(p.pspace)-min(p.pspace))/max(p.pspace)
        "SImbalance",
        count(distinct p.fgrp) "FailGrpCnt",
```

```
            sum(p.inactive)/2
        "Inactive"
    from
        v$asm_diskgroup g ,
        (
            select
                x.grp grp,
                x.disk disk,
                sum(x.active) cnt,
                greatest(sum(x.total_mb/d.total_mb),0.0001) pspace,
                d.failgroup fgrp,
                count(*)-sum(x.active) inactive
            from
                v$asm_disk d ,
                (
                    select
                        y.grp grp,
                        y.disk disk,
                        z.total_mb*y.active_kfdpartner total_mb,
                        y.active_kfdpartner active
                    from
                        x$kfdpartner y,
                        v$asm_disk z
                    where
                        y.number_kfdpartner = z.disk_number and
                        y.grp = z.group_number
                ) x
            where
                d.group_number = x.grp and
                d.disk_number = x.disk and
                d.group_number <> 0 and
                d.state = 'NORMAL' and
                d.mount_status = 'CACHED'
            group by
                x.grp, x.disk, d.failgroup
        ) p
    where
        g.group_number = p.grp
    group by     g.name
    /
```

Diskgroup Name	Partner Count Imbalance	Partner Space % Imbalance	Inactive Failgroup Count	Partnership Count
DATA_CM01	0	.0	3	0
DBFS_DG	1	12.5	3	0
RECO_CM01	0	.0	3	0
SDATA_CM01	0	.0	3	0

```
SQL>
```

As we can see, other than the DBFS_DG disk group, which contains our OCR and voting disks and resides on the cell disks that do not contain System Area storage, the partner disk counts are balanced evenly.

> **Note** To learn more about ASM partner disks, please see Recipe 9-5.

How It Works

One of the many design benefits of Oracle ASM is its inherent and automatic feature of balancing extents across disks in an ASM disk group. With many disks in a disk group, as is the case on Exadata, you should generally be able to measure a very even extent distribution across physical disks. A smooth extent distribution is one factor that enables high IOPs scalability in an Exadata storage grid as multiple physical disks typically work in tandem to service I/O requests.

On Exadata, you generally want to strive for extent balance across disks in Oracle ASM disk groups. By periodically examining the variance between V$ASM_DISK.FREE_MB for disks within the same ASM disk group, you can see this and take corrective rebalance actions if you see variances. Oracle ASM will automatically rebalance an ASM disk group when disks are added to or dropped from the disk group, but organic extent allocation and de-allocation, especially in cases when databases and their underlying tablespace segments are dropped and created, could cause an extent imbalance. Extent imbalances within an ASM disk group can impact I/O performance.

Additionally, as an administrator, it is ideal to create grid disks that are the same size. Doing so will result in more efficient space utilization across the disks in your Exadata storage grid, which also can have a downstream performance impact.

9-7. Rebuilding Cell Disks
Problem

You need to rebuild your Exadata cell disks to meet a specific requirement, such as introducing grid disk interleaving.

> **Note** You should *very* rarely need to rebuild cell disks. Depending on your situation, Exadata will automatically create and rebuild your cell disks for many types of storage server and disk failure. Please see the How It Works section of this recipe for additional details.

Recipe 9-8 discusses the concept of interleaving and interleaved grid disks.

Solution

In this recipe, we will show you how to rebuild your storage server's cell disks. Specifically, we will demonstrate how to do the following:

1. Prepare to recreate your ASM disk groups
2. Prepare to recreate your grid disks
3. Back up and validate your Oracle Cluster Registry (OCR) and voting disks prior to dropping ASM disk groups
4. Create local copies of your control files and server parameter file (spfile)

CHAPTER 9 ■ STORAGE ADMINISTRATION

5. Stop Oracle databases and ClusterWare resources on your compute nodes
6. Drop ASM disk groups and Exadata grid disks
7. Drop your Exadata cell disks
8. Create new cell disks and grid disks
9. Start Oracle services on the compute nodes
10. Create the DBFS_DG ASM disk group to store the OCR and voting disks
11. Restore your OCR and voting disks
12. Create your remaining ASM disk groups
13. Validate the health of your cluster

■ **Note** The steps provided in this recipe are destructive in nature and will cause a clusterwide outage. While you can perform these steps on an individual storage cell, we will elect to demonstrate rebuilding cell disks on all storage cells because you would typically only perform these steps to change your interleaving attributes, which should be consistent across storage cells.

Prepare to Recreate Your ASM Disk Groups

First, connect to an Oracle ASM instance via SQL*Plus as SYSASM and run the query in Listing 9-13 to display your ASM disk group configuration and disk group attributes.

Listing 9-13. lst09-13-asm-disk-details-prep.sql

```
SQL> select a.name,a.total_mb,a.free_mb,a.type,
    decode(a.type,'NORMAL',a.total_mb/2,'HIGH',a.total_mb/3) avail_mb,
    decode(a.type,'NORMAL',a.free_mb/2,'HIGH',a.free_mb/3) usable_mb,
    count(b.path) cdisks
    from v$asm_diskgroup a, v$asm_disk b
    where a.group_number=b.group_number
    group by a.name,a.total_mb,a.free_mb,a.type,
    decode(a.type,'NORMAL',a.total_mb/2,'HIGH',a.total_mb/3) ,
    decode(a.type,'NORMAL',a.free_mb/2,'HIGH',a.free_mb/3)
    order by 2,1
 /
```

Disk Group	Total MB Raw	Free MB Raw	Redund.	Total MB Usable	Free MB Usable	Cell Disks
DBFS_DG	894720	686876	NORMAL	447360	343438	30
SRECO_CM01	1352448	1351932	NORMAL	676224	675966	36
RECO_CM01	2469888	2257496	NORMAL	1234944	1128748	36
SDATA_CM01	5197824	5111392	NORMAL	2598912	2555696	36
DATA_CM01	10469376	2785132	NORMAL	5234688	1392566	36

5 rows selected.

Next, execute the following query to show how many grid disks are used per storage cell per ASM disk group:

```
SQL> select a.name,b.failgroup,count(*) cnt
    from v$asm_diskgroup a, v$asm_disk b
    where a.group_number=b.group_number
    group by a.name,b.failgroup
 /
```

Disk Group	Cell	Disks per Cell
DBFS_DG	CM01CEL01	10
DBFS_DG	CM01CEL02	10
DBFS_DG	CM01CEL03	10
DATA_CM01	CM01CEL01	12
DATA_CM01	CM01CEL02	12
DATA_CM01	CM01CEL03	12
RECO_CM01	CM01CEL01	12
RECO_CM01	CM01CEL02	12
RECO_CM01	CM01CEL03	12
SDATA_CM01	CM01CEL01	12
SDATA_CM01	CM01CEL02	12
SDATA_CM01	CM01CEL03	12
SRECO_CM01	CM01CEL01	12
SRECO_CM01	CM01CEL02	12
SRECO_CM01	CM01CEL03	12

15 rows selected.

Finally, list your ASM disk group attributes. These will be required to recreate our ASM disk groups:

```
SQL> select a.group_number,b.name dgname,a.name,a.value
     from v$asm_attribute a,
     v$asm_diskgroup b
     where a.name in ('au_size','disk_repair_time',
                    'compatible.rdbms','compatible.asm')
     and a.group_number=b.group_number
     order by b.name,a.name
 /
```

Group Number	DiskGroup Name	ASM Attribute Name	ASM Attribute Value
1	DATA_CM01	au_size	4194304
1	DATA_CM01	compatible.asm	11.2.0.3.0
1	DATA_CM01	compatible.rdbms	11.2.0.3.0
1	DATA_CM01	disk_repair_time	3.6h

... Other disk groups omitted for brevity

20 rows selected.

SQL>

With the information collected above, we recommended documenting your current configuration and building create diskgroup scripts to prepare for ASM disk group recreation.

Prepare to Recreate Your Grid Disks

Next, run CellCLI commands with dcli to list your Exadata grid disk configuration. Log in to a compute node and run the following command:

```
[oracle@cm01dbm01 ~]$ dcli -g ./cell_group cellcli -e list griddisk attributes
name,asmDiskGroupName,size | sort -u
cm01cel01: DATA_CD_00_cm01cel01          DATA_CM01        284G
cm01cel01: DATA_CD_01_cm01cel01          DATA_CM01        284G
cm01cel01: DATA_CD_02_cm01cel01          DATA_CM01        284G
... output omitted for brevity
[oracle@cm01dbm01 ~]$
```

■ **Note** Please see Recipes 7-6 and 7-7 for more information about using cellcli and dcli.

From the previous output, validate the grid disk names, associated ASM disk groups, and grid disk sizes. Pay special attention to grid disk prefix, which is the portion of each grid disk name preceding the CD string. Additionally, ensure that the grid disk sizes are uniform across cell disks and storage cells.

■ **Note** You should also capture the offset grid disk attribute to determine the order in which your grid disks were created on your cell disks. This is relevant from a performance standpoint as extents on the outer tracks of the physical hard disks will have shorter latencies and deliver better performance than the inner tracks. Recipe 9-8 discusses this in more detail.

Back Up and Validate Your Oracle Cluster Registry and Voting Disks

Once you have your ASM disk group and Exadata grid disk configuration understood and documented, you should back up your OCR and voting disks prior to destroying your Exadata grid disks and cell disks. This is necessary because we will be dropping the ASM disk group that stores the OCR and voting disks, DBFS_DG. Log in as root to your compute nodes and manually perform an OCR backup:

```
[root@cm01dbm01 ~]# /u01/app/11.2.0.3/grid/bin/ocrconfig -manualbackup

cm01dbm01     2012/09/12 23:22:28
                   /u01/app/11.2.0.3/grid/cdata/cm01-cluster/backup_20120912_232228.ocr
cm01dbm01     2011/05/03 16:11:19
                   /u01/app/11.2.0/grid/cdata/cm01-cluster/backup_20110503_161119.ocr
[root@cm01dbm01 ~]#
```

Once complete, validate your OCR backup using the `ocrconfig -showbackup` command. The line in bold represents the OCR file created from the manual backup above:

```
[root@cm01dbm01 ~]# /u01/app/11.2.0.3/grid/bin/ocrconfig -showbackup

cm01dbm01     2012/09/12 20:59:44     /u01/app/11.2.0.3/grid/cdata/cm01-cluster/backup00.ocr
cm01dbm01     2012/09/12 16:59:44     /u01/app/11.2.0.3/grid/cdata/cm01-cluster/backup01.ocr
cm01dbm01     2012/09/12 12:59:44     /u01/app/11.2.0.3/grid/cdata/cm01-cluster/backup02.ocr
cm01dbm01     2012/09/11 12:59:42     /u01/app/11.2.0.3/grid/cdata/cm01-cluster/day.ocr
cm01dbm01     2012/08/31 01:28:40     /u01/app/11.2.0.3/grid/cdata/cm01-cluster/week.ocr
cm01dbm01     2012/09/12 23:22:28     /u01/app/11.2.0.3/grid/cdata/cm01-cluster/
backup_20120912_232228.ocr
```
**cm01dbm01   2011/05/03 16:11:19   /u01/app/11.2.0/grid/cdata/cm01-cluster/
backup_20110503_161119.ocr**
```
[root@cm01dbm01 ~]#
```

You should also make it a practice to validate the health of your OCR file using the `ocrcheck` command as well as list the mirrored copies of your voting disks:

```
[root@cm01dbm01 bin]# /u01/app/11.2.0.3/grid/bin/ocrcheck
Status of Oracle Cluster Registry is as follows :
         Version                  :          3
         Total space (kbytes)     :     262120
         Used space (kbytes)      :       3464
         Available space (kbytes) :     258656
         ID                       : 1833511320
         Device/File Name         :    +DBFS_DG
                                    Device/File integrity check succeeded
                                    Device/File not configured
                                    Device/File not configured
                                    Device/File not configured
                                    Device/File not configured
         Cluster registry integrity check succeeded
         Logical corruption check succeeded
[root@cm01dbm01 bin]# /u01/app/11.2.0.3/grid/bin/crsctl query css votedisk
##  STATE   File Universal Id                 File Name                                    Disk group
--  -----   -----------------                 ---------                                    ----------
 1. ONLINE  948f35d3d9c44f94bfe7bb831758104a  (o/192.168.10.4/DBFS_DG_CD_06_cm01cel02)     [DBFS_DG]
 2. ONLINE  ac4207356f734f3cbff345397a9b217e  (o/192.168.10.5/DBFS_DG_CD_05_cm01cel03)     [DBFS_DG]
 3. ONLINE  8449ec381d9e4f8fbf6040fe4daa5bb3  (o/192.168.10.3/DBFS_DG_CD_05_cm01cel01)     [DBFS_DG]
Located 3 voting disk(s).
[root@cm01dbm01 bin]#
```

Create Local Copies of Your Control Files and Server Parameter Files

Prior to shutting down your Oracle databases, you should confirm that you have validated control file backups and a file system copy of your `spfile`, as both of these types of files will be stored in ASM disk groups that will be dropped as part of the procedure in this recipe. Let's start creating backups of each database's `spfile` to a file system directory.

Log in to a compute node as the Oracle software owner, launch SQL*Plus, connect as SYSDBA, and execute the following `create pfile` command. Repeat for each database on our Exadata Database Machine:

```
[oracle@cm01dbm01 ~]$ sqlplus / as sysdba

SQL*Plus: Release 11.2.0.3.0 Production on Wed Sep 12 23:34:52 2012

Copyright (c) 1982, 2011, Oracle.  All rights reserved.


Connected to:
Oracle Database 11g Enterprise Edition Release 11.2.0.3.0 - 64bit Production
With the Partitioning, Real Application Clusters, Automatic Storage Management, OLAP,
Data Mining and Real Application Testing options

SYS @ dwprd1> create pfile='/home/oracle/initdwprd.ora' from spfile;

File created.

Elapsed: 00:00:00.03
SYS @ dwprd1>
```

Stop Your Oracle Databases, ClusterWare Resources, and Drop ASM Disk Groups

Next, stop each of your Exadata databases using `srvctl stop database`. Log in as the Oracle software owner and run the following command:

```
[oracle@cm01dbm01 ~]$ srvctl stop database -d visy
[oracle@cm01dbm01 ~]$ srvctl stop database -d visx
[oracle@cm01dbm01 ~]$ srvctl stop database -d dwprd
[oracle@cm01dbm01 ~]$
```

When complete, log in to a compute node as the Grid Infrastructure owner and drop your ASM disk groups:

```
SQL> select name from v$asm_diskgroup;

NAME
------------------------------
DATA_CM01
DBFS_DG
RECO_CM01
SDATA_CM01
SRECO_CM01

SQL> drop diskgroup sreco_cm01 including contents;
Diskgroup dropped.
SQL> drop diskgroup sdata_cm01 including contents;
Diskgroup dropped.
SQL> drop diskgroup reco_cm01 including contents;
Diskgroup dropped.
SQL> drop diskgroup data_cm01 including contents;
Diskgroup dropped.
SQL>
```

Leave the DBFS_DG disk group available so that we can shut down our Oracle cluster services in the next step.

■ **Note** You *could* elect to stop your cluster resources and services using `crsctl stop cluster` and `crsctl stop crs`, followed by dropping your Exadata grid disks, but in this recipe, we will show the process of manually tearing down each storage component independently.

Now, stop you Oracle cluster services by logging in as root on one compute node and running the following crsctl command:

```
[root@cm01dbm01 ~]# /u01/app/11.2.0.3/grid/bin/crsctl stop cluster -f -all
CRS-2673: Attempting to stop 'ora.crsd' on 'cm01dbm01'
CRS-2790: Starting shutdown of Cluster Ready Services-managed resources on 'cm01dbm01'
CRS-2673: Attempting to stop 'ora.cm01dbm02.vip' on 'cm01dbm01'
CRS-2673: Attempting to stop 'ora.LISTENER.lsnr' on 'cm01dbm01'
CRS-2673: Attempting to stop 'ora.LISTENER_SCAN1.lsnr' on 'cm01dbm01'
CRS-2673: Attempting to stop 'ora.LISTENER_SCAN2.lsnr' on 'cm01dbm01'
CRS-2673: Attempting to stop 'ora.registry.acfs' on 'cm01dbm01'
CRS-2673: Attempting to stop 'ora.DBFS_DG.dg' on 'cm01dbm01'
CRS-2673: Attempting to stop 'ora.LISTENER_SCAN3.lsnr' on 'cm01dbm01'
... lines omitted for brevity
```

After the cluster is stopped, log in to each compute node as root and stop Oracle CRS:

```
[root@cm01dbm01 ~]# /u01/app/11.2.0.3/grid/bin/crsctl stop crs
CRS-2791: Starting shutdown of Oracle High Availability Services-managed resources on 'cm01dbm01'
CRS-2673: Attempting to stop 'ora.drivers.acfs' on 'cm01dbm01'
CRS-2673: Attempting to stop 'ora.crf' on 'cm01dbm01'
CRS-2673: Attempting to stop 'ora.mdnsd' on 'cm01dbm01'
CRS-2677: Stop of 'ora.drivers.acfs' on 'cm01dbm01' succeeded
CRS-2677: Stop of 'ora.mdnsd' on 'cm01dbm01' succeeded
CRS-2677: Stop of 'ora.crf' on 'cm01dbm01' succeeded
CRS-2673: Attempting to stop 'ora.gipcd' on 'cm01dbm01'
CRS-2677: Stop of 'ora.gipcd' on 'cm01dbm01' succeeded
CRS-2673: Attempting to stop 'ora.gpnpd' on 'cm01dbm01'
CRS-2677: Stop of 'ora.gpnpd' on 'cm01dbm01' succeeded
CRS-2793: Shutdown of Oracle High Availability Services-managed resources on 'cm01dbm01' has completed
CRS-4133: Oracle High Availability Services has been stopped.
[root@cm01dbm01 ~]#
```

■ **Note** The commands to control, stop, start, and manage Oracle cluster services and resources on Exadata are no different from the administration commands used in any Oracle 11gR2 cluster.

Drop Your Grid Disks and Cell Disks

Once all Oracle database and Grid Infrastructure processes are down on each compute node, proceed to dropping your Exadata grid disks. Following we will use dcli from a compute node to issue cellcli commands on each storage cell. First, list your Exadata grid disks:

■ **Note** In the example in this recipe, we will only be dropping and creating grid disks and cell disks on our SAS disks; flash disks will not be changed.

```
[oracle@cm01dbm01 ~]$ dcli -g ./cell_group cellcli -e list griddisk where disktype=harddisk
cm01cel01: DATA_CD_00_cm01cel01        active
cm01cel01: DATA_CD_01_cm01cel01        active
cm01cel01: DATA_CD_02_cm01cel01        active
cm01cel01: DATA_CD_03_cm01cel01        active
cm01cel01: DATA_CD_04_cm01cel01        active
... output omitted for brevity
```

Next, drop your grid disks. In the following example, we'll drop each grid disk using its disk prefix with the force option:

```
[oracle@cm01dbm01 ~]$ dcli -g ./cell_group cellcli -e drop griddisk all prefix=SDATA force
cm01cel01: GridDisk SDATA_CD_00_cm01cel01 successfully dropped
cm01cel01: GridDisk SDATA_CD_01_cm01cel01 successfully dropped
cm01cel01: GridDisk SDATA_CD_02_cm01cel01 successfully dropped
... output omitted for brevity

[oracle@cm01dbm01 ~]$ dcli -g ./cell_group cellcli -e drop griddisk all prefix=DATA force
cm01cel01: GridDisk DATA_CD_00_cm01cel01 successfully dropped
cm01cel01: GridDisk DATA_CD_01_cm01cel01 successfully dropped
cm01cel01: GridDisk DATA_CD_02_cm01cel01 successfully dropped
... output omitted for brevity

[oracle@cm01dbm01 ~]$ dcli -g ./cell_group cellcli -e drop griddisk all prefix=SRECO force
... output omitted for brevity

[oracle@cm01dbm01 ~]$ dcli -g ./cell_group cellcli -e drop griddisk all prefix=RECO force
... output omitted for brevity

[oracle@cm01dbm01 ~]$ dcli -g ./cell_group cellcli -e drop griddisk all prefix=DBFS_DG force
... output omitted for brevity
```

When complete, you will have no grid disks available:

```
[oracle@cm01dbm01 ~]$ dcli -g ./cell_group cellcli -e list griddisk where disktype=harddisk
[oracle@cm01dbm01 ~]$
```

Now, proceed to dropping your Exadata cell disks. First, query the cell disk name and interleaving attribute:

```
[oracle@cm01dbm01 ~]$ dcli -g ./cell_group cellcli -e list celldisk where diskType=HardDisk
attributes name,interleaving
cm01cel01: CD_00_cm01cel01        normal_redundancy
cm01cel01: CD_01_cm01cel01        normal_redundancy
cm01cel01: CD_02_cm01cel01        normal_redundancy
... output omitted
```

Next, issue the following `cellcli` command through `dcli` to drop your cell disks:

```
[oracle@cm01dbm01 ~]$ dcli -g ./cell_group cellcli -e drop celldisk all harddisk force
cm01cel01: CellDisk CD_00_cm01cel01 successfully dropped
cm01cel01: CellDisk CD_01_cm01cel01 successfully dropped
cm01cel01: CellDisk CD_02_cm01cel01 successfully dropped
cm01cel01: CellDisk CD_03_cm01cel01 successfully dropped
... output omitted for brevity
```

Create New Cell Disks and Grid Disks

After the cell disks are dropped, proceed to recreate them using the following `cellcli` command. In this example, we will not specify cell disk interleaving but cover this topic in Recipe 9-8.

```
[oracle@cm01dbm01 ~]$ dcli -g ./cell_group cellcli -e create celldisk all harddisk
cm01cel01: CellDisk CD_00_cm01cel01 successfully created
cm01cel01: CellDisk CD_01_cm01cel01 successfully created
cm01cel01: CellDisk CD_02_cm01cel01 successfully created
... output omitted for brevity
```

Validate your newly created cell disks using the following `cellcli` command:

```
[oracle@cm01dbm01 ~]$ dcli -g ./cell_group cellcli -e list celldisk where \
> disktype=HardDisk attributes name,interleaving
cm01cel01: CD_00_cm01cel01        none
cm01cel01: CD_01_cm01cel01        none
cm01cel01: CD_02_cm01cel01        none
cm01cel01: CD_03_cm01cel01        none
... output omitted
```

Next, you must rebuild your Exadata grid disks. Using information documented and captured from previous steps in this recipe, we will start by building our DATA, SDATA, RECO, and SRECO grid disks. Your grid disk prefixes may be different from these, but the DATA and RECO grid disk prefixes are common in many organizations. It is considered a best practice to create your grid disks uniformly across each storage cell in your Exadata storage grid, so this is what we will show:

```
[oracle@cm01dbm01 ~]$ dcli -g ./cell_group cellcli -e create griddisk all \
> harddisk prefix='DATA', size=284G
cm01cel01: GridDisk DATA_CD_00_cm01cel01 successfully created
cm01cel01: GridDisk DATA_CD_01_cm01cel01 successfully created
cm01cel01: GridDisk DATA_CD_02_cm01cel01 successfully created
... output omitted

[oracle@cm01dbm01 ~]$ dcli -g ./cell_group cellcli -e create griddisk all \
> harddisk prefix='SDATA', size=141G
```

```
cm01cel01: GridDisk SDATA_CD_00_cm01cel01 successfully created
cm01cel01: GridDisk SDATA_CD_01_cm01cel01 successfully created
cm01cel01: GridDisk SDATA_CD_02_cm01cel01 successfully created
... output omitted

[oracle@cm01dbm01 ~]$ dcli -g ./cell_group cellcli -e create griddisk all \
> harddisk prefix='RECO', size=67G
... output omitted

[oracle@cm01dbm01 ~]$ dcli -g ./cell_group cellcli -e create griddisk all \
> harddisk prefix='SRECO', size=36.6875G
... output omitted
```

Finally, create your DBFS_DG grid disks:

```
[oracle@cm01dbm01 ~]$ dcli -g ./cell_group cellcli -e create griddisk all \
> harddisk prefix='DBFS_DG'
cm01cel01: Cell disks were skipped because they had no freespace for grid disks:
CD_00_cm01cel01, CD_01_cm01cel01.
cm01cel01: GridDisk DBFS_DG_CD_02_cm01cel01 successfully created
cm01cel01: GridDisk DBFS_DG_CD_03_cm01cel01 successfully created
cm01cel01: GridDisk DBFS_DG_CD_04_cm01cel01 successfully created
```

Notice in this output that two cell disks were skipped on each storage server due to lack of free space; this is because the first two disks in each storage server reserve 29 GB of space in each of the first two SAS disks for Exadata's System Area. This is discussed in Recipe 1-4 and elsewhere in this text.

When complete, use cellcli to display grid disk details for one of your cell disks on one storage cell:

```
[oracle@cm01dbm01 ~]$ dcli -c cm01cel01 cellcli -e list griddisk where celldisk=CD_11_cm01cel01 \
> attributes name,size,offset
cm01cel01: DATA_CD_11_cm01cel01        284G       32M
cm01cel01: DBFS_DG_CD_11_cm01cel01     29.125G    528.734375G
cm01cel01: RECO_CD_11_cm01cel01        67G        425.046875G
cm01cel01: SDATA_CD_11_cm01cel01       141G       284.046875G
cm01cel01: SRECO_CD_11_cm01cel01       36.6875G   492.046875G
[oracle@cm01dbm01 ~]$
```

This output shows that we have five grid disks on this storage cell, each with the specified size and the byte offset corresponding to the order in which we created the grid disks. To confirm that your grid disks are evenly distributed and sized across all Exadata storage cells, run the Perl script in Listing 9-14.

Listing 9-14. lst09-14-griddisks.pl

```perl
#!/usr/bin/perl
open(F,"dcli -g ./cell_group cellcli -e list griddisk attributes name,size,offset|");
while (<F>) {
 $tgd++;
 ($cd,$gd,$sz,$offset)=split(' ',$_);
  $gd=substr $gd,0,index($gd,"_");
  $cell{$cd}++;
  $cell{$gd}++;
  push @CELLS, $cd ;
```

```
    push @GDS, $gd;
    push @DTL, "$gd".":\tSize "."$sz".":\tOffset ".$offset."\n";
}
print "Total grid disks: $tgd\n";
%seen = ();
@UNIQCELLS= grep { ! $seen{$_} ++ } @CELLS;
foreach (@UNIQCELLS) {
 print "$_ has $cell{$_} grid disks\n";
}
%seen = ();
@UNIQGDS= grep { ! $seen{$_} ++ } @GDS;
foreach (@UNIQGDS) {
 print "$_ is built on $cell{$_} grid disks\n";
}
%seen = ();
@UNIQDTL= grep { ! $seen{$_} ++ } @DTL;
foreach (@UNIQDTL) {
 print "Distinct size and offset for : $_";
}

[oracle@cm01dbm01 source]$ ./griddisks.pl
Total grid disks: 174
cm01cel01: has 58 grid disks
cm01cel02: has 58 grid disks
cm01cel03: has 58 grid disks
DATA is built on 36 grid disks
DBFS is built on 30 grid disks
RECO is built on 36 grid disks
SDATA is built on 36 grid disks
SRECO is built on 36 grid disks
Distinct size and offsets for : DATA:   Size 284G:       Offset 32M
Distinct size and offsets for : DBFS:   Size 29.125G:    Offset 528.734375G
Distinct size and offsets for : RECO:   Size 67G:        Offset 425.046875G
Distinct size and offsets for : SDATA:  Size 141G:       Offset 284.046875G
Distinct size and offsets for : SRECO:  Size 36.6875G:   Offset 492.046875G
[oracle@cm01dbm01 source]$
```

Start Oracle ClusterWare Resources on the Compute Nodes

With your grid disks rebuilt, it's time to get your Oracle cluster operational. Since your Oracle Cluster Registry will not be available because you've dropped your ASM disk group that stored it, you will need to start CRS in exclusive mode on one compute node and then manually start an ASM instance in order to recreate your DBFS_DG ASM disk group. We recommend first disabling the automatic restart of Oracle CRS by issuing the following command:

```
[root@cm01dbm01 ~]# /u01/app/11.2.0.3/grid/bin/crsctl disable crs
CRS-4621: Oracle High Availability Services autostart is disabled.
[root@cm01dbm01 ~]#
```

■ **Note** If you elect not to disable Oracle CRS from automatically starting, you can use the `crsctl stop res ora.crsd -init` command to stop CRS and prevent it from restarting.

Perform this step on each compute node and when complete, reboot your servers.

> **Note** Compute server reboots are not specifically required, but we recommend doing this to ensure that no Oracle ClusterWare resources are attempting to start.

Next, start Oracle CRS on one node with the -excl -nocrs flags. This will attempt to start CRS resources without CRS on a single node and will allow you to manually start an Oracle ASM instance. My Oracle Support note 1062983.1.1 provides more information on how and why this works:

```
[root@cm01dbm01 ~]# /u01/app/11.2.0.3/grid/bin/crsctl start crs -excl -nocrs
CRS-4123: Oracle High Availability Services has been started.
CRS-2672: Attempting to start 'ora.mdnsd' on 'cm01dbm01'
CRS-2676: Start of 'ora.mdnsd' on 'cm01dbm01' succeeded
CRS-2672: Attempting to start 'ora.gpnpd' on 'cm01dbm01'
CRS-2676: Start of 'ora.gpnpd' on 'cm01dbm01' succeeded
CRS-2672: Attempting to start 'ora.cssdmonitor' on 'cm01dbm01'
CRS-2672: Attempting to start 'ora.gipcd' on 'cm01dbm01'
CRS-2676: Start of 'ora.cssdmonitor' on 'cm01dbm01' succeeded
... output omitted for brevity
CRS-2676: Start of 'ora.cluster_interconnect.haip' on 'cm01dbm01' succeeded
CRS-2672: Attempting to start 'ora.asm' on 'cm01dbm01'
CRS-2676: Start of 'ora.asm' on 'cm01dbm01' succeeded
[root@cm01dbm01 ~]#
```

After CRS is started in exclusive mode, log in as your Grid Infrastructure owner, connect to SQL*Plus as SYSASM, and validate your ASM disk groups. At this point, you will not have any created:

```
[grid@cm01dbm01 ~]$ sqlplus / as sysasm
SQL*Plus: Release 11.2.0.3.0 Production on Thu Sep 13 14:38:38 2012
Copyright (c) 1982, 2011, Oracle.  All rights reserved.
Connected to:
Oracle Database 11g Enterprise Edition Release 11.2.0.3.0 - 64bit Production
With the Real Application Clusters and Automatic Storage Management options
SQL> select name from v$asm_diskgroup;
no rows selected
SQL>
```

Create the DBFS_DG ASM Disk Group to Store the OCR and Voting Disks

Next, create your DBFS_DG ASM disk group:

```
SQL> create diskgroup DBFS_DG
    normal redundancy
    disk 'o/*/DBFS_DG*'
    attribute   'compatible.rdbms' = '11.2.0.3.0',
                'compatible.asm' = '11.2.0.3.0',
```

```
                            'cell.smart_scan_capable' = 'TRUE',
                            'au_size' = '4M';
```

Diskgroup created.

SQL>

Restore Your OCR and Voting Disks and Restart Oracle CRS

After the disk group is created, restore your Oracle Cluster Registry using the manual OCR backup you created previously. Log in as root and run the following ocrconfig -restore command, followed by the ocrcheck command to validate that your OCR was restored properly:

```
[root@cm01dbm01 ~]# /u01/app/11.2.0.3/grid/bin/ocrconfig -restore \
> /u01/app/11.2.0.3/grid/cdata/cm01-cluster/backup_20120912_232228.ocr
[root@cm01dbm01 ~]#
[root@cm01dbm01 ~]# /u01/app/11.2.0.3/grid/bin/ocrcheck
Status of Oracle Cluster Registry is as follows :
         Version                  :          3
         Total space (kbytes)     :     262120
         Used space (kbytes)      :       3464
         Available space (kbytes) :     258656
         ID                       : 1833511320
         Device/File Name         :    +DBFS_DG
                                    Device/File integrity check succeeded
                                    Device/File not configured
                                    Device/File not configured
                                    Device/File not configured
                                    Device/File not configured
         Cluster registry integrity check succeeded
         Logical corruption check succeeded
[root@cm01dbm01 ~]#
```

Once your OCR is restored, proceed to restoring and validate your voting disks:

```
[root@cm01dbm01 ~]# /u01/app/11.2.0.3/grid/bin/crsctl replace votedisk +DBFS_DG
Successful addition of voting disk 3f2e37ba43b44f4fbf7e253d9288eea2.
Successful addition of voting disk 1393ac37d5544fffbf12c86c47312c75.
Successful addition of voting disk 4cab106752ef4f09bf2419705b98e650.
Successfully replaced voting disk group with +DBFS_DG.
CRS-4266: Voting file(s) successfully replaced

[root@cm01dbm01 ~]# /u01/app/11.2.0.3/grid/bin/crsctl query css votedisk
                                                                              Disk
##  STATE   File Universal Id                 File Name                       group
---  ------ --------------------------------  ------------------------------  ---------
 1.  ONLINE 3f2e37ba43b44f4fbf7e253d9288eea2  (o/192.168.10.5/DBFS_DG_CD_07_cm01cel03) [DBFS_DG]
 2.  ONLINE 1393ac37d5544fffbf12c86c47312c75  (o/192.168.10.4/DBFS_DG_CD_04_cm01cel02) [DBFS_DG]
 3.  ONLINE 4cab106752ef4f09bf2419705b98e650  (o/192.168.10.3/DBFS_DG_CD_10_cm01cel01) [DBFS_DG]
Located 3 voting disk(s).
[root@cm01dbm01 ~]#
```

After your voting disks and OCR are restored, enable Oracle High Availability services and restart Oracle CRS on each compute nodes without the exclusive option:

```
[root@cm01dbm01 ~]# /u01/app/11.2.0.3/grid/bin/crsctl stop crs
CRS-2791: Starting shutdown of Oracle High Availability Services-managed resources on 'cm01dbm01'
CRS-2673: Attempting to stop 'ora.mdnsd' on 'cm01dbm01'
CRS-2673: Attempting to stop 'ora.ctssd' on 'cm01dbm01'
CRS-2673: Attempting to stop 'ora.asm' on 'cm01dbm01'
... output omitted for brevity
[root@cm01dbm01 ~]# /u01/app/11.2.0.3/grid/bin/crsctl start crs
CRS-4123: Oracle High Availability Services has been started.
[root@cm01dbm01 ~]#
```

Create Your Remaining ASM Disk Groups

When Oracle CRS is started, log in as your Grid Infrastructure owner, connect to SQL*Plus as SYSASM, and create your remaining ASM disk groups:

```
SQL> create diskgroup DATA_CM01
    normal redundancy
    disk 'o/*/DATA*'
    attribute 'compatible.rdbms' = '11.2.0.3.0',
              'compatible.asm' = '11.2.0.3.0',
              'cell.smart_scan_capable' = 'TRUE',
              'au_size' = '4M';

Diskgroup created.

SQL>
SQL> create diskgroup SDATA_CM01
    normal redundancy
    disk 'o/*/SDATA*'
    attribute 'compatible.rdbms' = '11.2.0.3.0',
              'compatible.asm' = '11.2.0.3.0',
              'cell.smart_scan_capable' = 'TRUE',
              'au_size' = '4M';

Diskgroup created.
... Remaining ASM disk group creation statements omitted.
```

Validate the Health of Your Cluster

Once your Oracle ASM disk groups are all recreated, the remaining steps required to return your environment to an operational state are a combination of RMAN restore and recovery operations, combined with optionally placing your server parameter file in an ASM disk group. Start by placing your server parameter file back into the appropriate ASM disk group, using output from your preliminary validation steps. Since you have restored your Oracle Cluster

Registry, use the following command as the Oracle database owner to display the expected location of your server parameter file:

```
[oracle@cm01dbm01 ~]$ srvctl config database -d visx
Database unique name: visx
Database name: visx
Oracle home: /u01/app/oracle/product/11.2.0.3/dbhome_1
Oracle user: oracle
Spfile: +DATA_CM01/visx/spfilevisx.ora
... output omitted
```

Using the parameter file backed up previously in this recipe, start your database in nomount mode and create your server parameter file in the expected location, which in our case is +DATA_CM01/visx/spfilevisx.ora:

```
SQL> startup nomount pfile='/home/oracle/initvisx.ora';
ORACLE instance started.

Total System Global Area 1.7103E+10 bytes
Fixed Size                  2245480 bytes
Variable Size            2483031192 bytes
Database Buffers         1.4462E+10 bytes
Redo Buffers              155926528 bytes

SQL> create spfile='+DATA_CM01/visx/spfilevisx.ora' from pfile='/home/oracle/initvisx.ora';

File created.

SQL>
```

As your Oracle Grid Infrastructure owner, you can validate that Oracle successfully placed a server parameter file in the expected location using the following command:

```
[grid@cm01dbm01 ~]$ asmcmd ls DATA_CM01/VISX
PARAMETERFILE/
spfilevisx.ora
[grid@cm01dbm01 ~]$
```

Once your server parameter file has been created, start one of your instances in nomount mode using the spfile and restore your control file using RMAN.

Note The following example assumes that you have control file backups available. In our example, our control file is backed up to an external NFS-mounted NAS device.

```
[oracle@cm01dbm01 ~]$ rman target /
Recovery Manager: Release 11.2.0.3.0 - Production on Thu Sep 13 17:16:26 2012
Copyright (c) 1982, 2011, Oracle and/or its affiliates.  All rights reserved.
connected to target database: VISX (not mounted)
RMAN> shutdown immediate;
using target database control file instead of recovery catalog
```

```
Oracle instance shut down
RMAN> startup nomount;
connected to target database (not started)
Oracle instance started
Total System Global Area   17103163392 bytes
Fixed Size                     2245480 bytes
Variable Size               2483031192 bytes
Database Buffers           14461960192 bytes
Redo Buffers                 155926528 bytes

RMAN> restore controlfile from '/dump/visx_backup/cf_visx_k7nkfue1_1_1';

Starting restore at 13-SEP-12
allocated channel: ORA_DISK_1
channel ORA_DISK_1: SID=652 instance=visx1 device type=DISK
channel ORA_DISK_1: restoring control file
channel ORA_DISK_1: restore complete, elapsed time: 00:00:03
output file name=+DATA_CM01/visx/control01.ctl
output file name=+DATA_CM01/visx/control02.ctl
output file name=+DATA_CM01/visx/control03.ctl
Finished restore at 13-SEP-12

RMAN> alter database mount;

database mounted
released channel: ORA_DISK_1

RMAN>
```

Note The following example assumes that you have control file backups available. In our example, our control file is backed up to an external NFS-mounted NAS device.

The remaining steps to restore your environment entail using RMAN restore and recovery commands, which are outside the scope of this text. For details, please refer to Oracle's 11gR2 backup and recovery documentation, which can be found at http://docs.oracle.com/cd/E11882_01/backup.112/e10642/toc.htm.

When your restore is complete, your databases should be restored and healthy:

```
[oracle@cm01dbm01 ~]$ srvctl start database -d visx
[oracle@cm01dbm01 ~]$ srvctl status database -d visx
Instance visx1 is running on node cm01dbm01
Instance visx2 is running on node cm01dbm02
[oracle@cm01dbm01 ~]$
```

How It Works

Rebuilding Exadata cell disks is performed using the drop celldisk and create celldisk commands in the CellCLI interface. As this also will drop and destroy other database entities, such as grid disks, ASM disks, and database files (in the event you drop cell disks across all storage cells), you will need to be familiar with administering all storage-related components in your Exadata Database Machine to be successful.

Rebuilding Exadata storage cell disks is an activity you will likely not perform very often. Oracle automatically creates cell disks in many scenarios, including at time of installation, after replacing a damaged disk, and even after recovering from failed system volumes.

> **Note** Please see Recipe 8-9 to learn how to recover an Exadata cell from loss of your system volumes.

In our experience, the most common reason to perform a cell disk rebuild activity is if you wish to change the interleaving attribute of your cell disk, which is presented in Recipe 9-8 in detail.

To successfully rebuild your Exadata cell disks, you should understand the overall impact to your Exadata environment. Specifically:

- When you drop cell disks, you will be required to drop your grid disks.
- Dropping grid disks will offline or drop ASM disk group disks.
- When your ASM disks are unavailable, your databases will not be functional.
- If you drop your cell disks, grid disks, and ASM disk groups, you will need to restore your databases from a backup. Thus, a tested and validated backup strategy is critical when embarking on a cell disk rebuild exercise.
- If you drop the grid disks and associated ASM disk groups that store your Oracle Cluster Registry and voting disks, you will need to restore these as well prior to starting your Oracle cluster. By starting Oracle CRS in exclusive mode, as demonstrated in this recipe, you should be able to confidently perform your OCR and voting disk restoration.

In other words, when you drop and recreate your Exadata cell disks on a storage cell, you will lose access and destroy the data on the disks. Should you perform a cell disk rebuild across all storage cells, you will experience a clusterwide database outage.

An Oracle Exadata DMA should be well versed in each administration area covered in this recipe to successfully rebuild Exadata cell disks, including cell disk and grid disk management, ASM administration, Oracle Grid Infrastructure administration, Oracle 11gR2 database administration, and Oracle backup and recovery methods.

9-8. Creating Interleaved Cell Disks and Grid Disks

Problem

You wish to attain better levels of I/O performance balance across grid disks by configuring interleaved cell disks and grid disks.

Solution

Grid disk interleaving is a technique to interleave your grid disk extent ranges across Exadata cell disks to achieve evenly distributed extent balance across your Exadata cell disks. In this recipe, we will demonstrate how to validate your current disk interleaving attributes, configure your Exadata cell disks with interleaving, create grid disks on these cell disks, and measure the extent offsets for each grid disk created.

1. Begin by logging into a compute node or storage cell and using CellCLI to display your current cell disk interleaving attributes. In the following example, we will use `dcli` on a compute node to run the same `cellcli` command on each storage cell:

   ```
   [oracle@cm01dbm01 ~]$ dcli -g ./cell_group cellcli -e \
   > list celldisk where diskType=HardDisk attributes name,interleaving
   cm01cel01: CD_00_cm01cel01    none
   ... output omitted for brevity
   [oracle@cm01dbm01 ~]$
   ```

2. You can sort the output using the awk and sort commands to show your distinct cell disk interleaving attributes. Note that to ensure consistent performance, interleaving should be configured the same across each storage cell:

   ```
   [oracle@cm01dbm01 ~]$ dcli -g ./cell_group cellcli -e \
   > list celldisk where diskType=HardDisk attributes name,interleaving \
   > |awk '{print $3}' | sort -u
   none
   [oracle@cm01dbm01 ~]$
   ```

3. In the previous two examples, our cell disks are configured without interleaving. Now, examine your grid disk sizes and byte offsets using the Perl script in Listing 9-15, which runs `cellcli` commands on each storage server and reports your grid disk sizes and byte offsets.

■ **Note** The script in Listing 9-15 was introduced in Recipe 9-7 and is one that we use to gain a quick view of grid disk layouts on Exadata. With Exadata Half Rack and Full Rack deployments and many grid disks with different disk prefixes, sorting through the output of a list grid disk command can be time-consuming. The script is intended to summarize your grid disk configuration and display sizes and byte offsets.

Listing 9-15. lst09-15-griddisks.pl

```perl
#!/usr/bin/perl

open(F,"dcli -g ./cell_group cellcli -e list griddisk attributes name,size,offset|");
while (<F>) {
 $tgd++;
 ($cd,$gd,$sz,$offset)=split(' ',$_);
  $gd=substr $gd,0,index($gd,"_");
  $cell{$cd}++;
  $cell{$gd}++;
  push @CELLS, $cd ;
  push @GDS, $gd;
  push @DTL, "$gd".":\tSize "."$sz".":\tOffset ".$offset."\n";
}
print "Total grid disks: $tgd\n";
%seen = ();
@UNIQCELLS= grep { ! $seen{$_} ++ } @CELLS;
```

```
foreach (@UNIQCELLS) {
 print "$_ has $cell{$_} grid disks\n";
}
%seen = ();
@UNIQGDS= grep { ! $seen{$_} ++ } @GDS;
foreach (@UNIQGDS) {
 print "$_ is built on $cell{$_} grid disks\n";
}
%seen = ();
@UNIQDTL= grep { ! $seen{$_} ++ } @DTL;
foreach (@UNIQDTL) {
 print "Distinct size and offset for : $_";
}

[oracle@cm01dbm01 source]$ ./griddisks.pl
Total grid disks: 174
cm01cel01: has 58 grid disks
cm01cel02: has 58 grid disks
cm01cel03: has 58 grid disks
DATA is built on 36 grid disks
DBFS is built on 30 grid disks
RECO is built on 36 grid disks
SDATA is built on 36 grid disks
SRECO is built on 36 grid disks
Distinct size and offsets for : DATA:    Size 284G:     Offset 32M
Distinct size and offsets for : DBFS:    Size 29.125G:  Offset 528.734375G
Distinct size and offsets for : RECO:    Size 67G:      Offset 425.046875G
Distinct size and offsets for : SDATA:   Size 141G:     Offset 284.046875G
Distinct size and offsets for : SRECO:   Size 36.6875G: Offset 492.046875G
[oracle@cm01dbm01 source]$
```

In this output, we can glean the following information:

- Each storage cell has the same number of grid disks.
- There are five distinct types of grid disks across the cell disks, each with a different prefix and likely intended for different database storage purposes.
- The size of each of the grid disks is uniform across all cell disks and storage cells.
- The byte offset is in the same location per grid disk on each cell disk.
- The DATA grid disks were created first; the 32 MB offset means that the extents for each DATA* grid disk were formatted 32 MB from the outermost tracks of each cell disk and continued for 284 GB.
- The SDATA grid disks were created next at an offset of 284 GB, continuing for 141 GB.
- The RECO grid disks were created next, then our SRECO disks, and finally the DBFS_DG grid disks.

Now that you have a clear picture of where each grid disk's extents are physically located on your cell disks, you can begin your interleaving implementation.

4. Changing cell disk interleaving attributes requires that the cell disks be dropped and recreated. To prepare for this, you must first drop your grid disks. After dropping grid disks, you then drop your cell disks. To learn how to drop grid disks and cell disks, please refer to recipe 9-7.

5. Now, rebuild your cell disks with normal_redunancy interleaving. (We will demonstrate the impact of high_redundancy interleaving later in this recipe.)

    ```
    [oracle@cm01dbm01 ~]$ dcli -g ./cell_group cellcli -e create celldisk all harddisk \
    > interleaving='normal_redundancy'
    cm01cel01: CellDisk CD_00_cm01cel01 successfully created
    ... output omitted
    ```

6. Validate your cell disk interleaving using the following cellcli command:

    ```
    [oracle@cm01dbm01 ~]$ dcli -g ./cell_group cellcli -e list celldisk where
    disktype=HardDisk attributes name,interleaving
    cm01cel01: CD_00_cm01cel01       normal_redundancy
    ... output omitted
    ```

7. Recreate your grid disks using the cellcli create griddisk command. Following, we will only show the syntax for the first two sets of grid disks; you will have to rebuild all of the grid disks that your databases need.

    ```
    [oracle@cm01dbm01 ~]$ dcli -g ./cell_group cellcli -e create griddisk all \
    > harddisk prefix='DATA',size=284G
    cm01cel01: GridDisk DATA_CD_00_cm01cel01 successfully created
    ... output omitted
    [oracle@cm01dbm01 ~]$ dcli -g ./cell_group cellcli -e create griddisk all \
    > harddisk prefix='SDATA',size=141G
    cm01cel01: GridDisk SDATA_CD_00_cm01cel01 successfully created
    ... output omitted
    ```

8. When finished, examine the size and byte offset of your grid disks. Start by checking the grid disk configuration on a single cell disk:

    ```
    [oracle@cm01dbm01 ~]$ dcli -c cm01cel01 cellcli -e list griddisk where celldisk=CD_11_
    cm01cel01 attributes name,size,offset
    cm01cel01: DATA_CD_11_cm01cel01         284G            32M
    cm01cel01: DBFS_DG_CD_11_cm01cel01      29.125G         264.390625G
    cm01cel01: RECO_CD_11_cm01cel01         67G             212.546875G
    cm01cel01: SDATA_CD_11_cm01cel01        141G            142.046875G
    cm01cel01: SRECO_CD_11_cm01cel01        36.6875G        246.046875G
    [oracle@cm01dbm01 ~]$
    ```

In this output, note the following:

- The DATA_CD_11_cm01cel01 grid disk was the first grid disk created on the cell disk at a byte offset of 32 MB. It is still 284 GB in size, as was the case prior to rebuilding our cell disks and grid disks.

- SDATA_CD_11_cm01cel01 was the next grid disk created, but extents for this grid disk began at an offset of 142 GB. This is exactly half the size of the previous grid disk created, DATA_CD_11_cm01cel01.

- The RECO_CD_11_cm01cel01 grid disk was created next at a byte offset of 212 GB, which is half the size of the first two grid disks combined.
- This pattern continues with the remaining grid disks on the cell disk.

Figure 9-1 shows what your extent boundaries will look like for normal_redundancy interleaving with a grid disk configuration as previously created:

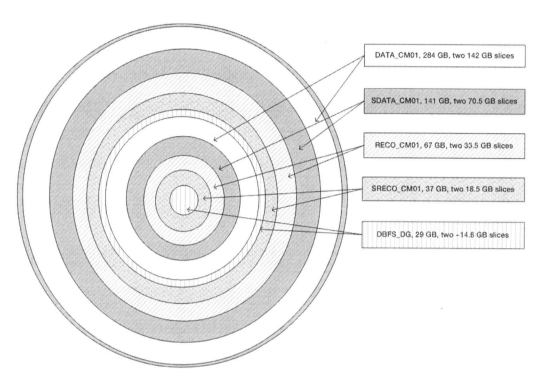

Figure 9-1. *Interleaving with normal_redundancy*

A summary of our grid disk configuration with normal_redunancy interleaving is provided, using the same Perl script used previously in this recipe:

```
[oracle@cm01dbm01 source]$ ./lst09-15-griddisks.pl
Total grid disks: 174
cm01cel01: has 58 grid disks
cm01cel02: has 58 grid disks
cm01cel03: has 58 grid disks
DATA is built on 36 grid disks
DBFS is built on 30 grid disks
RECO is built on 36 grid disks
SDATA is built on 36 grid disks
SRECO is built on 36 grid disks
```

```
Distinct size and offsets for : DATA:  Size 284G:      Offset 32M
Distinct size and offsets for : DBFS:  Size 29.125G:   Offset 264.390625G
Distinct size and offsets for : RECO:  Size 67G:       Offset 212.546875G
Distinct size and offsets for : SDATA: Size 141G:      Offset 142.046875G
Distinct size and offsets for : SRECO: Size 36.6875G:  Offset 246.046875G
[oracle@cm01dbm01 source]$
```

If you wish to understand how Oracle aligns extent boundaries with high_redundancy interleaving, drop your grid disks and cell disks and recreate the cell disks using the following command:

```
[oracle@cm01dbm01 ~]$ dcli -g ./cell_group cellcli -e create celldisk all harddisk
interleaving='high_redundancy'
cm01cel01: CellDisk CD_00_cm01cel01 successfully created
... output omitted
```

After creating grid disks in the same manner as previously in this recipe, our grid disk extent boundaries now look like this:

```
[oracle@cm01dbm01 source]$ ./lst09-15-griddisks.pl
Total grid disks: 174
cm01cel01: has 58 grid disks
cm01cel02: has 58 grid disks
cm01cel03: has 58 grid disks
DATA is built on 36 grid disks
DBFS is built on 30 grid disks
RECO is built on 36 grid disks
SDATA is built on 36 grid disks
SRECO is built on 36 grid disks
Distinct size and offsets for : DATA:  Size 284G:      Offset 32M
Distinct size and offsets for : DBFS:  Size 29.125G:   Offset 176.25G
Distinct size and offsets for : RECO:  Size 67G:       Offset 141.703125G
Distinct size and offsets for : SDATA: Size 141G:      Offset 94.703125G
Distinct size and offsets for : SRECO: Size 36.6875G:  Offset 164.03125G
[oracle@cm01dbm01 source]$
```

From the output above, you can see that high_redundancy interleaving splits the grid disk sizes into thirds before formatting other grid disk's extents. For example, the byte offset for the second grid disk created across each cell starts at 94.703 GB, which is one-third the size of the first grid disk created. Figure 9-2 displays this extent allocation.

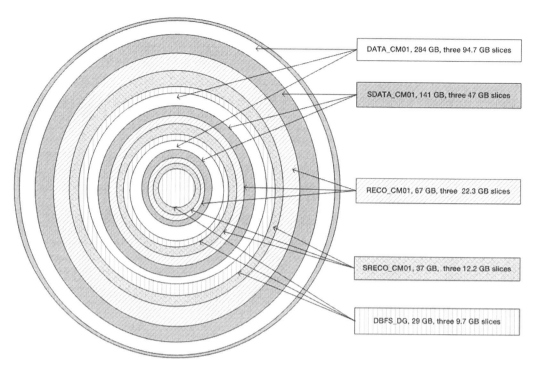

***Figure 9-2.** Interleaving with high_redundancy*

How It Works

Oracle provides the interleaving feature on Exadata cell disks to enable a cell's grid disks to be split and divided among different ranges of disk tracks. From a historical context, the reason why the cell disk layer exists to begin with is specifically to provide for this interleaving capability for a cell disk's grid disks.

In cases when cell disk interleaving is not configured, the first set of grid disks created will have their extents allocated on the outer tracks of the physical disk. The next set of grid disks created will reside on the inner tracks of the physical disk. In a standard Oracle ACS installation, there are typically two sets of grid disks created, DATA and RECO. This default design means that the DATA grid disks will reside on the outer tracks of the physical disk, RECO will reside on the inner tracks of the disk, and a third set of DBFS_DG grid disks will be placed on the innermost tracks.

Why is this important? It's important because the mechanics of a physical disk drive are such that the drive arms will travel a shorter distance to access tracks on the outer portion of a physical disk. Traveling a shorter distance equates to less time, which means that I/O seek times will be shorter to tracks on the outer portion of a physical disk with respect to the inner portion.

Let's pause to think about how a database's segments are physically stored on disk. When a segment's extents are created, they will be stored in the data files that are part of the tablespace to which the segment is assigned. The data files, in turn, are stored in Oracle ASM disk groups on Exadata. An ASM disk group is comprised of multiple Exadata grid disks, and as extents are placed on the grid disks, they are evenly distributed among the disks in units specified by the disk group's allocation unit size, or au_size. A grid disk is built upon an Exadata cell disk.

Without interleaving, the extents are placed with a range of disk tracks that begin at the grid disk's offset and end at the physical location specified by the offset value plus the grid disk size. So, if, for example, you are writing to the first grid disk created on the cell disk, your database extents will be distributed between tracks starting at the outer edge of the physical disk and terminate at the boundary specified by the grid disk offset plus the size of the grid disk.

With interleaving, Exadata will divide the grid disk into multiple sections of disk tracks. Grid disk extents will then be distributed evenly between each of the two or three ranges of available tracks for the grid disk. The impact of this configuration is that your database's segments will be spread a bit more evenly on the physical disks.

Cell disks can be defined with no interleaving, normal_redundancy interleaving, or high_redundancy interleaving. With normal_redundancy interleaving, Oracle will place one of two sets of extents on an outer set of disk tracks and the other set of extents on an inner set of tracks. In other words, you will have two ranges of disk tracks for your grid disk storage. With high_redundancy interleaving, Oracle divides the grid disk size into three equally sized ranges.

Note The cell disk interleaving terms normal_redundancy and high_redundancy may sound familiar to those familiar with Oracle ASM. In ASM, your redundancy configuration specifies how many mirrors will exist for each extent; normal redundancy means each extent will be mirrored once, and high redundancy means each extent will be mirrored twice. Do not confuse this with Exadata cell disk and grid disk interleaving; in the context of interleaving, redundancy does not refer to a mirroring or protection level but simply the number of equally sized disk track ranges within a cell disk.

Whether you choose to use no interleaving, normal_redundancy, or high_redundancy interleaving, Oracle will allocate the initial set of extents for a grid disk on the outer set of physical disk tracks for the first grid disk created on a cell disk. With interleaving based on your interleaving flavor, Oracle will divide your total grid disk size in half or in thirds, leaving "free" sets of tracks available for other grid disks on the cell disk. As additional grid disks are created on the cell disk, the grid disk's extents will again be split into either two or three sets of track ranges and be placed starting at the boundary of the previous grid disk's last extent. This pattern continues until the capacity on the cell disk is consumed.

After reading this recipe and Recipe 9-7, you may ask yourself whether grid disk interleaving is a deployment option you should consider and, specifically, whether it will address any real-world performance problems. As mentioned previously, Oracle ACS typically implements cell disks without interleaving, creates DATA grid disks first, RECO next, and DBFS_DG grid disks last. The intent of this implementation decision is to enable the lowest latency and best performance for data stored in the DATA grid disks.

In our experience, the default configuration without interleaving meets the needs of most Exadata customers. But there are some reasons why interleaving may be a good option for you. For example, if you have many databases consolidated on your Exadata Database Machine with competing performance service levels, interleaving your grid disks may satisfy these complex workload requirements and smooth your distribution of database extents across ranges of lower-performing and higher-performing tracks. Of course, there are other ways to handle workload management on Exadata for consolidated environments, such as I/O Resource Management.

Another reason for interleaving your grid disks is if you have multiple databases with equally important performance requirements but distinct security requirements that require the Exadata DMA to implement ASM scoped security. This security requirement will necessitate multiple sets of Exadata grid disks and interleaving is one technique to achieve a balanced I/O performance experience for each database.

Note To learn more about ASM scoped security on Exadata, please see Recipe 12-3.

9-9. Rebuilding Grid Disks

Problem

You wish to rebuild Exadata grid disks on your Exadata Storage Servers.

Solution

In this recipe, you will learn how to rebuild Exadata grid disks, and we will discuss considerations that must be accounted for in doing so. Specifically, we will demonstrate the following:

- How to capture your ASM disk group to Exadata grid disk mappings
- How to drop your grid disks and ASM disk groups
- How to build new Exadata grid disks
- How to recreate your ASM disk groups

First, log in to a compute node as the Oracle Grid Infrastructure owner and follow these steps:

1. Run the script in Listing 9-16 SQL*Plus while connected as SYSASM:

    Listing 9-16. lst09-16-asm-disks.sql

    ```
    SQL> select a.name,b.path,b.state,a.type,b.failgroup
        from v$asm_diskgroup a, v$asm_disk b
        where a.group_number=b.group_number
        and (a.name='&&diskgroup_name' or '&&diskgroup_name' is null)
        order by 2,1
    /
    Enter value for diskgroup_name: SRECO_CM01
    old    4: and (a.name='&&diskgroup_name' or '&&diskgroup_name' is null)
    new    4: and (a.name='SRECO_CM01' or 'SRECO_CM01' is null)

    Disk Group   Disk                                    State     Type     Failgroup
    ----------   -----------------------------------     --------  -------  ----------
    SRECO_CM01   o/192.168.10.3/SRECO_CD_00_cm01cel01    NORMAL    NORMAL   CM01CEL01
    SRECO_CM01   o/192.168.10.3/SRECO_CD_01_cm01cel01    NORMAL    NORMAL   CM01CEL01
    SRECO_CM01   o/192.168.10.3/SRECO_CD_02_cm01cel01    NORMAL    NORMAL   CM01CEL01
    ... output omitted
    36 rows selected.

    SQL>
    ```

2. The output in Listing 9-16 shows 36 grid disks for an ASM disk group named SRECO_CM01. Next, query your grid disks using `cellcli`:

    ```
    [oracle@cm01dbm01 ~]$ dcli -g ./cell_group cellcli -e list griddisk where \
    > asmDiskGroupName=SRECO_CM01 attributes name,celldisk,size,asmDiskName
    cm01cel01: SRECO_CD_00_cm01cel01   CD_00_cm01cel01   36.6875G   SRECO_CD_00_CM01CEL01
    cm01cel01: SRECO_CD_01_cm01cel01   CD_01_cm01cel01   36.6875G   SRECO_CD_01_CM01CEL01
    cm01cel01: SRECO_CD_02_cm01cel01   CD_02_cm01cel01   36.6875G   SRECO_CD_02_CM01CEL01
    [oracle@cm01dbm01 ~]$
    ```

CHAPTER 9 ■ STORAGE ADMINISTRATION

As you can see, our grid disks are 36.6875 GB in size and exist on each of three storage cells in our Exadata Quarter Rack.

3. Drop your ASM disk group by connecting to an ASM instance as SYSASM:

```
[grid@cm01dbm01 ~]$ sqlplus / as sysasm
SQL*Plus: Release 11.2.0.3.0 Production on Thu Sep 13 16:25:10 2012
Copyright (c) 1982, 2011, Oracle.  All rights reserved.

Connected to:
Oracle Database 11g Enterprise Edition Release 11.2.0.3.0 - 64bit Production
With the Real Application Clusters and Automatic Storage Management options

SQL> drop diskgroup sreco_cm01 including contents;

Diskgroup dropped.

SQL>
```

4. After this is complete, drop your grid disks using the `cellcli` command below:

■ **Note** If you drop your Exadata grid disks prior to dropping your ASM disk group, Exadata's automatic disk management features will automatically offline and drop your ASM disks.

```
[oracle@cm01dbm01 ~]$ dcli -g ./cell_group cellcli -e \
> drop griddisk all prefix=SRECO
cm01cel01: GridDisk SRECO_CD_00_cm01cel01 successfully dropped
cm01cel01: GridDisk SRECO_CD_01_cm01cel01 successfully dropped
cm01cel01: GridDisk SRECO_CD_02_cm01cel01 successfully dropped
... output omitted
[oracle@cm01dbm01 ~]$
```

■ **Note** If your grid disks have ASM disk groups created on them that you neglected to drop, you can use the `drop griddisk [options] force` syntax to forcibly drop your grid disks.

5. Once the grid disks are dropped, recreate them using the `create griddisk` command via cellcli:

```
[oracle@cm01dbm01 ~]$ dcli -g ./cell_group cellcli -e create griddisk all \
> harddisk prefix='SRECO', size=36.6875G
cm01cel01: GridDisk SRECO_CD_00_cm01cel01 successfully created
cm01cel01: GridDisk SRECO_CD_01_cm01cel01 successfully created
cm01cel01: GridDisk SRECO_CD_02_cm01cel01 successfully created
... output omitted
cm01cel02: GridDisk SRECO_CD_00_cm01cel02 successfully created
cm01cel02: GridDisk SRECO_CD_01_cm01cel02 successfully created
```

```
cm01cel02: GridDisk SRECO_CD_02_cm01cel02 successfully created
... output omitted
cm01cel03: GridDisk SRECO_CD_00_cm01cel03 successfully created
cm01cel03: GridDisk SRECO_CD_01_cm01cel03 successfully created
cm01cel03: GridDisk SRECO_CD_02_cm01cel03 successfully created
... output omitted
[oracle@cm01dbm01 ~]$
```

6. When complete, rebuild an Oracle ASM disk group on these newly created Exadata grid disks:

```
SQL> create diskgroup SRECO_CM01
    normal redundancy
    disk 'o/*/SRECO*'
    attribute 'compatible.rdbms' = '11.2.0.3.0',
              'compatible.asm' = '11.2.0.3.0',
              'cell.smart_scan_capable' = 'TRUE',
              'au_size' = '4M';

Diskgroup created.

SQL>
```

Note Please see Recipe 9-2 to learn more about appropriate settings for your au_size and other Exadata-related ASM disk group attributes.

How It Works

Exadata grid disks are the building blocks for Oracle ASM disks on Exadata. Oracle uses ASM for its database storage on Exadata. ASM disk groups consist of Exadata grid disks and grid disks are built on Exadata cell disks. Exadata grid disks represent the storage available for Oracle ASM disks. When you create ASM disk groups, the devices you use are grid disks, and grid disks are the disks exposed and available to Oracle ASM.

Dropping and creating Exadata grid disks is accomplished using the CellCLI drop griddisk and create griddisk commands, as demonstrated in the solution of this recipe.

Exadata DMAs should strive for equally sized, well-balanced grid disk configurations in order for an ASM disk group to contain extents on as many physical disks in your storage grid as possible. Doing so enables Exadata to maximize disk I/O bandwidth, I/Os per second, and ultimately ensure that you've got a well-balanced, high-performing storage platform on Exadata.

Oracle makes this effort easy on Exadata with its wildcard-capable CREATE GRIDDISK and CREATE DISKGROUP syntax. To create equally sized grid disks with the same prefix on each disk across all storage cells, you simply use the create griddisk all harddisk prefix='[prefix]', size=[size] syntax. You can also create single grid disks on a single storage cell disk using the more verbose syntax below:

```
CellCLI> create griddisk GDTEST celldisk=CD_08_cm01cel01, size=100M

cm01cel01: GridDisk GDTEST successfully created

CellCLI>
```

While this option is available to the Exadata DMA, it makes it more difficult to create ASM disk groups that span multiple Exadata grid disks, as you will need to either ensure that each of your individual grid disks are named similarly to allow for wildcard syntax on the `create diskgroup` command or individually list your Exadata grid disks in the ASM disk string.

To create Oracle ASM disk groups on your Exadata cell disks, use the `create diskgroup [disk group name] [redundancy clause] disk 'o/*/[prefix]*' attributes [attribute_list]` syntax, where:

- [disk group name] is your ASM disk group name
- [redundancy clause] is your choice of normal or high ASM disk group redundancy
- o is an instruction to Oracle ASM to search for its ASM disks over the InfiniBand storage interconnect
- * is an instruction to Oracle ASM to search for grid disks spanning each storage cell as listed in the /etc/oracle/cell/network-config/cellip.ora file on the compute node
- [prefix]* is your Exadata grid disk prefix
- [attribute list] is your list of ASM disk group attributes, such as au_size and compatible settings

You can also individually list each Exadata grid disk in your CREATE DISKGROUP command, which may be necessary if you do not employ consistent grid disk naming conventions and prefixes.

After you have created your Exadata grid disks and defined ASM disk groups on your grid disk entities, Exadata tracks several ASM-related attributes on each grid disk. You can retrieve these values using the `cellcli list griddisk` command below:

```
[oracle@cm01dbm01 ~]$ dcli -g ./cell_group cellcli -e list griddisk where celldisk=CD_00_cm01cel03 \
> attributes name,asmDiskGroupName,asmDiskName,availableTo,asmmodestatus
cm01cel03: DATA_CD_00_cm01cel03      DATA_CM01    DATA_CD_00_CM01CEL03     ONLINE
cm01cel03: RECO_CD_00_cm01cel03      RECO_CM01    RECO_CD_00_CM01CEL03     ONLINE
cm01cel03: SDATA_CD_00_cm01cel03     SDATA_CM01   SDATA_CD_00_CM01CEL03    ONLINE
cm01cel03: SRECO_CD_00_cm01cel03     SRECO_CM01   SRECO_CD_00_CM01CEL03    ONLINE
[oracle@cm01dbm01 ~]$
```

In this output, we are querying a specific cell disk to limit our output and choosing to display give attributes: name, asmDiskGroupName, asmDiskName, availableTo, and asmmodestatus:

- asmDiskGroupName indicates which ASM disk group a grid disk belongs do
- asmDiskName represents the grid disk as seen from Oracle ASM; note that it is the same as the grid disk name with the storage server in upper case
- availableTo is used for ASM scoped security and indicates which ASM disk groups are allowed to use the grid disk. Recipe 12-3 discusses ASM-scoped security on Exadata in detail. In the previous example, the output of this attribute is null as we do not have ASM scoped security configured.
- asmmodestatus displays the status of the grid disk as your Oracle ASM instance would see it; ONLINE indicates it is online, OFFLINE indicates it has been taken offline, and UNKNOWN typically indicates some sort of disk failure

9-10. Setting smart_scan_capable on ASM Disk Groups

Problem

You wish to configure your ASM disk groups to either enable or disable Exadata Smart Scan processing.

Solution

In this recipe, we will show you how to use the `smart_scan_capable` ASM disk group attributes to influence whether Exadata Smarts Scan will be enabled for I/O access to the extents resident on the disk group's files. Specifically, you will learn how to create an ASM disk group with Smart Scan enabled, how to create with Smart Scan disabled, how to alter your setting with the `alter diskgroup` command, and how to validate smart scans in both cases.

1. First, log in to your ASM instance as SYSASM and create an ASM disk group with `cell.smart_scan_capable` set to TRUE:

    ```
    SQL> create diskgroup DATA_CM01
        normal redundancy
        disk 'o/*/DATA*'
        attribute 'compatible.rdbms' = '11.2.0.3.0',
                  'compatible.asm' = '11.2.0.3.0',
                  'cell.smart_scan_capable' = 'TRUE',
                  'au_size' = '4M';

    Diskgroup created.

    SQL>
    ```

    The `cell.smart_scan_capable` configuration is an ASM disk group attribute and is configured using the attribute clause in the example above.

2. To create an ASM disk group with Smart Scan disabled, use the `'cell.smart_scan_capable'='FALSE'` syntax:

    ```
    SQL> create diskgroup SDATA_CM01
        normal redundancy
        disk 'o/*/SDATA*'
        attribute  'compatible.rdbms' = '11.2.0.3.0',
                   'compatible.asm' = '11.2.0.3.0',
                   'cell.smart_scan_capable' = 'FALSE',
                   'au_size' = '4M';

    Diskgroup created.

    SQL>
    ```

3. To modify your current disk group attribute, connect to your ASM instance as SYSASM and use the following `alter diskgroup` command:

    ```
    [grid@cm01dbm01 ~]$ sqlplus / as sysasm

    SQL*Plus: Release 11.2.0.3.0 Production on Fri Sep 14 01:29:21 2012
    ```

```
Copyright (c) 1982, 2011, Oracle.  All rights reserved.

Connected to:
Oracle Database 11g Enterprise Edition Release 11.2.0.3.0 - 64bit Production
With the Real Application Clusters and Automatic Storage Management options

SQL> alter diskgroup sdata_cm01
  2  set attribute 'cell.smart_scan_capable'='FALSE';

Diskgroup altered.

SQL>
```

4. Now, you can validate the impact of this by running a Smart Scan-eligible SQL statement on a table contained in a tablespace stored on both Smart Scan-enabled and Smart Scan-disabled ASM disk groups. Before running your test query, validate your ASM disk group attributes by connecting as SYSDBA to your database instance or ASM instance and running the script in Listing 9-17.

Listing 9-17. lst09-17-ss-enabled.sql

```
SQL> select a.group_number,b.name dgname,a.name,a.value
      from v$asm_attribute a,
      v$asm_diskgroup b
      where a.name = 'cell.smart_scan_capable'
      and b.name in ('&&dg_1','&&dg_2')
      and a.group_number=b.group_number
 /
Enter value for dg_1: DATA_CM01
Enter value for dg_2: SDATA_CM01
old   5:    and b.name in ('&&dg_1','&&dg_2')
new   5:    and b.name in ('DATA_CM01','SDATA_CM01')

   Group    DiskGroup       ASM Attribute                ASM Attribute
   Number   Name            Name                         Value
   -------  ------------    ------------------------     -------------
        2   DATA_CM01       cell.smart_scan_capable      TRUE
        3   SDATA_CM01      cell.smart_scan_capable      FALSE

SQL>
```

5. Next, identify or create tablespaces to use for your Smart Scan test case. In the following example, we will create two new tablespaces, TBS1 and TBS2. TBS1 will be stored in the DATA_CM01 disk group and TBS2 will have its data file placed in the SDATA_CM01 tablespace:

```
SYS @ visx1> create tablespace ts1 datafile '+DATA_CM01' size 4000m
  2  extent management local uniform size 4m;

Tablespace created.

SYS @ visx1> create tablespace ts2 datafile '+SDATA_CM01' size 4000m
  2  extent management local uniform size 4m;
```

Tablespace created.

SYS @ visx1>

6. Now, identify a table to conduct a full table scan against what will qualify for Exadata Smart Scan. In the following test, we will create two new tables for demonstration purposes, MMT_SS and MMT_NOSS:

    ```
    SYS @ visx1> create table apps.mmt_ss
        tablespace ts1 nologging
        as select /*+ full (mmt) */ * from inv.mtl_material_transactions mmt
    /

    Table created.

    SYS @ visx1>

    SYS @ visx1> create table apps.mmt_noss
        tablespace ts2 nologging
        as select /*+ full (mmt) */ * from inv.mtl_material_transactions mmt
    /

    Table created.

    SYS @ visx1>
    ```

■ **Note** Recipes in Chapter 15 discuss Smart Scan in detail. Please refer to these recipes for additional details about Exadata Smart Scan.

7. Once your tables are identified, run a query against them that performs a full table scan. Start by querying your table stored in the DATA_CM01 disk group with cell.smart_scan_capable=TRUE.

8. Next, execute a query that will benefit from Smart Scan:

    ```
    APPS @ visx1> select count(1) from (
      2  select /*+ full (x) */ *
      3  from mmt_ss x)
      4  ;

      COUNT(1)
    ----------
       8783431
    Elapsed: 00:00:03.30
    ```

CHAPTER 9 ■ STORAGE ADMINISTRATION

9. After your query completes, use the script in Listing 9-18 to validate your Smart Scan statistics:

Listing 9-18. lst09-18-examystats.sql

```sql
SQL> select * from
    (select phys_reads+phys_writes+redo_size mb_requested,
            offload_eligible mb_eligible_offload,
            interconnect_bytes interconnect_mb,
            storageindex_bytes storageindex_mb_saved, flashcache_hits flashcache_mb,
            round(((case
               when offload_eligible=0 then 0
               when offload_eligible> 0 then
             (100*(((phys_reads+phys_writes+redo_size)-interconnect_bytes) /
               (phys_reads+phys_writes+redo_size)))
            end)),2) smartscan_efficiency,
            interconnect_bytes/dbt interconnect_mbps,
            (phys_reads+phys_writes+redo_size)-(storageindex_bytes+flashcache_hits)
             cell_mb_processed,
            ((phys_reads+phys_writes+redo_size)-(storageindex_bytes+flashcache_hits))
             /dbt cell_mbps
    from (
     select * from (
        select name,mb,dbt from (
         select stats.name,tm.dbt dbt,
            (case
              when stats.name='physical reads' then (stats.value * dbbs.value)/1024/1024
              when stats.name='physical writes' then
                asm.asm_redundancy*((stats.value * dbbs.value)/1024/1024)
              when stats.name='redo size' then asm.asm_redundancy*((stats.value *
512)/1024/1024)
              when stats.name like 'cell physi%' then stats.value/1024/1024
              when stats.name like 'cell%flash%' then (stats.value * dbbs.value)/1024/1024
              else stats.value
            end) mb
         from (
           select b.name,
              value
           from    v$mystat a,
             v$statname b
           where  a.statistic# = b.statistic#
           and b.name in
             ( 'cell physical IO bytes eligible for predicate offload',
               'cell physical IO interconnect bytes',
               'cell physical IO interconnect bytes returned by smart scan',
               'cell flash cache read hits','cell physical IO bytes saved by storage index',
               'physical reads',
               'physical writes',
               'redo size')
             ) stats,
             (select value from v$parameter where name='db_block_size') dbbs,
             (select decode(max(type),'NORMAL',2,'HIGH',3,2) asm_redundancy
```

```
                    from v$asm_diskgroup ) asm,
                    (select b.value/100 dbt
                    from v$mystat b, v$statname a
                    where a.statistic#=b.statistic#
                    and a.name='DB time') tm
            )) pivot (sum(mb) for (name)
                in ('cell physical IO bytes eligible for predicate offload'  as offload_eligible,
                    'cell physical IO interconnect bytes'                    as interconnect_bytes,
                    'cell physical IO interconnect bytes returned by smart scan' as smartscan_returned,
                    'cell flash cache read hits'                             as flashcache_hits,
                    'cell physical IO bytes saved by storage index'          as storageindex_bytes,
                    'physical reads'                                         as phys_reads,
                    'physical writes'                                        as phys_writes,
                    'redo size'                                              as redo_size))
        ))
        unpivot
        (statval for stattype in
                (mb_requested as 'MB Requested',
                 mb_eligible_offload as 'MB Eligible for Offload',
                 smartscan_efficiency as 'Smart Scan Efficiency',
                 interconnect_mb as 'Interconnect MB',
                 interconnect_mbps as 'Interconnect MBPS',
                 storageindex_mb_saved as 'Storage Index MB Saved',
                 flashcache_mb as 'Flash Cache MB read',
                 cell_mb_processed as 'Cell MB Processed' ,
                 cell_mbps as 'Cell MBPS'))
  /

Statistic                          Statistic Value
-----------------------------      -----------------
MB Requested                              3277.79
MB Eligible for Offload                   3272.25
Smart Scan Efficiency                       95.69
Interconnect MB                            141.14
Interconnect MBPS                           42.77
Storage Index MB Saved                        .00
Flash Cache MB read                           .17
Cell MB Processed                         3277.62
Cell MBPS                                  993.22
```

In this output, you can see that the query requested approximately 3,277 MB of data of which 3,272 was eligible for Exadata Smart Scan and returned approximately 141 MB of data over the InfiniBand interconnect, yielding 95.69% Smart Scan efficiency. Additionally, note that the query returned in 3.3 seconds.

■ **Note** Chapter 15 will present additional details and explanations about measuring Smart Scan behavior and, specifically, Recipe 15-3 discusses how to measure Smart Scan metrics and overall I/O metrics from V$MYSTAT on Exadata.

10. Now we'll run the same tests against our `MMT_NOSS` table, which resides on an ASM disk group with `cell.smart_scan_capable` set to FALSE.

```
APPS @ visx1> select count(1) from (
    select /*+ full (x) */ *
    from mmt_noss x)
/

  COUNT(1)
----------
   8783431
Elapsed time: 16.61
APPS @ visx1> @lst09-18-examystats.sql
Statistic                      Statistic Value
------------------------------ ----------------
MB Requested                           3277.79
MB Eligible for Offload                   0.00
Smart Scan Efficiency                     0.00
Interconnect MB                        3273.68
... Output omitted for brevity
```

As you can see, zero bytes were eligible for Smart Scan, the offload efficiency was zero, and the query returned in 16.61 seconds.

How It Works

Setting the `cell.smart_scan_capable` ASM disk group attribute to TRUE will enable Smart Scan for qualifying SQL queries that access segments contained in the disk group, and setting the attribute to FALSE will disable Smart Scan. Exadata's storage server software examines this ASM disk group attribute as it ingests the iDB-encapsulated I/O request metadata from the SQL statements on the compute nodes and uses this attribute to determine whether to perform offload operations or act as a traditional block I/O server.

In real-world scenarios, we rarely see a non-academic business justification for setting `cell.smart_scan_capable` to FALSE. Exadata's most powerful performance feature is Smart Scan; disabling Smart Scan removes Exadata's biggest performance tool from the toolbox. This being said, using the ASM disk group `cell.smart_scan_capable` parameter can arguably be the most simple way to simply "turn off" Smart Scan, which in some cases may be interesting to do if you are conducting a "what if" analysis.

■ **Note** Use caution when disabling Smart Scan at the ASM disk group level and make sure to enable it unless you have a strong business justification to leave `cell.smart_scan_capable` set to FALSE. In our experience, ASM disk group attribute settings are one layer too deep in the technology stack for most traditional Oracle database administrators to consider when troubleshooting performance problems, and it can be maddening to try to figure out why Smart Scan isn't working on your Exadata environment if you have disabled it for an ASM disk group.

9-11. Creating Flash Grid Disks for Permanent Storage

Problem

You wish to utilize Exadata's storage server PCI Flash cards for permanent database file storage to improve I/O performance for specific database objects.

Solution

Generally speaking, database storage on Exadata is stored on the physical SAS disks inside the Exadata storage cells and the PCI flash is configured for Smart Flash Cache and Smart Flash Logging functionality. However, Oracle *does* allow an Exadata DMA to configure a storage server's PCI flash storage for use of *permanent* database storage in order to optimize specific types of I/O operations. This is achieved by creating flash-based grid disks in your storage cells and using these flash grid disks in Oracle ASM disk groups. In this recipe, we will show you how to do the following:

- Drop your flash cache in preparation for creating flash-based grid disks
- Create flash-based grid disks on your storage cells
- Recreating flash cache with the remaining flash capacity
- Build Oracle ASM disk groups on your flash storage
- Create an Oracle tablespace on your flash-based disk groups and test the performance impact of querying similar data from flash versus SAS disk storage

Follow these steps:

1. Begin by logging in to a compute node as an operating system account that has SSH trust configured with the storage cells and listing the details of your flash cache using `cellcli`; in the following example, we will use the `oracle` Linux account:

```
[oracle@cm01dbm01 ~]$ dcli -g ./cell_group cellcli -e list flashcache attributes name,size,celldisk
cm01cel01: cm01cel01_FLASHCACHE    364.75G
FD_05_cm01cel01,FD_02_cm01cel01,FD_06_cm01cel01,FD_07_cm01cel01,FD_13_cm01cel01,
FD_01_cm01cel01,FD_08_cm01cel01,FD_11_cm01cel01,FD_15_cm01cel01,FD_12_cm01cel01,
FD_14_cm01cel01,FD_10_cm01cel01,FD_00_cm01cel01,FD_04_cm01cel01,FD_03_cm01cel01,
FD_09_cm01cel01
cm01cel02: cm01cel02_FLASHCACHE    364.75G
FD_11_cm01cel02,FD_07_cm01cel02,FD_14_cm01cel02,FD_06_cm01cel02,FD_04_cm01cel02,
FD_05_cm01cel02,FD_02_cm01cel02,FD_01_cm01cel02,FD_10_cm01cel02,FD_08_cm01cel02,
FD_00_cm01cel02,FD_03_cm01cel02,FD_12_cm01cel02,FD_15_cm01cel02,FD_13_cm01cel02,
FD_09_cm01cel02
cm01cel03: cm01cel03_FLASHCACHE    364.75G
FD_02_cm01cel03,FD_15_cm01cel03,FD_04_cm01cel03,FD_07_cm01cel03,FD_13_cm01cel03,
FD_05_cm01cel03,FD_01_cm01cel03,FD_06_cm01cel03,FD_00_cm01cel03,FD_09_cm01cel03,
FD_11_cm01cel03,FD_10_cm01cel03,FD_03_cm01cel03,FD_12_cm01cel03,FD_08_cm01cel03,
FD_14_cm01cel03
[oracle@cm01dbm01 ~]$
```

2. In the output above, you can see that flash cache is enabled on each storage cell with a capacity of 364.75 GB. Next, drop your flash cache using the `cellcli` command below:

```
[oracle@cm01dbm01 ~]$ dcli -g ./cell_group cellcli -e drop flashcache all
cm01cel01: Flash cache cm01cel01_FLASHCACHE successfully dropped
```

CHAPTER 9 ■ STORAGE ADMINISTRATION

```
cm01cel02: Flash cache cm01cel02_FLASHCACHE successfully dropped
cm01cel03: Flash cache cm01cel03_FLASHCACHE successfully dropped
[oracle@cm01dbm01 ~]$
```

3. After this completes, recreate your flash cache with a smaller size, leaving room for flash grid disks. In the following example, we will create our flash disks with a capacity of 100 GB:

```
[oracle@cm01dbm01 ~]$ dcli -g ./cell_group cellcli -e create flashcache all size=100G
cm01cel01: Flash cache cm01cel01_FLASHCACHE successfully created
cm01cel02: Flash cache cm01cel02_FLASHCACHE successfully created
cm01cel03: Flash cache cm01cel03_FLASHCACHE successfully created
```

4. Create flash grid disks on the remaining free capacity on your flash storage by running the command below:

```
[oracle@cm01dbm01 ~]$ dcli -g ./cell_group cellcli -e create griddisk all flashdisk
prefix='FLASH'
cm01cel01: GridDisk FLASH_FD_00_cm01cel01 successfully created
cm01cel01: GridDisk FLASH_FD_01_cm01cel01 successfully created
cm01cel01: GridDisk FLASH_FD_02_cm01cel01 successfully created
... output omitted
```

5. Let's examine the attributes of one of our newly created flash grid disks using the `cellcli` command below:

```
[oracle@cm01dbm01 ~]$ dcli -c cm01cel01 cellcli -e list griddisk where
name=FLASH_FD_00_cm01cel01 detail
cm01cel01: name:                 FLASH_FD_00_cm01cel01
cm01cel01: asmDiskGroupName:
cm01cel01: asmDiskName:
cm01cel01: availableTo:
cm01cel01: cellDisk:              FD_00_cm01cel01
cm01cel01: comment:
cm01cel01: creationTime:          2012-09-14T14:26:09-04:00
cm01cel01: diskType:              FlashDisk
cm01cel01: errorCount:            0
cm01cel01: id:                    5ab896bf-61fc-4f79-b92d-384d511a7a54
cm01cel01: offset:                6.3125G
cm01cel01: size:                  16.546875G
cm01cel01: status:                active
[oracle@cm01dbm01 ~]$
```

You can see that the size of this specific grid disk is roughly 16.55 GB. With 16 flash disks per storage cell, our total grid disk capacity per cell is (16.55 GB) * (16) = 264.75 GB. On an Exadata X2-2 Quarter Rack, this equates to approximately 794.25 GB of capacity for our flash grid disks.

6. Log in to a compute node as the Grid Infrastructure software owner, launch SQL*Plus and connect as SYSASM to create an Oracle ASM disk group based on these grid disks, using the script in Listing 9-19.

293

Listing 9-19. lst09-19-create-flashdiskgroup.sql

```
SQL> create diskgroup FLASH_CM01
    normal redundancy
    disk 'o/*/FLASH*'
    attribute 'compatible.rdbms' = '11.2.0.3.0',
              'compatible.asm' = '11.2.0.3.0',
              'cell.smart_scan_capable' = 'TRUE',
              'au_size' = '4M';

Diskgroup created.

SQL>
```

7. Query v$asm_diskgroup to confirm the total and available size of your new ASM diskgroup:

```
SQL> select name,type,total_mb,free_mb from v$asm_diskgroup
    where (name ='&&diskgroup_name' or '&&diskgroup_name' is null)
  /
old   2: where (name ='&&diskgroup_name' or '&&diskgroup_name' is null)
new   2: where (name ='FLASH_CM01' or 'FLASH_CM01' is null)

NAME                     TYPE      TOTAL_MB     FREE_MB
------------------       ------    ----------   ----------
FLASH_CM01               NORMAL      813312       812712

SQL>
```

8. Connect to SQL*Plus from a database instance and build a tablespace using this ASM disk group:

```
SQL> create tablespace flash_tbs datafile '+FLASH_CM01'
  2  size 4000m extent management local uniform size 64m;

Tablespace created.

SQL>
```

9. To test the performance impact of storing tables permanently on flash storage, create your tables in the newly created tablespace and measure the query and DML performance against the traditional SAS storage. In the following example, we will copy a relatively large table to our new tablespace and measure full table scan performance. Our test table looks like the following:

```
SQL> select t.owner,t.table_name,t.blocks,
    t.tablespace_name,replace(substr(d.file_name,1,11),'/','') fn
    from dba_tables t, dba_data_files d
    where t.table_name in ('MMT_SS','MMT_FLASH')
    and t.tablespace_name=d.tablespace_name
  /
```

```
    Owner         Table         Blocks      Tablespace      Disk Group
    ----------    ----------    --------    ------------    ----------------
    APPS          MMT_FLASH     419580      FLASH_TBS       +FLASH_CM01
    APPS          MMT_SS        419736      TS1             +DATA_CM01

    SQL>
```

If we run a full-scan query against both of our tables, the results look like the following:

```
APPS @ visx1> select count(1) from (
     select /*+ full (x) */ *
     from mmt_ss x)
    ;

  COUNT(1)
----------
   8783431
APPS @ visx1> set echo off
Elapsed time: 1.27

                                                              Cell Disk    Cell Disk
Req. MB       Eligible MB    NB MB    Offload Effic.  NB MBPS    IO (MB)    MBPS
----------    -----------    -------  --------------  -------  ---------  ----------
   3284.00       3272.25      141.75           95.68   111.61    3282.68     2584.78
APPS @ visx1>

APPS @ visx1> select count(1) from (
  2    select /*+ full (x) */ *
  3    from mmt_flash x)
  4  ;

  COUNT(1)
----------
   8783431
APPS @ visx1> set echo off
Elapsed time: .61

                                                              Cell Disk    Cell Disk
Req. MB       Eligible MB    NB MB    Offload Effic.  NB MBPS    IO (MB)    MBPS
----------    -----------    -------  --------------  -------  ---------  ----------
   3273.45       3271.88      140.40           95.71   230.17    3273.25     5365.99
APPS @ visx1>
```

The results of these simple tests demonstrate a few things:

- Each query was eligible for and used Exadata Smart Scan.
- The disk bandwidth for the query against MMT_FLASH was more than double that of the query against MMT_SS.
- The query on flash disks completed in approximately half the time.

> **Note** Chapter 15 provides additional details and information about how to capture Smart Scan statistics and measure Smart Scan behavior. Please refer to recipes in Chapter 15 to learn more about this topic.

How It Works

Each Exadata storage cell in the X2-2 and X2-8 configurations is installed with four 96 GB PCIe Sun Flash Accelerator cards, *primarily* designed to provide flash storage for Exadata's Smart Flash Cache and Smart Flash Logging features. Each PCI flash card is partitioned into four sections, as discussed in Recipe 1-1, and each of these four FDOMs is presented as a cell disk; on a single storage server, you will see 16 cell disks of type `FlashDisk`.

> **Note** The Exadata X3-2 and X3-8 storage cells are configured with larger PCI flash cards, yielding significantly more flash storage. To learn more about the hardware configuration of Exadata's flash cards, please see Recipes 1-1 and 1-6. Chapter 18 also provides multiple recipes on the topics of Smart Flash Cache and Smart Flash Logging.

Exadata DMAs typically will elect to use all of the flash disk capacity for Smart Flash Cache and Smart Flash Logging, but you *can* choose to configure these flash cards for permanent database storage. This is achieved by building flash-based grid disks upon the flash disks to expose the storage to Oracle ASM, along with creating Oracle ASM disk groups on these flash-based grid disks.

Many Exadata DMAs entertain the idea of placing permanent storage on flash grid disks in order to improve performance. Our advice is that you should have a very specific I/O-latency business problem before proceeding with this decision because using flash storage for your database files reduces the capacity available for Smart Flash Cache.

Additionally, it is common for Exadata DMAs to *consider* placing online redo log files in flash grid disks to provide better redo log writer write times. With the advent of Smart Flash Logging and some general understanding of the DRAM cache on each SAS disk, we do not generally recommend this type of configuration.

> **Note** Recipe 18-7 discusses the topic of Smart Flash Logging in detail, along with the write-back versus write-through design details with Exadata storage.

CHAPTER 10

Network Administration

Exadata's compute nodes consist of a management network, a client access network, an InfiniBand network used for both the storage and Oracle RAC cluster interconnect, and an optional additional network. Exadata's storage cells are deployed with a similar management network as well as the InfiniBand storage network.

In this chapter, you will learn how to confidently manage and administer the various network components in the Exadata Database Machine.

10-1. Configuring the Management Network on the Compute Nodes

Problem

You wish to validate and modify the administrative network on the Exadata Compute Nodes.

Solution

In this recipe, you will learn how to validate your current administrative network configuration on the Exadata Compute Nodes and modify the administration network configuration.

The administration or management network is called the NET0 network and is used to provide shell access via SSH to the Exadata DMA. The NET0 network is enabled on interface eth0. To display the configuration, log in to a compute node and run the following `ifconfig` command:

```
[root@cm01dbm01 ~]# ifconfig eth0
eth0      Link encap:Ethernet  HWaddr 00:21:28:B2:17:02
          inet addr:172.16.1.10  Bcast:172.16.1.255  Mask:255.255.255.0
      ... Output omitted for brevity
[root@cm01dbm01 ~]#
```

This NET0/admin network is comprised of a single network interface and is not typically deployed with channel bonding, although in some rare cases clients choose to bond the eth0 interface with the NET3/eth3 interface to provide additional network interface redundancy.

When configuring DNS for your Exadata Database Machine, the host name of each compute node is registered with the IP address of the NET0/admin interface. Validate this by using `nslookup` from any host on your network and compare the IP address returned from the DNS query with that of the previous `ifconfig` output:

```
Macintosh-8:~ jclarke$ nslookup cm01dbm01
Server:         11.11.1.250
Address:        11.11.1.250#53
```

```
Name: cm01dbm01.centroid.com
Address: 172.16.1.10
Macintosh-8:~ jclarke$
```

To change the IP address of your NET0/admin network, edit /etc/sysconfig/network-scripts/ifcfg-eth0. A sample of this configuration file based on the previous ifconfig output is provided:

```
root@cm01dbm01 ~]# cat /etc/sysconfig/network-scripts/ifcfg-eth0
#### DO NOT REMOVE THESE LINES ####
#### %GENERATED BY CELL% ####
DEVICE=eth0
BOOTPROTO=static
ONBOOT=yes
IPADDR=10.16.1.10
NETMASK=255.255.255.0
NETWORK=10.16.1.0
BROADCAST=10.16.1.255
GATEWAY=10.16.1.1
HOTPLUG=no
IPV6INIT=no
HWADDR=00:21:28:b2:17:02
[root@cm01dbm01 ~]#
```

After changing ifcfg-eth0, determine if other network interfaces require changes as well as the ILOM interface, NET1-2 interfaces, and any other configuration files. Specifically, when changing the management network's IP address, you will need to locate the entry in /etc/hosts and make the necessary modification:

```
[root@cm01dbm01 ~]# grep cm01dbm01 /etc/hosts
192.168.10.1     cm01dbm01-priv.centroid.com     cm01dbm01-priv
10.16.1.10       cm01dbm01.centroid.com          cm01dbm01
192.168.10.1     cm01dbm01-priv.centroid.com     cm01dbm01-priv
[root@cm01dbm01 ~]#
```

Next, change the ListenAddress to match your new eth0 IP address in /etc/ssh/sshd_config. This will enable remote users to obtain shell access via SSH to the administrative network:

```
[root@cm01dbm01 ~]# grep Listen   /etc/ssh/sshd_config
#ListenAddress 0.0.0.0
#ListenAddress ::
ListenAddress 10.16.1.10
ListenAddress 192.168.10.1
```

After these changes are made, you must modify your routing rules for your management network in /etc/sysconfig/network-scripts/route-eth0. For example:

```
[root@cm01dbm01] # cd /etc/sysconfig/network-scripts
[root@cm01dbm01] # network-scripts]# ls route-eth0
route-eth0
[root@cm01dbm01 network-scripts]# cat route-eth0
172.16.1.0/24 dev eth0 table 220
default via 172.16.1.1 dev eth0 table 220
[root@cm01dbm01] #
```

After the changes are complete, restart your network services by running one of the following commands:

```
root@cm01dbm01 ~]# service network restart
... or
root@cm01dbm01 ~]# ifdown eth0
root@cm01dbm01 ~]# ifup eth0
```

■ **Note** Recipe 10-7 provides comprehensive steps to change your Exadata IP address information. Please see this recipe for the complete set of steps.

How It Works

Exadata Compute Nodes have at least three and typically four different networks. The administration or management network is called the NET0 network and is used to provide shell access via SSH to the Exadata DMA. The compute node administration network on each compute node is connected to the embedded Cisco 4948 switch. The compute node networks are explained as follows:

- The NET0/admin network allows for SSH connectivity to the server. It uses the eth0 interface, which is connected to the embedded Cisco switch.

- The NET1, NET2, NET1-2/Client Access network provides access to the Oracle RAC VIP address and SCAN addresses. It uses interfaces eth1 and eth2, which are typically bonded. These interfaces are connected to your data center network.

- The IB network connects two ports on the compute servers to both of the InfiniBand leaf switches in the rack. All storage server communication and Oracle RAC interconnect traffic uses this network.

- An optional "additional" network, NET3, which is built on eth3, is also provided. This is often used for backups and/or other external traffic.

The compute node administration network is also referred to as the NET0 network or management network. This network is configured during the initial installation process by Oracle ACS based on your site requirements and as provided in your configuration worksheet.

10-2. Configuring the Client Access Network
Problem

You wish to validate and modify the client access network and associated Oracle cluster-related network resources on the Exadata Compute Nodes.

Solution

In this recipe, we will provide a brief overview of the Exadata Compute Node client access network, show you how to validate your current network configuration, and modify your client access network configuration on the compute servers.

The client access network on the Exadata Compute Nodes is created on the NET1, NET2, or bonded NET1-2 network. The NET1-2 network is typically built on the eth1 and eth2 interfaces and is bonded to create the bondeth0 interface. Run the following `ifconfig` command to validate this:

```
[root@cm01dbm01 network-scripts]# ifconfig bondeth0
bondeth0  Link encap:Ethernet  HWaddr 00:21:28:B2:17:03
          inet addr:172.16.10.10  Bcast:172.16.10.255  Mask:255.255.255.0
... Output omitted for brevity
[root@cm01dbm01 network-scripts]#
```

This output shows that bondeth0 uses the 172.16.10.10 IP address; at your site, this IP address will be within the range of IP addresses provided in the client access network section of your configuration worksheet.

On each compute node, one or more additional bonded networks are typically established on this client access network, as depicted in the following `ifconfig` output:

```
bondeth0  Link encap:Ethernet  HWaddr 00:21:28:B2:17:03
          inet addr:172.16.10.10  Bcast:172.16.10.255  Mask:255.255.255.0
... Output omitted for brevity
bondeth0:1 Link encap:Ethernet  HWaddr 00:21:28:B2:17:03
          inet addr:172.16.10.12  Bcast:172.16.10.255  Mask:255.255.255.0
... Output omitted for brevity
bondeth0:2 Link encap:Ethernet  HWaddr 00:21:28:B2:17:03
          inet addr:172.16.10.16  Bcast:172.16.10.255  Mask:255.255.255.0
... Output omitted for brevity
```

In this output, the 172.16.10.12 interface is the node's VIP address and the 172.16.10.16 address is one of our SCAN addresses. You cannot tell this from the `ifconfig` output, but a simple series of DNS queries confirms this:

```
Macintosh-8:~ jclarke$ nslookup   172.16.10.12
Server:         11.11.1.250
Address:        11.11.1.250#53
12.10.16.172.in-addr.arpa    name = cm01dbm01-vip.centroid.com.
12.10.16.172.in-addr.arpa    name = cm0101-vip.centroid.com.
Macintosh-8:~ jclarke$ nslookup 172.16.10.16
Server:         11.11.1.250
Address:        11.11.1.250#53
16.10.16.172.in-addr.arpa         name = cm01-scan.centroid.com.
Macintosh-8:~ jclarke$
```

Since your client access network services multiple Oracle cluster networking purposes and functionality, changing your client access network entails a number of steps:

1. First, you must stop your Oracle cluster resources.

2. Edit /etc/sysconfig/network-scripts/ifcfg-bondeth0 and make the necessary IP address changes.

3. Change the GATEWAY in /etc/sysconfig/network.

4. Check your interface configuration using `oifcfg` from your Grid Infrastructure software installation, delete the bondeth0 network, and re-add it with the changed IP address.

5. Next, you will need to perform several steps to modify your Oracle cluster network resources.

Note Recipes 10-4, 10-5, and 10-7 provide detailed information about managing your cluster-related network resources and changing IP addresses on Exadata Compute Nodes.

How It Works

Exadata Compute Nodes have at least three and typically four different networks. The client access network is comprised of either or both the NET1 and NET2 network interfaces. Typically, organizations will choose to perform channel bonding on these two interfaces and create a NET1-2 network for the client access network.

The NET1 and NET2 interfaces are physically connected to your data center network. Their purpose is to provide network communications for your Oracle cluster-related network resources, such as Single Client Access Network (SCAN) networks and listeners, database listeners, and virtual IP addresses (VIPs).

The client access network on Exadata is configured and managed the same way it is on non-Exadata 11gR2 environments because Oracle Grid Infrastructure and Oracle RAC on Exadata works the same way as it does on other Oracle 11gR2 environments. With Exadata, Oracle provides two physical network interfaces for the client access network, NET1 (eth1) and NET2 (eth2). Organizations typically choose to bond these interfaces together for availability purposes. By default, the bondeth0 bond is configured in an active-backup configuration:

```
#### DO NOT REMOVE THESE LINES ####
#### %GENERATED BY CELL% ####
DEVICE=bondeth0
USERCTL=no
BOOTPROTO=none
ONBOOT=yes
IPADDR=172.16.10.10
NETMASK=255.255.255.0
NETWORK=172.16.10.0
BROADCAST=172.16.10.255
BONDING_OPTS="mode=active-backup miimon=100 downdelay=5000 updelay=5000 num_grat_arp=100"
IPV6INIT=no
GATEWAY=172.16.10.1
```

As is the case in all Oracle 11gR2 Grid Infrastructure and RAC environments, the VIP addresses and SCAN listener addresses are enabled on the client access network and need to be registered in DNS in order for your network to function.

10-3. Configuring the Private Interconnect on the Compute Nodes

Problem

You wish to validate your Exadata Compute Node's InfiniBand network configuration and confirm that your Oracle RAC interconnect is using the InfiniBand network.

Solution

In this recipe, you will learn how to list your InfiniBand network details on the compute nodes, understand how the InfiniBand network is built, and validate that your Oracle RAC interconnect is using the InfiniBand network.

On Exadata, the Oracle RAC private interconnect runs on the InfiniBand network, which is the same network that Exadata's storage network runs on. This InfiniBand private interconnect runs on a bonded InfiniBand interface, bondib0. To validate this, log in to your compute server as root and run ifconfig on the bonded InfiniBand interface:

```
[root@cm01dbm01 ~]# ifconfig bondib0
bondib0    Link encap:InfiniBand    HWaddr
80:00:00:48:FE:80:00:00:00:00:00:00:00:00:00:00:00:00:00:00
           inet addr:192.168.10.1  Bcast:192.168.11.255  Mask:255.255.252.0
... Additional interface details omitted
[root@cm01dbm01 ~]#
```

The Oracle RAC interconnect is deployed using Oracle's Cluster High Availability IP framework, or HAIP. We can find the details of the cluster HAIP by querying the relevant cluster resource:

```
[root@cm01dbm01 ~]# /u01/app/11.2.0.3/grid/bin/crsctl stat res -init -w "TYPE = ora.haip.type"
NAME=ora.cluster_interconnect.haip
TYPE=ora.haip.type
TARGET=ONLINE
STATE=ONLINE on cm01dbm01
[root@cm01dbm01 ~]#
```

> **Note** In this crsctl query, the -init argument lists the core Oracle CRS processes, such as ora.crsd, ora.cssd, ora.cluster_interconnect.haip, and so forth. The -w argument provides a means to display only a specific section of the resource, by name. In the previous example, we're displaying the Oracle CRS processes where TYPE = ora.haip.type.

Using oifcfg, you can find where Oracle places the InfiniBand network. Following, we see that the cluster interconnect is on network 192.168.8.0/22, the bondib0 interface. This is essentially a non-routable network dedicated for cluster interconnect traffic.

```
[root@cm01dbm01 ~]# /u01/app/11.2.0.3/grid/bin/oifcfg getif
bondib0    192.168.8.0   global   cluster_interconnect
bondeth0   172.16.10.0   global   public
[root@cm01dbm01 ~]#
```

You can also log in to either a database instance or ASM instance to validate the cluster_interconnects initialization parameter. Following, we see the 192.168.10.1 and 192.168.10.2 IP addresses, which in our case correspond to both of the compute nodes in our Exadata Quarter Rack.

```
[grid@cm01dbm01 ~]$ sqlplus / as sysasm
SQL*Plus: Release 11.2.0.3.0 Production on Fri Jul 27 17:54:42 2012
Copyright (c) 1982, 2011, Oracle.  All rights reserved.
```

```
Connected to:
Oracle Database 11g Enterprise Edition Release 11.2.0.3.0 - 64bit Production
With the Real Application Clusters and Automatic Storage Management options

SQL> select * from gv$cluster_interconnects;

   INST_ID NAME             IP_ADDRESS       IS_ SOURCE
---------- ---------------- ---------------- --- ------------------------
         1 bondib0          192.168.10.1     NO  cluster_interconnects parameter
         2 bondib0          192.168.10.2     NO  cluster_interconnects parameter
SQL>
```

As stated, the Oracle interconnect traffic is over the InfiniBand network. Confirm this by running skgxpinfo from the 11gR2 Grid Infrastructure software directory:

```
[grid@cm01dbm01 ~]$ which skgxpinfo
/u01/app/11.2.0.3/grid/bin/skgxpinfo
[grid@cm01dbm01 ~]$ /u01/app/11.2.0.3/grid/bin/skgxpinfo -v
Oracle RDS/IP (generic)
[grid@cm01dbm01 ~]$
```

This shows that the communication protocol is using Oracle RDS/IP—RDS is the InfiniBand protocol.

■ **Note** If you have a need to change your InfiniBand network configuration on Exadata, it is best to engage Oracle Support and/or follow My Oracle Support note 283684.1 to ensure that the cluster interconnect information is modified appropriately. Changing your interconnect information carries implications with your storage network as well.

How It Works

As documented in the Oracle Exadata Owner's Manual and other sources, the InfiniBand network serves as both the storage network and Oracle RAC private interconnect on Exadata. Oracle binaries in both the RDBMS and Grid Infrastructure homes are linked with the ipc_rds flags on Exadata, which you can see by examining the contents of $ORACLE_HOME/rdbms/lib/ins_rdbms.mk:

```
ipc_rds:
        -$(RMF) $(LIBSKGXP)
        $(CP) $(LIBHOME)/libskgxpr.$(SKGXP_EXT) $(LIBSKGXP)

ipc_relink:
        (if $(ORACLE_HOME)/bin/skgxpinfo | grep rds;\
        then \
        $(MAKE) -f $(MAKEFILE) ipc_rds; \
        else \
        $(MAKE) -f $(MAKEFILE) ipc_g; \
        fi)
```

Note than an Exadata DMA can mistakenly choose to relink binaries without RDS on Exadata; there is nothing on the compute nodes that prevents this from happening and, in fact, Oracle only decides to link with RDS if the output of the skgxpinfo command returns "RDS". When Oracle ACS installs the software on Exadata, the skgxpinfo.o object file is compiled with RDS enabled and after this, skgxpinfo is relinked. Once this is complete, Oracle binaries are linked with ipc_rds. If you check the contents of your /opt/oracle.SupportTools/onecommand/tmp directory, you will see evidence of this:

```
[root@cm01dbm01 tmp]# grep ipc_rds *
installActions2011-05-03_03-45-58PM.log:   make -f
/u01/app/11.2.0/grid/rdbms/lib/ins_rdbms.mk ipc_rds; \
installActions2011-05-03_04-01-33PM.log:   make -f
/u01/app/oracle/product/11.2.0/dbhome_1/rdbms/lib/ins_rdbms.mk ipc_rds; \
... Output omitted for brevity
```

10-4. Configuring the SCAN Listener

Problem

You are installing Oracle RAC on Exadata or changing network IP address information and wish to configure your Oracle SCAN listener.

Solution

In this recipe, you will learn how to list your Oracle SCAN listener configuration and modify your SCAN network and SCAN listener IP addresses.

Start by checking your current SCAN and SCAN listener configuration:

```
[grid@cm01dbm01 ~]$ srvctl config scan
SCAN name: cm01-scan, Network: 1/172.16.10.0/255.255.255.0/bondeth0
SCAN VIP name: scan1, IP: /cm01-scan/172.16.10.16
SCAN VIP name: scan2, IP: /cm01-scan/172.16.10.15
SCAN VIP name: scan3, IP: /cm01-scan/172.16.10.1
[grid@cm01dbm01 ~]$ srvctl config scan_listener
SCAN Listener LISTENER_SCAN1 exists. Port: TCP:1521
SCAN Listener LISTENER_SCAN2 exists. Port: TCP:1521
SCAN Listener LISTENER_SCAN3 exists. Port: TCP:1521
[grid@cm01dbm01 ~]$
```

When network resources are configured for an Exadata 11gR2 Grid Infrastructure installation, you are required to enter a SCAN name; in the previous example, we used a SCAN name of cm01-scan. The nslookup command below confirms the required three IP addresses for your SCAN network:

```
Macintosh-8:~ jclarke$ nslookup cm01-scan
Server:         11.11.1.250
Address:        11.11.1.250#53
Name: cm01-scan.centroid.com
Address: 172.16.10.16
Name: cm01-scan.centroid.com
Address: 172.16.10.15
Name: cm01-scan.centroid.com
Address: 172.16.10.14
Macintosh-8:~ jclarke$
```

If you wish to change your SCAN IP address information, you must first stop your cluster resources as outlined:

```
[grid@cm01dbm01 ~]$ srvctl stop scan_listener
[grid@cm01dbm01 ~]$ srvctl stop scan
```

Once down, you will need to modify the SCAN and ora.net1.network network. You will need to be logged in as root to perform these tasks:

```
[root@cm01dbm01 ~]# $CRS_HOME/bin/srvctl modify scan -n [scan name]
[root@cm01dbm01 ~]# $CRS_HOME/bin/srvctl modify network -S [new network]/[new subnet mask]/bondeth0
```

Next, modify the SCAN listener and the IP address information as the Grid Infrastructure owner and start your SCAN listeners:

```
[grid@cm01dbm01 ~]$ srvctl modify scan_listener -u
[grid@cm01dbm01 ~]$ srvctl start scan_listener
```

When finished, validate your configuration:

```
[grid@cm01dbm01 ~]$ srvctl config scan
[grid@cm01dbm01 ~]$ srvctl config scan_listener
```

■ **Note** Recipe 10-7 provides detailed information about how to change IP addresses on your Exadata Database Machine; changing SCAN network information is a piece of this process.

How It Works

In Oracle 11gR2 Grid Infrastructure with Oracle RAC on Exadata, Oracle requires a Single Client Access Network and SCAN listener to be created. The Grid Infrastructure installation will configure this and enable its network addresses on the client access network on each compute node upon which it starts a SCAN listener. The IP addresses for your SCAN listener must be registered in DNS as outlined in Recipes 6-2 and 6-3.

SCAN and SCAN listener configuration and management topics on Exadata are no different than on non-Exadata 11gR2 Grid Infrastructure environments. On Exadata:

- On the X2-2, X3-2 Eighth Rack, and X3-2 Quarter Rack, three SCAN listeners, two running one node and one running on the other node (if healthy), and a local listener running on the VIP address

- On the X2-2 and X3-2 Half Rack, three SCAN listeners, one running on three of the four compute nodes, one compute node without a SCAN listener, and a local listener running on the VIP address

- On the X2-2 and X3-2 Full Rack, three SCAN listeners, one running on three of the eight compute nodes, five compute nodes without a SCAN listener, and a local listener running on the VIP address

- On the X2-8 and X3-8 Full Rack, three SCAN listeners, two running one node and one running on the other node (if healthy), and a local listener running on the VIP address

10-5. Managing Grid Infrastructure Network Resources
Problem
You wish to validate the Oracle 11gR2 Grid Infrastructure network resources and configuration on Exadata in order to confidently manage your Grid Infrastructure network components.

Solution
In this recipe, you will learn how to identify and manage the following 11gR2 Grid Infrastructure network components and resources:

- The Oracle Cluster High Availability IP framework, or HAIP
- The ora.net1.network Oracle cluster resource
- The virtual IP addresses, or VIPs
- The SCAN network and SCAN listeners
- The database listeners

Validate your Oracle Cluster High Availability IP Framework
Start by examining your Oracle's Cluster High Availability IP framework, or HAIP. This is the interface upon which your Oracle RAC interconnect is deployed. You can find the details of the cluster HAIP by querying the relevant cluster resource:

```
[root@cm01dbm01 ~]# /u01/app/11.2.0.3/grid/bin/crsctl stat res -init -w "TYPE = ora.haip.type"
NAME=ora.cluster_interconnect.haip
TYPE=ora.haip.type
TARGET=ONLINE
STATE=ONLINE on cm01dbm01
[root@cm01dbm01 ~]#
```

Using oifcfg, you can find where Oracle places the InfiniBand network. Following, we see that the cluster interconnect is on network 192.168.8.0, using the bondib0 interface:

```
[root@cm01dbm01 ~]# /u01/app/11.2.0.3/grid/bin/oifcfg getif
bondib0  192.168.8.0  global  cluster_interconnect
bondeth0  172.16.10.0  global  public
[root@cm01dbm01 ~]#
```

Validate Your ora.net1.network Oracle Cluster Resource
Log in as the Grid Infrastructure owner and confirm the status of the ora.network.type cluster resource:

```
[grid@cm01dbm01 ~]$ crsctl stat res -w "TYPE = ora.network.type"
NAME=ora.net1.network
TYPE=ora.network.type
```

```
TARGET=ONLINE              , ONLINE
STATE=ONLINE on cm01dbm01, ONLINE on cm01dbm02
[grid@cm01dbm01 ~]$
```

Confirm the network that your ora.net1.network uses by running the srvctl config nodeapps and/or srvctl config network command; in the following output, you will see that the 172.16.10.0/24 network is in use. This represents your client access network, as discussed in Recipe 10-2:

```
[grid@cm01dbm01 ~]$ srvctl config nodeapps
Network exists: 1/172.16.10.0/255.255.255.0/bondeth0, type static
VIP exists: /cm0101-vip/172.16.10.12/172.16.10.0/255.255.255.0/bondeth0, hosting node cm01dbm01
VIP exists: /cm0102-vip/172.16.10.13/172.16.10.0/255.255.255.0/bondeth0, hosting node cm01dbm02
... Additional output omitted
[grid@cm01dbm01 ~]$ srvctl config network
Network exists: 1/172.16.10.0/255.255.255.0/bondeth0, type static
[grid@cm01dbm01 ~]$
```

Validating Your VIP and SCAN Addresses

Your Oracle client access network is used for your VIPs, SCAN network, and SCAN listeners. The VIP addresses can be found using nslookup, if registered in DNS, combined with the srvctl config nodeapps command above and a simple ifconfig -a command on each compute node. Each node should have a single VIP address enabled on it, and it should be enabled on the bondeth0:1 interface:

```
[grid@cm01dbm01 ~]$ /sbin/ifconfig -a bondeth0:1
bondeth0:1 Link encap:Ethernet   HWaddr 00:21:28:B2:17:03
          inet addr:172.16.10.12  Bcast:172.16.10.255  Mask:255.255.255.0
          UP BROADCAST RUNNING MASTER MULTICAST  MTU:1500  Metric:1

[grid@cm01dbm01 ~]$

Macintosh-8:~ jclarke$ nslookup cm01dbm01-vip
Server:         11.11.1.250
Address:        11.11.1.250#53
Name: cm01dbm01-vip.centroid.com
Address: 172.16.10.12
Macintosh-8:~ jclarke$
```

Check your SCAN network and SCAN listeners by running the following srvctl commands:

```
[grid@cm01dbm01 ~]$ srvctl config scan
SCAN name: cm01-scan, Network: 1/172.16.10.0/255.255.255.0/bondeth0
SCAN VIP name: scan1, IP: /cm01-scan/172.16.10.16
SCAN VIP name: scan2, IP: /cm01-scan/172.16.10.15
SCAN VIP name: scan3, IP: /cm01-scan/172.16.10.14
[grid@cm01dbm01 ~]$ srvctl config scan_listener
SCAN Listener LISTENER_SCAN1 exists. Port: TCP:1521
SCAN Listener LISTENER_SCAN2 exists. Port: TCP:1521
SCAN Listener LISTENER_SCAN3 exists. Port: TCP:1521
[grid@cm01dbm01 ~]$
```

Similar to the VIP addresses, the SCAN network interfaces will be enabled on the bondeth0 interface and typically are bondeth0:2 and/or bondeth0:3.

Validating Your Database and SCAN Listeners

The SCAN and database listener configuration information will reside in the Grid Infrastructure software home's $ORACLE_HOME/network/admin directory. On both Exadata and non-Exadata 11gR2 Grid Infrastructure installations, Oracle will automatically configure your network configuration during the Grid Infrastructure software installation and subsequent database installations will register their local_listener and remote_listener initialization parameter according to VIP address and SCAN listener provided via dbca during the database creation. A sample listener.ora and endpoints_listener.ora file is provided below:

■ **Note** Please see Oracle's documentation to learn more about 11gR2 Grid Infrastructure listener configuration details.

```
[grid@cm01dbm01 admin]$ pwd
/u01/app/11.2.0.3/grid/network/admin
[grid@cm01dbm01 admin]$ more listener.ora
LISTENER=(DESCRIPTION=(ADDRESS_LIST=(ADDRESS=(PROTOCOL=IPC)(KEY=LISTENER))))
# line added by Agent
LISTENER_SCAN3=(DESCRIPTION=(ADDRESS_LIST=(ADDRESS=(PROTOCOL=IPC)(KEY=LISTENER_SCAN3))))
        # line added by Agent
LISTENER_SCAN2=(DESCRIPTION=(ADDRESS_LIST=(ADDRESS=(PROTOCOL=IPC)(KEY=LISTENER_SCAN2))))
        # line added by Agent
LISTENER_SCAN1=(DESCRIPTION=(ADDRESS_LIST=(ADDRESS=(PROTOCOL=IPC)(KEY=LISTENER_SCAN1))))
        # line added by Agent
ENABLE_GLOBAL_DYNAMIC_ENDPOINT_LISTENER_SCAN1=ON          # line added by Agent
ENABLE_GLOBAL_DYNAMIC_ENDPOINT_LISTENER_SCAN2=ON          # line added by Agent
ENABLE_GLOBAL_DYNAMIC_ENDPOINT_LISTENER_SCAN3=ON          # line added by Agent
ENABLE_GLOBAL_DYNAMIC_ENDPOINT_LISTENER=ON                # line added by Agent
ADMIN_RESTRICTION_LISTENER=ON
SQLNET.EXPIRE_TIME=10

[grid@cm01dbm01 admin]$ more endpoints_listener.ora
LISTENER_CM01DBM01=(DESCRIPTION=(ADDRESS_LIST=(ADDRESS=(PROTOCOL=TCP)(HOST=cm0101-vip)(PORT=1521))
(ADDRESS=(PROTOCOL=TCP)(HOST=172.16.1.10)(PORT=1521)(IP=FIRST))))
        # line added
by Agent
[grid@cm01dbm01 admin]$
```

■ **Note** Recipe 21-1 walks you through using dbca, the Database Configuration Assistant, to create a new Oracle RAC database on Exadata.

Changing the various network interface IP addresses for the client access and Grid Infrastructure networks is a task that is best done cluster-wide, since cluster communications typically rely on consistent cluster networks. Recipe 10-7 provides an in-depth set of steps to accomplish this task.

How It Works

Grid Infrastructure network resources on Exadata are no different from those on non-Exadata 11gR2 Grid Infrastructure environments. Your Grid Infrastructure network is defined with the ora.net1.network Oracle Cluster resource and provides the network used for each client access network on your compute nodes.

The VIP addresses and SCAN addresses are added to DNS and used during the Grid Infrastructure installation to enable network connectivity on the NET1-2 Exadata client access network.

On Exadata, like all Oracle 11gR2 installations, there is a single Grid Infrastructure installation per compute node. As such, there is a single set of network configurations per node. The virtual IPs, SCAN network, SCAN listener, and database listeners all share a common network framework and utilize and enable IP addresses on the bondeth0 interface.

10-6. Configuring the Storage Server Ethernet Network
Problem

You wish to validate and configure the network on your Exadata storage cells.

Solution

In this recipe, we will show you how to identify the Exadata storage cell Ethernet network configuration, discuss Oracle's use of the cell.conf configuration file and how it's used with the ipconf utility, and provide some introductory guidance on how to modify your storage cell Ethernet networking.

■ **Note** Recipe 10-7 discusses the steps required to modify your storage cell Ethernet network in detail. Please refer to this recipe for a comprehensive discussion on the topic.

To display the Ethernet network configuration on your storage cells, log in to one of your storage cells and run the following ifconfig command:

```
[root@cm01cel02 ~]# ifconfig eth0
eth0      Link encap:Ethernet  HWaddr 00:21:28:B2:83:74
          inet addr:172.16.1.13  Bcast:172.16.1.255  Mask:255.255.255.0
          inet6 addr: fe80::221:28ff:feb2:8374/64 Scope:Link
          UP BROADCAST RUNNING MULTICAST  MTU:1500  Metric:1
          RX packets:2193649 errors:0 dropped:0 overruns:0 frame:0
          TX packets:2904578 errors:0 dropped:0 overruns:0 carrier:0
          collisions:0 txqueuelen:1000
          RX bytes:307325546 (293.0 MiB)  TX bytes:1153819741 (1.0 GiB)
          Memory:ddb60000-ddb80000
[root@cm01cel02 ~]#
```

The eth0 interface is connected to the internal Cisco Catalyst switch. Exadata's storage cells also have three additional interfaces, eth1, eth2, and eth3, all of which are unconfigured and not connected to the Cisco switch or data center network.

The Exadata storage cell network is managed automatically using the `ipconf` utility, located in /opt/oracle.cellos/ipconf. During system startup, `ipconf` is invoked from the /opt/oracle.cellos/cellFirstBoot.sh script and will read a configuration file called /opt/oracle.cellos/cell.conf. An example of a cell.conf file is displayed:

```
[root@cm01cel02 ~]# more /opt/oracle.cellos/cell.conf
$VAR1 = {
          'Internal' => {
                          'Interface infiniband prefix' => 'ib',
                          'Interface ethernet prefix' => 'eth'
                        },
          'Hostname' => 'cm01cel02.centroid.com',
          'Timezone' => 'America/Detroit',
          'Interfaces' => [
                          {
                            'IP address' => '192.168.10.4',
                            'Hostname' => 'cm01cel02-priv.centroid.com',
                            'Netmask' => '255.255.252.0',
                            'Net type' => 'Private',
                            'Slaves' => [
                                          'ib0',
                                          'ib1'
                                        ],
                            'Name' => 'bondib0',
                            'State' => 1
                          },
                          {
                            'Hostname' => 'cm01cel02.centroid.com',
                            'IP address' => '172.16.1.13',
                            'Netmask' => '255.255.255.0',
                            'Net type' => 'Management',
                            'Name' => 'eth0',
                            'State' => 1,
                            'Gateway' => '172.16.1.1'
... Additional information omitted
```

While the Exadata compute node networks are configured similarly to any Linux operating system, managing or modifying the network configuration on the storage cells should *only* be done by editing the contents of your cell.conf file; this is the configuration file that is read during system startup and during the system initialization. The host will read configuration details from cell.conf and alter or validate the network configuration accordingly.

You can validate a cell.conf network configuration file by running the `ipconf -verify` command:

```
[root@cm01cel02 ~]# /opt/oracle.cellos/ipconf -verify \
> -conf /opt/oracle.cellos/cell.conf
Verifying of Exadata configuration file /opt/oracle.cellos/cell.conf
Done. Configuration file /opt/oracle.cellos/cell.conf passed all verification checks
[root@cm01cel02 ~]#
```

In general, an Oracle Exadata DMA would not manually invoke `ipconf` unless changing the server's networking information. You can change multiple Ethernet networking attributes or configuration details by modifying your `cell.conf` configuration file, including the management network IP address and gateway, the NTP server configuration, the DNS server configuration, ILOM settings, as well as InfiniBand IP addresses and hostnames. The high level process to change your network configuration is as follows:

- Copy the cell.conf file to a backup configuration file, for example, "cp /etc/oracle.cellos/cell.conf /tmp/new.cell.conf"
- Make the desired modifications to the copy of your `cell.conf`
- Run `ipconf –verify` with your modified cell.conf file
- Run /opt/oracle.cellos/ipconf –force –newconf /tmp/new.cell.conf –reboot to load your new configuration file and reboot

As stated previously, Recipe 10-7 provides a detailed example of changing your network settings on the storage cells.

How It Works

The Exadata storage cells have one active Ethernet interface, eth0, designated for its management/administration network, and a bonded InfiniBand interface for the storage network. The NET0/admin network is used to log in to your storage cells via SSH as well as to remotely connect with `dcli` from other nodes.

> **Note** You can also use the InfiniBand IP address with `dcli` to run `cellcli` commands.

Oracle automates the configuration of your storage cell network by use of a standard `cell.conf` configuration file to ensure that your network configuration will remain persistent and healthy across reboots. The `cell.conf` file defines several network-related parameters, including IP addresses for the management and InfiniBand networks, DNS server information, NTP server information, ILOM configurations, and so forth. When the `ipconf` utility runs during the `FirstBoot.sh` process, it will examine the contents of `cell.conf` and take the following actions:

1. The hostname in /etc/sysconfig/network is set based on the hostname setting in cell.conf
2. The /etc/sysconfig/network-scripts/ifcfg-bondib0 file is modified with the InfiniBand network information from cell.conf and the interface is started
3. The /etc/sysconfig/network-scripts/ifcfg-eth0 file is modified with the management network information from cell.conf and the interface is started
4. The /etc/ntp.conf file is updated with the NTP server information from the NTP section of cell.conf
5. The /etc/resolv.conf file is updated with DNS information from the Nameservers section of cell.conf
6. The ILOM settings in /SP/network are modified with information from the ilom section of cell.conf

10-7. Changing IP Addresses on Your Exadata Database Machine

Problem

You would like to change IP addresses on your Exadata Database Machine and are looking for a step-by-step process to change the various network configurations across your storage cells, compute nodes, InfiniBand switches, KVM switch, internal Cisco Catalyst switch, and Power Distribution Units (PDUs).

Solution

Oracle provides step-by-step instructions for changing Exadata IP addresses for each node, switch, and component in the database machine at My Oracle Support document 1317159.1. In this recipe, we will demonstrate how to change IP addresses in an Exadata Quarter Rack; the same procedures can be expanded to Half Rack and Full Rack configurations. Specifically, we will show how to do the following:

- Prepare your Exadata Database Machine for network changes
- Change the InfiniBand switch Ethernet IP addresses
- Change network information in your KVM switch
- Change network information in the embedded Cisco switch
- Change the PDU IP addresses
- Change Ethernet IP addresses in the storage cells
- Change Ethernet IP addresses on the compute nodes
- Reconfigure Oracle RAC network resources to reflect IP address changes
- Perform post-change startup and validation

The examples in this recipe assume that we will be changing our administration, client access, and additional networks according to Table 10-1.

Table 10-1. Network Changes

Network	Old Network	New Network
Administration	172.16.1.0/24	10.16.1.0/24
Client Access	172.16.10.0/24	10.16.10.0/24
Additional	172.16.20.0/24	10.16.20.0.24

■ **Note** The scope of this recipe is restricted to changing Ethernet IP addresses on the nodes in your Exadata Database Machine. Changing hostnames and InfiniBand IP addresses is outside the scope of this text. This recipe also assumes that your business goal is to perform widespread network changes and change the IP addresses on all Exadata nodes to meet a specific network-addressing scheme. While individual servers or nodes can be re-addressed independently, this practice is not common.

Preparing Your Machine for the IP Address Changes

Changing Exadata IP address and network information requires an outage for all nodes in the Exadata.

1. If you are using DBFS and your DBFS mount is controlled via Oracle Clusterware, stop your DBFS resource on each node by logging in as root to the compute node and running the following command:

   ```
   [root@cm01dbm01 ~]# /u01/app/11.2.0.3/grid/bin/crsctl stop res dbfs_mount
   [root@cm01dbm01 ~]#
   ```

2. Next, shut down your databases:

   ```
   [root@cm01dbm01 ~]# su - oracle
   The Oracle base has been set to /u01/app/oracle
   [oracle@cm01dbm01 ~]$ srvctl stop database -d dwprd
   [oracle@cm01dbm01 ~]$ srvctl stop database -d visx
   [oracle@cm01dbm01 ~]$ srvctl stop database -d visy
   [oracle@cm01dbm01 ~]$
   ```

3. After this is complete, log in as root to one of your compute nodes and stop the cluster:

   ```
   [root@cm01dbm01 ~]# /u01/app/11.2.0.3/grid/bin/crsctl stop cluster -all
   CRS-2673: Attempting to stop 'ora.crsd' on 'cm01dbm01'
   CRS-2790: Starting shutdown of Cluster Ready Services-managed resources on 'cm01dbm01'
   CRS-2673: Attempting to stop 'ora.LISTENER_SCAN2.lsnr' on 'cm01dbm01'
   CRS-2673: Attempting to stop 'ora.oc4j' on 'cm01dbm01'
   CRS-2673: Attempting to stop 'ora.LISTENER.lsnr' on 'cm01dbm01'
   CRS-2673: Attempting to stop 'ora.LISTENER_SCAN3.lsnr' on 'cm01dbm01'
   CRS-2673: Attempting to stop 'ora.SRECO_CM01.dg' on 'cm01dbm01'
   .. output omitted for brevity
   ```

4. As later steps in this recipe will reboot the server at times when we do not wish for cluster services to automatically start, log in to a compute node as root and check to see if Oracle Clusterware is configured to automatically start:

   ```
   [root@cm01dbm01 ~]# cat dbs_group
   cm01dbm01
   cm01dbm02
   [root@cm01dbm01 ~]# dcli -g ./dbs_group -l root /u01/app/11.2.0.3/grid/bin/crsctl config crs
   cm01dbm01: CRS-4622: Oracle High Availability Services autostart is enabled.
   cm01dbm02: CRS-4622: Oracle High Availability Services autostart is enabled.
   [root@cm01dbm01 ~]#
   ```

5. In the previous output, we can see that Oracle High Availability Services are configured to automatically start, which is normal and expected. Disable and validate automatic restart using the following commands:

   ```
   [root@cm01dbm01 ~]# dcli -g ./dbs_group -l root /u01/app/11.2.0.3/grid/bin/crsctl disable crs
   cm01dbm01: CRS-4621: Oracle High Availability Services autostart is disabled.
   cm01dbm02: CRS-4621: Oracle High Availability Services autostart is disabled.
   [root@cm01dbm01 ~]# dcli -g ./dbs_group -l root /u01/app/11.2.0.3/grid/bin/crsctl config crs
   ```

```
cm01dbm01: CRS-4621: Oracle High Availability Services autostart is disabled.
cm01dbm02: CRS-4621: Oracle High Availability Services autostart is disabled.
[root@cm01dbm01 ~]#
```

6. At this point, you can power off the nodes in your machine and perform any re-cabling if necessary.

7. Finally, to prepare for the IP address changes, modify your DNS entries for each Exadata component registered in DNS. The steps to perform these changes are specific to your organization's specific DNS configuration and are outside the scope of this recipe.

Changing the InfiniBand Switch Ethernet Network

Now we'll change the InfiniBand switch Ethernet network:

1. Log in to your InfiniBand switches as root and run the spsh command to launch your ILOM shell, and check your current Ethernet network configuration:

```
[root@cm01sw-ib2 ~]# spsh
Oracle(R) Integrated Lights Out Manager
Version ILOM 3.0 r47111
Copyright (c) 2010, Oracle and/or its affiliates. All rights reserved.
-> show /SP/network

 /SP/network
    Targets:
   test
       Properties:
   commitpending = (Cannot show property)
   dhcp_server_ip = none
   ipaddress = 172.16.1.23
   ipdiscovery = static
   ipgateway = 172.16.1.1
   ipnetmask = 255.255.255.0
   macaddress = 00:E0:4B:32:67:A7
   pendingipaddress = 172.16.1.23
   pendingipdiscovery = static
   pendingipgateway = 172.16.1.1
   pendingipnetmask = 255.255.255.0
   state = enabled
   ... Output omitted for brevity
->
```

2. Next, issue the following command to change your IP address:

```
-> set /SP/network pendingipdiscovery=static pendingipaddress=10.16.1.23 \
pendingipgateway=10.16.1.1 pendingipnetmask=255.255.255.0
-> set /SP/network commitpending=true
-> exit
```

CHAPTER 10 ■ NETWORK ADMINISTRATION

3. After this is complete, update /etc/hosts to reflect your changes. When complete, update /etc/resolv.conf to change your DNS server IP address, if applicable.

4. Next, log back into the ILOM shell using spsh to modify your NTP server(s) and timezone, if applicable:

```
-> set /SP/clock timezone=timezone
-> set /SP/clients/ntp/server/1 address=NTP server 1
-> set /SP/clients/ntp/server/2 address=NTP server 2
-> set /SP/clock usentpserver=enabled
```

5. When finished, type reboot to reboot your switch. When it is back up, validate your firmware version, check the health of the switch, and perform an environment test:

```
[root@cm01sw-ib2 ~]# version
SUN DCS 36p version: 1.3.3-2
Build time: Apr  4 2011 11:15:19
SP board info:
Manufacturing Date: 2010.08.21
Serial Number: "NCD4V1753"
Hardware Revision: 0x0005
Firmware Revision: 0x0000
BIOS version: SUN0R100
BIOS date: 06/22/2010
[root@cm01sw-ib2 ~]# showunhealthy
OK - No unhealthy sensors
[root@cm01sw-ib2 ~]# env_test
Environment test started:
Starting Environment Daemon test:
Environment daemon running
Environment Daemon test returned OK
Starting Voltage test:
... output omitted for brevity
Fan 4 not present
FAN test returned OK
Starting Connector test:
Connector test returned OK
Starting Onboard ibdevice test:
Switch OK
All Internal ibdevices OK
Onboard ibdevice test returned OK
Environment test PASSED
[root@cm01sw-ib2 ~]#
```

6. Next, confirm that OpenSM is running; if not, use service opensmd restart to restart it:

```
[root@cm01sw-ib2 ~]# service opensmd status
opensm (pid 11504) is running...
[root@cm01sw-ib2 ~]#
```

315

7. Finally, validate that your Ethernet IP address has been changed using the following ifconfig command:

```
[root@cm01sw-ib2 ~]# ifconfig eth0
eth0      Link encap:Ethernet  HWaddr 00:E0:4B:32:67:A7
          inet addr:10.16.1.23  Bcast:10.16.1.255  Mask:255.255.255.0
          inet6 addr: fe80::2e0:4bff:fe32:67a7/64 Scope:Link
          UP BROADCAST RUNNING MULTICAST  MTU:1500  Metric:1
          RX packets:1337936 errors:2 dropped:0 overruns:0 frame:2
          TX packets:1373298 errors:0 dropped:0 overruns:0 carrier:0
          collisions:0 txqueuelen:1000
          RX bytes:178449962 (170.1 MiB)  TX bytes:283794470 (270.6 MiB)
[root@cm01sw-ib2 ~]#
```

Repeat the steps in this section for your other InfiniBand switches.

Changing KVM Switch Networking

To modify the IP address of the KVM switch, log on to the KVM web console as Admin and click on the Network-IPv4, as depicted in Figure 10-1, and change the IP address to the appropriate values.

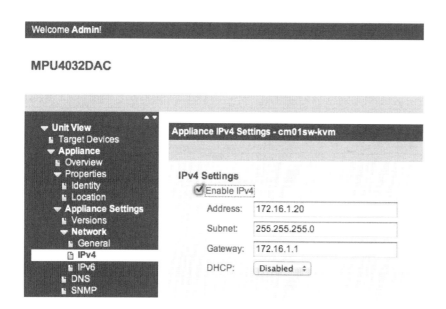

Figure 10-1. *Changing KVM switch IP address*

If you are changing DNS server information, click on the DNS link and modify the settings as displayed in Figure 10-2.

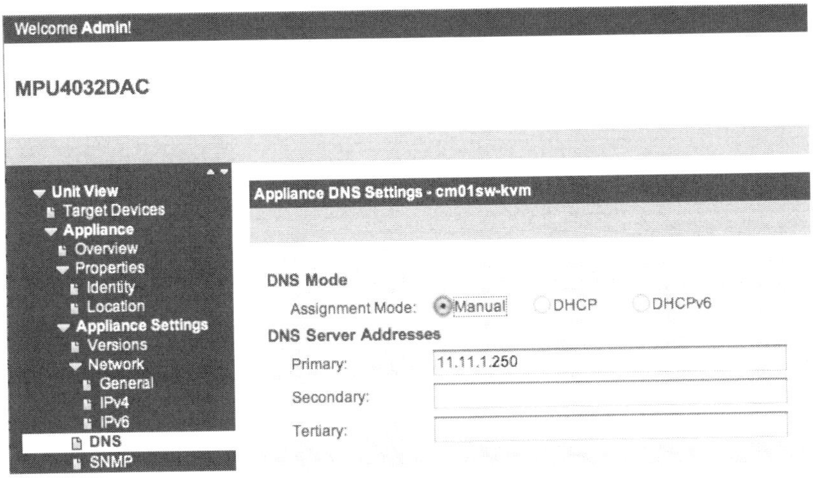

Figure 10-2. Changing KVM switch DNS server addresses

Changing Cisco Catalyst 4948 Networking

Connect a serial cable from the Cisco switch console to a laptop using the RJ45 to DB9 serial cable included with your Exadata package. Once you've got a serial connection, connect at 9600 baud, 8 bits, no parity, 1 stop bit, and no handshake.

Once connected, complete these steps:

1. Change to enable mode using the following command:

    ```
    Switch> enable
    Switch#
    ```

2. Enter configuration mode by entering the `configure terminal` command:

    ```
    Switch # configure terminal
    Enter configuration commands, one per line.End with CTRL/Z.
    Swich(config)#
    ```

3. If you wish to, for example, change your Name Server IP address, enter the following:

    ```
    Switch(config)# ip name-server 11.11.1.255
    Switch(config)# ip default-gateway 10.16.1.1
    Switch(config)# interface vlan1
    Switch(config)# ip address 10.16.1.121 255.255.255.0
    ```

4. To save changes, enter end and commit your changes by typing `write memory`:

    ```
    Switch(config)# end
    *Aug 27 18:01:26.155:%SYS-5-CONFIG_I:Configured from console by console
    Switch # write memory
    ```

CHAPTER 10 ■ NETWORK ADMINISTRATION

5. When finished, display your running configuration as displayed below:

```
Switch # show running-config
... output omitted for brevity
ip name-server 11.11.1.255
interface Vlan1
 ip address 10.16.1.121 255.255.255.0
 no ip route-cache
!
ip default-gateway 10.16.1.1
ip http server
!
snmp-server host 10.16.1.110 public
... output omitted for brevity
```

Changing Power Distribution Unit Networking

Open a web browser and connect to your PDU's current IP address. If the current network is not operational, you will have to connect a serial cable to an interface on your PDU and change your local network settings to that of the current PDU network. Once logged in to the PDU, click Net Configuration and change the IP addresses as depicted in Figure 10-3.

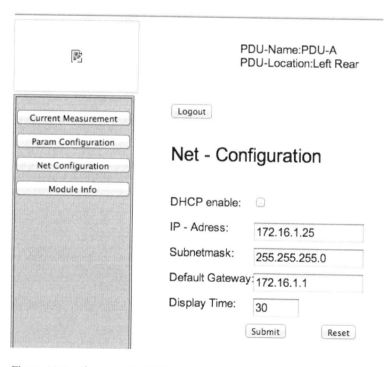

Figure 10-3. Changing the PDU network configuration

Repeat these steps on your other PDU when complete.

Changing Storage Cell Ethernet Networking

Now complete the following steps:

1. First, log in as root on each storage cell and stop your Cell Services software:

```
[root@cm01cel01 ~]# service celld stop
         Stopping the RS, CELLSRV, adn MS services...
               The SHUTDOWN of services was sucessful.
[root@cm01cel01 ~]#
```

2. Next, copy your active cell.conf file to a temporary directory to prepare for editing:

```
[root@cm01cel01 ~]# locate cell.conf
/opt/oracle.cellos/cell.conf
/opt/oracle.cellos/iso/lastGoodConfig/cell.conf
/root/ExadataRescued/lastGoodConfig/cell.conf
[root@cm01cel01 ~]# cp /opt/oracle.cellos/cell.conf /tmp/new.cell.conf
[root@cm01cel01 ~]#
```

3. Now you will need to change network address in your /tmp/new.cell.conf file. In the Interfaces stanza, find the Ethernet network section; you will find these by searching for the storage cell hostname. An example of this section follows:

```
{
  'Hostname' => 'cm01cel01.centroid.com',
  'IP address' => '172.16.1.12',
  'Netmask' => '255.255.255.0',
  'Net type' => 'Management',
  'Name' => 'eth0',
  'State' => 1,
  'Gateway' => '172.16.1.1'
},
```

4. Change the network settings to your new IP address. Next, find the ilom stanza in your /tmp/new.cell.conf file and make the necessary changes:

```
'ilom' => {
         'ILOM Nameserver' => '11.11.1.250',
         'ILOM Timezone' => 'America/Detroit',
         'ILOM Netmask' => '255.255.255.0',
         'ILOM IP address' => '10.16.1.17',
         'ILOM Search' => 'centroid.com',
         'ILOM Second NTP server' => '0.0.0.0',
         'ILOM Short Hostname' => 'cm01cel01-ilom',
         'ILOM Fully qualified hostname' => 'cm01cel01-ilom.centroid.com',
         'ILOM First NTP server' => 'pool.ntp.org',
         'ILOM Gateway' => '10.16.1.1',
         'ILOM Use NTP Servers' => 'enabled'
       }
```

5. When complete, ensure that you have made all the required changes by searching for your new network IP addresses:

```
[root@cm01cel01 ~]# grep 10.16 /tmp/new.cell.conf
                    'IP address' => '10.16.1.12',
                    'Gateway' => '10.16.1.1'
              'ILOM IP address' => '10.16.1.17',
              'ILOM Gateway' => '10.16.1.1',
[root@cm01cel01 ~]#
```

6. You should also confirm your timezone, DNS server, and NTP server settings:

```
[root@cm01cel01 ~]# egrep -i '(dns|ntp|timez)' /tmp/new.cell.conf
          'Timezone' => 'America/Detroit',
          'Ntp drift' => '/var/lib/ntp/drift',
          'Ntp servers' => [
                          'pool.ntp.org'
                'ILOM Timezone' => 'America/Detroit',
                'ILOM Second NTP server' => '0.0.0.0',
                'ILOM First NTP server' => 'pool.ntp.org',
                'ILOM Use NTP Servers' => 'enabled'
[root@cm01cel01 ~]#
```

7. Once all your entries look good, you use `ipconf` to validate your pending configuration:

```
[root@cm01cel01 ~]# /opt/oracle.cellos/ipconf -verify -conf /tmp/new.cell.conf -verbose
Verifying of Exadata configuration file /tmp/new.cell.conf
Configuration version is defined in Exadata configuration file
 : PASSED
Configuration version 11.2.2.3.0 has valid value in Exadata configuration file
 : PASSED
DNS server 11.11.1.250 has valid IP address syntax in the Exadata configuration file
 : PASSED
Canonical hostname is defined in Exadata configuration file
 : PASSED
Canonical hostname cm01cel02.centroid.com has valid syntax in Exadata configuration file
 : PASSED
Node type is defined in Exadata configuration file
 : PASSED
Node type cell is valid in Exadata configuration file
 : PASSED
This node type is cell
 : PASSED
... output omitted for brevity
```

You should see all of the tests completed with a PASSED status; if not, make adjustments and execute the `ipconf` command again.

8. After validating your modified cell.conf configuration file, save it to your cell's configuration by running the following ipconf command:

```
# /opt/oracle.cellos/ipconf -force -newconf /tmp/new.cell.conf -reboot
Logging started to /var/log/cellos/ipconf.log
Info. Started with the force option
Info. Loading new configuration from /tmp/new.cell.conf
Info. Run /opt/oracle.cellos/validations/init.d/saveconfig
Loading basic configuration settings from ILOM
... output omitted for brevity
```

9. This process will implement the changes and reboot your server. When the server is rebooted, validate your network configuration by running the following commands:

```
[root@cm01cel01 ~]# ifconfig eth0
eth0      Link encap:Ethernet  HWaddr 00:21:28:B2:84:1C
          inet addr:10.16.1.12  Bcast:172.16.1.255  Mask:255.255.255.0
          inet6 addr: fe80::221:28ff:feb2:841c/64 Scope:Link
          UP BROADCAST RUNNING MULTICAST  MTU:1500  Metric:1
          RX packets:63205 errors:0 dropped:0 overruns:0 frame:0
          TX packets:61642 errors:0 dropped:0 overruns:0 carrier:0
          collisions:0 txqueuelen:1000
          RX bytes:7673003 (7.3 MiB)  TX bytes:7456564 (7.1 MiB)
          Memory:ddb60000-ddb80000
[root@cm01cel01 ~]#

[root@cm01cel01 ~]# cat /etc/resolv.conf
# Search domain and name server
search centroid.com
nameserver 11.11.1.250
```

10. Next, validate that your services are up by running the following command while logged in as root:

```
[root@cm01cel01 ~]# service celld status
  rsStatus:                  running
  msStatus:                  running
  cellsrvStatus:             running
[root@cm01cel01 ~]#
```

Changing Compute Node Ethernet Networking

Each database server will need to be modified separately and manually.

1. First, log in as root on a compute node and use ipcalc to calculate the broadcast and network information for your new administration, client access, and additional networks:

```
[root@cm01dbm01 ~]# ipcalc -bnm 10.16.1.10 255.255.255.0
NETMASK=255.255.255.0
BROADCAST=10.16.1.255
NETWORK=10.16.1.0
```

```
[root@cm01dbm01 ~]# ipcalc -bnm 10.16.10.10 255.255.255.0
NETMASK=255.255.255.0
BROADCAST=10.16.10.255
NETWORK=10.16.10.0
[root@cm01dbm01 ~]# ipcalc -bnm 10.16.20.10 255.255.255.0
NETMASK=255.255.255.0
BROADCAST=10.16.20.255
NETWORK=10.16.20.0
[root@cm01dbm01 ~]#
```

2. With this information, you now need to manually edit the following files in /etc/sysconfig/network-scripts on each compute node and set the desired value for IPADDR, NETMASK, NETWORK, BROADCAST, and GATEWAY:

   - /etc/sysconfig/network-scripts/ifcfg-bondeth0
   - /etc/sysconfig/network-scripts/ifcfg-eth0
   - /etc/sysconfig/network-scripts/ifcfg-eth3

Note This section assumes that you have not altered the default Ethernet bonding; in other words, bondeth0 represents your client access network's bonded interface.

The following is an example of these changes:

```
[root@cm01dbm01 ~]# cat /etc/sysconfig/network-scripts/ifcfg-bondeth0
#### DO NOT REMOVE THESE LINES ####
#### %GENERATED BY CELL% ####
DEVICE=bondeth0
USERCTL=no
BOOTPROTO=none
ONBOOT=yes
IPADDR=10.16.10.10
NETMASK=255.255.255.0
NETWORK=10.16.10.0
BROADCAST=10.16.10.255
BONDING_OPTS="mode=active-backup miimon=100 downdelay=5000 updelay=5000 num_grat_arp=100"
IPV6INIT=no
GATEWAY=10.16.10.1
[root@cm01dbm01 ~]#

[root@cm01dbm01 ~]# cat /etc/sysconfig/network-scripts/ifcfg-eth0
#### DO NOT REMOVE THESE LINES ####
#### %GENERATED BY CELL% ####
DEVICE=eth0
BOOTPROTO=static
ONBOOT=yes
IPADDR=10.16.1.10
NETMASK=255.255.255.0
NETWORK=10.16.1.0
```

```
BROADCAST=10.16.1.255
GATEWAY=10.16.1.1
HOTPLUG=no
IPV6INIT=no
HWADDR=00:21:28:b2:17:02
[root@cm01dbm01 ~]#
```

3. Next, change the settings in /etc/sysconfig/network; specifically, change the GATEWAY address:

   ```
   [root@cm01dbm01 ~]# cat /etc/sysconfig/network
   NETWORKING=yes
   NETWORKING_IPV6=no
   NOZEROCONF=yes
   HOSTNAME=cm01dbm01.centroid.com
   GATEWAY=10.16.10.1
   GATEWAYDEV=bondeth0
   [root@cm01dbm01 ~]#
   ```

4. After this, modify entries in /etc/hosts:

   ```
   [root@cm01dbm01 ~]# grep cm01dbm01 /etc/hosts
   192.168.10.1     cm01dbm01-priv.centroid.com    cm01dbm01-priv
   10.16.1.10       cm01dbm01.centroid.com         cm01dbm01
   192.168.10.1     cm01dbm01-priv.centroid.com    cm01dbm01-priv
   [root@cm01dbm01 ~]#
   ```

5. Next, make any necessary changes in /etc/ssh/sshd_config, /etc/resolv.conf, and /etc/ntp.conf and make changes as listed:

   ```
   [root@cm01dbm01 ~]# grep Listen  /etc/ssh/sshd_config
   #ListenAddress 0.0.0.0
   #ListenAddress ::
   ListenAddress 10.16.1.10
   ListenAddress 192.168.10.1
   [root@cm01dbm01 ~]# cat /etc/resolv.conf
   # Search domain and name server
   search centroid.com
   # Commented it out, because OUI complains about it
   #domain centroid.com
   nameserver 11.11.1.250
   [root@cm01dbm01 ~]# grep pool /etc/ntp.conf
   # Use public servers from the pool.ntp.org project.
   # Please consider joining the pool (http://www.pool.ntp.org/join.html).
   restrict pool.ntp.org mask 255.255.255.255 nomodify notrap noquery
   server pool.ntp.org prefer
   [root@cm01dbm01 ~]#
   ```

6. After these changes are made, you must modify your routing rules for your management and additional networks in /etc/sysconfig/network-scripts/route* files. For example:

```
[root@cm01dbm01] # cd /etc/sysconfig/network-scripts
[root@cm01dbm01 network-scripts]# ls rout*
route-eth0   route-eth3
[root@cm01dbm01 network-scripts]# cat route-eth0
10.16.1.0/24 dev eth0 table 220
default via 10.16.1.1 dev eth0 table 220
[root@cm01dbm01 network-scripts]# cat route-eth3
10.16.20.0/24 dev eth3 table 223
default via 10.16.20.1 dev eth3 table 223
[root@cm01dbm01 network-scripts]#
```

7. If necessary, modify your timezone by adjusting /etc/sysconfig/clock:

```
[root@cm01dbm01 network-scripts]# cat /etc/sysconfig/clock
ZONE="America/Detroit"
UTC=true
ARC=false
[root@cm01dbm01 network-scripts]#
```

8. At this point, reboot your compute node. When the server is back up, display your current ILOM network configuration:

```
[root@cm01dbm01 network-scripts]# ipmitool sunoem cli "show /SP/network"
Connected. Use ^D to exit.
-> show /SP/network

 /SP/network
    Targets:
        interconnect
        ipv6
        test

    Properties:
        commitpending = (Cannot show property)
        dhcp_server_ip = none
        ipaddress = 172.16.1.15
        ipdiscovery = static
        ipgateway = 172.16.1.1
        ipnetmask = 255.255.255.0
        macaddress = 00:21:28:B2:17:06
        managementport = /SYS/SP/NET0
        outofbandmacaddress = 00:21:28:B2:17:06
        pendingipaddress = 172.16.1.15
        pendingipdiscovery = static
        pendingipgateway = 172.16.1.1
        pendingipnetmask = 255.255.255.0
        pendingmanagementport = /SYS/SP/NET0
        sidebandmacaddress = 00:21:28:B2:17:07
```

```
            state = enabled
    Commands:
        cd
        set
        show
-> Session closed
Disconnected
[root@cm01dbm01 network-scripts]# ipmitool sunoem cli "show /SP/clients/ntp/server/1"
Connected. Use ^D to exit.
-> show /SP/clients/ntp/server/1
 /SP/clients/ntp/server/1
    Targets:
    Properties:
        address = pool.ntp.org
    Commands:
        cd
        set
        show
-> Session closed
Disconnected
[root@cm01dbm01 network-scripts]# ipmitool sunoem cli "show /SP/clients/ntp/server/2"
Connected. Use ^D to exit.
-> show /SP/clients/ntp/server/2
 /SP/clients/ntp/server/2
    Targets:
    Properties:
        address = 0.0.0.0
    Commands:
        cd
        set
        show
-> Session closed
Disconnected
[root@cm01dbm01 network-scripts]# ipmitool sunoem cli "show /SP/clients/dns"
Connected. Use ^D to exit.
-> show /SP/clients/dns
 /SP/clients/dns
    Targets:
    Properties:
        auto_dns = enabled
        nameserver = 11.11.1.250
        retries = 1
        searchpath = centroid.com
        timeout = 5
    Commands:
        cd
        set
        show
-> Session closed
Disconnected
[root@cm01dbm01 network-scripts]#
```

9. Change your ILOM network settings using the following commands and repeat on all compute nodes:

```
[root@cm01dbm01]# ipmitool sunoem cli "set /SP/network \
> pendingipaddress=10.16.1.15 \
> pendingipgateway=10.16.1.1 \
> pendingipnetmask=255.255.255.0 \
> commitpending=true"
Connected. Use ^D to exit.
-> Session closed
Disconnected
[root@cm01dbm01]#
```

10. If you need to change your DNS server or NTP server addresses, use the following commands:

```
[root@cm01dbm01]# ipmitool sunoem cli "set /SP/clients/dns nameserver=11.11.1.250"
Connected. Use ^D to exit.
-> Session closed
Disconnected
[root@cm01dbm01]#

[root@cm01dbm01]# ipmitool sunoem cli "set /SP/clients/ntp/server/1 address=pool.ntp.org"
Connected. Use ^D to exit.

-> Session closed
Disconnected
[root@cm01dbm01]#
```

Configuring Oracle RAC Network Resources

After changing the network configuration on your computes node, you will be required to modify your Oracle RAC network resources.

1. The first step is to log in as root and start Oracle Clusterware on both nodes:

```
[root@cm01dbm01 ~]# /u01/app/11.2.0.3/grid/bin/crsctl start crs
CRS-4123: Oracle High Availability Services has been started.
[root@cm01dbm01 ~]#
```

2. Validate your CRS status by running the command below, as root:

```
[root@cm01dbm01 ~]# /u01/app/11.2.0.3/grid/bin/crsctl check crs
CRS-4638: Oracle High Availability Services is online
CRS-4537: Cluster Ready Services is online
CRS-4529: Cluster Synchronization Services is online
CRS-4533: Event Manager is online
[root@cm01dbm01 ~]#
```

3. Next, log in to a compute node as your Grid Infrastructure owner and check the network configuration using oifcfg:

```
[grid@cm01dbm01 ~]$ oifcfg getif
bondib0   192.168.8.0   global   cluster_interconnect
bondeth0  172.16.10.0   global   public
[grid@cm01dbm01 ~]$
```

4. You will need to delete the bondeth0 network and add it back into the cluster registry using the following commands:

```
[grid@cm01dbm01 ~]$ oifcfg delif -global bondeth0
[grid@cm01dbm01 ~]$ oifcfg setif -global bondeth0/10.16.10.0:public
[grid@cm01dbm01 ~]$ oifcfg getif
bondib0   192.168.8.0   global   cluster_interconnect
bondeth0  10.16.10.0    global   public
[grid@cm01dbm01 ~]$
```

5. Next, check your current SCAN and SCAN listener configuration:

```
[grid@cm01dbm01 ~]$ srvctl config scan
SCAN name: cm01-scan, Network: 1/172.16.10.0/255.255.255.0/bondeth0
SCAN VIP name: scan1, IP: /cm01-scan/172.16.10.16
SCAN VIP name: scan2, IP: /cm01-scan/172.16.10.15
SCAN VIP name: scan3, IP: /cm01-scan/172.16.10.14
[grid@cm01dbm01 ~]$ srvctl config scan_listener
SCAN Listener LISTENER_SCAN1 exists. Port: TCP:1521
SCAN Listener LISTENER_SCAN2 exists. Port: TCP:1521
SCAN Listener LISTENER_SCAN3 exists. Port: TCP:1521
[grid@cm01dbm01 ~]$
```

6. Oracle will automatically adjust your SCAN IP addresses based on your DNS settings. When complete, stop your SCAN listener:

```
[grid@cm01dbm01 ~]$ srvctl stop scan_listener
[grid@cm01dbm01 ~]$ srvctl stop scan
```

7. Once down, you will need to modify the SCAN and ora.net1.network network as listed below. You will need to be logged in as root to perform these tasks:

```
[root@cm01dbm01 ~]# $CRS_HOME/bin/srvctl modify scan -n cm01-scan
[root@cm01dbm01 ~]# $CRS_HOME/bin/srvctl modify network -S 10.16.10.0/255.255.255.0/bondeth0
```

8. Next, modify the SCAN listener and the IP address information as the Grid Infrastructure owner and start your SCAN listeners:

```
[grid@cm01dbm01 ~]$ srvctl modify scan_listener -u
[grid@cm01dbm01 ~]$ srvctl start scan_listener
```

9. When finished, validate your configuration:

```
[grid@cm01dbm01 ~]$ srvctl config scan
SCAN name: cm01-scan, Network: 1/10.16.10.0/255.255.255.0/bondeth0
SCAN VIP name: scan1, IP: /cm01-scan/10.16.10.16
SCAN VIP name: scan2, IP: /cm01-scan/10.16.10.15
SCAN VIP name: scan3, IP: /cm01-scan/10.16.10.14
[grid@cm01dbm01 ~]$ srvctl config scan_listener
SCAN Listener LISTENER_SCAN1 exists. Port: TCP:1521
SCAN Listener LISTENER_SCAN2 exists. Port: TCP:1521
SCAN Listener LISTENER_SCAN3 exists. Port: TCP:1521
[grid@cm01dbm01 ~]$
```

10. Repeat the process on each node and when complete, stop CRS on each node and enable Oracle High Availability Services to automatically start:

```
[root@cm01dbm01 bin]# ./crsctl stop cluster -f -all
CRS-2673: Attempting to stop 'ora.crsd' on 'cm01dbm01'
CRS-2790: Starting shutdown of Cluster Ready Services-managed resources on 'cm01dbm01'
CRS-2673: Attempting to stop 'ora.SRECO_CM01.dg' on 'cm01dbm01'
CRS-2673: Attempting to stop 'ora.registry.acfs' on 'cm01dbm01'
CRS-2673: Attempting to stop 'ora.DBFS_DG.dg' on 'cm01dbm01'
CRS-2673: Attempting to stop 'ora.SDATA_CM01.dg' on 'cm01dbm01'
CRS-2673: Attempting to stop 'ora.DATA_CM01.dg' on 'cm01dbm01'
... output omitted for brevity
[root@cm01dbm01 bin]# ./crsctl stop crs
CRS-2791: Starting shutdown of Oracle High Availability Services-managed resources on 'cm01dbm01'
CRS-2673: Attempting to stop 'ora.drivers.acfs' on 'cm01dbm01'
CRS-2673: Attempting to stop 'ora.crf' on 'cm01dbm01'
CRS-2673: Attempting to stop 'ora.mdnsd' on 'cm01dbm01'
CRS-2677: Stop of 'ora.drivers.acfs' on 'cm01dbm01' succeeded
CRS-2677: Stop of 'ora.mdnsd' on 'cm01dbm01' succeeded
CRS-2677: Stop of 'ora.crf' on 'cm01dbm01' succeeded
CRS-2673: Attempting to stop 'ora.gipcd' on 'cm01dbm01'
CRS-2677: Stop of 'ora.gipcd' on 'cm01dbm01' succeeded
CRS-2673: Attempting to stop 'ora.gpnpd' on 'cm01dbm01'
CRS-2677: Stop of 'ora.gpnpd' on 'cm01dbm01' succeeded
CRS-2793: Shutdown of Oracle High Availability Services-managed resources on 'cm01dbm01' has completed
CRS-4133: Oracle High Availability Services has been stopped.
[root@cm01dbm01 bin]#

[root@cm01dbm01 ~]# dcli -g ./dbs_group -l root /u01/app/11.2.0.3/grid/bin/crsctl enable crs
cm01dbm01: CRS-4621: Oracle High Availability Services autostart is enabled.
cm01dbm02: CRS-4621: Oracle High Availability Services autostart is enabled.
[root@cm01dbm01 ~]# dcli -g ./dbs_group -l root /u01/app/11.2.0.3/grid/bin/crsctl config crs
cm01dbm01: CRS-4621: Oracle High Availability Services autostart is enabled.
cm01dbm02: CRS-4621: Oracle High Availability Services autostart is enabled.
[root@cm01dbm01 ~]#
```

11. When complete, reboot your compute servers. After the nodes restart, check your Oracle CRS resources:

```
[root@cm01dbm01 ~]# /u01/app/11.2.0.3/grid/bin/crsctl stat res -t
--------------------------------------------------------------------------------
NAME           TARGET  STATE        SERVER                   STATE_DETAILS
--------------------------------------------------------------------------------
Local Resources
--------------------------------------------------------------------------------
... output omitted
ora.LISTENER.lsnr
               ONLINE  ONLINE       cm01dbm01
               ONLINE  ONLINE       cm01dbm02
... output omitted
ora.net1.network
               ONLINE  ONLINE       cm01dbm01
               ONLINE  ONLINE       cm01dbm02
... output omitted
ora.LISTENER_SCAN1.lsnr
      1        ONLINE  ONLINE       cm01dbm02
ora.LISTENER_SCAN2.lsnr
      1        ONLINE  ONLINE       cm01dbm01
ora.LISTENER_SCAN3.lsnr
      1        ONLINE  ONLINE       cm01dbm01
ora.cm01dbm01.vip
      1        ONLINE  ONLINE       cm01dbm01
ora.cm01dbm02.vip
      1        ONLINE  ONLINE       cm01dbm02
... output omitted
ora.scan1.vip
      1        ONLINE  ONLINE       cm01dbm02
ora.scan2.vip
      1        ONLINE  ONLINE       cm01dbm01
ora.scan3.vip
      1        ONLINE  ONLINE       cm01dbm01
... output omitted
 [root@cm01dbm01 ~]#
```

12. Once you have confirmed your network changes, start your database by logging in as the Oracle software owner and running srvctl start database:

```
[oracle@cm01dbm01 ~]$ srvctl start database -d dwprd
[oracle@cm01dbm01 ~]$ srvctl start database -d visx
[oracle@cm01dbm01 ~]$ srvctl start database -d visy
[oracle@cm01dbm01 ~]$
```

Post-Change Procedures

After the network changes are complete, there are a number of optional tasks that you may have to perform. For example, you should validate that your applications are functional, check your Enterprise Manager Grid Control/Cloud Control targets, and so forth. This post-change set of steps could vary from organization to organization.

How It Works

Changing Exadata IP addresses involves multiple steps on multiple nodes, many of which need to perform together to ensure a functional Exadata Database Machine. Generally speaking, when you have a requirement to change Ethernet IP address information on your Exadata nodes, you will likely be making changes to *all* of the components; for the tasks required to perform a single compute node, storage cell, or other Exadata component, you can refer to the appropriate section in the solution of this recipe.

This recipe focuses strictly on changing IP address and IP related network information. Changing server names is not supported by this process, but you can change domain names on each node by changing the HOSTNAME line in /etc/sysconfig/network on each compute node and storage cell.

Changing IP addresses on Exadata servers is accomplished by using a variety of tools and processes and requires a sound knowledge of Linux networking topics as well as the ability to confidently use utilities on your InfiniBand switches, storage cells, and compute nodes. Specifically:

- On the InfiniBand switches, you use ILOM shell commands to change your administration network settings

- On the KVM switch and PDU, you use the web interface

- With the embedded Cisco switch, you use Cisco IOS commands

- On the storage servers, you make changes to your cell.conf and use the ipconf utility to change your network information

- With the compute servers, you must manually reconfigure your IP addresses by editing Linux network configuration files for your NET0, NET1-2, and NET3 interfaces, and you use ipmitool to change your ILOM network addresses. Note that on the storage cells, these steps are handled by running ipconf

- For your Oracle RAC resources, you use standard Oracle 11gR2 cluster management utilities

CHAPTER 11

Patching and Upgrades

As Exadata is engineered as a complete and integrated system, Oracle periodically releases certified Exadata patches to facilitate patch and upgrade management on Exadata. Similar to other Oracle-engineered systems (and unlike traditional, disparate vendor solutions), Oracle's Exadata patches are pre-tested sets of patches designed to applied in a non-disruptive, rolling fashion and yield a comprehensive, validated end result. The goal of the Exadata patching is to remove uncertainty and non-compliance; for example, an Exadata DMA wouldn't download "one-off" patches for a database tier or storage server firmware. Exadata patches are intended to be all encompassing and typically include fixes for both the storage servers and compute servers, and optionally InfiniBand switches. In the real world, patching Exadata is typically one of the chief concerns of the Exadata administrator. The patches have a high likelihood of "touching everything," so properly planning and executing patch application is paramount to the availability of Exadata.

In this chapter, we will present an Exadata patching overview and provide real-world examples of how to apply patches on an Exadata Database Machine. This chapter will walk you through an Exadata patching exercise, recipe by recipe, giving you a comprehensive understanding of how to confidently patch your Exadata Database Machine.

11-1. Understanding Exadata Patching Definitions, Alternatives, and Strategies

Problem

You wish to better understand the landscape of patching on Exadata to enable yourself to confidently prepare for and apply patches to your Exadata environment.

Solution

In this recipe, we will provide an overview of how patching works on Exadata and present a list of Exadata patching definitions and use cases.

The first place to learn about how patching on Exadata works is My Oracle Support note 888828.1. Oracle continuously updates this support note, and it contains information about the latest Exadata patch updates, introduces new patching methods, and provides links to other patches and related software products.

Oracle provides patches for the Exadata compute nodes, storage cells, InfiniBand switches, and the associated Enterprise Manager agents and software. Table 11-1 outlines several key Exadata patching definitions and use cases.

Table 11-1. Exadata Patching Definitions

	Description and Definition
Storage server patches	Patches applied to Exadata Storage Servers using the `patchmgr` utility. Storage server patches apply operating system, firmware, and driver updates and update both the storage cells and compute nodes. These are usually released quarterly.
Database server yum channels	Database servers are patched using yum; there is a yum channel for each Exadata image version. Recently, this functionality replaced the "minimal pack."
Database "minimal pack"	The database minimal pack is defined as the minimal version of Oracle RDBMS, Grid Infrastructure, and diskmon software required to operate with a specific storage server patch. Minimal packs were phased out in favor of using yum channels for patching.
QDPE	QDPE = Quarterly Database Patch for Exadata. These patches are released quarterly in 11.2.0.2 and monthly in 11.2.0.3 and are applied using OPatch. Each QDPE patch includes three patches—one for the RDBMS binaries, one for the Grid Infrastructure binaries, and one for `diskmon`. QDPE patches are cumulative in nature and were previously called *bundle patches*. QDPE patches are always rolling patches and applied with the `opatch auto` command.
Bundle patches	Bundle patches are patches designed to patch Oracle RDBMS, Grid Infrastructure, and diskmon software. These have recently been renamed QDPE patches.
Patch set upgrades	These are full-upgrade patches on the compute node; for example, patching 11.2.0.2 to 11.2.0.3. Grid Infrastructure patches are always rolling in nature, and RDBMS patches require an outage.
InfiniBand patches	These are patches released annually that update your InfiniBand switches. These are always rolling in nature, and the patch mechanism depends on your InfiniBand version.
QFSDP	QFSDP = Quarterly Full Stack Download Patch. These patches contain all of the patches for each stack in your Exadata Database Machine, including your infrastructure, database, and Oracle Enterprise Manager. The patches inside a QFSDP patch are still applied individually, but they are downloadable from the same patch file.
OPlan	OPlan creates a patch deployment report customized for your environment and includes step-by-step instructions for patching your environment. Details of OPlan are discussed in MOS note 1306814.1 and delivered as part of patch 11846294.

When patching Exadata, we recommend following these steps:

1. Carefully read MOS note 888828.1 and become familiar with its contents. An Exadata DMA responsible for patching should bookmark note 888828.1 in his or her browser and refer to it often.
2. Determine if you will use a QFSDP patch or QDPE patches combined with storage server and other infrastructure patches.
3. Download the patches to a compute node and patch the storage servers first using `patchmgr`.
4. Apply the QDPE patches to the compute nodes.
5. Apply the QDPE patches to the compute nodes.

How It Works

Patching Exadata is generally a matter of carefully reading MOS note 888828.1 and fully understanding the various patch definitions, scope, and application methods. Table 11-1 in the Solution of this recipe provides a list of Exadata patching definitions and descriptions.

An example of the contents of a QFSDP patch are listed, along with descriptions about what each of the patch contents represent:

```
14207418                               -> Main QFSDP Patch
- Infrastructure/                      -> Storage server, InfiniBand, and PDU patches
       --ExadataStorageServer/         -> Storage server patches to be applied to cells and
                                              compute nodes
       --InfiniBandSwitchSoftware/     -> InfiniBand Switch patch
       --SunRackIIPDUMeteringUnitFirmware/   PDU patch
- Database/
       --11.2.0.3_QDPE_Jul2012/        -> Database QDPE patch
       --OPatch/                       -> Required OPatch
       --OPlan/                        -> Required OPlan
- SystemsManagement/                -> Enterprise Manager patches
       --CloudControl12/               -> EM patches for Cloud Control
            --OMS/
            --Agent/
            --WLS/
       --GridControl11/                -> EM patches for Grid Control
            --OMS/
            --Agent/
            --EMPlugins/
```

Recipes 11-2, 11-3, 11-4, and 11-5 provide detailed steps for patching the various Exadata components.

11-2. Preparing to Apply Exadata Patches

Problem

You wish to adequately prepare for patching your Exadata Database Machine.

Solution

In this recipe, you will learn how to find the most recent Exadata patches available from My Oracle Support, determine your current software, image, and firmware versions, download the Exadata patches, and prepare a plan for patching your Exadata Database Machine.

Start by logging in to My Oracle Support, opening document 888828.1, and clicking on the Latest Releases link as displayed at the bottom of Figure 11-1.

> **Database Machine and Exadata Storage Server 11g Release 2 (11.2) Supported Versions [ID 888828.1]**
> Modified: Oct 1, 2012   Type: REFERENCE   Status: PUBLISHED   Priority: 3   Comments (0)
>
> **In this Document**
>
> Purpose
> Scope
> Details
>   Latest Releases and Patching News
>   Exadata Patching Overview and Guidelines
>   Exadata Software and Hardware Maintenance Planning
>   Critical Issues
>   **Latest Releases**
>   Patch Release Frequency
>   Recommended Versions
>   Latest Releases

Figure 11-1. Latest releases from MOS Note 888828.1

As of October 2012, Quarterly Full Stack Download for Exadata (QFSDP) patch 14207418 was released. This is the version we will base our planning on in this recipe and the other recipes in this chapter. Under the Individual Components section on MOS note 888828.1, you can see the following:

- QFSDP patch 14207418 contains patch 14212264 for the Exadata storage cells
- The 11.2.0.3 QDPE patch 14084153 patch for Exadata
- Oracle 11gR2 Patch Set 2 (10404530)
- InfiniBand switch patch 12373676
- Patches for the PDUs and KVM switch

Download QFSDP patch 14207418, or the latest patch offered at the time you read this recipe, from My Oracle Support, and take some time to read the QFSDP patch README file as well as the individual README files in each component patch included in the QFSDP patch. To access the individual patch README files, download the patch from My Oracle Support and stage to a directory on your first compute node.

We typically recommend reading through the various patch README files in this order:

1. First read the contents of the `<patch>/ExadataStorageServer/<release>/README*.html`. For recent storage server patches, you will usually have two patches in this location, one for the storage server patch and one containing the ISO image for the compute node patches.

2. Look for references to required InfiniBand patches in the ExadataStorageServer patch `README.html` files. If your InfiniBand switch firmware version is lower than the recommended version, you should patch your InfiniBand switches first, as discussed in Recipe 11-5.

3. Next, examine the README contents in the `<patch>/Database/<QDPE Patch number>` directory.

4. Finally, read the `<patch>/SystemsManagement` README files and plan accordingly.

After reading through all the assorted README files under the QFSDP patch directories, compile a list of steps required for your specific environment. On our Exadata Quarter Rack running image version 11.2.2.4.2.111221 on both the compute and storage nodes and Oracle 11.2.0.3, our action plan is as follows:

1. Validate and apply required InfiniBand patches per instructions in README-13998727.html
2. Prepare your Exadata cells for patch application using the instructions in README-13998727.html
3. Apply the Exadata Storage Server patches using `patchmgr`
4. Apply the database server updates using yum, per instructions in README-13998727.html
5. Update PDU metering firmware
6. Apply 11.2.0.3_QDPE_Jul2012 patch to compute nodes using OPatch
7. Apply the Cloud Control OMS, WLS, and Agent patches to the Cloud Control management server and Exadata Compute Nodes

How It Works

My Oracle Support note 888828.1 is your first reference when planning for Exadata patching. This note contains the list of most recent patches, QDPEs, and QFSDPs.

We recommend reading all of the various patch README files prior to beginning the patch process to understand interdependencies and known issues. There will be a number of patches that make up a QFSDP patch, and many of these patches reference each other. In our experience, it is best to begin with the Exadata Storage Server patches, taking special care to ensure that your InfiniBand switches are patched first, followed by the database server QDPE patches, and finally, the systems management (Enterprise Manager) patches.

Note Recipes 11-3 through 11-6 will show patch application steps for QFSDP patch 14207418 and will guide you through a real-life Exadata patching exercise.

11-3. Patching Your Exadata Storage Servers

Problem

You wish to apply Exadata Storage Server patches and need step-by-step examples of how to prepare your storage servers for patching, using `patchmgr` to apply the patches, and how to confirm that the patches have been applied successfully.

Solution

In this recipe, you will learn how to prepare your Exadata storage cells and compute nodes for applying storage server patches, perform each of the steps required to apply storage software on your Exadata storage cells, and validate a successful patch application.

> **Note** In this recipe, as well as Recipes 11-4, 11-5, and 11-6, we will be showing examples for applying the July 2012 QFSDP, patch 14207418. The steps in this recipe are specific to the patch contents and README instructions of this patch, but they should provide an overview of a typical Exadata patching. Where possible, we will attempt to only present "common" storage server patching activities and leave it to the Exadata DMA to confirm specific patch steps required for specific Exadata software versions.

1. Start by transferring the QFSDP patch to a directory on your first compute node and unzipping the file. Using the instructions in the ExadataStorageServer/<version>/README-<version>.html file, go to Section 3: "Preparing Exadata Cells for Patch Application." The first paragraph in this section will likely say that your InfiniBand switches need to be on a specific version; before continuing, please see Recipe 11-5 for instructions on how to apply InfiniBand patches.

2. After ensuring that your InfiniBand switches are patched to the proper firmware level, a handful of preparation tasks are typically required. The first of these tasks is to start an ILOM console on each storage cell so that you can monitor the patch application log files and connect to the server in the event of patch failure or to troubleshoot. To start the ILOM console, log in to each storage cell's ILOM address and do the following:

```
Macintosh-8:~ jclarke$ ssh root@cm01cel01-ilom
Password:
Oracle(R) Integrated Lights Out Manager
Version 3.0.16.10 r65138
Copyright (c) 2011, Oracle and/or its affiliates. All rights reserved.
-> start /SP/console
Are you sure you want to start /SP/console (y/n)? y
Serial console started.  To stop, type ESC (
cm01cel01.centroid.com login: root
Password:
Last login: Wed Oct 10 13:46:59 from cm01dbm01
[root@cm01cel01 ~]#
```

3. The next step is usually to validate the version of the ofa package on your storage cells and take appropriate actions, per the patch README file, to ensure that your ofa binaries are at a high enough level to avoid file-system corruption. This step is typically done using the following rpm command, and if your version is lower than the expected version, you will be required to perform a number of steps to provide a workaround:

```
[root@cm01dbm01 ~]# rpm -qa|grep ofa
ofa-2.6.18-238.12.2.0.2.el5-1.5.1-4.0.53
[root@cm01dbm01 ~]#
```

4. Next, run ipconf -verify on your storage cells to validate your current configuration and address any issues prior to patching:

```
[root@cm01cel01 ~]# ipconf -verify
Verifying of Exadata configuration file /opt/oracle.cellos/cell.conf
Done. Configuration file /opt/oracle.cellos/cell.conf passed all
verification checks
[root@cm01cel01 ~]#
```

5. Before initiating the storage server patches, you will need to set up SSH equivalence from the compute node where the patches are staged with the root user on all of your storage cells. Use the following steps to set up and validate root SSH equivalence. In this example, the cell_group file is a text file containing the hostnames of each storage cell in your Exadata Database Machine:

```
[root@cm01dbm01 ~]# ssh-keygen -t rsa
Generating public/private rsa key pair.
Enter file in which to save the key (/root/.ssh/id_rsa):
Enter passphrase (empty for no passphrase):
Enter same passphrase again:
Your identification has been saved in /root/.ssh/id_rsa.
Your public key has been saved in /root/.ssh/id_rsa.pub.
The key fingerprint is:
77:79:b7:aa:65:86:ed:11:e7:fe:f7:de:1e:82:79:cd root@cm01dbm01.centroid.com
[root@cm01dbm01 ~]# dcli -g ./cell_group -l root -k
The authenticity of host 'cm01cel02 (172.16.1.13)' can't be established.
RSA key fingerprint is 29:6a:01:bb:67:c8:b9:6e:47:97:50:15:03:23:d4:46.
Are you sure you want to continue connecting (yes/no)? yes
Warning: Permanently added 'cm01cel02,172.16.1.13' (RSA) to the list of
known hosts.
root@cm01cel02's password:
... Output omitted for brevity
[root@cm01dbm01 ~]# dcli -g ./cell_group -l root 'hostname -i'
cm01cel01: 172.16.1.12
cm01cel02: 172.16.1.13
cm01cel03: 172.16.1.14
[root@cm01dbm01 ~]#
```

6. Next, unzip the QFSDP patch on your first compute node, navigate to the ExadataStorageServer patch directory, and run patchmgr to confirm that the patch can be applied in a rolling fashion. You should see SUCCESS on all operations:

```
[root@cm01dbm01 patch_11.2.3.1.1.120607]# pwd
/u01/stg/14207418/Infrastructure/ExadataStorageServer/11.2.3.1.1/
patch_11.2.3.1.1.120607
[root@cm01dbm01 patch_11.2.3.1.1.120607]# ./patchmgr -cells ~/cell_group
-patch_check_prereq -rolling
Linux cm01dbm01.centroid.com 2.6.18-238.12.2.0.2.el5 #1 SMP Tue Jun 28
05:21:19 EDT 2011 x86_64 x86_64 x86_64 GNU/Linux
2012-10-10 14:02:50        :Working: DO: Check cells have ssh equivalence
for root user. Up to 10 seconds per cell ...
2012-10-10 14:03:03        :SUCCESS: DONE: Check cells have ssh equivalence
for root user.
2012-10-10 14:03:03        :Working: DO: Check space and state of Cell
services on target cells. Up to 1 minute ...
2012-10-10 14:03:45        :SUCCESS: DONE: Check space and state of Cell
services on target cells.
2012-10-10 14:03:45        :Working: DO: Copy, extract prerequisite check
archive to cells. If required start md11 mismatched partner size correction.
Up to 40 minutes ...
```

```
2012-10-10 14:04:20 Wait correction of degraded md11 due to md partner size
mismatch. Up to 30 minutes.
2012-10-10 14:04:31          :SUCCESS: DONE: Copy, extract prerequisite check
archive to cells. If required start md11 mismatched partner size correction.
2012-10-10 14:04:31          :Working: DO: Check prerequisites on all cells.
Up to 2 minutes ...
2012-10-10 14:05:05          :SUCCESS: DONE: Check prerequisites on all cells.
[root@cm01dbm01 patch_11.2.3.1.1.120607]#
```

7. Before starting the patch application process, optionally adjust your disk_repair_time ASM disk group attribute on each of your ASM disk groups to a higher value than 3.6 hour default. This is often considered a "best practice" before patching to provide ASM more time before dropping ASM disks from a disk group in the event a patch runs longer than expected or encounters issues. Log in to your ASM instance as SYSASM and run the script in Listing 11-1.

Listing 11-1. lst11-01-asm-repairtime.sql

```
SQL> @lst11-01-asm-repairtime.sql
SQL> alter diskgroup &&diskgroup_name set attribute
'disk_repair_time'='&&disk_repair_time';
Enter value for diskgroup_name: DATA_CM01
Enter value for disk_repair_time: 3.6h
old   1: alter diskgroup &&diskgroup_name set attribute
'disk_repair_time'='&&disk_repair_time'
new   1: alter diskgroup DATA_CM01 set attribute 'disk_repair_time'='3.6h'
Diskgroup altered.
SQL>
```

8. At this point, you're ready to patch your storage cells. While logged in as root on the compute node, change directories to the ExadataStorageServer patch directory and run the following patchmgr command to patch your storage cells.

Note When applying storage server patches using the -rolling option, patchmgr will iteratively apply the patches to each storage cell defined in the cell_group file provided to the -cells command line argument. Storage server patches can take quite a bit of time to apply, so be patient while the patch is applying.

```
[root@cm01dbm01 patch_11.2.3.1.1.120607]# pwd
/u01/stg/14207418/Infrastructure/ExadataStorageServer/11.2.3.1.1/patch_11.2.3.1.1.120607
[root@cm01dbm01 patch_11.2.3.1.1.120607]#
[root@cm01dbm01 patch_11.2.3.1.1.120607]# ./patchmgr -cells ~/cell_group -patch -rolling
Linux cm01dbm01.centroid.com 2.6.18-238.12.2.0.2.el5 #1 SMP Tue Jun 28 05:21:19 EDT 2011
x86_64 x86_64 x86_64 GNU/Linux
Cells will reboot during the patch or rollback process.
For non-rolling patch or rollback, ensure all ASM instances using
the cells are shut down for the duration of the patch or rollback.
For rolling patch or rollback, ensure all ASM instances using
... Output omitted
```

```
2012-10-10 16:28:58 cm01cel03 Wait for patch finalization and reboot
2012-10-10 17:29:24 4 Done cm01cel03 :SUCCESS: Wait for cell to reboot and come online.
2012-10-10 17:29:24 5 Do cm01cel03 :Working: DO: Check the state of patch on cell.
Up to 5 minutes ...
2012-10-10 17:29:33 5 Done cm01cel03 :SUCCESS: Check the state of patch on cell.
2012-10-10 17:29:36 3-5 of 5 :SUCCESS: DONE: Finalize patch and check final status on cells.
[root@cm01dbm01 patch_11.2.3.1.1.120607]#
```

9. After the patches are applied and the storage cells are rebooted, validate the image on each of the cells to confirm a successful patch application:

```
[root@cm01cel02 ~]# imageinfo

Kernel version: 2.6.18-274.18.1.0.1.el5 #1 SMP Thu Feb 9 19:07:16 EST 2012 x86_64
Cell version: OSS_11.2.3.1.1_LINUX.X64_120607
Cell rpm version: cell-11.2.3.1.1_LINUX.X64_120607-1
Active image version: 11.2.3.1.1.120607
Active image activated: 2012-10-10 16:25:12 -0400
Active image status: success
Active system partition on device: /dev/md5
Active software partition on device: /dev/md7
In partition rollback: Impossible
Cell boot usb partition: /dev/sdm1
Cell boot usb version: 11.2.3.1.1.120607
Inactive image version: 11.2.2.4.2.111221
Inactive image activated: 2012-02-11 20:58:06 -0500
Inactive image status: success
Inactive system partition on device: /dev/md6
Inactive software partition on device: /dev/md8
Boot area has rollback archive for the version: 11.2.2.4.2.111221
Rollback to the inactive partitions: Possible

[root@cm01cel02 ~]# imagehistory
Version                              : 11.2.2.2.0.101206.2
Image activation date                : 2011-02-21 11:20:58 -0800
Imaging mode                         : fresh
Imaging status                       : success
... Multiple historical images omitted for brevity
Version                              : 11.2.2.4.2.111221
Image activation date                : 2012-02-11 20:58:06 -0500
Imaging mode                         : out of partition upgrade
Imaging status                       : success
Version                              : 11.2.3.1.1.120607
Image activation date                : 2012-10-10 16:25:12 -0400
Imaging mode                         : out of partition upgrade
Imaging status                       : success
[root@cm01cel02 ~]#
```

10. Next, run the following `cellcli` command with `dcli` to ensure that all of your Exadata grid disks are online. The `grep -v` will omit all lines that do not contain the text ONLINE; in other words, you want to confirm that the following command returns no output:

```
[root@cm01dbm01 ~]# dcli -g ./cell_group -l root cellcli -e list griddisk
attributes name,status,asmmodestatus | grep -v ONLINE
[root@cm01dbm01 ~]#
```

11. Confirm that there are no errors reported by the storage cell's validation framework using the following `dcli` command. The command should show no output:

```
[root@cm01dbm01 ~]# dcli -g cell_group -l root grep -i fail \
/var/log/cellos/validations.log
[root@cm01dbm01 ~]#
```

12. After confirming a successful patch application, run the patch cleanup utility using `patchmgr` to delete any interim patch files from each storage cell:

```
[root@cm01dbm01 patch_11.2.3.1.1.120607]# ./patchmgr -cells ~/cell_group -cleanup
Linux cm01dbm01.centroid.com 2.6.18-238.12.2.0.2.el5 #1 SMP Tue Jun 28
    05:21:19 EDT 2011 x86_64 x86_64 x86_64 GNU/Linux
2012-10-10 18:18:57 :DONE: Cleanup
[root@cm01dbm01 patch_11.2.3.1.1.120607]#
```

13. The last step is typically to check your InfiniBand switch software and OpenSM configuration from each storage cell using the following `CheckSWProfile.sh` command:

```
[root@cm01cel01 ~]# /opt/oracle.SupportTools/CheckSWProfile.sh -I \
cm01sw-ib2,cm01sw-ib3
Checking if switch cm01sw-ib2 is pingable...
Checking if switch cm01sw-ib3 is pingable...
Use the default password for all switches? (y/n) [n]: n
Use same password for all switches? (y/n) [n]: y
Enter admin or root password for All_Switches:
Confirm password:
[INFO] SUCCESS Switch cm01sw-ib2 has correct software and firmware version:
        SWVer: 1.3.3-2
[INFO] SUCCESS Switch cm01sw-ib2 has correct opensm configuration:
            controlled_handover=TRUE polling_retry_number=5 routing_engine=ftree
                sminfo_polling_timeout=1000 sm_priority=5
[INFO] SUCCESS Switch cm01sw-ib3 has correct software and firmware version:
        SWVer: 1.3.3-2
[INFO] SUCCESS Switch cm01sw-ib3 has correct opensm configuration:
            controlled_handover=TRUE polling_retry_number=5 routing_engine=ftree
                sminfo_polling_timeout=1000 sm_priority=5
[INFO] SUCCESS All switches have correct software and firmware version:
        SWVer: 1.3.3-2
```

```
[INFO] SUCCESS All switches have correct opensm configuration:
         controlled_handover=TRUE polling_retry_number=5 routing_engine=ftree
             sminfo_polling_timeout=1000 sm_priority=5 for non spine and 8
for spine switch5
[root@cm01cel01 ~]#
```

How It Works

Exadata Storage Servers are patched using the `patchmgr` utility. `patchmgr` is included with each storage server patch and is located in the `<staging directory>/Infrastructure/ExadataStorageServer/<version>/patch_<version>` directory.

Prior to applying Exadata Storage Server patches, you typically need to perform a few prerequisite tasks, including the following:

1. Starting an ILOM console on each storage cell
2. Running `ipconf -verify` to validate your storage cell network configuration
3. Establishing SSH user equivalence between `root` on your compute node and `root` on each storage cell
4. Running `patchmgr` with the `-check_prereq -rolling` option to ensure that your cells can be patched in a rolling manner
5. Adjusting your ASM disk group's `disk_repair_time` attribute

Applying the Exadata Storage Server patches on the storage cells is performed using the `patchmgr` utility, as presented in the solution of this recipe. As the storage servers are patched, Oracle will first apply the patch to the inactive system partition, which is part of Exadata's System Area or system volumes. If the patch fails for whatever reason, the cells are still bootable from the active, unpatched partition. If a patch succeeds, the inactive partition, patched via `patchmgr`, is made the active partition and the active partition that holds the previous image is swapped to the active partition. `patchmgr` performs these tasks automatically and also performs one or more reboots during the process.

■ **Note** In the README for each storage server patch, Oracle provides detailed rollback instructions that are to be followed in the event of a patch failure. We will not discuss these steps in this recipe, as the nature of the failure could vary from one patch to the next. Our recent experience has shown that it is becoming increasingly rare for a storage server patch to fail.

The steps in this recipe have only covered the storage cell components of an Exadata Storage Server patch. When storage cells are patched, there is almost always a set of storage server patches that need to be applied to the Exadata Compute Nodes as well. Historically, these were called "minimal packs," but recent improvements to the compute node patching process deliver these updates using yum channels on Oracle's Unbreakable Linux Network (ULN). Regardless, these patches on the compute nodes update software binaries and libraries, RPMs, and install a new image on the compute node that is certified with the images on the storage cells. When patching a storage server, always make sure you understand the compute node patching requirements and apply accordingly. Recipe 11-4 presents details on how to patch Exadata Compute Nodes using yum and Oracle's ULN.

11-4. Patching Your Exadata Compute Nodes and Databases

Problem

You wish to apply Exadata Storage Server patches to your compute nodes, apply a Quarterly Database Patch for Exadata (QDPE), and apply the latest PSU patches to your Oracle software homes on the compute nodes.

Solution

In this recipe, you will learn how to install the latest operating system patches and images on your compute nodes using yum and Oracle's ULN, how to apply the QDPE patches on your Exadata Compute Nodes using OPatch, how to apply the latest PSU patches to your Oracle databases, and how to validate the patch installation.

> **Note** In this recipe, as well as Recipes 11-3, 11-5, and 11-6, we will be showing examples for applying the July 2012 QFSDP, patch 14207418. The steps in this recipe are specific to the patch contents and README instructions of this patch, but they should provide an overview of a typical Exadata patching. Where possible, we will attempt to only present "common" storage server patching activities and leave it to the Exadata DMA to confirm specific patch steps required for specific Exadata software versions.

Registering with ULN and Setting Up a yum Repository

The first step required to update your compute node image, kernel, and RPMs is to register your compute nodes with Oracle's ULN and set up a yum repository. Follow the instructions in www.oracle.com/technetwork/topics/linux/yum-repository-setup-085606.html to register your compute nodes with ULN. Detailed instructions for how to configure a yum repository and register your systems with ULN are provided both in the previous link as well as the README file with patch 13741363.

> **Note** As the specific instructions, patch numbers, and configuration details are subject to change, we will omit the steps required to register your systems with ULN and configure a yum repository; refer to the patch instructions in your QFSDP or storage server patch README files for recent, version-specific information.

Once your compute nodes are registered with ULN, you need to define which channels you wish to subscribe to using the Manage Subscriptions link on the ULN web site. The storage server patch README will instruct you which channels to subscribe to; in Figure 11-2, we are subscribing to the Enterprise Linux 5 Add ons (x86_64), Exadata release 11.2 Latest (x86_64), and Oracle Linux 5 Latest (x86_64) channels based on instructions in the QFSDP storage server README file.

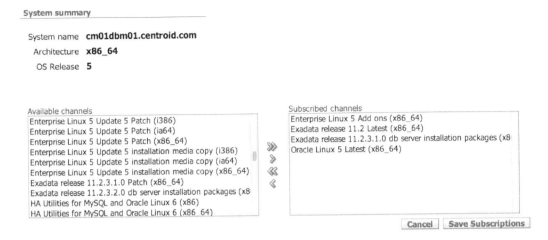

Figure 11-2. *ULN subscriptions for compute node patching*

After your system is registered and subscribed to the proper channels, you will need to create the following directory on each compute node:

```
[root@cm01dbm01 11.2.3.1.0]# mkdir -p /var/www/html/yum
```

Once this is complete, download script 167283.sh from www.oracle.com/technetwork/topics/linux/yum-repository-setup-085606.html to retrieve the RPMs based on the channels you've subscribed to and run the script on each compute node. Following is an example execution of 167283.sh:

```
[root@cm01dbm01 stg]# sh ./167283.sh
Fetching Obsoletes list for channel: el5_x86_64_addons...
########################################
Fetching Obsoletes list for channel: ol5_x86_64_latest...
########################################
Fetching rpm headers...
######
... output omitted
Digesting rpms 98 % complete: xz-devel-4.999.9-0.3.beta.20091007git.el5.x86_64.rDigesting rpms
98 % complete: xz-libs-4.999.9-0.3.beta.20091007git.el5.x86_64.rpDigesting rpms 99 % complete:
xz-lzma-compat-4.999.9-0.3.beta.20091007git.el5.x8Digesting rpms 99 % complete:
yum-NetworkManager-dispatcher-1.1.16-21.el5.noarchDigesting rpms 100 % complete:
zsh-html-4.2.6-6.el5.x86_64.rpm
   Total: 3696
   Used: 3696
   Src: 0
Writing header.info file
## END PROCESSING ol5_x86_64_latest ##
[root@cm01dbm02 stg]#
```

Next, enable HTTP on your compute nodes in preparation for using yum to download updates:

```
[root@cm01dbm01 ~]# chkconfig --add httpd
[root@cm01dbm01 ~]# chkconfig httpd on
```

```
[root@cm01dbm01 ~]# service httpd start
Starting httpd:                                                     [  OK  ]
[root@cm01dbm01 ~]#
```

After this is complete, open a browser and ensure you can navigate to
http://yourserver.yourdomain.com/yum/unknown/EXADATA/dbserver/11.2/latest/x86_64.

The patch instructions may, at this point, require you to remove some or many existing RPMs on your system; as these requirements may vary for different patches, please following the instructions in the README file to identify and remove any packages that the patch requires removing.

Typically, after removing unnecessary patches, the README will instruct you to install yum support. This is accomplished by installing a number of packages in the yum_essential_rpms directory from patch 13741363:

```
[root@cm01dbm02 yum_essential_rpms]# pwd
/u01/stg/13741363/11.2.3.1.0/yum_essential_rpms
[root@cm01dbm02 yum_essential_rpms]# rpm -Uvh --force --nodeps *rpm
-nodeps: unknown option
[root@cm01dbm02 yum_essential_rpms]# rpm -Uvh --force --nodeps *rpm
Preparing...                ########################################### [100%]
   1:rpm-python             ########################################### [ 13%]
   2:yum-metadata-parser    ########################################### [ 25%]
   3:rhpl                   ########################################### [ 38%]
   4:curl                   ########################################### [ 50%]
   5:gnupg                  ########################################### [ 63%]
   6:rhnlib                 ########################################### [ 75%]
   7:up2date                ########################################### [ 88%]
   8:yum                    ########################################### [100%]
[root@cm01dbm02 yum_essential_rpms]#
```

After this is complete, import the RPM key for signature validation and remove the yum_rhn plugin:

```
[root@cm01dbm02]#  rpm --import /usr/share/rhn/RPM-GPG-KEY
[root@cm01dbm02 yum_essential_rpms]# rpm -q yum-rhn-plugin
package yum-rhn-plugin is not installed
[root@cm01dbm02 yum_essential_rpms]#
```

The next step is to copy the repository file from the yum patch, 13741363, to /etc/yum.repos.d/Exadata-computenode.repo and edit it to match Oracle's instructions in the storage server README file.

■ **Note** When editing the information in the following file, use the instructions supplied in the Exadata Storage Server patch, not those in patch 13741363. The latter patch provides generic instructions that are not release-specific to the Exadata patch you are applying, and the patch you are applying should have instructions in its README file that identify alternative steps to those in 13741363.

```
[root@cm01dbm02 11.2.3.1.0]# cp etc_yum.repos.d_Exadata-computenode.repo \
/etc/yum.repos.d/Exadata-computenode.repo

[root@cm01dbm01 ~]# cat /etc/yum.repos.d/Exadata-computenode.repo
[exadata_dbserver_11.2_x86_64_latest]
```

```
name=Oracle Exadata DB server 11.2 Linux $releasever - $basearch - latest
baseurl=http://cm01dbm01.centroid.com/yum/unknown/EXADATA/dbserver/11.2/latest/x86_64/
gpgcheck=1
enabled=1
[root@cm01dbm01 ~]#
```

Next, empty your yum cache using the following command:

```
[root@cm01dbm02 11.2.3.1.0]# yum clean all
Cleaning up Everything
[root@cm01dbm02 11.2.3.1.0]#
```

Next, enable your repository using a command similar to the following command based on instructions in the storage server's patch README:

```
[root@cm01dbm02 11.2.3.1.0]# yum --enablerepo=exadata_dbserver_11.2_x86_64_latest repolist
exadata_dbserver_11.2_x86_64_latest                                      | 1.9 kB     00:00
exadata_dbserver_11.2_x86_64_latest/primary_db                           | 1.1 MB     00:00
repo id                         repo name                                           status
exadata_dbserver_11.2_x86_64_latest Oracle Exadata DB server 11.2 Linux 5 - x86_64
     - latest   enabled: 482
repolist: 482
[root@cm01dbm02 11.2.3.1.0]#
```

When this is complete, you may be instructed to install RPMs that are missing, as listed:

```
[root@cm01dbm02 11.2.3.1.0]# yum --enablerepo=exadata_dbserver_11.2_x86_64_latest \
 install elfutils-libelf.i386 libstdc++-devel.i386 libX11.i386 \
 libXau.i386 libXdmcp.i386 libXext.i386 libXp.i386 libXtst.i386
Setting up Install Process
Package elfutils-libelf-0.137-3.el5.i386 already installed and latest version
Package libXp-1.0.0-8.1.el5.i386 already installed and latest version
Package libXtst-1.0.1-3.1.i386 already installed and latest version
Resolving Dependencies
--> Running transaction check
---> Package libX11.i386 0:1.0.3-11.el5_7.1 set to be updated
---> Package libXau.i386 0:1.0.1-3.1 set to be updated
---> Package libXdmcp.i386 0:1.0.1-2.1 set to be updated
---> Package libXext.i386 0:1.0.1-2.1 set to be updated
```

Updating Your Compute Nodes Using yum

Prior to applying the latest firmware and package updates on the compute nodes, stop and disable CRS on the node you wish to patch.

■ **Note** Exadata storage patches are typically applied one compute node at a time, and we recommend following all of the steps in this section's recipe on a single node first before continuing to the next one.

```
[root@cm01dbm02 bin]# $GI_HOME/bin/crsctl stop crs
[root@cm01dbm02 bin]# $GI_HOME/bin/crsctl disable crs
```

Once your cluster resources are down, update your kernel using a command similar to the following:

```
[root@cm01dbm02 11.2.3.1.0]# yum --enablerepo=exadata_dbserver_11.2_x86_64_latest install
kernel-2.6.18-308.8.2.0.1.el5
Setting up Install Process
Resolving Dependencies
--> Running transaction check
---> Package kernel.x86_64 0:2.6.18-308.8.2.0.1.el5 set to be installed
--> Finished Dependency Resolution
--> Running transaction check
---> Package kernel.x86_64 0:2.6.18-194.3.1.0.3.el5 set to be erased
--> Finished Dependency Resolution
Dependencies Resolved
... Kernel dependency information omitted
Install      1 Package(s)
Upgrade      0 Package(s)
Remove       1 Package(s)
Reinstall    0 Package(s)
Downgrade    0 Package(s)

Total download size: 21 M
Is this ok [y/N]: y
... Additional output omitted
```

When this is complete, you are ready to install the main Exadata database server RPMs. Run the following command, which will download all software updates, resolve dependencies, and reboot your compute node:

```
# yum --enablerepo=exadata_dbserver_11.2_x86_64_latest install exadata-sun-computenode
  Dependency Updated:
  Lib_Utils.noarch 0:1.00-09          MegaCli.noarch 0:8.02.21-1          compat-dapl.x86_64
... Detailed information omitted for brevity
Replaced:
  kernel-headers.x86_64 0:2.6.18-238.12.2.0.2.el5
Complete!
[root@cm01dbm02 11.2.3.1.0]#
Remote broadcast message (Thu Oct 11 02:07:51 2012):
Exadata post install steps started.
It may take up to 2 minutes.
The db node will be rebooted upon successful completion.
Remote broadcast message (Thu Oct 11 02:08:15 2012):
Exadata post install steps completed.
Initiate reboot in 10 seconds to apply the changes.
```

When finished, log in to your compute node and validate your kernel version:

```
[root@cm01dbm02 ~]# uname -r
2.6.32-400.1.1.el5uek
[root@cm01dbm02 ~]#
```

Assuming that your versions are correct and expected, update the remaining RPMs using the following command:

```
# yum --enablerepo=exadata_dbserver_11.2_x86_64_latest update
```

After a successful validation, you will typically be required to verify your kernel and ofa versions, clear the yum cache, relink your Oracle binaries, and reboot your server.

Applying QDPE Patches

In this section, you will learn how to apply a typical QDPE patch to the Oracle RDBMS, Grid Infrastructure (GI), and diskmon binaries on the Exadata Compute Nodes. First, change directories to the database patch staging directory and install the OPatch patch into each of your RDBMS and GI homes. OPatch is delivered in p6880880_112000_Linux-x86-64.zip; you will very likely already have OPatch installed in each Oracle home, but before applying the QDPE patches, you will need the version that is included in the QDPE patch installed in each home.

Once OPatch is installed, create your Oracle Configuration Management response file in each RDBMS and GI home to avoid being prompted for your My Oracle Support credentials when opatch runs:

```
[oracle@cm01dbm01 bin]$ cd $ORACLE_HOME/OPatch/ocm/bin
[oracle@cm01dbm01 bin]$ ./emocmrsp
OCM Installation Response Generator 10.3.4.0.0 - Production
Copyright (c) 2005, 2010, Oracle and/or its affiliates.  All rights reserved.
Provide your email address to be informed of security issues, install and
initiate Oracle Configuration Manager. Easier for you if you use your My
Oracle Support Email address/User Name.
Visit http://www.oracle.com/support/policies.html for details.
Email address/User Name: john.clarke@centroid.com
Provide your My Oracle Support password to receive security updates via your My Oracle
Support account.
Password (optional):
The OCM configuration response file (ocm.rsp) was successfully created.
[oracle@cm01dbm01 bin]$
... Repeat on all nodes for both the RDBMS and GI Home
```

Next, validate the inventory on each RDBMS and GI home using the following commands. Use the Oracle software owner when validating the RDBMS Oracle Home and the Grid Infrastructure owner when validating the GI Home, and run the validation against each patch contained under the unzipped patch directory according to the patch README file:

```
[grid@cm01dbm02 ]$  $GI_HOME/OPaych/opatch lsinventory -detail -oh /u01/app/11.2.0.3/grid
[oracle@cm01dbm01 ~]$ $ORACLE_HOME/OPatch/opatch lsinventory -detail -oh \
/u01/app/oracle/product/11.2.0.3/dbhome_1
```

After unzipping the individual QDPE patch contents, check for patch conflicts using opatch on both the RDBMS and GI Oracle Homes:

```
[grid@cm01dbm01 ~]$ /u01/app/11.2.0.3/grid/OPatch/opatch prereq CheckConflictAgainstOHWithDetail \
> -phBaseDir /u01/stg/14207418/Database/11.2.0.3_QDPE_Jul2012/14103267/14103267
Oracle Interim Patch Installer version 11.2.0.3.0
... Output omitted
Invoking prereq "checkconflictagainstohwithdetail"
```

```
Prereq "checkConflictAgainstOHWithDetail" passed.
OPatch succeeded.

[oracle@cm01dbm01 ~]$ /u01/app/oracle/product/11.2.0.3/dbhome_1/OPatch/opatch prereq \
CheckConflictAgainstOHWithDetail \
> -phBaseDir /u01/stg/14207418/Database/11.2.0.3_QDPE_Jul2012/14103267/14103267
Oracle Interim Patch Installer version 11.2.0.3.0
... Output omitted
Prereq "checkConflictAgainstOHWithDetail" passed.
OPatch succeeded.
[oracle@cm01dbm01 ~]
```

After this, you will typically be required to validate that enough disk space is required to apply the patches using opatch's prereq `CheckSystemSpace` argument. Run the following command for each patch as both the RDBMS and GI software owner:

```
[grid@cm01dbm01 ~]$ /u01/app/11.2.0.3/grid/OPatch/opatch prereq CheckSystemSpace -phBaseDir \
> /u01/stg/14207418/Database/11.2.0.3_QDPE_Jul2012/14103267/14103267
[oracle@cm01dbm01 ~]$ /u01/app/oracle/product/11.2.0.3/dbhome_1/OPatch/opatch prereq \
CheckSystemSpace -phBaseDir \
> /u01/stg/14207418/Database/11.2.0.3_QDPE_Jul2012/14103267/14103267
```

Now, you are ready to apply the patches. We recommend using opatch auto to apply each patch to each RDBMS or GI tier with a single command, per compute node server. Log in as root, ensure that opatch is in root's PATH, and run the following opatch auto command:

```
[root@cm01dbm01 ~]# export PATH=$PATH:/u01/app/11.2.0.3/grid/OPatch/
[root@cm01dbm01 ~]# which opatch
/u01/app/11.2.0.3/grid/OPatch/opatch
[root@cm01dbm01 ~]#
[root@cm01dbm01 ~]# opatch auto /u01/stg/14207418/Database/11.2.0.3_QDPE_Jul2012/14103267/
Executing /usr/bin/perl /u01/app/11.2.0.3/grid/OPatch/crs/patch112.pl -patchdir
/u01/stg/14207418/Database/11.2.0.3_QDPE_Jul2012 -patchn 14103267 -paramfile
/u01/app/11.2.0.3/grid/crs/install/crsconfig_params
opatch auto log file location is
/u01/app/11.2.0.3/grid/OPatch/crs/../../cfgtoollogs/opatchauto2012-10-11_12-32-57.log
Detected Oracle Clusterware install
Using configuration parameter file: /u01/app/11.2.0.3/grid/crs/install/crsconfig_params
... Output omitted for brevity.
```

When complete, check your patch log files for errors and proceed to the next compute node. Iterate through your compute nodes until all the patches are applied successfully and at the same version. You should see successful completion messages like these:

```
patch /u01/stg/14207418/Database/11.2.0.3_QDPE_Jul2012/14103267/14103267   apply successful for home
/u01/app/oracle/product/11.2.0.3/dbhome_1
patch /u01/stg/14207418/Database/11.2.0.3_QDPE_Jul2012/14103267/13919095/custom/server/13919095
apply successful for home   /u01/app/oracle/product/11.2.0.3/dbhome_1
patch /u01/stg/14207418/Database/11.2.0.3_QDPE_Jul2012/14103267/14184077   apply successful for home
/u01/app/oracle/product/11.2.0.3/dbhome_1
Successfully unlock /u01/app/11.2.0.3/grid
```

```
patch /u01/stg/14207418/Database/11.2.0.3_QDPE_Jul2012/14103267/14103267   apply successful for home
/u01/app/11.2.0.3/grid
patch /u01/stg/14207418/Database/11.2.0.3_QDPE_Jul2012/14103267/13919095   apply successful for home
/u01/app/11.2.0.3/grid
patch /u01/stg/14207418/Database/11.2.0.3_QDPE_Jul2012/14103267/14184077   apply successful for home
/u01/app/11.2.0.3/grid
```

Updating Your Oracle Databases

After your Oracle binaries have been patched with the QDPE patches, you typically will need to update your Oracle registry information. Log in to a compute node as the Oracle software owner, change directories to $ORACLE_HOME, and for each database log in to SQL*Plus as SYSDBA and run the following:

```
SQL> connect / as sysdba

SQL> @rdbms/admin/catbundle.sql exa apply
```

How It Works

When patching your Exadata Database Machine using a QFSDP or other storage server patch, there are generally three distinct activities required for patching your compute nodes:

1. First, you must update your compute nodes with the image, RPMs, and software required to coexist with the images on your storage cells. As discussed in Recipe 11-1, these were historically referred as "minimal packs," but Oracle has phased out the minimal pack concept in preference of using Oracle's ULN and yum.

2. Next, you would typically apply patches to your RDBMS, Grid Infrastructure, and diskmon binaries using OPatch. These patches are usually delivered as part of a QPDE (Quarterly Database Patch for Exadata).

3. Finally, you would update each database's registry using catbundle.sql exa apply.

The QDPE patches are not necessarily required to coexist with the updated versions of your compute node firmware, kernel, and RPMs unless specified in the patch README file, but we generally recommend that when applying a QFSDP patch that the Exadata DMA apply the QDPE patches along with storage server and compute node updates.

11-5. Patching the InfiniBand Switches

Problem

You wish to patch your InfiniBand switches.

Solution

In this recipe, you will learn how to patch your InfiniBand switches. We will demonstrate by showing an example of applying an InfiniBand patch.

Note In this recipe, as well as Recipes 11-3, 11-4, and 11-6, we will be showing examples for applying the July 2012 QFSDP, patch 14207418. The steps in this recipe are specific to the patch contents and README instructions of this patch, but they should provide an overview of a typical Exadata patching.

1. Begin by reading the patch README file. Unzip the patch contents from the <patch_stage>/14207418/Infrastructure/InfiniBandSwitchSoftware/1.3.3-2 directory and transfer to your first InfiniBand switch's /tmp directory, as outlined:

```
[root@cm01dbm01 1.3.3-2]# unzip p11891229_133_Generic.zip
    Archive:  p11891229_133_Generic.zip
  inflating: NM2_SW_1.3.3_THIRDPARTYLICENSE.txt
  inflating: readme_SUN_DCS_36p_1.3.3.txt
  inflating: SUN_DCS_36p_1.3.3.tar.gz
[root@cm01dbm01 1.3.3-2]# unzip p12373676_112100_Linux-x86-64.zip
    Archive:  p12373676_112100_Linux-x86-64.zip
   creating: 12373676/
  inflating: 12373676/ibswitchcheck.sh
  inflating: 12373676/README.txt
[root@cm01dbm01 1.3.3-2]#
[root@cm01dbm01 1.3.3-2]# tar -zxvf SUN_DCS_36p_1.3.3.tar.gz
ENTITY-MIB.txt
SUN-DCS-IB-MIB.txt
SUN-HW-TRAP-MIB.mib
SUN-ILOM-CONTROL-MIB.mib
SUN-ILOM-PET-MIB.mib
SUN-PLATFORM-MIB.txt
sundcs_36p_repository_1.3.3_2.pkg
[root@cm01dbm01 1.3.3-2]#
[root@cm01dbm01 1.3.3-2]# scp -r 12373676/ root@cm01sw-ib2:/tmp
The authenticity of host 'cm01sw-ib2 (172.16.1.23)' can't be established.
RSA key fingerprint is be:6b:01:27:90:91:0a:f9:ab:7f:fd:99:81:76:4a:45.
Are you sure you want to continue connecting (yes/no)? yes
Warning: Permanently added 'cm01sw-ib2,172.16.1.23' (RSA) to the list of known hosts.
root@cm01sw-ib2's password:
ibswitchcheck.sh                          100%   14KB   13.6KB/s   00:00
README.txt                                100% 8634    8.4KB/s   00:00
[root@cm01dbm01 1.3.3-2]# scp sundcs_36p_repository_1.3.3_2.pkg root@cm01sw-ib2:/tmp
root@cm01sw-ib2's password:
sundcs_36p_repository_1.3.3_2.pkg         100%  112MB   5.3MB/s   00:21
[root@cm01dbm01 1.3.3-2]#
```

2. Log in as root to your InfiniBand switch and disable your InfiniBand subnet manager:

```
[root@cm01sw-ib2 12373676]# disablesm
Stopping partitiond daemon.                              [ OK ]
Stopping IB Subnet Manager..                             [ OK ]
[root@cm01sw-ib2 12373676]#
```

3. Run the patch prerequisite steps by executing ibswitchchecksh pre from the /tmp directory:

```
[root@cm01sw-ib2 12373676]# ./ibswitchcheck.sh pre|grep ERROR
[ERROR]    Switch is at target patching level
[ERROR]    Entry in /etc/hosts for FQN cm01sw-ib2.centroid.com does not
match hostname=cm01sw-ib2
Overall status of pre check is ERROR
[root@cm01sw-ib2 12373676]#
```

In the previous output, we see errors with fully qualified name resolution in /etc/hosts as well as a message indicating that our switch is already at the current patch level. You can ignore the FQN error message. Normally, if your switch is already at the proper patch level, you would stop now, but for the purposes of this recipe we will apply the patch anyway. To proceed, type spsh to enter the ILOM command line interface and load the patch:

```
[root@cm01sw-ib2 tmp]# spsh
Oracle(R) Integrated Lights Out Manager
Version ILOM 3.0 r47111
Copyright (c) 2010, Oracle and/or its affiliates. All rights reserved.
-> load -source /tmp/sundcs_36p_repository_1.3.3_2.pkg
NOTE: Firmware upgrade will upgrade the SUN DCS 36p firmware.
      ILOM will enter a special mode to load new firmware. No
      other tasks should be performed in ILOM until the firmware
      upgrade is complete.
Are you sure you want to load the specified file (y/n)? y
Setting up environment for firmware upgrade. This will take few minutes.
Starting SUN DCS 36p FW update
==========================
Performing operation: I4 A
==========================
I4 A: I4 is already at the given version.
==========================
Summary of Firmware update
==========================
I4 status                : FW UPDATE - SUCCESS
I4 update succeeded on   : none
I4 already up-to-date on : A
I4 update failed on      : none
========================================
Performing operation: SUN DCS 36p firmware update
========================================
INFO: SUN DCS 36p is already at the given version.
Firmware update is complete.
->
```

These messages indicate that our switch is already patched to this firmware level. Upon successful completion and based on directions in the README file, validate that /conf/configvalid file contains a single line with the number 1 in it:

```
[root@cm01sw-ib2 tmp]# cat /conf/configvalid
1
[root@cm01sw-ib2 tmp]#
```

Different subnet manager priorities need to be set based on whether the patched switch is a spine switch or leaf switch. Make sure to follow the instructions in the patch README based on which type of switch you are patching. When complete, reboot your switch and enable the subnet manager by typing enablesm:

```
[root@cm01sw-ib2 tmp]# enablesm
Starting IB Subnet Manager.                              [  OK  ]
Starting partitiond daemon.                              [  OK  ]
[root@cm01sw-ib2 tmp]#
```

4. Finally, run ibswitchcheck.sh post to validate that your switch is healthy and patched to the proper firmware level.

How It Works

Patching Exadata's InfiniBand switches is a relatively straightforward process. After downloading and staging the patches, the following steps are typically required:

- Run ibswitchcheck.sh pre to perform a pre-patching validation
- Disable the subnet manager
- Load the patch package file using the ILOM CLI
- Configure or reset subnet manager priorities
- Reboot your switch
- Enable the subnet manager
- Run ibswitchcheck.sh post to validate the switch

As mentioned in Recipe 11-1, InfiniBand patches are released relatively infrequently and though they are always included with QFSDPs and storage server patches, you will likely not need to apply them very often.

11-6. Patching Your Enterprise Manager Systems Management Software

Problem

You wish to patch the various Enterprise Manager systems management software deployments on your Exadata Database Machine.

Solution

In this recipe, you will learn some general guidelines for patching the Systems Management software along with an Exadata patch.

The Systems Management (that is, Enterprise Manager) software patches are typically included in the SystemsManagement directory under your Exadata patch, as listed in bold:

```
[root@cm01dbm01 14207418]# pwd
/u01/stg/14207418
[root@cm01dbm01 14207418]# ls
```

```
Database  Infrastructure  README.html  README.txt  SystemsManagement
[root@cm01dbm01 14207418]#
```

Under the SystemsManagement directory, you will find a number of individual patches, each with their own README and patch application instructions:

```
[root@cm01dbm01 14207418]# find SystemsManagement/ -type d
SystemsManagement/
SystemsManagement/GridControl11
SystemsManagement/GridControl11/OMS
SystemsManagement/GridControl11/OMS/11727299
... Output omitted
SystemsManagement/GridControl11/Agent
SystemsManagement/GridControl11/Agent/9482559
... Output omitted
SystemsManagement/GridControl11/EMPlugins
SystemsManagement/GridControl11/EMPlugins/KVM
... Output omitted
SystemsManagement/CloudControl12
SystemsManagement/CloudControl12/WLS
SystemsManagement/CloudControl12/WLS/13470978
... Output omitted
SystemsManagement/CloudControl12/OMS
SystemsManagement/CloudControl12/OMS/14037537
... Output omitted
SystemsManagement/CloudControl12/Agent
SystemsManagement/CloudControl12/Agent/13550565
... Output omitted
[root@cm01dbm01 14207418]#
```

First, determine if you wish or need to apply the Enterprise Manager patches. These are not critical to the functionality of your Exadata databases, but they could be important for monitoring or management purpose.

Next, identify whether you use Enterprise Manager Grid Control or Enterprise Manager Cloud Control. For both types of deployments, there will be a number of "one-off" patches for the Enterprise Manager agents and Oracle Management Server (OMS). For Cloud Control, there will also be a number of one-off Web Logic Server (WLS) patches.

If you are using Grid Control, you will have a number of Exadata-specific Grid Control plugins available, but for 12c Cloud Control, the plugins are downloadable and installable from your EM Cloud Control web interface.

The patches for the EM agents, OMS, and WLS are typically applied using OPatch. Many of the patches have specific custom pre-install and post-install steps.

Since the steps for applying Enterprise Manager patches on Exadata will vary from patch to patch, read the README file for each patch under the SystemsManagement directory for instructions on how to apply a specific patch.

How It Works

When Oracle releases QFSDP, QDPE, or other Exadata patches, there are typically a number of Enterprise Manager patches released and delivered with the patch bundle. These Enterprise Manager patches do not necessarily need to be applied at the same time as the storage server or compute node patches, but they are included to enable your Enterprise Manager agents and repository to take advantage of any additional features or updates with the cell or compute node updates.

CHAPTER 12

Security

When you install your Exadata Database Machine, there are a number of security-related configurations performed. In your configuration worksheet, you specified an Oracle RDBMS software owner and Grid Infrastructure software owner. By default, Oracle ACS typically installs a single Grid Infrastructure and a single, separate Oracle RDBMS Oracle Home on each compute node, each owned by the Linux account specified in the configuration worksheet. The operating system account that owns the Grid Infrastructure binaries can be the same account as the Oracle RDBMS software owner, but, in most cases, organizations elect to use separate accounts.

Oracle does allow you, however, to secure your Oracle software, database, and storage entities at a more granular level to ensure that your environment is secured according to your organization's policies. For example, you can choose to install multiple Oracle RDBMS Homes with different operating system accounts, secure access to your Oracle ASM storage to restrict access for Exadata grid disks to specific clusters on your compute node (ASM-scoped security), and limit a database's access to specific sets of Exadata grid disks in an ASM disk group (Database-scoped security).

In this chapter, you will learn how to configure multiple software owners on your Exadata Compute Nodes, install multiple Oracle RDBMS Homes on your compute nodes, configure ASM-scoped security, and configure Database-scoped security on Exadata.

12-1. Configuring Multiple Oracle Software Owners on Exadata Compute Nodes

Problem

You wish to create multiple Oracle software owners and segregate management responsibilities for databases consolidated on your Exadata Database Machine. In other words, you wish to configure role-separated authentication on Exadata with unique Oracle software owners for different databases on Exadata.

Solution

In this recipe, you will learn the differences between standard OS authentication and role-separated authentication on Exadata and build on this knowledge to create a custom, role-separated Oracle RDBMS software deployment with different operating system accounts for different Oracle RDBMS Home software installations. You will specifically learn how to create operating system groups and users, configure limits, enable sudo access from non-DBA accounts, and restrict SSH logins from your Oracle software owners.

> **Note** Please refer to Recipe 12-2 for additional information about how to install multiple Oracle RDBMS Homes on Exadata.

Most customers choose, at a minimum, to configure role-separated authentication for the Oracle RDBMS and Grid Infrastructure installations. While you can elect to use the same operating system account and group structure for both the RDBMS and Grid Infrastructure binaries, in this recipe, we will assume you are running Grid Infrastructure software under a user called grid and the Oracle Database software under a different operating system user called oracle. In the How It Works section of this recipe, we will show the operating system accounts and groups used in a typical role-separated Exadata environment.

> **Note** When you fill out your configuration worksheet prior to installing Exadata, you can change these defaults to suit your needs, but, in our experience, customers typically perform role-separated authentication initially.

Start by defining the security policies. For example, let's assume you will deploy three databases on your Exadata Database Machine, PROD, TEST, and DEV, and further assume that the Exadata DMAs responsible for administering these databases will be from different organizations in your IT department. Also, we will assume that your security policies mandate that each IT organization's scope of administration responsibility aligns with the three databases. Under this requirement, the first task to perform is to create a different operating system group for each database. In the example in Listing 12-1, we will set up six operating system groups, two for each of the three databases with one of these two being the default group for each OS account and one representing the OS group targeted for the OSDBA role, which will provide SYSDBA access.

Listing 12-1. lst12-01-setup-osgroups.sh

```
#!/bin/sh -x
# Name: lst12-01-setup-osgroups.sh
groupadd dba_prod -g 1010
groupadd dba_test -g 1011
groupadd dba_dev  -g 1012
groupadd oraprod -g 1110
groupadd oratest -g 1111
groupadd oradev  -g 1112
```

Next, create three additional database users using the script in Listing 12-2. In this script, we will create a Linux account using the useradd command and modify /etc/security/limits.conf to properly configure operating system limits for Oracle 11gR2 on Exadata.

Listing 12-2. lst12-02-setup-dbausers.sh

```
#!/bin/bash
# Name: lst12-02-setup-dbausers.sh
export PASSWD=welcome1
export USER_LIST="oraprod oratest oradev"
export USER_ID=3001
export LC=/etc/security/limits.conf
cp $LC ${LC}_`date +%Y-%m-%d_%H:%M:%S`
#
for username in `echo $USER_LIST`
do
export user_suffix=`echo $username | cut -f2 -da`
useradd -u ${USER_ID} -g oinstall -G dba_${user_suffix},oinstall,asmdba -d /home/${username} ${username}
```

```
echo "${username}:${PASSWD}" | chpasswd
chown -R ${username}:oinstall /home/${username}
echo " " >> ${LC}
echo "$username soft core unlimited" >> $LC
echo "$username soft core unlimited" >> $LC
echo "$username soft nproc 131072" >> $LC
echo "$username hard nproc 131072" >> $LC
echo "$username soft nofile 131072" >> $LC
echo "$username hard nofile 131072" >> $LC
echo "$username soft memlock 55520682" >> $LC
echo "$username hard memlock 55520682" >> $LC
(( USER_ID+=1 ))
done
```

You will likely need to create these operating system groups and user accounts on each Exadata Compute Node, so use dcli with the previous scripts to run the scripts in Listing 12-1 and 12-2 on each node. Following, we will show an example dbs_group file containing the names of each compute node in an Exadata Quarter Rack and the dcli command to execute the scripts on both compute nodes:

```
[root@cm01dbm01 source]# cat dbs_group
cm01dbm01
cm01dbm02
[root@cm01dbm01 source]# dcli -g ~/dbs_group -l root -x lst12-01-setup-osgroups.sh
+ groupadd dba_prod -g 1010
+ groupadd dba_test -g 1011
... Additional groupadd output omitted
[root@cm01dbm01 source]# dcli -g ~/dbs_group -l root -x lst12-02-setup-dbausers.sh
[root@cm01dbm01 source]# dcli -g ~/dbs_group -l root grep ora /etc/passwd
cm01dbm01: oracle:x:1001:1001::/home/oracle:/bin/bash
cm01dbm01: oraprod:x:1001:1001::/home/oracle:/bin/bash
cm01dbm01: oratest:x:1001:1001::/home/oracle:/bin/bash
... Additional lines from /etc/passwd omitted
```

At this point, if your business requirements demand it, you can also elect to create additional Linux groups and user accounts for non-DBA access. Many organizations require named user logins to database servers and prevent SSH access from privileged accounts, forcing named users to sudo to the Oracle database accounts. If this matches your security requirement, you can create a named user account or accounts for each database. In the example in Listing 12-3, we will create three additional accounts, userprod, usertest, and userdev. You would likely want to use dcli to propagate these accounts to your other compute nodes, as demonstrated previously.

Listing 12-3. lst12-03-setup-osusers.sh

```
#!/bin/bash
# Name: lst12-03-setup-osusers.sh
export PASSWD=welcome1
export USER_LIST="userprod usertest userdev"
# Set USER_ID to the next available id from /etc/passwd or an unused value
export USER_ID=3004
#
for username in `echo $USER_LIST`
do
useradd ${username} -u ${USER_ID} -d /home/${username}
```

```
echo "$username:$PASSWD" | chpasswd
(( USER_ID+=1 ))
done
```

Next, set up sudo access for each of these accounts and enable them to sudo to your database accounts. Run the visudo command to make the following entries (output is omitted for brevity):

```
User_Alias  PROD    = userprod
User_Alias  TEST    = usertest
User_Alias  DEV     = userdev
Cmnd_Alias  PROD_SU = /bin/su - oraprod, /bin/su oraprod
Cmnd_Alias  TEST_SU = /bin/su - oratest, /bin/su oratest
Cmnd_Alias  DEV_SU  = /bin/su - oradev, /bin/su oradev
PROD   ALL = PROD_SU
TEST   ALL = TEST_SU
DEV    ALL = DEV_SU
```

Finally, restrict SSH access from your database owner accounts by editing /etc/ssh/sshd_config on each compute node, adding the DenyUsers line as provided below, and restarting your SSH daemon:

```
[root@cm01dbm01 source]# grep Deny /etc/ssh/sshd_config
DenyUsers oraprod oratest oradev
[root@cm01dbm01 source]# service sshd restart
Stopping sshd:                                             [  OK  ]
Starting sshd:                                             [  OK  ]
[root@cm01dbm01 source]#
```

When complete, you can proceed to install additional Oracle RDBMS software binaries under each of these new operating system accounts.

How It Works

Operating system user and group administration on Exadata is no different than administering users and groups on a non-Exadata Linux environment, but as many organizations consolidate different types of databases on a single Exadata Database Machine, it is important to understand how to customize your standard security deployment to meet your business requirements. Even if you do not wish to create different OS accounts and users or install additional Oracle Homes, it is common to prevent SSH access from the oracle operating system account; the last several steps in the solution of this recipe can be applied to the oracle OS account as well.

When you install a default, role-separated authentication strategy on Exadata, you will typically use the grid operating system account for Grid Infrastructure and the oracle account for your RDBMS software. The standard operating system groups typically used are oinstall, dba, asmadmin, asmdba, and asmoper for your oracle and grid software owner, each of which serves a distinct purpose as outlined in your Exadata Owner's Guide. The steps in this recipe extend your base installation and create additional operating system groups and user accounts to provide compute grid capable of segregating authentication and responsibility for different Oracle software installations and databases.

If you follow the steps in this recipe, the natural next course of action would be to install different Oracle RDBMS Homes on your Exadata Compute Nodes and use the newly created users and groups to install your software. Recipe 12-2 discusses installing additional Oracle RDBMS Homes on Exadata.

12-2. Installing Multiple Oracle Homes on Your Exadata Compute Nodes

Problem

You wish to install additional Oracle RDBMS Homes on your Exadata Compute Nodes to isolate your Oracle software binaries.

Solution

In this recipe, we will provide the steps necessary to install an additional Oracle RDBMS software home on your Exadata Compute Nodes.

First, determine whether you will use an existing set of operating system groups and users to install the Oracle software. If you are installing an additional Oracle Home for security, manageability, or operational practices reasons, create a new set of OS groups and operating system accounts using instructions in Recipe 12-1.

Next, determine whether you will install your new Oracle RDBMS Home under the existing /u01 file system or use additional local storage on your compute nodes to create and mount another file system. The existing /u01 file system is created by default on Exadata Compute Nodes and is 100 GB in size. The size of a single Oracle RDBMS and Grid Infrastructure software installation will not typically consume more than 20–25 GB initially, but log files, trace files, diagnostics, and other files will likely cause it to consume larger percentages of disk space over time. Depending on how many additional Oracle RDBMS Homes you intend to create on the /u01 file system and how much free space is currently available, there are a few ways to handle disk-space constraints. One of these methods is to extend the size of your current /u01 file system using unallocated available storage on your local compute node disks using lvextend. To extend the logical volume upon which your /u01 file system is mounted, determine the amount of free space on the VGExaDb volume group using the following vgdisplay command:

```
[root@cm01dbm01 ~]# vgdisplay VGExaDb | grep Free
  Free  PE / Size       103327 / 403.62 GB
[root@cm01dbm01 ~]#
```

This output shows that we have over 400 GB of free space on our existing VGExaDB volume group. To increase the size of the /u01 file system, stop all Oracle databases and cluster services on your compute node using `crsctl stop crs` and then unmount the /u01 file system using umount. Then determine the name of your logical volume used for /u01 and use `lvm lvextend` to increase the size of your logical volume. In the following code, we will increase our size by 200 GB:

```
[root@cm01dbm01 ~]# lvdisplay|grep "LV Name"
  LV Name                /dev/VGExaDb/LVDbSys1
  LV Name                /dev/VGExaDb/LVDbSwap1
  LV Name                /dev/VGExaDb/LVDbOra1
[root@cm01dbm01 ~]# lvm lvextend -L +200G -verbose
/dev/VGExaDB/LVdbOra1   Finding volume group VGExaDb
Archiving volume group "VGExaDb" metadata (seqno 10).
Extending logical volume LVDbOra1 to 300.00 GB
... Output omitted for brevity
```

When complete, run e2fsck on your logical volume, resize your file system using `resize2fs`, and mount your file system:

```
[root@cm01dbm01 ~]# e2fsck -f /dev/VGExaDb/LVDbOra1
e2fsck 1.39 (29-May-2006)
Pass 1: Checking inodes, blocks, and sizes
Pass 2: Checking directory structure
Pass 3: Checking directory connectivity
Pass 4: Checking reference counts
Pass 5: Checking group summary information
DBORA: 3638421/13107200 files (3.3% non-contiguous), 19506778/26214400 blocks
... Output omitted

[root@cm01dbm01 ~]# resize2fs -p /dev/VGExaDb/LVDbOra1
resize2fs 1.39 (29-May-2006)
Resizing the filesystem on /dev/VGExaDb/LVDbOra1 to 78643200 (4k) blocks.
Begin pass 1 (max = 1600)
Extending the inode table     XXXXXXXXXXXXXXXXXXXXXXXXXXXXXXXXXXXXXXXXXXXX
... Output omitted

[root@cm01dbm01 ~]# mount /u01
```

An alternative to extending your /u01 file system is to NFS mount external storage and symbolically link your Oracle 11gR2 diagnostics directories for each of your database to external storage.

■ **Note** We recommend installing new Oracle Homes in a subdirectory under /u01 rather than using available disk storage to create a new volume and mount point. Changing the default file system layout on Exadata can lead to challenges performing LVM-snapshot-based recovery and compute-node reimaging; both of these features will still work with a custom file-system layout, but they introduce risk and additional steps.

Next, download and stage the Oracle 11gR2 software from My Oracle Support or the Oracle Technology Network (OTN). Installing Oracle on Exadata is similar to installing Oracle on non-Exadata, and you will need to stage your installation software on a directory on one of your compute nodes.

■ **Note** When Oracle ACS performs the initial Exadata installation, the Oracle 11gR2 binaries are pre-staged on /opt/oracle.SupportTools/onecommand<version> and Step 19 of the installation process uses the Oracle Installer to install your first Oracle GI and RDBMS Home on your compute nodes. This installation uses a seeded response file for input parameters based on your configuration worksheet. You can attempt to adjust this response file and run the /opt/oracle.SupportTools/onecommand/tmp/dbm-dbsw.sh script, which is called from Step 19 of the installation process, but in many cases organizations patch and/or upgrade their binaries over time. We recommend downloading current, supported software from Oracle and manually launching the installer to complete your installation.

After downloading, staging, and unzipping your software, log in as your Oracle software owner, navigate to the database directory, and launch `runInstaller` to install your new Oracle RDBMS Home.

When prompted, choose to do an Oracle RAC installation using the existing Grid Infrastructure and enter the appropriate inventory location, operating system groups, Oracle Home location, Oracle Home name, and so forth. Make sure to enter a new directory when installing your new Oracle RDBMS Home.

■ **Note** In Oracle 11gR2, only one Grid Infrastructure installation can exist on a database server; as such, this recipe only pertains to an additional Oracle RDBMS Home installation. All databases and Oracle RBDMS Homes on Exadata share a common Grid Infrastructure.

After completing your software installation, you must patch your new Oracle RDBMS Home with the latest QDPE or bundle patch that currently exists on your compute nodes. In other words, if you are installing a new Oracle Home on a server that has been patched either during the initial installation or any time after with Exadata patches, you need to download and apply these patches using the instructions in the patch README file. Recipe 11-4 discusses patching the compute nodes in detail.

After the software is installed, you should run skgxpinfo from your new $ORACLE_HOME/bin directory to ensure that the binaries are compiled using the Reliable Datagram Sockets protocol, or rds. If not, relink your Oracle binary by issuing the following command:

```
[oracle@cm01dbm01 ~]$ make -f $ORACLE_HOME/rdbms/lib/ins_rdbms.mk ipc_rds ioracle
```

When complete, you can create databases using your new Oracle RDBMS Home using the 11gR2 Database Configuration Assistant, dbca, following the steps in Recipe 21-1.

How It Works

Installing additional Oracle RDBMS Homes on Exadata is similar to installing Oracle 11gR2 on non-Exadata systems. Typically, you would elect to create additional Oracle Homes for the following reasons:

- To provide more granular security control over your database instances when consolidating on Exadata
- To enable a more controlled means to patch and upgrade Oracle RDBMS binaries

---

■ **Note** Operations' and IT systems' life-cycle policies often mandate separating software binaries between production and non-production systems, which often poses a challenge with consolidating on Exadata. In our experience, it is beneficial to explore the topic of "rolling patches" and weigh the benefit of iterating patching across multiple environments simultaneously against the *true* risk of patching an Oracle Home that services multiple databases.

- To provide a supported Oracle RDBMS infrastructure to meet application-specific implementation requirements. For example, Oracle e-Business Suite deploys a set of software under the RDBMS $ORACLE_HOME to support AutoConfig; while many environments can share a single Oracle RDBMS Home with AutoConfig, the Oracle Applications teams and support generally recommend isolated homes for each database.

One of the potential challenges with installing multiple Oracle RDBMS Homes that some organizations face is a disk-space limitation on the compute node. In the solution of this recipe, we have provided an example for extending your volume size using available local storage on the compute node.

12-3. Configuring ASM-Scoped Security

Problem

You wish to restrict access to Exadata grid disks to specific Oracle ASM instances or Grid Infrastructure clusters.

Solution

In this recipe, you will learn how to configure ASM-scoped security on Exadata to allow or restrict ASM instances to and from access specific Exadata grid disks. Figure 12-1 shows an example of ASM-scoped security in which the Oracle cluster on the first two compute nodes for the QA database is restricted to three Exadata cells and the production cluster on the other two compute nodes is restricted to four Exadata cells.

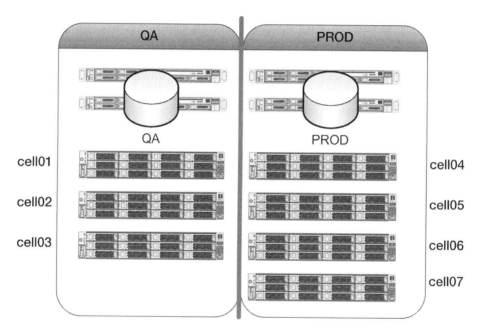

Figure 12-1. ASM-scoped security on Exadata

1. Query the db_unique_name from one of your Oracle ASM instances:

   ```
   [grid@cm01dbm01 ~]$ sqlplus /nolog
   SQL*Plus: Release 11.2.0.3.0 Production on Sat Oct 13 01:14:16 2012
   Copyright (c) 1982, 2011, Oracle.  All rights reserved.
   SQL> conn / as sysasm
   Connected.
   SQL> show parameter unique
   NAME                                 TYPE        VALUE
   ------------------------------------ ----------- ------------------------------
   db_unique_name                       string      +ASM
   SQL>
   ```

2. Stop your Oracle databases and cluster resources using srvctl and/or crsctl.

3. Launch cellcli from any storage cell in your Exadata storage grid and create a key:

```
CellCLI> create key
        f3eda381ef98b0dcc1a1d89b6249d042
CellCLI>
```

4. With this key, create a cellkey.ora with the key generated above on one of the compute nodes as the Grid Infrastructure owner. In the following example, the cellkey.ora file is placed in the grid account's home directory:

```
[grid@cm01dbm01 ~]$ cat cellkey.ora
key=f3eda381ef98b0dcc1a1d89b6249d042
asm=+ASM
#realm=my_realm
[grid@cm01dbm01 ~]$
```

5. Use dcli to alter each of your grid disks and make them available to the +ASM db_unique_name:

```
[oracle@cm01dbm01 ~]$ dcli -g ./cell_group "cellcli -e \
alter griddisk all availableTo=\'+ASM\'"
cm01cel01: GridDisk DATA_CD_00_cm01cel01 successfully altered
cm01cel01: GridDisk DATA_CD_00_cm01cel02 successfully altered
... Additional output omitted
```

■ **Note** In the this command, we're making all grid disks available to the "+ASM" ASM instance; you can opt to choose only a subset of the grid disks, if so desired.

6. Copy the cellkey.ora file created previously to /etc/oracle/cell/network-config directory on each compute node and set permissions to 600:

```
[grid@cm01dbm01 ~]$ dcli -g ./dbs_group "cellcli -l grid -f \
/home/grid/cellkey.ora -d /etc/oracle/cell/network-config/
[grid@cm01dbm01 ~]$ dcli -g ./dbs_group "cellcli -l grid -f \
chmod 600 /etc/oracle/cell/network-config/cellkey.ora
[grid@cm01dbm01 ~]$
```

7. Finally, start CRS on each compute node and validate your environment.

How It Works

ASM-scoped security on Exadata is a means to restrict Exadata grid disks to specific Oracle RAC clusters on the Exadata compute grid. In other words, in situations in which you have an Exadata Full Rack or Half Rack and elected to build separate Oracle clusters of subsets of the servers, you can use ASM-scoped security to isolate grid disk storage for different sets of clustered environments.

ASM-scoped security is accomplished by the following:

- Creating a cell key for each unique Oracle RAC cluster; this assumes that different db_unique_name instances are assigned to each set of ASM instances on multiple Oracle RAC clusters on an Exadata Database Machine

- Copying the key to /etc/oracle/cell/network-config/cellkey.ora on the compute nodes

- Altering grid disks and assigning them to an ASM db_unique_name

When would this configuration typically be done? Consider an organization that purchases an Exadata Full Rack and intends to consolidate production and non-production environments. ASM-scoped security can be beneficial or required under the following business requirements:

- When the required compute node power for production is a subset of the available resources on the eight-node Full Rack compute grid

- When you want the flexibility to leverage physical storage from each of the 14 storage cells; in other words, you want to carve your compute grid into multiple Oracle clusters but allow each of your compute grid to access each cell

- When you desire to have your production database always use grid disks built on the outer tracks of the Exadata cell disks, for performance

- When you have patching or systems life-cycle requirements in which multiple Oracle Grid Infrastructure installations on a single Exadata Database Machine

- When you want to prevent non-production ASM instances from accessing production storage and vice versa

- When you wish to physically isolate I/O calls based on site security requirements

12-4. Configuring Database-Scoped Security

Problem

You wish to restrict database storage for different Exadata databases to specific sets of Exadata grid disks.

Solution

In this recipe, you will learn how to configure Database-scoped security on Exadata to allow or restrict Oracle databases instances to and from access specific Exadata grid disks. Figure 12-2 shows an example of Database-scoped security in which different databases in an Exadata cluster are restricted to specific sets of grid disks.

CHAPTER 12 ■ SECURITY

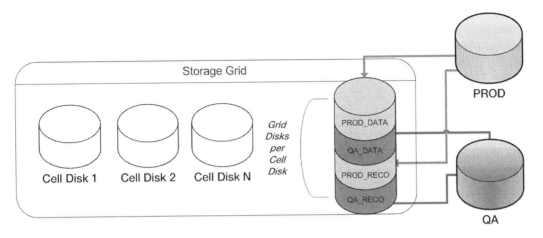

Figure 12-2. Database-scoped security on Exadata

Follow these steps:

1. Shut down your databases and Oracle cluster resources. Similar to ASM-scoped security in Recipe 12-3, your compute node resources need to be stopped in order to implement Database-scoped security.

2. Launch cellcli from any Exadata storage cell and create a key for each database that you wish to configure Database-scoped security for. In the following example, we will create two keys, one for a database called VISX and one for a database called EDW:

    ```
    CellCLI> create key
            2ee72ba501b5884615292616c2c85095
    CellCLI> create key
            23067149d2eb022aa61c39222148cbea
    CellCLI>
    ```

3. Create a cellkey.ora file under $ORACLE_HOME/admin/<DB name>/pfile directory for each database you generated a key for. Unless you have previously configured Database-scoped security, you will likely need to create the $ORACLE_HOME/admin/<DB name>/pfile directory first. In the cellkey.ora file, enter the key created above as well as a line with the string "asm=+ASM", where +ASM is our ASM instance's db_unique_name:

    ```
    [oracle@cm01dbm01 ~]$ dcli -g ./dbs_group -l oracle \
    mkdir -p $ORACLE_HOME/admin/visx/pfile
    [oracle@cm01dbm01 ~]$ dcli -g ./dbs_group -l oracle \
    mkdir -p $ORACLE_HOME/admin/edw/pfile
    [oracle@cm01dbm01 ~]$

    [oracle@cm01dbm01 ~]$ dcli -g ./dbs_group -l oracle cat $ORACLE_HOME/admin/
    visx/pfile/cellkey.ora
    cm01dbm01: key=2ee72ba501b5884615292616c2c85095
    cm01dbm01: asm=+ASM
    cm01dbm02: key=2ee72ba501b5884615292616c2c85095
    cm01dbm02: asm=+ASM
    ```

```
[oracle@cm01dbm01 ~]$ dcli -g ./dbs_group -l oracle cat $ORACLE_HOME/admin/
edw/pfile/cellkey.ora
cm01dbm01: key=23067149d2eb022aa61c39222148cbea
cm01dbm01: asm=+ASM
cm01dbm02: key=23067149d2eb022aa61c39222148cbea
cm01dbm02: asm=+ASM
[oracle@cm01dbm01 ~]$
```

4. Assign your keys to database clients using dcli:

```
[oracle@cm01dbm01 ~]$ dcli -g ./cell_group "cellcli -e \
assign key for visx=\'2ee72ba501b5884615292616c2c85095\', \
   edw=\' 23067149d2eb022aa61c39222148cbea\'"
cm01cel01: Key for visx successfully created
cm01cel01: Key for edw successfully created
... Additional output omitted
```

5. When finished, validate your keys using dcli and cellcli:

```
[oracle@cm01dbm01 ~]$ dcli -g ./cell_group cellcli -e list key
cm01cel01: visx      2ee72ba501b5884615292616c2c85095
cm01cel01: edw   23067149d2eb022aa61c39222148cbea
cm01cel02: visx      2ee72ba501b5884615292616c2c85095
cm01cel02: edw   23067149d2eb022aa61c39222148cbea
cm01cel03: visx      2ee72ba501b5884615292616c2c85095
cm01cel03: edw   23067149d2eb022aa61c39222148cbea
[oracle@cm01dbm01 ~]$
```

6. At this point, you will need to alter your grid disks and assign them to each of your databases. You will likely have a large number of grid disks to assign to databases and, assuming you can easily map your grid disk prefixes to Oracle databases, use the script in Listing 12-4 to generate the appropriate cellcli commands. The script accepts two arguments, the grid disk prefix and database name, which can be a single database name or comma-separated list of databases.

Listing 12-4. lst12-04-gen-db-sec.sh

```
#!/bin/sh
# Name: lst12-04-gen-db-sec.sh
dcli -g ./cell_group -l celladmin "cellcli -e list griddisk where name   \
like \'$1.*\'" | awk -F: '{print $1 " " $2}' | awk '{print "dcli -c  \
" $1 " -l celladmin \"cellcli -e alter griddisk " $2 " availableTo="   \
"\x5c\x27" "+ASM,'$2'" "\x5c\x27" "\""}'
dcli -c  cm01cel01 -l celladmin "cellcli -e alter griddisk DATA_CD_00_cm01cel01
    availableTo=\'+ASM,edw\'"
dcli -c  cm01cel01 -l celladmin "cellcli -e alter griddisk DATA_CD_01_cm01cel01
    availableTo=\'+ASM,edw\'"
dcli -c  cm01cel01 -l celladmin "cellcli -e alter griddisk DATA_CD_02_cm01cel01
    availableTo=\'+ASM,edw\'"
dcli -c  cm01cel01 -l celladmin "cellcli -e alter griddisk DATA_CD_03_cm01cel01
    availableTo=\'+ASM,edw\'"
```

7. Run the script in Listing 12-4, validate the output, and execute each line. You can copy and paste the output or redirect it to a text file. When complete, validate your Database-scoped security using `dcli` or `cellcli` commands:

```
[oracle@cm01dbm01 ~]$ dcli -g ./cell_group cellcli -e list griddisk
attributes name,availableTo
cm01cel01:   DATA_CD_00_cm01cel01    +ASM,edw
cm01cel01:   DATA_CD_01_cm01cel01    +ASM,edw
... Output omitted for brevity
```

8. When complete, start CRS and your Oracle databases.

9. To validate that Database-scoped security is working normally, log in to a database without access to a specific set of grid disks and attempt to create a tablespace using the ASM disk group containing the grid disks. For example, following we will connect to the VISX database and attempt to create a tablespace in the DATA_CM01 ASM disk group, which contains grid disks with the DATA prefix assigned to +ASM,edw above:

```
SYS@VISX SQL> create tablespace test datafile '+DATA_CM01'
size 100m;
create tablespace test datafile '+DATA_CM01'
*
ERROR at line 1:
ORA-01119: error in creating database file '+DATA_CM01'
ORA-15045: ASM file name '+DATA_CM01' is not in reference form
ORA-17052: ksfdcre:5 Failed to create file +DATA_CM01
ORA-15081: failed to submit an I/O operation to a disk
```

How It Works

Database-scoped security on Exadata is a means to restrict Exadata grid disks to specific Oracle databases and is configured by the following:

- Creating a cell key for each database you wish to secure with Database-scoped security
- Copying the key to `$ORACLE_HOME/admin/<DB name>/pfile/cellkey.ora` for each database
- Altering grid disks and assigning them to specific databases and your ASM instance

Database-scoped security is most often implemented when the Exadata DMA chooses to install multiple Oracle software owners and Oracle RDBMS Homes, as presented in Recipes 12-1 and 12-2. By default, each Oracle database, regardless of whether you are configured with a single Oracle RDBMS Home or multiple homes, a single operating system account or multiple accounts, has access to each Exadata grid disk in the storage grid. Database-scoped security provides a means to isolate database access to specific grid disks on the storage grid.

PART 4

Monitoring Exadata

Exadata runs the Oracle Database and, specifically, Oracle 11gR2. On Exadata, your database storage uses Oracle ASM and your instances will typically be deployed into an Oracle RAC cluster. With Oracle 11gR2, Oracle has seeded a number of Exadata-specific performance statistics and wait events into its kernel.

In addition to your Oracle 11gR2 databases, Exadata's architecture is configured with a number of storage servers, or storage cells, that comprise the Exadata Storage Grid. Each storage cell captures alerts, metrics, and I/O request information.

Successfully monitoring Exadata environments is a matter of identifying which statistics or metrics Oracle has introduced into its software and knowing how to interpret the values from these statistics. The chapters in this section present a number of Exadata-monitoring techniques and solutions geared to solving real-life monitoring challenges so that, as an Exadata DMA, you will know how to find the information you need and, further, how to interpret the data.

CHAPTER 13

Monitoring Exadata Storage Cells

Each Exadata storage cell can be monitored, configured, and managed using the CellCLI command line interface. With CellCLI, you can monitor active cell server requests, report on a wide range of storage cell metrics, monitor alert conditions, and monitor each of the storage cell objects including the cell itself, cell disks, grid disks, I/O Resource Management, as well as Flash Cache, Flash Logging, and your InfiniBand interconnect. Additionally, Exadata provides the ability to set and modify various metric and alert thresholds.

The Exadata DMA will often monitor storage cells using CellCLI commands as part of an overall performance and health monitoring strategy. CellCLI monitoring commands generate such a great deal of output that it is often difficult for the Exadata DMA to summarize the information and make intelligent decisions about its output. Oracle simplifies this with Exadata plug-ins for Oracle Enterprise Manager, but in situations when Enterprise Manager is not available, it is still imperative that the Exadata DMA be familiar with CellCLI monitoring techniques in order to properly support the Exadata Database Machine.

In this chapter, we'll cover some CellCLI and `dcli` monitoring basics, demonstrate how to list current and historical metrics, and provide real-world examples demonstrating useful Exadata Storage Server monitoring tasks for a variety of storage cell objects and metrics. With nearly 200 metrics available in recent versions of Exadata, we will not cover all possible monitoring queries or techniques but, rather, provide a series of recipes that you can expand upon based on your monitoring needs.

13-1. Monitoring Storage Cell Alerts
Problem
You wish to monitor and report on Exadata Storage Server alert conditions.

Solution
In this recipe, you will learn how to monitor alerts on your Exadata Storage Servers using CellCLI's `list alerthistory` command, add `cellcli where` conditions to limit the output from the `list alerthistory` command, flag alerts with the `examinedBy` attribute, and drop alerts from the alert repository.

Displaying Your Alert History
Log in to CellCLI from an Exadata storage cell and run the following command to display your storage cell's alert history:

```
CellCLI> list alerthistory
     1         2012-10-10T14:41:37-04:00       info       "Factory defaults restored for Adapter 0"
     2_1       2012-10-17T05:00:33-04:00       info       "The disk controller battery is executing a
```

learn cycle and may temporarily enter WriteThrough Caching mode as part of the learn cycle. Disk write throughput might be temporarily lower during this time. The flash drives are not affected. The battery learn cycle is a normal maintenance activity that occurs quarterly and runs for approximately 1 to 12 hours. Note that many learn cycles do not require entering WriteThrough caching mode. When the disk controller cache returns to the normal WriteBack caching mode, an additional informational alert will be sent. Battery Serial Number : 467   Battery Type : iBBU08   Battery Temperature   : 40 C   Full Charge Capacity   : 1417 mAh   Relative Charge : 96 %   Ambient Temperature   : 27 C"
         2_2   2012-10-17T10:22:13-04:00   clear   "All disk drives are in WriteBack caching mode. Battery Serial Number : 467   Battery Type   : iBBU08   Battery Temperature   : 45 C   Full Charge Capacity   : 1408 mAh   Relative Charge   : 69 %   Ambient Temperature   : 27 C"

CellCLI>

You can see three distinct alerts with names 1, 2_1, and 2_2. Alerts 2_1 and 2_2 are related to each other; 2_1 indicates an informational alert showing that the disk controller battery is undergoing a "learn cycle," and Alert 2_2 indicates that the message is cleared after the completion of the cycle. Each alert object has multiple attributes. Use the following `list alerthistory` command with the detail option to display each attribute of an alert:

```
CellCLI> list alerthistory 2_1 detail
         name:                   2_1
         alertMessage:           "The disk controller battery is executing a learn cycle and may
temporarily enter WriteThrough Caching mode as part of the learn cycle. Disk write throughput
might be temporarily lower during this time. The flash drives are not affected. The battery
learn cycle is a normal maintenance activity that occurs ... output omitted for brevity
         alertSequenceID:        2
         alertShortName:         Hardware
         alertType:              Stateful
         beginTime:              2012-10-17T05:00:33-04:00
         endTime:                2012-10-17T10:22:13-04:00
         examinedBy:
         metricObjectName:       LUN_LEARN_CYCLE_ALERT
         notificationState:      0
         sequenceBeginTime:      2012-10-17T05:00:33-04:00
         severity:               info
         alertAction:            Informational.

CellCLI>
```

Stateful and Stateless Alerts

In the above output, the `alertType` indicates that this is a `Stateful` alert, which means that it can, at a later date, be tested to detect whether the alert condition or state has changed. Alert 2_2 is the partner of Alert 2_1 and, in this case, at the completion of the operation, the alert will be cleared. Exadata also raises `Stateless` alerts. These alerts indicate point-in-time events that do not reflect a persistent condition—they simply communicate that an event occurred.

In addition, for Alert 2_1 the severity is marked info and the alertAction is Informational. This would indicate that the Exadata DMA would likely not need to perform any specific tasks to rectify the condition. If we run the same list alerthistory command for Alert 1, you can see that Oracle provides corrective action measures in the alertAction attribute:

```
CellCLI> list alerthistory 1 detail
         name:                    1
         alertMessage:            "Factory defaults restored for Adapter 0"
         alertSequenceID:         1
         alertShortName:          Hardware
         alertType:               Stateless
         beginTime:               2012-10-10T14:41:37-04:00
         endTime:
         examinedBy:
         notificationState:       0
         sequenceBeginTime:       2012-10-10T14:41:37-04:00
         severity:                info
         alertAction:             "If this change is unintentional, contact Oracle Support."
CellCLI>
```

Listing Your alerthistory Using dcli

Exadata DMAs typically monitor storage cell alerts for each cell in the storage grid. Use the following dcli command to list your alert history for each of your storage cells:

```
[oracle@cm01dbm01 ~]$ dcli -g ./cell_group cellcli -e list alerthistory
cm01cel01: 1     2012-10-10T14:41:37-04:00    info     "Factory defaults restored for Adapter 0"
cm01cel01: 2_1   2012-10-17T05:00:33-04:00    info     "The disk controller battery is executing a
... Output omitted for brevity
cm01cel01: 2_2   2012-10-17T10:22:13-04:00    clear    "All disk drives are in WriteBack caching
mode.  Battery Serial Number : 467  Battery Type      : iBBU08  Battery Temperature  : 45 C
Full Charge Capacity  : 1408 mAh  Relative Charge     : 69 %  Ambient Temperature    : 27 C"
cm01cel02: 1     2012-10-10T15:44:57-04:00    info     "Factory defaults restored for Adapter 0"
cm01cel02: 2_1   2012-10-17T02:00:40-04:00    info     "The disk controller battery is executing a
... Output omitted for brevity
cm01cel02: 2_2   2012-10-17T07:34:02-04:00    clear    "All disk drives are in WriteBack caching
mode.  Battery Serial Number : 224  Battery Type      : iBBU08  Battery Temperature  : 43 C
Full Charge Capacity  : 1382 mAh  Relative Charge     : 70 %  Ambient Temperature    : 26 C"
cm01cel03: 1     2012-10-10T16:45:26-04:00    info     "Factory defaults restored for Adapter 0"
cm01cel03: 2_1   2012-10-17T02:01:05-04:00    info     "The disk controller battery is executing a
... Output omitted for brevity
cm01cel03: 2_2   2012-10-17T08:29:26-04:00    clear    "All disk drives are in WriteBack caching
mode.  Battery Serial Number : 3767  Battery Type     : iBBU08  Battery Temperature  : 45 C
Full Charge Capacity  : 1268 mAh  Relative Charge     : 77 %  Ambient Temperature    : 26 C"
[oracle@cm01dbm01 ~]$
```

To report on your critical storage cell alerts, use the following dcli/cellcli command:

```
[oracle@cm01dbm01 ~]$ dcli -g ./cell_group cellcli -e list alerthistory where severity='critical'
[oracle@cm01dbm01 ~]$
```

Next, use the following `dcli/cellcli` command to display alerts generated after a specific time:

```
[oracle@cm01dbm01 ~]$ dcli -c cm01cel01 \
"cellcli -e list alerthistory where beginTime \> \'2012-10-17T02:00:42-04:00\'"
cm01cel01: 2_1     2012-10-17T05:00:33-04:00     info        "The disk controller battery is executing a
.. Output omitted for brevity
cm01cel01: 2_2     2012-10-17T10:22:13-04:00     clear       "All disk drives are in WriteBack caching
... Output omitted for brevity
[oracle@cm01dbm01 ~]$
```

■ **Note** Please see Recipe 13-5 for additional information about using `dcli` with escape sequences to handle single quotes and special characters.

Assigning and Dropping Alerts

In organizations with multiple Exadata DMAs and different administration roles and responsibilities, you can mark specific Exadata alerts with the `examinedBy` attribute to a specific administrator using the following `alter alerthistory` command. In this command, we will set the `examinedBy` attribute to john for Alert 1:

```
CellCLI> alter alerthistory 1 examinedBy='john'
Alert 1 successfully altered
CellCLI>
```

You can then query your alert history based on specific `examinedBy` attributes using the following command:

```
CellCLI> list alerthistory where examinedBy='john'
     1    2012-10-10T14:41:37-04:00    info        "Factory defaults restored for Adapter 0"
CellCLI>
```

After clearing or otherwise handling an alert, you can drop the alert from Exadata's alert history using the `drop alerthistory` CellCLI command. In this case, we will drop Alert 1:

```
CellCLI> drop alerthistory 1
Alert 1 successfully dropped
CellCLI> list alerthistory where examinedBy='john'
```

To drop alerts across all storage cells, use `dcli/cellcli` commands. Following, we will use the `list alerthistory` command to display alerts with a severity of `info` and `clear` and then use this output to drop the alerts:

```
[oracle@cm01dbm01 ~]$ dcli -g ./cell_group cellcli -e list alerthistory where severity='info'
attributes name
cm01cel01: 2_1
cm01cel02: 2_1
cm01cel03: 2_1
[oracle@cm01dbm01 ~]$
[oracle@cm01dbm01 ~]$ dcli -g ./cell_group cellcli -e list alerthistory where severity='clear'
attributes name
cm01cel01: 2_2
```

```
cm01cel02: 2_2
cm01cel03: 2_2
[oracle@cm01dbm01 ~]$
[oracle@cm01dbm01 ~]$ dcli -c cm01cel01 cellcli -e drop alerthistory 2_1, 2_2
cm01cel01: Alert 2_1 successfully dropped
cm01cel01: Alert 2_2 successfully dropped
[oracle@cm01dbm01 ~]$
```

In this output, we've specified two comma-separated alerts in our drop alerthistory command. This is required because the alerts are related as part of an alert sequence. If you attempt to drop a single alert that is part of a sequence, an error message will be raised:

```
[oracle@cm01dbm01 ~]$ dcli -c cm01cel02 cellcli -e drop alerthistory 2_1
cm01cel02:
cm01cel02: CELL-02643: DROP ALERTHISTORY command did not include all members of the alert sequence
for 2_1. All members of the sequence must be dropped together.
[oracle@cm01dbm01 ~]$
```

To drop all of your alerts, use the drop alerthistory all command:

```
[oracle@cm01dbm01 ~]$ dcli -g ./cell_group cellcli -e drop alerthistory all
cm01cel01: No alerts qualified for this drop operation
cm01cel02: Alert 2_1 successfully dropped
cm01cel02: Alert 2_2 successfully dropped
cm01cel03: Alert 2_1 successfully dropped
cm01cel03: Alert 2_2 successfully dropped
[oracle@cm01dbm01 ~]$
```

■ **Note** With the drop alerthistory CellCLI command, you cannot use a where condition; alerts need to either be dropped by their specific name, a comma-separated list of alerts names, or with the all clause.

How It Works

Similar to how Exadata Storage Servers capture metrics as discussed in Recipe 13-3, Exadata triggers alerts on the storage servers when events occur that compromise the function of the storage cell. Exadata's MS process is responsible for capturing alert conditions when it discovers a cell hardware issue, software or configuration issues, a CELLSRV internal error, or when a metric has exceeded an alert threshold. Exadata DMAs can view these triggered alerts using the CellCLI list alerthistory command, via Oracle Enterprise Manager, and/or optionally configure the cell to automatically send e-mail and/or SNMP messages when an alert is raised.

Exadata Storage Servers come with a number of predefined alerts. You can use the list alertdefinition detail command from CellCLI to display information about each alert, as displayed in the following code:

```
CellCLI> list alertdefinition detail
        name:                ADRAlert
        alertShortName:      ADR
        alertSource:         "Automatic Diagnostic Repository"
        alertType:           Stateless
        description:         "Incident Alert"
        metricName:
```

```
            name:                HardwareAlert
            alertShortName:      Hardware
            alertSource:         Hardware
            alertType:           Stateless
            description:         "Hardware Alert"
            metricName:
... Additional output omitted
```

Exadata uses a Baseboard Management Controller, or BMC, to control the components in the cell, and the BMC raises alerts and publishes these alerts to the alert repository in the Exadata System Area when an alert event is captured. Hardware alerts that are captured by the BMC are rarely serviceable automatically by the Exadata DMA; in most cases, an Oracle Service Request is the proper escalation path to take. The BMC should be running at all times on the Exadata cells and can be queried using the CellCLI `list cell` command:

```
CellCLI> list cell attributes name,bmcType
         cm01cel01       IPMI
CellCLI>
```

Exadata storage cells trigger and store alerts in the following manner:

- The BMC captures hardware faults and sends to alert repository.
- CELLSRV sends software errors to MS.
- CELLSRV also sends internal errors to ADR, the Automatic Diagnostics Repository.
- The MS process writes alert information to disk so it can be externalized with the `list alerthistory` CellCLI command.
- Additionally, MS can optionally send e-mail or SNMP messages to an Exadata DMA or management server.

13-2. Monitoring Cells with Active Requests

Problem

You wish to report active I/O operations on your Exadata storage cells in order to troubleshoot Exadata storage cell I/O performance.

Solution

In this recipe, you will learn how to monitor active I/O requests on the Exadata storage cells. Specifically, you will learn how to use CellCLI's `list activerequest` command to provide a point-in-time performance report on the Exadata storage cells and use the `activerequest` object to summarize actively running I/O requests.

Begin by logging in to one of your storage cells as `root`, `celladmin`, or `cellmonitor` and launch `cellcli`:

■ **Note** You can also execute the `list activerequest` command using `dcli` from a compute node, as discussed in Recipe 7-7. If you elect to use `dcli`, ensure that you have established SSH equivalency as outlined in Recipe 7-2.

```
[celladmin@cm01cel01 ~]$ cellcli
CellCLI: Release 11.2.3.1.1 - Production on Tue Oct 23 00:03:05 EDT 2012
Copyright (c) 2007, 2011, Oracle.  All rights reserved.
Cell Efficiency Ratio: 197
CellCLI>
```

Next, run the list activequest command:

```
CellCLI> list activerequest
0    OTHER_GROUPS    EDW    "Smart scan"    "Predicate Pushing"    "Queued for Predicate Disk"
0    OTHER_GROUPS    EDW    "Smart scan"    PredicateFilter        "Queued for Filtered Backup"
0    OTHER_GROUPS    EDW    "Smart scan"    "Predicate Pushing"    "Predicate Computing"
... Additional list activequest detail omitted
```

Without supplying an attributes clause or providing additional selection criteria, the list activerequest command will display the request name, the consumer group name, database name, the I/O reason and I/O type, and the current request state. In the previous output, you can see that the database EDW is executing a number of Smart Scan operations with Predicate Pushing and Predicate Filtering, with a request state represented in the rightmost column of the output.

Some of the more common types of list activerequests queries involve reporting I/O operations that are performing Smart Scans, listing I/O operations that are conducting Smart Scan predicate filtering, reporting on I/O operations for a specific Oracle session or SQL_ID, listing active I/O operations issued from a specific database, and others. To list your current Smart Scan I/O requests conducting predicate filtering operations, issue the following command from CellCLI:

```
CellCLI> list activerequest where ioReason="Smart scan" attributes dbName,ioReason,ioType,requestState
         EDW    "Smart scan"    "Predicate Pushing"    "Predicate Computing"
         EDW    "Smart scan"    "Predicate Pushing"    "Queued for Predicate Disk"
         EDW    "Smart scan"    PredicateFilter        "Queued for Filtered Backup"
         EDW    "Smart scan"    "Predicate Pushing"    "Predicate Computing"
         EDW    "Smart scan"    PredicateFilter        "Queued for Filtered Backup"
         EDW    "Smart scan"    PredicateFilter        "Queued for Filtered Backup"
         EDW    "Smart scan"    PredicateFilter        "Queued for Filtered Backup"
... Additional output omitted
```

On busy Exadata environments, listing active I/O requests with list activerequest can display a great deal of information. In order to summarize your active I/O requests information, execute the Perl script in Listing 13-1 from a node in your Exadata Database Machine.

■ **Note** The script in Listing 13-1 assumes that you have a cell_group file created containing a list of each Exadata storage cell and that you have established SSH trust. Please see Recipe 7-2 to learn how to configure this.

Listing 13-1. lst13-01-activereq.pl

```perl
#!/usr/bin/perl
# Name: lst13-01-activereq.pl
# Usage: ./lst13-01-ar.pl [-g|-c] [cell group file|list of cells] [-s|-v]
use Getopt::Std;
use Text::ParseWords;
```

```perl
sub usage {
 print "Usage: ./lst13-01-ar.pl [-g|-c] [cell group file|list of cells] [-s|-v]\n";
}
sub prtheader {
printf "%-90s\n","-"x90;
}
sub prtreport {
 my $header=$_[1];
 print "\n$header\n";&prtheader;
 my(%currarray) = %{$_[0]};
 foreach my $key (sort keys %currarray) {
  printf "%10s %-8.0f\n", "$key", "$currarray{$key}";
 }
}
## Command line argument handling     ##
getopts("svg:c:",\%options);
die usage unless ((defined $options{s}) || (defined $options{v}));
die usage unless ((defined $options{c}) || (defined $options{g}));
$dclipref="-g $options{g}" if defined $options{g};
$dclipref="-c $options{c}" if defined $options{c};
$dclitail="attributes dbName,ioReason,ioType,ioBytes,\
                     requestState" if defined $options{s};
$dclitail="attributes dbName,ioReason,ioType,ioBytes,\
                     requestState,sqlID,sessionID,objectNumber" if defined $options{v};
## End Command line argument handling ##
open(F,"dcli ${dclipref} cellcli -e list activerequest ${dclitail}|");
while (<F>) {
 @words= quotewords('\\s+', 0, $_);
 $ars++;                          # Total active requests
 ## Build various arrays to store cellcli output ##
 unless (/Heartbeat/) {
 if (/PredicateCacheGet/) {
    $cell{$words[0]}++;                         # cell name
    $dbnm{$words[1]}++;                         # db name
    $as=sprintf "%-10s %-18s %-25s %-30s", \
             "$words[1]","Null","$words[2]","$words[4]";
    $asqlid=sprintf "%-10s %-15s", \
             "$words[1]", "$words[5]";
    $aobj=sprintf "%-10s %-15s", "$words[1]", "$words[7]";
    $bytesperop{$as}+=$words[3]/1048576;
    $cntperop{$as}++;
    $bytespersql{$asqlid}+=$words[3]/1048576;
    $cntpersql{$asqlid}++;
    $bytesperobj{$aobj}+=$words[3]/1048576;
    $cntperobj{$aobj}++;
    $tbytes+=$words[3];
 } else {
    $cell{$words[0]}++;
    $dbnm{$words[1]}++;
    $as=sprintf "%-10s %-18s %-25s %-30s", \
             "$words[1]","$words[2]","$words[3]","$words[5]";
```

```
            $asqlid=sprintf "%-10s %-15s", \
                     "$words[1]", "$words[6]";
            $aobj=sprintf "%-10s %-15s", "$words[1]", "$words[8]";
            $bytesperop{$as}+=$words[4]/1048576;
            $cntperop{$as}++;
            $bytespersql{$asqlid}+=$words[4]/1048576;
            $cntpersql{$asqlid}++;
            $bytesperobj{$aobj}+=$words[4]/1048576;
            $cntperobj{$aobj}++;
            $tbytes+=$words[4];
   }}
   ## End various arrays to store cellcli output ##
}
## Print output ##
if ($ars > 0) {
 $hdr=sprintf "%-10s %-10s", "Cell", "#Requests"; &prtreport(\%cell, $hdr);
 $hdr=sprintf "%-10s %-10s", "DB", "#Requests";   &prtreport(\%dbnm, $hdr);
 $hdr=sprintf "%-10s %-18s %-25s %-30s %-10s", \
        "DB", "ioReason", "ioType", "requestState", "MB";\
              &prtreport(\%bytesperop, $hdr); $hdr=sprintf "%-10s %-18s %-25s %-30s %-10s", \
        "DB", "ioReason", "ioType", "requestState", "#Requests"; \
              &prtreport(\%cntperop, $hdr);
  if (defined $options{v}) {
    $hdr=sprintf "%-10s %-15s %-10s", "DB", "SqlID", "MB"; &prtreport(\%bytespersql, $hdr);
    $hdr=sprintf "%-10s %-15s %-10s", "DB", "SqlID", "#Requests"; &prtreport(\%cntpersql, $hdr);
    $hdr=sprintf "%-10s %-15s %-10s", "DB", "Object", "MB"; &prtreport(\%bytesperobj, $hdr);
    $hdr=sprintf "%-10s %-15s %-10s", "DB", "Object", "#Requests"; &prtreport(\%cntperobj, $hdr);
  }
}
## End Print output ##

[oracle@cm01dbm01 source]$ ./lst13-01-activereq.pl -g ~/cell_group -s
Cell        #Requests
--------------------------------------------------------------------------------
cm01cel01:  123
cm01cel02:  109
cm01cel03:  110


DB          #Requests
--------------------------------------------------------------------------------
EDW         342


DB      ioReason        ioType                  requestState                 MB
--------------------------------------------------------------------------------
EDW     Null            PredicateCacheGet       Queued for Predicate Disk    1
EDW     Null            PredicateCacheGet       Queued for Predicate Read    6
EDW     Smart scan      Predicate Pushing       Predicate Computing          208
EDW     Smart scan      Predicate Pushing       Queued for Predicate Disk    77
EDW     Smart scan      PredicateFilter         Queued for Filtered Backup   48
```

DB	ioReason	ioType	requestState	#Requests
EDW	Null	PredicateCacheGet	Queued for Predicate Disk	1
EDW	Null	PredicateCacheGet	Queued for Predicate Read	8
EDW	Smart scan	Predicate Pushing	Predicate Computing	208
EDW	Smart scan	Predicate Pushing	Queued for Predicate Disk	77
EDW	Smart scan	PredicateFilter	Queued for Filtered Backup	48

```
[oracle@cm01dbm01 source]$
```

In this output, we see 342 active I/O requests across all of our storage cells as well as a breakdown of I/O megabytes and active request counts per database, ioReason, ioType, and requestState. You can also run the script in Listing 13-1 with a –v option to report summarized active request information on per SQL_ID and per object basis:

```
[oracle@cm01dbm01 source]$ ./lst13-01-activereq.pl -g ~/cell_group -v
... Output omitted for brevity
```

DB	SqlID	MB
EDW	brd3nyszkb4v3	339

DB	SqlID	#Requests
EDW	brd3nyszkb4v3	340

DB	Object	MB
EDW	20274	22
EDW	20275	22

... Additional output omitted

DB	Object	#Requests
EDW	20274	22
EDW	20275	22

... Additional output omitted
```
[oracle@cm01dbm01 source]$
```

How It Works

Active requests are one of three classifications of objects that you can monitor using CellCLI on the Exadata storage cells, along with metrics and alerts. Active requests provide point-in-time information about actively running I/O requests as processed by Exadata's cell services software. Active I/O request information can be queried using the CellCLI list activerequest command and, similar to other storage cell objects, you can limit the output to display specific activerequest attributes.

In recent versions of Exadata, there are 25 distinct activerequest attributes. You can use the CellCLI describe command to list the available activerequest attributes, as displayed:

```
CellCLI> describe activerequest
    name
    asmDiskGroupNumber
```

```
  ... Additional activerequest attributes omitted
        sqlID
        tableSpaceNumber
CellCLI>
```

Most of the `activerequest` attributes are self-explanatory in name, but some of the more common `activerequest` attributes that we suggest building a monitoring strategy around are outlined below:

- The `dbName` attribute contains the name of your database and is useful when you wish to query I/O information for specific databases.

- The `ioReason` describes the reason for the I/O request and is useful when you wish to query on Smart Scan operations, block I/O requests, and so forth.

- The `ioType` attribute lists the specific I/O operation being performed; the values will vary based on the `ioReason` attribute.

- The `requestState attribute` displays the current state of the I/O request. Here, large numbers of queued I/O requests could indicate I/O performance bottlenecks on your storage cell.

- The `consumerGroupName` attribute will display the associated consumer group for the I/O request and, along with `dbName`, it provides insight into the different types of sessions performing I/O requests.

- The `sqlID` attribute can be used to measure I/O operations from specific SQL cursors.

- The `objectNumber` attribute represents the object number that the I/O request is servicing.

- The `sessionNumber` and `sessionSerNumber` attributes represent the unique session identifier information from a specific database instance.

13-3. Monitoring Cells with Metrics

Problem

You wish to report current or historical performance, configuration, or alert conditions on the Exadata storage cells and storage cell components and, specifically, learn how to navigate Exadata's metric "data model" to enable you to build a robust monitoring strategy.

Solution

In this recipe, you will learn how to do the following:

- Use CellCLI to display Exadata Storage Server metric definitions
- Identify the different metric object types present in the Exadata storage cells
- Query current cell server metrics
- Report on historical storage server metrics
- Identify metric alert conditions
- Recognize how Exadata tracks storage server metrics

You will begin by learning about the metricdefinition object and build upon your understanding of the metric object attributes to construct CellCLI queries against current and historical storage server metrics. The examples in this recipe will focus on specific storage server metrics and outline commonly used CellCLI list commands to demonstrate the relationships and meanings between the metrics objects, limit list output using where conditions, and customize column output using the attributes clause.

Listing Storage Server Metrics

Launch cellcli from any Exadata storage cell and run the following describe metricdefinition command:

```
CellCLI> describe metricdefinition
        name
        description
        metricType
        objectType
        persistencePolicy
        unit
CellCLI>
```

Next, run the list metricdefinition command to display the available storage server metrics:

```
CellCLI> list metricdefinition
        CD_IO_BY_R_LG
        CD_IO_BY_R_LG_SEC
        CD_IO_BY_R_SM
... Additional metrics omitted
```

With recent versions of Exadata, you will have nearly 200 metrics available to you. Each of these metrics tracks information for different components in your Exadata Storage Servers. The previous output shows a single attribute, or column—this corresponds to the name attribute in the metricdefinition object. You can list information about a specific metric using the list command with the metric name supplied, as listed:

```
CellCLI> list metricdefinition CL_CPUT
        CL_CPUT
CellCLI>
```

Above, we're displaying a specific storage server metric, CL_CPUT. What does this metric represent? Add the detail clause at the end of your CellCLI list command to display all of the metric's attributes:

```
CellCLI> list metricdefinition CL_CPUT detail
        name:            CL_CPUT
        description:     "Percentage of time over the previous minute that the system CPUs were
                          not idle."
        metricType:      Instantaneous
        objectType:      CELL
        unit:            %
CellCLI>
```

As you can see, CL_CPUT represents the CPU utilization of the storage cell. The attributes displayed are the same as those reported from the describe metricdefinition CellCLI command. Next, use the attributes clause to display a subset of your metric's attributes:

```
CellCLI> list metricdefinition CL_CPUT attributes name,metricType,objectType
         CL_CPUT         Instantaneous     CELL
CellCLI>
```

Metric Object Types

Each Exadata Storage Server metric is associated with a specific object type and is assigned to an objectType attribute. The objectType attribute specifies which Exadata component the metric is related to. To display a list of distinct metric objectType attributes, run the following cellcli command:

```
[celladmin@cm01cel01 ~]$ cellcli -e list metricdefinition attributes objectType|sort -u
         CELL
         CELLDISK
         CELL_FILESYSTEM
         FLASHCACHE
         FLASHLOG
         GRIDDISK
         HOST_INTERCONNECT
         IORM_CATEGORY
         IORM_CONSUMER_GROUP
         IORM_DATABASE
[celladmin@cm01cel01 ~]$
```

Each objectType name is relatively self-explanatory. Using the CL_CPUT metric example above, you can expand on this to list each metric associated with the CELL objectType attribute by adding the following where objectType clause:

```
CellCLI> list metricdefinition attributes name,metricType,description where objectType='CELL'
    CL_BBU_CHARGE    Instantaneous    "Disk Controller Battery Charge"
    CL_BBU_TEMP      Instantaneous    "Disk Controller Battery Temperature"
    CL_CPUT          Instantaneous    "Percentage of time over the previous minute that the system
CPUs were not idle."
    CL_CPUT_CS       Instantaneous    "Percentage of CPU time used by CELLSRV"
    CL_CPUT_MS       Instantaneous    "Percentage of CPU time used by MS"
... Additional CELL metrics omitted
```

The metriccurrent Object

Now that you have an understanding of the metricdefinition object and its attributes, run the following describe command to show the object definition of the metriccurrent object:

```
CellCLI> describe metriccurrent
         name
         alertState
         collectionTime
         metricObjectName
```

```
                metricType
                metricValue
                objectType
CellCLI>
```

The metriccurrent object contains observable metrics as of the *current* time; in other words, it stores information about each metric as of the time the object is queried. Using the same CL_CPUT metric provided above, run the following command to display your current storage cell CPU utilization:

```
CellCLI> list metriccurrent CL_CPUT
        CL_CPUT         cm01cel01    0.4 %
CellCLI>
```

We see the current CPU utilization of our storage cell is 0.4%. Next, add the detail condition to your list command to display each metriccurrent attribute:

```
CellCLI> list metriccurrent CL_CPUT detail
        name:                   CL_CPUT
        alertState:             normal
        collectionTime:         2012-10-25T00:15:01-04:00
        metricObjectName:       cm01cel01
        metricType:             Instantaneous
        metricValue:            0.9 %
        objectType:             CELL
CellCLI>
```

The detailed output shows some additional attributes:

- alertState is the current alert status of the metric; valid values include normal, warning, and critical.

- collectionTime is the time at which the metric was collected.

- metricValue represents the value of the metric; in the previous case, it displays 0.9%.

- metricType represents the unit, or scope, upon which the metric's metricValue is based. Valid values for metricType include Instantaneous (typically presented as a percentage or raw data value), Cumulative, Rate (units per time interval), or Transition.

- metricObjectName represents the specific object to which the metric is scoped; for example, for each CELL objectType, the metricObjectName will be the name of the storage cell.

- objectType represents the type of the metric.

To illustrate the different types of CellCLI output, use the following list metriccurrent command to display current metrics for the CELL objectType:

```
CellCLI> list metriccurrent where objectType='CELL' attributes -
> name,metricObjectName,metricValue,metricType
        CL_BBU_CHARGE           cm01cel01    91.0 %        Instantaneous
        CL_BBU_TEMP             cm01cel01    41.0 C        Instantaneous
        CL_CPUT                 cm01cel01    0.2 %         Instantaneous
... Additional Instaneous metrics omitted
```

```
        N_HCA_MB_RCV_SEC        cm01cel01       0.156 MB/sec    Rate
        N_HCA_MB_TRANS_SEC      cm01cel01       0.151 MB/sec    Rate
... Additional metrics omitted
CellCLI>
```

The metrichistory Object

The metrichistory object contains, by default, seven days of historical metrics sampled over one-minute intervals. To display the attributes of the metrichistory object, use the following describe command in CellCLI:

```
CellCLI> describe metrichistory
        name
        alertState
        collectionTime
        metricObjectName
        metricType
        metricValue
        metricValueAvg
        metricValueMax
        metricValueMin
        objectType
CellCLI>
```

You will notice that the metrichistory object contains the same attributes as the metriccurrent object, plus average, minimum, and maximum values of the metricValue attribute. Using the same CL_CPUT metric demonstrated previously, run the following CellCLI command to display your historical storage server CPU utilization:

```
CellCLI> list metrichistory CL_CPUT
        CL_CPUT         cm01cel01       3.6 %   2012-10-18T00:00:59-04:00
        CL_CPUT         cm01cel01       0.4 %   2012-10-18T00:01:59-04:00
        CL_CPUT         cm01cel01       1.7 %   2012-10-18T00:02:59-04:00
... Additional output omitted for brevity
```

As mentioned, Exadata's storage server historical metrics store information at one-minute intervals and the volume of information that an Exadata DMA would need to analyze can often be challenging. You can add where conditions on the collectionTime attribute to limit the output to specific date ranges. Using our CL_CPUT metric, execute the following CellCLI command to introduce a date-based search criteria:

```
CellCLI> list metrichistory CL_CPUT where collectionTime < '2012-10-18T00:07:59-04:00';
        CL_CPUT         cm01cel01       3.6 %   2012-10-18T00:00:59-04:00
        CL_CPUT         cm01cel01       0.4 %   2012-10-18T00:01:59-04:00
        CL_CPUT         cm01cel01       1.7 %   2012-10-18T00:02:59-04:00
CellCLI>
```

Experienced Exadata DMAs typically employ a number of techniques to make the volume of metrichistory data easier to cope with. Recipe 13-6 includes some techniques for summarizing large amounts of metrichistory data.

The alertState Attribute

One of the more important metric object attributes, from a monitoring standpoint, is the alertState attribute. Exadata DMAs often will build reporting or monitoring strategies that include reporting on some or all metrics with an abnormal alertState. You can find any metrics in an abnormal state from current metrics (that is, metriccurrent) or for any given time from your metric history (in other words, `metrichistory`). To list any metrics currently in an abnormal state, run the following CellCLI command:

```
CellCLI> list metriccurrent where alertState != 'Normal'
CellCLI>
```

Here, we see no evidence of abnormal metric conditions. Next, query your `metrichistory` object to list all abnormal metrics:

```
CellCLI> list metrichistory where alertState != 'Normal'
CellCLI>
```

■ **Note** The `alertState` of a metric is governed by seeded or customized metric *thresholds*. To learn more about metric thresholds, please see Recipe 13-4.

How It Works

Exadata Storage Server metrics are recorded observations of important runtime properties or internal instrumentation values of the storage cell and its components. Exadata's CELLSRV (Cell Services) and MS (Management Services) processes work in tandem to track and store metric information.

- Exadata's Cell Services software, CELLSRV, is instrumented to track several hundred metrics and stores these in storage server memory. When you execute a `list metriccurrent` command from CellCLI, you are accessing the in-memory storage server metrics.

- Every hour, the MS process writes the in-memory metric information to disk and flushes current metrics from memory. Once written to disk, the data is available through the CellCLI `metrichistory` object.

- MS retains seven days of metrics on disk and automatically ages out information older than seven days.

The three main objects that contain metric information are `metricdefinition`, `metriccurrent`, and `metrichistory`. In the Problem section of this recipe, we used the term "data model"; the metric hierarchy is not actually stored in a relational model, but the attributes of each object are related.

As mentioned, there are a number of metric object types, each of which is associated with a specific component of the storage server infrastructure. You can report current or past metrics for each metric and each classification of `objectType` using the same `list metriccurrent` and `list metrichistory` commands. In the following sections, we provide some additional detail and monitoring recommendations per `objectType`:

Cell Disks (objectType = CELLDISK)

Cell disks metrics are broken down into two main categories: I/O requests and I/O throughput. These are further provided for both small I/O and large I/O requests, and each of these is also classified based on a cumulative and rate metrics.

- Look for a relatively smooth distribution of I/O requests, MB per second, and I/O latencies across each cell disk and Exadata storage cell.

- Look for relatively low I/O latencies; under 10ms is generally considered an ideal target for small I/Os, but larger I/O operations can have higher values.

- Monitor your I/O load using the `CD_IO_LOAD` metric and watch for high utilization.

Grid Disks (objectType = GRIDDISK)

Exadata grid disk metrics are broken down into two main categories: I/O requests and I/O throughput. These metrics are further broken down into operations for small I/O and large I/O, and each of these is also classified based on a cumulative count and rate metric.

Monitoring grid disk metric values can be a bit more complex than monitoring cell disk metrics because your databases can be spread unevenly across your Exadata grid disks depending on your deployment. We recommend combining a grid disk metric monitoring strategy with an IORM Database monitoring strategy, as presented in Recipe 13-12.

Host Interconnect (objectType = HOST_INTERCONNECT)

Exadata tracks a number of InfiniBand interconnect metrics using the HOST_INTERCONNECT metric objectType:

- Watch for drops, retransmissions, and resend metrics using the N_MB_DROP*, N_MB_RDMA_DROP*, N_MB_RESENT*, and N_RDMA_RETRY* metrics. Ideally, you should not see non-zero values for these metrics.

- Look for the number of MB sent and received to and from the compute nodes to be smoothly distributed.

IORM Databse (objectType = IORM_DATABASE)

Many IORM_DATABASE metrics are collected whether you have an IORM plan enabled or not; Exadata automatically tags the I/O request metadata instructions with the database sending the I/O request to the Exadata storage cells.

- Measure the DB_IO_LOAD metric, which reports the disk I/O load per database. This is a good way to measure which database and application are generating the highest I/O workload.

- Measure the DB_IO_UTIL* metric, which reports the disk I/O utilization for small and large I/Os per database. This is a good way to measure which database and application is generating the highest disk utilization.

- If you have implemented an IORM plan, monitor the DB_IO_WT* metrics. These metrics will show you which databases are suffering wait time based on IORM plan I/O queuing and can be used to validate or adjust your IORM plan.

IORM Consumer Group (objectType = IORM_CONSUMER_GROUP)

Oracle automatically collects IORM consumer group performance metrics on each storage server for each database and consumer group deployed on your Exadata Database Machine when an IORM plan is enabled.

- Measure the CG_IO_LOAD metric, which reports the disk I/O load per database per consumer group. This is a good way to measure which database, application, and resource consumer are generating the highest I/O workload.

- Measure the CG_IO_UTIL* metrics, which report the disk I/O utilization for small and large I/Os per database per consumer group. This is a good way to measure which database and resource consumer group are generating the highest disk utilization.

- If you have implemented an IORM plan, monitor the CG_IO_WT* metrics. These metrics will show you which consumer groups are suffering wait time based on IORM plan I/O queuing and can be used to validate or adjust your IORM plan.

IORM Category (objectType = IORM_CATEGORY)

Oracle automatically collects IORM category performance metrics on each storage server for each database and consumer group deployed on your Exadata Database Machine when an IORM plan is enabled.

- Measure the CT_IO_LOAD metric, which reports the disk I/O load per resource category. This is a good way to measure which classifications of resource consumers are generating the highest I/O workload.

- Measure the CT_IO_UTIL* metric, which reports the disk I/O utilization for small and large I/Os per database per category. This is a good way to measure which classifications of resource consumers are generating the highest disk utilization.

- If you have implemented an IORM plan, monitor the CT_IO_WT* metrics. These metrics will show you which resource categories are suffering wait time based on IORM plan I/O queuing and can be used to validate or adjust your IORM plan.

Flash Cache (objectType = FLASHCACHE)

Exadata's Flash Cache metrics are classified into two main metric buckets: bandwidth and I/O requests. The FC*BY* metrics report on the number of MB processed, skipped, or pushed out of Flash Cache for a variety of reasons, and the FC*RQ* metrics contain I/O request metrics for a variety of conditions. In addition to the bandwidth and I/O requests classification, there is generally a metric for each Flash Cache "hit" reason and a Flash Cache "miss" reason.

- Look for high numbers for the FC_BYKEEP* metrics; these indicate that data was pushed out of Flash Cache in order to load objects tagged with a Flash Cache "keep" attribute.

- If you have elected to pin objects in Flash Cache, examine the FC_IO_BYKEEP* and FC_IO_RQKEEP* metrics to measure the effectiveness of your caching strategy.

- Measure the FC*SKIP* metrics to measure the amount of data and number of requests that needed to be satisfied from hard disks because the nature of the requests bypassed Smart Flash Cache.

- Measure the FC*MISS* metrics to report the number of MB and I/O requests that required I/O to be satisfied from hard disks because not all of the data was loaded into the Flash Cache.

Like all data-caching solutions, the goal of Flash Cache is to reduce the need to perform disk I/O on physical hard disks. As such, you would ideally like to see a relatively high percentage of your database's I/O requests be satisfied from Flash Cache (if not from the database instance buffer cache). However, as large I/O requests generally bypass Flash Cache, your benefit from Flash Cache is truly dependent on your database, application, and workload.

Flash Logging (objectType = FLASHLOG)

Many of Exadata's FLASHLOG metrics are cumulative, which makes measuring Smart Flash Logging behavior relatively simple to measure and monitor.

- Look for a high ratio of FL_FLASH_FIRST to FL_DISK_FIRST; the higher the metric values are for FL_FLASH_FIRST, the more often Exadata is writing to flash before disk. While this is the purpose of Smart Flash Logging, it could indicate that your application is performing a very high number of commits.

- To measure the overall effectiveness and impact of Smart Flash Logging, monitor the value of FL_PREVENTED_OUTLIERS and FL_ACTUAL_OUTLIERS. These represent the number of redo write requests that were cushioned, or "saved", Flash Logging and the number that could not be serviced *either* flash or disk, respectively.

Smart Flash Logging in Exadata X3 configurations can play an even greater and more beneficial role as the X3 storage cells have significantly more PCI flash. This decreases the probability of witnessing FL_ACTUAL_OUTLIERS metrics of significance.

13-4. Configuring Thresholds for Cell Metrics

Problem

You wish to create custom thresholds for specific Exadata metrics in order to generate alerts tailored to meet your business requirements.

Solution

In this recipe, you will learn how to create a custom metric threshold to trigger alerts based on a desired condition. This recipe will walk you through the steps to create a single threshold on a specific alert and show you how to create the threshold, validate the threshold configuration using the list threshold CellCLI command, and confirm that the threshold is working as planned.

1. First, determine which metric you wish to customize the metric threshold for. In the following example, we will use the DB_IO_UTIL_LG metric, which captures the I/O utilization for a specific database on your Exadata Database Machine.

2. Next, validate whether custom thresholds are configured by using the list threshold CellCLI command. You will see that we currently have no thresholds created:

   ```
   CellCLI> list threshold
   CellCLI>
   ```

3. Use the list metriccurrent CellCLI command to determine the metricObjectName to create the threshold for. Since the DB_IO_UTIL_LG metric is scoped to an Oracle database name, you will see one or more database names in the metricObjectName attribute:

   ```
   CellCLI> list metriccurrent DB_IO_UTIL_LG attributes name,metricObjectName
            DB_IO_UTIL_LG    DWPRD
            DB_IO_UTIL_LG    EDW
            DB_IO_UTIL_LG    VISX
            DB_IO_UTIL_LG    VISY
            DB_IO_UTIL_LG    _OTHER_DATABASE_
   CellCLI>
   ```

4. Above, we see four distinct named databases. Once you have decided which metricObjectName to create your threshold for, issue the following command to create your threshold:

   ```
   CellCLI> create threshold DB_IO_UTIL_LG.EDW -
   > warning=50,critical=70,comparison='>',occurrences=2,observation=5
   Threshold DB_IO_UTIL_LG.EDW successfully created
   CellCLI>
   ```

In this command:

- The first line creates a threshold on the DB_IO_UTIL_LG metric for the EDW database. The hyphen (-) at the end of the first line represents the line continuation character.

- In the second line, we're specifying to trigger a warning condition when the CPU utilization for the EDW database exceeds 50% and a critical message when it exceeds 70%.

- In the second line, the occurrences attribute signifies to raise an alert if two consecutive alerts are raised.

- Also in the second line, the observation attribute indicates the number of measurements over which the measured values are averaged. In other words, in this case an alert would be raised if more than two conditions exceeded the threshold over five measurements.

5. To validate your threshold, run the list threshold command from CellCLI:

```
CellCLI> list threshold detail
         name:                DB_IO_UTIL_LG.EDW
         comparison:          >
         critical:            70.0
         observation:         5
         occurrences:         2
         warning:             50.0
CellCLI>
```

6. Assuming you have a workload condition that causes the measurements for this metric to be exceeded, run the list metriccurrent and list alerthistory command to display the alerts generated from this current threshold:

```
CellCLI> list metriccurrent DB_IO_UTIL_LG where metricObjectName='EDW'
         DB_IO_UTIL_LG     EDW      72 %

CellCLI> list alerthistory
         1_1     2012-10-27T01:06:01-04:00     warning     "The warning threshold for the
following metric has been crossed. Metric Name    : DB_IO_UTIL_LG  Metric Description :
Percentage of disk resources utilized by large requests from this database  Object Name :
EDW  Current Value    : 72.0 %  Threshold Value    : 50.0 % "
CellCLI>
```

As you can see, I/O workload from our EDW database caused the alert to be raised based on the threshold we created.

7. If you wish to drop the threshold, use the following drop threshold command in CellCLI:

```
CellCLI> drop threshold DB_IO_UTIL_LG.EDW
Threshold DB_IO_UTIL_LG.EDW successfully dropped
CellCLI>
```

How It Works

Exadata comes delivered with a number of seeded alerts and their corresponding thresholds. To adjust the metric threshold, the Exadata DMA uses the CellCLI create threshold command. If a metric value exceeds your user-defined thresholds, Exadata will trigger an alert.

Metrics can be associated with warning and critical thresholds. Thresholds relate to extreme values in the metric and may indicate a problem or other event of interest to the Exadata DMA.

Thresholds are supported on a number of cell disk, grid disk, cell server, and I/O Resource Management utilization metrics and apply to Stateful alerts. The CellCLI list alertdefinition command lists all the metrics for which thresholds can be set:

```
CellCLI> list alertdefinition where alertType='Stateful'
        StatefulAlert_CD_IO_BY_R_LG
        StatefulAlert_CD_IO_BY_R_LG_SEC
... Additional stateful alerts omitted
```

We recommend following these guidelines when creating metric thresholds:

- The threshold name needs to be of the format name.metricObjectName, where name is the name of the metric and metricObjectName is the scope to which the metric applies.
- Use the list metriccurrent or list metrichistory command to validate the metricObjectName for your threshold.
- Unless your goal is simply to test thresholds and alerts, do not arbitrarily create metric thresholds without a business case. We recommend aligning your metric threshold strategy with known monitoring needs and using list metrichistory to determine metric names, collection times, and measurement values as your inputs to the warning, critical, occurrences, and observations attributes.

13-5. Using dcli with Special Characters

Problem

Using dcli, you wish to execute a CellCLI command that contains one or more special characters, such as a single quote, the > sign, or the < sign.

Solution

In this recipe, you will learn how to issue dcli commands that contain "special characters" by using the backslash (\) character and double quotes. In this recipe, we will provide several examples with different special characters, and we will also provide explanations and comparisons between using dcli and cellcli to issue the same command.

■ **Note** To learn more about using dcli, the Distributed Command Line Interface, please see Recipe 7-7.

We will begin by demonstrating a simple example using single quotes. In the following CellCLI example, you can see that single quotes are allowed when, for example, you wish to qualify a list command to restrict output to a specific attribute:

```
CellCLI> list griddisk where diskType='HardDisk'
        DATA_CD_00_cm01cel01         active
        DATA_CD_01_cm01cel01         active
... Additional grid disks omitted
```

As you learned from your Exadata Owner's Guide or Recipe 7-7, the dcli command to list the same information for a specific storage cell looks like this:

```
[oracle@cm01dbm01 ~]$ dcli -c cm01cel01 cellcli -e list griddisk where diskType='HardDisk'
cm01cel01: DATA_CD_00_cm01cel01          active
cm01cel01: DATA_CD_01_cm01cel01          active
... Additional grid disks omitted
```

In this specific case, the special character is the single quote ('), and in situations when the CellCLI list command is simple, no escape sequences are required. If, however, you enclose your dcli command in double quotes, as is sometimes required based on the CellCLI or host command you are executing, you need to escape the single quotes with a backslash character. Run the following dcli command to list the same information, this time enclosing the entire cellcli command in double quotes and escaping the single quotes with a backslash:

```
[oracle@cm01dbm01 ~]$ dcli -c cm01cel01 "cellcli -e list griddisk where diskType=\'HardDisk\'"
cm01cel01: DATA_CD_00_cm01cel01          active
cm01cel01: DATA_CD_01_cm01cel01          active
... Additional grid disks omitted
```

When is it required to enclose your dcli commands in single quotes? With dcli, double quotes are required any time the command contains punctuation marks or special characters. For example, consider the following CellCLI list alerthistory command, which displays alerts generated after a specific time:

```
CellCLI> list alerthistory attributes name,severity -
> where beginTime > '2012-10-17T02:00:42-04:00';
         1_1     warning
         1_2     critical
         1_3     clear
CellCLI>
```

Try running the above cellcli command using dcli without using the backslash special character and double quotes:

```
[oracle@cm01dbm01 ~]$ dcli -c cm01cel01 cellcli -e list alerthistory \
> attributes name,severity where beginTime > '2012-10-17T02:00:42-04:00'
[oracle@cm01dbm01 ~]$
```

As you can see, no errors were reported but, unfortunately, no output was returned. To generate the proper output, enclose the entire cellcli command with double quotes and use the backslash to escape the > and single quote characters:

```
[oracle@cm01dbm01 ~]$ dcli -c cm01cel01 "cellcli -e \
> list alerthistory attributes name,severity where beginTime \> \'2012-10-17T02:00:42-04:00\'"
cm01cel01: 1_1     warning
cm01cel01: 1_2     critical
cm01cel01: 1_3     clear
[oracle@cm01dbm01 ~]$
```

Notice the double quotes surrounding the entire cellcli command as well as the escape character preceding the greater than symbol and each single quote. In the next example, we will demonstrate using escape characters to implement an I/O Resource Management plan on each of our storage cells. In this example, you will see backslash characters preceding both single quotes and open and close parentheses, as well as double quotes enclosing the entire cellcli command:

```
[oracle@cm01dbm01 ~]$ dcli -g ./cell_group "cellcli -e \
> alter iormplan objective=\'auto\', \
> dbplan=\(\(name=visx,level=1,allocation=55\), \
> \(name=prod1,level=1,allocation=25\),    \
> \(name=prod2,level=1,allocation=65\),  \
> \(name=other,level=2,allocation=100\)\), \
> catplan=\(\(name=CAT_HIGH,level=1,allocation=70\), \
> \(name=CAT_MEDIUM,level=1,allocation=20\),      \
> \(name=CAT_LOW,level=2,allocation=80\),         \
> \(name=other,level=3,allocation=100\)\)\)"
cm01cel01: IORMPLAN successfully altered
cm01cel02: IORMPLAN successfully altered
cm01cel03: IORMPLAN successfully altered
[oracle@cm01dbm01 ~]$
```

How It Works

When using dcli to execute either CellCLI commands or host commands, there are two important considerations:

- If the command contains any special characters or punctuation marks, the entire command needs to be enclosed in double quotes.
- To escape special characters, use the backslash character (\).

With dcli, the following characters are considered *special characters*:

- The dollar sign: $
- The single quote: '
- The less than sign: <
- The greater than sign: >
- Open and close parentheses: (and)

Failure to properly escape special characters in dcli could lead to either an error being raised or no output being returned.

13-6. Reporting and Summarizing metrichistory Using R

Problem

You wish to summarize historical Exadata Storage Server metrics in order to recognize performance trends.

Solution

In this recipe, you will learn how to generate metrichistory metric values for specific Exadata metrics and summarize the information using a simple shell script combined with an R script.

Since the scripts in this recipe include reporting statistical metric information using R and using an R script to plot metric information, the first step you must perform is to install R on one of your Exadata Compute Nodes.

> **Note** With Exadata X3 models, Oracle delivers Oracle R Enterprise at the compute node operating system level as well as Oracle R functions and packages inside the database. The following examples will show you how to install R in an Exadata X2-2 environment. By default, R is not installed on the Exadata Compute Nodes or storage cells and although Oracle discourages installing additional software on the compute nodes, http://docs.oracle.com/cd/E11882_01/doc.112/e26499/install.htm#BABCEACI provides instructions specific for Exadata. If your organization does not allow you to install R on a compute node, an alternative approach is to extract cellcli data to a different server or workstation and analyze the results from there.

Prior to executing the scripts provided in this recipe, you will need to install R on an Exadata Compute Node. To accomplish this, first download the public-yum-el5.repo file from http://public-yum.oracle.com/public-yum-el5.repo and place it under /etc/yum.repos.d. Disable the current Exadata repository by renaming the existing repository with the **.disabled** suffix:

```
[root@cm01dbm01 yum.repos.d]# ls -l
total 12
-rw-r----- 1 root root  220 Oct 11 03:17 Exadata-computenode.repo.disabled
-r--r----- 1 root root 1160 Jul 13 13:39 Exadata-computenode.repo.sample
-rw-r--r-- 1 root root 3974 Oct 30 02:20 public-yum-el5.repo
[root@cm01dbm01 yum.repos.d]#
```

Next, set enabled=1 for the el5_addons and el5_oracle_addons stanzas in the pubic-yum-el5.repo file:

```
[el5_addons]

name=Enterprise Linux $releasever Add ons ($basearch)
baseurl=http://public-yum.oracle.com/repo/EnterpriseLinux/EL5/addons/$basearch/
gpgkey=http://public-yum.oracle.com/RPM-GPG-KEY-oracle-el5
gpgcheck=1
enabled=1
```

When this is complete, run yum install R as root on your compute node:

```
[root@cm01dbm01 yum.repos.d]# yum install R
el5_addons                                       | 1.2 kB     00:00
el5_latest                                       | 1.4 kB     00:00
el5_oracle_addons                                |  951 B     00:00
... Output omitted
```

After R is installed, you can validate it by launching R:

```
[root@cm01dbm01 yum.repos.d]# R
Oracle Distribution of R version 2.13.2 (2011-09-30)
Copyright (C) 2011 The R Foundation for Statistical Computing
ISBN 3-900051-07-0
Platform: x86_64-redhat-linux-gnu (64-bit)
... Output omitted for brevity
```

As the scripts in this recipe will use the ggplot2 package, you must download ggplot2 version 8.9 and install it using the following command:

```
[root@cm01dbm01 yum.repos.d]# R CMD INSTALL ./ggplot2_0.9.2.1.tar.gz
```

■ **Note** At the time of this writing, the version of R installed with the el5_addons channel is 2.13-2. The ggplot2 package does not exist for 2.13-2, so you will not be able to simply run `install.packages('ggplot2')` from the R command prompt; this is why we're showing you how to download a version compatible with R version 2.13-2 and manually install it.

Once R, Rscript, and the ggplot2 package are installed, you use the scripts in Listings 13-2 and 13-3 to summarize your metrichistory data. Listing 13-2 accepts a cell server or cell group file and a specific Exadata Storage Server as input parameters and feeds the output into an R script to summarize the statistical minimum, median, mean, and maximum values. Additionally, the script in Listing 13-3 will generate both a line plot and frequency histogram plot based for the metric values extracted via `cellcli`:

Listing 13-2. lst13-02-metricsum.sh

```
#!/bin/sh
# Name: lst13-02-metricsum.sh
# Usage: ./lst13-02-metricsum.sh [-c|-g] [cell|cell_group] -m [metric]
export rscript=./lst13-03-metricsum.r
usage() {
 echo "Usage: 'basename $0' [-c|-g] [cell|cell_group] -m [metric]"
 echo "Invalid metric: $1"
 exit 1
}
case $# in
4)
   if [ "$1" == "-c" ] && [ "$3" == "-m" ]; then
      scp=$1; cells=$2; metric=$4
      export a4=$4
   elif [ "$1" == "-g" ] && [ "$3" == "-m" ]; then
      scp=$1; cells=$2; metric=$4
   else
        usage
   fi
metricdesc='dcli ${scp} ${cells} cellcli -e list metricdefinition ${metric} \
      attributes description|head -1 | awk 'BEGIN { FS = "\"" } ; { print $2 }''
unit='dcli ${scp} ${cells} cellcli -e list metricdefinition ${metric} \
      attributes unit|head -1 | sed 's/IO requests/IORequests/g'| \
        awk '{ print $2 }''
   if [ -z "${metricdesc}" ]; then
      usage ${metric}
   fi
   case $metric in
   CD*|GD*) plt=1;;
   *) plt=2;;
   esac
   echo "Reporting on ${metric}: ${metricdesc}"
```

```bash
        echo "This could take awhile ..."
        dcli --serial ${scp} ${cells} cellcli -e list metrichistory ${metric} \
            attributes name,metricObjectName,metricValue,collectionTime | \
            sed 's/,//g' | sed 's/IO requests/IORequests/g'  | \
            ${rscript} ${metric} ${unit} ${plt}
    ;;
*)
    usage;;
esac
```

Listing 13-3. lst13-03-metricsum.r

```r
#!/usr/bin/env Rscript
# Name:  lst13-03-metricsum.r
# Usage: (output) | ./lst13-03-metricsum.r [metric] [unit] [1|2]
msg.trap <- capture.output(suppressMessages(library("ggplot2")))
msg.trap <- capture.output(suppressMessages(library("RColorBrewer")))
args <- commandArgs(trailingOnly = TRUE)
local.plt    <- c(as.numeric(args[3]));
local.title  <- paste(args[1],"in",args[2])
fn.line <- args[1]
fn.hist <- paste(fn.line,"_FREQ",sep="")
df <- read.table("stdin")   # main df frame
colnames(df) <- c('cell','metric', 'metricObjectName','metricValue','myx','collectionTime')
cat("Cell Summary information\n")
by(df[,c('metricValue')],df$cell,summary)
cat("\n\nMetric Object Summary information\n")
by(df[,c('metricValue')],df$metricObjectName, summary)
if (local.plt == 1) {
 pline <- ggplot(df,aes(collectionTime,metricValue,colour=cell))
 pline <- pline + geom_line(aes(colour=cell,group=1))
 pline <- pline + facet_grid(cell ~ .)
 pline <- pline + opts(title=local.title)
 phist <- ggplot(df, aes(metricValue, fill=cell)) + geom_bar(binwidth=50)
 phist <- phist + facet_grid(cell ~ .)
 phist <- phist + opts(title=local.title)
} else {
 pline <- ggplot(df,aes(collectionTime,metricValue,colour=metricObjectName))
 pline <- pline + geom_line(aes(colour=metricObjectName,group=1))
 pline <- pline + facet_grid(metricObjectName ~ .)
 pline <- pline + opts(title=local.title)
 phist <- ggplot(df, aes(metricValue, fill=metricObjectName)) + geom_bar(binwidth=50)
 phist <- phist + facet_grid(metricObjectName ~ .)
 phist <- phist + opts(title=local.title)
}
pdf(paste(fn.line,".pdf",sep=""))
print(pline)
pdf(paste(fn.hist,".pdf",sep=""))
print(phist)
```

Run `lst13-02-metricsum.sh` as demonstrated below, which we will demonstrate using the CL_CPUT metric:

```
[oracle@cm01dbm01 source]$ ./lst13-02-metricsum.sh -g ~/cell_group -m CL_CPUT
Reporting on CL_CPUT: Percentage of time over the previous minute that the system CPUs were not
idle.
This could take awhile ...

Cell Summary information
df$cell: cm01cel01:
   Min. 1st Qu.  Median    Mean 3rd Qu.    Max.
  0.100   0.400   0.600   1.317   0.900  99.000
------------------------------------------------------------
df$cell: cm01cel02:
   Min. 1st Qu.  Median    Mean 3rd Qu.    Max.
  0.100   0.400   0.600   1.264   0.900  98.800
------------------------------------------------------------
df$cell: cm01cel03:
   Min. 1st Qu.  Median    Mean 3rd Qu.    Max.
   0.10    0.40    0.60    1.23    0.80   98.70

Metric Object Summary information
df$metricObjectName: cm01cel01
   Min. 1st Qu.  Median    Mean 3rd Qu.    Max.
  0.100   0.400   0.600   1.317   0.900  99.000
------------------------------------------------------------
df$metricObjectName: cm01cel02
   Min. 1st Qu.  Median    Mean 3rd Qu.    Max.
  0.100   0.400   0.600   1.264   0.900  98.800
------------------------------------------------------------
df$metricObjectName: cm01cel03
   Min. 1st Qu.  Median    Mean 3rd Qu.    Max.
   0.10    0.40    0.60    1.23    0.80   98.70
[oracle@cm01dbm01 source]$
```

The R script displays statistical minimum, median, mean, and maximum values for both the Exadata storage cell and `metricObjectName` corresponding to the metric, which in this case is the same as the cell name. Additionally, the R script will generate two plots, one showing a line graph for the metric broken out by `metricObjectName`, and one displaying the frequency histogram for the measured values. Figure 13-1 shows these plots.

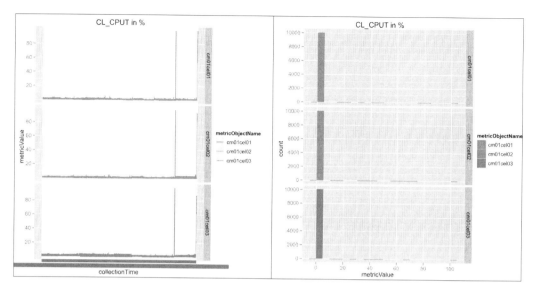

Figure 13-1. *R plots for CL_CPUT metric*

How It Works

Exadata DMAs generally employ a number of techniques to summarize historical Exadata Storage Server metrics, including the following:

- Saving `cellcli` output to a text file, importing to Excel, and building graphs
- Saving `cellcli` output to a text file and using external tables to load the data into Oracle tables and then using SQL to report on the metric values
- Saving `cellcli` output to a text file and using SQL*Loader to load to Oracle tables
- Using Enterprise Manager with Exadata plug-ins to display Exadata Storage Server performance
- Using R to generate statistical information and plots from `cellcli` output

Although the script in Listing 13-3 is very simple by R standards, we prefer using R to summarize Exadata metric information for a number of reasons. First, it is relatively easy to incorporate your analysis into a small subset of server-side scripts, thus reducing the time required to transfer files and prepare independent analysis. Second, R provides a rich set of statistical analysis and plotting features that are often difficult and time-consuming to replicate using other scripting languages, SQL, or Excel.

> **Note** Programming in the R language is beyond the scope of this text. To learn more about R and Oracle's direction with R, please see www.r-project.org and www.oracle.com/technetwork/database/options/advanced-analytics/r-enterprise/index.html.

13-7. Reporting and Summarizing metrichistory Using Oracle and SQL

Problem

You wish to summarize historical Exadata Storage Server metrics in order to recognize performance trends using Oracle tables and SQL.

Solution

In this recipe, you will learn how to load `metrichistory` information into an Oracle table or tables to use SQL to report on your metrics. We will provide sample scripts for extracting `metrichistory` information to a flat file and build an Oracle external table from this table.

To begin, scope your analysis to one or more metrics, run the `list metrichistory` command from `dcli` or `cellcli`, and save the output to a text file:

```
[oracle@cm01dbm01 cellscr]$ dcli -g ./cell_group list metrichistory \
where name='DB_IO_LOAD' > ./db_io_load.dat
```

Next, create an external table using this data and displayed in Listing 13-4:

Listing 13-4: lst13-04-bld-ext-tab.sql

```
SQL> create table celliorm.db_metrics_ext
 (cell_server varchar2(100),
  metric_name varchar2(100),
  metric_dtl  varchar2(256),
  dtl_value   number,
  dtl_unit    varchar2(36),
  sample_time varchar2(256))
 organization external
 (type oracle_loader
 default directory my_dir
  access parameters
 (records delimited by newline
 fields terminated by whitespace)
 location ('db_io_load.dat')
 ) reject limit 100000000
/
Table created
```

This script assumes that you have created an Oracle directory named `my_dir` that contains your extract file and also assumes you have a schema named `celliorm` created; you can change these names to meet your needs.

At this point, you can run SQL statements against this external table to report your performance metrics or, optionally, load this external table into a more "permanent" table and use this for a historical storage cell metrics repository.

How It Works

Exadata DMAs generally employ a number of techniques to summarize historical Exadata Storage Server metrics, including the following:

- Saving `cellcli` output to a text file, importing to Excel, and building graphs
- Saving `cellcli` output to a text file and using external tables to load the data into Oracle tables and then using SQL to report on the metric values
- Saving `cellcli` output to a text file and using SQL*Loader to load to Oracle tables
- Using Enterprise Manager with Exadata plug-ins to display Exadata Storage Server performance
- Using R to generate statistical information and plots from `cellcli` output, as discussed in Recipe 13-6

Many Exadata DMAs are comfortable with SQL and elect to save metric history information to an Oracle database in order to retain metric history information beyond the default seven-day retention period. Beyond this, DMAs sometimes prefer a "design once, report many times" strategy that allows them to periodically load `metrichistory` information into database tables rather than remember `cellcli` syntax. While the solution in this recipe is certainly not required for your storage cell monitoring strategy, it is a common approach adapted by many DMAs.

■ **Note** For a more comprehensive tool to create an Oracle repository for IORM metrics, please see `lst13-10-cellscr.zip`. The contents of this zip file include a utility called `celliormbundle.sh`, which extracts I/O Resource Management information from your storage cells, loads the data into an external table, populates a permanent table from this external table, and includes SQL scripts to report on your permanent table. Installation instructions are included in the `README_cellscr.txt` file.

The `lst13-10-cellscr.zip` file also includes two other utilities, `celldig.sh` and `cellstats.sh`. `celldig.sh` provides a menu-driven interface to CellCLI and `cellstats.sh` is a wrapper to `cellcli` that offers a simpler command-line syntax. We have purposefully left the details of these utilities out of this chapter so that you can become familiar with Exadata Storage Server monitoring techniques using native Oracle-supplied tools, but once you are familiar listing and reporting storage server metrics, we encourage you to test these utilities.

13-8. Detecting Cell Disk I/O Bottlenecks

Problem

You wish to determine whether you have Exadata cell disk I/O bottlenecks on your storage grid.

Solution

In this recipe, you will learn how to use Exadata's `CELLDISK` metrics to report I/O bottlenecks. In this context, "I/O bottlenecks" refers to any measured cell disk I/O condition in which a specified threshold value is crossed.

Execute the script in Listing 13-5. This script will display current I/O statistics for small I/O disk bandwidth per second, large I/O disk bandwidth per second, small I/O requests per second, large I/O requests per second, small I/O latency per second, and large I/O latency per second.

Listing 13-5. lst13-05-celldisk-iostats.sh

```
#!/bin/sh
# Name: lst13-06-celldisk-iostats.sh
# Purpose: Show current cell disk metrics
# Usage: ./lst13-06-celldisk-iostats.sh [metriccurrent|metrichistory]
SCOPE=$1                    # run with either metriccurrent or metrichistory
# Adjust the following to suit your needs
CELLGROUP=/home/oracle/cell_group
MBMIN=125                ## 125 MB/second per disk
IORQMIN=120              ## 120 IOPs per disk
LATMIN=10000             ## 10 ms latency
########################################

## Metrics list per type #################################################
MBPS="CD_IO_BY_R_LG_SEC CD_IO_BY_R_SM_SEC CD_IO_BY_W_LG_SEC CD_IO_BY_W_SM_SEC"
IORQ="CD_IO_RQ_R_LG_SEC CD_IO_RQ_R_SM_SEC CD_IO_RQ_W_LG_SEC CD_IO_RQ_W_SM_SEC"
LAT="CD_IO_TM_R_LG_RQ CD_IO_TM_R_SM_RQ CD_IO_TM_W_LG_RQ CD_IO_TM_W_SM_RQ"
##########################################################################

# dcli/cellcli commands
for met in $MBPS
do
echo "Listing ${SCOPE} for ${met} when IO rate > ${MBMIN} MB/second"
dcli -g ${CELLGROUP} "cellcli -e list ${SCOPE} \
      where objectType=\'CELLDISK\' and name=\'${met}\' \
      and metricValue \> ${MBMIN}"
done
for met in $IORQ
do
echo "Listing ${SCOPE} for ${met} when #requests > ${IORQMIN} IO requests/second"
dcli -g ${CELLGROUP} "cellcli -e list ${SCOPE} \
      where objectType=\'CELLDISK\' and name=\'${met}\' \
      and metricValue \> ${IORQMIN}"
done
for met in $LAT
do
echo "Listing ${SCOPE} for ${met} when IO latency > ${LATMIN} microseconds"
dcli -g ${CELLGROUP} "cellcli -e list ${SCOPE} \
      where objectType=\'CELLDISK\' and name=\'${met}\' \
      and metricValue \> ${LATMIN}"
done
[oracle@cm01dbm01 source]$ ./lst13-04-celldisk-iostats.sh metriccurrent
Listing metriccurrent for CD_IO_BY_R_LG_SEC when IO rate > 125 MB/second
... Additional output omitted for brevity
cm01cel02: CD_IO_RQ_R_LG_SEC     CD_00_cm01cel02           152 IO/sec
... Additional output omitted for brevity
Listing metriccurrent for CD_IO_RQ_R_SM_SEC when #requests > 120 IO requests/second
```

```
... Additional output omitted for brevity
Listing metriccurrent for CD_IO_RQ_W_LG_SEC when #requests > 120 IO requests/second
cm01cel01: CD_IO_TM_R_LG_RQ      CD_OO_cm01cel01        275,905 us/request
... Additional output omitted for brevity
Listing metriccurrent for CD_IO_TM_R_SM_RQ when IO latency > 10000 microseconds
cm01cel01: CD_IO_TM_R_SM_RQ      CD_OO_cm01cel01        208,588 us/request
... Additional output omitted for brevity
Listing metriccurrent for CD_IO_TM_W_LG_RQ when IO latency > 10000 microseconds
Listing metriccurrent for CD_IO_TM_W_SM_RQ when IO latency > 10000 microseconds
cm01cel01: CD_IO_TM_W_SM_RQ      CD_OO_cm01cel01         31,724 us/request
... Additional output omitted for brevity
[oracle@cm01dbm01 source]$
```

In Listing 13-5, we are reporting on cell disk metrics in which the I/O bandwidth exceeds 125 MB/second, the number if I/O requests exceeds 120 I/Os per second, and when the average I/O latency exceeds 10 milliseconds, or 10,000 microseconds. These thresholds are defined at the beginning of the script—you can change these values to report on different values as needed.

With the script in Listing 13-5, you can also pass the string `metrichistory` as a command line argument. Doing so will report historical metrics for each of the cell disk metrics defined by the MBPS, IOQQ, and LAT environment variables.

How It Works

The example in this recipe uses the `list metriccurrent` or `list metrichistory` command on a variety of cell disk metrics using a `cellcli` where condition based on a specified set of modifiable thresholds. In Listing 13-5, we used the `where metricValue >` clause to generate a report for all situations that crossed the thresholds hard-coded in the variable declaration section at the top of the script.

Note As an alternative to the script in Listing 13-5, it may be worthwhile to establish cell disk metric thresholds. Please see Recipe 13-4 to learn how to configure metric thresholds for your Exadata cells.

13-9. Measuring Small I/O vs. Large I/O Requests

Problem

You wish to measure the balance of small I/O vs. large I/O requests on Exadata to provide a picture of the balance of I/O requests.

Solution

In this recipe, you will learn how to report the ratio between small I/O and large I/O requests on your Exadata storage grid. Execute the script in Listing 13-6 to measure this ratio.

Listing 13-6. lst13-06-celldisk-smallvslarge.pl

```
#!/usr/bin/perl
# Name: lst13-07-celldisk-smallvslarge.pl
# Usage: ./lst13-07-celldisk-smallvslarge.pl [--g|--c]=[cell group file|list of cells]
```

```perl
use Getopt::Long;
use Text::ParseWords;
sub usage {
 print "Usage: ./lst13-05-celldisk-smallvslarge.pl [--g|--c]=[cell group file|list of cells]\n";
}
## Command line argument handling      ##
GetOptions(
  'cell=s' => \$c,
  'grp=s'  => \$g,
) or die usage;
die usage unless defined($g) || defined ($c);
$dclipref="-g $g" if defined($g);
$dclipref="-c $c" if defined($c);
## End Command line argument handling ##
foreach $metric ("CD_IO_RQ_R_SM","CD_IO_RQ_R_LG") {
 open(F,"dcli ${dclipref} \"cellcli -e list metriccurrent where name like \'${metric}\'\"|");
 while (<F>) {
  @words=quotewords('\\s+', 0, $_);
  $words[3]=~ s/,//g;
  $iot{total} += $words[3];
  $ios{HardDisk} += $words[3] if ($words[2]=~ /^CD/) && ($metric=~/SM/);
       # assumes hard disks start with CD
  $ios{FlashDisk} += $words[3] if ($words[2]=~ /^FD/) && ($metric=~/SM/);
       # assumes flash disks start with FD
  $iol{HardDisk} += $words[3]  if ($words[2]=~ /^CD/) && ($metric=~/LG/);
       # assumes hard disks start with CD
  $iol{FlashDisk} += $words[3] if ($words[2]=~ /^FD/) && ($metric=~/LG/);
       # assumes flash disks start with FD
 }
 close(F);
}
printf "%-40s=%8.0f\n", "Small IO Requests for Hard Disks", $ios{HardDisk};
printf "%-40s=%8.0f\n", "Small IO Requests for Flash Disks", $ios{FlashDisk};
printf "%-40s=%8.0f\n", "Large IO Requests for Hard Disks", $iol{HardDisk};
printf "%-40s=%8.0f\n", "Large IO Requests for Flash Disks", $iol{FlashDisk};
printf "%-40s=%8.2f%\n", "% of Large IO Requests for Hard Disks",
                                100*($iol{HardDisk}/($iol{HardDisk} + $ios{HardDisk}));
printf "%-40s=%8.2f%\n", "% of Large IO Requests for All Disks",
                                100*(($iol{HardDisk}+$iol{FlashDisk})/$iot{total});


[oracle@cm01dbm01 source]$ ./lst13-03-celldisk-smallvslarge.pl --c=cm01cel01

Small IO Requests for Hard Disks         = 11332358
Small IO Requests for Flash Disks        = 17426074
Large IO Requests for Hard Disks         = 22468541
Large IO Requests for Flash Disks        = 0
% of Large IO Requests for Hard Disks    = 66.47%
% of Large IO Requests for All Disks     = 43.86%
[oracle@cm01dbm01 source]$
```

How It Works

On Exadata Storage Servers, small I/O requests are defined as I/O requests smaller than 128 KB and large I/O requests are larger than 128 KB. Each cell disk I/O metric has both a small I/O and large I/O measurement. This is important on Exadata because large I/O requests are more likely to yield cell offload and Smart Scan performance savings. Measuring the ratio of small I/O requests to large I/O requests, then, can be a mechanism to measure the likelihood of your workload from being able to leverage some of Exadata's important performance features.

In the solution of this recipe, we used CellCLI's `list metriccurrent` command for the small I/O and large I/O IOPs-related metrics for both hard disks and flash disks and reported on the total number of requests along with the ratio between the two types.

13-10. Detecting Grid Disk I/O Bottlenecks
Problem

You wish to diagnose Exadata grid disk I/O bottlenecks on your Exadata storage grid.

Solution

In this recipe, you will learn how to use Exadata's `GRIDDISK` metrics to measure I/O bottlenecks for your Exadata grid disks. Execute the script in Listing 13-7, which will display I/O statistics for your grid disks in which the metric values exceed predefined thresholds.

Listing 13-7. lst13-07-griddisk-iostats.sh

```
#!/bin/sh
# Name: lst13-08-griddisk-iostats.sh
# Purpose: Show current grid disk metrics
# Usage: ./lst13-08-griddisk-iostats.sh [metriccurrent|metrichistory]

SCOPE=$1                # run with either metriccurrent or metrichistory

# Adjust the following to suit your needs
CELLGROUP=/home/oracle/cell_group
MBMIN=1                 ## 1 MB/second per disk
IORQMIN=120             ## 10 IOPs per disk
LATMIN=10000            ## 10 ms latency
#########################################

## Metrics list per type ####################################################
MBPS="GD_IO_BY_R_LG_SEC GD_IO_BY_R_SM_SEC GD_IO_BY_W_LG_SEC GD_IO_BY_W_SM_SEC"
IORQ="GD_IO_RQ_R_LG_SEC GD_IO_RQ_R_SM_SEC GD_IO_RQ_W_LG_SEC GD_IO_RQ_W_SM_SEC"
LAT="GD_IO_TM_R_LG_RQ GD_IO_TM_R_SM_RQ GD_IO_TM_W_LG_RQ GD_IO_TM_W_SM_RQ"
#############################################################################

# dcli/cellcli commands
for met in $MBPS
do
echo "Listing ${SCOPE} for ${met} when IO rate > ${MBMIN} MB/second"
dcli -g ${CELLGROUP} "cellcli -e list ${SCOPE} \
```

```
        where objectType=\'GRIDDISK\' and name=\'${met}\' \
        and metricValue \> ${MBMIN}"
done
for met in $IORQ
do
echo "Listing ${SCOPE} for ${met} when #requests > ${IORQMIN} IO requests/second"
dcli -g ${CELLGROUP} "cellcli -e list ${SCOPE} \
        where objectType=\'GRIDDISK\' and name=\'${met}\' \
        and metricValue \> ${IORQMIN}"
done
for met in $LAT
do
echo "Listing ${SCOPE} for ${met} when IO latency > ${LATMIN} microseconds"
dcli -g ${CELLGROUP} "cellcli -e list ${SCOPE} \
        where objectType=\'GRIDDISK\' and name=\'${met}\' \
        and metricValue \> ${LATMIN}"
done

[oracle@cm01dbm01 source]$ ./lst13-06-griddisk-iostats.sh metriccurrent
Listing metriccurrent for GD_IO_BY_R_LG_SEC when IO rate > 1 MB/second
... Output omitted
Listing metriccurrent for GD_IO_RQ_R_LG_SEC when #requests > 10 IO requests/second
... Output omitted
Listing metriccurrent for GD_IO_TM_R_LG_RQ when IO latency > 10000 microseconds
... Output omitted
 [oracle@cm01dbm01 source]$
```

In Listing 13-7, we are reporting on grid disk metrics in which the I/O bandwidth exceeds 1 MB/second, the number if I/O requests exceeds 10 I/Os per second, and when the average I/O latency exceeds 10 milliseconds, or 10,000 microseconds. These thresholds are defined at the beginning of the script—you can change these values to report on different values as needed.

How It Works

The example in this recipe uses the `list metriccurrent` or `list metrichistory` command on a variety of grid disk metrics using a `cellcli where` condition based on a specified set of modifiable thresholds. In Listing 13-7, we used the `where metricValue >` clause to generate a report for all situations that crossed the thresholds hard-coded in the variable declaration section at the top of the script.

■ **Note** As an alternative to the script in Listing 13-7, it may be worthwhile to establish grid disk metric thresholds. Please see Recipe 13-4 to learn how to configure metric thresholds for your Exadata cells.

13-11. Detecting Host Interconnect Bottlenecks

Problem

You wish to diagnose host interconnect performance issues or bottlenecks.

Solution

In this recipe, you will learn how to use HOST_INTERCONNECT metrics to identify network bottlenecks on your Exadata storage grid. Execute the script in Listing 13-8, which will display network metrics for network drops, RDMA network drops, and resent/RDMA retry operations in units of MB per second. If the script displays output, it is an indication that you have a network issue of some sort.

Listing 13-8. lst13-08-interconnect-probs.sh

```
#!/bin/sh
# Name: lst13-09-interconnect-probs.sh
# Purpose: Show host interconnect metrics above threshold
# Usage: ./lst13-09-interconnect-probs.sh [metriccurrent|metrichistory]

SCOPE=$1                      # run with either metriccurrent or metrichistory

# Adjust the following to suit your needs
CELLGROUP=/home/oracle/cell_group
MBMIN=0                       ## 0 MB/second for each type of dtop
#########################################

## Metrics list per type #####################################################
MBPS="N_MB_DROP_SEC N_MB_RDMA_DROP_SEC N_MB_RESENT_SEC"
##############################################################################

# dcli/cellcli commands
for met in $MBPS
do
echo "Listing ${SCOPE} for ${met} when IO rate > ${MBMIN} MB/second"
dcli -g ${CELLGROUP} "cellcli -e list ${SCOPE} \
        where objectType=\'HOST_INTERCONNECT\' and name=\'${met}\' \
        and metricValue \> ${MBMIN}"
done

[oracle@cm01dbm01 source]$ ./lst13-07-interconnect-probs.sh metriccurrent
Listing metriccurrent for N_MB_DROP_SEC when IO rate > 0 MB/second
Listing metriccurrent for N_MB_RDMA_DROP_SEC when IO rate > 0 MB/second
Listing metriccurrent for N_MB_RESENT_SEC when IO rate > 0 MB/second
[oracle@cm01dbm01 source]$
```

In Listing 13-8, we are reporting on HOST_INTERCONNECT metrics in which the network drops and retransmission rates are above 0 MB per second; ideally, your machine should not experience network drops. These thresholds are defined at the beginning of the script—you can change these values to report on different values as needed.

How It Works

The example in this recipe uses the `list metriccurrent` or `list metrichistory` command on a variety of HOST_INTERCONNECT metrics using a `cellcli` where condition based on a specified set of modifiable thresholds. In Listing 13-8, we used the `where metricValue >` clause to generate a report for all situations that crossed the thresholds hard-coded in the variable declaration section at the top of the script.

> **Note** As an alternative to the script in Listing 13-8, it may be worthwhile to establish host interconnect metric thresholds. Please see Recipe 13-4 to learn how to configure metric thresholds for your Exadata cells.

13-12. Measuring I/O Load and Waits per Database, Resource Consumer Group, and Resource Category

Problem

You wish to measure the I/O resource load per database, resource consumer group, or resource category on your Exadata Database Machine.

Solution

In this recipe, you will learn how to use IORM_DATABASE, IORM_CONSUMER_GROUP, and IORM_CATEGORY metrics to measure the I/O load and IORM-induced waits for your databases, resource consumer groups, and resource categories.

> **Note** To learn more about I/O Resource Management, please see Chapter 17.

Measuring I/O Load and I/O Waits per Database

To determine which databases are generating the most I/O load, run the following `cellcli` command from `dcli` using the DB_IO_LOAD metric:

```
[oracle@cm01dbm01 ~]$ dcli -g ./cell_group "cellcli -e list metriccurrent \
> where name=\'DB_IO_LOAD\'"
cm01cel01: DB_IO_LOAD      DWPRD           1
cm01cel01: DB_IO_LOAD      EDW             9
cm01cel01: DB_IO_LOAD      VISX            1
cm01cel01: DB_IO_LOAD      VISY            2
... Output omitted for brevity
```

To measure the small and large I/O waits per request per database, use the DB_IO_WT_.*_RQ metrics with the following `dcli` command:

```
[oracle@cm01dbm01 ~]$ dcli -g ./cell_group "cellcli -e list metriccurrent \
> where objectType=\'IORM_DATABASE\'  \
> and name like \'DB_IO_WT_.*_RQ\'"
```

```
cm01cel01: DB_IO_WT_LG_RQ        DWPRD           0.0 ms/request
cm01cel01: DB_IO_WT_LG_RQ        EDW             0.0 ms/request
... Output omitted
cm01cel01: DB_IO_WT_SM_RQ        DWPRD           0.0 ms/request
cm01cel01: DB_IO_WT_SM_RQ        EDW             0.0 ms/request
... Output omitted
```

Measuring I/O Load and I/O Waits per Resource Consumer Group

To determine which consumer groups are contributing the most to your Exadata I/O load to your hard disks, run the following cellcli command using the CG_IO_LOAD metric:

```
[oracle@cm01dbm01 ~]$ dcli -g ./cell_group "cellcli -e list metriccurrent \
where objectType=\'IORM_CONSUMER_GROUP\' \
and name=\'CG_IO_LOAD\'"
... Output omitted
```

To measure the small and large I/O waits per resource consumer group, use the CG_IO_WT_.*_RQ metrics with the following dcli command:

```
[oracle@cm01dbm01 ~]$ dcli -g ./cell_group "cellcli -e list metriccurrent \
> where objectType=\'IORM_CONSUMER_GROUP\' \
> and name like \'CG_IO_WT_.*_RQ\'"
cm01cel01: CG_IO_WT_LG_RQ        DWPRD.OTHER_GROUPS              0.0 ms/request
cm01cel01: CG_IO_WT_LG_RQ        DWPRD.SYS_GROUP                 0.0 ms/request
cm01cel01: CG_IO_WT_LG_RQ        DWPRD._ORACLE_LOWPRIBG_GROUP_   0.0 ms/request
cm01cel01: CG_IO_WT_LG_RQ        DWPRD._ORACLE_LOWPRIFG_GROUP_   0.0 ms/request
... Output omitted
```

Measuring I/O Load and I/O Waits per Resource Category

To determine which resource categories are contributing the most to your Exadata I/O load to your hard disks, run the following cellcli command using the CT_IO_LOAD metric:

```
[oracle@cm01dbm01 ~]$  dcli -g ./cell_group "cellcli -e list metriccurrent \
> where objectType=\'IORM_CATEGORY\' \
> and name=\'CT_IO_LOAD\'"
cm01cel01: CT_IO_LOAD    CAT_HIGH        0
cm01cel01: CT_IO_LOAD    CAT_LOW         0
cm01cel01: CT_IO_LOAD    CAT_MEDIUM      0
cm01cel01: CT_IO_LOAD    OTHER           0
cm01cel01: CT_IO_LOAD    _ASM_           0
[oracle@cm01dbm01 ~]$
```

To measure the small and large I/O waits per resource consumer group, use the CT_IO_WT_.*_RQ metrics with the following dcli command:

```
[oracle@cm01dbm01 ~]$ dcli -g ./cell_group "cellcli -e list metriccurrent \
> where objectType=\'IORM_CATEGORY\' \
> and name like \'CT_IO_WT_.*_RQ\'"
```

```
cm01cel01:  CT_IO_WT_LG_RQ        CAT_HIGH                0.0 ms/request
cm01cel01:  CT_IO_WT_LG_RQ        CAT_LOW                 0.0 ms/request
cm01cel01:  CT_IO_WT_LG_RQ        CAT_MEDIUM              0.0 ms/request
cm01cel01:  CT_IO_WT_LG_RQ        OTHER                   0.0 ms/request
```

How It Works

Exadata provides three types of metrics for I/O resource management: database, consumer group, and category. With few exceptions, the metrics for each of these object types are the same and provide utilization, wait, and load information for databases, consumer groups, and categories.

Monitoring I/O load and I/O wait statistics per database and consumer provides an excellent means to measure the relative contribution to your overall I/O workload on your database machine. Database IORM statistics are populated regardless of whether you have an IORM plan enabled on your storage cells because Exadata tags each I/O request with the database name.

CHAPTER 14

Host and Database Performance Monitoring

Performance monitoring for databases, compute nodes, and storage cells in an Exadata Database Machine can be performed using a number of available operating system tools, Oracle scripts, and Oracle Enterprise Manager. Exadata's compute nodes run either Oracle Linux or Solaris 11 Express, and Exadata Storage Servers run Oracle Linux. As such, both traditional Linux and Solaris performance-monitoring tools are available to the Exadata DMA to monitor server performance. Additionally, Exadata runs the Oracle 11gR2 database and is capable of being integrated with Oracle Enterprise Manager, so an Exadata DMA's traditional performance monitoring tools will likely be the same as the tools, software, and utilities used in a non-Exadata environment.

In this chapter, we will provide guidance for how to monitor Exadata-specific performance aspects using operating system tools and utilities, Oracle scripts, and Oracle Enterprise Manager. Throughout this chapter, we will demonstrate performance-monitoring techniques that are applicable for Oracle 11g, whether you are running on an Exadata Database Machine or not. Since many organizations implement Exadata to address database performance, it is important for the Exadata DMA to build a well-developed tool set of performance tools and processes in order to quickly identify and triage performance issues.

14-1. Collecting Historical Compute Node and Storage Cell Host Performance Statistics

Problem

You wish to collect historical CPU statistics, virtual memory statistics, disk device level I/O statistics, Ethernet network statistics, disk drive statistics on the compute nodes, summarized I/O statistics on the storage cells, top resource-consuming operating system process information, and InfiniBand protocol network statistics on your Exadata's compute nodes and storage cells.

Solution

In this recipe, you will learn how to identify and locate output generated by Oracle's OSWatcher utility to examine historical performance statistics for various hardware, operating systems, and process information spanning your processors, memory, disks, and network interfaces in the Exadata infrastructure stack. We will specifically show you how to locate the specific output files generated by OSWatcher for each of the aforementioned components and provide a brief explanation about the tasks each OSWatcher subprogram executes.

Note This recipe does not provide an in-depth explanation for how to interpret the results of each OSWatcher subprogram. We assume that an Exadata DMA will already be familiar with most, if not all, of these utilities. If this is not the case, please refer to the man page for each referenced utility or perform a Google search to learn more about the output each utility generates.

OSWatcher spawns multiple subprograms, each of which collects performance statistics for a different component of the machine. Each subprogram is located in the /opt/oracle.oswatcher/osw directory and spawns its command output to a subdirectory under /opt/oracle.oswatcher/osw/archive, as displayed below, on both the compute nodes and storage cells:

```
[root@cm01dbm01 ~]# ls /opt/oracle.oswatcher/osw/archive
ExadataOSW       oswdiskstats   oswmpstat     oswps         oswvmstat
ExadataRDS       oswiostat      oswnetstat    oswslabinfo
Oswcellsrvstat   oswmeminfo     oswprvtnet    oswtop
[root@cm01dbm01 ~]#
```

Locate the output files for the performance metric of your choice by referring to Table 14-1.

Table 14-1. *Summarized OSWatcher Information*

Component	Subprogram	Command Used	Sample	Runs on . . .	Output
CPU statistics	Exadata_mpstat.sh	mpstat	5 sec	Both node types	oswmpstat
Virtual memory statistics	Exadata_vmstat.sh	vmstat	5 sec	Both node types	oswvmstat
Ethernet network statistics	Exadata_netstat.sh	netstat	15 sec	Both node types	oswnetstat
Device I/O statistics	Exadata_iostat.sh	iostat	5 sec	Both node types	oswiostat
Disk statistics	Exadata_diskstats.sh	/proc/diskstats	5 sec	Compute nodes	oswdiskstats
Top sessions	Exadata_top.sh	top	5 sec	Both node types	oswtop
InfiniBand RDS statistics	ExadataRdsInfo.sh	rds-ping	10 sec	Both node types	ExadataRDS
Summarized cell server statistics	Exadata_cellsrvstat.sh	cellsrvstat	10 sec	Cell servers	oswcellsrvstat
Host memory usage	OSWatcher.sh	/proc/meminfo	15 sec	Both node type	oswmemstat
Process listing	OSWatcher.sh	ps	15 sec	Both node types	oswps
Kernel slab allocator statistics	OSWatcher.sh	/proc/slabinfo	15 sec	Both node types	oswslabinfo

Using the output file directories provided in the rightmost column in Table 14-1, you will find a number of files in each archive output directory. Older files will be compressed with bzip2 and the most recent statistics will have a .dat file extension. View the file of your choice using vi, more, tail, less, or the editor/viewer of your choice. Following are the first ten lines of our CPU statistics from an Exadata Compute Node:

```
[root@cm01dbm01 oswmpstat]# head -5 cm01dbm01.centroid.com_mpstat_12.11.06.1200.dat
zzz ***Tue Nov 6 12:03:56 EST 2012 Sample interval: 5 seconds
Linux 2.6.32-400.1.1.el5uek (cm01dbm01.centroid.com)      11/06/12
12:03:56    CPU   %user   %nice   %sys %iowait   %irq  %soft  %steal  %idle   intr/s
12:04:01    all    0.52    0.00   0.51    0.00   0.00   0.01    0.00  98.95 11620.44
12:04:06    all    0.36    0.00   0.36    0.01   0.00   0.00    0.00  99.27 11234.06
[root@cm01dbm01 oswmpstat]#
```

To view an older, compressed file, use the following bzcat command:

```
[root@cm01dbm01 oswmpstat]# bzcat cm01dbm01.centroid.com_mpstat_12.11.06.1200.dat.bz2 \
> head -10
zzz ***Tue Nov 6 12:03:56 EST 2012 Sample interval: 5 seconds
Linux 2.6.32-400.1.1.el5uek (cm01dbm01.centroid.com)      11/06/12
12:03:56    CPU   %user   %nice   %sys %iowait   %irq  %soft  %steal  %idle   intr/s
12:04:01    all    0.52    0.00   0.51    0.00   0.00   0.01    0.00  98.95 11620.44
12:04:06    all    0.36    0.00   0.36    0.01   0.00   0.00    0.00  99.27 11234.06
[root@cm01dbm01 oswmpstat]#
```

How It Works

Exadata automatically runs a pre-configured set of operating system performance monitoring tools with the OSWatcher utility. OSWatcher is spawned at system initialization as follows:

1. At run levels 2, 3, 4, and 5, the compute nodes and storage cells invoke S99local

2. S99local calls /etc/rc.d/rc.Oracle.Exadata

3. /etc/rc.d/rc.Oracle.Exadata runs Exadata's validation framework, /opt/oracle.cellos/vldrun

4. vldrun performs a number of tasks, including invoking /opt/oracle.cellos//validations/init.d/oswatcher

5. /opt/oracle.cellos/validations/init.d/oswatcher starts the OSWatcher utility and spawns the subprograms to collect each of the performance statistics

When OSWatcher starts, it will automatically spawn multiple subprograms. Using the following pstree listing, you can see the operating system process hierarchy:

```
[root@cm01dbm01 etc]# pstree -aAhlup 'pgrep OSWwatcher'|more
init,1

  |-OSWatcher.sh,16601 ./OSWatcher.sh 15 168 bzip2 3
  |   |-OSWatcherFM.sh,16894 ./OSWatcherFM.sh 168 3
  |   |-oswsub.sh,16914 ./oswsub.sh HighFreq ./Exadata_vmstat.sh
  |   |    '-Exadata_vmstat.,16920 ./Exadata_vmstat.sh HighFreq
  |   |         '-vmstat,24750 5 720
```

```
        |    |-oswsub.sh,16915 ./oswsub.sh HighFreq ./Exadata_mpstat.sh
        |    |    '-Exadata_mpstat.,16922 ./Exadata_mpstat.sh HighFreq
        |    |         '-mpstat,25319 5 720
        |    |-oswsub.sh,16916 ./oswsub.sh HighFreq ./Exadata_netstat.sh
        |    |    '-Exadata_netstat,16924 ./Exadata_netstat.sh HighFreq
        |    |         '-sleep,16069 15
        |    |-oswsub.sh,16917 ./oswsub.sh HighFreq ./Exadata_iostat.sh
        |    |    '-Exadata_iostat.,16926 ./Exadata_iostat.sh HighFreq
        |    |         '-iostat,24694 -t -x 5 720
        |    |-oswsub.sh,16918 ./oswsub.sh HighFreq ./Exadata_diskstats.sh
        |    |    '-Exadata_disksta,16928 ./Exadata_diskstats.sh HighFreq
        |    |         '-sleep,16064 5
        |    |-oswsub.sh,16919 ./oswsub.sh HighFreq ./Exadata_top.sh
        |    |    '-Exadata_top.sh,16930 ./Exadata_top.sh HighFreq
        |    |         '-top,31419 -b -c -d 5 -n 720
        |    '-oswsub.sh,16927 ./oswsub.sh HighFreq /opt/oracle.oswatcher/osw/ExadataRdsInfo.sh
        |         '-ExadataRdsInfo.,16941 /opt/oracle.oswatcher/osw/ExadataRdsInfo.sh HighFreq
```

As part of its normal operation, OSWatcher will automatically compress older output files using `bzip2` and retain seven days of compressed statistics files in the `/opt/oracle.oswatcher/osw/archive/*` directories.

It is worth mentioning that OSWatcher is not an Exadata-specific utility. Oracle has modified the default OSWatcher utility that is shipped with Exadata to include Exadata-specific metrics and output. The stand-alone version of OSWatcher is currently described in My Oracle Support document 301137.1 and includes references to a graphical tool called the OSWBB, or OSWatcher Black Box Analyzer. This current OSWBB plotting utility will unfortunately not work on Exadata's customized OSWatcher output files, so graphing your host performance metrics generally requires manual scripting and graphing. We recommend using Perl and R to perform these tasks, but specific examples are beyond the scope of this recipe.

14-2. Displaying Real-Time Compute Node and Storage Cell Performance Statistics

Problem

You wish to perform real-time performance monitoring for multiple performance metrics on your Exadata Compute Nodes and storage cells without having to independently execute and collect output for individual host commands such as `sar`, `iostat`, and `vmstat`.

Solution

In this recipe, you will learn how to install and use `collectl` on your Exadata Compute Nodes and storage cells to report on various performance utilization metrics.

Note The `collectl` utility is not installed by default on Exadata. Oracle prohibits installing unsupported software on your Exadata Compute Nodes and storage cells and, as such, the steps contained in this recipe are not strictly supported. Having said this, in our experience, `collectl` is a tool used by many experienced Exadata DMAs and Oracle employees and poses no risk to your environment.

Download and Install collectl and collectl-utils

The collectl and collectl-utils software is located at collectl.sourceforge.net and collectl-utils.sourceforge.net, respectively. Download the software from these locations, transfer the files to each node in your Exadata Database Machine to a directory of your choice, uncompress and untar the contents, and install them using the INSTALL program as root. Refer to the README files for each utility for more information.

Installing collectl and its utilities will place Perl scripts in /usr/bin on each node. The /usr/bin/collectl script is the main collectl program and, in this recipe, we will also demonstrate using /usr/bin/colmux to collate collectl information from multiple Exadata nodes.

■ **Note** gnuplot is not installed on the Exadata Compute Nodes or storage cells, so the installation of collectl-utils will generate a warning message. You can safely ignore this message, but bear in mind that plotting functionality with colplot will not be available. To graph collectl output, you can use Excel, plot using R scripts, or use the graphing tool of your choice.

Execute collectl with No Command Line Options

To get a feel for collectl's output, simply execute collectl while logged in as any user on the nodes that you have installed the software on. When you execute the collectl program without arguments, the default output will display CPU utilization statistics, disk I/O statistics, and Ethernet network performance statistics:

```
[root@cm01dbm01 ~]# collectl
waiting for 1 second sample...
#<----CPU[HYPER]-----><----------Disks-----------><----------Network---------->
#cpu sys inter  ctxsw KBRead  Reads KBWrit Writes  KBIn PktIn  KBOut  PktOut
   0   0 11554  18592      0      0      0      0     1    11      6       8
   1   0 12013  19333      0      0      0      0     4    18      2      19
   0   0 10767  18487      0      0    824     32     1     8      7       8
   1   0 12195  20860      0      0      0      0     0     3      0       3
... Output omitted for brevity
[root@cm01dbm01 ~]#
```

Running collectl on a Single Node

collectl includes a number of command line arguments and switches to tailor the output to your needs. By default, collect uses the **-scdn** command line switch, where s represents the switch arguments, c denotes CPU utilization, d indicates disk I/O statistics, and n represents Ethernet network information. As you can see, collectl allows you to report multiple operating system performance statistics on a single line in real time.

Use collectl -showoptions and collectl -x to display the collectl help and command line switches that are available. Additionally, you can find this information in collectl's man page.

On Exadata Database Machines, several performance metrics may be important to monitor. With collectl, these are referred to as subsystems. Some of the more commonly monitored subsystems with collectl are CPU utilization, disk I/O, InfiniBand interconnect statistics, and memory information. To collect data from these subsystems, issue the following `collectl` command:

```
[root@cm01dbm01 ~]# collectl -sdcmx
waiting for 1 second sample...
#<--CPU[HYPER]--><-----------Memory------------><----------Disks----------><----InfiniBand---->
                                                                                           Pkt
#cpu sys inter ctxsw Free Buff Cach Inac Slab Map KBRd Rds KBWrit Wrts KBIn PktIn KBOut Out Errs
   1   0 13017 20251   3G   1G  23G   5G  11G 12G    0   0    364   15  193   417   204 430    0
   0   0 12533 20474   3G   1G  23G   5G  11G 12G    0   0    540   30  473   524   401 488    0
   0   0 11359 18804   3G   1G  23G   5G  11G 12G    0   0      0    0  167   272   420 385    0
   0   0 11214 18838   3G   1G  23G   5G  11G  2G    0   0      0    0  468   476   153 327    0
   1   0 11886 18775   3G   1G  23G   5G  11G 12G    0   0      0    0 1515  1193   572 762    0
..Output omitted for brevity
```

As you can see, the more subsystems you provide to the `collectl` switch argument, the wider the output becomes; by default, `collectl` will report all metrics on a single line.

Run collectl to Report Verbose Information for a Subsystem or Subsystems

To collect more granular performance metrics, execute `collectl` with capitalized subsystem command line switches. For example, the following command will report per-thread CPU utilization metrics using the –sD switch:

```
[root@cm01dbm01 ~]# collectl -sC
waiting for 1 second sample...
# SINGLE CPU[HYPER] STATISTICS
#   Cpu  User Nice  Sys Wait IRQ  Soft Steal  Idle
      0     0    0    0    0   0     0     0   100
      1     0    0    1    0   0     0     0    99
      2     0    0    0    0   0     0     0    99
... Output omitted
```

Monitoring Exadata Compute Nodes and Storage Cells Simultaneously

To report performance metrics for various subsystems across multiple Exadata nodes in parallel, use the `colmux` utility, delivered with `collectl-utils`. The following command reports CPU and disk I/O statistics for each compute node and storage cell in an Exadata Quarter Rack:

```
[oracle@cm01dbm01 ~]$colmux -addr cm01dbm01,cm01dbm02,celladmin@cm01cel01,celladmin@cm01cel02, \
-> celladmin@cm01cel03 -command "-scd" -column 0
# Tue Nov  6 17:53:45 2012  Connected: 5 of 5
#              <-----CPU[HYPER]----->         <--------------Disks-------------->
#Host          cpu sys inter   ctxsw       KBRead     Reads    KBWrit     Writes
cm01dbm02       27   0 22333   25120            0         0         0          0
cm01dbm01       33   5 24016   26147            0         0         0          0
cm01cel03       88   1 21282   14473        1787K      1832       283         57
cm01cel02       84   4 27150  115435        1747K      1772       147         11
cm01cel01       93   2 16448   12263        1641K      1678      2026         97
^C
[oracle@cm01dbm01 ~]$
```

In this command, the following things have occurred:

- We chose to run `colmux` from an Exadata Compute Node as the `oracle` operating system account because this account has SSH keys distributed to each node in our Exadata cluster.
- The `-addr` command line argument specifies a comma-separated list of hosts to collect performance information from. For our storage cells, we used the format `celladmin@<cell>` to allow for password-less authentications
- We specified the `-scd` command line arguments, which cause `colmux` to run `collectl` with the same switches and display CPU and I/O subsystem statistics.

Saving collectl Output to a File

To save `collectl` output to a text file, use the `-f` command line argument to `collectl`. This is useful when you wish to perform additional analysis on your performance output, including graphing or plotting.

How It Works

The `collectl` utility is designed to efficiently collect system performance data across a variety of subsystems on a machine or machines. Because of its depth of performance analysis scope, flexibility of terminal or file output, and ability to simultaneously report performance statistics across multiple machines, many Exadata DMAs view `collectl` as an invaluable tool to collect performance metrics.

Oracle ships a modified version of `OSWatcher` on each Exadata Compute Node and storage cell, as discussed in Recipe 14-1. `OSWatcher` is Oracle's officially supported tool of choice for host level performance data collection, but since `OSWatcher` is simply a wrapper around individual host-monitoring commands, it lacks the ability to report on multiple types of metrics (or subsystems, in `collectl` vernacular) simultaneously. `OSWatcher` also lacks the ability to continuously display performance metrics over a specified interval and duration, as is possible with `collectl` command line switches; with `OSWatcher`, the DMA needs to modify the sampling intervals and retroactively assimilate and report on various operating system utilization and performance metrics.

As mentioned in the solution of this recipe, the `collectl-utils` package includes several additional `collectl` utilities including `colmux`. `colmux` enables you to simultaneously collect metrics from one or more subsystems across nodes in an Exadata Database Machine, which makes it an ideal tool for larger racks.

Gathering performance data is typically the first step in building a host-performance-monitoring strategy. Summarizing and plotting output is also typically required to round out your host-monitoring portfolio, and in lieu of tools such as Oracle Enterprise Manager, raw data from `collectl` and `colmux` can be used to feed the summary and graphing tool of your choice.

14-3. Monitoring Exadata with Enterprise Manager
Problem

You have Oracle Enterprise Manager 12c Cloud Control installed in your organization, and you wish to monitor Exadata performance using Enterprise Manager.

Solution

In this recipe, you will learn how to use the Enterprise Manager 12c Cloud Control browser interface to monitor Exadata-specific performance information. You will specifically learn how to locate your Exadata targets in 12c Cloud Control, use the Resource Utilization features, display the overall topology of your Exadata Database Machine, view the InfiniBand switch topology, monitor performance of your Exadata Storage Grid and its components, and display Exadata-specific database performance information.

■ **Note** This recipe assumes a working knowledge of Oracle Enterprise Manager and a general grasp of Enterprise Manager terminology. We will not present Enterprise Manager "basics" in this recipe; rather, we will focus on Exadata-specific Enterprise Manager monitoring. This recipe also assumes that the Exadata DMA has discovered an Exadata Database Machine in EM 12c Cloud Control. If you have not yet done this, please refer to Recipe 20-1.

Locating Your Exadata Targets in Cloud Control

Log in to Enterprise Manager 12c Cloud Control and navigate to Targets-Exadata as displayed in Figure 14-1.

Figure 14-1. *Locating Exadata targets in Enterprise Manager Cloud Control*

After selecting Exadata, your Exadata Database Machine (or Machines) will be displayed. Click on the target name to open the main Exadata Database Machine page. Once you select your database machine, a number of panes will be displayed including a target navigation pane, the target availability overview window, and a database machine schematic.

Viewing Performance Information on Your Exadata Storage Grid

To view performance and configuration information for your Exadata Storage Grid, or storage cells, select the Exadata Grid from the main Exadata target navigation page. The Exadata Storage Grid page displays Overview, Performance, Capacity, Workload Distribution by Database, ASM Diskgroup summary, and Incidents panes. Figure 14-2 shows the Performance pane, which includes a portion of the I/O load, CPU utilization, network utilization, and response time statistics for your storage cells.

CHAPTER 14 ■ HOST AND DATABASE PERFORMANCE MONITORING

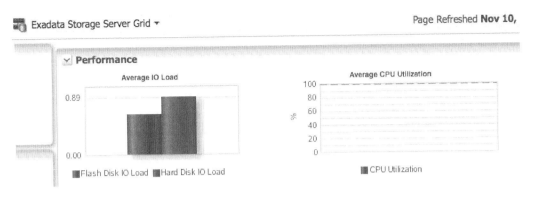

Figure 14-2. Exadata Storage Grid performance summary

Next, drill down on the Exadata Storage Server Grid drop-down and select Performance. From this window, you can view more granular performance information from your storage cells. Figure 14-3 shows a portion of a two-day workload distribution per database.

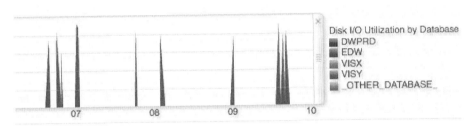

Figure 14-3. Workload distribution per database

Viewing Exadata-Specific Performance Information for Your Databases

The methods to monitor and view performance information for Exadata databases with Enterprise Manager is similar to what you would use for non-Exadata databases, with a few interesting exceptions. First, choose a cluster database target from Enterprise Manager and select one of your instances, and then navigate to the main performance page for the instance by selecting the Performance Home option under the Performance menu. Below the Average Active Sessions window, you will find four tabs that read *Throughput, I/O, Parallel Execution*, and *Services*. Select the *I/O* tab, as displayed in Figure 14-4.

419

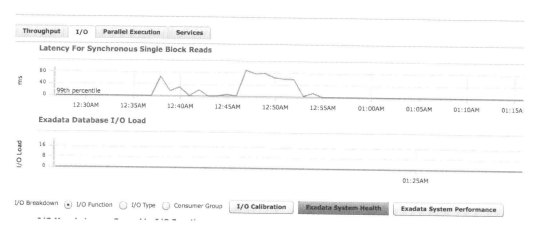

Figure 14-4. *I/O tab on Performance Home page*

You will see two interesting buttons, Exadata System Health and Exadata System Performance. Click the Exadata System Health button and you will be taken to the I/O Load page that displays disk I/O statistics for your storage cells, as displayed in Figure 14-5.

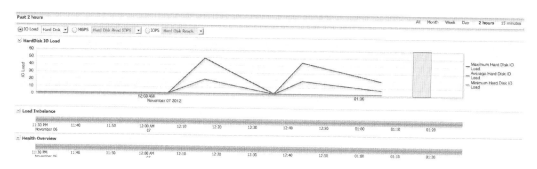

Figure 14-5. *Hard disk I/O load on storage cells*

From the Performance Home page under the I/O tab, select the Exadata System Performance button. Figure 14-6 shows you the total cell disk I/Os per second and I/O load for all cell disks in your storage grid.

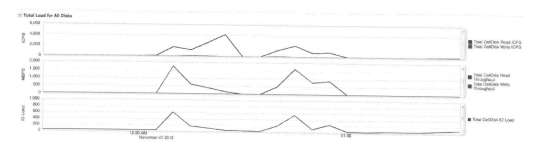

Figure 14-6. *Cell disk IOPs and I/O load*

Finally, from the Performance Home page select below the I/O load section, look at the I/O Megabytes per Second by I/O Function and I/O Requests per Second by I/O Function sections. These portions of the main performance page display data transfer rates and I/Os per second, broken down by the type of I/O being performed. With Exadata, this is a great place to view the use of smart scan and graphically compare the volume and percentage of smart scan I/O requests versus other I/O functions. Figure 14-7 displays that for a specific database we experienced a high volume of smart scan I/O megabytes for a period of time.

Figure 14-7. *I/O megabytes per second by I/O function*

How It Works

Enterprise Manager 12c Cloud Control provides a feature-rich and robust set of solutions for monitoring your Oracle Exadata Database Machine. In this recipe, we have provided a number of solutions to view specific Enterprise Manager monitoring features for Exadata, but what we've provided is by no means exhaustive or comprehensive—the range and depth of monitoring functionality provided by Enterprise Manager for Exadata is a broad topic and worth a text on its own.

To learn more about monitoring Exadata with Enterprise Manager 12c Cloud Control, we recommend reading through Oracle's documentation at www.oracle.com/technetwork/oem/exa-mgmt/exadata-mgmt-twp-1662642.pdf.

14-4. Monitoring Performance with SQL Monitoring
Problem

You wish to perform Real-Time SQL Monitoring on your Oracle 11gR2 Exadata databases in order to gain an in-depth picture of your database's SQL workload.

Solution

In this recipe, you will learn how to use Oracle's 11g Real-Time SQL Monitoring tool to view performance information for SQL statements running on Exadata. We will demonstrate both how to use SQL Monitoring from Enterprise Manager as well as provide methods to use DBMS_SQLTUNE to generate SQL Monitoring reports.

■ **Note** Real-Time SQL Monitoring is not unique to Exadata; it is an Oracle 11g database feature. We are including a SQL Monitoring recipe in this chapter because of its applicability to the topic of performance optimization on Exadata. We believe Real-Time SQL Monitoring is one of the best features introduced into Oracle 11g and with Exadata's "Extreme Performance" promise, provides the best method for visualizing your Oracle SQL statement performance behavior.

Viewing SQL Monitor from Enterprise Manager

Log in to Oracle Enterprise Manager 12c Cloud Control and select a database target that resides on Exadata. By default, the main database page will display a SQL Monitor window similar to Figure 14-8.

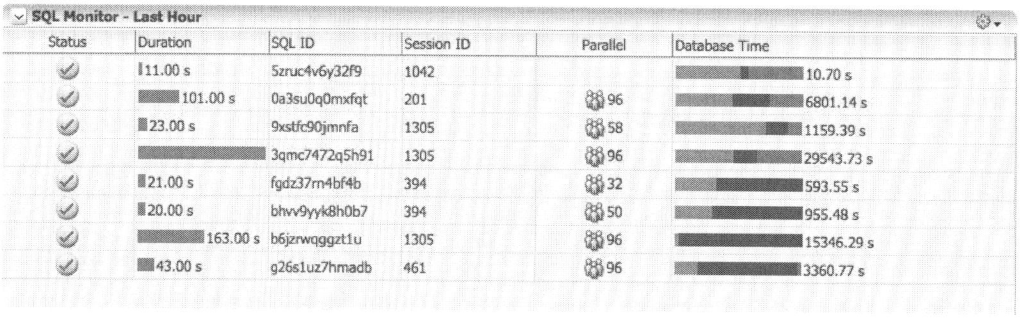

Figure 14-8. SQL Monitor pane from database target landing page

The rightmost column in Figure 14-8 shows the database time per SQL ID and can be used to determine which SQL statements are consuming the most time. From this SQL Monitor window, click a specific SQL ID to drill down into the performance aspects of the SQL cursor. After selecting a SQL ID, you will be presented with the `Monitored SQL Execution Details` page. The Overview panes, displayed in Figure 14-9, show summarized statistics for the SQL execution. In Figure 14-9, we are mousing over the purple area in the `Wait Activity %` section to show the percentage of time spent waiting on smart scans.

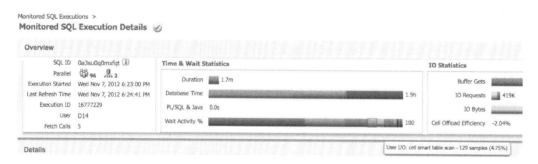

Figure 14-9. Monitored SQL execution details

Below the Overview section, you will see the execution plan for the SQL statement, which we will cover in the next section.

Viewing Monitored SQL Executions and Execution Details

Navigate to the `Performance - Performance Home` page for a specific instance or cluster and then click on the SQL Monitoring link to open the `Monitored SQL Executions` window. Alternatively, navigate directly to the `Performance-SQL Monitoring` page from the main database target window. Regardless of how you access the `Monitored SQL Executions` window, this page differs from the example in the previous section because from here, you can see Real Time SQL Monitoring details, not historical SQL Monitor data. Figure 14-10 displays the Monitored SQL Executions window.

CHAPTER 14 ■ HOST AND DATABASE PERFORMANCE MONITORING

Figure 14-10. Monitored SQL executions

Similar to in the previous section, you can not only see a number of SQL execution details from this main page, but you can also select a SQL ID to drill down into the Monitored SQL Execution Details page. The Overview sections are similar to the examples above, but in Figure 14-11, we are displaying an excerpt showing the SQL execution plan. As you can see, each operation is color-coded and weighted based on time, I/O requests, CPU activity, and so on.

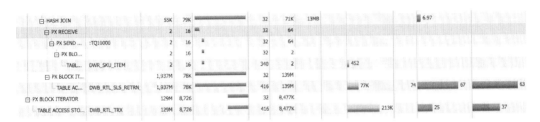

Figure 14-11. SQL plan details from SQL Monitor

Generating SQL Monitoring Reports with dbms_sqltune

If you do not have Enterprise Manager or want an alternative to using the Enterprise Manager, you can use DBMS_SQLTUNE.REPORT_SQL_MONITOR to produce a text- or HTML-based SQL Monitoring report. Use Listing 14-1 to display a SQL Monitor report for a specific SQL ID.

Listing 14-1. lst14-01-sqlmon-sqlid-html.sql

```
SQL> set pagesize 0 echo on timing off
SQL>set linesize 1000 trimspool on trim on
SQL>set long 2000000 longchunksize 2000000
SQL>set echo on
SQL>spool output.html
SQL>select DBMS_SQLTUNE.REPORT_SQL_MONITOR( sql_id=>'&&p_sqlid',
event_detail=>'YES',
report_level=>'ALL',
type=>'HTML')
from dual;
spool off
```

The type parameter is used to specify the report output, which in this case is HTML. If you wish to generate a text file report, you can omit the type attribute or specify the type=>'TEXT' argument.

To report on the current SQL Monitoring data without a specific SQL ID, execute the script in Listing 14-2. This is analogous to navigating to the SQL Monitoring window in Enterprise Manager but generates a point-in-time SQL Monitoring report for active SQL statements.

Listing 14-2. lst14-02-sqlmon-list-text.sql

```
SQL> set pagesize 0 echo on timing off
SQL> set linesize 1000 trimspool on trim on
SQL> set long 2000000 longchunksize 2000000
SQL> select dbms_sqltune.report_sql_monitor_list(
type=>'TEXT',
report_level=>'ALL') as report
from dual;
```

How It Works

Starting with 11g, Oracle introduced a new tool to add to the performance optimizer's toolkit called "Real-Time SQL Monitoring." Real-Time SQL Monitoring, or simply SQL Monitoring, enables you to view and analyze detailed performance statistics for SQL statements.

SQL Monitoring is enabled any time a statement runs in parallel or when it consumes more than five seconds of CPU or I/O time. For large databases on Exadata, these conditions are common. The SQL Monitoring browser interface, text output, and HTML output is externalized from two data dictionary views, V$SQL_MONITOR and V$SQL_PLAN_MONITOR. Oracle populates V$SQL_MONITOR and V$SQL_PLAN_MONITOR views with performance characteristics of running SQL statements and stores these for as long as the SQL_ID remains in the library cache.

The V$SQL_MONITOR view contains key performance statistics for each qualifying SQL statement (a subset of what's in V$SQL) and V$SQL_PLAN_MONITOR provides statistics for each execution path step for the statement. This allows tools such as Enterprise Manager Grid Control to provide a graphical, intuitive representation of the time taken at each step in the path, as well as I/O consumption, CPU consumption, and so on.

Contrary to VSQL, VSQL_MONITOR tracks performance statistics for each execution of a SQL statement, not a summary of accumulated statistics.

As presented in the solution of this recipe, you can view SQL Monitoring data from Enterprise Manager or by using DBMS_SQLTUNE.REPORT_SQL_MONITOR. Whether you use an Enterprise Manager browser interface or use DBMS_SQLTUNE directly, there are a number of nice features with Real-Time SQL Monitoring:

- SQL Monitoring provides intuitive visual feedback that shows you exactly how much time each operation in an execution plan is taking. This is very helpful for an Oracle performance engineer, DBA, or Exadata DMA because it shows you exactly which step or steps to focus your optimization efforts on.

- SQL Monitoring shows not only estimated rows, but also actual rows, for qualifying operations. This helps in determining if the optimizer is not estimating cardinality optimally.

- SQL Monitoring provides the best and most information for parallel query operations, period. All SQL statements with a degree of parallelism greater than 1 are captured in V$SQL_MONITOR, and with SQL Monitoring you see a lot of detail about parallel execution.

- In the Enterprise Manager user interface, the SQL Monitoring details allow for intuitive drill-downs into the query execution plan, query statistics, and so forth.

- The DBMS_SQLTUNE.REPORT_SQL_MONITOR report output displays activity detail for each operation. This activity detail shows statistics including wait event information, CPU information, and so forth, so you can determine which events or statistics contributed time to each operation.

- SQL Monitoring reports on Exadata-specific features such as smart scan and offload efficiency. This provides the Exadata DMA with valuable insight to the benefit of Exadata's performance features for a currently running SQL workload.

CHAPTER 14 ■ HOST AND DATABASE PERFORMANCE MONITORING

Specific to Exadata, one of the SQL execution characteristics commonly monitored is the SQL statement's offload efficiency. The offload efficiency is reported from the `Monitored SQL Execution Details` window in both the I/O statistics section of the Overview pane as well as at a per-operation level in the SQL execution plan, as shown in Figure 14-12.

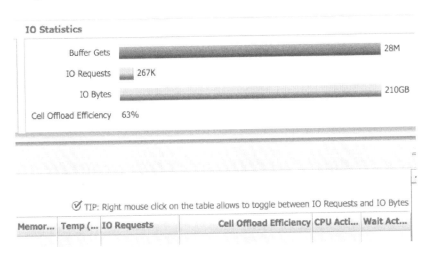

Figure 14-12. Cell offload efficiency from SQL Monitoring

14-5. Monitoring Performance by Database Time

Problem

You wish to collect recent and historical performance statistics for your Exadata databases, focusing on database time and the Average Active Sessions (AAS) metric.

Solution

In this recipe, you will learn how to extract database time-based and AAS performance information using Active Session History (ASH) views.

Monitoring Historical Summarized Database Time and AAS Metrics from ASH

To report on summarized database time and AAS metrics from ASH views for an Oracle 11gR2 database running on Exadata, log in to SQL*Plus and execute the script in Listing 14-3.

Listing 14-3. lst14-03-dbt-ashpast-bytype.sql

```
... Formatting options omitted for brevity
SQL> col bt NEW_VALUE _bt NOPRINT
SQL> col et NEW_VALUE _et NOPRINT
SQL> alter session set nls_date_format='DD-MON-RR HH24:MI:SS';
SQL> select min(cast(sample_time as date)) bt,
  from  dba_hist_active_sess_history
 where to_date(to_char(sample_time,'DD-MON-RR HH24:MI:SS'),'DD-MON-RR HH24:MI:SS')
```

CHAPTER 14 ■ HOST AND DATABASE PERFORMANCE MONITORING

```
between (sysdate-&&days_ago)
        and ((sysdate-&&days_ago)+(&&duration_min/1440));

SQL> WITH xtimes (xdate) AS
  (SELECT to_date('&_bt') xdate FROM dual
  UNION ALL
  SELECT xdate+(&&interval_mins/1440) FROM xtimes
        WHERE xdate+(&&interval_mins/1440) <= to_date('&_et')
  )
select to_char(xdate,'DD-MON-RR HH24:MI:SS') samplestart,
       (sum(decode(wait_class,null,0,dbtw)) over
         (partition by to_char(xdate,'DD-MON-RR HH24:MI:SS'))) smpcnt,
       (sum(decode(wait_class,null,0,dbtw)) over
         (partition by to_char(xdate,'DD-MON-RR HH24:MI:SS')))/60/&&interval_mins aas,
       nvl(wait_class,'*** IDLE *** ') tc,
       decode(wait_class,null,0,dbtw) dbtw,
       decode(wait_class,null,0,dbtw)/60/&&interval_mins aas_comp
from (
       select s1.xdate,wait_class,10*count(*) dbtw,count(ash.smpcnt) smpcnt
         from ( select sample_id, sample_time, session_state,
                       decode(session_state,'ON CPU','CPU + CPU Wait',wait_class) wait_class,
                       10*(count(sample_id) over (partition by sample_id)) smpcnt
                from dba_hist_active_sess_history
                where to_date(to_char(sample_time,'DD-MON-RR HH24:MI:SS'),'DD-MON-RR HH24:MI:SS')
                      between to_date('&_bt') and to_date('&_et'))  ash,
              (select xdate from xtimes ) s1
       where ash.sample_time(+) between s1.xdate and s1.xdate+(&&interval_mins/1440)
       group by s1.xdate,wait_class)
order by 1,dbtw desc
/
BeginTime           DBTimeTotal    AAS    Component         DBTPerMetric   AASPerMetric
------------------  -----------  ------   ---------------   ------------   ------------
08-NOV-12 01:11:46        20.00     .07   CPU + CPU Wait           20.00            .07
08-NOV-12 01:16:46        10.00     .03   System I/O               10.00            .03
08-NOV-12 01:21:46          .00     .00   *** IDLE ***               .00            .00
08-NOV-12 01:26:46        20.00     .07   CPU + CPU Wait           20.00            .07
08-NOV-12 01:31:46        70.00     .23   CPU + CPU Wait           70.00            .23
08-NOV-12 01:36:46        10.00     .03   CPU + CPU Wait           10.00            .03
08-NOV-12 01:41:46     14100.00   47.00   User I/O              11790.00          39.30
                                          CPU + CPU Wait         2210.00           7.37
                                          System I/O               50.00            .17
                                          Scheduler                20.00            .07
                                          Concurrency              20.00            .07
                                          Other                    10.00            .03
08-NOV-12 01:46:46     26870.00   89.57   User I/O              24150.00          80.50
... Output omitted for brevity
```

This script accepts several input variables:

- &&days_ago = the number of days ago to report from. For example, if you enter the number 3, it will limit the output to three days from the time you execute the script.
- &&duration_min = the number of minutes to report on
- &&interval_mins = the number of minutes to summarize the report by

In this output, the first column represents the beginning of the time interval specified by the &&interval_mins input parameter, the second column lists the total database time per time interval, the third column is the total AAS, and the remaining columns list the breakdown of database time and AAS per time "component"; a component, in this context, is defined as either CPU time or wait class.

Monitoring Detailed Historical Database Time and AAS Metrics from ASH

To report detailed database time and AAS metrics, run the script in Listing 14-4. This script is similar to that in Listing 14-3, but it provides additional grouping and detail output including the SQL ID and wait event information.

Listing 14-4. lst14-04-dbt-ashpast-details.sql

```
... Column formatting omitted
SQL> col bt NEW_VALUE _bt NOPRINT
SQL col et NEW_VALUE _et NOPRINT
SQL> select min(cast(sample_time as date)) bt,
max(cast(sample_time as date)) et
from dba_hist_active_sess_history
where to_date(to_char(sample_time,'DD-MON-RR HH24:MI:SS'),'DD-MON-RR HH24:MI:SS')
between (sysdate-&&days_ago)
        and ((sysdate-&&days_ago)+(&&duration_min/1440));

SQL> WITH xtimes (xdate) AS
  (SELECT to_date('&_bt') xdate FROM dual
  UNION ALL
  SELECT xdate+(&&interval_mins/1440) FROM xtimes
        WHERE xdate+(&&interval_mins/1440) <= to_date('&_et')
  )
select to_char(xdate,'DD-MON-RR HH24:MI:SS') samplestart,
       nvl(sql_id,'NULL') sql_id,
       (sum(decode(event,null,0,dbtw)) over
              (partition by to_char(xdate,'DD-MON-RR HH24:MI:SS'))) smpcnt,
       (sum(decode(event,null,0,dbtw)) over
              (partition by to_char(xdate,'DD-MON-RR HH24:MI:SS')))/60/&&interval_mins aas,
       nvl(event,'*** IDLE *** ') tc,
       decode(event,null,0,dbtw) dbtw,
       decode(event,null,0,dbtw)/60/&&interval_mins aas_comp
from (
        select s1.xdate,event,10*count(*) dbtw,sql_id,count(ash.smpcnt) smpcnt
          from (
                select  sample_id,
                        sample_time,
                        session_state,sql_id,
```

```
                decode(session_state,'ON CPU','CPU + CPU Wait',event) event,
                10*(count(sample_id) over (partition by sample_id)) smpcnt
           from dba_hist_active_sess_history
           where to_date(to_char(sample_time,'DD-MON-RR HH24:MI:SS'),
'DD-MON-RR HH24:MI:SS')
                   between to_date('&_bt') and to_date('&_et'))  ash,
           (select xdate from xtimes ) s1
      where ash.sample_time(+) between s1.xdate and s1.xdate+(&&interval_mins/1440)
      group by s1.xdate,event,sql_id)
order by 1,dbtw desc
/


Begin Time         SQL ID          DBT      AAS  Component                DBTPerMetric AASPerMetric
-----------------  -------------  --------  ----  --------------------   ------------ ------------
08-NOV-12 01:41:44 brd3nyszkb4v3  40980.00 68.30  cell smart table scan      15860.00        26.43
                   b6jzrwqggzt1u                  cell smart table scan      14740.00        24.57
                   g26s1uz7hmadb                  cell smart table scan       2850.00         4.75
                   brd3nyszkb4v3                  CPU + CPU Wait              2680.00         4.47
                   cp7daugwu0s3q                  cell smart table scan       1340.00         2.23
                   g26s1uz7hmadb                  CPU + CPU Wait               760.00         1.27
                   b6jzrwqggzt1u                  CPU + CPU Wait               480.00          .80
... Output omitted for brevity
```

In this output, during the sampled time interval, SQL ID brd3nyszkb4v3 had 26.43 AAS waiting on the cell smart table scan wait event. On Exadata, you can use the "cell smart%" component details to understand the cell offload AAS metrics.

Monitoring Historical Database Time and AAS metrics for Specific SQL Statements or Wait Events

Limit your report output to a specific SQL statement and/or component by placing additional logic in the script. Run the script in Listing 14-5 for a specific SQL ID in your environment, searching for database time and AAS metrics representing Exadata smart scans.

Listing 14-5. lst14-05-dbt-ashpast-bydtl.sql

```
... Column formatting omitted
SQL> col bt NEW_VALUE _bt NOPRINT
SQL> col et NEW_VALUE _et NOPRINT
SQL> select min(cast(sample_time as date)) bt,
max(cast(sample_time as date)) et
from dba_hist_active_sess_history
where to_date(to_char(sample_time,'DD-MON-RR HH24:MI:SS'),'DD-MON-RR HH24:MI:SS')
between (sysdate-&&days_ago)
       and ((sysdate-&&days_ago)+(&&duration_min/1440));

SQL> WITH xtimes (xdate) AS
  (SELECT to_date('&_bt') xdate FROM dual
  UNION ALL
```

```
    SELECT xdate+(&&interval_mins/1440) FROM xtimes
         WHERE xdate+(&&interval_mins/1440) <= to_date('&_et')
   )
  select * from (
 select to_char(xdate,'DD-MON-RR HH24:MI:SS') samplestart,
         nvl(sql_id,'NULL') sql_id,
         (sum(decode(event,null,0,dbtw)) over
                  (partition by to_char(xdate,'DD-MON-RR HH24:MI:SS'))) smpcnt,
         (sum(decode(event,null,0,dbtw)) over
                  (partition by to_char(xdate,'DD-MON-RR HH24:MI:SS')))/60/&&interval_mins aas,
         nvl(event,'*** IDLE *** ') tc,
         decode(event,null,0,dbtw) dbtw,
         decode(event,null,0,dbtw)/60/&&interval_mins aas_comp
  from (
          select s1.xdate,event,10*count(*) dbtw,sql_id,count(ash.smpcnt) smpcnt
            from (
                 select  sample_id,
                         sample_time,
                         session_state,sql_id,
                         decode(session_state,'ON CPU','CPU + CPU Wait',event) event,
                         10*(count(sample_id) over (partition by sample_id)) smpcnt
                 from dba_hist_active_sess_history
                 where to_date(to_char(sample_time,'DD-MON-RR HH24:MI:SS'),'DD-MON-RR
                      HH24:MI:SS')
                         between to_date('&_bt') and to_date('&_et'))  ash,
                 (select xdate from xtimes ) s1
          where ash.sample_time(+) between s1.xdate and s1.xdate+(&&interval_mins/1440)
          group by s1.xdate,event,sql_id)
  order by 1,dbtw desc)
  where (sql_id='&&sql_id' or '&&sql_id' is null)
  and   (tc='&&event_descr' or  '&&event_descr' is null)
  ... Code from LIsting 14-5
  Enter value for sql_id: brd3nyszkb4v3
  old  33: where (sql_id='&&sql_id' or '&&sql_id' is null)
  new  33: where (sql_id='brd3nyszkb4v3' or 'brd3nyszkb4v3' is null)
  Enter value for event_descr: cell smart table scan
  old  34: and   (tc='&&event_descr' or  '&&event_descr' is null)
  new  34: and   (tc='cell smart table scan' or  'cell smart table scan' is null)

  Begin Time         SQL ID          DBT      AAS  Component              DBTPerMetric AASPerMetric
  ------------------ ------------- -------- -----  ---------------------- ------------ ------------
  07-NOV-12 18:05:21 brd3nyszkb4v3  4660.00  15.53 cell smart table scan       3110.00        10.37
  07-NOV-12 18:10:21 brd3nyszkb4v3 27450.00  91.50 cell smart table scan      12250.00        40.83
```

This query displays two intervals in which cursor brd3nyszkb4v3 performed Exadata smart scans and waited on the `cell smart table scan` wait event.

Monitoring Recent, Detailed Database Time and AAS Metrics

To report detailed database time and AAS metrics from the in-memory Oracle ASH buffer, which displays granular, un-summarized ASH data, run the script in Listing 14-6. This script is similar to the script in Listing 14-4 but extracts its data from V$ACTIVE_SESSION_HISTORY instead of DBA_HIST_ACTIVE_SESS_HISTORY.

Listing 14-6. lst14-06-dbt-ashcurr-details.sql

```
... Column formatting omitted
SQL> col bt NEW_VALUE _bt NOPRINT
SQL> col et NEW_VALUE _et NOPRINT
SQL> select min(cast(sample_time as date)) bt,
max(cast(sample_time as date)) et
from v$active_session_history
where to_date(to_char(sample_time,'DD-MON-RR HH24:MI:SS'),'DD-MON-RR HH24:MI:SS')
between (sysdate-&&days_ago)
        and ((sysdate-&&days_ago)+(&&duration_min/1440));
SQL> WITH xtimes (xdate) AS
  (SELECT to_date('&_bt') xdate FROM dual
  UNION ALL
  SELECT xdate+(&&interval_mins/1440) FROM xtimes
        WHERE xdate+(&&interval_mins/1440) <= to_date('&_et')
  )
select to_char(xdate,'DD-MON-RR HH24:MI:SS') samplestart,
        nvl(sql_id,'NULL') sql_id,
        (sum(decode(event,null,0,dbtw)) over
                (partition by to_char(xdate,'DD-MON-RR HH24:MI:SS'))) smpcnt,
        (sum(decode(event,null,0,dbtw)) over
                (partition by to_char(xdate,'DD-MON-RR HH24:MI:SS')))/60/&&interval_mins aas,
        nvl(event,'*** IDLE *** ') tc,
        decode(event,null,0,dbtw) dbtw,
        decode(event,null,0,dbtw)/60/&&interval_mins aas_comp
from (
        select s1.xdate,event,count(*) dbtw,sql_id,count(ash.smpcnt) smpcnt
          from (
                select  sample_id,
                        sample_time,
                        session_state,sql_id,
                        decode(session_state,'ON CPU','CPU + CPU Wait',event) event,
                        (count(sample_id) over (partition by sample_id)) smpcnt
                from v$active_session_history
                where to_date(to_char(sample_time,'DD-MON-RR HH24:MI:SS'),'DD-MON-RR
                        HH24:MI:SS')
                            between to_date('&_bt') and to_date('&_et'))  ash,
                (select xdate from xtimes ) s1
        where ash.sample_time(+) between s1.xdate and s1.xdate+(&&interval_mins/1440)
        group by s1.xdate,event,sql_id)
order by 1,dbtw desc;
```

Begin Time	SQL ID	DBT	AAS	Component	DBTPerMetric	AASPerMetric
08-NOV-12 13:40:54	NULL	3.00	.02	CPU + CPU Wait	2.00	.01
	c3rvcbu8r3zx8			CPU + CPU Wait	1.00	.01
08-NOV-12 13:43:54	NULL	2.00	.01	CPU + CPU Wait	2.00	.01
08-NOV-12 13:46:54	NULL	4.00	.02	CPU + CPU Wait	4.00	.02
08-NOV-12 13:49:54	NULL	3.00	.02	CPU + CPU Wait	1.00	.01
	NULL			ASM file metadata operation	1.00	.01
	NULL			control file sequential read	1.00	.01

... Output omitted for brevity

How It Works

Over the years, Oracle DBAs, performance engineers, and developers have used a number of techniques to identify and optimize Oracle performance. In recent years, the Oracle Database Performance Method, described in docs.oracle.com/cd/E11882_01/server.112/e10822/tdppt_method.htm has become increasingly adopted and utilized to focus performance monitoring and optimization because it is based on the most important metric from an end user's or application's perspective: time. While statistics, counters, ratios, wait events, and a number of other types of information are valuable inputs to an overall performance assessment analysis, the most important aspect of performance is time, or time per interval.

In this recipe, we demonstrated using Oracle's ASH framework as the basis for time-based performance monitoring. At a high level, Oracle's ASH buffer is externalized in the V$ACTIVE_SESSION_HISTORY view and, at one-hour intervals, Oracle summarizes this information and publishes to the WRH$_ tables. The DBA_HIST_ACTIVE_SESS_HISTORY view can then be used to query AWR data from the WRH$_ tables. When Oracle writes ASH data from the ASH buffer to the WRH$_ tables, one of every ten in-memory samples is captured, which is why the historical ASH queries in the solution of this recipe multiply the sample counts by ten.

The AAS metrics is a reflection of the number of sessions actively consuming CPU resources or actively waiting on a named Oracle wait event over a time interval; in other words, the AAS metric is a reflection of the average Oracle database load for a time range. AAS can be formulated as follows:

$$AAS = \Delta(\text{Database Time}) / \text{Elapsed clock time}$$
$$AAS = \Sigma(\text{ASH samples, where } \Delta=1 \text{ second}) / \text{Elapsed clock time}$$

This metric is important for a number of reasons and is often used to size and/or validate whether your underlying compute node infrastructure is capable of handling your workload. With Exadata, this is especially important because most organizations make the Exadata investment for performance reasons. Oracle places such a high value on the AAS metric and database time methodology that it uses the underlying ASH data for the main chart on the Performance landing page in Enterprise Manager, as displayed in Figure 14-13. In Figure 14-13, the line on the Y-axis represents AAS and the area under the curve represents database time, broken apart by the various components of time that make up the workload. The red line at the top of this chart shows the total number of CPU cores for your cluster; Oracle displays this because as AAS approaches your processor ceiling, it is typically an indication that performance could be impacted.

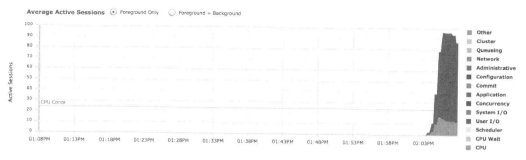

Figure 14-13. Average Active Sessions from Enterprise Manager

The scripts listed in this recipe provide a means to summarize database time and AAS performance information from SQL scripts, and they can be used to plot key performance information over a user-defined time range, similar to what you can achieve with Enterprise Manager.

There are a number of resources available to learn more about the Oracle's database performance methodology and AAS. We suggest consulting Oracle's documentation first and then expanding to a Google search, as there are many white papers and blogs available to the public.

14-6. Monitoring Smart Scans by Database Time and AAS

Problem

You wish to monitor recent and historical performance information specific to Exadata smart scans in order to measure the frequency and time consumed by Smart Scans relative to your overall database workload.

Solution

In this recipe, you will learn how to query Oracle's ASH views to report detailed smart scan behavior based on the database time and AAS performance method, as initially introduced in Recipe 14-5.

Monitoring Recent and Current Smart Scan Performance Metrics from ASH

To measure recent and current smart-scan-related AAS metrics from ASH, run the script in Listing 14-7. In this script, we will report on summarized AAS data related to Smart Scan and cell offload queries and group the output on the SQL ID and a user-entered sample interval.

Listing 14-7. lst14-07-ss-ashcurr-details.sql

```
SQL> alter session set nls_date_format='DD-MON-RR HH24:MI:SS';
SQL> col bt NEW_VALUE _bt NOPRINT
SQL> col et NEW_VALUE _et NOPRINT
SQL> select min(cast(sample_time as date)) bt,
max(cast(sample_time as date)) et
from v$active_session_history
where to_date(to_char(sample_time,'DD-MON-RR HH24:MI:SS'),'DD-MON-RR HH24:MI:SS')
> (sysdate-&&mins_ago/1440);
SQL> WITH xtimes (xdate) AS
  (SELECT to_date('&_bt') xdate FROM dual
```

```
   UNION ALL
   SELECT xdate+(&&interval_mins/1440) FROM xtimes
          WHERE xdate+(&&interval_mins/1440) <= to_date('&_et')
   )
 select * from (
 select to_char(xdate,'DD-MON-RR HH24:MI:SS') samplestart,
         nvl(sql_id,'NULL') sql_id,
         (sum(decode(event,null,0,dbtw)) over
                (partition by to_char(xdate,'DD-MON-RR HH24:MI:SS'))) smpcnt,
         (sum(decode(event,null,0,dbtw)) over
                (partition by to_char(xdate,'DD-MON-RR HH24:MI:SS')))/60/&&interval_mins aas,
         nvl(event,'*** IDLE *** ') tc,
         decode(event,null,0,dbtw) dbtw,
         decode(event,null,0,dbtw)/60/&&interval_mins aas_comp
 from (
         select s1.xdate,event,count(*) dbtw,sql_id,count(ash.smpcnt) smpcnt
           from (
                select  sample_id,
                        sample_time,
                        session_state,sql_id,
                        decode(session_state,'ON CPU','CPU + CPU Wait',event) event,
                        (count(sample_id) over (partition by sample_id)) smpcnt
                from v$active_session_history
                where to_date(to_char(sample_time,'DD-MON-RR HH24:MI:SS'),'DD-MON-RR
                    HH24:MI:SS')
                        between to_date('&_bt') and to_date('&_et'))  ash,
                (select xdate from xtimes ) s1
         where 1=1
         and ash.sample_time(+) between s1.xdate and s1.xdate+(&&interval_mins/1440)
         group by s1.xdate,event,sql_id)
 order by 1,dbtw desc)
 where tc like 'cell smart%'
 /
 Begin Time         SQL ID        DBT       AAS   Component              DBTPerMetric AASPerMetric
 -----------------  ------------- --------- ----- ---------------------- ------------ ------------
 09-NOV-12 14:01:27 brd3nyszkb4v3 20848.00  34.75 cell smart table scan       7837.00        13.06
                    b6jzrwqggzt1u                 cell smart table scan       7379.00        12.30
                    g26s1uz7hmadb                 cell smart table scan       1517.00         2.53
 ... Output omitted for brevity
```

In this output, the DBT and AAS columns indicate the total database time per sample interval, including both smart scan and non-smart scan operations, and the DBTPerMetric and AASPerMetric represent the database time and AAS value specific to events classified by the "cell smart%" wait event for a specific SQL ID within the interval.

Monitoring Historical Smart Scan Performance Metrics from ASH

To report historical smart scan performance metrics from ASH data, use the script in Listing 14-8. In this script, we have changed our data source from V$ACTIVE_SESSION_HISTORY and modified the time component by multiplying by 10 since Oracle summarizes in-memory ASH data in 10 second buckets when publishing to the ASH views in the AWR repository. In this script, similar to the logic in Listing 14-4 in Recipe 14-5, you will be prompted for sample start time with the &&days_ago parameter, a sample duration with the &&duration_min parameter, and a sampling window as specified by the &&interval_mins parameter:

Listing 14-8. lst14-08-ss-ashpast-details.sql

```
... Column formatting and min/max dates identical to Listing 14-7
SQL> WITH xtimes (xdate) AS
  (SELECT to_date('&_bt') xdate FROM dual
  UNION ALL
  SELECT xdate+(&&interval_mins/1440) FROM xtimes
       WHERE xdate+(&&interval_mins/1440) <= to_date('&_et')
  )
select * from (
select to_char(xdate,'DD-MON-RR HH24:MI:SS') samplestart,
       nvl(sql_id,'NULL') sql_id,
       (sum(decode(event,null,0,dbtw)) over
               (partition by to_char(xdate,'DD-MON-RR HH24:MI:SS'))) smpcnt,
       (sum(decode(event,null,0,dbtw)) over
               (partition by to_char(xdate,'DD-MON-RR HH24:MI:SS')))/60/&&interval_mins aas,
       nvl(event,'*** IDLE *** ') tc,
       decode(event,null,0,dbtw) dbtw,
       decode(event,null,0,dbtw)/60/&&interval_mins aas_comp
from (
       select s1.xdate,event,10*count(*) dbtw,sql_id,count(ash.smpcnt) smpcnt
         from (
              select  sample_id,
                      sample_time,
                      session_state,sql_id,
                      decode(session_state,'ON CPU','CPU + CPU Wait',event) event,
                      10*(count(sample_id) over (partition by sample_id)) smpcnt
              from dba_hist_active_sess_history
              where to_date(to_char(sample_time,'DD-MON-RR HH24:MI:SS'),'DD-MON-RR
                  HH24:MI:SS')
                     between to_date('&_bt') and to_date('&_et'))  ash,
              (select xdate from xtimes ) s1
       where ash.sample_time(+) between s1.xdate and s1.xdate+(&&interval_mins/1440)
       group by s1.xdate,event,sql_id)
order by 1,dbtw desc)
where tc like 'cell smart%'
/
```

How It Works

Oracle database performance method and the AAS metrics, as introduced in Recipe 14-5, are important for the Exadata DMA to be familiar with. Specific to measuring time-based smart scan behavior, the key is to capture session-history-related information from ASH using the cell smart table scan and cell smart index scan Oracle wait events.

Oracle has introduced additional Exadata-related wait events in 11gR2 to capture Exadata-related instrumentation values. When sessions enter a state in which they are waiting for I/O as a result of a smart scan request, the session will post a wait on the cell smart table scan event for table scans and cell smart index scan event for offloadable index scans. You may also witness sessions waiting on the cell single block physical read or cell multiblock physical read events; these are not smart-scan-related events but rather traditional block I/O wait events that are raised when Oracle requires a non-buffered physical read to satisfy a request and the nature of the query and data is such that smart scan is not used. Recipe 14-7 and recipes in Chapter 15 discuss this is more detail.

14-7. Monitoring Exadata with Wait Events

Problem

You wish to monitor database performance using the wait event method and collect Exadata-specific wait event information in order to diagnose performance problems.

Solution

In this recipe, you will learn how to query Oracle's wait interface, ASH, and AWR views using Exadata-specific wait events. First, run the following query to list Exadata wait events introduced in Oracle 11gR2:

```
SQL> select name from v$event_name where name like 'cell%';
NAME
-------------------------------------------------------------
cell smart table scan
cell smart index scan
cell statistics gather
... Additional cell related wait events omitted
cell manager cancel work request
17 rows selected.

SQL>
```

As you can see, Oracle introduced 17 Exadata-specific wait events in Oracle 11gR2. There are a number of dynamic performance views that can be used to query Exadata wait event information and, in the following sections, we will provide scripts to monitor your Exadata wait events.

Monitoring Current Wait Events from v$session

To monitor session-level Exadata wait events, use GV$SESSION and focus on the events that begin with the string cell. Execute the script in Listing 14-9 to display information for sessions currently waiting on an Exadata wait I/O event.

Listing 14-9. lst14-09-exawait-sess.sql

```
SQL> select  sess.inst_id,sess.sid,sess.sql_id,
        sess.event event,
        cell.cell_path,
        (case when event like '%block%'
        then (select path from v$asm_disk where hash_value=sess.p2)
        else 'N/A'
        end) asm_disk,
        p3,
        decode(sess.state,'WAITING',sess.seconds_in_wait,
                'WAITED UNKNOWN TIME',-999, 'WAITED SHORT TIME',sess.wait_time,
                'WAITED KNOWN TIME',sess.wait_time) wt,
```

```
                substr(nvl(sess.module,sess.program),1,15) pgm
    from        gv$session sess,
                v$cell cell
    where       sess.state in ('WAITING','WAITED KNOWN TIME')
    and         sess.status='ACTIVE'
    and         sess.event like 'cell%'
    and         sess.p1=cell.cell_hashval
    order by 8 desc
    /
    Inst  Sess  SQL_ID         Wait Event               Cell          Columns headings omitted..
    ----  ----  -------------  -----------------------  ------------  -----  -----  -----  ---------
       2   528  fgdz37rn4bf4b  cell smart table scan    192.168.10.3  N/A        0     13  SQL*Plus
       2  1175  fgdz37rn4bf4b  cell smart table scan    192.168.10.3  N/A        0      2  SQL*Plus
       2   850  fgdz37rn4bf4b  cell smart table scan    192.168.10.3  N/A        0      0  SQL*Plus
       2   787  fgdz37rn4bf4b  cell smart table scan    192.168.10.3  N/A        0      0  SQL*Plus
```

For each Exadata wait event, the p1 column in V$SESSION and other wait interface views refers to the storage cell hash value from v$cell. For block I/O-related wait events, such as `cell single block physical read` waits, the p2 column represents the ASM disk hash value and the p3 column lists the number of bytes or blocks involved in the wait event. For smart scan wait operations, the p2 and p3 columns will be zero. This information is useful when measuring balance of I/O waits across your available storage cell disk resources. For ideal performance, you should expect to see the I/O waits distributed evenly across your storage cells and the block I/O waits relatively evenly distributed across grid disks.

Monitoring Exadata Wait Events from ASH

Oracle's ASH views can be used to extract the same type of wait event information as the example above from GV$SESSION, but with ASH you can scope your analysis to time ranges in the past and summarize your results according to any number of ASH dimensions, including the session ID, SQL ID, and more. You have a great deal of flexibility for monitoring wait event information from ASH and can adapt your script repository to meet your needs, but one method we find useful is to measure wait times for block I/O requests per ASM disk using ASH data. To generate this report, execute the script in Listing 14-10.

Listing 14-10. lst14-10-exawait-ashcurr.sql

```
SQL> alter session set nls_date_format='DD-MON-RR HH24:MI:SS';
SQL> select min(cast(sample_time as date)) bt,
max(cast(sample_time as date)) et
from v$active_session_history
where to_date(to_char(sample_time,'DD-MON-RR HH24:MI:SS'),'DD-MON-RR HH24:MI:SS')
> (sysdate-&&mins_ago/1440);

SQL> WITH xtimes (xdate) AS
  (SELECT to_date('&_bt') xdate FROM dual
   UNION ALL
   SELECT xdate+(&&interval_mins/1440) FROM xtimes
        WHERE xdate+(&&interval_mins/1440) <= to_date('&_et')
  )
select samplestart,sql_id,tc,dbtw,aas_comp,tw from (
select to_char(xdate,'DD-MON-RR HH24:MI:SS') samplestart,
       nvl(sql_id,'NULL') sql_id,
```

```
        (sum(decode(event,null,0,dbtw)) over
             (partition by to_char(xdate,'DD-MON-RR HH24:MI:SS'))) smpcnt,
        (sum(decode(event,null,0,dbtw)) over
             (partition by to_char(xdate,'DD-MON-RR HH24:MI:SS')))/60/&&interval_mins aas,
        nvl(event,'*** IDLE *** ') tc,
        decode(event,null,0,dbtw) dbtw,
        decode(event,null,0,dbtw)/60/&&interval_mins aas_comp,tw
from (
       select s1.xdate,event,count(*) dbtw,sql_id,count(ash.smpcnt) smpcnt,sum(time_waited) tw
         from (
             select  ash.sample_id,
                     ash.sample_time,
                     ash.session_state,sql_id,
                     decode(ash.session_state,'ON CPU','CPU + CPU Wait',ash.event) event,
                     (count(ash.sample_id) over (partition by ash.sample_id)) smpcnt,
                     (sum(ash.time_waited/1000000) over (partition by sample_id)) time_waited
                from v$active_session_history ash
               where  to_date(to_char(ash.sample_time,'DD-MON-RR HH24:MI:SS'),'DD-MON-RR
                  HH24:MI:SS')
                      between to_date('& bt') and to_date('& et')
                and ash.event like 'cell%block%') ash,
            (select xdate from xtimes ) s1
       where ash.sample_time(+) between s1.xdate and s1.xdate+(&&interval_mins/1440)
       group by s1.xdate,event,sql_id)
order by 1,dbtw desc)
where tc like 'cell%'
/

Begin Time           SQL ID          Event                              AshDBTime    AAS   TimeWaited
-----------------    -------------   -----------------------------      ----------   -----  ----------
09-NOV-12 14:11:16   fgdz37rn4bf4b   cell multiblock physical read          74.00    .12       140.90
                     0a3su0q0mxfqt   cell multiblock physical read          36.00    .06        12.25
                     0a3su0q0mxfqt   cell single block physical read        28.00    .05        11.97
                     fgdz37rn4bf4b   cell single block physical read         6.00    .01        10.82
                     fgdz37rn4bf4b   cell list of blocks physical read       6.00    .01        13.07
                     3626j8qpgf20s   cell single block physical read         1.00    .00          .20
                     ajymgnp1qnruw   cell list of blocks physical read       1.00    .00          .02
                     cbaqspgygz94n   cell list of blocks physical read       1.00    .00          .37
09-NOV-12 15:21:16   bt4gw911p5vf0   cell multiblock physical read          39.00    .07         7.81
                     bt4gw911p5vf0   cell single block physical read        11.00    .02         1.43
... Ouptut omitted
```

In this output, notice the discrepancy between the ASH database time and the TIME_WAITED value from V$ACTIVE_SESSION_HISTORY. This occurs because Oracle only populates the last sample after event completes. For these reasons, it is not useful to perform any calculations with the TIME_WAITED column from ASH; we have constructed the query in Listing 14-10 to include this column to demonstrate why it should not be trusted when querying ASH data.

Monitoring Exadata Wait Events from AWR

To gather wait event information from AWR, generate an AWR report from either Enterprise Manager or $ORACLE_HOME/rdbms/admin/awrrpt.sql. We will assume that most experienced Oracle DBAs should be familiar with the steps required to generate an AWR report and, as such, will not provide instructions.

> ■ **Note** To learn how to generate an AWR report using Oracle Enterprise Manager or via the standard SQL*Plus scripts provided in the Oracle RDBMS software installation directory, please consult Oracle documentation.

If you are interested in collecting Exadata wait-specific information from Oracle's AWR views, however, execute the script in Listing 14-11. This script accepts a starting and ending snapshot ID and generates a snapshot-based summary of Exadata wait event metrics.

Listing 14-11. lst14-11-exawait-awr.sql

```
SQL> break on snaptime
SQL> select snaptime,event_name,wtdelta,todelta,twdelta from (
 select snap_id,snaptime,event_name,therank,
  (waits-lag(waits,1,0)
                over (partition by event_name order by snap_id)) wtdelta,
  (timeouts-lag(timeouts,1,0)
                over (partition by event_name order by snap_id)) todelta,
  (time_waited-lag(time_waited,1,0)
                over (partition by event_name order by snap_id)) twdelta
 from (
   select s.snap_id,
          to_char(s.begin_interval_time,'DD-MON-RR HH24:MI') snaptime,
          event_name, sum(e.total_waits) waits,
          sum(e.total_timeouts) timeouts,
          sum(e.time_waited_micro)/1000000 time_waited,
          (rank() over (order by s.snap_id)) therank
     from dba_hist_system_event e,
          dba_hist_snapshot    s
    where s.snap_id = e.snap_id
    and s.snap_id between (&&snap_low-1) and &&snap_hi
    and s.dbid           =e.dbid
    and s.instance_number=e.instance_number
    and e.event_name like 'cell%'
    group by s.snap_id,
         to_char(s.begin_interval_time,'DD-MON-RR HH24:MI'),event_name
 )
 order by snap_id, twdelta desc)
where therank>1;
```

```
BeginTime         Event                              Waits      Timeouts    SecsWaited
---------------   ---------------------------------  ---------  ---------   ----------
09-NOV-12 14:00   cell smart table scan              2540318    1244278     42749
                  cell multiblock physical read      92429      0           531
                  cell single block physical read    92592      0           176
                  cell list of blocks physical read  739        0           39
                  cell statistics gather             0          0           0
09-NOV-12 15:00   cell smart table scan              2567750    1263377     41534
                  cell multiblock physical read      87860      0           437
                  cell single block physical read    91367      0           109
                  cell list of blocks physical read  800        0           21
                  cell statistics gather             0          0           0
... Output omitted
```

How It Works

As many experienced DBAs and performance engineers know, Oracle instruments a large number of named wait events. In Oracle 11.2.0.3, for example, there are 1,152 specific named wait events. With Exadata, Oracle has added 17 wait events, each which begins with the string cell.

Wait-event-based monitoring and performance optimization is generally conducted using the following approaches, all of which are valid and have their merits:

- Querying the V$SESSION_WAIT, V$SESSION_EVENT, and V$SESSION performance views
- Querying the Oracle ASH views, V$ACTIVE_SESSION_HISTORY and DBA_HIST_ACTIVE_SESS_HISTORY views
- Using Oracle AWR data

Wait-event-based monitoring on Exadata is no different than the wait-event-based performance methodology on non-Exadata systems. As is the case with other wait events, the key for the Exadata DMA is to know what each Exadata wait event means and how to interpret the p1, p2, and p3 columns. Oracle's documentation and the V$EVENT_NAME view can be used to gather this information, but a summary of what you need to know is provided:

- Each Exadata wait event begins with the string cell.
- Some of the common events are cell smart table scan, cell smart index scan, cell single block physical read, cell multiblock physical read, and cell list of physical blocks read.
- The cell smart% waits indicate that cell offload and smart scan is taking place.
- The cell%block% wait events indicate that traditional block I/O-related waits are occurring, such as those caused by index scans and any scans that do not qualify for smart scan.
- The p1 column in the various wait interface views always represents the storage cell's hash value, which is mapped to V$CELL.CELL_HASHVAL.
- For the block I/O-related wait events, p2 corresponds to the ASM grid disk involved with the wait operation and can be mapped to V$ASM_DISK.HASH_VALUE.
- For block I/O wait events, p3 indicates either the number of blocks or number of bytes. You can determine this by querying V$EVENT_NAME.PARAMETER3 for the wait event in question.

14-8. Monitoring Exadata with Statistics and Counters

Problem

You wish to monitor database performance using statistics and counter metrics in a similar manner so that you may measure performance for other Oracle features or performance behavior.

Solution

In this recipe, you will learn about the new system, session, and SQL statistics that Oracle introduced for Exadata and how to build a framework or reference for designing queries and scripts for Exadata database performance monitoring.

Begin by running the following query, which will list all of the Exadata statistics available in 11gR2:

```
SQL> select name from v$statname
    where (name like 'cell%'
    or name like 'flash %')
/
cell IO uncompressed bytes
cell flash cache read hits
cell index scans
cell physical IO bytes eligible for predicate offload
cell physical IO bytes saved by storage index
... Ouput omitted
cell physical IO bytes sent directly to DB node to balance CPU
cell physical IO interconnect bytes
... Ouput omitted
flash cache insert skip: corrupt
... Ouput omitted
56 rows selected.
SQL>
```

As you can see, there are roughly 56 Exadata-specific statistics available in our database, which is running Oracle 11.2.0.3. Each of these statistics is a counter-based statistic; each time an Oracle session encounters the condition that triggers the statistic, the statistic's value is incremented. Run the following query to report on the number of bytes eligible for predicate offload, systemwide, since the instance was started:

```
SQL> select name,value/1024/1024/1024 val
    from v$sysstat
    where name='cell physical IO bytes eligible for predicate offload'
/

Stat Name                                                    GB
----------------------------------------------------  ---------
cell physical IO bytes eligible for predicate offload    57,415
SQL>
```

We see that in our instance, over 56 TB of data was eligible for predicate offload. You can query or monitor statistics information at the system level using V$SYSSTAT, at the session level with V$SESSTAT, using AWR reports or data, or in the case of specific offload information at a per SQL ID level. As listed above, Oracle tracks many Exadata-specific performance statistics. Table 14-2 displays some of the more commonly monitored statistics and their meanings.

Table 14-2. *Common Exadata Statistics*

Statistic	Meaning
cell physical I/O interconnect bytes	Number of bytes transmitted over the InfiniBand interconnect
cell physical I/O bytes eligible for predicate offload	Number of bytes eligible for predicate offload, an indication of smart scan
cell physical I/O interconnect bytes returned by smart scan	Numbers of bytes transmitted over the storage interconnect as a result of smart scan
cell physical I/O bytes saved by storage index	Number of bytes saved by a storage index; this is a reflection of how many physical disk I/O bytes (and by proxy, requests) were saved due to a storage index eliminating candidate blocks
cell flash cache read hits	Number of read requests satisfied in Smart Flash Cache

■ **Note** This recipe is noticeably void of scripts and examples because in Chapters 15 through 19, we will demonstrate using Exadata statistics and counters to measure specific characteristics of Exadata performance in Chapters 15 through 19.

How It Works

Monitoring with statistics and counters is a performance methodology with a long history. Combined with the database time and wait event performance methodologies, the counter-based performance monitoring strategy rounds out the performance engineer's monitoring tool set.

When painted with a broad stroke, monitoring with statistics and counters typically has limited benefits for the performance engineer because statistics alone often have no bearing on what an application or user experiences. Users are concerned with how long it takes to complete an operation or run a program and when performance is unacceptable, the questions that need to be answered are the following:

- Where is the program or session spending its time?
- What resources is the program or session waiting on, if any, and can these bottlenecks be addressed?
- Is the program or session issuing SQL statements to the database efficiently?

As is evident for most experienced Oracle DBAs and performance engineers, raw, counter-based statistics do not answer these questions beyond a hypothetical or correlative level.

Exadata statistics and counters, however, do provide some value to the Exadata DMA. With Exadata, you presumably wish to unleash the power of the software that runs on the storage cells. The cell offload statistics can present a nice means to measure the effectiveness of the storage server software and help determine whether your workload, programs, sessions, or system is benefiting from Exadata's features.

In Chapters 15 through 19, we will demonstrate statistics-based techniques to measure the effectiveness and use of these Exadata software features.

14-9. Measuring Cell I/O Statistics for a SQL Statement

Problem

You wish to report a comprehensive set of storage cell I/O statistics for a given SQL statement, including smart scan behavior, storage index impact, flash cache impact, and the overall storage cell I/O statistics in order to quantify the I/O workload contribution.

Solution

In this recipe, you will learn how to measure the overall I/O load generated by a SQL statement and quantify the impact of Exadata smart scans, storage indexes, and Smart Flash Cache. Start by executing a query of your choice and then execute the script in Listing 14-12.

```
SQL> select count(*) from d14.myobj_uncomp;

  COUNT(*)
----------
  20423000


Elapsed: 00:00:00.61
```

Listing 14-12. lst14-12-myiostats.sql

```
SQL> select * from
    (select phys_reads+phys_writes+redo_size mb_requested,
            offload_eligible mb_eligible_offload,
            interconnect_bytes interconnect_mb,
            storageindex_bytes storageindex_mb_saved, flashcache_hits flashcache_mb,
            round(((case
              when offload_eligible=0 then 0
              when offload_eligible> 0 then
                 (100*(((phys_reads+phys_writes+redo_size)-interconnect_bytes) /
                    (phys_reads+phys_writes+redo_size)))
            end)),2) smartscan_efficiency,
            interconnect_bytes/dbt interconnect_mbps,
            (phys_reads+phys_writes+redo_size)-(storageindex_bytes+flashcache_hits)
               cell_mb_processed,
            ((phys_reads+phys_writes+redo_size)-(storageindex_bytes+flashcache_hits))/dbt
               cell_mbps
    from (
      select * from (
        select name,mb,dbt from (
          select stats.name,tm.dbt dbt,
            (case
              when stats.name='physical reads' then (stats.value * dbbs.value)/1024/1024
              when stats.name='physical writes' then
                    asm.asm_redundancy*((stats.value * dbbs.value)/1024/1024)
              when stats.name='redo size' then asm.asm_redundancy*((stats.value * 512)
                  /1024/1024)
              when stats.name like 'cell physi%' then stats.value/1024/1024
```

```
              when stats.name like 'cell%flash%' then (stats.value * dbbs.value)/1024/1024
              else stats.value
            end) mb
      from (
        select b.name,
            value
        from     v$mystat a,
                 v$statname b
        where    a.statistic# = b.statistic#
        and b.name in
        ( 'cell physical IO bytes eligible for predicate offload',
                'cell physical IO interconnect bytes',
                'cell physical IO interconnect bytes returned by smart scan',
                'cell flash cache read hits','cell physical IO bytes saved by storage
                    index',
                'physical reads',
                'physical writes',
          'redo size')
          ) stats,
          (select value from v$parameter where name='db_block_size') dbbs,
          (select decode(max(type),'NORMAL',2,'HIGH',3,2) asm_redundancy
          from v$asm_diskgroup ) asm,
          (select b.value/100 dbt
           from v$mystat b, v$statname a
           where a.statistic#=b.statistic#
           and a.name='DB time') tm
  )) pivot (sum(mb) for (name)
         in ('cell physical IO bytes eligible for predicate offload'  as offload_eligible,
             'cell physical IO interconnect bytes'                    as interconnect_bytes,
             'cell physical IO interconnect bytes returned by smart scan' as smartscan_returned,
             'cell flash cache read hits'                             as flashcache_hits,
             'cell physical IO bytes saved by storage index'          as storageindex_bytes,
             'physical reads'                                         as phys_reads,
             'physical writes'                                        as phys_writes,
             'redo size'))                                            as redo_size))
))
unpivot
(statval for stattype in
         (mb_requested as 'MB Requested',
          mb_eligible_offload as 'MB Eligible for Offload',
          smartscan_efficiency as 'Smart Scan Efficiency',
          interconnect_mb as 'Interconnect MB',
          interconnect_mbps as 'Interconnect MBPS',
          storageindex_mb_saved as 'Storage Index MB Saved',
          flashcache_mb as 'Flash Cache MB read',
          cell_mb_processed as 'Cell MB Processed' ,
          cell_mbps as 'Cell MBPS'))
/
```

```
Statistic                      Statistic Value
-----------------------------  ---------------
MB Requested                           2255.27
MB Eligible for Offload                2255.09
Smart Scan Efficiency                    89.20
Interconnect MB                         243.53
Interconnect MBPS                       386.56
Storage Index MB Saved                     .00
Flash Cache MB read                      19.02
Cell MB Processed                      2236.25
Cell MBPS                              3549.60
```

The script in Listing 14-12 queries a number of I/O statistics and displays the number of megabytes requested for your session, the number of megabytes eligible for predicate offload (in other words, smart scan), the volume of data transmitted over the storage interconnect, the amount of I/O processed on the storage cells, Smart Flash Cache statistics, as well as Storage Index savings.

How It Works

If you are reading this book sequentially, this recipe is a preview to topics covered in Chapters 15 through 19. In these chapters, we discuss how to measure smart scan and cell offload statistics, storage index savings, and flash cache metrics. In this recipe, we have combined each of these statistics and metrics into a simple script that measures the overall I/O load for your individual SQL statement.

Listing 14-12 queries a number of statistics for your current session and derives the rate-based measurements, such as storage interconnect megabytes per second, by dividing the MB values by the amount of database time consumed for your session. In the script, we use Oracle's PIVOT statement to align row values in a columnar fashion so to easily perform calculations on a number of different values without having to join multiple times to the statistic view, V$MYSTAT. We then UNPIVOT the final results to display the output in row format.

While not displayed in this recipe, Listing 14-13, lst14-13-sessiostats.sql uses the same logic to display Exadata I/O statistics given a specific session, and it is included in the source code repository.

■ **Note** To learn more about smart scan, storage indexes, Exadata's smart flash cache, and other storage server software features, please read Chapters 15 through 19.

PART 5

Exadata Software

Exadata's most important feature is the unique software deployed on the storage servers, or storage cells. While it's true that Oracle delivers a fast combination of redundant hardware components at each layer in the Exadata technology stack, it is through Exadata's software that organizations can truly realize extreme performance. In short, the hardware infrastructure is fast, capable, and balanced, and the software features enable Exadata to maximize utilization and reduce the demand for physical compute or storage resources.

The chapters in this section present real-life solutions for understanding and leveraging Exadata's software features, including Smart Scan, Hybrid Columnar Compression, I/O Resource Management, Smart Flash Cache and Smart Flash Logging, and Storage Indexes. These software features primarily execute with the cell services software on each Exadata storage cell and, while some of the features work automatically, several require planning and a step-by-step approach in order to successfully deploy and realize the benefits from. In this section, we will arm you with the information needed to identify when and how the software features are used, measure the performance gains, and confidently plan and configure your databases to take advantage of each software component.

CHAPTER 15

Smart Scan and Cell Offload

Smart Scan is probably the most important performance component in Exadata's software offering in terms of delivering extreme performance. Smart Scan is a cell offload feature whose goal is to offload processing to storage cells instead of performing block I/O requests in the database tier. The goal of Smart Scan processing is to do all the "heavy lifting", I/O-wise, in the storage cell and only send back data to the compute nodes that is actually needed and requested. This reduces interconnect traffic between the storage grid and database tier, reduces the clutter in the database buffer cache, improves query performance, and improves concurrency for multiple full-scan types of queries happening at once. With smart scan processing, row filtering, column filtering, some join processing, and other functions are performed in the Exadata cells.

In this chapter we'll present several examples of Smart Scan, show how to control it, provide tips on how to measure it and calculate its effectiveness, and discuss various qualifying conditions for Smart Scan to be used.

15-1. Identifying Cell Offload in Execution Plans

Problem

You wish to identify Smart Scan and cell offload behavior in SQL execution plans.

Solution

In this recipe, you will learn how to identify cell offload or Smart Scan behavior in SQL execution plans and in an EXPLAIN PLAN output. There are a number of ways to display SQL plans, including using DBMS_XPLAN, extracting the plans from Enterprise Manager, querying and formatting data from V$SQL_PLAN, and so forth, but in this recipe we use AUTOTRACE from SQL*Plus for simplicity. Identify a table to conduct a full table scan query against, enter a hint if necessary to bypass index access, and execute the following statements from a database running on Exadata:

```
SQL> set lines 200
SQL> set autotrace on
SQL> select /*+ full (f) */ count(*)
  2  from fnd_user f;
```

```
  COUNT(*)
----------
      2840

Execution Plan
----------------------------------------------------------
Plan hash value: 2973321430
--------------------------------------------------------------------------------
| Id  | Operation                  | Name     | Rows  | Cost (%CPU)| Time     |
--------------------------------------------------------------------------------
|   0 | SELECT STATEMENT           |          |     1 |     4   (0)| 00:00:01 |
|   1 |  SORT AGGREGATE            |          |     1 |            |          |
|   2 |   TABLE ACCESS STORAGE FULL| FND_USER |  2840 |     4   (0)| 00:00:01 |
--------------------------------------------------------------------------------
```

The TABLE ACCESS STORAGE FULL operation in the above execution plan indicates that the SQL statement was eligible for cell offload. The differentiating text between cell offload and traditional full-scan operations is STORAGE FULL. Oracle introduced this SQL plan operation specifically for Exadata and, when you see this in an execution plan, you know that the optimizer has chosen a full scan and that if Oracle elects to perform a direct read for the table access, the query will be eligible for Smart Scan and cell offload.

You may have noticed in the previous query that the table we're conducting a full table scan on is small—only 2,840 rows in size—and if you are an Oracle e-Business Suite customer, you'll know that this table is physically very small as well. In reality, Oracle will almost never actually perform a smart scan on a table of this size unless you have taken measures to force smart scans because smart scans are only performed when Oracle adaptively performs direct path read operations; this is predicated by the segment's size.

Note Please see Recipe 15-6 for additional details about direct reads and Smart Scan.

How It Works

With Oracle 11gR2, the `cell_offload_plan_display` initialization parameters determine whether SQL plans will display STORAGE FULL operations for full table or full index scans. This parameter is set to AUTO by default, which will display STORAGE FULL operations for databases running on Exadata. For non-Exadata databases, the similar operation will be displayed as TABLE ACCESS FULL or INDEX ACCESS FULL. There are three available choices for `cell_offload_plan_display`:

- AUTO will display STORAGE FULL operations in the plan display if an Exadata storage cell is present, the segments being scanned reside on the cell, and the SQL statement is offloadable.
- ALWAYS will display STORAGE FULL operations for full scans if the SQL statement is offloadable whether or not the storage is on Exadata cells. This is sometimes useful when conducting an Exadata assessment and you wish to simulate cell offload behavior.
- NEVER will revert the plan display to show the traditional, ACCESS FULL operations. The following example illustrates this behavior on an Exadata database:

```
SQL> alter session set cell_offload_plan_display=NEVER;
Session altered.
SQL> select /*+ full (f) */ count(*)
  2  from fnd_user f;
```

```
  COUNT(*)
----------
      2840

Execution Plan
----------------------------------------------------------
Plan hash value: 2973321430

---------------------------------------------------------------------------
| Id  | Operation          | Name     | Rows  | Cost (%CPU) | Time     |
---------------------------------------------------------------------------
|   0 | SELECT STATEMENT   |          |     1 |     4   (0) | 00:00:01 |
|   1 |  SORT AGGREGATE    |          |     1 |             |          |
|   2 |   TABLE ACCESS FULL| FND_USER |  2840 |     4   (0) | 00:00:01 |
---------------------------------------------------------------------------
```

As mentioned in the solution of this recipe, the fact that a SQL plan operation shows a STORAGE FULL operation does *not* imply that the operation was actually offloaded and was satisfied via Smart Scan; rather, it simply implies that it *could* be depending on whether a direct read operation was performed. This behavior can be confusing for an Exadata DMA and one of the reasons why additional diagnostics measures are required to confirm that smart scans are actually taking place for your queries. Additional recipes in this chapter will arm you with these diagnostics techniques.

In the solution of this recipe, we presented the concept of a "SQL operating being offloadable." Oracle enables cell offload for full table scans, fast full index scans, fast full IOT scans, and a subset of SQL functions. These functions are visible in the V$SQLFN_METADATA view, and V$SQLFN_METADATA.OFFLOADABLE contains a YES or NO value indicating whether the function is offloadable on the storage cells. You can query V$SQLFN_METADATA to find all offloadable and non-offloadable functions. In Oracle 11gR2, there are 393 offloadable operations and the following query lists some of these:

```
SQL> select name,offloadable
from v$sqlfn_metadata
where offloadable='YES'
/

NAME                    OFF
--------------------    ---
>                       YES
<                       YES
>=                      YES
<=                      YES
=                       YES
... Output omitted for brevity
```

If you are not seeing offload operations in your SQL plan, check the Predicate Information from your plan and look for functions that are not offloadable, as outlined in bold:

```
Predicate Information (identified by operation id):
---------------------------------------------------

   2 - storage("ORG_ID"=TO_NUMBER(SYS_CONTEXT('multi_org2','current_org_id')))
       filter("ORG_ID"=TO_NUMBER(SYS_CONTEXT('multi_org2','current_org_id')))
```

15-2. Controlling Cell Offload Behavior
Problem
You wish to control cell offload and Smart Scan behavior for a particular session or SQL statement.

Solution
In this recipe, you will learn how to employ techniques to force or prevent cell offload functionality systemwide, at a session level, for specific SQL statements, and at the ASM disk group level.

Enabling or Disabling Cell Offload Systemwide

To disable cell offload for all sessions in your database, issue the following SQL statement while connected as a database user with the ALTER SYSTEM system privilege:

```
SQL> alter system set cell_offload_processing=false;
System altered.
SQL>
```

To enable cell offload for all sessions in your database, issue the following SQL statement:

```
SQL> alter system set cell_offload_processing=false;
System altered.
SQL>
```

Enabling or Disabling Cell Offload for a Session

To disable or enable cell offload for your individual session, execute the following commands:

```
SQL> alter session set cell_offload_processing=false;
Session altered.
SQL> alter session set cell_offload_processing=true;
Session altered.
SQL>
```

Enabling or Disabling Cell Offload for a Specific SQL Statement

To control cell offload behavior for individual SQL statements, use the opt_param hint. Following is a sample SQL statement that is hinted to disable cell offload:

```
SQL> select /*+ opt_param('cell_offload_processing','false') */ count(1)
  2  from mtl_material_transactions;
  COUNT(1)
----------
   8783431
SQL>
```

To enable cell offload, use the the following SQL statement:

```
SQL> select /*+ opt_param('cell_offload_processing','true') */ count(1)
  2  from mtl_material_transactions;
COUNT(1)
----------
   8783431
SQL>
```

Enabling and Disabling Smart Scan for an ASM Disk Group

There may be cases in which you wish to disable or enable Smart Scan operations for an entire ASM disk group and all its segments. This is accomplished by altering the ASM disk group attribute cell.smart_scan_capable. While connected as SYSASM to an ASM instance, execute the following command:

```
SQL> alter diskgroup sdata_cm01
 set attribute 'cell.smart_scan_capable'='FALSE';
Diskgroup altered.
SQL>
```

How It Works

There are a number of techniques available to control Smart Scan behavior at a variety of levels. Table 15-1 summarizes these techniques.

Table 15-1. Controlling Cell Offload Behavior

Technique	Scope	Example
cell_offload_processing initialization parameter	System or session	alter system set cell_offload_processing=false;
		alter session set cell_offload_processing=true;
opt_param hint	SQL statement	select /*+ opt_param('cell offload processing','true' */ ...
		select /*+ opt_param('cell offload processing','false' */ ...
alter diskgroup set attribute	ASM disk group	alter diskgroup [DG] set attribute 'cell.smart_scan_capable'='[TRUE|FALSE]';

15-3. Measuring Smart Scan with Statistics

Problem

You wish to determine whether a SQL query, session, or system processed SQL statements using Exadata Smart Scan.

Solution

In this recipe you will learn how to use Oracle's Smart Scan related statistics to determine whether Smart Scan was utilized and measure the I/O bytes transmitted over the storage interconnect. We will focus on measuring Smart Scan at four levels: systemwide, for a specific session, within your own Oracle session, and from Oracle's Automatic Workload Repository (AWR). In each section, we will provide scripts that report on the cell physical IO interconnect bytes, cell physical IO bytes eligible for predicate offload, and cell physical IO interconnect bytes returned by Smart Scan statistics.

Measuring Smart Scan Statistics Systemwide

To measure Smart Scan statistics systemwide, execute the script in Listing 15-1.

Listing 15-1. lst15-01-exass-system.sql

```
SQL> select  inst.instance_name,
         b.name,
         a.value/1024/1024/1024 value
    from  gv$sysstat a, gv$statname b, gv$instance inst
    where a.statistic# = b.statistic#
    and   b.name in
                 ('cell physical IO bytes eligible for predicate offload',
                     'cell physical IO interconnect bytes',
                  'cell physical IO interconnect bytes returned by Smart Scan')
    and    inst.inst_id=a.inst_id
    and    inst.inst_id=b.inst_id
    order by 1,2;
Instance   Statistic                                                          Value (GB)
----------  ------------------------------------------------------------       ------------
edw1       cell physical IO bytes eligible for predicate offload                 59,080
edw1       cell physical IO interconnect bytes                                   28,048
edw1       cell physical IO interconnect bytes returned by Smart Scan            25,791
edw2       cell physical IO bytes eligible for predicate offload                 58,914
edw2       cell physical IO interconnect bytes                                   27,968
edw2       cell physical IO interconnect bytes returned by Smart Scan            25,702
```

In this query, we can see that for this database, each instance had almost 60 TB of data eligible for Smart Scan, approximately 28 TB transmitted over the storage interconnect, and about 25 TB returned via Smart Scan queries.

Measuring Smart Scan for a Specific Session

To measure Smart Scan statistics for a specific session, identify an Oracle session and execute the script in Listing 15-2.

Listing 15-2. lst15-02-exass-session.sql

```
SQL> select sess.sid,
        stat.name,
        round(sess.value/1024/1024/1024,2) value
   from  v$sesstat sess,
         v$statname stat
   where stat.statistic# = sess.statistic#
     and sess.sid = '&&sid'
     and stat.name in
                 ('cell physical IO bytes eligible for predicate offload',
                  'cell physical IO interconnect bytes',
                   'cell physical IO interconnect bytes returned by Smart Scan')
union
```

```
select -1,
       stat.name,
       round(sum(sess.value)/1024/1024/1024,2) value
from   v$sesstat sess,
       v$statname stat
where  stat.statistic# = sess.statistic#
  and  sess.sid  in (select sid from v$px_session where qcsid='&&sid')
  and  stat.name in
                  ('cell physical IO bytes eligible for predicate offload',
                   'cell physical IO interconnect bytes',
                   'cell physical IO interconnect bytes returned by Smart Scan')
group by stat.name
order by 1 desc,2;
```

```
                                                                        Value (GB)
SID    Statistic
-----  ------------------------------------------------------------     ------------
  914  cell physical IO bytes eligible for predicate offload                 2,648
  914  cell physical IO interconnect bytes                                     749
  914  cell physical IO interconnect bytes returned by Smart Scan              749
```

The script accepts a &&sid input parameter and uses V$SESSTAT to report on Smart Scan statistics. In addition to listing statistics from V$SESSTAT for the specific session ID, the script will report summarized Smart Scan statistics for all parallel query slaves in the event that the session is a parallel query coordinator and is actively running a parallel query operation. Oracle increments system statistics for the parallel query coordinator at the completion of the parallel query, while the counters for each parallel query slave are incremented in real time.

Measuring Smart Scan Statistics for Your Session

To collect Smart Scan statistics from your own session, use the V$MYSTAT view. While logged in to to SQL*Plus and ideally, after running a query or two, execute the script in Listing 15-3.

Listing 15-3. lst15-03-exass-mysess.sql

```
SQL> select stat.name,
            round(sess.value/1024/1024/1024,2) value
     from   v$mystat sess,
            v$statname stat
     where  stat.statistic# = sess.statistic#
       and  stat.name in
                    ('cell physical IO bytes eligible for predicate offload',
                     'cell physical IO interconnect bytes',
                     'cell physical IO interconnect bytes returned by Smart Scan')
     order by 1;
```

```
                                                                  Value (GB)
Statistic
------------------------------------------------------------      ------------
cell physical IO bytes eligible for predicate offload                    883
cell physical IO interconnect bytes                                      346
cell physical IO interconnect bytes returned by Smart Scan               346
```

Measuring Smart Scan Statistics from AWR

To measure your Smart Scan statistics per AWR interval over a period of snapshots, execute the script in Listing 15-4.

Listing 15-4. lst15-04-exass-awr.sql

```
select stime,icgb,eliggb,ssgb from (
        select  distinct
                to_char(snap.begin_interval_time,'DD-MON-RR HH24:MI') stime,
                snaps.icbytes/1024/1024/1024 icgb,
                snaps.eligbytes/1024/1024/1024 eliggb,
                snaps.ssbytes/1024/1024/1024 ssgb,
                myrank
        from (
                select ss1.snap_id,
                  (sum(ss1.value) - lag(sum(ss1.value),1,0) over (order by ss1.snap_id)) icbytes,
                  (sum(ss2.value) - lag(sum(ss2.value),1,0) over (order by ss2.snap_id))
                                                                                       eligbytes,
                  (sum(ss3.value) - lag(sum(ss3.value),1,0) over (order by ss3.snap_id)) ssbytes,
                        rank() over (order by ss1.snap_id) myrank
from
     dba_hist_sysstat ss1,
     dba_hist_sysstat ss2,
     dba_hist_sysstat ss3
where    ss1.snap_id=ss2.snap_id
and      ss2.snap_id=ss3.snap_id
and      ss1.snap_id between &&snap_low-1 and &&snap_hi
and      ss2.dbid=ss1.dbid
and       ss3.dbid=ss2.dbid
and      ss1.stat_name='cell physical IO interconnect bytes'
and      ss2.stat_name='cell physical IO bytes eligible for predicate offload'
and      ss3.stat_name='cell physical IO interconnect bytes returned by Smart Scan'
group by ss1.snap_id,ss2.snap_id,ss3.snap_id
        order by ss1.snap_id) snaps,
        dba_hist_snapshot snap
where    snap.snap_id=snaps.snap_id
        order by 1)
where myrank>1;


SnapStart           InterconnectGB    SmartScanEligibleGB    SmartScanReturnedBytes
---------------     --------------    -------------------    ----------------------
10-NOV-12 17:00                  3                      0                         0
10-NOV-12 18:00               1887                   6660                      1884
10-NOV-12 19:00               2496                   7463                      2495
```

How It Works

Oracle tracks I/O statistics specific to the Exadata storage interconnect three main statistics, as explained in Table 15-2.

Table 15-2. Smart Scan Statistic Descriptions

Statistic	Meaning
cell physical IO interconnect bytes	Represents the number of bytes transmitted over the storage interconnect. Oracle increments this counter for all physical I/Os, regardless of whether satisfied via smart scans or block I/O requests. As such, this statistic provides a mechanism to measure the amount of data being serviced over your InfiniBand interconnect and ingested on the compute nodes by the database instances.
cell physical IO bytes eligible for predicate offload	Represents the number of bytes eligible for Smart Scan. For queries that qualify for Smart Scan, this statistic provides an indication of how much interconnect I/O you will save as a result of cell offload.
cell physical IO interconnect bytes returned by Smart Scan	Represents the number of bytes returned by Smart Scan. For queries in which the majority of I/O is serviced via Smart Scan, this statistic is often very close in size to the cell physical IO interconnect bytes statistic.

Using these statistics and their meanings, you can design scripts to measure Smart Scan behavior and quantify the volume of I/O bytes transmitted over the storage interconnect. One of the ways that an Exadata DMA can quantify the savings provided by Smart Scan is to compare the ratio of bytes eligible for predicate offload to the number of actual bytes transmitted over the storage interconnect. This is commonly referred to as the Exadata storage cell offload efficiency and is the subject of Recipe 15-5.

15-4. Measuring Offload Statistics for Individual SQL Cursors

Problem

You wish to gather I/O interconnect and cell offload statistics on a per SQL statement basis in order to understand whether the statement benefited from Exadata Smart Scan.

Solution

In this recipe, you will learn how to extract cell I/O interconnect and offload statistics from V$SQL and SQL Monitor views.

Querying SQL Cursor Cell I/O Statistics from V$SQL

To report cell I/O and offload statistics for individual SQL statements, run the script in Listing 15-5. This script accepts a single sql_id as an input parameter.

CHAPTER 15 ■ SMART SCAN AND CELL OFFLOAD

Listing 15-5. lst15-05-exass-vsql.sql

```
SQL> select sql_id,
            (elapsed_time/1000000)/executions avgelapsed,
            decode(io_cell_offload_eligible_bytes,0,'No','Yes') eligible,
            io_interconnect_bytes/1024/1024/1024 icgb,
            io_cell_offload_returned_bytes/1024/1024/1024 ssgb,
            sql_text
     from   gv$sql s
     where  sql_id='&&sql_id'
     order by 1, 2, 3;
  /
SqlID          ChildN AvgSecs Offloaded IO(GB) SS(GB) SqlText
-------------- ------ ------- --------- ------ ------ ----------------------------------------
1xxbw6b88uc77       0    2.46 Yes          .14    .14 select /* jc1 */ /*+ full (mmt) */ count
```

In this output, we are displaying the SQL ID, child cursor number, the average elapsed seconds, a Yes or No indication of whether the SQL statement was offloaded, the number of I/O gigabytes transmitted over the interconnect, the number of gigabytes transmitted via Smart Scan, and a bit of the SQL statement text. For example, if you wish to report cell I/O and offload statistics for a given SQL text, use the V$SQL.SQL_TEXT column in your query predicate. To list the top ten SQL statements by average elapsed time and report on their cell I/O and offload eligibility, execute the script in Listing 15-6. This type of analysis is helpful in determining what your top time-consuming SQL statements are (in cache) but also identify whether they were offloaded.

Listing 15-6. lst15-06-exass-allvsql.sql

```
SQL> select  sql_id, child_number,
             (elapsed_time/1000000)/
             executions/
             decode(px_servers_executions,0,1,px_servers_executions) avgelapsed,
              decode(io_cell_offload_eligible_bytes,0,'No','Yes') eligible,
             io_interconnect_bytes/1024/1024/1024 icgb,
             io_cell_offload_returned_bytes/1024/1024/1024 ssgb,
             sql_text
       from gv$sql s
      where executions > 0
      order by 3 desc
  /

SqlID          ChildN AvgSecs Offloaded IO(GB)    SS(GB)   SqlText
-------------- ------ ------- --------- --------- -------- ----------------------------------------
6tdgz7h966hnv       1  159.71 Yes          173.15   173.25 select count(*) from d14.DWB_
3qmc7472q5h91       2  121.75 Yes        1,485.66 1,494.09 select sum(qty) from dwb_rtl_sls_retrn_l
3qmc7472q5h91       1   83.62 Yes        2,178.07 2,191.16 select sum(qty) from dwb_rtl_sls_retrn_l
3qmc7472q5h91       2   43.82 Yes        3,529.50 3,543.58 select sum(qty) from dwb_rtl_sls_retrn_l
... Output omitted for brevity
```

Using Real-Time SQL Monitoring to Report Cell I/O and Offload Statistics for a SQL Statement

Oracle's Real-Time SQL Monitoring feature, discussed in Recipe 14-4, can be used to not only report cell I/O statistics for a SQL statement but also at a SQL plan operation level, providing more granularity for your analysis. Oracle Enterprise Manager provides the most intuitive interface to view this information, but you can also use DBMS_SQLTUNE.REPORT_SQL_MONITOR to collect the same information. For a specific SQL cursor, execute the script in Listing 15-7 to execute a SQL Monitoring report.

Listing 15-7. lst15-07-exass-sqlmon.sql

```
SQL> select dbms_sqltune.report_sql_monitor( sql_id=>'&&p_sqlid',
    event_detail=>'YES',
    report_level=>'ALL')
    from dual;
Enter value for p_sqlid: 3qmc7472q5h91
```

When you generate a SQL Monitor report, the offload statistics are reported as offload efficiencies; raw cell I/O statistics are not displayed. SQL Monitor calculates this efficiency by dividing the V$SQL_PLAN_MONITOR.IO_INTERCONNECT_BYTES by V$SQL_PLAN_MONITOR.PHYSICAL_READ_BYTES columns. What this tells us is that the SQL Monitor views do not contain offload eligible or offload returned columns; Oracle measures the offload efficiency strictly based on the number of bytes returned from the storage cells and the number of physical bytes read.

How It Works

Oracle tracks four storage cell I/O statistics in multiple SQL-related performance views, including VSQL, VSQLAREA, VSQL_STATS, VSQL_AREA_PLAN_HASH, V$SQL_STATS_PLAN_HASH, V$SQL_MONITOR and V$SQL_PLAN_MANAGER. In these views, you can find the IO_CELL_OFFLOAD_ELIGIBLE_BYTES, IO_INTERCONNECT_BYTES, IO_CELL_UNCOMPRESSED_BYTES, and IO_CELL_OFFLOAD_RETURNED_BYTES columns, all of which are populated with self-explanatory values based on the column name. SQL statistics are summarized into the AWR view DBA_HIST_SQLSTAT, which contains summarized and delta values for each of these columns.

Querying the cell I/O and offload statistics on a SQL cursor or SQL plan operation level allows you to not only measure the number of bytes transmitted over the storage interconnect, but also determine the degree to which they used Smart Scan. These statistics provide a more granular mechanism to understand the Smart Scan behavior for your workload than session- or system-level statistics discussed in Recipe 15-3, and they can be used to understand Smart Scan behavior, Smart Scan efficiencies, and overall I/O processing statistics for individual SQL cursors.

15-5. Measuring Offload Efficiency

Problem

You wish to measure the I/O savings provided by Smart Scan and cell offload to determine the impact that Smart Scan is having on your database.

Solution

In this recipe, you will learn how to calculate the cell offload efficiency for a SQL statement, session, or the entire system. The offload efficiency is defined as the number of bytes saved by Exadata Smart Scan offload.

Calculating Offload Efficiency for a SQL Statement

To measure the offload efficiency for an individual SQL statement, execute the script in Listing 15-8. In this script, we are reporting the offload efficiency in two ways: first, by dividing the number of bytes sent over the storage interconnect by the number of bytes eligible for predicate offload and, second, but dividing the number of bytes set over the interconnect to the total read and write bytes for the SQL cursor. This is done to not only account for the fact that not all SQL statements will be offloadable and additionally, but also recognize that there are times when SQL statements are only partially offloadable or may incur write I/O as a result of sort operations.

Listing 15-8. lst15-08-offloadeff-sqlid.sql

```
SQL> select    sql_id,
               (case when io_cell_offload_eligible_bytes = 0 then 0
                  else 100*(1-(io_interconnect_bytes/io_cell_offload_eligible_bytes))
               end) offload1,
               (case when phybytes = 0 then 0
                  else 100*(1-(io_interconnect_bytes/phybytes))
               end) offload2
   from (
    select  sql_id,
            physical_read_bytes+physical_write_bytes phybytes,
            io_cell_offload_eligible_bytes,
            io_interconnect_bytes
     from v$sql
     where sql_id='&&sqlid');

Enter value for sqlid: 9ygh669cakd8c
SqlID              EstOffloadEfficiency%    TrueOffloadEfficiency%
-------------      ---------------------    ----------------------
9ygh669cakd8c                      95.62                      95.62
```

Calculating Offload Efficiencies for Multiple SQL Statements

To generate a report of all of your cached SQL statements and their corresponding offload efficiencies, execute the script in Listing 15-9. In this script, we are only displaying the "Top N" queries by elapsed time, which is provided as an input prompt to the script.

Listing 15-9. lst15-09-offloadeff-sqls.sql

```
SQL> select    sql_id, avgelapsed,
               (case when io_cell_offload_eligible_bytes = 0 then 0
                  else 100*(1-(io_interconnect_bytes/io_cell_offload_eligible_bytes))
               end) offload1,
               (case when phybytes = 0 then 0
                  else 100*(1-(io_interconnect_bytes/phybytes))
               end) offload2
   from (
    select  sql_id,
            physical_read_bytes+physical_write_bytes phybytes,
            io_cell_offload_eligible_bytes,
```

```
                io_interconnect_bytes,
                (elapsed_time/1000000)/
                executions/
                   decode(px_servers_executions,0,1,px_servers_executions) avgelapsed
    from v$sql
    where executions > 0
    order by avgelapsed desc)
   where rownum < &&rows_to_display + 1;
Enter value for rows_to_display: 6

SqlID             AvgElaspedSecs    EstOffloadEfficiency%    TrueOffloadEfficiency%
-------------     --------------    ---------------------    ----------------------
6tdgz7h966hnv             159.71                    60.86                     60.85
3qmc7472q5h91             121.75                    32.41                     32.15
3qmc7472q5h91              83.62                    29.33                     29.03
cnwarupsx3z3k              26.49                    71.69                     71.69
b6usrg82hwsa3              24.06                      .00                     -2.62
b6jzrwqggzt1u              22.90                    60.85                     60.84
```

The fifth row in the output above illustrates an interesting offload efficiency case. In this query, our offload efficiency as measured by the io_cell_offload_eligible_bytes column is zero, indicating that it was not a candidate for Smart Scan. However, the true offload efficiency, which is a reflection of the interconnect bytes divided by physical read plus physical writes, shows a negative number. How can this be? The answer lies in the fact that our script is not accounting correctly for mirrored writes to Oracle ASM disk groups. On our Exadata Database Machine, each of our ASM disk groups is configured with normal ASM redundancy, so when write I/Os take place, they are mirrored. With this knowledge, it is safe to say that SQL ID b6usrg82hwsa3 likely performed direct path writes as a result of a large sort operation. You can confirm this by running the following query:

```
SQL> select sql_id,direct_writes,physical_write_bytes,physical_read_bytes,io_interconnect_bytes
     from v$sql where sql_id='b6usrg82hwsa3'
     /

SqlID            DirectWrites    WriteBytes       ReadBytes         InterconnectBytes
-------------    ------------    --------------   --------------    -----------------
b6usrg82hwsa3          15,728       128,843,776    4,782,235,648          5,039,923,200
SQL>
```

Once you've confirmed that you have performed direct writes and you know your ASM disk group redundancy level, you can multiply the physical_write_bytes by the redundancy level to calculate the true number of write bytes. The following script multiplies the write bytes by two and, as you can see, the statistics match:

```
SQL> select sql_id,(physical_read_bytes + physical_write_bytes*2) totbytes, io_interconnect_bytes
     from v$sql where sql_id='b6usrg82hwsa3'
     /
SqlID            Total Bytes         InterconnectBytes
-------------    ---------------     -----------------
b6usrg82hwsa3      5,039,923,200         5,039,923,200
SQL>
```

This illustrates an important point when you are analyzing cell offload efficiencies from homegrown scripts or via Oracle Enterprise Manager. When you see negative offload efficiencies or offload efficiencies that don't seem to make sense, determine whether your queries are performing direct writes and, if so, multiple the physical_write_bytes statistic by two or three depending on whether your ASM disk groups are configured with normal or high redundancy.

Calculating Offload Efficiency for a Session

To measure offload efficiencies for a specific Oracle session, use Exadata cell statistics from V$SESSTAT. Execute the script in Listing 15-10.

Listing 15-10. lst15-10-offloadeff-sess.sql

```
SQL> select ic_bytes.sid,
            (case when offload_elig.value = 0 then 0
              else 100*(1-(ic_bytes.value/offload_elig.value))
            end) offload1,
            (case when totbytes.value = 0 then 0
              else 100*(1-(ic_bytes.value/totbytes.value))
            end) offload2
              from
              (select sess.sid,stat.name,sess.value
               from   v$sesstat sess, v$statname stat
               where  sess.sid='&&sid' and sess.statistic#=stat.statistic#
               and    stat.name='cell physical IO interconnect bytes') ic_bytes,
              (select sess.sid,stat.name,sess.value
               from v$sesstat sess, v$statname stat
               where  sess.sid='&&sid' and sess.statistic#=stat.statistic#
               and    stat.name='cell physical IO bytes eligible for predicate offload')
                    offload_elig,
              (select sess.sid,sum(sess.value) value
               from v$sesstat sess, v$statname stat
               where  sess.sid='&&sid' and sess.statistic#=stat.statistic#
               and    stat.name in ('physical read bytes','physical write bytes')
               group by sess.sid) totbytes
   where ic_bytes.sid=offload_elig.sid
     and   ic_bytes.sid=totbytes.sid;
Enter value for sid: 847

SID    EstOffloadEfficiency%    TrueOffloadEfficiency%
-----  ---------------------    ----------------------
847                    91.05                     91.08
```

How It Works

The Exadata cell offload efficiency is defined as a percentage of I/O saved as a result of cell offload, or Smart Scan. Using SQL, session, or system statistics, you can determine this offload efficiency by dividing the cell physical IO interconnect bytes statistic by the cell physical IO bytes eligible for predicate offload *or* physical read bytes statistic, depending on whether the statement or session's SQL statements were eligible for offload.

The number of bytes eligible for predicate offload will be non-zero if the SQL statement qualifies for Smart Scan; if not and if Exadata reverts to a normal block I/O server, this statistic will be zero and the physical read bytes (and possibly physical write bytes, in the event of a sorting operation) will indicate the amount of physical I/O performed. In these cases, the cell physical I/O interconnect bytes statistic will closely match the physical read bytes statistic.

When reporting offload efficiencies in this recipe, the higher the efficiency percentage, the greater the I/O savings as a result of offload operations.

As described in the solution of this recipe, the offload efficiencies can sometimes show negative values or report efficiencies that are difficult to explain. If you find this to be the case, check whether your SQL statements are performing physical writes and direct path writes and, if so, multiple the write values by the ASM redundancy of your ASM disk groups. This behavior sometimes manifests itself in Enterprise Manager and with Real-Time SQL Monitoring reports. With SQL Monitoring, it is also important to note that the offload efficiency calculations are based on the physical_read_bytes and physical_write_bytes columns in the V$SQL_MONITOR and V$SQL_PLAN_MONITOR views; SQL Monitoring does not track the cell physical IO bytes eligible for predicate offload statistic.

One final note about cell offload efficiencies—if you have ever launched CellCLI from a storage cell, you have undoubtedly noticed the Cell Efficiency Ratio display:

```
[celladmin@cm01cel01 ~]$ cellcli
CellCLI: Release 11.2.3.1.1 - Production on Sun Nov 11 03:14:57 EST 2012
Copyright (c) 2007, 2011, Oracle.  All rights reserved.
Cell Efficiency Ratio: 5
CellCLI>
```

This efficiency ratio is often difficult to explain, and we recommend you ignore it as it has no practical value for the Exadata DMA when assessing offload and Smart Scan performance behavior.

15-6. Identifying Smart Scan from 10046 Trace Files

Problem

You have generated an extended trace file using event 10046 and wish to identify Smart Scan operations in the trace file.

Solution

In this recipe, you will learn how to identify Smart Scan wait events as well as traditional block I/O wait events inside a 10046 trace file generated for a database running on Exadata.

1. Begin by enabling extended SQL trace in your session:

   ```
   APPS @ visx1> alter session set events '10046 trace name context forever, level 8';
   Session altered.
   Elapsed: 00:00:00.00
   APPS @ visx1>
   ```

   We have enabled event 10046 with level 8, which enables tracing for our session with wait events enabled. There are a number of ways to capture wait event information with extended SQL trace, but additional methods are beyond the scope of this Recipe.

2. Next, execute a series of SQL statements and locate your trace file in your diagnostic_dest location.

3. When complete, turn tracing off and open your 10046 trace file using the viewer or editor of your choice.

4. To locate Smart Scan wait events, search for lines that display the cell smart table scan wait event:

```
[oracle@cm01dbm01 trace]$ grep "cell smart table scan" visx1_ora_23639.trc |head -5
WAIT #140715485923920: nam='cell smart table scan' ela= 126 cellhash#=2520626383 ...
output truncated
WAIT #140715485923920: nam='cell smart table scan' ela= 112 cellhash#=88802347... output
truncated
WAIT #140715485923920: nam='cell smart table scan' ela= 136 cellhash#=398250101  ..
output truncated
WAIT #140715485923920: nam='cell smart table scan' ela= 502 cellhash#=2520626383 ...
output truncated
WAIT #140715485923920: nam='cell smart table scan' ela= 494 cellhash#=88802347 ... output
truncated
[oracle@cm01dbm01 trace]$
```

5. To find wait event lines corresponding to block I/O, execute the following command:

```
[oracle@cm01dbm01 trace]$ grep "cell" visx1_ora_23639.trc|grep block|head -5
WAIT #140715485923920: nam='cell single block physical read' ela= 607 cellhash#=88802347 ...
WAIT #140715485923920: nam='cell multiblock physical read' ela= 820 cellhash#=88802347 ...
WAIT #140715485922944: nam='cell single block physical read' ela= 515 cellhash#=2520626383 ...
WAIT #140715485923920: nam='cell single block physical read' ela= 529 cellhash#=88802347 ...
WAIT #140715485923920: nam='cell multiblock physical read' ela= 1632 cellhash#=88802347 ...
[oracle@cm01dbm01 trace]$
```

The bottom of a tkprof output will show a summary of wait events and their corresponding statistics. The line in bold indicates Smart Scan operations:

```
Elapsed times include waiting on following events:
  Event waited on                         Times   Max. Wait  Total Waited
  ----------------------------------      Waited  ---------  ------------
  cell single block physical read          104      0.00         0.05
  cell smart table scan                   8356      0.01         1.15
  cell list of blocks physical read         11      0.00         0.01
... Output omitted for brevity
```

How It Works

As presented in Recipe 14-7, Smart Scan wait events begin with the cell smart% string. Any wait event that begins with cell and has the text block inside it represents a traditional I/O-related wait event on Exadata.

Extended SQL trace is enabled by setting event 10046 for a session or SQL statement. There are a number of ways to enable SQL trace with wait event information. As most experienced Oracle DBAs are familiar with extended SQL trace and its application and use, a detailed explanation is outside the scope of this text. To learn more, consult Oracle's documentation at docs.oracle.com/cd/E11882_01/server.112/e16638/sqltrace.htm#PFGRF94998 or Google using the search term "extended sql trace with event 10046".

15-7. Qualifying for Direct Path Reads

Problem

You wish to determine whether a SQL statement or workload will qualify for direct path reads in order to assess whether Exadata Smart Scan will be leverage for full scans against the tables in your query.

Solution

In this recipe, you will learn how to determine the conditions and thresholds upon which direct path reads are invoked for your SQL workload. Smart scans require full scans and either serial or parallel direct path read operations, so it is important to be able to predict whether a query will execute with direct path reads to qualify for Smart Scan.

Measuring Your Direct Read Threshold

In 11gR2, when a SQL statement executes with a full table scan or fast full index scan operation, Oracle will attempt to use direct path reads instead of buffered reads when the number of blocks in the table or index exceeds the _small_table_threshold initialization parameter. This parameter defaults to 2% of the size of your database buffer cache. Use the following script to determine your small table threshold and database buffer cache size:

```
SYS @ visx1> select a.ksppinm name, b.ksppstvl value, b.ksppstdf isdefault
    from x$ksppi a, x$ksppsv b
    where a.indx = b.indx
    and (a.ksppinm ='_small_table_threshold'
    or a.ksppinm='__db_cache_size')
    order by 1,2
/
__db_cache_size                  14294188032           FALSE
_small_table_threshold                  32389           TRUE
2 rows selected.
SYS @ visx1>
SYS @ visx1> show parameter db_block_size
db_block_size                    integer      8192
SYS @ visx1>
```

In this output, our database buffer cache size is approximately 13.3 GB and, with an 8 KB block size, we can see that our _small_table_threshold value is roughly 2% of the size of the database buffer cache. For our database, we have sga_target set and db_cache_size unset, so Oracle has dynamically adjusted the buffer cache size based on its Automatic Shared Memory Management (ASMM) calculations based on the database's workload:

_small_table_threshold = 2% * (14294188032 / 8192) = 34898 =~ 32389

What this means for our database is that for objects access via full-scan operations, Oracle will attempt to use direct path reads if the number of blocks exceeds 32,389.

■ **Note** In Oracle 11gR1, direct reads were invoked when the size of the object exceeded five times the small table threshold value. With 11gR2, Oracle is more aggressive with direct reads and uses the _small_table_threshold setting as the threshold.

Testing Direct Path Reads Based on Your _small_table_threshold Setting

For testing purposes, select a few tables whose number of blocks is a little bit below and a little bit above your _small_table_threshold setting:

```
SYS @ visx1> select owner,table_name,
blocks from dba_tables where blocks between 31000 and 33000;

OWNER       TABLE_NAME                      BLOCKS
--------    ----------------------------    ----------
MSC         MSC_RESOURCE_REQUIREMENTS       32560
FEM         FEM_BALANCES                    31328
```

In our test cases, we will use FEM.FEM_BALANCES to confirm buffer read access and MSC.MSC_RESOURCE_REQUIREMENTS to validate direct reads. To validate, query the physical reads direct statistic before and after running a full table scan on the segment. An example is provided:

```
APPS @ visx1> alter system flush buffer_cache;
System altered.
APPS @ visx1> select /*+ full (t) */ count(*) from fem.fem_balances t;

  COUNT(*)
----------
   1217591
1 row selected.
APPS @ visx1> select     stat.name,sess.value
  2  from       v$statname stat, v$mystat sess
  3  where      stat.statistic#=sess.statistic#
  4  and        stat.name='physical reads direct';

NAME                            VALUE
----------------------------    ----------
physical reads direct                    0

1 row selected.
APPS @ visx1>

APPS @ visx1> alter system flush buffer_cache;

System altered.

Elapsed: 00:00:00.14
APPS @ visx1> select /*+ full (t) */ count(*) from msc.msc_resource_requirements t;

  COUNT(*)
----------
   1057766
1 row selected.
APPS @ visx1> select     stat.name,sess.value
  2  from       v$statname stat, v$mystat sess
  3  where      stat.statistic#=sess.statistic#
  4  and        stat.name='physical reads direct';
```

```
NAME                              VALUE
------------------------------    ----------
physical reads direct                  31867
1 row selected.
APPS @ visx1>
```

As you can see, our query performed direct path reads when we scanned the larger of the tables and used a traditional buffered read mechanism to access the data for our smaller full table scan.

Validating That Smart Scan Is Used for Full-Scan Operations

There are a number of ways to confirm whether your SQL statements are using Smart Scan and in Recipes 15-3 and 15-4, we provide several techniques. From our example in the previous section, in Listing 15-11 we will query V$SQL and measure the offload efficiency for each of the SQL statements above.

Listing 15-11. lst15-11-offloadeff-sqltext.sql

```
SQL> select    sql_id,
  2            (case when io_cell_offload_eligible_bytes = 0 then 0
  3              else 100*(1-(io_interconnect_bytes/io_cell_offload_eligible_bytes))
  4            end) offload1,
  5            (case when phybytes = 0 then 0
  6              else 100*(1-(io_interconnect_bytes/phybytes))
  7            end) offload2,
  8            sql_text
  9   from (
 10     select   sql_id,
 11              physical_read_bytes+physical_write_bytes phybytes,
 12              io_cell_offload_eligible_bytes,
 13              io_interconnect_bytes, sql_text
 14     from v$sql
 15     where sql_text like '%full (t)%' and
 16     sql_text not like '%sql_id%')
 17  ;

SqlID           EstOffloadEfficiency%  TrueOffloadEfficiency%  SqlText
-------------   ---------------------  ----------------------  --------------------------------
9ms95j9bzjxp1                     .00                     .00  select /*+ full (t) */ count(*)
                                                               from fem.fem_balances t
13p3231c8uxza                   93.29                   93.35  select /*+ full (t) */ count(*)
                                                               from msc.msc_resource_requirements t
```

Adaptive Direct Reads and the Cached Block Threshold

In addition to examining the _small_table_threshold parameter in order to determine whether full scans will be serviced via direct path reads, Oracle employs an *adaptive direct read* mechanism that assesses whether the number of cached blocks in the database buffer cache exceeds a threshold, prior to making a decision to use buffered reads or direct reads. This cached block threshold, or the "stop cached" threshold, is defined as 50% of the number of object's blocks for Oracle 11gR2; in other words, if more than 50% of an object's blocks reside in the database buffer cache, subsequent queries that perform full table scans on the object will use buffered reads.

To determine how many of an object's blocks are cached in the database buffer cache, execute the script in Listing 15-12. This script uses the X$KCBOQH fixed table and references its NUM_BUF column.

Listing 15-12. lst15-12-cached-blocks.sql

```
SQL> select co.object_name object_name,
            nvl(co.subobject_name,'N/A') partition_name,
            co.cachedblocks, 100*(co.cachedblocks/seg.blocks) cachepct
     from (
       select owner, object_name,
           subobject_name, object_type, sum(num_buf) cachedblocks
       from
           dba_objects, x$kcboqh
       where obj# = data_object_id
         and   upper(object_name) =upper('&&object_name')
         and   upper(owner)=upper('&&owner')
         group by owner, object_name, subobject_name, object_type) co,
       (select owner,segment_name,partition_name,blocks
       from dba_segments
       where upper(owner)=upper('&&owner') and upper(segment_name)=upper('&&object_name')) seg
       where co.owner=seg.owner and co.object_name=seg.segment_name
         and nvl(co.subobject_name,'ZZZ')=nvl(seg.partition_name,'ZZZ');
Enter value for object_name: MSC_RESOURCE_REQUIREMENTS
Enter value for owner: MSC

Object                         Partition                      CachedBlk    Cached%
------------------------------ ------------------------------ ---------- ---------
MSC_RESOURCE_REQUIREMENTS      RESOURCE_REQUIREMENTS__21               9     30.47
MSC_RESOURCE_REQUIREMENTS      RESOURCE_REQUIREMENTS_0                 1      6.25
MSC_RESOURCE_REQUIREMENTS      RESOURCE_REQUIREMENTS_999999         7767     23.95
MSC_RESOURCE_REQUIREMENTS      RESOURCE_REQUIREMENTS_1                 1      6.25
SQL>
```

From this output, we can see the number of cached blocks for our table and its partitions from the X$KCBOQH.NUM_BUF column. If the value in this column exceeds 50% of the number of blocks in the object, direct reads will not take place for full scans.

Adaptive Direct Reads and the Dirty Block Threshold

Similar to the descriptions and example in the previous section, Oracle employs an *adaptive direct read* mechanism that assesses whether the number of *dirty* blocks in the database buffer cache exceeds a threshold, prior to making a decision to use buffered reads or direct reads. This dirty block threshold, or the "stop dirty" threshold, is defined as 25% of the number of an object's blocks for Oracle 11gR2; in other words, if more than 25% of an objects blocks are dirty in the buffer cache, subsequent queries that perform full table scans will use buffered reads.

To determine how many of an object's blocks are dirty in the database buffer cache, execute the script in Listing 15-13. This script counts the number of blocks from V$BH where the DIRTY flag is set to Y.

Listing 15-13. lst15-13-dirty-blocks.sql

```sql
SQL> select object.object_name, object.partition_name,object.dirty dirty,
       100*(object.dirty/seg.blocks) dirtypct
     from
     (select owner,object_name,subobject_name partition_name,count(1) dirty
          from dba_objects obj, v$bh bh
          where obj.data_object_id=bh.objd
          and upper(obj.object_name)=upper('&&object_name')
          and upper(obj.owner)=upper('&&owner')
          and bh.dirty='Y'
         group by owner,object_name,subobject_name) object,
     (select owner,segment_name,partition_name,blocks
      from dba_segments
      where upper(owner)=upper('&&owner') and upper(segment_name)=upper('&&object_name')) seg
    where object.owner=seg.owner and object.object_name=seg.segment_name
    and nvl(object.partition_name,'ZZZ')=nvl(seg.partition_name,'ZZZ');
Enter value for object_name: MSC_RESOURCE_REQUIREMENTS
Enter value for owner: MSC
Object                         Partition                         DirtyBlk     Dirty%
-------------------------      ----------------------------      ---------    --------
MSC_RESOURCE_REQUIREMENTS      RESOURCE_REQUIREMENTS__21               12        9.38
MSC_RESOURCE_REQUIREMENTS      RESOURCE_REQUIREMENTS_999999           292         .90
```

Statistics-Driven Direct Read Decisions

How does Oracle determine the segment block counts to determine whether the number of blocks is above the _small_table_threshold value? Prior to Oracle 11.2.0.2, this was determined by examining the segment header block and using the *actual* number of blocks below the segment's highwater mark. In other words, a segment's object statistics had no bearing on the direct path read algorithm.

With 11.2.0.2 and above, Oracle introduced a hidden parameter called _direct_read_decision_statistics_driven. By default, this parameter is set to TRUE, which means that Oracle will query the object statistics (specifically, TAB$.BLKCNT and TABPART$.BLKCNT for tables and indexes, respectively) as its basis for determining how many blocks exist for a segment. When set to FALSE, Oracle will scan the segment header to determine the actual number of blocks.

Test this behavior by seeding misrepresentative statistics for one of your tables. In the following script, we are seeding a block count of 20 for the MSC_RESOURCE_REQUIREMENTS table used in the previous examples and running a direct read test. Recall that previously in this recipe, we measured that full scans against this table utilized direct path reads and benefited from Smart Scan:

```
APPS @ visx1> begin
    dbms_stats.set_table_stats('MSC','MSC_RESOURCE_REQUIREMENTS',
        numblks=>20);
    end;
/
PL/SQL procedure successfully completed.
APPS @ visx1>
APPS @ visx1> alter system flush buffer_cache;
System altered.
APPS @ visx1> select /*+ full (t) */ count(*) from msc.msc_resource_requirements t;
```

```
  COUNT(*)
----------
   1057766
1 row selected.
APPS @ visx1> select    stat.name,sess.value
  2  from       v$statname stat, v$mystat sess
  3  where      stat.statistic#=sess.statistic#
  4  and        stat.name='physical reads direct';
NAME                              VALUE
------------------------------    ----------
physical reads direct                      0
1 row selected.
APPS @ visx1>
```

If you gather or seed object statistics with accurate block count numbers and if the block count is larger than the small table threshold, full scans will be performed with direct path reads assuming that the cached block and dirty block thresholds discussed in the previous sections are not surpassed.

How It Works

On Exadata, smart scans require direct path reads—this logic resides in Oracle's I/O code path. Direct path reads come in two flavors: parallel direct reads and serial direct reads. Parallel query operations perform parallel direct reads unless In Memory Parallel Execution buffers parallel read blocks, as discussed in Recipe 21-8. Serial direct reads occur when an object is accessed via full scan in serial and is subject to the small table threshold and adaptive direct read algorithms. Direct reads work by fetching the required data into the foreground session's PGA. With buffered reads, blocks are loaded into the database buffer cache.

In 11g, Oracle introduced the serial direct read functionality to improve performance for full table scan operations and mitigate the impact of polluting the database buffer cache with blocks accessed via full scans. This direct read functionality for full scans is generic to Oracle 11g, but Exadata's Smart Scan code exploits this generic performance feature.

The choice of whether to perform a direct path read is made at runtime by Oracle. The optimizer itself has no influence on whether or not direct reads are performed, but rather, the number of blocks in the object combined with the number of cached or dirty blocks is used to determine whether to perform direct reads. This choice is made on a per SQL statement basis for each object upon which the optimizer elects to perform a full scan.

Why are direct path reads so important on Exadata? The answer is that smart scans depend on direct path reads, and Smart Scan is probably the most important performance feature delivered by Exadata. So, for smart scans to take place, the following steps need to be taken:

1. The optimizer must elect to perform a full table scan or fast full index scan. This choice is dependent on a number of factors including the existence of indexes on a table, query predicates, and recently, Exadata-specific system statistics that effectively reduce the cost of a full table scan (see Recipe 21-8 for additional details).

2. The size of the object being scanned must be larger than 2% of the size of the database buffer cache, and fewer than 50% of the blocks are cached in the buffer cache and fewer than 25% of the blocks are dirty in the buffer cache.

3. If the previous conditions are met, the object can be accessed with direct path reads when accessed in serial. When using parallel query, direct reads are used unless In Memory Parallel Execution is used.

For the new Exadata DMA, the influence of direct path reads on smart scans often presents a challenging puzzle. Many DMAs know how to determine whether smart scans are taking place and are often faced with trying to answer the following question: "Why didn't my query offload?" In our experience, one of the most common reasons (other than situations when the query didn't perform a full scan) is because Oracle elected to do a buffered read based on the object's size being under the small table threshold. One factor that compounds this issue is for organizations that, during the move to Exadata, increase the size of their buffer cache significantly beyond the pre-Exadata sizing; a larger buffer cache means that the small table threshold is higher and direct path reads will be less common.

You can force direct path reads using a number of techniques, which we will cover in Recipe 15-8. Keep in mind though that in many situations, a traditional buffered read may be what you want. Depending on your queries and workloads, local buffer cache access is often preferred over offloaded smart scans and physical disk I/O on your storage cells.

15-8. Influencing Exadata's Decision to Use Smart Scans

Problem

You have a query that is either not using Smart Scan and you believe it should or it is using Smart Scan and you believe it shouldn't and you are looking for techniques to enable or disable Smart Scan.

Solution

In this recipe, you will learn about some techniques to encourage or discourage Smart Scan behavior.

> **Note** The examples in this recipe should not be implemented without proper testing. Some of the tips are "hacks" to force behavior that Oracle would not otherwise perform and could have performance, scalability, or concurrency implications depending on your workload.

Forcing Full Table Scans with Hints

If you have a query on a table with a predicate that supports an index lookup and the optimizer decides that an index scan is preferable to a full table scan, you can use a full table scan hint in your query assuming you have access to the source code. When you do this, Oracle should elect to perform a full scan and, assuming the object qualifies for direct path reads, you should benefit from Smart Scan:

```
APPS @ visx1> select /*+ full (tab) */ ...
```

Dropping Indexes

If your queries are performing index scans and you believe that full scans with cell offload are preferable, you can drop your indexes. This advice was one of the early Exadata marketing claims that caught the attention of many Oracle DBAs, and for good reason. Our opinion on the topic is that you should know, through comprehensive testing, that you do not need your indexes before dropping them. There are a number of techniques to validate your index usage including enabling monitoring for your indexes and checking the V$OBJECT_USAGE view, querying SYS.COL_USAGE$ for your query predicates on indexed columns, and so forth.

Making Indexes Invisible

In lieu of dropping your indexes, you can make them invisible by running the ALTER INDEX [INDEX] INVISIBLE command. This command makes the index invisible to the optimizer, so when queries are parsed for the table and indexed columns, Oracle will exclude an index access path and could favor a full table scan operation. Following is a before-and-after example of running a query with a visible and invisible index and autotrace enabled to capture the execution plan:

```
APPS @ visx1> select count(*) from mmt_temp
  2  where transaction_id between 100 and 999;
1 row selected.
Execution Plan
----------------------------------------------------------
Plan hash value: 980181954
------------------------------------------------------------------
| Id | Operation         | Name   | Rows | Bytes | .... 
------------------------------------------------------------------
|  0 | SELECT STATEMENT  |        |   1  |   6   | ...
|  1 |  SORT AGGREGATE   |        |   1  |   6   | ...
|* 2 |   INDEX RANGE SCAN| MMT_N1 |  49  |  294  | ...
------------------------------------------------------------------

APPS @ visx1> alter index apps.mmt_n1 invisible;
Index altered.
APPS @ visx1>
APPS @ visx1> select count(*) from mmt_temp
  2  where transaction_id between 100 and 999;
  COUNT(*)
----------
         1
1 row selected.
Execution Plan
----------------------------------------------------------
Plan hash value: 3452543490
------------------------------------------------------------------
| Id | Operation                 | Name     | Rows | Bytes |
------------------------------------------------------------------
|  0 | SELECT STATEMENT          |          |   1  |   6   | ...
|  1 |  SORT AGGREGATE           |          |   1  |   6   | ...
|* 2 |   TABLE ACCESS STORAGE FULL| MMT_TEMP|  49  |  294  | ...
------------------------------------------------------------------
```

■ **Note** Making indexes invisible only prevents the optimizer from considering the index in an access path decision. The entries in the index will continue to be updated as DML is issued to the table. For these reasons, the invisible indexes approach often provides a relatively low-risk option when considering a longer-term option to drop unnecessary indexes.

Ignoring Optimizer Hints

If you have a query or queries that contain hints that favor index access, you can instruct Oracle to ignore all SQL hints by setting the _optimizer_ignore_hints initialization parameter. This can be set for a session and at the system level:

```
APPS @ visx1> alter session set "_optimizer_ignore_hints"=TRUE;
Session altered.
APPS @ visx1>
```

■ **Note** As you can probably surmise, this option is relatively drastic and could cause performance problems. Unless you are confident that there are no "valuable" hints in your application code base, we recommend extensive testing before using this solution. One of the scenarios in which disabling all optimizer hints may be worthwhile is if your application has been extensively hinted to account for optimizer deficiencies from older versions of Oracle and this legacy code base has been carried forward over the years.

Forcing Direct Reads

By default, direct reads are controlled by the _serial_direct_read initialization parameter. This underscore parameter defaults to auto in Oracle 11g, which means that Oracle will automatically and adaptively determine when to perform direct path reads.

■ **Note** Please see Recipe 15-7 to learn more about direct path reads and smart scan.

To force direct path reads, set _serial_direct_read to always:

```
APPS @ visx1> alter session set "_serial_direct_read"=always;
```

To prevent direct path reads, set _serial_direct_read to never:

```
APPS @ visx1> alter session set "_serial_direct_read"=never;
```

In these examples, we altered this initialization parameter at the session level, but we could also perform an alter system to change the behavior systemwide. Take caution when doing this as it could create a detrimental impact on performance based on your workload.

Influence Direct Reads by Adjusting Your Block Counts

As presented in Recipe 15-7, direct path reads will be enabled when the number of blocks in the table or index you are scanning exceeds the _small_table_threshold parameter. Direct path reads are disabled if the number of blocks is below this threshold, the percentage of blocks cached in the buffer cache exceeds 50% of the number of blocks for the object, or if greater than 25% of the blocks for the object are dirty in the buffer cache. While there is no way to influence the "stop cache" and "stop dirty" threshold without changing the way DML is issued in your application, you can influence the block count calculation by manually seeding statistics for the object to a lower value using

DBMS_STATS.SET_TABLE_STATS or DBMS_STATS.SET_INDEX_STATS. The following example demonstrates how to set your number of blocks in the table to a value higher than your small table threshold:

```
APPS @ visx1> select    a.ksppinm name, b.ksppstvl value, b.ksppstdf isdefault
    from x$ksppi a, x$ksppsv b
    where a.indx = b.indx
    and a.ksppinm ='_small_table_threshold'
    order by 1,2
/
_small_table_threshold              32389                         TRUE
1 row selected.
APPS @ visx1> exec dbms_stats.set_table_stats('APPS','MMT_TEMP',numblks=>32390);
PL/SQL procedure successfully completed.
APPS @ visx1>
```

In situations where you want to discourage direct path reads and smart scans, you can reduce your block count to a number less than your small table threshold.

■ **Note** In order for these steps to provide the desired result, _direct_read_decision_statistics_driven must be set to TRUE. This is the default in Oracle 11gR2 and is discussed in Recipe 15-7.

Influencing Direct Reads by Adjusting _small_table_threshold

You can manually increase or decrease the _small_table_threshold parameter, systemwide, by executing the following command:

```
SQL> alter system set "_small_table_threshold"=1000 scope=spfile;
System altered.
SQL>
```

When altered with the ALTER SYSTEM command, you will need to write your changes to an spfile (or manually edit a parameter file if you are not using an spfile) and bounce your database. You can also change this for your individual session using the ALTER SESSION command.

Adjusting your _small_table_threshold parameter is a means to influence when direct path reads start. To learn more about direct path reads, please see Recipe 15-7.

Using the cell_offload_processing Parameter

If you wish to disable or enable cell offload processing for your session or system, you can use the cell_offload_processing initialization parameter. This is dynamically modifiable at the session or system level. To learn more about cell_offload_processing, please see Recipe 15-2.

Using the opt_param Hint

If you wish to disable or enable cell offload processing for a specific SQL statement, you can use the opt_param hint. To learn more about this hint, please see Recipe 15-2.

Gathering System Statistics for Exadata

Starting with Exadata patch bundle 18 for 11.2.0.2 and patch bundle 8 with 11.2.0.3, Oracle introduced a new option to DBMS_STATS.GATHER_SYSTEM_STATS to account for the better performance of full table scans. If you are patched up to or beyond the versions above, gather your system statistics with the following option:

```
SYS @ visx1> exec dbms_stats.gather_system_stats('EXADATA');
PL/SQL procedure successfully completed.
SYS @ visx1>
```

This will cause the optimizer to effectively reduce the cost of full table scans when evaluating potential access paths, favoring full table scans over index scan options.

How It Works

Recall from Oracle's documentation that smart scans happen in the following instances:

- Your query performs a full table scan or fast full index scan.
- The object or objects that you are scanning qualify for direct path reads. Please see Recipe 15-7 to learn about direct path reads and smart scans.
- Your query does not contain any functions that are not offloadable as is visible in V$SQLFN_METADATA.OFFLOADABLE.
- Your database storage resides on Exadata cells.

At times, you may be faced with situations when you want Exadata to perform smart scans when it is not or not perform smart scans when it is. Some of the techniques in this recipe are relatively common for the Exadata DMA, such as the process of making indexes invisible. Before Exadata's smart I/O and cell offload capabilities, many Oracle databases were plagued by I/O problems and DBAs and developers attempted to address these issues by over-indexing their tables in hopes of discouraging full table scans. By testing with invisible indexes, you can confirm whether your indexes are actually needed for your current workload or SQL statements.

Other tips in this solution are less common and certainly discouraged without extensive testing as they could impose performance risk to your application and database. Like all Oracle performance advice, there is rarely a "silver bullet" recommendation that meets the needs of all databases and applications.

15-9. Identifying Partial Cell Offload

Problem

You have a query that you believe should be benefiting significantly from Smart Scan but measures lower than expected offload efficiencies and evidence of block I/O access methods.

Solution

Partial cell offload takes place when Oracle is able to access some of its requested data via Smart Scan and is required to access other rows via block shipping. In this recipe, you will learn how to identify whether partial cell offload is taking place under a variety of conditions.

Measuring Partial Cell Offload Due to Consistent Reads for a Session

Check for the following conditions for a specific session:

- Look for `cell single block physical read` or `cell multiblock physical read` wait events from V$SESSION_EVENT or other wait interface views and compare to the `cell smart table scan` or `cell smart index scan` wait events
- Look for `consistent gets` and `session logical reads` from V$SESSTAT

Measuring Partial Cell Offload Due to Consistent Reads for a SQL Statement

To determine whether you are experiencing partial cell offload for a specific SQL statement, examine V$SQL and V$SQLSTAT for non-zero values for `io_cell_offload_eligible_bytes` combined with large non-zero values for `buffer_gets`.

Measuring Partial Cell Offload Due to Chained Rows

Check for the following conditions for a specific session:

- Look for `cell single block physical read` or `cell multiblock physical read` wait events from V$SESSION_EVENT or other wait interface views and compare to the `cell smart table scan` or `cell smart index scan` wait events
- Look for `consistent gets` and `session logical reads` from V$SESSTAT
- Look for non-zero values for the table fetch continued row statistic

Measuring Partial Cell Offload Due to Overloaded Storage Cells

When Oracle determines that the storage cells are too busy to perform smart scans, the `cell num smart IO sessions in rdbms block IO due to no cell mem` or `cell num smart IO sessions in rdbms block IO due to big payload` system or session counters will be incremented. You can check V$SYSSTAT or V$SESSTAT to confirm if this is the case.

How It Works

Partial cell offload happens when a portion of the data requested is serviced via Smart Scan and a portion is fetched with traditional block I/O methods. At a very simplistic level, the following two statements are true:

- Exadata is a row and column server when data is accessed via Smart Scan.
- Exadata is a block server when data is accessed without Smart Scan.

There are a number of situations in which Exadata reverts to block shipping mode, even for situations in which smart scans should be performed. Exadata can choose or be forced to revert to block shipping mode any time a situation occurs in which Oracle has to read another block to complete its unit of work. One of the more common events is when a chained row is accessed; when Oracle reads a block that contains a chained row, it will follow the pointer to the block containing the row piece to complete the operation. Since this row piece could physically reside on a different storage cell, Oracle must perform a block I/O request and load the blocks into the database buffer cache. Individual storage cells do not communicate with each other so, in this case, Oracle simply ships the entire block back to the database tier and allows the database instance to handle the I/O processing.

Another common situation in which Exadata reverts to block shipping is when dealing with read consistency. If Oracle finds a newer block in cache than the current query, the process of finding the proper block to present to the user is handled in Oracle's read consistency algorithms. These lie at a layer in the kernel that requires Oracle to be operating on blocks in the buffer cache, not rows and columns in the PGA.

15-10. Dealing with Fast Object Checkpoints

Problem

You are noticing significant wait times and wait occurrences for the `enq: KO - fast object checkpoint` wait and wish to troubleshoot and resolve the wait occurrences and times.

Solution

If you are experiencing significant wait times on the `enq: KO - fast object checkpoint` wait event, ensure that you are not forcing direct path reads and bypassing Oracle's adaptive direct read mechanism. Oracle performs a fast object checkpoint when attempting to perform direct path reads and finds dirty blocks in the buffer cache; if this is the case, the foreground process will trigger CKPT to flush the blocks to disk, and the CKPT process asks DBWR to perform the writes.

A good way to put yourself in a position to worry about fast object checkpoints is to have a busy OLTP application with a mix of DML and full scans against busy tables, and force direct reads using the `alter system set "_serial_direct_read"=always` command.

The solution is to *not* bypass adaptive direct reads. Rather, allow Oracle to revert to buffered reads when the percentage of dirty blocks exceeds 25% of the number of blocks in the table, as discussed in Recipe 15-7.

How It Works

When Oracle begins a direct path read operation as a result of a full scan, any blocks for the object that are dirty in the database buffer cache must be checkpointed before being loaded via direct path to protect Oracle's consistent read policy. Sessions that wait many times or long amounts of time on the `enq: KO - fast object checkpoint` wait are usually doing so because DBWR can't write fast enough to disk or too many blocks are dirty in the buffer cache and you have implemented means to bypass Oracle's adaptive direct read algorithms, perhaps by employing techniques from Recipe 15-8.

If you force direct reads for operations that Oracle would otherwise not perform direct reads on, you are opening the door for concurrency bottlenecks and I/O bottlenecks of this sort. Our recommendation is to stick with Oracle's default direct path read decisions if this becomes a problem for your database.

CHAPTER 16

Hybrid Columnar Compression

Exadata Hybrid Columnar Compression, or HCC, is a type of segment compression first made available by Oracle on the Exadata Database Machine. HCC is designed to provide the highest levels of database segment compression.

With HCC, data is organized for storage by columns. Oracle uses the concept of a "compression unit" (CU) with HCC, which stores data by columns but only for a set of rows—this collection of groups of rows organized and compressed together is what leads to the "hybrid" tag in the feature name.

HCC offers very high compression ratios for QUERY compression and even higher compression ratios for ARCHIVE compression. Higher compression ratios mean two things: less disk space is required to store large objects and there is potential for better I/O performance.

But HCC comes at a cost if not implemented appropriately. In this chapter, we'll cover HCC basics, compare it with other compression alternatives, show when to use HCC and when not to, and show you how to measure the impact of Hybrid Columnar Compression for your database.

16-1. Estimating Disk Space Savings for HCC

Problem

You wish to estimate the disk space savings you will attain by compressing a table with Hybrid Columnar Compression.

Solution

In this recipe, you will learn how to use the compression advisor to estimate the disk space requirements and compression ratio for an existing, uncompressed table. Start by logging in to SQL*Plus in an existing Oracle 11g database and execute the script in Listing 16-1. This script will prompt you for a "scratch" tablespace (which cannot be defined with uniform extent allocation), a table owner, and table name.

■ **Note** When you execute the compression advisor, Oracle will temporarily create and subsequently drop an actual physical segment in your database, based on the input compression type supplied to DBMS_COMPRESSION.GET_COMPRESSION_RATIO. This segment could very well be large, based on the size of the table you are performing the analysis with, so you should make sure you have sufficient disk space to execute the advisor and, ideally, execute the advisor during off-peak hours.

Another topic worth mentioning is that while HCC is only available on Exadata and other Oracle storage products (ZFS Storage Appliance and Pillar Axiom), the compression advisor is shipped with Oracle 11g and can be executed from a non-Exadata database.

Listing 16-1. lst16-01-compadv.sql

```
SQL> declare
       l_blkcnt_cmp        binary_integer;
       l_blkcnt_uncmp      binary_integer;
       l_row_cmp           binary_integer;
       l_row_uncmp         binary_integer;
       l_cmp_ratio         number;
       l_comptype_str      varchar2(200);
     begin
       dbms_compression.get_compression_ratio(scratchtbsname=>'&&tbs',
           ownname=>upper('&tab_owner'),
           tabname=>upper('&table'),
           partname=>null,
           comptype=>dbms_compression.comp_for_query_low,
           blkcnt_cmp=>l_blkcnt_cmp,
           blkcnt_uncmp=>l_blkcnt_uncmp,
           row_cmp=>l_row_cmp,
           row_uncmp=>l_row_uncmp,
           cmp_ratio=>l_cmp_ratio,
           comptype_str=>l_comptype_str);
       dbms_output.put_line('Blocks, Compressed='||l_blkcnt_cmp);
       dbms_output.put_line('Blocks, Uncompressed='||l_blkcnt_uncmp);
       dbms_output.put_line('Rows, Compressed='||l_row_cmp);
       dbms_output.put_line('Rows, Uncompressed='||l_row_uncmp);
       dbms_output.put_line('Compression Ratio='||l_cmp_ratio);
       dbms_output.put_line('Compression Type='||l_comptype_str);
     end;
/
Enter value for tbs: SYSAUX
Enter value for tab_owner: INV
Enter value for table: MTL_MATERIAL_TRANSACTIONS
Compression Advisor self-check validation successful. select count(*) on both
Uncompressed and EHCC Compressed format = 1000001 rows
Blocks, Compressed=2592
Blocks, Uncompressed=47639
Rows, Compressed=386
Rows, Uncompressed=20
Compression Ratio=18.3
Compression Type="Compress For Query Low"
PL/SQL procedure successfully completed.
SQL>
```

In this output, we have noted several lines in bold:

- The comptype argument specifies which flavor of compression you wish to run your compression advisor with. In our example, we chose DBMS_COMPRESSION.COMP_FOR_QUERY_LOW, which means to compress for Query Low.

- The number of estimated compressed blocks is 2,592 and the number of uncompressed blocks is 47,639.

- The compression ratio equals 47,639 / 2,592, or approximately 18:3.

How It Works

DBMS_COMPRESSION.GET_COMPRESSION_RATIO performs the following tasks:

- Samples data from the input table and creates a 1,000,001 row uncompressed table in your scratch tablespace
- Samples the same input table and creates a 1,000,001 row compressed table with the HCC compression flavor specified in the comptype argument
- Compares the storage results using several other temporary tables, which it drops at the completion of the procedure
- Reports the estimated number of rows, blocks, and the compression ratio

Because the compression advisor samples a million rows from your source table, the estimated block counts and compression ratio will likely be very accurate; the compression advisor performs an intermediate set of uncompressed and compressed tables using PARALLEL CREATE TABLE AS (PCTAS).

In the solution of this recipe, we demonstrated using the compression advisor to estimate the HCC compression statistics when compressing with Compress For Query Low. You can execute the DBMS_COMPRESSION procedure using the following choices as well:

- COMPTYPE=>DBMS_COMPRESSION.COMP_FOR_QUERY_HIGH = Query High
- COMPTYPE=>DBMS_COMPRESSION.COMP_FOR_ARCHIVE_LOW = Archive Low
- COMPTYPE=>DBMS_COMPRESSION.COMP_FOR_ARCHIVE_HIGH = Archive High
- COMPTYPE=>DBMS_COMPRESSON.COMP_NOCOMPRESS = No Compression
- COMPTYPE=>DBMS_COMPRESSION.COMP_FOR_OLTP = OLTP compression. Note that this compression flavor is *not* one of the HCC compression types, but rather a feature of Oracle Advanced Compression.

16-2. Building HCC Tables and Partitions

Problem

You wish to build Hybrid Columnar Compressed tables or partitions in your Exadata database.

Solution

In this recipe, you will learn how to create HCC tables and partitions in your database using the COMPRESS FOR storage clause in the CREATE statement as well as setting the default compression level for tablespaces.

Creating a HCC Table Compressed for Query High

Execute the following CREATE TABLE statement, with the HCC clauses in **bold**:

```
SQL> create table mytab_compqueryhigh
        (empname varchar2(30)
    ,empno number
    ,empdescr varchar2(100)
    ,hire_date date)
    tablespace apps_ts_tx_idx compress for query high;
Table created.
SQL>
```

Creating a HCC Table Compressed for Query High Using Create Table as Select (CTAS)

Execute the following SQL statement, with the HCC clause in **bold**:

```
SQL> create table mmt_compqueryhigh
    nologging tablespace apps_ts_tx_data
    compress for query high
    as select * from mtl_material_transactions;
Table created.
SQL>
```

Creating a Table with HCC Partitions

To create a partitioned table with HCC-compressed partitions, choose a table name and partitioning strategy and execute a SQL statement similar to the following one. In this example, we are using CREATE TABLE to build our compressed partitioned table:

```
SQL> create table xla.xla_ae_lines_t1
    partition by list (application_id)
    subpartition by range (accounting_date)
    (partition AP values (200)
     (subpartition ap_1995 values less than (to_date('01-JAN-1996','dd-MON-yyyy')),
...Output omitted for brevity
     subpartition ap_2011 values less than (to_date('01-JAN-2012','dd-MON-yyyy')),
     subpartition ap_max values less than (maxvalue)
    ),
    partition AR values (222)
     (subpartition ar_1995 values less than (to_date('01-JAN-1996','dd-MON-yyyy')),
...Output omitted for brevity
    ), partition partother values (default))
  tablespace apps_ts_tx_data nologging
  compress for query high
as select * from xla.xla_ae_lines
/
Table created.
SQL>
```

Creating a Table with a Mix of Uncompressed and HCC-Compressed Partitions

To create a partitioned table with some of its partitions compressed with HCC and some uncompressed, issue a SQL statement like the one that follows. In this CREATE TABLE statement, we are specifying the compression clause at the partition level, not at the table level:

```
SQL> create table xla.xla_ae_lines_t1
    partition by list (application_id)
    subpartition by range (accounting_date)
    (partition AP values (200)
     (subpartition ap_1995 values less than (to_date('01-JAN-1996','dd-MON-yyyy'))
                                                    compress for query high,
```

```
    subpartition ap_1996 values less than (to_date('01-JAN-1997','dd-MON-yyyy'))
                                                        compress for query high,
... Output omitted for brevity
    subpartition ap_2011 values less than (to_date('01-JAN-2012','dd-MON-yyyy'))),
    subpartition ap_max values less than (maxvalue)
... Output omitted for brevity
    subpartition ap_jan2010 values less than (to_date('01-FEB-2010','dd-MON-yyyy'))),
  ), partition partother values (default))
... Output omitted for brevity
    subpartition ap_jan2010 values less than (to_date('01-FEB-2010','dd-MON-yyyy'))),
  tablespace apps_ts_tx_data nologging
  as
  select * from xla.xla_ae_lines;
Table created.
SQL>
```

Specifying Compression Attributes for a Tablespace

You can also specify default compression settings at the tablespace level using the DEFAULT COMPRESS FOR clause in your CREATE TABLESPACE command. Doing so will enable HCC compression for rows inserted or loaded via Oracle's direct path insert/load operations. The following is an example of using the CREATE TABLESPACE command to set a tablespace's default compression:

```
SQL> create bigfile tablespace rtl3 datafile '+DATA_CM01'
        size 2g         autoextend on next 1m
        extent management local autoallocate
        segment space management auto
        default compress for query low;
Tablespace created.
SQL>
```

To list your tablespace's default compression settings, run the SQL statement in Listing 16-2.

Listing 16-2. lst16-02-tbs-compsettings.sql

```
SQL> select tablespace_name,
            def_tab_compression,
            nvl(compress_for,'NONE') compress_for
     from dba_tablespaces;

Tablespace              CompSetting         CompressType
----------------------  ------------------  --------------------
SYSTEM                  DISABLED            NONE
SYSAUX                  DISABLED            NONE
.. Output omitted for brevity
TBS_TEST                DISABLED            NONE
TBS_OLTPCOMP            ENABLED             OLTP
TBS_QUERYHIGH           ENABLED             QUERY HIGH
```

Note Rows inserted via conventional insert or load operations to tablespaces with a default compression type set will revert to uncompressed data for HCC compression. This is in contrast with OLTP or standard compression, in which conventional inserts will result in rows compressed according to the tablespace's configuration parameters.

How It Works

Creating HCC tables or partitions is achieved by using the COMPRESS FOR syntax in the storage clause of the SQL statement. The following compression clauses are available for HCC:

- COMPRESS FOR QUERY LOW
- COMPRESS FOR QUERY HIGH
- COMPRESS FOR ARCHIVE LOW
- COMPRESS FOR ARCHIVE HIGH

The HCC-specific compression types are Query Low, Query High, Archive Low, and Archive High. The COMPRESS FOR QUERY compression types are referred to as warehouse compression and the COMPRESS FOR ARCHIVE types are called archive compression. Each flavor of HCC compression offers its own compression algorithm and is designed for different business purposes. Depending on your data, Query Low offers the lowest compression ratio, followed by Query High, then Archive Low, with Archive High yielding the best compression ratios. Along with this increased space savings comes increased CPU usage when creating the compressed objects and an increasingly detrimental performance impact should you need to modify data in your tables. Recipe 16-8 discusses the DML impact on HCC segments and Oracle's documentation at docs.oracle.com/cd/E11882_01/server.112/e17120/tables_002.htm#CJAGFBFG, a good resource to learn more about Oracle's HCC alternatives.

16-3. Contrasting Oracle Compression Types

Problem

You wish to measure the differences between HCC warehouse compression, HCC archive compression, and OLTP compression, a compression solution offered by Advanced Compression in Oracle 11g.

Solution

In this recipe, you will learn how to use the compression advisor to compare the space savings differences and compression ratios between the four different HCC compression types as well as OLTP compression. We will use a test table created by using a row generator function to generate 200+ million rows and over 87,000 blocks based on the DBA_OBJECTS view:

```
SQL> create table d14.myobj_uncomp
     tablespace tbs_test
     nologging as
     select * from
      (select * from dba_objects) obj,
      (select rownum from dual connect by level<=1000)
/
Table created.
SQL> exec dbms_stats.gather_table_stats('D14','MYOBJ_UNCOMP');
PL/SQL procedure successfully completed.
```

```
SQL> select num_rows, blocks from dba_tables
where table_name='MYOBJ_UNCOMP';

NUM_ROWS       BLOCKS
----------   ----------
20423000       289446
SQL>
```

Using this uncompressed table as the baseline, we will use the compression advisor to estimate the compression ratio, create HCC and OLTP compressed tables using CREATE TABLE AS with the COMPRESS FOR clause, compare the actual compression ratio and block counts to the compression advisor's output, and capture the time it takes to create our compressed tables. Table 16-1 provides a summary of the findings on an Exadata X2-2 Quarter Rack.

Table 16-1. Compression Comparisons

Table	Compression Type	Advisor Ratio	Actual Ratio/Blks	Create Time
MYOBJ_UNCOMP	Uncompressed	N/A	Ratio: 1 to 1 Blks: 289,446	N/A
MYOBJ_COMPQL	Warehouse Query Low	8.6 to 1	Ratio: 8.59 to 1 Blks: 33,821	20 seconds
MYOBJ_COMPQH	Warehouse Query High	19.6 to 1	Ratio: 19.06 to 1 Blks: 15,188	35 seconds
MYOBJ_COMPAL	Archive Low	19.7 to 1	Ratio: 19.22 to 1 Blks: 15,058	36 seconds
MYOBJ_COMPAH	Archive High	31.5 to 1	Ratio: 27.76 to 1 Blks: 10,426	225 seconds
MYOBJ_COMPOLTP	OLTP compression	2.9 to 1	Ratio: 2.9 to 1 Blks: 97,490	31 seconds

■ **Note** Please see Recipe 16-1 to learn about Oracle's compression advisor and Recipe 16-2 to learn how to build compressed tables using CREATE TABLE AS SELECT.

As you can see in Table 16-1, the actual compression ratios closely matched the estimated compression ratios generated with the compression advisor. This is not surprising, based on how the compression advisor executes, as described in Recipe 16-1. The time required to build the compressed tables is generally relative to the type of compression being performed; the higher compression level, the more CPU resources are required to compress the data and the longer the build operations takes.

In our example, notice the nonlinear compression ratios and build times as we go from Query High to Archive Low compression; in this case, the fact that Archive Low compression only yielded a marginally better compression ratio and relatively the same amount of time to build is related to the distribution of data in our source table and the degree of duplicity of column values in the table.

How It Works

When data is inserted into HCC segments, Oracle examines the input stream of data from the direct path insert/load operation and divides this stream into arrays of columns. It then employs a compression algorithm, based on the HCC type, on these columnar values and formats a collection of blocks into a logical construct called the compression unit (CU) for ranges of rows to be inserted. Each CU contains multiple blocks, each of which contains columnar subsets of the entire range of columns in the segment. When the first CU is filled with its rows (again, organized by column), a second CU will be established, then a third, and so on until all of the rows are inserted. Using the test tables from the solution of this recipe, which are based on SYS.OBJ$, Figure 16-1 provides a simplified graphical representation of how the CUs would be established in the case of QUERY HIGH compression.

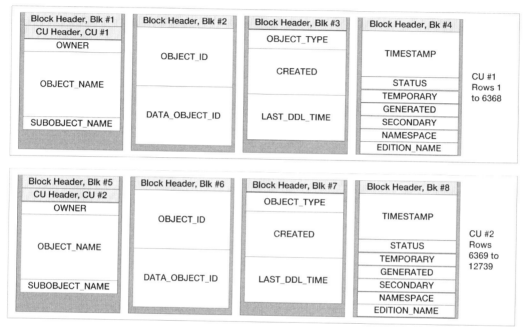

Figure 16-1. Compression unit and block layout for HCC table

Figure 16-1 shows a logical representation of how the first two CUs are used on an HCC table. The sizes of each column in the blocks for each CU indicate the number of distinct values for the column; the more distinct values, the more space the columnar values use within each CU's block. When the CU's blocks become full, a new CU and new set of blocks is formatted to store the data.

Technically speaking, a CU is physically stored in a chained row of a fixed-size pseudo-column. This column is actually a CU-specific pseudo-column. The CU has a small header section that contains byte offsets to the compressed columns, which store compressed values for your table's actual columns. When data is inserted into a CU, Oracle creates a single chained row for a single CU column (not to be confused with the actual columns). Each physical block inside the CU has a block header and row directory, and every row directory has an entry that refers to the single row piece inside the block. Each row piece has a row header and, also, if it's not the last block in the CU, a "next rowid" pointer to the next row piece. When accessing data from an HCC segment, Oracle will read the entire CU in one I/O and, to read all of the actual columns in the row, it will be required to follow the chained row from CU block to CU block until the last physical block is read.

In the example in Figure 16-1, each CU stores roughly 6,368 rows and contains each of the columns defined in the table. You can confirm the physical storage details of your HCC segments by performing a block dump. To do this, determine your absolute file number and block number for a rowid in your table as follows:

```
SQL> select 'alter system dump datafile '||fno||' block '||blk||';'
  2  from (
  3    select dbms_rowid.rowid_to_absolute_fno(rowid,'D14','MYOBJ_COMPQH') fno,
```

```
   4            dbms_rowid.rowid_block_number(rowid,'BIGFILE') blk
   5    from d14.myobj_compqh
   6    where object_name='SOURCE$'
   7    and rownum < 2)
   8  /
------------------------------------------------------------------------
alter system dump datafile 9 block 303236;
SQL>
SQL> alter system dump datafile 9 block 303236;
System altered.
SQL>
```

Once you've dumped an HCC data block, locate the trace file in your diagnostics destination and search for the block_row_dump string. The following is an excerpt from our trace file, with line numbers and descriptions after it:

```
1. block_row_dump:
2. tab 0, row 0, @0x30
3. tl: 8016 fb: --H-F--N lb: 0x0  cc: 1
4. nrid:  0x0004a085.0
5. col  0: [8004]
6. Compression level: 02 (Query High)
7.  Length of CU row: 8004
8. kdzhrh: ------PC CBLK: 0 Start Slot: 00
9.  NUMP: 04
10.   PNUM: 00 POFF: 7954 PRID: 0x0004a085.0
11.   PNUM: 01 POFF: 15970 PRID: 0x0004a086.0
12.   PNUM: 02 POFF: 23986 PRID: 0x0004a087.0
13.   PNUM: 03 POFF: 32002 PRID: 0x0004a088.0
14. CU header:
15. CU version: 0   CU magic number: 0x4b445a30
16. CU checksum: 0x90834fdb
17. CU total length: 33416
18. CU flags: NC-U-CRD-OP
19. ncols: 16
20. nrows: 6368
21. algo: 0
22. CU decomp length: 32534     len/value length: 576331
23. row pieces per row: 1
24. num deleted rows: 0
```

- Line 3 indicates that this block contains the *first* row piece for the CU based on the H in the --H-F--N string.

- Line 4 displays the address of the second row piece in the CU (and if we were to perform a block dump on this block, we would see a line that looks like **fb: ------PN)**.

- Line 6 indicates that the rows in this block are HCC compressed for Query High.

- Lines 9 through 13 indicate the number of blocks in the CU, in this case four.

- Lines 17 and 22 indicate the length of the CU, in bytes. You will typically see up to 32 KB compression length.

- Line 19 indicates that there are 16 columns in the block.
- Line 20 states that there are 6,638 rows in the CU blocks.

The fundamental *storage* differences between HCC and standard or OLTP compression is the unit upon which the compression takes place and whether the data is aligned by column or by row. With standard and advanced compression, the unit of compression is a database block. As rows are inserted into OLTP or standard-compressed segments, duplicate values are inserted into an area in the block called the symbol table. The symbol table is a structure in compressed blocks that stores metadata about the compression inside the block; the symbol table contains a single copy of duplicate column values and the row directory contains a short reference to the location in the symbol table.

■ **Note** Oracle's Standard Compression and 11g Advanced Compression features are beyond the scope of this text, but to learn more please see www.oracle.com/technetwork/database/storage/advanced-compression-whitepaper-130502.pdf and www.oracle.com/technetwork/database/performance/oow-adv-compression-1-130322.pdf.

As you learned in the solution of this recipe, different HCC compression types yield different compression ratios and have different performance characteristics during data loads. Oracle uses LZO compression for Query Low, ZLIB/gzip compression for Query High and Archive Low, and bzip2 compression for Archive High.

■ **Note** To validate which compression algorithm is used for each HCC compression type, you can perform an oradebug short_stack on the process compressing the data or, alternatively, using the operating system pstack command. An example call stack for a session performing Archive High compression is provided below (note the BZip2 entries in the call stack):

<-copy_input_until_stop()+102<-handle_compress()+61<-**BZ2_bzCompress()+77<-kgccbzip2do()+141<-kgccbzip2pseudodo**()+9<-kgccdo()+51<-kdzc_comp_buffer()+227<-kdzc_comp_col_analyzer()+165<-kdza_compress_col()+95<-kdza_analyze_col_trans()+179<-kdza_best_col_trans()+265<-kdzanalyze()+763<-kdzains()+775<-

My Oracle Support note 1058210.6 provides information about how to attach to a processing using oradebug. Use caution when using oradebug as some of the functionality provided with the interface could cause outages. As is the case with anything, if you don't know what a command does, do not execute it in production!

Each of HCC's compression types organizes and compresses data by column; the difference between them is the compression algorithm used to perform the actual compression and the number of blocks in the CU. If you examine a block dump from an HCC compressed table, you will see the differences between each of the HCC compression types; in the following, we display the number of blocks and rows per CU in each of the four HCC tables built in the solution of this recipe:

```
[oracle@cm01dbm01 hcc]$ egrep '(NUMP|nrows)' *trc
edw1_ora_3237.trc: NUMP: 04      <- Query Low, 4 blocks per compression unit
edw1_ora_3237.trc:nrows: 2779    <- Query Low, 2779 rows per CU
edw1_ora_3937.trc: NUMP: 04      <- Query High, 4 blocks per compression unit
```

```
edw1_ora_3937.trc:nrows: 6368    <- Query High, 6368 rows per CU
edw1_ora_5357.trc: NUMP: 05      <- Archive Low, 5 blocks per compression unit
edw1_ora_5357.trc:nrows: 8222    <- Archive Low, 8222 rows per CU
edw1_ora_4219.trc: NUMP: 07      <- Archive High, 7 blocks per compression unit
edw1_ora_4219.trc:nrows: 32759   <- Archive High, 32759 rows per CU
```

16-4. Determining the Compression Type of a Segment

Problem

You wish to determine whether a table or partition is compressed, decide which type of compression the segment is using, and identify the compression attributes for individual rows within a table or partition.

Solution

In this recipe, you will learn how to query a table's compression settings and determine the compression type for individual rows in a table.

To determine which type of compression is used for a table, query the COMPRESSION and COMPRESSED_FOR columns in DBA_TABLES or DBA_TAB_PARTITIONS. In the following, we are showing the settings for two tables with different compression configurations:

```
SQL> select table_name, compression,compress_for
  2  from user_tables
  3  where table_name in ('MTL_MATERIAL_TRANSACTIONS','MMT_COMPQUERYHIGH');
TABLE_NAME                      COMPRESSION     COMPRESS_FOR
------------------------------  -----------     ------------
MMT_COMPQUERYHIGH               ENABLED         QUERY HIGH
MTL_MATERIAL_TRANSACTIONS       DISABLED
SQL>
```

The default compression type for MMT_COMPQUERYHIGH is compressed for Query High and MTL_MATERIAL_TRANSACTIONS is uncompressed. For the compressed table, this means that if rows are inserted via direct path load, they will be formatted into an HCC compression unit and compressed using the HCC Query High algorithms.

If rows are individually inserted into an HCC segment via conventional inserts, the resulting rows will be loaded as uncompressed. Use the DBMS_COMPRESSION.GET_COMPRESSION_TYPE function to display the compression type for individual rows in a table. The example in Listing 16-3 demonstrates querying HCC-compressed rows from one of the tables in the previous example.

Listing 16-3. lst16-03-comptype.sql

```
SQL> select '&&owner' owner, '&&table_name' tabname, rowid myrowid,
        decode(dbms_compression.get_compression_type('&&owner','&&table_name',rowid),
              1,'No Compression', 2,'Basic/OLTP', 4,'HCC Query High',8,'HCC Query Low',
              16,'HCC Archive High', 32,'HCC Archive Low',64,'Block') comptype
    from "&&owner"."&&table_name"
    where &&predicate
/
Enter value for owner: D14
Enter value for table_name: OBJ_COMP1
Enter value for predicate: ROWNUM < 2
```

Owner	Table	RowId	CompType
D14	OBJ_COMP1	AAAGzKAAEAAPcCDAAA	HCC Query High

If rows in an HCC table or partition are updated, the row will be migrated and re-inserted using block compression. Recipe 16-8 discusses this topic is detail.

How It Works

When you create a compressed table, the SPARE1 column in SYS.SEG$ is populated with a value that is decoded and externalized to the *_TABLES views. The COMPRESS column shows whether the segment is compressed and the COMPRESS_FOR column will show the compression type.

These segment-level compression settings refer to the segment's default compression behavior. As rows are inserted into the table or partition, Oracle will elect to compress these with HCC compression as long as they are loaded via direct path load, as presented in Recipe 16-6.

The DBMS_COMPRESSION.GET_COMPRESSION_TYPE function can be used to determine the compression type for individual rows in a table or partition, and it is useful when trying to identify whether a row has been migrated due to DML or inserted via conventional load. The script in Listing 16-3 in the solution of this recipe uses a decode function on the return value from DBMS_COMRPESSION.GET_COMPRESSION_TYPE to derive the compression type for the rows queried. This decode is based on constants specified inside $ORACLE_HOME/rdbms/admin/dbmscomp.sql:

```
COMP_NOCOMPRESS            CONSTANT NUMBER := 1;
COMP_FOR_OLTP              CONSTANT NUMBER := 2;
COMP_FOR_QUERY_HIGH        CONSTANT NUMBER := 4;
COMP_FOR_QUERY_LOW         CONSTANT NUMBER := 8;
COMP_FOR_ARCHIVE_HIGH      CONSTANT NUMBER := 16;
COMP_FOR_ARCHIVE_LOW       CONSTANT NUMBER := 32;
COMP_BLOCK                 CONSTANT NUMBER := 64;
```

As presented in Recipes 16-6, 16-7, and 16-8, HCC is only applied to inserts or data loads performed using direct path insert or load operations. Updates cause rows to be migrated to a block or OLTP compressed format depending on whether the block is full.

Altering a segment's compression type will only affect the rows inserted after the compression type has been changed; existing records will remain in their original compression format unless you rebuild the segment with an ALTER ... MOVE command. This is the reason why using DBA_TABLES and DBA_TAB_PARTITIONS alone is not sufficient to determine the compression type for your rows as it only provides the current default compression settings for the table. Using DBMS_COMPRESSION.GET_COMPRESSION_TYPE or examining block dumps is the correct means to identify the compression type for individual rows in a table or partition.

16-5. Measuring the Performance Impact of HCC for Queries

Problem

You wish to measure the performance of queries against HCC tables and partitions and contrast with performance characteristics of queries against similar, uncompressed tables.

Solution

In this recipe, you will learn how to use a number of Exadata-specific system statistics and columns from V$SQL to measure the performance benefits from HCC tables. Start by identifying a HCC table and an uncompressed table with similar characteristics and sizes; in the following example, we will use the test tables created in Recipe 16-4:

```
SQL> select table_name,num_rows,blocks,
  compression,compress_for
    from dba_tables
    where table_name in ('MYOBJ_UNCOMP','MYOBJ_COMPQH')
    and owner='D14';

Table                 Rows            Blocks        Compressed         Compressed For
-------------------   -----------     ----------    ---------------    --------------
MYOBJ_UNCOMP          20423000        289446        DISABLED
MYOBJ_COMPQH          20423000         15188        ENABLED            QUERY HIGH
SQL>
```

Next, run a full table scan against each table and measure its statistics using the query in Listing 16-4. In our test cases, we selected the MAX(OBJECT_NAME) from each of three tables, without a query predicate.

Listing 16-4. lst16-04-exahcc-mysess.sql

```
SQL> select stat.name,
            sess.value value
from    v$mystat sess,
            v$statname stat
where   stat.statistic# = sess.statistic#
and     stat.name in ('physical read total bytes',
            'cell IO uncompressed bytes',
            'cell physical IO interconnect bytes')
and sess.value > 0
order by 1;
```

Table 16-2 provides the results of our full table scan tests.

Table 16-2. *Query Test Results against Uncompressed and HCC Compressed Tables*

Statistic	MYOBJ_UNCOMP	MYOBJ_COMPQH	MYOBJ_COMPAH	MYOBJ_COMPQH with Smart Scan
Compression Type	Uncompressed	Query High	Archive High	Query High
Query Response	1.75 seconds	4.04 seconds	3.06 seconds	1.87 seconds
physical read total bytes	2,364,825,600	123,101,184	84,205,568	123,559,936
cell physical I/O interconnect bytes	541,298,056	123,101,184	84,205,568	407,969,576
cell I/O uncompressed bytes	2,367,651,840	0	0	2,181,193,193
CPU used by this session	145	289	1,009	175

Table 16-2 points out some interesting performance aspects of our queries against HCC tables and uncompressed tables:

- The amount of physical I/O bytes required for the compressed tables was less than the uncompressed table, which is to be expected since the compressed tables are smaller in size.

- Without Smart Scan, the number of bytes transmitted over the storage interconnect both the MYOBJ_COMPQH and MYOBJ_COMPAH queries was equal to the number of bytes physical read from disks.

- The cell IO uncompressed bytes statistic is a measure of how many uncompressed bytes the storage grid processes after decompression; in other words, it reflects how much data was decompressed on the storage cells prior to sending in uncompressed format to the compute nodes. Note that without Smart Scan enabled in Columns 3 and 4, no data was uncompressed on the storage cells. This means that all of the decompression occurred on the compute node.

- When forcing Smart Scan, which we accomplished by setting _serial_direct_read=always at the session level, our query on MYOBJ_COMPQH in the rightmost column performed roughly the same amount of physical I/O as the traditional scan but transmitted almost four times more data over the interconnect. This is an indication that the storage servers performed at least some of the required decompression before sending data to the compute nodes.

- The query execution times were longer when accessing HCC data without smart scans as compared to querying on the uncompressed table; this was the case because the compute nodes were forced to process uncompressed data from the storage cells and decompress on the compute node.

- CPU usage was higher when accessing data from HCC tables; in these tests, this was due to where the decompression occurred.

The same type of analysis can also be achieved by querying V$SQL for our SQL statements. Listing 16-5 provides an example showing the same behavior for the previous test cases.

Listing 16-5. lst16-05-exahcc-sqls.sql

```
SQL> select    sql_id ,avgelapsed,phybytes/1024/1024 phymb,
            io_cell_uncompressed_bytes/1024/1024 celluncompmb,
            io_interconnect_bytes/1024/1024 icmb,
             sql_text
    from (
     select  sql_id,
             physical_read_bytes+physical_write_bytes phybytes,io_interconnect_bytes,
             (elapsed_time/1000000)/
             executions/
             decode(px_servers_executions,0,1,px_servers_executions) avgelapsed,
             substr(sql_text,1,30) sql_text,
             io_cell_uncompressed_bytes
    from v$sql
    where executions > 0
    and sql_text like '%'||'&&sql_text'||'%'
    order by avgelapsed desc);
Enter value for sql_text: hcc_myobj
```

```
SqlID           AvgElasped  PhysIOMb  CellUncompMB  InterconnectMB  SQL
-------------   ----------  --------  ------------  --------------  ------------------------------
4m958qrfphdqy        10.94        81             0              81  select /* hcc_myobj_compah */
13jh8dfsb5sam         1.86       118         2,080             389  select /* hcc_myobj_compqh*/ m
3mwrbh4cmbf3v         1.80     2,256         2,258             517  select /* hcc_myobj_uncomp */
```

How It Works

In this recipe, we demonstrated using statistics to measure the amount of I/O physical read from disk (`physical read total bytes`), the amount of I/O sent over the Exadata storage grid (`cell physical IO interconnect bytes`), and the amount of uncompressed data processed on the cell (`cell_io_uncompressed_bytes`). The statistics were queried from V$MYSTAT in Listing 16-4, but you can use V$SESSTAT, V$SYSSTAT, or AWR and ASH views to collect the same information at a different scope.

On a per SQL ID basis, V$SQL also contains the IO_CELL_UNCOMPRESSED_BYTES, IO_INTERCONNECT_BYTES, and multiple physical I/O statistics. You can query VSQL, VSQLSTATS, or DBA_HIST_SQLSTAT to report on the same information for a broader scope or historical time periods.

When tables are compressed with HCC, they consume less physical disk space. Less disk space means less I/O required to access the data from disk and, ideally, better performance. But, as demonstrated, there is often a performance trade-off between I/O and CPU.

As data is retrieved from HCC tables or partitions, the unit of I/O that Oracle performs is the CU. A single I/O against an HCC table will read an entire CU, which typically is four or more blocks depending on the compression type and your data.

The tests in this recipe demonstrated that archive compression yielded a better compression ratio than the QUERY HIGH compressed table but took more time to execute the query, despite the I/O savings on the storage cells. This unveils a potential performance "gotcha" for HCC; when data is compressed, upon retrieval it will need to be uncompressed at some layer in the infrastructure. HCC aims to perform as much decompression as it can on the storage cells and utilize the ample number of processors to do so, but even so, the higher the compression ratio, the more work required to uncompress the data. Exadata's choice on where to decompress data (compute servers or storage cells) is dependent on the amount of data requested and the access method used to retrieve the data. Single-row lookups via index scans will pass uncompressed data to the compute nodes. These are important considerations when designing your HCC strategy.

Note Recipe 16-9 discusses compression and decompression behavior in detail and provides you with information to understand and measure the performance impact of HCC decompression.

One other important point from the tests provided in this recipe has to do with cell offload and Smart Scan. When using HCC, your table or partition segments will likely be smaller in size. The fewer blocks your segments have, the less likely it is that your scans will qualify for direct path reads. Direct path reads are required for smart scans and, if disabled, not only will your storage cells send more data to the compute grid and bypass Oracle's cell offload functionality, but the CUs will be shipped in compressed format. This means that your database servers will be responsible for decompression.

Note Please see Recipe 15-7 to learn more about direct path reads and their impact on Smart Scan and Recipe 16-9 to learn more about HCC decompression.

16-6. Direct Path Inserts into HCC Segments

Problem

You wish to know how to insert rows into your HCC tables in order to ensure that they are compressed according to your desired compression type.

Solution

In order to populate rows into HCC segments, you need to load or insert via direct path inserts or loads. There are a number of ways to load data into Oracle tables or partitions and, in this recipe, you will learn how to use a few of these techniques. Additionally, you will learn how to use DBMS_COMPRESSION.GET_COMPRESSION_TYPE to determine the compression type for the inserted rows. The sections in this recipe will be based on an example in which we use SYS.OBJ$ as the source and methods introduced in Recipe 16-4 (see Listing 16-3) to determine the compression type of the loaded rows.

Create Table as Select

In the following, we will create a sample table using SYS.OBJ$ as our source:

```
SQL> create table myobj1
    nologging compress for query high
    as select * from sys.obj$;
Table created.
SQL>
```

Using Listing 16-6, we can measure the compression type for one of the rows in the table.

Listing 16-6. lst16-06-comptype.sql

```
SQL> SQL> select '&&owner' owner, '&&table_name' tabname, rowid myrowid,
    decode(dbms_compression.get_compression_type('&&owner','&&table_name',rowid),
           1,'No Compression', 2,'Basic/OLTP', 4,'HCC Query High',8,'HCC Query Low',
          16,'HCC Archive High', 32,'HCC Archive Low',64,'Block') comptype
  from "&&owner"."&&table_name"
  where &&predicate
/
Enter value for owner: SYS
Enter value for table_name: MYOBJ1
Enter value for predicate: ROWNUM < 2
Owner           Table                               RowId                 CompType
--------------- ----------------------------------- --------------------- ---------------------
SYS             MYOBJ1                              AAM6zZABZAAAeocAAA    HCC Query High
SQL>
```

INSERT /*+ APPEND */

In the following script, we will create a second table, MYOBJ2, and load data with direct path insert using the APPEND hint. When finished, we will use the script in Listing 16-6 to determine the compression type:

```
SQL> create table myobj2
   nologging tablespace apps_ts_tx_data
   compress for archive low
   as select * from sys.obj$ where 1=2;
Table created.
SQL> insert /*+ append */ into myobj2
  2  select * from sys.obj$;
427692 rows created.
SQL> commit;

Owner             Table                          RowId                   CompType
---------------   ----------------------------   ---------------------   ---------------------
SYS               MYOBJ2                         AAM6zaABZAAAeosAAA      HCC Archive Low
SQL>
```

Using Tablespace Compression Settings

If you have specified default compression settings at the tablespace level, as presented in Recipe 16-3, direct path inserts will be loaded based on the tablespace's compression attributes of the segment's tablespace; you will not need to use the COMPRESS FOR clause during segment creation.

If you insert rows via conventional load or conventional inserts, the data will be loaded as uncompressed.

How It Works

Data needs to be loaded into HCC segments using direct path load operations in order for the rows to be compressed according to your desired compression type. There are a number of ways to perform direct path loads, including ALTER TABLE MOVE, Data Pump import, CREATE TABLE AS, direct path INSERT using the APPEND or APPEND_VALUES hint, and direct path SQL*Loader.

Note To learn more about Oracle's direct path load and insert mechanics, please consultant Oracle's documentation.

When rows are inserted via conventional inserts into a HCC table or partition, the resulting rows will be inserted uncompressed into normal data blocks (in other words, not with an HCC compression unit). This is an important consideration when designing your HCC strategy as it impacts your compression ratio and space savings. Knowing which segments to compress, then, is not only a matter of targeting your large tables but also understanding the nature of how your applications load or insert data into your HCC segments. Additionally, there is a potentially significant performance impact when DML is issued against HCC segments. Recipe 16-8 will discuss this topic in detail.

16-7. Conventional Inserts to HCC Segments
Problem

You wish to insert data into HCC tables using conventional insert or load operations and measure the compression type on the rows after being loaded.

Solution

In this recipe, you will learn how to insert data via conventional INSERT statements into your HCC segments and identify the compression type on the inserted rows. In the following examples, we will create two empty tables, HCC-compressed for query high, in two different tablespaces with different default compression attributes.

> **Note** Please see Recipe 16-2 to learn more about setting default compression attributes for your tablespaces.

Our tablespace's default compression attributes are specified as follows:

```
SQL>    select tablespace_name,
               def_tab_compression,
               nvl(compress_for,'NONE') compress_for
    from dba_tablespaces
    where tablespace_name like 'TBS%';
```

Tablespace	CompSetting	CompressType
TBS_TEST	DISABLED	NONE
TBS_QUERYHIGH	ENABLED	QUERY HIGH

Using these tablespaces, we will create two empty tables, each compressed for query high:

```
SQL> create table d14.myobj_tab1
     tablespace tbs_test compress for query high
     as select * from dba_objects where 1=2;
Table created.
SQL> create table d14.myobj_tab2
     tablespace tbs_queryhigh compress for query high
     as select * from dba_objects where 1=2;
Table created.
SQL>
```

Now, we will insert rows via conventional insert into these tables and use the script in Listing 16-7 to determine the compression type of the rows:

```
SQL> insert into d14.myobj_tab1 select * from dba_objects;
20430 rows created.
SQL> insert into d14.myobj_tab2 select * from dba_objects;
20430 rows created.
SQL> commit;
Commit complete.
SQL>
```

Listing 16-7. lst16-07-comptype.sql

```
SQL> select '&&owner' owner, '&&table_name' tabname, rowid myrowid,
     decode(dbms_compression.get_compression_type('&&owner','&&table_name',rowid),
            1,'No Compression', 2,'Basic/OLTP', 4,'HCC Query High',8,'HCC Query Low',
            16,'HCC Archive High', 32,'HCC Archive Low',64,'Block') comptype
```

```
    from "&&owner"."&&table_name"
    where &&predicate
/
Enter value for owner: D14
Enter value for table_name: MYOBJ_TAB1
Enter value for predicate: ROWNUM < 2

Owner             Table                   RowId                  CompType
---------------   ---------------------   --------------------   --------------------
D14               MYOBJ_TAB1              AAAG2mAAAAABcyDAAA     No Compression
/
Enter value for owner: D14
Enter value for table_name: MYOBJ_TAB2
Enter value for predicate: ROWNUM < 2

Owner             Table                   RowId                  CompType
---------------   ---------------------   --------------------   --------------------
D14               MYOBJ_TAB2              AAAG2nAAAAAAACDAAA     No Compression
```

How It Works

Oracle allows you to use conventional insert or load mechanisms to populated HCC tables or partitions, but it is important to understand the compression impact when doing so. If you have applications or data load strategies that cannot be tailored to perform direct path inserts, your code will function without change and without generating error messages, but the data will be inserted as uncompressed to your tables and/or partitions.

Using DBMS_COMPRESSION.GET_COMPRESSION_TYPE for individual row and comparing against DBA_TABLES.COMPRESS_FOR and/or DBA_TAB_PARTITIONS.COMPRESS_FOR is a good way to determine whether you have HCC segments that are being populated via conventional inserts or loads.

If your application inserts data via conventional inserts or loads to your HCC segments, over time your compression ratios and expected storage and I/O savings will be diminished. If you deem it worthwhile, you can correct this behavior by rebuilding your tables or partitions with the ALTER ... MOVE DDL statement.

16-8. DML and HCC

Problem

You have learned through Oracle's documentation or other sources that performing DML on HCC tables is discouraged for performance reasons, and you wish to measure and identify situations in which DML has taken place on your HCC segments.

Solution

In this recipe, you will learn about various aspects of DML and HCC tables, including how to determine whether a row in an HCC table has been updated, how to determine the percentage of a segment's rows that have been updated, and how to measure concurrency and locking issues that may arise due to DML on HCC segments. We will focus primarily on the impact of UPDATE statements in this section, as INSERT mechanics were presented in Recipes 16-6 and 16-7.

We will start with a test table, compressed for QUERY HIGH. The sections in this recipe will perform UPDATE statements on this table and use it to demonstrate features of DML on HCC tables:

```
SQL> create table d14.myobj_dmltest
  2   tablespace tbs_queryhigh compress for query high
  3   as select * from dba_objects;
Table created.
SQL>
```

Determining the Compression Type of an Updated Row

First, we will use DBMS_COMPRESSION.GET_COMPRESSION_TYPE to identify the compression type for a single row in our test table. Listing 16-8 can be used for this purpose.

Listing 16-8. lst16-08-comptype.sql

```
SQL> select '&&owner' owner, '&&table_name' tabname, rowid myrowid,
        decode(dbms_compression.get_compression_type('&&owner','&&table_name',rowid),
               1,'No Compression', 2,'Basic/OLTP', 4,'HCC Query High',8,'HCC Query Low',
               16,'HCC Archive High', 32,'HCC Archive Low',64,'Block') comptype
      from "&&owner"."&&table_name"
      where &&predicate
/
Enter value for owner: D14
Enter value for table_name: MYOBJ_DMLTEST
Enter value for predicate: OBJECT_NAME='SOURCE$'
Owner           Table                    RowId                 CompType
--------------  ----------------------   -------------------   --------------------
D14             MYOBJ_DMLTEST            AAAG2pAAAAAAACDADe    HCC Query High
```

Now we will update the row and re-run the query in Listing 16-8:

```
SQL> update d14.myobj_dmltest
  2   set object_name=object_name where object_name='SOURCE$';
1 row updated.
SQL> commit;
Commit complete.
SQL> @lst16-08-comptype.sql
... Output omitted for brevity, see above
Enter value for owner: D14
Enter value for table_name: MYOBJ_DMLTEST
Enter value for predicate: OBJECT_NAME='SOURCE$'

Owner           Table                    RowId                 CompType
--------------  ----------------------   -------------------   --------------------
D14             MYOBJ_DMLTEST            AAAG2pAAAAAAACUAAA    No Compression
```

Note that our ROWID changed from AAAG2pAAAAAAACDADe to AAAG2pAAAAAAACUAAA; this is an indication that row migration has occurred. Additionally, the compression type on the new row is "1", or uncompressed. This happens because Oracle re-inserted the row and has not yet compressed it because the block is not yet full. Let's update *all* of our rows in the table and re-execute the same query to check our compression type:

```
SQL> update d14.myobj_dmltest
  2  set object_name=object_name where object_name <> 'SOURCE$';
20428 rows updated.
SQL> commit;
Commit complete.
SQL>
```

Now, we'll re-run the query in Listing 16-8 and extract the compression type for a number of rows:

```
Enter value for owner: D14
Enter value for table_name: MYOBJ_DMLTEST
Enter value for predicate: object_name='SOURCE$' or object_name like 'x%'

Owner           Table                    RowId                   CompType
--------------  -----------------------  ----------------------  --------------------
D14             MYOBJ_DMLTEST            AAAG2pAAAAAAACUAAA      No Compression
D14             MYOBJ_DMLTEST            AAAG2pAAAAAAADUABJ      Block
D14             MYOBJ_DMLTEST            AAAG2pAAAAAAADUABM      Block
D14             MYOBJ_DMLTEST            AAAG2pAAAAAAADUABZ      Block
```

As you can see, we now have a combination of uncompressed and block-compressed rows in our table.

What happened to the original row? You can still see find the old ROWID and compare it with the new one and look for indication that row migration has taken place:

```
SQL> select object_name from d14.myobj_dmltest
  2  where rowid='AAAG2pAAAAAAACDADe';
ObjectName
------------------------------
SOURCE$
SQL> select rowid from d14.myobj_dmltest
  2  where object_name='SOURCE$';
ROWID
------------------
AAAG2pAAAAAAACUAAA
SQL>
```

Examining a Block Dump

An HCC segment's block dump will also provide insight into whether a row in the block was updated and migrated. In Listing 16-9, we will rebuild our test table used in the previous section, determine the absolute file number and block number for a specific row, update the row, and perform a block dump on the original block.

Listing 16-9. lst16-09-getrowidinfo.sql

```
SQL> select object_name,rowid,
            dbms_rowid.rowid_to_absolute_fno(rowid,'D14','MYOBJ_DMLTEST') fno,
            dbms_rowid.rowid_block_number(rowid,'BIGFILE') blk
```

```
    from d14.myobj_dmltest
    where object_name='SOURCE$'
    /

ObjectName           RowID                   File# Blk#
-------------------- ----------------------- ----- --------
SOURCE$              AAAG2tAAAAAAACDADe        12    131

SQL> update d14.myobj_dmltest
  2  set object_name=object_name
  3  where object_name='SOURCE$';
1 row updated.
SQL> commit;
Commit complete.
SQL>
```

Now, using the *original* absolute file number and block number, we'll dump the block:

```
SQL> alter system dump datafile 12 block 131;
System altered.
SQL>
```

After locating the trace file in your diagnostics dump destination, you can determine that the compression format of the original block and the number of rows deleted from the block as a result of row migration by running the following command:

```
[oracle@cm01dbm01 trace]$ egrep '(Compression level|num deleted rows)' edw1_ora_32231.trc
Compression level: 02 (Query High)      <- Indicates that the original block was compressed for
query high
num deleted rows: 1     <- Indicates that one row was deleted from the original block
[oracle@cm01dbm01 trace]$
```

If you dump the block that the new row is in, you will see that it is not in a compressed block:

```
SQL> select object_name,rowid,
  2         dbms_rowid.rowid_to_absolute_fno(rowid,'D14','MYOBJ_DMLTEST') fno,
  3         dbms_rowid.rowid_block_number(rowid,'BIGFILE') blk
  4  from d14.myobj_dmltest
  5  where object_name='SOURCE$'
  6  /
ObjectName           RowID                   File# Blk#
-------------------- ----------------------- ----- --------
SOURCE$              AAAG2tAAAAAAADkAAA        12    228      <- Note the new block number


SQL> alter system dump datafile 12 block 228;
System altered.
SQL>
[oracle@cm01dbm01 trace]$ egrep '(Compression level|num deleted rows)' edw1_ora_3532.trc
[oracle@cm01dbm01 trace]$
```

Identify Migrated Rows from Statistics

To measure whether queries accessing this update block are accessing the data via a migrated row, examine the `table fetch continued row` statistic. We will query the new rowid after the update and compare with a single-row query using the old rowid using the script in Listing 16-10.

```
SQL> select 'x' from d14.myobj_dmltest
  2  where rowid='AAAG2tAAAAAAADkAAA';    <- New rowid
-
x
```

Listing 16-10. lst16-10-tbcr.sql

```
SQL> select stat.name,
  2         sess.value value
  3  from   v$mystat sess,
  4         v$statname stat
  5  where  stat.statistic# = sess.statistic#
  6  and    stat.name like 'table fetch%'
  7  and sess.value > 0
  8  order by 1
  9  /

Statistic                                    Value
------------------------------------------  ---------
table fetch by rowid                             1

SQL> select 'x' from d14.myobj_dmltest
     where rowid='AAAG2tAAAAAAACDADe';    <- Old rowid
-
x
SQL> select stat.name,
   ... Code from Listing 16-10

Statistic                                    Value
------------------------------------------  ---------
table fetch by rowid                             1
table fetch continued row                        4    <- Indicates row migration
```

> **Note** You may be wondering why the previous query showed a 4 instead of a 1 for the `table fetch continued row` statistic. This has to do with how the rows are physically stored inside an HCC compression unit (CU). A row in an HCC CU is chained across the multiple blocks that comprise the CU. A single-row read operation follows the `nrid` pointer from block-to-block inside a CU to retrieve each of the row pieces for the row. Each time it does so, the `table fetch continued row` statistic is incremented. To learn more about how data is physically stored in an HCC CU, please see the How It Works section in Recipe 16-3.

Finding Percentage of Updated Rows

To find the number of update rows in an HCC table that have been updated or inserted via conventional inserts, execute the script in Listing 16-11.

> **Note** The script in Listing 16-11 will execute DBMS_COMPRESSION.GET_COMPRESSION_TYPE for all rows in your table and could take a long time to execute and consume a large amount of CPU resources on your machine, so proceed with caution if you attempt to run against a large table.

Listing 16-11. lst16-11-allcomptypes.sql

```
SQL> select comptype,count(*) cnt,100*(count(*)/rowcount) pct
   from (
    select '&&owner' owner, '&&table_name' tabname, rowid myrowid,
    decode(dbms_compression.get_compression_type('&&owner','&&table_name',rowid),
           1,'No Compression', 2,'Basic/OLTP', 4,'HCC Query High',
           8,'HCC Query Low', 16,'HCC Archive High', 32,'HCC Archive Low',
           64,'Block') comptype,
    (count(*) over ()) rowcount
    from "&&owner"."&&table_name"
  ) group by comptype,rowcount;
Enter value for owner: D14
Enter value for table_name: MYOBJ_DMLTEST

CompType                #Rows          %ofTotal
--------------------    ------------   --------
Block                          4,862      23.80
HCC Query High                15,560      76.17
No Compression                     7        .03
SQL>
```

Concurrency and Locking

Oracle's documentation states that updates to a single row in an HCC table will lock the entire CU containing the row. If you are suffering from lock contention and have HCC tables in your database that are updated, you can validate this by mapping the block containing the first row being updated to the block containing the second row updated and determining if they belong to the same compression unit. First, we will set up a test casing using the MYOBJ_DMLTEST table created previously in this recipe, and query a handful of relevant pieces of information:

```
SQL> select * from (
  2    select object_id,rowid,
  3           dbms_rowid.rowid_to_absolute_fno(rowid,'D14','MYOBJ_DMLTEST') fno,
  4           dbms_rowid.rowid_block_number(rowid,'BIGFILE') blk
  5    from d14.myobj_dmltest
  6    order by object_id)
  7  where rownum < 5;
```

OBJECT_ID	RowID	File#	Blk#
2	AAAG2vAAAAABcyDAAw	9	380035
3	AAAG2vAAAAABcyDAAF	9	380035
4	AAAG2vAAAAABcyDAAx	9	380035
5	AAAG2vAAAAABcyDAAa	9	380035

When using DBMS_ROWID.ROWID_BLOCK_NUMBER on HCC tables, the block refers to the compression unit so we know that all of the rows above are located in the same CU. Next, let's update the first row with OBJECT_ID=2 from one session, leaving the transaction uncommitted:

```
SQL> update d14.myobj_dmltest
  2   set object_name='X123'
  3   where object_id=2;
1 row updated.
SQL>
```

From a different session, let's attempt to perform a SELECT FOR UPDATE NOWAIT on OBJECT_ID 3:

```
SQL> select object_id from d14.myobj_dmltest
  2   where object_id=3 for update nowait;
select object_id from d14.myobj_dmltest
ERROR at line 1:
ORA-00054: resource busy and acquire with NOWAIT specified or timeout expired
SQL>
```

As you can see, the SELECT FOR UPDATE failed—not because the row with OBJECT_ID=3 was locked, but because the entire CU containing this row had an uncommitted update on a different row being held.

If you find yourself waiting on row locks (enq: TX - row lock contention waits), run the script in Listing 16-12 to identify the lock holder and CU block information.

Listing 16-12. lst16-12-hcclocks.sql

```
SQL> select row_wait_block#,row_wait_row#,
  2   blocking_instance,blocking_session
  3   from v$session
  4   where sid='&&waiting_sid'
  5   /
Enter value for waiting_sid: 1237
old   4: where sid='&&waiting_sid'
new   4: where sid='1237'
```

ROW_WAIT_BLOCK#	ROW_WAIT_ROW#	BLOCKING_INSTANCE	BLOCKING_SESSION
380035	5	1	394

How It Works

There a few important design characteristics for HCC segments with respect to DML. First, as discussed in Recipes 16-6 and 16-7, data in HCC segments is only compressed according to the segment's compression type when loaded via direct path insert operations. Second, when data is updated, the updated row is migrated to another block and re-inserted initially as uncompressed. When the newly formatted block becomes full, Oracle transitions the block to a "block-compressed" block. In addition, DML against rows on HCC tables locks the entire compression unit, or CU.

The impact of migrated rows in the context of HCC tables is similar to the query impact for traditional tables—extra I/Os are required to access the data when retrieved via a SELECT statement. Additionally, if many updates occur, over time the percentage of compressed blocks will decrease and the segment's compression ratio will decrease.

Perhaps of more significant importance is the locking mechanics when DML occurs on HCC rows. As demonstrated in the solution of this recipe, Oracle locks the entire CU when updates are made to a row. Updates to other rows in the blocks are forced to wait for any pending transactions to commit or roll back. This is certainly not Oracle's normal locking behavior, in which locks are only held for individual rows. This, of course, means that extra care must be taken when your application is designed to update HCC segments in order to avoid excessive lock-related waits.

16-9. Decompression and the Performance Impact

Problem

You wish to measure the performance impact of decompressing data when selecting rows from an HCC segment.

Solution

In this recipe, you will learn how Oracle decompresses HCC data on Exadata, where the decompression takes place depending on your query conditions, and measure the performance impact related to HCC decompression.

To demonstrate where Oracle decompresses data when accessing rows from HCC segments, we will conduct a number of test cases and measure HCC-related statistics using the script in Listing 16-13. The tests were executed on an Exadata Quarter Rack with a set of 20+ million row tables and a flushed database buffer cache between each execution as summarized:

- Test #1: Access approximately 1 million rows for a single column in a 20 million row table compressed for Query High using Smart Scan

- Test #2: Access approximately 1 million rows for a single column in a 20 million row table compressed for Archive High using Smart Scan

- Test #3: Access 1,000 rows for a single column in a 20 million row table compressed for Query High using Smart Scan

- Test #4: Access 1,000 rows for a single column in a 20 million row table compressed for Archive High using Smart Scan

- Test #5: Access approximately 1 million rows for a single column in a 20 million row table compressed for Query High *without* smart scans

- Test #6: Access approximately 1 million rows for a single column in a 20 million row table compressed for Archive High *without* smart scans

Listing 16-13 provides the script used to collect the results, which are listed in Table 16-3.

Table 16-3. *Decompression Behavior under Multiple Test Scenarios*

Statistic	Test 1	Test 2	Test 3	Test 4	Test 5	Test 6
CPU used by this session	9	7	5	5	329	1166
cell physical I/O bytes eligible for predicate offload (MB)	117	81	117	81	0	0
physical read total bytes (MB)	117	81	117	81	117	81
cell physical I/O interconnect bytes (MB)	2	1	0.31	.20	117	81
cell I/O uncompressed bytes (MB)	1879	1880	1879	1880	0	0
cell CUs processed for uncompressed	3847	731	1000	630	0	0
cell CUs sent uncompressed	3847	731	1000	630	0	0
% Uncompressed on compute node	0%	0%	0%	0%	100%	100%

Listing 16-13. lst16-13-exahcc-decompstats.sql

```
SQL> select stat.name,
            sess.value value
     from   v$mystat sess,
            v$statname stat
     where  stat.statistic# = sess.statistic#
     and    stat.name in ('physical read total bytes', 'CPU used by this session',
                'cell CUs sent uncompressed',
                'cell CUs processed for uncompressed',
                'cell physical IO bytes eligible for predicate offload',
                'cell IO uncompressed bytes', 'cell physical IO interconnect bytes')
     and sess.value > 0
     order by 1;
```

Table 16-3 illustrates some important points about how Oracle decompresses data when accessing via Smart Scan versus traditional block I/O:

- When HCC data is accessed via Smart Scan, decompression occurs on the storage cells as indicated by the cell CUs sent uncompressed and cell IO uncompressed bytes statistics.

- When accessed *without* Smart Scan, the storage cells do *not* perform any decompression and send compressed blocks back to the compute node's database buffer cache.

- Database server CPU requirements are much lower when the storage cells can perform the decompression, as indicated in test cases 5 and 6.

Is it possible for compression to occur on the database tier even with smart scans? The answer is yes, and this is largely due to the nature of your data and queries. The following example processed 1254 CUs on the storage cells and transmitted 735 of these CUs back to the compute nodes, which means that the database server was required to uncompress 1-(735/1254) =~ 42% of the CUs.

```
SQL> select count(object_name) from d14.myobj_compah;
------------------
         20423000
Statistic                                                          Value
------------------------------------------------------------  ----------------
CPU used by this session                                                   142
... Output omitted for brevity
cell CUs processed for uncompressed                                       1254
cell CUs sent uncompressed                                                 735
cell IO uncompressed bytes                                          3600680935
cell physical IO bytes eligible for predicate offload                 84197376
cell physical IO interconnect bytes                                  370107624
physical read total bytes                                             84221952
```

Note from this example that the number of bytes sent over the storage interconnect exceeded the bytes eligible for predicate offload and the `physical read total bytes`; this is because 735 CUs were transmitted uncompressed.

How It Works

With HCC, compression operations always occur on the compute nodes as data is inserted via direct path load/insert. Decompression can take place on either the storage cells or the compute servers, depending on the access method, volume of data being returned, rows and columns being retrieved, and so forth. In general, the following statements are true:

- When smart scans are used to access HCC segments, decompression occurs for the selected rows and columns on the storage cells.

- When smart scans are *not* used, decompression takes place on the compute nodes; entire compression units (think in terms of multiple blocks and many rows-per-block) are sent over the storage interconnect, loaded into the database buffer cache, and uncompressed.

This second bullet implies that index access to HCC segments means that decompression will take place on the compute nodes, and there is also a 1 MB boundary upon which Exadata will choose to decompress on the storage cell. If the amount of data is greater than 1 MB and smart scans are used, decompression takes place on the storage cells. Any I/O requests smaller than 1 MB in size cause the storage cells to ship compressed CUs to the compute node.

The script used in the solution of this recipe queries several Exadata and HCC-specific performance statistics, including CPU usage, interconnect and physical I/O, cell I/O, and cell CU-related statistics. Together, these statistics can help paint a picture of where decompression is taking place and how much it is costing your database tier CPUs. The script in Listing 16-13 can certainly be expanded to report on systemwide HCC information by using V$SYSSTAT, sessionwide by using V$SESSTAT, as well various AWR views.

Why is it important to know where HCC decompression is taking place? The numbers in Table 16-3 tell the story; decompression is expensive from a CPU perspective, and decompressing HCC data on the database servers can be costly, cause performance issues, or create scalability challenges. Oracle software licensing on the compute servers costs you more than three times as much as the processor licenses on the storage cells—keep this in mind as you begin deploying HCC for your databases. If your HCC tables or partitions will be queried, it is best to do so using smart scans and, as covered in Chapter 15, smart scans require that the compressed form of your segments be large.

■ **Note** To learn more about Exadata Smart Scan, please see recipes in Chapter 15.

CHAPTER 17

I/O Resource Management and Instance Caging

I/O Resource Management (IORM) provides a means to govern I/O from different workloads in the Exadata Database Machine. Database consolidation is a key driver to customer adoption of Exadata, and consolidation means that multiple databases and applications will typically share Exadata storage. Different databases in a shared storage grid typically have different I/O performance requirements, and one of the common challenges with shared storage infrastructures, in general, is that of competing I/O workloads. Non-Exadata Oracle environments historically have attempted to address this challenge by over-provisioning storage, but this can become expensive and yield performance behavior that it is difficult to measure and predict.

IORM is Exadata's answer to protecting your I/O performance investment. IORM is similar to Oracle Database Resource Manager (DBRM) in that it provides a means for controlling allocation of system resources. Where DBRM's primary goals are to control CPU resources, limit the degree of parallelism, and impose resource consumption constraints for different types of sessions *within* an Oracle database, IORM's goal is to govern I/O resource allocations *between* databases on a shared storage infrastructure. When consolidating Oracle databases on Exadata, IORM can be used to ensure that I/O is controlled between databases as well as classifications of consumes that utilize the same ASM disk infrastructure and, as such, provide resource control capabilities beyond what DBRM provides within a database.

In this chapter, we will discuss how IORM works, show examples of how to define IORM plans, and provide guidance for how to measure I/O resource utilization when an IORM plan is enabled.

In addition to controlling I/O utilization on the Exadata storage cells, Oracle also allows you to limit CPU resource utilization on the compute nodes using a technique called *instance caging*. This chapter will also include a recipe that will show you how to configure instance caging for your Exadata database instances.

17-1. Prioritizing I/O Utilization by Database

Problem

You wish to define storage cell I/O resource allocations for your databases in order to prioritize I/O resources between different databases deployed on your Exadata Database Machine.

Solution

In this recipe, you will learn how to configure an Interdatabase IORM plan, which is typically the easiest IORM plan to conceptualize and implement.

CHAPTER 17 ■ I/O RESOURCE MANAGEMENT AND INSTANCE CAGING

1. First, determine the percentage of I/O resource utilizations to assign to each database on your database machine. In this recipe, we will assume that a database named EDW will be allocated 55% of I/O resources, VISX will be allotted 25% of I/O resources, DWPRD will have 15%, and VISY will have the remaining 5% of I/O resources.

2. Next, disable the currently enabled IORM plans on your storage cells, if applicable. In the following, we will use `dcli` to run the CellCLI `alter iormplan inactive` command to disable any enabled plans:

```
[oracle@cm01dbm01 iorm]$ dcli -g ./cell_group cellcli -e list iormplan
cm01cel01: cm01cel01_IORMPLAN  active
cm01cel02: cm01cel02_IORMPLAN  active
cm01cel03: cm01cel03_IORMPLAN  active
[oracle@cm01dbm01 iorm]$ dcli -g ./cell_group cellcli -e alter iormplan inactive
cm01cel01: IORMPLAN successfully altered
cm01cel02: IORMPLAN successfully altered
cm01cel03: IORMPLAN successfully altered
[oracle@cm01dbm01 iorm]$ dcli -g ./cell_group cellcli -e list iormplan
cm01cel01: cm01cel01_IORMPLAN  inactive
cm01cel02: cm01cel02_IORMPLAN  inactive
cm01cel03: cm01cel03_IORMPLAN  inactive
[oracle@cm01dbm01 iorm]$
```

3. Now, create and enable an Interdatabase IORM plan using the following CellCLI command from `dcli`:

```
[oracle@cm01dbm01 iorm]$ dcli -g ./cell_group "cellcli -e \
> alter iormplan objective=\'auto\', \
> dbplan=\(\(name=edw,level=1,allocation=55\), \
> \(name=visx,level=1,allocation=25\),     \
> \(name=dwprd,level=1,allocation=15\),    \
> \(name=visy,level=1,allocation=5\),      \
> \(name=other,level=2,allocation=100\)\)"
cm01cel01: IORMPLAN successfully altered
cm01cel02: IORMPLAN successfully altered
cm01cel03: IORMPLAN successfully altered
[oracle@cm01dbm01 iorm]$ dcli -g ./cell_group "cellcli -e alter iormplan active"
cm01cel01: IORMPLAN successfully altered
cm01cel02: IORMPLAN successfully altered
cm01cel03: IORMPLAN successfully altered
[oracle@cm01dbm01 iorm]$
```

In these commands we are doing the following:

- We are first setting the IORM plan objective to auto, which instructs IORM to automatically tailor I/O scheduling based on workload. Exadata's IORM algorithms will monitor large and small I/O requests and adjust I/O scheduling based on the mix of low latency I/O requests (small) and high throughput (large) requests.

- We are specifying the resource utilizations for each of our databases at level=1. You can specify utilization percentages at multiple levels in a similar manner to how you control resource utilization for consumer groups in a database resource management plan.

506

> **Note** Please see docs.oracle.com/cd/E11882_01/server.112/e25494/dbrm.htm#g1021210 to learn more about Database Resource Manager.

- The other database allocation in the last line of our dbplan section shows an allocation of 100 at level=2. This is required to enable unnamed databases, in our Interdatabase IORM plan, to be able to issue I/O. If you do not specify an other database, the dbplan implementation will raise an error.
- The second dcli command issues an alter iormplan active CellCLI command and is required to enable your plan.
- We used dcli to implement the Interdatabase IORM plan to ensure that each storage cell had an identical plan definition. This is not required; you can choose to implement IORM plans on a per-cell basis and even create IORM plans with different definitions on different cells.

How It Works

Deploying Interdatabase IORM plans is achieved by using the alter iormplan command with the dbplan I/O resource utilization syntax; in other words, Interdatabase IORM is established with the dbplan directive in an alter iormplan statement.

Database I/O resource utilizations are expressed as percentages, so in the example in the solution of this recipe, allocation=55 would equate to "allow this database to utilize 55% of I/O resources in the event that I/O is saturated on the storage cell." As Oracle's documentation states, IORM begins prioritizing and scheduling I/O requests as needed and not until I/O queues become full on the Exadata storage cell disks.

> **Note** Recipe 17-5 provides a complete IORM plan scenario with a combination of Interdatabase and Category IORM plans. In the How It Works section of Recipe 17-5 we will discuss several architecture details about IORM in general, including a discussion on when IORM "kicks in."

17-2. Limiting I/O Utilization for Your Databases
Problem

You wish to restrict a database's I/O utilization to a specific utilization "ceiling" across your storage cells.

Solution

In this recipe, you will learn how to use the limit clause for an Interdatabase IORM Plan to impose a disk I/O utilization cap for specific databases.

Select a target database to configure an I/O utilization percentage limit condition on and then issue the alter iormplan commands to introduce the limit. Notice the limit clause in **bold** below:

```
[oracle@cm01dbm01 iorm]$ dcli -g ./cell_group "cellcli -e \
> alter iormplan objective=\'auto\', \
> dbplan=\(\(name=edw,level=1,allocation=55,limit=70\), \
```

```
>  \(name=visx,level=1,allocation=25\),      \
>  \(name=dwprd,level=1,allocation=15\),     \
>  \(name=visy,level=1,allocation=5,limit=5\),      \
>  \(name=other,level=2,allocation=100\)\)"
cm01cel01: IORMPLAN successfully altered
cm01cel02: IORMPLAN successfully altered
cm01cel03: IORMPLAN successfully altered
[oracle@cm01dbm01 iorm]$ dcli -g ./cell_group "cellcli -e alter iormplan active"
cm01cel01: IORMPLAN successfully altered
cm01cel02: IORMPLAN successfully altered
cm01cel03: IORMPLAN successfully altered
[oracle@cm01dbm01 iorm]$
```

In this dbplan directive, we are specifying an I/O resource utilization limit of 70% for the EDW database and 5% of the VISY database.

How It Works

Interdatabase IORM plan limits are a means to establish a resource utilization ceiling for specific databases. By default, IORM plans are only engaged in the event that cell disk I/O utilization is at capacity, so the I/O utilization percentages introduced for each database via the dbplan directive do not, by themselves, impose hard limits on I/O resource utilizations. In other words, IORM resource allocation directives govern and control I/O resource utilization in the event of I/O saturation, whereas *limits* impose a hard ceiling on cell disk I/O resource allotment regardless of whether I/O is saturated on the cell disks.

The limit clause enforces a hard utilization ceiling on a per-database scope, restricting utilization to a fixed percentage of I/O resources whether or not the cell disks are saturated.

17-3. Managing Resources within a Database
Problem

You wish to create a resource management plan within a database or databases in order to either control storage cell I/O utilization for different consumer groups in a single database or to control I/O resource utilization for classifications of resource consumers across your Exadata databases.

Solution

In this recipe, you will learn how to create Database Resource Manager (DBRM) plans, consumer groups, and resource plan directives; assign specific types of sessions to DBRM consumer groups; and enable a DBRM plan. We will demonstrate using the DBMS_RESOURCE_MANAGER PL/SQL API and a database named VISX to create three separate consumer groups, CG_SHIPPING, CG_FINANCE, and CG_REPORTING. The consumer group names and resource allocations are arbitrarily selected for demonstration purposes; in a realistic environment, these would be configured based on your business requirements.

1. Create a pending area, resource plan, consumer groups, and resource plan directives. In the following, we are creating a resource plan called visx_plan, creating three consumer groups, and assigning 50%, 40%, and 10% CPU utilizations to the CG_SHIPPING, CG_FINANCE, and CG_REPORTING consumer groups, respectively:

```
SYS @ visx1> begin
    dbms_resource_manager.create_pending_area();
    dbms_resource_manager.create_plan(plan=>'visx_plan',
            comment=>'VISX Plan');
    dbms_resource_manager.create_consumer_group(consumer_group=>'CG_SHIPPING',
            comment=>'CG_SHIPPING');
    dbms_resource_manager.create_consumer_group(consumer_group=>'CG_FINANCE',
            comment=>'CG_FINANCE');
    dbms_resource_manager.create_consumer_group(consumer_group=>'CG_REPORTING',
            comment=>'CG_REPORTING');
    dbms_resource_manager.create_plan_directive(plan=>'visx_plan',
            comment=>'CG_SHIPPING_50_L1',group_or_subplan=>'CG_SHIPPING', mgmt_p1=>50);
    dbms_resource_manager.create_plan_directive(plan=>'visx_plan',
            comment=>'CG_FINANCE_40_L1',group_or_subplan=>'CG_FINANCE',mgmt_p1=>40);
    dbms_resource_manager.create_plan_directive(plan=>'visx_plan',
            comment=>'CG_REPORTING_10_L1',group_or_subplan=>'CG_REPORTING',mgmt_p1=>10);
    dbms_resource_manager.create_plan_directive(plan=>'visx_plan',
            comment=>'OTHER_GROUPS_L2',group_or_subplan=>'OTHER_GROUPS',
              mgmt_p1=>0,mgmt_p2=>100);
    dbms_resource_manager.validate_pending_area();
    dbms_resource_manager.submit_pending_area();
  end;
 /
PL/SQL procedure successfully completed.
SYS @ visx1>
```

2. Assign sessions to the consumer groups. In the following example, we are assigning a USR1 Oracle user to the CG_SHIPPING consumer group, USR2 to CG_FINANCE, and USR3 to the CG_REPORTING consumer group:

```
SYS @ visx1> begin
    dbms_resource_manager.create_pending_area();
    dbms_resource_manager.set_consumer_group_mapping(dbms_resource_manager.oracle_user,
            'USR1','CG_SHIPPING');
    dbms_resource_manager.set_consumer_group_mapping(dbms_resource_manager.oracle_user,
            'USR2','CG_FINANCE');
    dbms_resource_manager.set_consumer_group_mapping(dbms_resource_manager.oracle_user,
            'USR3','CG_REPORTING');
    dbms_resource_manager_privs.grant_switch_consumer_group(
      grantee_name=>'USR1',consumer_group=>'CG_SHIPPING',grant_option=>TRUE);
    dbms_resource_manager_privs.grant_switch_consumer_group(
      grantee_name=>'USR2',consumer_group=>'CG_FINANCE',grant_option=>TRUE);
    dbms_resource_manager_privs.grant_switch_consumer_group(
      grantee_name=>'USR3',consumer_group=>'CG_REPORTING',grant_option=>TRUE);
```

```
                    dbms_resource_manager.submit_pending_area();
                    end;
                    /
        PL/SQL procedure successfully completed.
        SYS @ visx1>
```

3. Enable your resource plan:

```
        SYS @ visx1> alter system set resource_manager_plan='visx_plan' scope=both sid='*';
```

> **Note** The steps provide a very simplistic DBRM plan with three consumer groups, designed to govern CPU utilization by resource consumer, and maps three database schemas to these consumer groups. DBRM provides a tremendous amount of resource control flexibility that is obviously not covered in this recipe. To learn more about DBRM, please see docs.oracle.com/cd/E11882_01/server.112/e25494/dbrm.htm#g1021210.

How It Works

Intradatabase IORM on Exadata is an extension of DBRM plans configured in your databases. DBRM is a method used to impose resource controls for different resource consumers inside your databases.

There are a few reasons why this may be important for you on Exadata:

- If you only have a single database deployed on an Exadata Database Machine and wish to control I/O resource utilization on your storage cells based on your database resource plan, IORM automatically performs I/O resource prioritization and scheduling based on your DBRM plan and calls this an Intradatabase IORM plan.

- If you have classifications, or categories, of resource consumers that span multiple databases on your Exadata Database Machine, a DBRM plan is required in order to assign resource consumer groups to resource categories. These categories are then outlined in a category plan, as presented in Recipe 17-4.

In short, if you wish to govern I/O resource utilization for a single database, simply create a DBRM plan based on your business needs and IORM will schedule and prioritize I/O requests according to the DBRM plan. Furthermore, if you have DBRM categories assigned to resource consumer groups for multiple databases, these categories will need to be assigned to consumer groups in order for an IORM category plan to work.

In contrast to Interdatabase IORM and Category IORM, Intradatabase IORM is not established with CellCLI `alter iormplan` commands; Category IORM is, and Category IORM relies on your consumer group to category mappings.

> **Note** To learn more about Category IORM and Intradatabase IORM, please see Recipes 17-4 and 17-1.

17-4. Prioritizing I/O Utilization by Category of Resource Consumers

Problem

You wish to govern I/O resource utilization on your Exadata storage cells based on database resource categories, or classifications of consumer workload across multiple databases.

Solution

In this recipe, you will learn how to assign DBRM consumer groups to resource categories and use these categories to create a Category IORM plan. We will demonstrate Category IORM implementation by using DBRM consumer groups created in Recipe 17-3. To learn more about resource consumer group creation and the steps to create an Intradatabase IORM plan, please refer to Recipe 17-3.

1. First, create DBRM categories in each of your databases using the DBMS_RESOURCE_MANAGER PL/SQL API. In the following, we will create three resource categories, CAT_HIGH, CAT_LOW, and CAT_MEDIUM.

    ```
    SYS @ visx1> begin
        dbms_resource_manager.create_pending_area();
        dbms_resource_manager.create_category(category=>'CAT_HIGH', comment=>'CAT_HIGH');
        dbms_resource_manager.create_category(category=>'CAT_MEDIUM',comment=>'CAT_MEDIUM');
        dbms_resource_manager.create_category(category=>'CAT_LOW',comment=>'CAT_LOW');
        dbms_resource_manager.validate_pending_area();
        dbms_resource_manager.submit_pending_area();
        end;
      /

    PL/SQL procedure successfully completed.
    SYS @ visx1>
    ```

2. After the DBRM categories are created, assign your DBRM resource consumer groups to the desired categories created in the previous step:

    ```
    SYS @ visx1> begin
        dbms_resource_manager.create_pending_area();
        dbms_resource_manager.update_consumer_group(consumer_group=>'CG_SHIPPING',
              new_category=>'CAT_HIGH');
        dbms_resource_manager.update_consumer_group(consumer_group=>'CG_FINANCE',
              new_category=>'CAT_MEDIUM');
        dbms_resource_manager.update_consumer_group(consumer_group=>'CG_REPORTING',
              new_category=>'CAT_LOW');
        dbms_resource_manager.validate_pending_area();
        dbms_resource_manager.submit_pending_area();
        end;
      /
    SYS @ visx1>
    ```

3. As an alternative to Step 2, you can assign categories to consumer groups at the time the consumer groups are created. The following is an example:

   ```
   dbms_resource_manager.create_consumer_group(consumer_group=>'CG_SHIPPING,
          comment=>'CG_SHIPPING',category=>'CAT_HIGH');
   ```

4. Create a Category IORM plan using the `alter iormplan` CellCLI statement with the `catplan` directive. In the next example, we will use `dcli` to implement our Category IORM plan to ensure that each storage cell has an identical plan definition. Additionally, we will also delete any currently implemented Interdatabase IORM plan by providing an empty `dbplan` directive. In our Category IORM plan, we will allocate 100% of I/O resources to the CAT_HIGH category at level 1, 80% for CAT_MEDIUM at level 2, 20% for CAT_LOW at level 2, and 100% of all other categories at level 3:

   ```
   [oracle@cm01dbm01 iorm]$ dcli -g ./cell_group "cellcli -e \
   > alter iormplan objective=\'auto\', \
   > dbplan=\'\', \
   > catplan=\(\(name=CAT_HIGH,level=1,allocation=100\), \
   > \(name=CAT_MEDIUM,level=2,allocation=80\),      \
   > \(name=CAT_LOW,level=2,allocation=20\),         \
   > \(name=other,level=3,allocation=100\)\)"
   cm01cel01: IORMPLAN successfully altered
   cm01cel02: IORMPLAN successfully altered
   cm01cel03: IORMPLAN successfully altered
   [oracle@cm01dbm01 iorm]$ dcli -g ./cell_group "cellcli -e alter iormplan active"
   cm01cel01: IORMPLAN successfully altered
   cm01cel02: IORMPLAN successfully altered
   cm01cel03: IORMPLAN successfully altered
   [oracle@cm01dbm01 iorm]$
   ```

How It Works

Category IORM is implemented by issuing the `alter iormplan` CellCLI command with the `catplan` directive, as outlined in the solution of this recipe. In this recipe, we demonstrated the process of assigning resource categories to resource consumer groups in a DBRM plan, which is a required step if you wish your category classifications to be controlled with a Category IORM plan.

Category IORM is the first classification of I/O resource allocation settings that IORM evaluates, and it can be enabled with or without Interdatabase IORM or even Intradatabase. As an Exadata DMA, you are allowed to create a category plan without named categories actually mapped to your database's resource consumer groups; in this case, each consumer group will fall under the OTHER category.

While Interdatabase IORM is often the simplest and most often used IORM type, Category IORM combined with Interdatabase IORM provides the finest level of control of your Exadata storage cell I/O resources. Recipe 17-5 provides instructions for how to configure an IORM plan, which is defined by Oracle as a combination of Category IORM and Interdatabase IORM. In the How It Works section of Recipe 17-5, we will provide a more comprehensive discussion about how IORM prioritizes and schedules I/O to the cell disks, the order in which IORM plan types are evaluated in a complex IORM plan, and an overview of how IORM determines utilization restrictions and caps in the event of storage cell I/O saturation.

17-5. Prioritizing I/O Utilization by Categories of Resource Consumers and Databases

Problem

You wish to implement I/O resource utilization control on your Exadata storage cells across categories of resource consumers and Exadata databases.

Solution

In this recipe, you will learn how to implement an IORM plan, which is defined as a Category IORM plan plus an Interdatabase IORM plan.

Creating an IORM plan is achieved by using the `alter iormplan` CellCLI command with both the `dbplan` and `catplan` directives. Before creating your IORM plan, you must do the following:

1. Gather business requirements for your databases, resource consumers within each database, and classifications of resources (in other words, categories) across each database.

2. Build your Intradatabase plans on each of the databases that you wish to control resources on DBRM. Recipe 17-3 provides instructions on how to accomplish these steps using the `DBMS_RESOURCE_MANAGER` PL/SQL package procedures.

3. Create resource categories in each of your databases using the `DBMS_RESOURCE_MANAGER.CREATE_CATEGORY` and assign your categories to the proper resource consumer groups.

4. Review the expected I/O utilization capacity numbers using tips provided in the How It Works section of this recipe or by consulting Oracle's IORM documentation.

5. Implement your IORM plan across your storage cells.

Following is an example that uses `dcli` with the `alter iormplan` CellCLI command to enable an IORM plan across all of your storage cells. We will number each of the lines and provide a description of what each line accomplishes after the listing output:

```
1.  [oracle@cm01dbm01 iorm]$ dcli -g ./cell_group "cellcli -e alter iormplan inactive"
2.  cm01cel01: IORMPLAN successfully altered
3.  cm01cel02: IORMPLAN successfully altered
4.  cm01cel03: IORMPLAN successfully altered
5.  [oracle@cm01dbm01 iorm]$ dcli -g ./cell_group "cellcli -e \
6.  > alter iormplan objective=\'auto\', \
7.  > dbplan=\(\(name=edw,level=1,allocation=55\), \
8.  > \(name=visx,level=1,allocation=25\), \
9.  > \(name=dwprd,level=1,allocation=15\), \
10. > \(name=visy,level=1,allocation=5\), \
11. > \(name=other,level=2,allocation=100\)\), \
12. > catplan=\(\(name=CAT_HIGH,level=1,allocation=100\), \
13. > \(name=CAT_MEDIUM,level=2,allocation=80\), \
14. > \(name=CAT_LOW,level=2,allocation=20\), \
```

```
15. > \(name=other,level=3,allocation=100\)\)"
16. cm01cel01: IORMPLAN successfully altered
17. cm01cel02: IORMPLAN successfully altered
18. cm01cel03: IORMPLAN successfully altered
19. [oracle@cm01dbm01 iorm]$ dcli -g ./cell_group "cellcli -e alter iormplan active"
20. cm01cel01: IORMPLAN successfully altered
21. cm01cel02: IORMPLAN successfully altered
22. cm01cel03: IORMPLAN successfully altered
23. [oracle@cm01dbm01 iorm]$
```

- In line 1, we are disabling any current IORM plan. This is not required, but it is something we prefer to do in order to avoid confusion should the new IORM plan have any errors.

- In line 5, we are using `dcli` to launch `cellcli` on each storage cell.

- In line 6, we are specifying `auto` as our plan objective; we will discuss this in more detail in the How It Works section of this recipe.

- Lines 7 through 11 contain our Interdatabase IORM plan objectives. Here, we assign a specific I/O utilization target for four different databases, each at level 1, as well as a 100% utilization at level 2.

- Lines 12 through 15 contain our Category IOR plan objectives. Here we are assigning 100% for `CAT_HIGH` at level 1, 80% and 20% for `CAT_MEDIUM` and `CAT_LOW` at level 2, and all other categories 100% at level 3.

- Line 19 enables our IORM Plan.

How It Works

Although it is common for Exadata DMAs to refer to any implementation of `iormplan` as "IORM," Oracle defines an IORM plan as a combination of Category IORM and Interdatabase IORM plans. IORM plans are created by using the `alter iormplan` command to implement both a Category Plan (catplan) and Interdatabase Plan (dbplan). In short:

- An IORM plan is a combination of a Category plan and an Interdatabase plan.

- A Category plan specifies resource allocations per classification, or category, of resource consumer groups. Categories with the same names are assigned to consumer groups across *multiple* Exadata databases, and IORM sees these as requests that have the same I/O characteristics from a prioritization perspective.

- Categories are assigned to consumer groups and consumer groups are created as part of a DBRM or Intradatabase plan within a database.

- An Interdatabase plan specifies I/O resource allocations on a per database level.

If you are reading the recipes in this chapter sequentially, you may have noticed that, thus far, we have not described how IORM actually "works." Here, we will attempt to provide a concise explanation of how IORM functions, when it is engaged, the order in which IORM rules are evaluated, and the information needed to understand the "math" of IORM.

We have stated in several recipes in this chapter that IORM is only engaged "when I/O is saturated on the storage cells." More accurately speaking, IORM kicks in when there are "full" disk I/O queues (and when IORM is enabled, of course). Figure 17-1 provides a graphical representation of how IORM works.

CHAPTER 17 ■ I/O RESOURCE MANAGEMENT AND INSTANCE CAGING

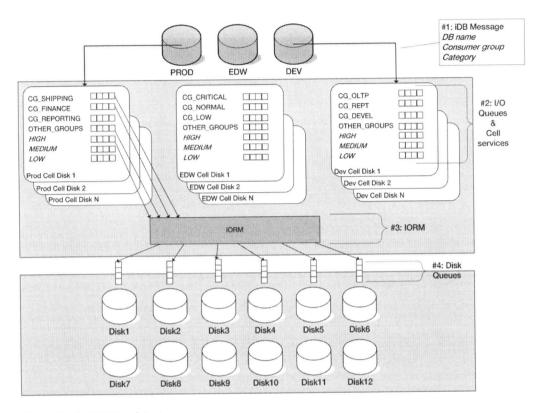

Figure 17-1. IORM architecture

The process flow for I/O requests with IORM can be described as follows:

1. Each I/O request submitted by a database sends an iDB message to each storage cell. The iDB message includes the list of extents required to satisfy the operation as well as several pieces of metadata, including the database name associated with the request, the consumer group name (or "other" if DBRM is not in place), the resource and the resource category (or "other" if categories are not assigned to consumer groups).

2. The I/O request is placed on an I/O queue, managed by cell services. Each cell disk maintain an I/O queue for each database and each consumer group per database.

3. IORM intercepts the I/O requests from the I/O queues before placing them on a disk queue. If the disk queue(s) is full, IORM will evaluate the IORM plan rules for each incoming I/O request and place the I/O request in the proper, prioritized order on the disk queue.

4. I/Os on the disk queues are processed in a FIFO basis; at this point, IORM would have already executed its logic to properly prioritize I/O requests.

Without IORM, I/Os are serviced on each cell disk based on a first-in-first-out (FIFO) algorithm; whichever request is issued first gets priority, then the second request, followed by the third, and so on. When an IORM plan is enabled, it evaluates the rules configured in the IORM plan and prioritizes disk I/Os accordingly by placing them in the proper slot on the disk queue.

IORM is an integral software component of the Exadata Storage Server software and runs within the Cell Services (`cellsrv`) software stack on each cell. This design allows for IORM to efficiently perform I/O prioritization in line with the I/O request; disk queues and disk I/O requests are facilitated directly by IORM in accordance with the IORM plan configurations established by the DMA. If cell disk I/O is *not* saturated, IORM will place I/O requests on the disk queues in a FIFO basis and the disks are made available to all workloads. From an architecture and design perspective, the following are key concepts to understand about IORM:

- Each cell disk maintains an I/O queue for each consumer group and each database, as depicted in Figure 17-1, as well as three background queues: High, Medium, and Low.
- If no Intradatabase (DBRM) plans are set for an I/O request, non-background I/O requests are mapped to the OTHER_GROUPS consumer group I/O queue.
- Background I/O queues are mapped to High, Medium, and Low based on different I/O types.
- Redo log file and control file writes are always prioritized at the highest level; they fall into the High priority consumer group on each database's I/O queue for each cell disk.
- Background I/O and DBWR I/O is scheduled at the same priority as user I/O. This means, for example, that DBWR writes for a specific database will be prioritized according to the database's Interdatabase IORM plan configuration, if any.
- You can configure an Intradatabase IORM, Interdatabase IORM, Category IORM, and any combination of the three. IORM will automatically adjust its I/O scheduling policies based on the configuration you create.

One of the important aspects to understand about IORM is the order in which different IORM operations are evaluated. Category IORM is evaluated first, then Interdatabase IORM, and finally, Intradatabase IORM. In the event of cell disk saturation, IORM will engage and the following formula can be used to determine the percentage resource utilization for an I/O request:

CG% = (Intra CG%) / Σ(x)) * db% * cat%

Where:

- CG% = the IORM-calculated resource allocation for a database's consumer group sessions
- Intra CG% = resource allocation for a consumer group within an Intradatabase resource plan
- x = the sum of Intradatabase resource allocations for all consumer groups in the same category within a database
- db% = the Interdatabase resource allocation for a database
- cat% = the percentage utilization for the category in which the consumer group belongs

■ **Note** Calculating the IORM resource allocations for complex plans involves a number of calculations, and we believe that fully understanding this "IORM math" is critical when deploying IORM to ensure that each of your key database sessions is allotted the proper amount of I/O resource utilization. The IORMPlanningCalculatorV1.xlsx spreadsheet, included in the code repository for this text, can be used to calculate your IORM resource allocations for a desired IORM plan.

To close out this recipe, we will offer a brief summary of IORM objectives. As you may have noticed in the Solution section of this recipe as well as in Recipes 17-1 through 17-4, we used the `objective=auto` clause in our `alter iormplan` CellCLI statements. This is one of a number of IORM objectives that are allowed:

- `auto`: Used to allow IORM to determine the best optimization method when prioritizing I/O requests. Exadata's Cell Services software (`cellsrv`) will continuously monitor your I/O utilization and, if greater than 75% of requests are small I/O requests less than 128 KB in size, IORM will treat the workload as a "low latency" workload. Otherwise, IORM will treat the I/O profile as a high throughput profile. The next bullets describe these terms in the context of IORM.
- `low_latency`: Used to limit disk utilization to the greatest extent possible and is used when workloads require low I/O latency. This is typically configured for databases that are primarily characterized by OLTP workload profiles.
- `high_throughput`: Used to maximize disk throughput and is typically configured for data warehouse environments.
- `balanced`: Use when you have mixed workloads. Exadata limits disk utilization to the greatest extent possible for small I/O operations and provides greater utilization for large I/O operations.

17-6. Monitoring Performance When IORM Is Enabled

Problem

You wish to monitor database performance after an IORM plan is enabled.

Solution

In this recipe, you will learn how to query IORM-related storage cell metrics to measure the I/O performance impact when an IORM plan is enabled. In the test cases in this recipe, we will enable an IORM plan consisting of both an Interdatabase plan as well as a Category IORM plan covering multiple resource consumers across each of four databases.

> **Note** We will not display our IORM and DBRM configuration in this recipe for sake of brevity. To learn how to create Category IORM plans, Interdatabase IORM plans, and Intradatabase IORM plans, please refer to Recipes 17-1 through 17-5.

Using Storage Cell Metrics to Measure IORM Performance Impact

Exadata provides a number of performance metrics for each of the Category, Interdatabase, and Intradatabase IORM types. As presented initially in Chapter 13, you can find these metric and their descriptions using the following CellCLI commands:

```
CellCLI> list metricdefinition where objectType='IORM_CATEGORY' attributes name,description
CellCLI> list metricdefinition where objectType='IORM_DATABASE' attributes name,description
CellCLI> list metricdefinition where objectType='IORM_CONSUMER_GROUP' attributes name,description
```

With a representative database workload running and after your IORM plan has been created, use the `list metriccurrent` or `list metrichistory` CellCLI command to report your current or historical IORM metrics. In the following, we will display the current I/O throughput statistics, measured in megabytes per second, for each category, database, and consumer group using the CT_IO_BY_SEC, DB_IO_BY_SEC, and CG_IO_BY_SEC metrics, respectively:

```
[oracle@cm01dbm01 iorm]$ dcli -c cm01cel01 cellcli -e list metriccurrent where name=CT_IO_BY_SEC
cm01cel01: CT_IO_BY_SEC    CAT_HIGH                911 MB/sec
cm01cel01: CT_IO_BY_SEC    CAT_LOW                 165 MB/sec
cm01cel01: CT_IO_BY_SEC    CAT_MEDIUM              426 MB/sec
[oracle@cm01dbm01 iorm]$ dcli -c cm01cel01 cellcli -e list metriccurrent where name=DB_IO_BY_SEC
cm01cel01: DB_IO_BY_SEC    DWPRD                   366 MB/sec
cm01cel01: DB_IO_BY_SEC    EDW                     470 MB/sec
cm01cel01: DB_IO_BY_SEC    VISX                    424 MB/sec
cm01cel01: DB_IO_BY_SEC    VISY                    242 MB/sec
[oracle@cm01dbm01 iorm]$ dcli -c cm01cel01 cellcli -e list metriccurrent where name=CG_IO_BY_SEC
cm01cel01: CG_IO_BY_SEC    DWPRD.CG_HIGH           192 MB/sec
cm01cel01: CG_IO_BY_SEC    DWPRD.CG_LOW             33 MB/sec
... Output omitted for brevity
[oracle@cm01dbm01 iorm]$
```

In this output, you should expect to see higher I/O transfer numbers for the databases, categories, and consumer groups with higher resource allocations. For example, the CAT_HIGH category, at the time of the measurement, was reporting almost double the I/O transfer rate as the CAT_MEDIUM consumer category.

Since IORM can introduce I/O waits under periods of high load, you can measure the average I/O wait time per request for categories, databases, and consumer groups using the [CT|DB|CG]_IO_WT* metrics. In the following, we will run a workload on each of our databases and display the average wait time per request for each of these IORM types for large I/O requests, using the CT_IO_WT_LG_SEC, DB_IO_WT_LG_RQ, and CG_IO_WT_LG_RQ metrics:

```
[oracle@cm01dbm01 iorm]$ dcli -c cm01cel01 cellcli -e list metriccurrent where name=CT_IO_WT_LG_RQ
cm01cel01: CT_IO_WT_LG_RQ       CAT_HIGH              40.9 ms/request
cm01cel01: CT_IO_WT_LG_RQ       CAT_LOW            2,990 ms/request
cm01cel01: CT_IO_WT_LG_RQ       CAT_MEDIUM           639 ms/request
cm01cel01: CT_IO_WT_LG_RQ       OTHER                  0.0 ms/request
cm01cel01: CT_IO_WT_LG_RQ       _ASM_                  6.3 ms/request
[oracle@cm01dbm01 iorm]$ dcli -c cm01cel01 cellcli -e list metriccurrent where name=DB_IO_WT_LG_RQ
cm01cel01: DB_IO_WT_LG_RQ       DWPRD                749 ms/request
cm01cel01: DB_IO_WT_LG_RQ       EDW                  350 ms/request
cm01cel01: DB_IO_WT_LG_RQ       VISX                 452 ms/request
cm01cel01: DB_IO_WT_LG_RQ       VISY                 716 ms/request
cm01cel01: DB_IO_WT_LG_RQ       _OTHER_DATABASE_       6.3 ms/request
[oracle@cm01dbm01 iorm]$ dcli -c cm01cel01 cellcli -e list metriccurrent where name=CG_IO_WT_LG_RQ
cm01cel01: CG_IO_WT_LG_RQ       DWPRD.CG_HIGH         73.1 ms/request
cm01cel01: CG_IO_WT_LG_RQ       DWPRD.CG_LOW       4,220 ms/request
cm01cel01: CG_IO_WT_LG_RQ       DWPRD.CG_MEDIUM      843 ms/request
... Output omitted for brevity
[oracle@cm01dbm01 iorm]$
```

As you can see, the `list metriccurrent` command for the *WT_LG_RQ* metrics will display the average I/O wait time per request, and under periods of high I/O load, you will see that IORM types with higher resource allocations will show smaller wait times per request than the types with lower resource allocations.

In these outputs, note that we restricted our output to a single storage cell, cm01cel01; you could also execute these queries for all storage cells using the `dcli -g [cell group file]` command. Of course, you could also report historical IORM metrics using the `list metrichistory` CellCLI command and summarize the data using techniques presented in Chapter 13.

In this section of the recipe, we have only displayed a subset of the available IORM metrics. Please refer to the `list metricdefinition` output to obtain a complete list of available metrics and the How It Works section of this recipe to learn what we consider to be the most commonly monitored IORM-related storage cell metrics.

Using metric_iorm.pl to Measure IORM Performance Impact

Another way to measure IORM performance statistics is via the `metric_iorm.pl` Perl script, which you can download from My Oracle Support note 1337265.1. This script collects performance statistics from multiple IORM metrics and summarizes into an easy-to-read report, as displayed:

```
[root@cm01cel01 ~]# ./metric_iorm.pl
... Additional database detail omitted for brevity
Database:         VISY
Utilization:      Small=0%      Large=4%
Flash Cache:      IOPS=6.1
Throughput:       MBPS=110
Small I/O's:      IOPS=4.7      Avg qtime=5.1ms
Large I/O's:      IOPS=108      Avg qtime=347ms
Consumer Group: CG_ADHOC
Utilization:      Small=0%      Large=1%
Flash Cache:      IOPS=0.0
Throughput:       MBPS=33
Small I/O's:      IOPS=0.2      Avg qtime=22.9ms
Large I/O's:      IOPS=33.1     Avg qtime=1111ms
... Other consumer groups omitted for brevity
Consumer Group: CG_FINANCE
Utilization:      Small=0%      Large=1%
Flash Cache:      IOPS=0.0
Throughput:       MBPS=44
Small I/O's:      IOPS=2.1      Avg qtime=8.1ms
Large I/O's:      IOPS=43.0     Avg qtime=5.2ms
Consumer Group: CG_PROJECTS
Utilization:      Small=0%      Large=1%
Flash Cache:      IOPS=0.0
Throughput:       MBPS=32
Small I/O's:      IOPS=0.4      Avg qtime=3.6ms
Large I/O's:      IOPS=31.7     Avg qtime=12.7ms
... Other consumer groups omitted for brevity

DISK LATENCY METRICS
Avg small read latency:        37.70 ms
Avg small write latency:        0.86 ms
Avg large read latency:        79.87 ms
Avg large write latency:        0.00 ms
[root@cm01cel01 ~]#
```

The output in the `metric_iorm.pl` script is separated by database, with database-wide performance statistics provided including the I/O utilization broken down by small I/O and large I/O, Flash Cache I/Os per second, I/O bandwidth measured in megabytes per second, as well as small I/O and large I/O per second and average queue times. The average queue times are a reflection of I/O waits or queues introduced as a result of an IORM plan. After the database statistics, `metric_iorm.pl` reports the same performance statistics for each consumer group within the database. At the bottom of the report, `metric_iorm.pl` provides small and large I/O disk latency metrics, which are extracted from cell disk metrics (not IORM metrics).

> **Note** In addition to displaying current IORM metric summaries and reports from a single cell, `metric_iorm.pl` can also summarize historical information and be executed across multiple cells using `dcli`. MOS Note 1337265.1 provides syntax and examples for these scenarios.

How It Works

As presented in Chapter 13, Exadata is preconfigured with a number of storage server metrics and continuously collects IORM metrics. Category IORM metrics are contained in the `IORM_CATEGORY` objectType, Interdatabase IORM metrics are part of the `IORM_DATABASE` objectType, and Intradatabase IORM metrics are part of the `IORM_CONSUMER_GROUP` objectType.

The `list metriccurrent` command can be used to display current IORM metrics and the `list metrichistory` command can be used to retrieve historical IORM metrics. As described in the solution of this recipe, you can use the `list metricdefinition` command to list all of your IORM-related storage cell metrics. In Table 17-1, we provide what we consider to be the most relevant metrics related to IORM.

Table 17-1. Important IORM Metrics

Metric	Description	Metric	Description
CT_IO_BY_SEC DB_IO_BY_SEC CG_IO_BY_SEC	I/O load in MB/second for categories, databases, and consumer groups	CT_IO_RQ_[LG|SM]_SEC DB_IO_RQ_[LG|SM]_SEC CG_IO_RQ_[LG|SM]_SEC	Small and large I/O requests per second for categories, databases, and consumer groups
CT_IO_UTIL_[SM_LG] DB_IO_UTIL_[SM_LG] CG_IO_UTIL_[SM_LG]	Small and large I/O disk utilization for categories, databases, and consumer groups	CT_IO_WT_[LG|SM]_RQ DB_IO_WT_[LG|SM]_RQ CG_IO_WT_[LG|SM]_RQ	Small and large I/O average waits per second for categories, databases, and consumer groups

> **Note** Chapter 13 discusses the topic of monitoring Exadata storage cells with metrics in more detail, including several recipes that present techniques for summarizing metric data. These summarization techniques can be especially helpful when building a performance statistics repository for IORM, as IORM metrics closely align with databases and resource consumers in your databases.

If you have read other recipes in this book, you will have learned that we use Perl to summarize storage server metrics with regularity; this is largely due to how `cellcli` generates text listings of metric output. With `metric_iorm.pl`, Oracle has delivered an IORM-specific reporting tool that uses this same approach. `metric_iorm.pl` extracts many of the same metrics listed in Table 17-1 and, additionally, a handful of metrics not specifically associated with IORM including cell disk latency metrics, and it generates an easy-to-read report. Since `metric_iorm.pl` is a relatively self-documented Perl script, we encourage you to view its contents to understand the specific storage server metrics that it uses.

CHAPTER 17 ■ I/O RESOURCE MANAGEMENT AND INSTANCE CAGING

17-7. Obtaining IORM Plan Information

Problem

You wish to list the details of your currently enabled IORM plan in order to understand how your plan is configured.

Solution

In this recipe, you will learn how to display your currently enabled IORM plan details using two methods, with CellCLI's `list iormplan` command and by generating a Cell Services statedump.

Begin by running the following CellCLI command from one of your storage cells:

```
CellCLI> list iormplan detail
         name:              cm01cel01_IORMPLAN
         catPlan:           name=CAT_HIGH,level=1,allocation=100
                            name=CAT_MEDIUM,level=2,allocation=80
                            name=CAT_LOW,level=2,allocation=20
                            name=other,level=3,allocation=100
         dbPlan:            name=edw,level=1,allocation=55
                            name=visx,level=1,allocation=25
                            name=dwprd,level=1,allocation=15
                            name=visy,level=1,allocation=5
                            name=other,level=2,allocation=100
         objective:         auto
         status:            active
CellCLI>
```

We see an active IORM plan with a combination of Category IORM and Interdatabase IORM configured using the auto IORM plan objective. Recipes 17-1 through 17-5 walk you through examples of how to create these types of IORM plans and, in the How It Works section of Recipe 17-5, we elaborate on the details of how Exadata implements I/O resource management functionality with IORM.

To provide a more comprehensive picture of your IORM plans, execute the following command from CellCLI to generate a cell services (`cellsrv`) statedump:

```
CellCLI> alter cell events = "immediate cellsrv.cellsrv_statedump(0,0)"
Dump sequence #1 has been written to /opt/oracle/cell11.2.3.1.1_LINUX.X64_120607/log/diag/asm/cell/
cm01cel01/trace/svtrc_12910_71.trc
Cell cm01cel01 successfully altered
CellCLI>
```

The `cellsrv statedump` is written to a text file reported in the output of your `alter cell events` command. Open this file with a text editor and look for the following:

1. Search for the text "IORM state dump" to find the beginning of your IORM configuration. In the following, we see that an IORM plan is currently enabled and I/O is being "throttled" based on the plan's rules:

    ```
    ----------------------------------------------------------------
    IORM state dump
    ----------------------------------------------------------------
    Time: 11-25-2012 23:49:52.084883000
    IORM Enabled: Active Plan, Throttling
    Current IORM Plans
    ```

2. The next section displays any configured Category IORM plans; the fact that this section is listed first is a good indication that cell services software evaluates Category IORM first. In the next section, you will see a number of IORM categories listed, including three custom categories and a number of Oracle background process-related queries with descriptions of these seeded categories provided:

```
Category Plan
  number of categories: 8
    id 0: CAT_HIGH
    id 1: CAT_MEDIUM
    id 2: CAT_LOW
    id 3: OTHER
    id 4: _ORACLE_BG_CATEGORY_
    id 5: _ORACLE_MEDPRIBG_CATEGORY_
    id 6: _ORACLE_LOWPRIBG_CATEGORY_
    id 7: _ASM_
  other category index: 3
  ASM category index: 7
  emergency/background category index: 4
  medium-priority background category index: 5
  low-priority background category index: 6
```

3. Underneath the Category Plan section, you will also see a listing of database-to-consumer group-to-category mappings:

```
map of database and consumer group indicies to category index
    database 0 <EDW>, consumer group 0 <ORA$DIAGNOSTICS> maps to category 3 <OTHER>
    database 0 <EDW>, consumer group 1 <SYS_GROUP> maps to category 3 <OTHER>
    database 0 <EDW>, consumer group 2 <OTHER_GROUPS> maps to category 3 <OTHER>
    ... Mappings omitted for brevity
    database 1 <VISX>, consumer group 0 <CG_REPORTING> maps to category 2 <CAT_LOW>
    database 1 <VISX>, consumer group 1 <CG_SHIPPING> maps to category 0 <CAT_HIGH>
... Additional mappings omitted for brevity
```

4. Below the Category Plan section, the trace file will display your Interdatabase IORM plan details. This section shows your I/O resource allocation per database as well as indications of whether Flash Cache and Flash Logging are enabled for your database and the resource limits for each database. Recipe 17-2 discusses resource allocation limits with IORM, and Recipe 17-8 shows you how to enable or disable Flash Cache and/or Flash Logging for a database:

```
Inter-Database Plan
  number of databases: 5
    id 0: EDW
    id 1: VISX
    id 2: DWPRD
    id 3: VISY
    id 4: OTHER
```

```
    other database index: 4
    map of database id to database index
       id 4075123336 <VISX> maps to index 1 <VISX> has FlashCache=on, FlashLog=on, Limit=0
       id 3369927204 <VISY> maps to index 3 <VISY> has FlashCache=on, FlashLog=on, Limit=0
       id 849012303 <DWPRD> maps to index 2 <DWPRD> has FlashCache=on, FlashLog=on, Limit=0
       id 2273376219 <EDW> maps to index 0 <EDW> has FlashCache=on, FlashLog=on, Limit=0
```

5. Below the Inter-Database Plan section, the trace file displays your Intradatabase IORM details. This section is broken down into subsections for each of your databases and provides mappings to Category mappings, as indicated in bold:

```
Intra-Database Plan
   database index: 3
   database id: 3369927204
   database name: VISY
   plan name: VISY_PLAN
   number of consumer groups: 8
   other consumer group index: 3
   background consumer group index: 4
   medium-priority background consumer group index: 5
   low-priority background consumer group index: 6
   low-priority foreground consumer group index: 7
   map of consumer group id to index:
     CG_FINANCE maps to index 0
     CG_PROJECTS maps to index 1
     CG_ADHOC maps to index 2
     OTHER_GROUPS maps to index 3
      _ORACLE_BACKGROUND_GROUP_ maps to index 4
      _ORACLE_MEDPRIBG_GROUP_ maps to index 5
      _ORACLE_LOWPRIBG_GROUP_ maps to index 6
      _ORACLE_LOWPRIFG_GROUP_ maps to index 7
   bitmasks:
     plan VISY_PLAN:
.. Bitmasks omitted for brevity
```

6. Further down in the trace file, you will find sections for each of your cell disks that contain IORM statistics and workload information specific to the I/O queues on each cell disk, as presented in the How It Works section in Recipe 17-5. Following is a section of the IORM_STATS for a single cell disk using physical device /dev/sda3:

1. ******** IORM STATS ******** Sun Nov 25 23:49:52 2012
2. IORM stats for disk=/dev/sda3
3. Heap stats: Inuse=2240KB Total=4141KB
4. --------- IORM Workload State & Characterization ---------
5. IORM: Solo Workload
6. Solo workload (no db or cg): 26 transitions
7. IORM boost =119.000000 (cnt = 92929, amt = 11108520)
8. #Bypassedios=49
9. #served=24 bitmap=0 #queued=0 adtime=0ms asmrdtime=0ms #cumulserved=10195937
   #pending=0 #lpending=0

```
10.     #max_conc_io=5 write_cache_hit_rate=94% iocost=55834574849ms
11.        catidx=0 bitmap=0 CAT_HIGH
12.        catidx=1 bitmap=0 CAT_MEDIUM
13.        catidx=2 bitmap=0 CAT_LOW
14.        catidx=3 bitmap=0 OTHER
15.        catidx=4 bitmap=0 _ORACLE_BG_CATEGORY_
16.          SIO:#served=16 #queued=0 Util=0% aqtime=0ms adtime=0ms
17.             dbidx=0 bitmap=0 EDW
18.             dbidx=1 bitmap=0 VISX
19.             dbidx=2 bitmap=0 DWPRD
20.             dbidx=3 bitmap=0 VISY
21.                SIO:#served=16 #queued=0 Util=0% aqtime=0ms adtime=0ms
22.                   cgidx=0 bitmap=0 cgname=CG_FINANCE
23.                   cgidx=1 bitmap=0 cgname=CG_PROJECTS
24.                   cgidx=2 bitmap=0 cgname=CG_ADHOC
25.                   cgidx=3 bitmap=0 cgname=OTHER_GROUPS
26.                   cgidx=4 bitmap=0 cgname=_ORACLE_BACKGROUND_GROUP_
27.                     SIO:#served=16 #queued=0 Util=0% aqtime=0ms adtime=0ms
28.                       #concios=43652, #fragios=0 #starvedios=0 #maxcapwaits=0
29.                   cgidx=5 bitmap=0 cgname=_ORACLE_MEDPRIBG_GROUP_
30.                   cgidx=6 bitmap=0 cgname=_ORACLE_LOWPRIBG_GROUP_
31.                   cgidx=7 bitmap=0 cgname=_ORACLE_LOWPRIFG_GROUP_
32.             dbidx=4 bitmap=0 _OTHER_DATABASE_
33.        catidx=5 bitmap=0 _ORACLE_MEDPRIBG_CATEGORY_
34.        catidx=6 bitmap=0 _ORACLE_LOWPRIBG_CATEGORY_
35.        catidx=7 bitmap=0 _ASM_
36.          SIO:#served=8 #queued=0 Util=0% aqtime=0ms adtime=0ms
... Output omitted for brevity
```

This section is the `cellsrv statedump`'s representation of the I/O queues discussed in Recipe 17-5 and logically presented in Figure 17-1 in this chapter. Here is a brief description of some of the important lines in the previous output:

- Line 1 marks the beginning of the IORM statistics for a specific cell disk.
- Line 2 lists the physical device for the cell disk.
- Line 7 displays `IORM boost=119`; this represents the ratio of I/Os skipped to I/Os scheduled and is an indication of how "active" IORM is rescheduling I/O operations.
- Lines 11 through 15 mark your Category IORM section.
- Lines 17–20 indicate your Interdatabase IORM index mappings.
- Line 21 shows that for database VISX, 16 I/Os were being serviced at the time of the `cellsrv statedump` with no queuing.
- Lines 22 through 31 display the consumer groups for the VISX database and, in line 27, we see the I/O requests for the `_ORACLE_BACKGROUND_GROUP_` consumer group equal the total active I/O requests for the database.
- The output in this entire section is telling us this: for disk /dev/sda3, at the time the `cellsrv statedump` was taken, only a single database (VISX) had active I/O requests being serviced and these fell into a background consumer group I/O queue.

CHAPTER 17 ■ I/O RESOURCE MANAGEMENT AND INSTANCE CAGING

How It Works

The `list iormplan [detail]` CellCLI command can be used to display your current IORM configuration for any or all cells in your Exadata storage grid, and this is a good way to quickly see your IORM configuration. To obtain a more granular picture of your IORM configuration, a `cellsrv statedump` trace file can be a valuable tool. The `cellsrv statedump` trace file can be used to not only display your IORM configuration, but also display active I/O queues on each cell disk for each database and consumer group. The trace file is arranged as follows:

```
-------------------------------------------------------------------
IORM state dump
-------------------------------------------------------------------
Category Plan

... List of categories and category mappings

... Map of database and consumer group indicies to category index

Inter-Database Plan

... List of databases and their resource allocations

Intra-Database Plan

... List of databases, consumer groups per database, and category mappings for each consumer group

QUEUED IO REQUESTS for cellDisk /dev/sda3

... IORM statistics for each cell disk

... Category index mappings for each I/O queue on each cell disk

... Database and consumer group I/O information

... Active I/O requests and queueing information for each I/O queue

QUEUED IO REQUESTS for cellDisk /dev/sdaa
QUEUED IO REQUESTS for cellDisk /dev/sdc
```

From the `cellsrv statedump`, it is relatively simple to not only see how IORM is configured and how each consumer is mapped to categories and databases, but also view the individual I/O queues for each entity on each cell disk.

17-8. Controlling Smart Flash Cache and Smart Flash Logging with IORM

Problem

You wish to disable Smart Flash Cache or Smart Flash Logging for a database on your Exadata Database Machine.

Solution

In this recipe, you will learn how to use an Interdatabase IORM plan to disable Exadata's Smart Flash Cache or Smart Flash Logging for a specific database.

■ **Note** Flash Cache and Flash Logging are enabled by default for your databases so, in this recipe, we will only show how to disable these features.

After selecting a database to disable Flash Cache or Flash Logging on, execute the following CellCLI command. We will use `dcli` to disable both Flash Cache and Flash Logging for a database named VISY and leave the other databases with the default, enabled behavior:

```
[oracle@cm01dbm01 iorm]$ dcli -g ./cell_group "cellcli -e \
> alter iormplan objective=\'auto\', \
> dbplan=\(\(name=edw,level=1,allocation=55\), \
> \(name=dwprd,level=1,allocation=15\), \
> \(name=visx,level=1,allocation=25\), \
> \(name=visy,level=1,allocation=5,flashcache=off,flashlog=off\), \
> \(name=other,level=2,allocation=100\)\)"
cm01cel01: IORMPLAN successfully altered
cm01cel02: IORMPLAN successfully altered
cm01cel03: IORMPLAN successfully altered
[oracle@cm01dbm01 iorm]$
```

The `flashcache=off` and `flashlog=off` IORM plan directives disable Smart Flash Cache and Smart Flash Logging.

How It Works

Smart Flash Cache and Smart Flash Logging are Exadata Storage Server software features designed to intelligently cache data and redo log writes in Exadata's PCI flash cards installed on each Exadata Storage Server. You can disable this on a per-database level using IORM as part of the Interdatabase IORM plan's `dbplan` directive.

As discussed in Recipe 17-5, Exadata's cell services software is able to leverage IORM for this purpose because IORM functionality resides within the `cellsrv` software and is "in-line" with the I/O call. If an I/O request from a database with `flashcache` or `flashlog` disabled is sent to the storage cells, IORM simply tags these I/O requests as non-cacheable and bypasses any Flash Cache and/or Flash Logging code paths.

■ **Note** To learn more about Smart Flash Cache and Smart Flash Logging, please refer to Chapter 18.

17-9. Limiting CPU Resources with Instance Caging

Problem
You wish to limit the number of processors that an Oracle instance can use on the compute nodes.

Solution
In this recipe, you will learn how to use the `cpu_count` database initialization parameter to restrict the number of CPUs a database instance can use.

1. After selecting an instance to limit CPU resources for, log in to SQL*Plus as SYSDBA and execute the following command. In this example, we will restrict the number of processors on each database in the cluster to four and update the parameter in memory as well as the server parameter file.

   ```
   SQL> alter system set cpu_count=4 scope=both sid='*';
   System altered.
   SQL>
   ```

2. Next, ensure that you have a resource manager plan enabled in your database. If you are using Intradatabase IORM as presented in Recipes 17-4 and 17-5, this will suffice to complete your instance caging setup. If you do not have specific Intradatabase (DBRM) plans designed, you can simply enable the default plan using the following command:

   ```
   SQL> alter system set resource_manager_plan='default_plan'
     2  scope=both sid='*';
   System altered.
   SQL>
   ```

How It Works

Adjusting `cpu_count` is a means to limit compute node processor availability on per-instance basis and, when used in combination with a DBRM plan, is also referred to as "instance caging."

By default, Oracle will set `cpu_count` to the number of CPU cores times the number of threads per core in a threaded architecture; on Exadata X2-2 models, this equates to 24 per compute node and on the X3 configurations, 32.

Historically, the Oracle DBA would typically not configure the `cpu_count` initialization parameter to anything other than the default value, as it would impact a number of other performance-related configuration parameters and would not restrict compute node CPU resources for an instance. With Oracle 11gR2, which is the database version used for Exadata, setting `cpu_count` in combination with a DBRM plan places a hard ceiling on the number of processor threads a single instance can use.

Why would you implement instance caging? When consolidating databases on Exadata, it is common for a combination of production, non-production, critical, and less critical instances to be deployed across your compute nodes. Instance caging enables you to protect your processor investment by restricting processor threads from less critical databases, and it is commonly used in conjunction with I/O Resource Management.

CHAPTER 18

Smart Flash Cache and Smart Flash Logging

Smart Flash Cache and Smart Flash Logging make the Exadata Database Machine the first flash-optimized Oracle database platform by providing intelligent caching algorithms to cache "appropriate" data in flash-based storage. Exadata's use of flash storage is named "smart" due to the intelligence of Oracle's caching algorithms. The Exadata storage cell software automatically and intelligently determines which data to cache on the storage cell flash cards based on the nature of the data being requested. This typically includes frequently accessed data and index blocks, control file reads and writes, file header blocks, and any object the Exadata DMA chooses to cache with use of the flash-based KEEP clause.

Why is this intelligence important and what differentiates the solution from storage vendor solutions? It's a matter of economics. By Oracle *only* caching what Oracle considers to be reusable and not one-time or limited-use data, Exadata has a much better chance of storing important, relevant data. The software design of the Exadata Database Machine uniquely equips it with in-depth insight of the nature of each I/O request—when Oracle issues a request for I/O and ships the I/O messages to the storage cells, the cell services software is provided with metadata that defines the nature of the I/O request. With this information, Smart Flash Cache and Smart Flash Logging are able to determine whether the requested data is suitable for caching. So, not only does Exadata deliver a large amount of PCI flash storage on each storage cell (384 GB on the Exadata X2 models and 1.6 TB on the X3 configurations), but it also ensures that only *important* data is stored in Smart Flash.

As most readers will know, Oracle's marketing folks have named recent X3 configuration the Oracle Exadata X3 Database In-Memory Machine. The "in-memory" part of the new name is based on the combination of large amounts of physical DRAM on the compute and storage cells but, more specifically, the 1.6 TB of PCI flash configured on each storage cell. Technically speaking, the flash storage on the cells is not actually Random Access Memory, but flash on PCIe cards. This PCI flash can deliver orders of magnitude higher I/O bandwidth and I/Os per second than traditional SAS disks.

In this chapter, we'll cover Smart Flash Cache basics, including how Oracle populates flash for read and write operations, how to monitor your flash storage, and how to measure performance gains delivered with Smart Flash Cache. We will also present Smart Flash Logging, a software feature provided in recent releases/patches, which provides the ability to satisfy redo log write requests from storage cell PCI flash.

18-1. Managing Smart Flash Cache and Smart Flash Logging
Problem
You wish to drop, create, size, or view configuration details for your Smart Flash Cache (SFC) and Smart Flash Logging (SFL) storage.

CHAPTER 18 ■ SMART FLASH CACHE AND SMART FLASH LOGGING

■ **Note** Smart Flash Cache and Smart Flash Logging are both Exadata software features designed to improve database performance by intelligently caching specific types of data in Exadata's PCI flash cards. The How It Works section of this recipe provides additional detail about these software features.

Solution

In this recipe, you will learn how to display configuration and sizing details for Exadata's Smart Flash Cache and Smart Flash Logging storage, drop your SFC and SFL storage, create SFC/SFL storage using all of the available capacity on your flash disks, and create SFC/SFL using a portion of your flash storage.

Start by logging in to a compute node with an account with SSH keys established and run the following command to list your SFC/SFC storage configuration:

```
[oracle@cm01dbm01 ~]$ dcli -g ./cell_group cellcli -e list flashcache attributes name,size,status
cm01cel01: cm01cel01_FLASHCACHE    364.75G    normal
cm01cel02: cm01cel02_FLASHCACHE    364.75G    normal
cm01cel03: cm01cel03_FLASHCACHE    364.75G    normal
[oracle@cm01dbm01 ~]$
[oracle@cm01dbm01 ~]$ dcli -g ./cell_group cellcli -e list flashlog attributes name,size,status
cm01cel01: cm01cel01_FLASHLOG     512M     normal
cm01cel02: cm01cel02_FLASHLOG     512M     normal
cm01cel03: cm01cel03_FLASHLOG     512M     normal
[oracle@cm01dbm01 ~]$
```

You can see that in our Exadata X2-2 environment, each storage cell has 364.75 GB of storage allocated to SFC and 512 MB of capacity allocated to SFL. You can drop your SFC and SFL storage across all storage cells by using the drop flashcache all and drop flashlog all CellCLI commands from dcli:

```
[oracle@cm01dbm01 ~]$ dcli -g ./cell_group cellcli -e drop flashcache all
cm01cel01: Flash cache cm01cel01_FLASHCACHE successfully dropped
cm01cel02: Flash cache cm01cel02_FLASHCACHE successfully dropped
cm01cel03: Flash cache cm01cel03_FLASHCACHE successfully dropped
[oracle@cm01dbm01 ~]$
[oracle@cm01dbm01 ~]$ dcli -g ./cell_group cellcli -e drop flashlog all
cm01cel01: Flash log cm01cel01_FLASHLOG successfully dropped
cm01cel02: Flash log cm01cel02_FLASHLOG successfully dropped
cm01cel03: Flash log cm01cel03_FLASHLOG successfully dropped
[oracle@cm01dbm01 ~]$
```

To recreate your SFC and SFL storage, first create SFL storage using the create flashlog all and then create your SFC storage with create flashcache all:

```
[[oracle@cm01dbm01 ~]$ dcli -g ./cell_group cellcli -e create flashlog all
cm01cel01: Flash log cm01cel01_FLASHLOG successfully created
cm01cel02: Flash log cm01cel02_FLASHLOG successfully created
cm01cel03: Flash log cm01cel03_FLASHLOG successfully created
[oracle@cm01dbm01 ~]$ dcli -g ./cell_group cellcli -e list flashlog attributes name,size
cm01cel01: cm01cel01_FLASHLOG     512M
cm01cel02: cm01cel02_FLASHLOG     512M
cm01cel03: cm01cel03_FLASHLOG     512M
```

```
[oracle@cm01dbm01 ~]$ dcli -g ./cell_group cellcli -e create flashcache all
cm01cel01: Flash cache cm01cel01_FLASHCACHE successfully created
cm01cel02: Flash cache cm01cel02_FLASHCACHE successfully created
cm01cel03: Flash cache cm01cel03_FLASHCACHE successfully created
[oracle@cm01dbm01 ~]$
```

> **Note** If you issue a `create flashcache all` statement prior to creating your SFL storage, Exadata will allocate all of the PCI flash storage for SFC and leave none for SFL. For this reason, we recommend creating SFL first. When you do so, Exadata wll automatically allocate 512 MB of storage from the available PCI flash for SFL, leaving the rest unallocated for SFC or pehaps permanent flash-based grid disk storage.

You can also elect to manually size a subset of your PCI flash for SFC by specifying the size attribute. In the following script, we are specifying to allocate 100 GB of storage for SFC:

```
[oracle@cm01dbm01 ~]$ dcli -g ./cell_group cellcli -e create flashcache all size=100g
cm01cel01: Flash cache cm01cel01_FLASHCACHE successfully created
cm01cel02: Flash cache cm01cel02_FLASHCACHE successfully created
cm01cel03: Flash cache cm01cel03_FLASHCACHE successfully created
[oracle@cm01dbm01 ~]$
```

How It Works

Smart Flash Cache and Smart Flash Logging are Exadata software features that utilize PCI flash storage to intelligently cache data. SFC is designed to provide an extra layer of flash-based cache for data, and SFL is designed to cushion redo log writes.

With SFL, when the storage cells receive a redo log write request, Exadata will perform a parallel write to both the on-disk redo logs as well as a small amount of flash storage carved out from the available PCI flash storage. When *either* of these writes completes successfully, the database issuing the I/O request will receive a write acknowledgement. This design allows for Exadata to provide smooth redo log write I/O performance in the event that either writes to permanent storage or flash storage is slow. SFL is not permanent storage; it is simply a temporary store designed to provide fast redo log write response times.

Both SFC and SFL utilize the same PCI flash storage on each cell. SFL capacity defaults to 512 MB and is not subject to resizing, but SFC can be configured to use any or all of the remaining storage on your flash cards. While they use the same physical storage, SFC and SFL storage is managed (that is, dropped and created) independently.

SFC is typically configured to use all of the available flash storage above the 512 MB chunk reserved for SFL, but the Exadata DMA can elect to only allocate a subset of available storage based on business needs. Typically, DMAs would only limit the size of SFC when deciding to configure permanent grid disk storage on flash, as discussed in Recipe 9-11.

SFL hasn't always existed on the Exadata storage cells; it was introduced with storage cell image 11.2.2.4.2 as a means to provide a flash-based "cushion" for redo log write activity in situations when `LGWR` is unable to write redo entries to disk (or the disk's DRAM cache) fast enough. For DML-intensive workloads, SFC can provide a high-speed storage solution to reduce write I/O wait times. To learn more about the performance benefits of SFC, please see Recipe 18-7.

Data in Smart Flash Cache is managed automatically by the Exadata Storage Server software using a least recently used algorithm. As the flash storage becomes full, Exadata will age lesser-used data from cache in a similar manner to how blocks are aged from the database buffer cache. One thing that is unique about cached data in Smart Flash Cache is that it is persistent across database instance restarts, so even if you bounce your instances, SFC will still contain copies of cached data unless the data has been aged or SFC has been dropped.

CHAPTER 18 ■ SMART FLASH CACHE AND SMART FLASH LOGGING

■ **Note** To learn more about the physical characteristics and configuration of the PCI flash storage on the Exadata storage cells, please refer to Recipes 1-6 and 3-3.

18-2. Determining Which Database Objects Are Cached
Problem
You wish to determine which database objects are currently cached in Smart Flash Cache.

Solution
In this recipe, you will learn how to use the list flashcachecontent CellCLI command to report the objects currently stored in Smart Flash Cache and map these to database object names.

Using dcli or cellcli from a storage cell, run the following command:

```
[oracle@cm01dbm01 ~]$ dcli -g ./cell_group cellcli -e list flashcachecontent \
> attributes dbUniqueName,hitCount,missCount,cachedSize,objectNumber
cm01cel01:   EDW          0    2    98304      3
cm01cel01:   DWPRD        0    0    57344      8
cm01cel01:   VISY         0    0     8192      8
cm01cel01:   EDW          9   15   729088     18
cm01cel01:   DWPRD        0    0    16384     18
... Output omitted for brevity
```

Here, we are listing the database name that the object belongs to, the SFC hit count, SFC miss count, the cached size (in bytes), and the objectNumber. This objectNumber corresponds to the DATA_OBJECT_ID from the %_TABLES data dictionary views in your database. Using the fourth row from this output, we can see that objectNumber 18 from a database called EDW has experienced 9 SFC hits and 15 SFC misses, and has had a total of 729088 bytes. To map this to the actual object name, query DBA_OBJECTS while logged in to the appropriate database. In the following script, we can see that objectNumber 18 is the SYS.OBJ$ table:

```
SQL> select data_object_id dobject_id,object_name,owner
  2  from dba_objects
  3  where data_object_id=18;

DataObjId   Object                      Owner
---------   -------------------------   --------------
       18   OBJ$                        SYS
```

If you have a specific object that you wish to determine the cache status for, you can add where conditions to your list flashcachecontent command:

```
SQL> select data_object_id
  2  from dba_objects where owner='PO' and object_name='RCV_TRANSACTIONS';
DataObjId
--------------
  3010199
```

```
SQL> select name from v$database;
NAME
---------
VISX
SQL>
[oracle@cm01dbm01 ~]$ dcli -g ./cell_group "cellcli -e list flashcachecontent \
> attributes dbUniqueName,hitCount,missCount,cachedSize,objectNumber \
> where objectNumber=3010199 and dbUniqueName=\'VISX\'"
cm01cel01: VISX     0      321     11501568       3010199
cm01cel02: VISX     0      557     20996096       3010199
cm01cel03: VISX     0      284     9437184        3010199
[oracle@cm01dbm01 ~]$
```

Notice that each cell in our storage grid contains cached data for the PO.RCV_TRANSACTIONS table and, further, the amount of space in cache varies from cell to cell. Exadata automatically manages cache Smart Flash Cache depending on your workload and data distribution between cells, so it is common to see variances with the amount of cached content for a single object across cells.

How It Works

Exadata's storage server software automatically captures Smart Flash Cache statistics and stores these in the flashcachecontent object. As database sessions request data from the Exadata disks, the storage cells examine the metadata of the I/O request to determine whether the data being accessed is suitable for Smart Flash Cache. If so, several flashcachecontent attributes are populated or incremented. In this recipe, we demonstrated the following:

- The dbUniqueName attribute represents the database name from which the I/O initiated.
- The objectNumber attribute is the object ID (or more specifically, data_object_id) for the object.
- The cachedSize attribute represents the number of cached bytes for the object.
- The hitCount attribute reflects whether the I/O request was satisfied in SFC.
- The missCount attribute reflects whether the I/O request for the specific objectNumber/dbUniqueName combination resulted in a cache miss; in these cases, disk I/O was required to satisfy the request.

You may be wondering if a physical disk I/O were required to satisfy an I/O request, why would Smart Flash Cache track "miss" statistics at all? The answer is twofold:

1. If SFC software determines that the data is a candidate for caching and the data is not yet populated to cache, SFC will do so. In doing so, the number of I/O requests required to populate the cache is tabulated and the missCount statistic is incremented.
2. If an I/O request is issued for a segment and SFC finds some of the necessary blocks in cache and some of the blocks uncached, the missCount statistic will be incremented for each read request not satisfied from cache.

If you have executed the list flashcachecontent command on your Exadata Database Machine, you may notice that there is a single row for each object stored in cache per storage cell. The counter-based attributes are incremented or decremented over time as requests are satisfied from cache or data is aged from cache. The cachedSize attribute will always reflect the total number of bytes in cache per storage cell.

As stated in the introduction to this chapter, not all I/O requests are eligible for Smart Flash Cache; this is what makes SFC intelligent. Specifically, you will not typically find data from "large" segments populated in cache, nor will you find large amounts of cached content from segments that are frequently accessed via sequential reads (that is, full scans). Simply speaking, Smart Scan is designed for dealing with large, sequential scans, and Smart Flash Cache is designed for random-access data that SFC considers is likely to be requested in the future.

> **Note** Oracle considers a segment to be "large" if its block count is greater than _small_table_threshold, as discussed in Recipe 15-7. The _small_table_threshold parameter defaults to 2% the size of your database buffer cache. You can, however, elect to "pin" large segments in flash cache by using the CELL_FLASH_CACHE KEEP storage clause on your larger segments, and you can also use this mechanism to prevent any object from aging out of flash cache. Recipe 18-6 provides more information on this topic.

18-3. Determining What's Consuming Your Flash Cache Storage

Problem

You wish to identify how much free space exists in flash cache, which segments are consuming the most space, and how frequently these consumers are yielding flash cache hits.

Solution

In this recipe, you will learn how to measure your available flash cache capacity, identify the top storage consumers, and measure how much benefit is being delivered from these top consumers. Listing 18-1 queries the flashcachecontent objects across the storage cells and summarizes the total flash cache usage and capacity utilization, reports the cache utilization per database, and lists the "Top N" segments in cache in terms of space consumption.

Listing 18-1. lst18-01-sfcconsumer.pl

```perl
#!/usr/bin/perl
# Name:   lst18-01-sfcconsumer.pl
# Usage: ./lst18-01-sfcconsumer.pl [-g|-c] [cell group file|list of cells] -n [topN]

use Getopt::Std;
use Text::ParseWords;

sub usage {
 print "Usage: /lst18-01-sfcconsumer.pl [-g|-c] [cell group file|list of cells] -n [topN]\n";
}
## Command line argument handling     ##
getopts("g:c:n:",\%options);
die usage unless (defined $options{n});
die usage unless ((defined $options{c}) || (defined $options{g}));
$dclipref="-g $options{g}" if defined $options{g};
$dclipref="-c $options{c}" if defined $options{c};
$dclitail="attributes cachedSize,dbUniqueName,hitCount,missCount,objectNumber";
## End Command line argument handling ##
```

```perl
open(F,"dcli ${dclipref} cellcli -e list flashcache attributes name,size|");
while (<F>) {
 @words=quotewords('\\s+', 0, $_);
 $words[2]=~s/G//; $cbytes=1024*1024*1024*$words[2];
 $cell{$words[0]}+=$cbytes;
}
close(F);
open(F,"dcli ${dclipref} cellcli -e list flashcachecontent ${dclitail}|");
while (<F>) {
 @words=quotewords('\\s+', 0, $_);
 $cached{$words[0]}+=$words[1];   # Array for storage by cell
 $db{$words[2]}+=$words[1];       # Array for storage by DB
 $mb=$words[1]/1024/1024;
 $objd=sprintf "%-8.2f %8s %8.0f %8.0f %8.0f", "$mb", "$words[2]", "$words[3]", "$words[4]",
"$words[5]"; # Bld string
 push @DTL, $objd;
}
close(F);
$tcellused=0;
$rc=0;
printf "%-10s %8s %8s %8s\n", "Cell", "Avail", "Used", "%Used";
printf "%-10s %-8s %-8s %8s\n", "-"x10, "-"x8, "-"x8, "-"x5;
foreach my $key (sort keys %cell) {
 $celltot=$cell{$key}/1024/1024/1024;
 $cellused=$cached{$key}/1024/1024/1024;
 $tcellused=$tcellused + $cellused;
 $pctused=100 * ($cellused / $celltot);
 printf "%10s %8.2f %8.2f %8.3f\n", "$key", $celltot, $cellused,$pctused;
}
printf "\n%20s %-8.2f\n\n", "Total GB used:", $tcellused;
printf "%-10s %8s %8s\n", "DB",   "DBUsed", "%Used";
printf "%-10s %8s %8s\n", "-"x10, ,"-"x8, "-"x6;
foreach my $key (sort keys %db) {
 $dbused=$db{$key}/1024/1024/1024;
 $pctused=100 * ($dbused / $tcellused);
 printf "%-10s %8.2f %8.3f\n", "$key",  $dbused,$pctused;
}
printf "\n%-8s %8s %8s %8s %8s\n", "CachedMB",  "DB", "HitCount", "MissCnt", "objNo";
printf "%-8s %8s %8s %8s %8s\n", "-"x8, "-"x8, "-"x8, "-"x8, "-"x8;
foreach my $line (sort { $b <=> $a } @DTL) {
 last if $rc eq $options{n};
 print "$line\n";
 $rc++;
}
```

```
Cell          Avail      Used      %Used
------------- --------  --------  --------
cm01cel01:    364.75       5.28     1.447
cm01cel02:    364.75       5.27     1.445
cm01cel03:    364.75       5.35     1.468

    Total GB used: 15.90
```

```
DB           DBUsed      %Used
----------   ---------   --------
DWPRD           0.07      0.410
EDW             0.44      2.738
UNKNOWN         0.01      0.051
VISX            7.98     50.211
VISY            7.41     46.588
VISYVISX        0.00      0.001


CachedMB         DB        HitCount   MissCnt    objNo
-------------  --------    --------   ---------  ------------
72.07          VISX               4       1272      3081977
68.11          VISX               0       1875      3037737
66.25          VISX               0       1799      3037737
66.02          VISY               0       1689      3037737
65.68          VISY               4       1124      3081977
```

To determine the object name for the objectNumber column in the rightmost column of the last section above, query DBA_OBJECTS on DATA_OBJECT_ID, as outlined in Recipe 18-2.

How It Works

As described in Recipe 18-2, the flashcachecontent cell object contains current information about the database segments stored in Exadata's flash cache. SFC is able to satisfy I/O requests from flash for data stored in flash cache. The information in the flashcachecontent object contains a cachedSize attribute, which stores the number of bytes per objectNumber per database.

In this recipe, we provided a simple Perl script that uses dcli to fetch flashcachecontent data, but you could also manually retrieve the same information using the following command and sort or format the information to meet your needs:

```
$ dcli -g [cell group file] cellcli -e list flashcachecontent attributes \
cachedSize,dbUniqueName,hitCount,missCount,objectNumber
```

18-4. Determining What Happens When Querying Uncached Data
Problem

You wish to identify what happens when SFC-eligible I/Os are issued and the requested data is not yet available in flash cache.

Solution

In this recipe, you will learn how to use information from CellCLI's flashcachecontent object and flash cache database statistics to see what happens when an Oracle session issues a request for data *not yet* stored in flash cache. In this recipe, we present a test in which we query a single row using an index for a table, measure the relevant statistics, bounce our database, and repeat the test. Our test consists of running the following SQL statement. With this, we're displaying a portion of the execution plan:

```
SQL> select customer_id,x.transaction_id from po.rcv_transactions
where transaction_id=2298598;
```

```
| Id  | Operation                     | Name               | Rows | Bytes |
------------------------------------------------------------------------------
|   0 | SELECT STATEMENT              |                    |    1 |     8 |
|   1 |  TABLE ACCESS BY INDEX ROWID  | RCV_TRANSACTIONS   |    1 |     8 |
|*  2 |   INDEX UNIQUE SCAN           | RCV_TRANSACTIONS_U1|    1 |       |
Statistics
----------------------------------------------------------
.. Output omitted
         4  consistent gets
         4  physical reads
... Output omitted
```

As you can see, our query used an index called RCV_TRANSACTIONS_U1 followed by a TABLE ACCESS BY ROWID operation to access the RCV_TRANSACTIONS table. We then determined the DATA_OBJECT_ID for the index and table and ran the following CellCLI command to display flashcachecontent measurements for these objects:

```
SQL> select data_object_id dobject_id,object_name,owner
  2  from dba_objects
  3  where owner='PO' and object_name in ('RCV_TRANSACTIONS','RCV_TRANSACTIONS_U1');

DataObjId   Object                          Owner
---------   ------------------------------  --------------
  3010199   RCV_TRANSACTIONS                PO
  3080102   RCV_TRANSACTIONS_U1             PO

[oracle@cm01dbm01 ]$ dcli -g ~/cell_group cellcli -e list flashcachecontent attributes
        dbUniqueName,hitCount,missCount,cachedSize,objectNumber where objectNumber=3080102

[oracle@cm01dbm01 ]$ dcli -g ~/cell_group cellcli -e list flashcachecontent attributes
        dbUniqueName,hitCount,missCount,cachedSize,objectNumber where objectNumber=3010199

[oracle@cm01dbm01 ]$
```

As you can see, the cellcli command showed no evidence of our segments existing in flash cache. Prior to running the tests, we bounced our database and recreated our SFC storage in order to conduct a "clean" test; you would not do this in a production environment, of course, but, here, it is helpful to demonstrate the goal of this recipe.

Note To learn how to drop and create Smart Flash Cache storage, please refer to Recipe 18-1.

Prior to executing our previous test query, we ran the script in Listing 18-2 to measure a handful of relevant statistics.

Listing 18-2. lst18-02-sfc-mysess.sql

```
select  stat.name,
        sess.value value
from    v$mystat sess,
        v$statname stat
where   stat.statistic# = sess.statistic#
and     stat.name in ('cell flash cache read hits','physical read total bytes',
                'physical reads','consistent gets','db block gets',
                'physical read IO requests','session logical reads')
order by 1;
```

Before executing the query against the RCV_TRANSACTIONS table, our session level statistics from Listing 18-2 looked like this:

```
Statistic                                Value
---------------------------------------- ----------------
cell flash cache read hits                              0
consistent gets                                         3
db block gets                                           0
physical read IO requests                               2
physical read total bytes                           16384
physical reads                                          2
session logical reads                                   3
```

Note in this output that our session had measured zero cell flash cache read hits. This database statistic is our measuring for SFL cache hits. After executing the query for the first time, our session statistics showed these values:

```
Statistic                                Value
---------------------------------------- ----------------
cell flash cache read hits                              0
consistent gets                                         7
db block gets                                           0
physical read IO requests                               6
physical read total bytes                           49152
physical reads                                          6
session logical reads                                   7
```

This output shows that we still witnessed zero cell flash cache read hits, but it also shows that we performed (6-2) = 4 physical read I/O requests. These I/O requests were satisfied from disk. Now, we'll examine the metrics from the flashcachecontent object on the storage cells:

```
[oracle@cm01dbm01 ]$ dcli -g ~/cell_group cellcli -e list flashcachecontent attributes
        dbUniqueName,hitCount,missCount,cachedSize,objectNumber where objectNumber=3080102
cm01cel02: VISX      0      3       98304  3080102

[oracle@cm01dbm01 ]$ dcli -g ~/cell_group cellcli -e list flashcachecontent attributes
        dbUniqueName,hitCount,missCount,cachedSize,objectNumber where objectNumber=3010199
cm01cel02: VISX      0      1       32768  3010199

[oracle@cm01dbm01 ]$
```

This output shows us the following information:

- For our index (DATA_OBJECT_ID=3080102), 3 flash cache misses were registered on cell cm01cel02 and a total of 98,304 bytes of data was written to our flash storage.
- For the table (DATA_OBJECT_ID=3010199), 1 flash cache miss was observed on cm01cel02 for a total of 32,768 bytes.
- The storage cells recorded zero flash cache hits; this was expected because, at the time the query was executed, flash cache had not been populated.
- The total number of flash cache misses equaled 4: three for the index and 1 for the table. The count matches our total expected physical I/O count based on the execution plan listed above and the height of our index (I/Os required = DBA_INDEXES.BLEVEL + index leaf node blocks + table blocks = 2 + 1 + 1 = 4):

```
SQL> select index_name,blevel
  2  from dba_indexes
  3  where index_name='RCV_TRANSACTIONS_U1';

INDEX_NAME                         BLEVEL
------------------------------     ----------
RCV_TRANSACTIONS_U1                         2
```

The main thing to understand from this test is that uncached physical reads, if Exadata deems suitable, will populate data in flash cache.

What happens if we execute the same query again after flushing our database buffer cache? Following are the system statistics and flashcachecontent statistics on the next execution:

```
Statistic                                Value
---------------------------------------  ----------------
cell flash cache read hits                            6
consistent gets                                       7
db block gets                                         0
physical read IO requests                             6
physical read total bytes                         49152
physical reads                                        6
session logical reads                                 7
[oracle@cm01dbm01 ]$ dcli -g ~/cell_group cellcli -e list flashcachecontent attributes
        dbUniqueName,hitCount,missCount,cachedSize,objectNumber where objectNumber=3080102
cm01cel02: VISX    3     3      98304  3080102

[oracle@cm01dbm01 ]$ dcli -g ~/cell_group cellcli -e list flashcachecontent attributes
        dbUniqueName,hitCount,missCount,cachedSize,objectNumber where objectNumber=3010199
cm01cel02: VISX    1     1      32768  3010199

[oracle@cm01dbm01 ]$
```

We can see that each of our physical read I/O requests was satisfied from flash cache; both the `cell flash cache read hits` and `physical read IO requests` statistics showed a value of 6. Additionally, our flashcachecontent statistics shows three flash cache hits for our index and one for our table, and zero flash cache misses as compared to the initial execution.

How It Works

Similar to how Oracle's database buffer cache caches blocks, Smart Flash Cache inserts candidate blocks into flash assuming that Exadata considers the data worthy of caching and the flash cache capacity is not exhausted based on reservations specified by CELL_FLASH_CACHE KEEP objects, presented in Recipe 18-8. The first physical I/O against a segment may not be fulfilled from flash, but subsequent queries on the same data stand a good chance of seeing benefits from Smart Flash Cache.

By using the cell flash cache read hits and physical read IO requests database statistics, you can determine whether your sessions or system is benefiting from SFC. You can also use the list flashcachecontent CellCI command to display SFC statistics at a granular level as published by the storage cells.

One thing worth mentioning is that Smart Flash Cache behaves the same way for writes (that is, DML) as it does reads. If a DML operation is deemed suitable for caching, Exadata's storage server software will instantiate flash cache with the appropriate data. For example, consider a simple table with objectNumber=3386692 with an index with objectNumber=3386693:

```
[oracle@cm01dbm01 ]$ dcli -g /home/oracle/cell_group cellcli -e list flashcachecontent \
> attributes dbUniqueName,hitCount,missCount,cachedSize,objectNumber where objectNumber=3386693

[oracle@cm01dbm01 ]$ dcli -g /home/oracle/cell_group cellcli -e list flashcachecontent \
> attributes dbUniqueName,hitCount,missCount,cachedSize,objectNumber where objectNumber=3386692

[oracle@cm01dbm01 ]$
```

If you insert data into the table, flash cache will be populated:

```
SQL> insert into my_user
  2  select * from applsys.fnd_user;
2840 rows created.
SQL>
[oracle@cm01dbm01 ]$ dcli -g /home/oracle/cell_group cellcli -e list flashcachecontent \
> attributes dbUniqueName,hitCount,missCount,cachedSize,objectNumber where objectNumber=3386693
cm01cel03: VISX    1      2       8192     3386693
[oracle@cm01dbm01]$ dcli -g /home/oracle/cell_group cellcli -e list flashcachecontent \
> attributes dbUniqueName,hitCount,missCount,cachedSize,objectNumber where objectNumber=3386692
cm01cel02: VISX    0      2       57344    3386692
[oracle@cm01dbm01 sfc]$
```

Updates to the data could cause additional blocks to be populated in flash cache as well as increment hit counts:

```
SQL> update my_user set user_name='X'||user_name
  2  where user_name between 'A' and 'F';
1632 rows updated.
SQL>
[oracle@cm01dbm01 sfc]$ dcli -g /home/oracle/cell_group cellcli -e list flashcachecontent \
> attributes dbUniqueName,hitCount,missCount,cachedSize,objectNumber where objectNumber=3386693
cm01cel03: VISX    1      2       8192     3386693
[oracle@cm01dbm01 sfc]$ dcli -g /home/oracle/cell_group cellcli -e list flashcachecontent \
> attributes dbUniqueName,hitCount,missCount,cachedSize,objectNumber where objectNumber=3386692
cm01cel01: VISX    0      12      589824   3386692
cm01cel02: VISX    3      16      868352   3386692
cm01cel03: VISX    0      5       360448   3386692
[oracle@cm01dbm01 sfc]$
```

■ **Note** Deleting data or even dropping segments does not *initially* have any impact whatsoever on cached content for Smart Flash Cache. Smart Flash Cache software automatically employs a modified LRU mechanism to age data from flash cache, however, so this type of data has a high probability of being aged from cache over time.

18-5. Measuring Smart Flash Cache Performance
Problem
You wish to measure Smart Flash Cache performance statistics and determine the benefit provided by Smart Flash Cache both databasewide and on a per-SQL statement basis.

Solution
In this recipe, you will learn how to use various system and SQL statistics to measure Smart Flash Cache behavior on your system. Additionally, you will learn how to query the cell's flashcachecontent object to identify segments that have experienced high "hit counts," an indication that Smart Flash Cache is providing benefits.

Measuring SFC Usage for Your Database
To measure the use of Smart Flash Cache for your database instance, query V$SYSSTAT using the script in Listing 18-3.

Listing 18-3. lst18-03-sfc-sysstat.sql

```
SQL> select i.instance_name,
            ss.name, ss.value
     from         gv$sysstat ss,
            gv$instance i
     where  i.inst_id=ss.inst_id
     and    ss.name in ('cell flash cache read hits',
                   'physical read total bytes',
                   'physical read total bytes optimized',
                   'physical read total IO requests',
                   'physical read requests optimized')
     order by 2,1 asc
/
Instance    Statistic                                  Value
----------  -----------------------------------------  ------------
visx1       cell flash cache read hits                        19358
visx2       cell flash cache read hits                        17198
visx1       physical read requests optimized                  19358
visx2       physical read requests optimized                  17198
visx1       physical read total IO requests                   41128
visx2       physical read total IO requests                   25202
visx1       physical read total bytes                    2755176960
visx2       physical read total bytes                     517865984
visx1       physical read total bytes optimized           326631424
visx2       physical read total bytes optimized           252706816
```

This script allows you to compare total read requests and bytes with "optimized" read requests and bytes. Optimized reads are reads satisfied from Smart Flash Cache. In the previous output, notice that the cell flash cache read hits and physical read requests optimized statistics are the same on each instance; these statistics are measuring the same thing—flash cache read hits. You can modify the query in Listing 18-3 to query V$SESSTAT or V$MYSTAT if you are interested in session level Smart Flash Cache statistics as well.

As you are likely thinking, one question that most Exadata DMAs ask is "What percentage of my reads or total bytes is satisfied by Smart Flash Cache?" To calculate this, simply divide (physical read requests optimized) by (physical read total IO requests) and/or (physical read total bytes optimized) by (physical read total bytes). Using the statistics above, our flash cache hit ratio across our cluster was the following:

```
SFCHitRatio = (19358 +17198) / (41128 + 25202) = 55%
```

To conduct an arguably more beneficial analysis, run the script in Listing 18-4. This script reports the total number of physical read I/Os per second, physical read I/O bandwidth (MB), optimized I/Os per second, optimized I/O bandwidth, and a flash cache utilization percentage for both I/Os bandwidth and I/Os per second.

Listing 18-4. lst18-04-sfc-awrstat.sql

```sql
SQL> select id,tm,dur,prtb,prtbo,
        100*(prtbo/prtb) byteshr,
        priops,priopso,
        100*(priopso/priops) iopshr
    from (
     select  snaps.id, snaps.tm,snaps.dur,snaps.instances,
           ((sysstat.fcrh -
                lag (sysstat.fcrh,1) over (order by snaps.id)))/dur/60   fcrh,
           ((sysstat.prtb -
                lag (sysstat.prtb,1) over (order by snaps.id)))/dur/60/1024/1024   prtb,
           ((sysstat.prtbo -
                lag (sysstat.prtbo,1) over (order by snaps.id)))/dur/60/1024/1024   prtbo,
           ((sysstat.priops -
                lag (sysstat.priops,1) over (order by snaps.id)))/dur/60   priops,
           ((sysstat.priopso-
                lag (sysstat.priopso,1) over (order by snaps.id)))/dur/60   priopso
     from
     ( /* DBA_HIST_SNAPSHOT */
     select distinct id,dbid,tm,instances,max(dur) over (partition by id) dur from (
     select distinct s.snap_id id, s.dbid,
           to_char(s.end_interval_time,'DD-MON-RR HH24:MI') tm,
           count(s.instance_number) over (partition by snap_id) instances,
1440*((cast(s.end_interval_time as date) - lag(cast(s.end_interval_time as date),1)
over (order by s.snap_id))) dur
      from      dba_hist_snapshot s,
           v$database d
     where s.dbid=d.dbid)
     ) snaps,
      ( /* DBA_HIST_SYSSTAT */
        select * from
            (select snap_id, dbid, stat_name, value from
            dba_hist_sysstat
         ) pivot
```

```
          (sum(value) for (stat_name) in
              (
               'cell flash cache read hits' as fcrh, 'physical read total bytes' as prtb,
               'physical read total bytes optimized' as prtbo,
               'physical read total IO requests' as priops,
               'physical read requests optimized' as priopso))
      ) sysstat
    where dur > 0
    and snaps.id=sysstat.snap_id
    and snaps.dbid=sysstat.dbid)
    order by id asc;

SnapID  SnapStart         Mins    ReadMB     OptMB     %MB      ReadIOPs    OptIOPs    %IOPs
------  ---------------   -----   --------   -------   ------   ---------   --------   ------
1352    12-NOV-12 02:00   60.25      0.08      0.08    99.75         5.47       5.42   99.16
1353    12-NOV-12 03:00   60.20      0.09      0.08    99.76         5.47       5.43   99.18
1354    12-NOV-12 04:00   60.20      0.08      0.08    99.76         5.43       5.38   99.17
1355    12-NOV-12 05:00   60.03     28.20      0.08      .30        37.23       5.38   14.45
1356    12-NOV-12 06:00   59.38      0.08      0.08    99.75         5.43       5.38   99.16
... Ouput omitted for brevity
1424    15-NOV-12 02:00   59.53   1983.15      9.58      .48      2925.25     282.90    9.67
1425    15-NOV-12 03:00   59.95      0.10      0.10    94.22         6.99       6.80   97.32
```

Measuring SFC Usage for SQL Statements

To determine which SQL statements in your library cache were optimized with Smart Flash Cache, run the query in Listing 18-5. Oracle defines "optimized reads" and reads that were fulfilled via Smart Flash Cache, such as indexed reads and small I/O requests.

Listing 18-5. lst18-05-sfc-sqls.sql

```
SQL> select sql_Id,prr,oprr,100*(oprr/prr) orate,sql_text from (
     select sql_id,sum(physical_read_requests) prr,
            sum(optimized_phy_read_requests) oprr,
       substr(sql_text,1,40) sql_text
       from gv$sql
       group by sql_Id,sql_text
       order by 2 desc)
     where rownum < &&num_rows + 1 ;
Enter value for num_rows: 5

SQL_ID             PhysRds     OptRds     Flash%    SQL
--------------    --------    --------    ------    ----------------------------------------
05s9358mm6vrr       73012       64997      89.02    begin dbms_feature_usage_internal.exec_d
1cq3qr774cu45       44002       43965      99.92    insert into WRH$_IOSTAT_FILETYPE (sna
8m2sw3z7kt6ph       26884       26884     100.00    select p, NULL, NULL from (select count(
2d1p0p5k3f8fu       26884       26884     100.00    select p, NULL, NULL from (select count(
6phrcjjvtbhjj       15705         974       6.20    SELECT ATTR_NO, ATTR_NAME, ATTR_TYPE_NAM
```

This script queries the OPTIMIZED_PHY_READ_REQUESTS and PHYSICAL_READ_REQUESTS columns from V$SQL, which represent optimized and total physical read requests. As you can see in the fourth column, a flash cache hit percentage is displayed.

To perform this same type of analysis using Oracle's AWR repository, query DBA_HIST_SQLSTAT on the OPTIMIZED_PHYSICAL_READS column and compare against your total reads. Listing 18-6 provides an example.

Listing 18-6. lst18-06-sfc-sqlawr.sql

```
SQL> select sql_id,prr,oprr,100*(oprr/prr) orate from (
    select sql_id,sum(physical_read_requests_total) prr,
            sum(optimized_physical_reads_total) oprr
    from dba_hist_sqlstat
    where physical_read_requests_total is not null
    group by sql_Id
    order by 2 desc)
    where rownum < &&num_rows + 1 ;
Enter value for num_rows: 5
SQL_ID            PhysReads     OptPhysReads    Flash%
--------------   -----------   -------------   -------
1cq3qr774cu45    507077882       507067843     100.00
934ur8r7tqbjx     42566664        42566387     100.00
6m2ckkhmmqctb     36371819        36367782      99.99
bpmt7gm1bbd4u     20814431        20814241     100.00
9ybhpsssm2zhn     16379002        15273896      93.25
```

Measuring Smart Flash Cache Hits per Object

To measure your Smart Flash Cache hit counts per object, interrogate the cell server's flashcachecontent object. Following, we are listing flash cache hits where the number of hits per object exceeded 1,000:

```
[oracle@cm01dbm01 ~]$ dcli -g ./cell_group "cellcli -e list flashcachecontent \
> attributes dbUniqueName,hitCount,missCount,cachedSize,objectNumber \
> where hitCount \> 1000"
cm01cel01: VISX      1397      573    20979712      3321189
cm01cel01: VISY    490628     2572      851968   4294967294
cm01cel01: EDW      74968     2617      163840   4294967294
cm01cel01: DWPRD     1470        2      147456   4294967294
cm01cel01: VISX     24629      345      892928   4294967294
... Output omitted for brevity
[oracle@cm01dbm01 ~]$
```

Once you have this information, you can map objectNumber to your object names using steps presented in Recipe 18-2.

You can also query V$SEGSTAT or its AWR counterpart, DBA_HIST_SEG_STAT, to measure the number of optimized reads per segment. Use the script in Listing 18-7 to display your current and historical physical reads, optimized physical reads, and a flash read hit percentage.

Listing 18-7. lst18-07-sfc-seg.sql

```
SQL> @lst18-07-sfc-seg.sql
Current segment statistics
SQL> select obj.owner, obj.object_name,
            segstat.pr prd, segstat.opr oprd,
            100*(segstat.opr/segstat.pr) pct
```

```
      from
        (select * from
        (select obj#,dataobj#,statistic_name,value
            from v$segstat) pivot
              (sum(value) for (statistic_name) in
                ('optimized physical reads' as opr,
                 'physical reads' as pr))) segstat,
        (select owner,object_name,object_id,data_object_id
            from dba_objects
            where owner=upper('&&owner') and object_name=upper('&&object_name')) obj
     where segstat.obj#=obj.object_id
     and segstat.dataobj#=obj.data_object_id;
Enter value for owner: PO
Enter value for object_name: RCV_TRANSACTIONS

Owner         Object                PhysReads    OptPhysReads    %FlashReads
----------    ----------------      ----------   ------------    -----------
PO            RCV_TRANSACTIONS          17602              2           0.01

    Historical segment statistics from AWR

SnapTime              Owner     Object              PhysReads    OptPhysReads    %FlashReads
------------------    -------   ----------------    ----------   ------------    -----------
18-NOV-12 23:49       PO        RCV_TRANSACTIONS       175984             24           0.01
19-NOV-12 00:00       PO        RCV_TRANSACTIONS        70900            122           0.17
```

Measuring Flash Cache with Storage Server Metrics

Recipe 13-3 in Chapter 13 introduces the topic of monitoring Exadata with storage server metrics. Exadata provides a number of Smart Flash Cache and Smart Flash Logging metrics with the FLASHCACHE and FLASHLOG objectTypes. To list the available flash cache metrics and their descriptions, execute the following command from CellCLI:

```
CellCLI> list metricdefinition where objectType='FLASHCACHE' attributes name,description
... Output omitted for brevity
FC_BYKEEP_USED           "Number of megabytes used for 'keep' objects on FlashCache"
FC_BY_USED               "Number of megabytes used on FlashCache"
FC_IO_BYKEEP_R           "Number of megabytes read from FlashCache for 'keep' objects"
... Output omitted for brevity
CellCLI>
```

There are a number of flash cache metrics that you may find worthwhile to monitor; the following example shows just one, the number of I/O requests satisfied from flash cache since the storage cell has started and Smart Flash Cache has been created:

```
CellCLI> list metriccurrent where name='FC_IO_RQ_R'
         FC_IO_RQ_R      FLASHCACHE     34,505,666 IO requests
CellCLI>
```

Perhaps of more use is a query displaying the number of flash cache I/O hits per second, using the list metrichistory command. Execute the following CellCLI command and refer to Recipes 13-6 and 13-7 to employ techniques to summarize your metrichistory output:

```
CellCLI> list metrichistory where name='FC_IO_RQ_R_SEC'
        FC_IO_RQ_R_SEC    FLASHCACHE      6.1 IO/sec     2012-11-15T00:00:22-05:00
        FC_IO_RQ_R_SEC    FLASHCACHE      6.2 IO/sec     2012-11-15T00:01:22-05:00
        FC_IO_RQ_R_SEC    FLASHCACHE      6.8 IO/sec     2012-11-15T00:02:22-05:00
        FC_IO_RQ_R_SEC    FLASHCACHE      7.2 IO/sec     2012-11-15T00:03:22-05:00
... Output omitted for brevity
```

The IORM_DATABASE, IORM_CATEGORY, and IORM_CONSUMER_GROUP metrics also contain flash cache specific metrics, which you can learn about using the list metricdefinition detail command, looking at the description attribute in a similar manner to the previous example. To report on your flash disk I/O load per database, query the DB_FD_IO_LOAD metric:

```
CellCLI> list metriccurrent where name='DB_FD_IO_LOAD'
        DB_FD_IO_LOAD    DWPRD      0
        DB_FD_IO_LOAD    EDW        0
        DB_FD_IO_LOAD    VISX       1
        DB_FD_IO_LOAD    VISY       0
CellCLI>
```

How It Works

Oracle provides several statistics that enable the Exadata DMA to determine whether physical reads or read requests are serviced from Smart Flash Cache. You will see the statistic "optimized physical reads" used throughout various statistics names, AWR reports, and assorted Enterprise Manager screens; this is Oracle's terminology for read requests and bytes satisfied from flash.

In addition to database-centric flash cache statistics, the storage servers also collect information about Smart Flash Cache usage in the flashcachecontent object. As presented initially in Recipe 18-2, this is a great place to look to understand the makeup of your flash cached data segments.

Finally, Exadata provides numerous flash-cache-specific counter and rate-based metrics in the FLASHCACHE metric objectType. On top of this, a number of flash cache, flash logging, and flash disk metrics are stored in the three IORM objectType classifications. Using methods presented in the solution of this recipe as well as in Chapter 13, the Exadata DMA has a wealth of flash-cache-related performance information at his or her fingertips to analyze flash utilization and performance behavior.

18-6. Pinning Specific Objects in Smart Flash Cache

Problem

You wish to pin specific segments in flash in order to encourage I/O being serviced from flash cache.

Solution

In this recipe, you will learn how to use the CELL_FLASH_CACHE storage clause to KEEP database segments in Smart Flash Cache. In this example, we will use a large table that Smart Flash Cache would normally not cache with Smart Flash Cache due to it size:

CHAPTER 18 ■ SMART FLASH CACHE AND SMART FLASH LOGGING

```
SQL> select data_object_id, object_name,owner
  2  from dba_objects
  3  where object_name in ('MYOBJ_UNCOMP')
  4  /
DataObjId   Object                           Owner
---------   ----------------------------     --------------
    27880   MYOBJ_UNCOMP                     D14

SQL> select blocks from dba_tables where table_name='MYOBJ_UNCOMP';
    BLOCKS
----------
    289446
SQL>
```

We see a table with nearly 290,000 blocks with a DATA_OBJECT_ID=27880. If we execute a full scan against this table multiple times in attempts to garner flash cache hits, we can see that none of our queries are benefitting from Smart Flash Cache. In the following example, we are using an adaptation of Listing 18-5, introduced in Recipe 18-5:

```
SQL> select sql_id,executions,sum(physical_read_requests) prr,
            sum(optimized_phy_read_requests) oprr,
    substr(sql_text,1,40) sql_text
    from gv$sql
    where upper(sql_text) like '%MYOBJ_UNCOMP%'
    group by sql_Id,sql_text,executions
    order by 2 desc
  /

SQL_ID          Execs   Reads       OptReads    SQL
-------------   -----   ---------   ---------   ----------------------------------------
18bkv3d4w0kak       3        7016          0    select count(*) from d14.myobj_uncomp
```

Furthermore, if we query flashcachecontent as presented in Recipe 18-2, we see some data cached in flash cache but zero cache hits:

```
[oracle@cm01dbm01 sfc]$ dcli -g ~/cell_group cellcli -e list flashcachecontent \
> attributes dbUniqueName,hitCount,missCount,cachedSize,objectNumber where objectNumber=27880
cm01cel03:  EDW      0      2260    32768   27880
[oracle@cm01dbm01 sfc]$
```

This behavior demonstrates one of Smart Flash Cache's features—SFC is not caching the data because the I/O request is large.

To change this behavior, you can rebuild your object using the CELL_FLASH_CACHE KEEP storage clause:

```
SQL> alter table d14.myobj_uncomp
  2  move nologging storage (cell_flash_cache keep);
Table altered.
SQL> select data_object_id from dba_objects where object_name='MYOBJ_UNCOMP';
DATA_OBJECT_ID
--------------
         28689
SQL>
```

Here, we have rebuilt the table using the ALTER TABLE MOVE command, but you could use CREATE TABLE depending on your needs; the key is the CELL_FLASH_CACHE KEEP storage clause. We also re-queried our new DATA_OBJECT_ID in order to validate with flashcachecontent later. If we execute full-scan select statements on our newly created table, you can see in the bold text below that the I/O requests were being serviced from flash:

```
SQL> select sql_id,executions,sum(physical_read_requests) prr,
          sum(optimized_phy_read_requests) oprr,
     substr(sql_text,1,40) sql_text
     from gv$sql
     where upper(sql_text) like 'SELECT%MYOBJ_UNCOMP%'
     group by sql_Id,sql_text,executions
     order by 2 desc
  /
SQL_ID          Execs    Reads       OptReads     SQL
-------------   ------   ----------  ------------ ----------------------------------------
18bkv3d4w0kak      3        7452         6920     select count(*) from d14.myobj_uncomp
```

Once you have cached a segment using CELL_FLASH_CACHE KEEP, the flashcachecontent object will display additional information in the cachedKeepSize attribute:

```
[oracle@cm01dbm01 ~]$ dcli -g ./cell_group "cellcli -e list flashcachecontent \
> attributes dbUniqueName,hitCount,missCount,cachedKeepSize,cachedSize \
> where objectNumber=28689"
cm01cel01: EDW   2158    118      796917760       796917760
cm01cel02: EDW   2029    262      793575424       793575424
cm01cel03: EDW   2140    101      780476416       780476416
[oracle@cm01dbm01 ~]$
```

In this output, note that in the fifth column, we see nearly 800 MB of data cached on each storage cell and in the hitCount column, we now see non-zero flash hit counts.

How It Works

The CELL_FLASH_CACHE KEEP segment creation storage clause causes Exadata to "pin" an object's data in flash and be eligible for Smart Flash Cache read hits. By using measuring and monitoring techniques presented throughout this chapter as well as the cachedKeepSize flashcachecontent attribute, you can determine which database segments are marked for KEEP in flash.

As is the case with caching database objects in the database buffer cache, pinning a segment's data in flash could produce some negative side effects. Keeping large segments in cache will reduce the effective capacity used by other, unkept segments and limit the overall effectiveness of Smart Flash Cache because, as a DMA, you're asking the software to not act as intelligently as it thinks it should. Luckily, there are a number of ways to measure your overall flash usage for KEEP objects using various CellCLI commands:

- list metriccurrent where name=FC_BYKEEP_OVERWR will tell you how many megabytes of data were pushed out of flash cache to make room for KEEP objects.

- list metriccurrent where name=FC_BYKEEP_USED will tell you how much data exists in flash for KEEP objects.

- list flashcachecontent where cachedKeepSize > 0 will display statistics for each of the KEEP objects.

You may be asking yourself the following question: "Should I pin objects in flash or allow Smart Flash Cache to make its own judgments about whether a segment should be cached or not?" Like many performance-related configuration decisions, it truly depends on your workload and performance SLAs. There are cases when specific segments have very stringent performance requirements that cell offload alone may not be able to provide, hence motivating you to KEEP large segments. More commonly, however, are situations in very busy environments in which OLTP-type I/O access requests need to be satisfied from flash, and the data access patterns are such that the data is very uncommonly accessed, such as a month-end period close process. In cases such as these, the blocks required to satisfy a program may be unlikely to reside in Oracle's database buffer cache, and it may be beneficial to KEEP these in flash.

18-7. Quantifying Benefits of Smart Flash Logging

Problem

You are experiencing performance issues related to heavy redo log write activity and wish to quantify the benefit of Exadata's Smart Flash Logging behavior, introduced in storage cell version 11.2.2.4.2.

Solution

In this recipe, you will learn how to query Exadata's Smart Flash Logging (FLASHLOG) metrics in order to measure the performance impact and redo write I/O savings provided by Smart Flash Logging. To demonstrate the behavior of Smart Flash Logging, we will execute a simple anonymous PL/SQL block that issues 20 million single-row inserts and performs 20 million single commits:

```
SQL> declare
    myrec d14.myobj_uncomp%rowtype;
     cursor mycursor is select * from d14.myobj_uncomp;
    begin
    for myrec in mycursor loop
            insert into d14.myobj_u2
            values myrec;
            commit;
    end loop;
  end;
/
```

> **Note** If you have an application that is actually designed in this manner, we advise sitting down with the developers and discussing alternative strategies.

To measure the impact of Smart Flash Logging, query the FL_DISK_FIRST, FL_FLASH_FIRST, FL_ACTUAL_OUTLIERS, and FL_PREVENTED_OUTLIERS FLASHLOG metrics. The script in Listing 18-8 summarizes this information.

```
#!/bin/sh
# Name:    lst13-10-flashlog-eff.sh
# Purpose: Show Smart Flash Logging effiency
# Usage: ./lst13-10-flashlog-eff.sh
# Adjust the following to suit your needs
CELLGROUP=/home/oracle/cell_group
```

```
disktot=0
flashtot=0
realout=0
prevout=0
CELLCMD="dcli -g ${CELLGROUP} cellcli -e list metriccurrent "
#########################################
for diskfirst in '${CELLCMD} FL_DISK_FIRST|awk '{print $4}'|sed 's/,//g''
do
 disktot='echo "scale=2; $disktot + $diskfirst"|bc'
done
for flashfirst in '${CELLCMD} FL_FLASH_FIRST|awk '{print $4}'|sed 's/,//g''
do
 flashtot='echo "scale=2; $flashtot + $flashfirst"|bc'
done
for outl in '${CELLCMD} FL_ACTUAL_OUTLIERS|awk '{print $4}'|sed 's/,//g''
do
 realout='echo "scale=2; $realout + $outl"|bc'
done
for outl in '${CELLCMD} FL_PREVENTED_OUTLIERS|awk '{print $4}'|sed 's/,//g''
do
 prevout='echo "scale=2; $prevout + $outl"|bc'
done
flashpct='echo "scale=2; 100*($flashtot / ($disktot+$flashtot))"|bc'
echo "$diskfirst redo writes satisfied to Disk first"
echo "$flashfirst redo writes satisfied to Flash first"
echo "$flashpct% satisfied in Flash first"
echo "Prevented outliers: $prevout"
echo "Actual outliers: $realout"

[oracle@cm01dbm01 source]$ ./lst18-08-flashlog-eff.sh
3042177 redo writes satisfied to Disk first
52074 redo writes satisfied to Flash first
1.00% satisfied in Flash first
Prevented outliers: 1601
Actual outliers: 1
[oracle@cm01dbm01 source]$
```

In this script, we measured 1% of our redo write requests (52,074 total redo log writes) being satisfied to flash first via Smart Flash Logging and 1,601 redo writes being prevented from being classified as redo log write "outliers."

How It Works

Exadata's Smart Flash Logging functionality was introduced with image version 11.2.2.4.2 and is used to cushion redo log writer activity when the throughput to the physical disks becomes a bottleneck. Exadata carves a small chunk of space from flash cache and reserves for redo writes; when the DRAM cache on the SAS disks becomes saturated, redo write activity can be staged to flash first.

Monitoring the FLASHLOG metrics provided in the solution of this recipe can enable you to measure the ratio of writes satisfied to disk first versus flash first as well as show you the number of conditions under which flash logging enabled you to satisfy writes without queuing to disk.

Smart Flash Logging works automatically, as long as the flash log storage has been created and you are running on a patch level that supports it. Oracle allocates 512 MB of storage on each cell for flash logging, and it is our experience that this is often more than enough to adequately cushion bursty and high redo log write activity.

> **Note** The undocumented _enable_flash_logging initialization parameter provides another means to disable Smart Flash Logging, but we see no reason to alter the default setting of this parameter.

Smart Flash Logging represents a relatively significant improvement for Exadata X2 and X3 systems. Prior to SFL, it was sometimes common for Exadata DMAs to build their online redo log files on flash-based grid disks using techniques presented in Recipe 9-11, which had the effect of reducing the available capacity for Smart Flash Cache. With Smart Flash Logging, this practice is no longer required.

CHAPTER 19

Storage Indexes

Storage indexes are a feature unique to Exadata. A storage index is a memory-based structure that reduces the amount of physical I/O required by the cell when accessing data via Exadata Smart Scan. A storage index tracks the minimum and maximum values retrieved based on your application's WHERE clause predicates and builds storage indexes based on usage.

In contrast to traditional B*Tree indexes, which tell Oracle exactly where to find a segment's extents, storage indexes behave like "anti-indexes"; their purpose is to tell Oracle with absolute certainty that a requested extent *does not* exist in specific locations, and Exadata uses this information to bypass I/O requests to the physical storage locations.

By default, storage indexes are created and maintained automatically by Exadata's cell services software. As an Exadata DMA, you can influence storage index behavior using a number of methods, including forcing direct path reads with full table scans, disabling storage indexes using the _kcfis_storageidx_enabled undocumented initialization parameter, or reordering the data in your tables to make storage indexes more beneficial.

In this chapter, we'll talk about conditions required for storage indexes to be used, present cases for different types of queries and storage indexes, and show various tracing and diagnosis methods.

19-1. Measuring Performance Impact of Storage Indexes

Problem

You wish to measure the performance impact when Exadata Storage Indexes are used.

Solution

In this recipe, you will learn how to measure the I/O savings provided by storage indexes using the cell physical IO bytes saved by storage index statistic.

Begin by issuing a SQL statement that qualifies for Exadata Smart Scan and run the script in Listing 19-1 to display the I/O savings as a result of storage indexes:

```
SQL> select count(*) from d14.myobj_uncomp
  2  where object_id between 100 and 200;
  COUNT(*)
----------
    101000
Elapsed: 00:00:00.16
```

Listing 19-1. lst19-01-exastorind-mysess.sql

```
SQL> select stat.name,
            sess.value/1024/1024 value
    from    v$mystat sess,
            v$statname stat
    where   stat.statistic# = sess.statistic#
    and stat.name in
          ('cell physical IO bytes eligible for predicate offload',
           'cell physical IO interconnect bytes',
           'cell physical IO bytes saved by storage index',
           'cell physical IO interconnect bytes returned by smart scan')
order by 1;

Statistic                                                          Value (MB)
----------------------------------------------------------------   ----------
cell physical IO bytes eligible for predicate offload                2,255.09
cell physical IO bytes saved by storage index                        1,344.27
cell physical IO interconnect bytes                                      1.51
cell physical IO interconnect bytes returned by smart scan               1.49
SQL>
```

In this output, we can see that our query completed in under a second and we saved over 1,344 megabytes of I/O to Exadata's cell disks by use of storage indexes. Part of the reason for the very fast performance was certainly related to Smart Scan, but a large part of this was related to I/O savings via storage indexes.

■ **Note** To learn more about Exadata's Smart Scan feature and ways to measure the performance impact of Smart Scan, please refer to Chapter 15.

One important consideration to be aware of with storage indexes is that in order for Exadata to produce storage index I/O savings, the data in these indexes will need to be written to the index's storage regions. In other words, storage index data needs to be "primed" on the cell server's region index memory structures in order for them to be utilized. If we were to run the previous query the first time, you would see no storage index I/O savings because the region indexes would contain no relevant data. In the following example, we will bounce our database and execute the same test case twice to demonstrate the point:

```
[oracle@cm01dbm01 source]$ srvctl stop database -d edw
[oracle@cm01dbm01 source]$ srvctl start database -d edw
SQL> select count(*) from d14.myobj_uncomp
  2  where object_id between 100 and 200;
  COUNT(*)
----------
    101000
Elapsed: 00:00:18.95                                                     <- First execution
SQL> set echo off
SQL> @lst19-01-exastorind-mysess.sql
```

```
Statistic                                                   Value (MB)
----------------------------------------------------------  ----------
cell physical IO bytes eligible for predicate offload         2,255.09
cell physical IO bytes saved by storage index                      .00    <- First execution
cell physical IO interconnect bytes                               1.72
cell physical IO interconnect bytes returned by smart scan        1.68

SQL> select count(*) from d14.myobj_uncomp
  2  where object_id between 100 and 200;
  COUNT(*)
----------
    101000
Elapsed: 00:00:00.21                                                      <- Second execution
SQL> @ lst19-01-exastorind-mysess.sql
Statistic                                                   Value (MB)
----------------------------------------------------------  ----------
cell physical IO bytes eligible for predicate offload         2,255.09
cell physical IO bytes saved by storage index                 1,344.27    <- Second execution
cell physical IO interconnect bytes                               1.51
cell physical IO interconnect bytes returned by smart scan        1.49
```

As you can see from these two tests, both queries took advantage of Smart Scan but, in the first query, there was zero I/O savings are a result of storage indexes. The next query, however, ran in a fraction of the time (00.21 seconds as compared to almost 19 seconds) as a result of 1,344 megabytes of savings via storage indexes.

The query in Listing 19-1 measures storage index savings for your specific session by querying the V$MYSTAT view. Like many statistics-based performance queries, you can also broaden the scope to capture storage index statistics at a session level, system level, and from historical AWR data. We will not display the results of these scenarios in this recipe, but the following script listings are provided in the source code repository for these purposes:

- `lst19-02-exastorind-sess.sql` displays storage index and Smart Scan statistics for a specific session.
- `lst19-03-exastorind-system.sql` displays systemwide storage index and Smart Scan statistics for each instance in your cluster.
- `lst19-04-exastorind-awr.sql` displays a Smart Scan and storage index statistics for a user-entered range of AWR snapshots.
- `lst19-05-examystats.sql` displays not only storage index statistics for your session, but also Smart Scan, Smart Flash Cache, and cell disk I/O statistics.
- `lst19-06-exasesstats.sql` displays storage index, Smart Scan, Flash Cache, and cell disk I/O statistics for a specific session.

How It Works

Storage indexes are a feature unique to the Exadata Database Machine whose primary goal is to reduce the amount of I/O required to service I/O requests for Exadata Smart Scan. By using the `cell physical IO bytes saved by storage index` statistic, you can measure the I/O savings as a result of storage indexes.

Storage indexes are used during direct path read operations, when the queries contain predicates (that is, a WHERE clause) and if the underlying ASM disk group has the `cell.smart_scan_capable=TRUE` attribute set. In other words, storage indexes compliment Exadata Smart Scan for SQL statements with query predicates. Additionally, storage indexes yield the greatest performance savings when your data is well ordered with respect to the columns in your query predicates.

CHAPTER 19 ■ STORAGE INDEXES

■ **Note** Please see Recipe 15-7 to learn more about Smart Scan and direct path reads, Recipe 9-10 to learn how to enable or disable Smart Scan at the ASM disk group level, and Recipe 19-2 to learn more about the impact of ordered data and storage indexes.

From a design perspective, it is important to understand that storage indexes are nothing at all like traditional Oracle B*Tree indexes or other index types. They are not a physical structure stored as a segment inside your databases but, rather, memory structures that reside on the Exadata storage cells. While the goal of traditional indexes is to assist Oracle in rapidly finding rows in a table, the goal of storage indexes is to provide a very efficient means to instruct the cell services software to *skip* physical reads to sets of extents if the values in the storage index indicate that the requested data is not contained therein.

On the Exadata storage cell disks, your database's data is physically stored inside an Oracle ASM allocation unit. ASM allocation units are comprised of a set of 1 MB chunks called *storage regions*, and as I/O is issued, Exadata's cell services software conducts I/O requests in 1 MB units based on these storage regions.

Each storage region has a small memory structure associated with it that is used to store a *region index*, which is another name for a storage index. Region indexes are populated as data is requested via Smart Scan, and based on the query predicates used to access the data, the region indexes are populated with the high and low values found when servicing the I/O request. These region indexes track the high and low values for up to eight columns per segment, based on the nature of the query predicates. So, in the example provided in the solution of this recipe, the following statements can be made.

1. The first time that each cell's cell services software issued an I/O request to access extents from the D14.MYOBJ_UNCOMP table, Exadata populated a region index for each storage index with the high and low values found for the OBJECT_ID column, based on the WHERE OBJECT_ID BETWEEN 100 AND 200 query predicate.

2. Subsequent queries against this table generated an iDB message instructing Exadata's cell services software to read the same sets of extents as the first query, but in this case the region indexes would have been populated based on the I/Os read from the first query.

3. Prior to issuing a physical disk read, cellsrv checks the high and low values stored in the region index and if it determines that a storage region does not contain any values meeting the query predicate, bypasses the physical I/O to the region.

Bypassing I/O equates to skipping physical reads, and skipping physical reads means generally means you will save time. Figure 19-1 provides a logical representation of how storage indexes work.

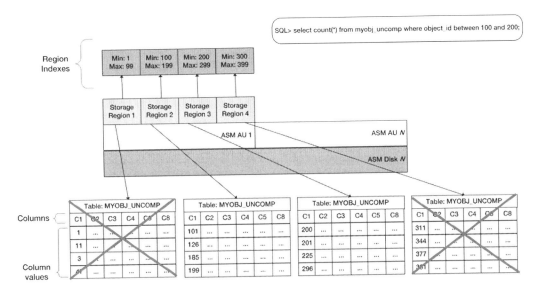

Figure 19-1. *Storage indexes in action*

In Figure 19-1, we are showing the storage regions that comprise a single ASM allocation unit for the table used in the solution of this recipe. The first storage region contains a minimum value for OBJECT_ID of 1 and a maximum of 99, the second has a minimum of 100 and maximum of 199, the third has values between 200 and 299, and the fourth has values between 300 and 399. When I/Os for this table are issued using the predicate condition supplied in the SQL statement above, Exadata will examine the region indexes for each storage region and bypass physical I/O requests to storage regions 1 and 4. Region 3 has a minimum value of 200, so based on the between predicate, cellsrv will perform a physical I/O to this region.

It is worth mentioning that Exadata automatically maintains storage indexes over time based on your application usage. There is nothing an Exadata DMA can do to influence storage index behavior outside of potentially ordering your data to encourage their use or change your application's query predicates. Recipe 19-2 discusses the impact of ordered data with respect to storage indexes.

19-2. Measuring Storage Index Performance with Not-So-Well-Ordered Data

Problem

You wish to measure and contrast the storage index performance savings with well-ordered and randomly ordered data.

Solution

In this recipe, you will learn how to measure and contrast storage index I/O savings for queries that retrieve data from tables with well-ordered data and tables with randomly ordered data. In the following test case, we will use the table introduced in Recipe 19-1 and create two identical tables, ordering our data on the OBJECT_NAME column for one table and, randomly, using the ORDER BY DBMS_RANDOM.VALUE clause, for the second table. We will then issue the same query against each table using a query predicate on the OBJECT_NAME table. First, we'll create our test tables:

```
SQL> create table d14.myobj_ordered
  2  tablespace tbs_test nologging
  3  as select * from d14.myobj_uncomp
  4  order by object_name
  5  /
Table created.
SQL> create table d14.myobj_unordered
  2  tablespace tbs_test nologging
  3  as select * from d14.myobj_uncomp
  4  order by dbms_random.value;
Table created.
SQL>
```

Next, we will run a full table scan that uses Smart Scan against both of our tables, searching for the number of rows that match a range of OBJECT_NAME values and measure the storage index savings using the script in Listing 19-1, introduced in Recipe 19-1:

```
SQL> select count(*) from d14.myobj_ordered
  2  where object_name between 'a' and 'b';
  COUNT(*)
----------
      3000
Elapsed: 00:00:00.09
SQL> @lst19-01-exastorind-mysess.sql
```

Statistic	Value (MB)
cell physical IO bytes eligible for predicate offload	2,254.73
cell physical IO bytes saved by storage index	**2,242.82**
cell physical IO interconnect bytes	.06
cell physical IO interconnect bytes returned by smart scan	.04

```
SQL>

SQL> select count(*) from d14.myobj_unordered
  2  where object_name between 'a' and 'b';
  COUNT(*)
----------
      3000
Elapsed: 00:00:00.80
SQL> SQL> @lst19-01-exastorind-mysess.sql
```

Statistic	Value (MB)
cell physical IO bytes eligible for predicate offload	2,254.38
cell physical IO bytes saved by storage index	**.00**
cell physical IO interconnect bytes	.77
cell physical IO interconnect bytes returned by smart scan	.74

```
SQL>
```

As you can see from these results, the ordering of data inside your blocks (and more specifically, storage regions) has an impact on Exadata's ability to use storage indexes. Both of our test queries were offloadable and used Smart Scan, and both ran in under one second, but the query on D14.MYOBJ_UNORDERED took nearly nine times as long to complete and saved zero bytes of I/O via storage indexes.

How It Works

As presented in the How It Works section of Recipe 19-1, Exadata's cellsrv software tracks high and low values for columns in your query predicates for each storage region inside your ASM allocation unit.

If a segment's data in a storage region is relatively well ordered for a given column typically used in a query predicate, storage indexes will enable the cellsrv processes to bypass physical I/O requests and save I/O; the cell physical IO bytes saved by storage index is a system statistic that can be used to measure this I/O savings benefit. If, on the other hand, the data is not well ordered, storage indexes will provide limited or no benefit as each storage region has a higher probability of containing a large range of potential values for a given column. Like traditional B*Tree indexes, clustering is an important consideration for storage indexes.

One of the interesting things to point out about storage indexes is that Exadata's cellsrv processes will only use them if the predicate values in a query fall outside the high and low values tracked in the region indexes for each storage region, regardless of whether the storage region actually contains data within the tracked ranges. Consider a simplistic example in which a storage region contains data for ten rows in a table. Within these ten rows, let's assume there is a column called FIRST_NAME and within this column, the region contains rows with the FIRST_NAME containing "john", "anto", "max", "leigh", "theo", "rachel", "lauren", "bob", "denise", and "jen". If you were to issue a query searching for FIRST_NAME="chris", any existing storage indexes for this table would not disqualify this region from being accessed because "chris" falls between "anto" and "theo". If you were to query based on FIRST_NAME="victor", cellsrv would bypass a physical I/O to this storage region because the value falls outside the high and low values. In short, this means that storage index functions can return false positives (with respect to allowing I/O requests to be issued), but they will never return false negatives.

As an Exadata DMA or developer, then, tables that are accessed with known query predicates may benefit well from storage indexes by ordering your data to encourage them.

■ **Note** Ordering tables for benefit of storage indexes, while sometimes beneficial, could pose challenges in the event that your application relies on index range scans with clustered data. Before re-ordering the data in hopes of leveraging storage indexes, you should have a firm understanding of the query predicates issued on behalf of your applications and ensure that clustering-related scans will not be adversely impacted.

19-3. Testing Storage Index Behavior with Different Query Predicate Conditions

Problem

You wish to measure the storage index I/O savings for queries that use various query predicate conditions, including use of bind variables, LIKE, BETWEEN, wildcards, range predicates, situations when your queried columns contain null values, and multicolumn query predicates.

Solution

In this recipe, you will learn how storage indexes behave when accessing data under a variety of query predicate conditions. In each subsection of this recipe, we will use the same table as our test case, the MYOBJ_ORDERED table created in Recipe 19-2, and query the table based on a number of conditions. After each query, we will measure our storage index savings using the previously introduced script in Listing 19-1.

The purpose of this recipe is primarily to demonstrate how storage indexes are or are not used under a variety of query predicate and data conditions in attempts to arm you with information to troubleshoot storage index usage in your environment. We have previously demonstrated how to measure storage index I/O savings in Recipe 19-1 and will use this technique to measure our results. Each section in this recipe will start with a script, measure the storage index I/O savings, and comment on the output.

Storage Indexes and Bind Variables

In this section, we will demonstrate a test in which bind variables are used in a query predicate and measure whether Exadata uses storage indexes:

```
SQL> variable objname varchar2(256);
SQL> exec :objname :='SOURCE$';
PL/SQL procedure successfully completed.
SQL> select count(*) from d14.myobj_ordered
  2  where object_name = :objname;
  COUNT(*)
----------
      1000
Elapsed: 00:00:00.52
SQL> @lst19-01-exastorind-mysess.sql

Statistic                                                              Value (MB)
---------------------------------------------------------------------  ----------
cell physical IO bytes eligible for predicate offload                    2,254.73
cell physical IO bytes saved by storage index                            1,007.05
cell physical IO interconnect bytes                                           .22
cell physical IO interconnect bytes returned by smart scan                    .19
```

As you can see, storage indexes function when using bind variables in your query predicates as indicated by the nearly 1 GB of I/O savings.

Storage Indexes and BETWEEN Predicates

In this section, we will demonstrate two cases of BETWEEN predicates, one with a narrow range of values and one with a wider range of values, and display our storage index I/O savings results. First, we will execute a query with a narrow range of selected values:

```
SQL> select count(*) from d14.myobj_ordered
  2  where object_name between 'A' and 'B';
  COUNT(*)
----------
   1174000
Elapsed: 00:00:00.14
SQL> @lst19-01-exastorind-mysess.sql
```

```
Statistic                                                          Value (MB)
----------------------------------------------------------------   ----------
cell physical IO bytes eligible for predicate offload                2,254.73
cell physical IO bytes saved by storage index                        2,060.34
cell physical IO interconnect bytes                                      14.01
cell physical IO interconnect bytes returned by smart scan               13.99
```

Next, we will query a wider range of values:

```
SQL> select count(*) from d14.myobj_ordered
  2  where object_name between 'A' and 'M';
  COUNT(*)
----------
   9057000
Elapsed: 00:00:00.56
SQL> @lst19-01-exastorind-mysess.sql

Statistic                                                          Value (MB)
----------------------------------------------------------------   ----------
cell physical IO bytes eligible for predicate offload                2,254.73
cell physical IO bytes saved by storage index                          599.85
cell physical IO interconnect bytes                                    107.75
cell physical IO interconnect bytes returned by smart scan             107.73
```

As you can see, when querying wide ranges of values, the storage index I/O savings is not as much as when selecting a narrower range of values, as expected.

Storage Indexes and Null Values

In this section, we will update roughly 10% of the rows in our test table with null values for cases when OBJECT_NAME='SOURCE$' and execute a query selecting the unmodified rows:

```
SQL> select count(*) from d14.myobj_ordered
  2  where object_name = 'SOURCE$';

  COUNT(*)
----------
       901

Elapsed: 00:00:00.56
SQL> @lst19-01-exastorind-mysess.sql

Statistic                                                          Value (MB)
----------------------------------------------------------------   ----------
cell physical IO bytes eligible for predicate offload                2,254.73
cell physical IO bytes saved by storage index                        1,007.05
cell physical IO interconnect bytes                                       .22
cell physical IO interconnect bytes returned by smart scan                .19
```

Now, we will run tests searching for conditions when our OBJECT_NAME column is null:

```
SQL> select count(*) from d14.myobj_ordered
  2  where object_name is null;

  COUNT(*)
----------
        99
Elapsed: 00:00:00.06
SQL> @lst19-01-exastorind-mysess.sql

Statistic                                                         Value (MB)
----------------------------------------------------------------- ----------
cell physical IO bytes eligible for predicate offload               2,254.73
cell physical IO bytes saved by storage index                       2,252.82
cell physical IO interconnect bytes                                      .03
cell physical IO interconnect bytes returned by smart scan               .00
```

Not only does Exadata use storage indexes for our first query, but it also benefits significantly when querying our 99 rows with null values. This means that cellsrv handles null values and can eliminate I/O requests successfully in situations when null values exist in the predicate column as well as eliminate I/O requests when the IS NULL clause is used.

Storage Indexes and Unbounded Range Scans

In the first section of this recipe, we demonstrated how storage indexes can be used when supplying a range criteria with the BETWEEN predicate. What happens when you execute a query with an unbounded range criterion?

```
SQL> select count(*) from d14.myobj_ordered
  2  where object_name > 'T';

  COUNT(*)
----------
   4247000

Elapsed: 00:00:00.47
SQL> @lst19-01-exastorind-mysess.sql

Statistic                                                         Value (MB)
----------------------------------------------------------------- ----------
cell physical IO bytes eligible for predicate offload               2,254.73
cell physical IO bytes saved by storage index                       1,375.70
cell physical IO interconnect bytes                                    50.98
cell physical IO interconnect bytes returned by smart scan             50.95
```

As you can see, storage indexes are used with unbounded range criteria and the I/O savings is proportional to the number of rows selected in this case, in which our data is well ordered with respect to the query predicate.

Storage Indexes with LIKE and Wildcard Predicates

What happens when your query predicates use the LIKE condition with wildcards?

```
SQL> select count(*) from d14.myobj_ordered
  2  where object_type like 'SOU%';
  COUNT(*)
----------
         0
Elapsed: 00:00:00.84
SQL> @lst19-01-exastorind-mysess.sql
Statistic                                                         Value (MB)
---------------------------------------------------------------   ----------
cell physical IO bytes eligible for predicate offload               2,254.73
cell physical IO bytes saved by storage index                            .00
cell physical IO interconnect bytes                                      .35
cell physical IO interconnect bytes returned by smart scan               .33
```

In this output, we can see that when using LIKE conditions with wildcards, storage indexes are not used.

Storage Indexes and MultiColumn Predicates

We will demonstrate the impact of using multiple predicates for a single table query. First, we will show the performance statistics when using a single predicate:

```
SQL> select count(*) from d14.myobj_ordered
  2  where object_name between 'S' and 'T';
  COUNT(*)
----------
   2858901
SQL>
SQL> @lst19-01-exastorind-mysess.sql
Statistic                                                         Value (MB)
---------------------------------------------------------------   ----------
cell physical IO bytes eligible for predicate offload               2,254.73
cell physical IO bytes saved by storage index                         888.61
cell physical IO interconnect bytes                                    34.52
cell physical IO interconnect bytes returned by smart scan             34.35
```

Now, we will add another predicate condition:

```
SQL> select count(*) from d14.myobj_ordered
  2  where object_name between 'S' and 'T'
  3  and object_type='TABLE';
  COUNT(*)
----------
    186901
SQL>
SQL> @lst19-01-exastorind-mysess.sql
```

```
Statistic                                                             Value (MB)
--------------------------------------------------------------------  ----------
cell physical IO bytes eligible for predicate offload                   2,254.73
cell physical IO bytes saved by storage index                           1,266.39
cell physical IO interconnect bytes                                         2.42
cell physical IO interconnect bytes returned by smart scan                  2.38
```

As you can see, the I/O savings was greater in the multicolumn predicate test, an indication that storage index I/O savings can be additive when multiple column predicate conditions are listed in the WHERE clause.

How It Works

Exadata is able to successfully use storage indexes under a variety of query predicate conditions, including bind variables, BETWEEN predicates, situations when null values exist in your columns, and both bounded and unbounded range scans. One of the situations under which storage indexes will *not* be used is when you use wildcard values with LIKE operations, however. In our tests, the LIKE condition is not the storage index disabler—the wildcard is. A simple test confirms this:

```
SQL> select count(*) from d14.myobj_ordered
  2  where object_name like 'SOURCE$';
  COUNT(*)
----------
         0

Elapsed: 00:00:00.63
SQL> @lst19-01-exastorind-mysess.sql
Statistic                                                             Value (MB)
--------------------------------------------------------------------  ----------
cell physical IO bytes eligible for predicate offload                   2,254.73
cell physical IO bytes saved by storage index                           1,006.05
cell physical IO interconnect bytes                                          .22
cell physical IO interconnect bytes returned by smart scan                   .20
```

In addition to the importance of ordered data with respect to storage index usability as presented in Recipe 19-2 (especially with BETWEEN clauses) and the previous wildcard example, there are a number of other situations in which storage indexes will either not work at all, or not work "reliably":

- Queries that use the != clause in the predicate will not benefit from storage indexes.
- Queries on columns that contain CLOB data will not benefit from storage indexes.
- Queries with implicit conversions on date/time-based columns may or may not benefit from storage indexes depending on how the data is actually stored and what the date format is in the query predicate.

19-4. Tracing Storage Index Behavior
Problem

You wish to diagnose storage index behavior to better understand how Exadata maintains storage indexes.

Solution

In this recipe, you will learn how to enable tracing for storage indexes and interpret the storage index trace files.

1. First, set the undocumented _kcfis_storageidx_diag_mode parameter to 2 in your current session using the ALTER SESSION command. This will enable storage index tracing in debug mode:

   ```
   SQL> alter session set "_kcfis_storageidx_diag_mode"=2;
   ```

2. Next, execute a query that you believe should benefit from storage indexes. In the following, we will execute one of the queries introduced in a previous recipe in this chapter:

   ```
   SQL> select count(*) from d14.myobj_ordered
     2  where object_name between 'a' and 'm';
     COUNT(*)
   ----------
        38000
   Elapsed: 00:00:00.10
   SQL>
   ```

3. After the query completes, log in to one of your storage cells and navigate to your diagnostics/trace file directory. In all of the versions of Exadata that we have worked on, this is located in $ADR_BASE/diag/asm/cell/[cell server name]/trace and symbolically linked to /var/log/oracle/diag/asm/cell/[cell server name]/trace:

   ```
   [root@cm01cel01 ~]# cd $ADR_BASE/diag/asm/cell/cm01cel01/trace
   [root@cm01cel01 trace]# pwd
   /opt/oracle/cell11.2.3.1.1_LINUX.X64_120607/log/diag/asm/cell/cm01cel01/trace
   [root@cm01cel01 trace]#
   ```

■ **Note** Storage index trace information is stored on the storage cell, not the diagnostics directory on your database server. The context of the trace files is the cell services operating system processes on the storage cells, not your database instance.

---

4. You will find a number of trace files that begin with the svtrc*; examine the contents of one the recently created files:

   ```
   [root@cm01cel01 trace]# ls -alrt svtrc*|tail -5
   -rw-r----- 1 root celladmin 3363 Nov 28 00:38 svtrc_12910_75.trc
   -rw-r----- 1 root celladmin  265 Nov 28 00:38 svtrc_12910_71.trm
   -rw-r----- 1 root celladmin 1414 Nov 28 00:38 svtrc_12910_71.trc
   -rw-r----- 1 root celladmin  260 Nov 28 00:38 svtrc_12910_43.trm
   -rw-r----- 1 root celladmin 1414 Nov 28 00:38 svtrc_12910_43.trc
   [root@cm01cel01 trace]# vi svtrc_12910_43.trc
   ```

> **Note** The Exadata storage cells will generate a fixed number of cellsrv trace files for storage index tracing, as established by the cell server initialization parameter _cell_si_max_num_diag_mode_dumps. This parameter defaults to 20, and Oracle limits this to protect against filling up your trace file directory with hundreds or thousands of files.

   5. Search for the string RIDX in the trace file. RIDX stands for "region index," as introduced in the How It Works section of Recipe 19-1. The contents of the trace file below the RIDX section will contain information about your region indexes (in other words, storage indexes):

```
2012-11-28 01:41:21.235089*: RIDX (0x2aacf77f1d64) for SQLID 81mxd5muz2543 filter 0
2012-11-28 01:41:21.237399*: RIDX (0x2aacf77f1d64) : st 2 validBitMap 0 tabn 0 id
{29336 12         2273376219}
2012-11-28 01:41:21.237399*: RIDX: strt 0 end 2048 offset 218594541568 size 1048576
rgnIdx 208468         RgnOffset 0 scn: 0x0000.0617dc23 hist: 0x92
2012-11-28 01:41:21.237399*: RIDX validation history: 0:FullRead 1:FullRead 2:FullRead
3:Undef 4:Undef 5:Undef 6:Undef 7:Undef 8:Undef 9:Undef
2012-11-28 01:41:21.237399*: Col id [2] numFilt 11 flg 2:
2012-11-28 01:41:21.237399*: lo: 4d 47 4d 54 5f 44 45 4c
2012-11-28 01:41:21.237399*: hi: 78 64 62 2d 6c 6f 67 31
2012-11-28 01:41:21.237399*: Col id [4] numFilt 3 flg 2:
2012-11-28 01:41:21.237399*: lo: c3 2 31 0 0 0 0 0
2012-11-28 01:41:21.237399*: hi: c3 2 5a 48 0 0 0 0
2012-11-28 01:41:21.243399*: Col id [6] numFilt 4 flg 2:
2012-11-28 01:41:21.243399*: lo: 53 59 4e 4f 4e 59 4d 0
2012-11-28 01:41:21.243399*: hi: 54 59 50 45 0 0 0 0
```

Here is how to interpret the trace file:

- Each line in the region index section is prefaced by a timestamp at which the trace file line was generated. The top row contains the SQL ID for the SQL statement that searched the storage index:

  RIDX (0x2aacf77f1d64) for SQLID **81mxd5muz2543** filter 0

- You can query V$SQL to confirm which SQL statement was issued that generated this section of the storage index trace file by running the following SQL statement:

  ```
  SQL> select sql_text from v$sql where sql_id='81mxd5muz2543';
  SQL_TEXT
  --------------------------------------------------------------------------------
  select count(*) from d14.myobj_ordered where object_name between 'a' and 'm'
  SQL>
  ```

- The next line, which contains the string tabn, contains your object information details in curly brackets:

  RIDX (0x2aacf77f1d64) : st 2 validBitMap 0 tabn 0 id {**29336 12**   2273376219}

CHAPTER 19 ■ STORAGE INDEXES

- In the previous line, 29336 represents the data object ID for the segment and the 12 represents the tablespace ID:

  ```
  SQL> select dataobj#, name from obj$ where dataobj#=29336;
       29336 MYOBJ_ORDERED
  SQL> select ts#,name from ts$ where ts#=12;
          12 TBS_TEST
  SQL>
  ```

- The line beginning with the string RIDX: strt contains a number of pieces of information about the physical attributes of the storage region. Specifically, the size attribute displays 1048576 for each storage region, or 1 MB:

  ```
  RIDX: strt 0 end 2048 offset 218594541568 size 1048576 rgnIdx 208468 RgnOffset 0 scn:
  0x0000.0617dc23 hist: 0x92
  ```

- Beneath this header information, you will find one or more sections that begin with the string Col, followed by a lo and a hi line. The line containing the Col string indicates the column number for the segment provided in the tabn line, the line containing the string lo represents the hexadecimal representation of the low values for this region, and the hi list represents the high values for this region.

  ```
  Col id [2] numFilt 11 flg 2:
  lo: 4d 47 4d 54 5f 44 45 4c
  hi: 78 64 62 2d 6c 6f 67 31
  Col id [4] numFilt 3 flg 2:
  lo: c3 2 31 0 0 0 0 0
  hi: c3 2 5a 48 0 0 0 0
  Col id [6] numFilt 4 flg 2:
  lo: 53 59 4e 4f 4e 59 4d 0
  hi: 54 59 50 45 0 0 0 0
  ```

This output tells us that for this specific storage region, there were three different column predicates that had been issued to populate high and low values for this specific database segment, and these predicates were issued on columns 2, 4, and 6. You can use the following query to map these column numbers to column names:

```
SQL> select obj.name, col.segcol#,col.name
  2  from obj$ obj, col$ col
  3  where obj.name='MYOBJ_ORDERED'
  4  and obj.obj#=col.obj#
  5  and col.segcol# in (2,4,6)
  6  /
MYOBJ_ORDERED                          2 OBJECT_NAME
MYOBJ_ORDERED                          4 OBJECT_ID
MYOBJ_ORDERED                          6 OBJECT_TYPE
SQL>
```

As stated, the high and low values for each column in the region index are listed in hexadecimal format in the trace file. If you are able to convert hexadecimal values to string characters in your head, more power to you but, if not, you can use the following simple Perl one-liner to find the low and high values for our OBJECT_NAME column:

```
$ perl -e '$str="4d474d545f44454c";$str =~ s/([a-fA-F0-9][a-fA-F0-9])/chr(hex($1))/eg;print "$str\n"'
MGMT_DEL        <- Low value
$ perl -e '$str="7864622d6c6f6731";$str =~ s/([a-fA-F0-9][a-fA-F0-9])/chr(hex($1))/eg;print "$str\n"'
xdb-log1        <- HIgh Value
```

567

How It Works

You can set the _kcfis_storageidx_diag_mode parameter, at both the session and system level, to enable storage index tracing. When you set this value to 2, cellsrv will enable storage index tracing in debug mode and generate a trace file for each cellsrv process thread that performs I/O and uses storage indexes.

> **Note** The default value for _kcfis_storageidx_diag_mode is 0. Setting to 1 disables tracing.

Why would you want to trace storage index behavior? Other than the pure academic joy of the endeavor, storage indexes are unique in that they are structures that you have no *direct* means of managing, yet provide potentially dramatic performance gains to your applications. These significant performance gains are at times accompanied by some unexpected results. As stated in Oracle's documentation, Exadata maintains region indexes for up to eight columns on a table and, as such, a storage index trace file can provide you with insight into which columns have associated storage indexes and which ones do not. This can be vital information for a performance engineer tasked with explaining why queries sometimes run for a minute and sometimes execute in a fraction of a second.

> **Note** One thing you may observe from storage index trace files is that only the first eight bytes of the column values are tracked. So, if your columns are populated with a common set of characters in the first eight bytes, storage indexes will *not* be effective as cellsrv will have no way of distinguishing different ranges of high and low values for your columns.

19-5. Tracing Storage Indexes When More than Eight Columns Are Referenced

Problem

You wish to measure and understand how Exadata dynamically maintains storage indexes when your applications issue queries with predicate conditions on more than eight columns for a table.

Solution

In this recipe, you will learn how to trace storage indexes, similar to the examples provided in Recipe 19-4 and identify how Exadata dynamically adjusts region index contents when more than eight columns are used in query predicates for a specific table.

1. Begin by identifying or creating a test case. In this recipe, we will create a test table called MYOBJ_TEST and populate it with two NUMBER columns and eight VARCHAR2 columns, each containing a value from DBA_OBJECTS.OBJECT_NAME. We will load the table with over 20 million rows to encourage Smart Scan and make the queries issued against it eligible for storage indexes:

```
SQL> create table d14.myobj_test
  2  tablespace tbs_test nologging as
  3  select * from (
  4  select rownum  as col1 from dual connect by level <=1000),
```

```
  5  (select mod(abs(dbms_random.random),50000)+1 col2,
  6      object_name col3, object_name col4, object_name col5,
  7      object_name col6, object_name col7, object_name col8,
  8      object_name col9, object_name col10
  9  from dba_objects
 10  order by 3) obj
 11  /
Table created.
SQL>
```

2. Next, we'll query the object and column number values from SYS.OBJ# and SYS.COL$ so that we can identify the relevant rows in our trace files:

```
SQL> select obj.name, obj.dataobj#,col.segcol#,col.name colname
  2    from obj$ obj, col$ col
  3    where obj.name='MYOBJ_TEST'
  4    and obj.obj#=col.obj#
  5    order by col.segcol#
  6  /
Table                   DataObj#    Col#   ColName
--------------------    --------    ----   --------------------
MYOBJ_TEST                29606        1   COL1
MYOBJ_TEST                29606        2   COL2
MYOBJ_TEST                29606        3   COL3
MYOBJ_TEST                29606        4   COL4
MYOBJ_TEST                29606        5   COL5
MYOBJ_TEST                29606        6   COL6
MYOBJ_TEST                29606        7   COL7
MYOBJ_TEST                29606        8   COL8
MYOBJ_TEST                29606        9   COL9
MYOBJ_TEST                29606       10   COL10
```

3. After this, execute a series of SQL statements with different where conditions for each of the columns in your table. In the test below, we are executing queries using each of the ten columns in our MYOBJ_TEST table in order to force Exadata to make decisions about which columns to retain region index data for and which columns to "purge" from the region indexes. Prior to executing our test script, we will enable storage index tracing by setting the _kcfis_storageidx_diag_mode parameter to 2 at the session level, as introduced in Recipe 19-4:

```
SQL> alter session set "_kcfis_storageidx_diag_mode"=2;
Session altered.
SQL> declare
  2    cnt number;
  3    xtr varchar2(100);
  4    str varchar2(80):='select count(*) from d14.myobj_test where col';
  5  begin
  6    for x in 1..10 loop
  7      for i in 1..10 loop
  8        execute immediate 'alter system flush buffer_cache';
  9        if i>2 then
```

```
         10    xtr:=str||to_char(i)||' between ''A'' and ''B''';
         11    else
         12    xtr:=str||to_char(i)||' between 100 and 110';
         13    end if;
         14    dbms_output.put_line(xtr);
         15    execute immediate xtr into cnt;
         16    end loop;
         17    end loop;
         18    end;
         19    /
     select count(*) from d14.myobj_test where col1 between 100 and 110
     select count(*) from d14.myobj_test where col2 between 100 and 110
     select count(*) from d14.myobj_test where col3 between 'A' and 'B'
     select count(*) from d14.myobj_test where col4 between 'A' and 'B'
     ... Output omitted for brevity
     PL/SQL procedure successfully completed.
     SQL>
```

4. When complete, a number of trace files will be written to the trace file directory on each storage cell. Use the script in Listing 19-2 to display pertinent information related to storage indexes, passing the DATAOBJ# as an argument as outlined.

Listing 19-2. *./lst19-07-storindsum.pl*

```perl
#!/usr/bin/perl
# Name: lst19-07-storindsum.pl
# Usage: ./lst19-07-storindsum.pl -o [dataobj#]
# To do: do the pattern matching
use Getopt::Std;
use Text::ParseWords;
use Env;
sub usage {
 print "Usage: /lst19-07-storindsum.pl -o [dataobj#]\n";
}
getopts("o:",\%options);
die usage unless (defined $options{o});
$hostname=$ENV{HOSTNAME};
$hostname=~s/\..*//;
$trcdir="/var/log/oracle/diag/asm/cell/$hostname/trace";
$p=0;
open(F,"cat $trcdir/svtrc*trc|") ;
while (<F>) {
$p=1 if ((/tabn/) && (/\{$options{o}/)) ;
$p=0 if /SQLID/;
 if (/tabn/) {
  ($day,$tm,$x3,$x4,$x5,$x6,$x7,$x8,$x9,$x10,$x11,$x12,$obj,$tbs,$x15)=split(' ',$_);
  print "Object: $obj $tbs $x15\n" if $p;
 }
 if (/rgnIdx/) {
  ($day,$tm,$x3,$x4,$x5,$x6,$x7,$x8,$x9,$x10,$x11,$x12,$rgnIdx,
         $x14,$x15,$x16,$x17,$x18,$x19)=split(' ',$_);
```

```
  print "\t$day $tm: Region Idx => $rgnIdx\n" if $p;
 }
 if (/Col id/) {
   print "\t\t$_" if $p;
 }
}
close(F);

[root@cm01cel01 source]# ./lst19-07-storindsum.pl -o 29606 | more
Object: {29606 12 2273376219}
        2012-11-29 01:17:09.324738*:: Region Idx => 208787
                2012-11-29 01:17:09.324738*: Col id [1] numFilt 14 flg 2:
                2012-11-29 01:17:09.324738*: Col id [3] numFilt 0 flg 2:
                2012-11-29 01:17:09.324738*: Col id [4] numFilt 0 flg 2:
                2012-11-29 01:17:09.324738*: Col id [5] numFilt 1 flg 2:
                2012-11-29 01:17:09.324738*: Col id [6] numFilt 2 flg 2:
                2012-11-29 01:17:09.324738*: Col id [7] numFilt 3 flg 2:
                2012-11-29 01:17:09.324738*: Col id [8] numFilt 4 flg 2:
Object: {29606 12 2273376219}
        2012-11-29 01:17:09.325352*:: Region Idx => 208790
                2012-11-29 01:17:09.325352*: Col id [1] numFilt 14 flg 2:
                2012-11-29 01:17:09.325352*: Col id [3] numFilt 0 flg 2:
                2012-11-29 01:17:09.325352*: Col id [4] numFilt 0 flg 2:
                2012-11-29 01:17:09.325352*: Col id [5] numFilt 1 flg 2:
                2012-11-29 01:17:09.325352*: Col id [6] numFilt 2 flg 2:
                2012-11-29 01:17:09.325352*: Col id [7] numFilt 3 flg 2:
                2012-11-29 01:17:09.325352*: Col id [8] numFilt 4 flg 2:
... Output omitted for brevity
```

In the script output, you will find sections for each timestamp and region index accessed for the object provided. This output will help you understand which columns are being tracked in the region index over time. For example, in the first section of output above, region index 208787 contains values for columns 1, 3, 4, 5, 6, 7, and 8. Further down in the script output, you will find different columns for this specific region index as Exadata dynamically adjusts which columns to track. In the following trace file output, which was generated an hour and a half after the first values for the region index were written to a trace file, we can see that column number 3 no longer resides in the storage index and column number 10 has replaced it:

```
Object: {29606 12 2273376219}
        2012-11-29 02:39:57.330536*:: Region Idx => 208787
                2012-11-29 02:39:57.330536*: Col id [1] numFilt 14 flg 2:
                2012-11-29 02:39:57.330536*: Col id [4] numFilt 1 flg 2:
                2012-11-29 02:39:57.330536*: Col id [5] numFilt 2 flg 2:
                2012-11-29 02:39:57.330536*: Col id [6] numFilt 3 flg 2:
                2012-11-29 02:39:57.330536*: Col id [7] numFilt 4 flg 2:
                2012-11-29 02:39:57.330536*: Col id [8] numFilt 0 flg 2:
                2012-11-29 02:39:57.330536*: Col id [9] numFilt 0 flg 2:
                2012-11-29 02:39:57.330536*: Col id [10] numFilt 0 flg 2:
```

How It Works

Oracle's documentation states that Exadata creates storage indexes for up to eight columns in a table based on the nature of query predicates issued against the table, and dynamically adjusts the storage indexes based on your query workload.

More accurately though, cellsrv maintains high and low values for up to eight columns in a table for a *specific storage region*, and not all storage regions will necessarily have the same storage indexes on the same columns for a table. The nature of the data, as stored on disk, in combination with the mix of query predicates, will dictate which columns will have storage indexes created for them at any given point in time. Contrast the following excerpt from the lst19-07-storindsum.pl script, which displays a different set of columns for different storage regions at nearly the same point in time. The differences are outlined in bold:

```
Object: {29606 12 2273376219}
        2012-11-29 02:40:02.993332*:: Region Idx => 208643
                2012-11-29 02:40:02.993332*: Col id [1] numFilt 14 flg 2:
                2012-11-29 02:40:02.993332*: Col id [2] numFilt 4 flg 2:
                2012-11-29 02:40:02.993332*: Col id [4] numFilt 0 flg 2:
                2012-11-29 02:40:02.993332*: Col id [5] numFilt 0 flg 2:
                2012-11-29 02:40:02.993332*: Col id [6] numFilt 0 flg 2:
                2012-11-29 02:40:02.993332*: Col id [7] numFilt 1 flg 2:
                2012-11-29 02:40:02.993332*: Col id [9] numFilt 0 flg 2:
                2012-11-29 02:40:02.993332*: Col id [10] numFilt 2 flg 2:
Object: {29606 12 2273376219}
        2012-11-29 02:40:03.004267*:: Region Idx => 208685
                2012-11-29 02:40:03.004267*: Col id [1] numFilt 1 flg 2:
                2012-11-29 02:40:03.004267*: Col id [3] numFilt 1 flg 2:
                2012-11-29 02:40:03.004267*: Col id [4] numFilt 2 flg 2:
                2012-11-29 02:40:03.004267*: Col id [5] numFilt 3 flg 2:
                2012-11-29 02:40:03.004267*: Col id [6] numFilt 4 flg 2:
                2012-11-29 02:40:03.004267*: Col id [8] numFilt 0 flg 2:
                2012-11-29 02:40:03.004267*: Col id [9] numFilt 0 flg 2:
                2012-11-29 02:40:03.004267*: Col id [10] numFilt 0 flg 2:
```

You may be asking yourself whether this entire topic is worthwhile to understand or what practical use you would have for knowing how to trace storage index behavior in general. In our opinion, the likelihood of needing to know this information is relatively low, but it comes in handy when attempting to diagnose performance variances for your applications over time. For example, a full offloaded table scan that sometimes runs in 30 seconds but other times has sub-second response times is frequently a result of storage index benefits on Exadata. This response time variance may be acceptable, but in the event it isn't, being able to diagnose how cellsrv is "using" storage indexes can be useful.

■ **Note** As documented and stated a number of times in this chapter, the Exadata DMA has no direct way to influence storage indexes, only indirect means such as ordering data intelligently, limiting your query predicates, and so forth. Additionally, storage indexes are not persistent across storage cell reboots and also need to be "primed" before Exadata can leverage them. For these reasons, we like to tell people that storage indexes are great to have when Exadata decides it can use them, but do not rely on them as an optimization tool to guarantee a performance SLA.

19-6. Tracing Storage Indexes when DML Is Issued against Tables

Problem

You wish to identify how Exadata maintains storage indexes as data is updated or deleted from a table.

Solution

In this recipe, you will learn how to use storage index tracing to identify how Exadata maintains storage indexes when data is updated or deleted from a table. We will start by executing a query that benefits from storage indexes, measure the storage index savings, and trace using the _kcfis_storageidx_diag_mode parameter, as presented in Recipes 19-4 and 19-5.

> **Note** Please refer to Recipes 19-4 and 19-5 to learn how to trace storage indexes, identify where Exadata generates the trace files on the storage cells, and interpret the results.

Our query and storage index performance information is provided below:

```
SQL> select count(*) from d14.myobj_test where col5 ='SOURCE$';
  COUNT(*)
----------
      1000
SQL> @lst19-05-examystats.sql
Statistic                        Statistic Value
-------------------------------- ---------------
MB Requested                              3841.16
MB Eligible for Offload                   3840.94
Smart Scan Efficiency                       99.99
Interconnect MB                               .53
Interconnect MBPS                             .63
Storage Index MB Saved                    1844.75
Flash Cache MB read                           .02
Cell MB Processed                         1996.38
Cell MBPS                                 2376.65
```

An excerpt from the diagnostics trace file confirms that column number 5 has a storage index, and for this specific cellsrv trace file, there were two filter operations using this column as indicated by the numFilt flag:

```
2012-11-29 03:33:37.529441*: RIDX (0x2aacfd1c1d40) : st 2 validBitMap 0 tabn 0 id {29606 12 2273376219}
2012-11-29 03:33:37.529441*: RIDX: strt 0 end 2048 offset 218739245056 size 1048576 rgnIdx 208606 RgnOffset 0 scn: 0x0000.0623baea hist: 0x92492492
2012-11-29 03:33:37.529441*: RIDX validation history: 0:FullRead 1:FullRead 2:FullRead 3:FullRead 4:FullRead 5:FullRead 6:FullRead 7:FullRead 8:FullRead 9:FullRead
... Output omitted for brevity
2012-11-29 03:33:37.529441*: Col id [5] numFilt 2 flg 2:
2012-11-29 03:33:37.529441*: lo: 4d 47 4d 54 5f 43 4f 4e
```

```
2012-11-29 03:33:37.529441*: hi: 53 59 53 5f 4c 4f 42 30
... Output omitted for brevity
```

Now, we will update all rows for COL5 in our table and append a 'Z':

```
SQL> update d14.myobj_test
  2  set col5=col5||'Z';
20439000 rows updated.
SQL
```

Finally, we will execute the same type of query and measure whether storage indexes were used:

```
SQL> select count(*) from d14.myobj_test where col5 ='SOURCE$Z';
  COUNT(*)
----------
      1000
SQL>
SQL> @lst19-05-examystats.sql
Statistic                      Statistic Value
-----------------------------  ---------------
MB Requested                          3841.16
MB Eligible for Offload               3840.94
Smart Scan Efficiency                   99.98
Interconnect MB                           .80
Interconnect MBPS                         .63
Storage Index MB Saved                    .00
Flash Cache MB read                       .02
Cell MB Processed                     3841.13
Cell MBPS                             3048.52
```

From the same `cellsrv` trace file, we still see that column 5 has a storage index entry but the `numFilt` flag shows 0, indicating that no filter operations (that is, storage index I/O savings) have been performed on this column. Additionally, if you examine the `lo` and `hi` values for the column, you will notice different values as compared to before the UPDATE:

```
2012-11-29 03:49:25.446618*: Col id [5] numFilt 0 flg 2:
2012-11-29 03:49:25.446839*: lo: 41 42 53 50 41 54 48 0
2012-11-29 03:49:25.446839*: hi: 78 64 62 2d 6c 6f 67 31
```

How It Works

When data is updated, the storage indexes are maintained but the usability is initially "invalidated". Subsequent queries against using the same columns in the query predicates will benefit from storage indexes. If you think about the mechanics of how storage indexes work, this should come as no surprise—they are dynamically built based on the high and low values of columns queried from your tables, and if the data changes the regions, indexes will change in concert with the data in the storage regions.

In real-world Exadata workloads, this rarely presents a performance "problem" for a number of reasons. First, as explained in Recipe 19-5, you probably shouldn't be relying on storage indexes for performance reasons to begin with due to their nondeterministic performance benefit. Additionally, as mentioned in Recipe 19-1 and presented throughout Oracle's documentation, storage indexes are used when data is accessed via smart scans. Smart scans occur for full scans on large tables and, generally speaking, most Oracle environments do not typically UPDATE data in large tables. If they do, the workload is most often characterized as an OLTP workload, which generally means that the queries issued against these tables are often single-row lookups and serviced without a physical read (or Smart Scan).

> **Note** We acknowledge that all Oracle database workloads are different, but, generally speaking, if you are *relying* on storage indexes for performance and your applications are issuing smart scans, and *if* the usability of storage indexes were being adversely impacted by DML, we would hazard to guess that you likely have a larger application design issue to address.

19-7. Disabling Storage Indexes
Problem
You wish to disable storage indexes to mitigate potential performance variability for your Oracle database workloads.

Solution
In this recipe, you will learn how to disable storage indexes. Before disabling storage indexes, we will execute a test query and show the storage index I/O savings:

```
SQL> select count(*) from d14.myobj_test where col4 ='SOURCE$';
  COUNT(*)
----------
      1000
SQL>@ lst19-01-exastorind-mysess.sql
Statistic                                                            Value (MB)
-------------------------------------------------------------------- ----------
cell physical IO bytes saved by storage index                          1,844.75
... Output omitted for brevity
```

Now, execute the following ALTER SYSTEM command to disable storage indexes for your database:

```
SQL> alter system set "_kcfis_storageidx_disabled"=TRUE scope=both sid='*';
System altered.
SQL>
```

If you re-execute the same query, you will see that there are no I/O savings from storage indexes:

```
SQL> select count(*) from d14.myobj_test where col4 ='SOURCE$';
  COUNT(*)
----------
      1000
SQL>@ lst19-01-exastorind-mysess.sql
Statistic                                                            Value (MB)
-------------------------------------------------------------------- ----------
cell physical IO bytes saved by storage index                              0.00
```

How It Works

Exadata enables storage indexes by default when queries execute with Smart Scan, and `cellsrv` can determine that storage indexes are created on the storage regions being accessed, as discussed in multiple recipes in this chapter. To disable storage indexes for a specific database, simply use the `ALTER SYSTEM` command and set `_kcfis_storageidx_disabled` to TRUE.

Why would you ever want to do this? Outside of a purely academic exercise, there are cases in which organizations consider *consistent* application performance to be of higher importance than variable performance, even when the variable performance is always "for the positive." Storage indexes are unique for many reasons, but one of the interesting features is that their use will never make performance worse, only better. Simply put, the goal of storage indexes is to avoid issuing physical I/Os when not needed. Avoiding work means less work to do, and less work means your queries will run faster.

19-8. Troubleshooting Storage Indexes
Problem

You have determined that your query is *not* benefiting from storage indexes and you would like to determine why this is the case.

Solution

In this recipe, you will learn how to identify conditions under which Exadata will not use storage indexes and determine whether your query is subject to these limitations.

1. Ensure that your query contains a query predicate, or WHERE clause. Storage indexes will only be used for queries imposing a limiting condition on the rows returned.

2. Ensure that your query is using Smart Scan. Recipe 15-3, 15-4, and other recipes in Chapter 15, along with the script in Listing 19-1, demonstrate how to use the `cell physical IO bytes eligible for predicate offload` statistic to determine whether your query was Smart Scan eligible.

3. Ensure that the ASM disk group that stores your segment has the `cell.smart_scan_capable attribute` set to TRUE. Recipe 9-10 demonstrates how to measure this.

4. Ensure that your query does not use LIKE operations in the query predicate with wildcard literals.

5. If your storage index savings is minimal or zero and all of the above conditions are met, ensure that the data in your segment is well ordered with respect to the query predicate. Recipe 19-2 discusses the importance of ordered data and storage indexes in more detail.

6. Generate a storage index trace file and examine the number of columns in use for your segment. Recipe 19-4 outlines the steps required to generate and understand the contents of a `cellsrv` trace file with storage index diagnostics.

How It Works

As discussed in the How It Works section of Recipe 19-1, storage indexes are used in the following situations:

- During direct path read operations
- With smart scans
- When the queries contain predicates (in other words, a WHERE clause) and do not contain wildcards

Furthermore, storage indexes are most beneficial in terms of performance when the data is well ordered with respect to the query predicate and the WHERE clause is able to eliminate large numbers of rows from the result set.

PART 6

Post Implementation Tasks

After successfully installing your Exadata Database Machine, it's time to start migrating databases to the machine and begin realizing the benefits of Exadata. A solid understanding of Exadata's architecture and unique software features is a great starting point for the Exadata Database Machine administrator, but in addition, there are a number of configuration alternatives that are important to understand and optionally deploy in order to get the most from your investment.

The chapters in this section outline a number of these optional tasks, including a step-by-step approach for integrating your Exadata Database Machine with Oracle Enterprise Manager, configuring your machine with Automated Service Requests, as well as a number of compute node and database-specific performance tasks. Not all of the recipes in the chapters in this section will be relevant to every organization, nor is the list of recipes comprehensive in nature, but, hopefully, you will gain some insight into some of the most useful and common post-implementation tasks that you can perform to get the most out of your Exadata Database Machine.

CHAPTER 20

Post-Installation Monitoring Tasks

Successfully administering, monitoring, and managing Exadata often requires use of interfaces, tools, and utilities delivered with Exadata and other Oracle software. In this chapter, we will provide solutions for performing additional, optional post-installation tasks to improve the manageability and monitoring capabilities of your Exadata Database Machine.

20-1. Installing Enterprise Manager 12c Cloud Control Agents for Exadata

Problem

You wish to register and discover your Exadata Database Machine with Enterprise Manager 12c Cloud Control to monitor your entire Oracle Exadata Database Machine, including the compute servers, storage cells, InfiniBand switches, KVM switch, embedded Cisco switch, Oracle Grid Infrastructure Services, and Oracle database.

Solution

There are two options for installing the Enterprise Manager Cloud Control agents on your Exadata servers:

- Using the agent push method from the Enterprise Manager Cloud Control UI
- Using the Exadata Agent Kit

In this recipe, we will present the steps required when using the Exadata Agent Kit method. The steps in this recipe assume you already have an Enterprise Manager Cloud Control environment installed. If not, you can follow instructions in the Exadata Agent Kit README.txt to set up a stand-alone Cloud Control environment or install an Enterprise Manager Cloud Control environment; either way, you will need a functional 12c Cloud Control environment prior to using the Exadata Agent Kit to install agents.

The Exadata Agent Kit is provided via an Oracle patch, and you can find the latest version of this patch by referring to My Oracle Support Note 1440951.1. After reading MOS note 1440951.1, download the latest version of the patch.

After you have downloaded the patch, stage the Agent Kit patch to /tmp/emkit directory on your first compute node, unzip it, and extract the contents using these commands:

```
[oracle@cm01dbm01 stg]$ cd emkit
[oracle@cm01dbm01 emkit]$ unzip ./p13551607_121010_Linux-x86-64.zip
Archive:  ./p13551607_121010_Linux-x86-64.zip
 extracting: CloudControl_Agent_12.1.0.1.1_LINUX.X64.tar.Z
  inflating: README.txt
```

```
[oracle@cm01dbm01 emkit]$  tar xBvpf CloudControl_Agent_12.1.0.1.1_LINUX.X64.tar.Z
common/
common/sshSetup.sh
... Output omitted
```

Next, gather Cloud Control OMS details from your Enterprise Manager 12c Cloud Control information. The important pieces of information to gather are your OMS host name, HTTPS upload port, and your admin password:

```
[oracle@emcc bin]$ ./emctl status oms -details
Oracle Enterprise Manager Cloud Control 12c Release 12.1.0.1.0
Copyright (c) 1996, 2012 Oracle Corporation.  All rights reserved.
Enter Enterprise Manager Root (SYSMAN) Password :
Console Server Host : emcc.centroid.com
HTTP Console Port   : 7790
HTTPS Console Port  : 7803
HTTP Upload Port    : 4890
```
HTTPS Upload Port   : 4904
```
OMS is not configured with SLB or virtual hostname
Agent Upload is locked.
OMS Console is locked.
Active CA ID: 1
Console URL: https://emcc.centroid.com:7803/em
Upload URL: https://emcc.centroid.com:4904/empbs/upload
WLS Domain Information
Domain Name        : GCDomain
```
Admin Server Host: emcc.centroid.com
```
Managed Server Information
Managed Server Instance Name: EMGC_OMS1
Managed Server Instance Host: emcc.centroid.com
[oracle@emcc bin]$
```

Using information from your Enterprise Manager Cloud Control OMS environment, adjust and/or configure parameter settings in the /opt/oracle.SupportTools/onecommand/em.param file. The DB Configurator would have created this file during installation, but if you installed your Exadata prior to version 112, the em.param file may be missing on your system. If so, you can either re-run the configurator or manually create your em.param file. An example em.param file will look like the following:

EM_VERSION=1.0
OMS_LOCATION=emcc
EM_BASE=/u01/app/oracle/product/agent12c
OMS_HOST=emcc.centroid.com
OMS_PORT=4904
EM_USER=oracle
EM_PASSWORD=<password>
```
EM_CELLS=(cm01cel01 cm01cel02 cm01cel03)
EM_COMPUTE_ILOM_NAME=(cm01dbm01-ilom cm01dbm02-ilom)
EM_COMPUTE_ILOM_IP=(172.16.1.15 172.16.1.16)
machinemodel="X2-2 Quarter rack"
swikvmname=cm01sw-kvm
swikvmip=172.16.1.20
swiib2name=cm01sw-ib2
swiib2ip=172.16.1.23
```

```
swiib3name=cm01sw-ib3
swiib3ip=172.16.1.24
pduaname=cm01-pdua
pduaip=172.16.1.25
pdubname=cm01-pdub
pdubip=172.16.1.26
```

Once you've validated or created your em.param file, log in to the compute node as root, change directories to /tmp/emkit, and run the following command:

```
# (sh setupem.sh | tee /tmp/setupag.log) 3>&1 1>&2 2>&3 | tee /tmp/setupag.err
```

When the setupem.sh script runs, it will ask whether you wish to establish and exchange SSH keys between your compute node and the other nodes in your database machine; we typically recommend that you configure SSH keys to allow for a smooth installation.

Assuming your em.param file is correct and you have node connectivity available, the setupem.sh script will deploy Enterprise Manager 12c Cloud Control agents on your nodes. When the installation is complete, the /tmp/setupag.log file should resemble the following:

```
[INFO] - Enterprise Manager Base location '/u01/app/oracle/product/agent12c' found in
/opt/oracle.SupportTools/onecommand/em.param, will be used
[INFO] - /u01/app/oracle/product/agent12c exist..skipping creating it
[INFO] - Changing permission on /u01/app/oracle/product/agent12c
[INFO] - AGENT_HOME=/u01/app/oracle/product/agent12c/core/12.1.0.1.0
[INFO] - Checking free space on ' /u01/app/oracle/product/agent12c '...........
<< output omitted >>
[INFO] - Searching for ILOM IPS information by key EM_COMPUTE_ILOM_IP from
/opt/oracle.SupportTools/onecommand/em.param
[INFO] - Do you want this kit to setup the SSH connectivity among the nodes? Note: If you choose
'yes' this script will setup the new SSH connectivity and cleanup the same at the end of the
installation and choose 'no' if you already have SSH connectivity among the nodes and this
script will not remove any SSH connectivity at the end of the installation. (yes/no)
[INFO] - Chose to setup and remove root ssh setup.
[INFO] - Setting up SSH for root
[INFO] - Running command sh sshSetup.sh -user root -advanced -hostfile all_hosts -confirm
-noPromptPassphrase
The output of this script is also logged into /tmp/sshUserSetup_2012-08-24-01-39-30.log
Hosts are cm01dbm01 cm01dbm02 cm01cel01 cm01cel02 cm01cel03
user is root
Platform:- Linux
Checking if the remote hosts are reachable
PING cm01dbm01.centroid.com (172.16.1.10) 56(84) bytes of data.
64 bytes from cm01dbm01.centroid.com (172.16.1.10): icmp_seq=1 ttl=64 time=0.017 ms
<< output omitted >>
======================================
cm01dbm01
cm01dbm02
[INFO] - Exadata Storage Nodes are:
[INFO] - ======================================
cm01cel01
cm01cel02
cm01cel03
```

```
[INFO] - Expected time for agent setup on 2 nodes is 10 mins
[INFO] - Setting write permission on cm01dbm01 for /u01/app/oracle/product/agent12c
[INFO] - Setting write permission on cm01dbm02 for /u01/app/oracle/product/agent12c
[INFO] - ==========================Setup EM/Agent start=======================
[INFO] - User has selected to setup Enterprise Manager Agent
[INFO] - Using Enterprise Manager user as oracle
[INFO] - Proceeding with additional agent setup on local node
[INFO] - Creating Exadata Machine provisioning directory on local node: /opt/oracle.SupportTools/emkit
[INFO] - Contents will be copied to the local folders /opt/oracle.SupportTools/emkit and /opt/oracle.SupportTools/onecommand
[INFO] - Finished copying common and exadata directories to /opt/oracle.SupportTools/emkit
[INFO] - /opt/oracle.SupportTools/emkit/archives does not exist, proceeding to create
[INFO] - Copying files from /tmp/emkit/archives, this could take a while
[INFO] - Copy completed. Cleaning /tmp/emkit/archives ...
[INFO] - EM software owner OS username: oracle
[INFO] - EM agent install zip file to be used: /opt/oracle.SupportTools/emkit/archives/12.1.0.1.0_AgentCore_226.zip
Enter Management Agent Registration Password :
Confirm password:
[INFO] - Agent home root directory: /u01 existing, skipping create...
[INFO] - Initializing stage location: /u01/app/oracle/product/agent12c/tmp/stage
[INFO] - Staging Additional agent install kit zip file: /opt/oracle.SupportTools/emkit/archives/12.1.0.1.0_AgentCore_226.zip to location: /u01/app/oracle/product/agent12c/tmp/stage. This could take a while
[INFO] - Stage area: /u01/app/oracle/product/agent12c/tmp/stage has been prepared for Additional agent install
[INFO] - Response file: /tmp/additional_agent.response has been initialized
[INFO] - Central inventory pointer exists.
... Output omitted
```

Upon successful installation of your agents, you should be able to check the status by logging in as the agent owner (as specified in em.param):

```
[oracle@cm01dbm01 ~]$ cd /u01/app/oracle/product/agent12c/core/12.1.0.1.0/bin
[oracle@cm01dbm01 bin]$ ./emctl status agent
Oracle Enterprise Manager 12c Cloud Control 12.1.0.1.0
Copyright (c) 1996, 2011 Oracle Corporation.  All rights reserved.
---------------------------------------------------------------
Agent Version          : 12.1.0.1.0
OMS Version            : 12.1.0.1.0
Protocol Version       : 12.1.0.1.0
Agent Home             : /u01/app/oracle/product/agent12c/agent_inst
Agent Binaries         : /u01/app/oracle/product/agent12c/core/12.1.0.1.0
Agent Process ID       : 20715
Parent Process ID      : 20615
Agent URL              : https://cm01dbm01.centroid.com:1830/emd/main/
Repository URL         : https://emcc.centroid.com:4904/empbs/upload
Started at             : 2012-08-24 01:48:17
Started by user        : oracle
Last Reload            : (none)
Last successful upload                       : 2012-08-24 11:33:20
Last attempted upload                        : 2012-08-24 11:33:20
```

```
Total Megabytes of XML files uploaded so far : 10.37
Number of XML files pending upload           : 0
Size of XML files pending upload(MB)         : 0
Available disk space on upload filesystem    : 39.89%
Collection Status                            : Collections enabled
Last attempted heartbeat to OMS              : 2012-08-24 11:35:50
Last successful heartbeat to OMS             : 2012-08-24 11:35:50

---------------------------------------------------------------
Agent is Running and Ready
[oracle@cm01dbm01 bin]$
```

At this point, you will need to log in to your Enterprise Manager 12c Cloud Control web interface and perform Exadata Discovery. Navigate to Setup RA Add Target RA Add Targets Manually as displayed in Figure 20-1.

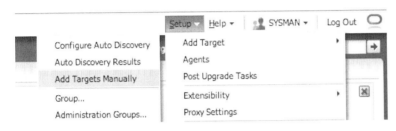

Figure 20-1. Adding Exadata targets manually from Cloud Control

Next, choose to add non-host targets using the guided discovery process as shown in Figure 20-2.

Add Targets Manually
- Add Host Targets
- ● Add Non-Host Targets Using Guided Process (Also Adds Related Targets)
- Add Non-Host Targets by Specifying Target Monitoring Properties

Target Types: Oracle Exadata Database Machine

[Add Using Guided Discovery ...]

Figure 20-2. Adding non-host targets using guided discovery

Then, choose to discover a new database machine and its components as shown in Figure 20-3.

Oracle Exadata Database Machine Discovery

This process allows you to add the hardware components (such as Oracle Exadata Storage Servers, Exadata Database Machine as managed targets. Compute Nodes should have been added as host ta discovery process. Please select one of the following tasks:
- ● Discover a new Database Machine and its hardware components as targets
- Discover newly added hardware components in an existing Database Machine as targets

[Cancel] [Discover Targets]

Figure 20-3. Discover a new database machine and its components

CHAPTER 20 ■ POST-INSTALLATION MONITORING TASKS

Next, select the Grid Control agent on the first compute node as depicted in Figures 20-4 and 20-5.

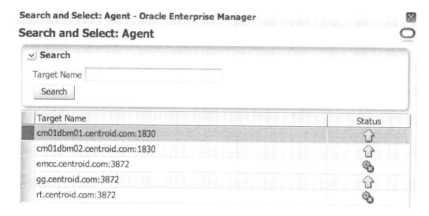

Figure 20-4. Select the agent on the first compute node

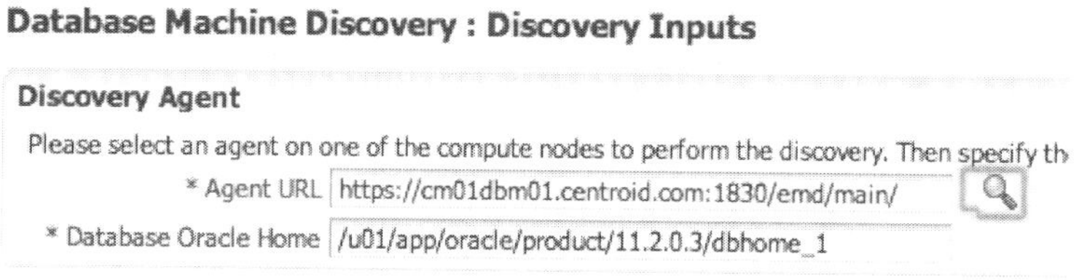

Figure 20-5. Select the agent and database home

Once the discovery process starts, it may fail during InfiniBand discovery; if so, ensure that the nm2user password is correct and set under the discovery credentials as depicted in Figure 20-6.

Figure 20-6. InfiniBand Discovery

After clicking Next in the discovery wizard, you should see a list of the components in your database machine (Figure 20-7).

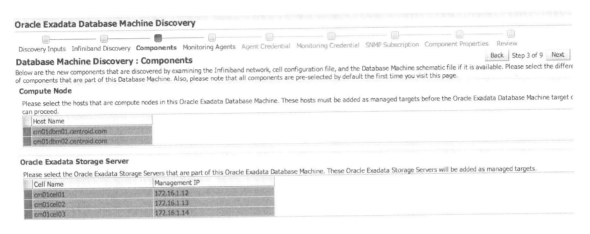

Figure 20-7. Discovery components

The next screen will show the agents used for each of the database machine components. (See Figure 20-8.)

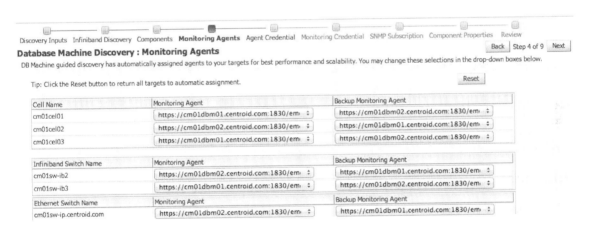

Figure 20-8. Monitoring agents

Next, enter or confirm your agent host credentials as displayed in Figure 20-9.

CHAPTER 20 ■ POST-INSTALLATION MONITORING TASKS

Figure 20-9. Agent host credentials

Enter or confirm the monitoring credentials. (See Figure 20-10.)

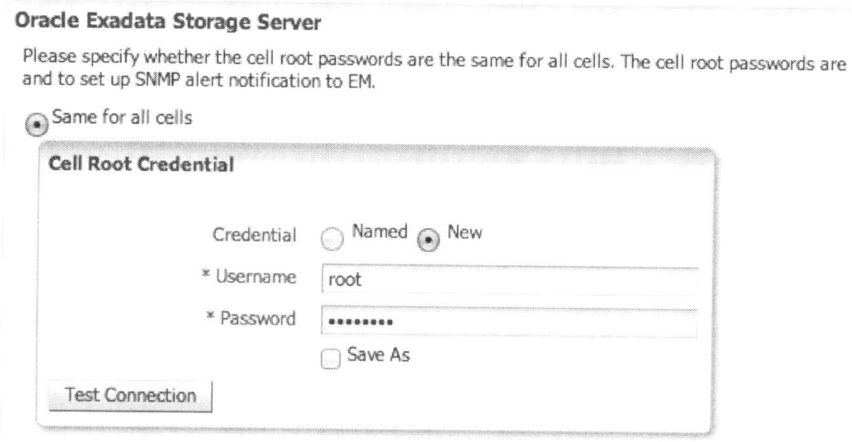

Figure 20-10. Monitoring credentials

If you choose, you can enable SNMP subscriptions to your Exadata nodes as displayed in Figure 20-11.

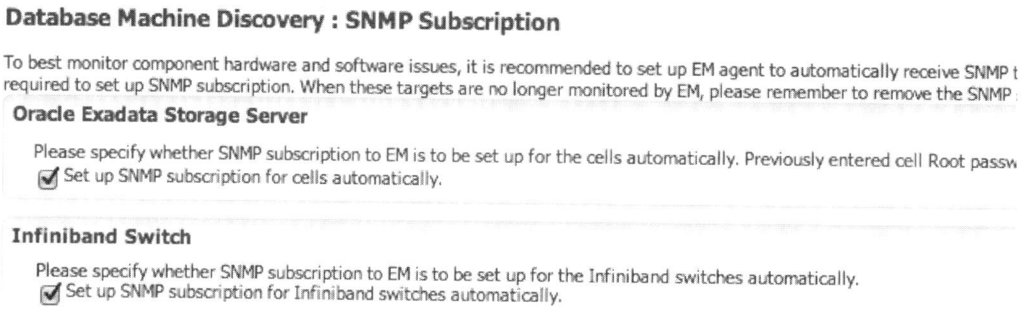

Figure 20-11. SNMP subscription

586

Figure 20-12 shows the next discovery screen, which displays your component properties. Check the values and if they look right, click Next.

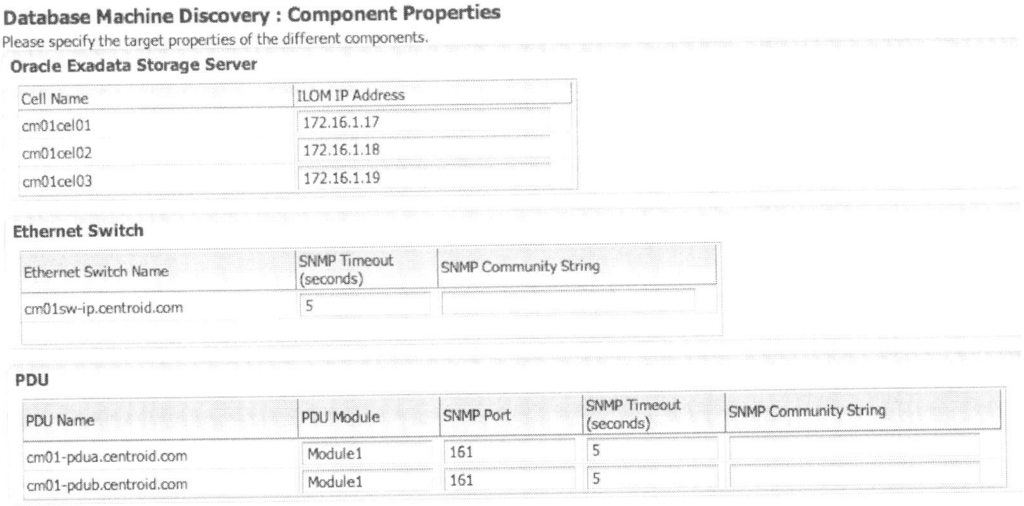

Database Machine Discovery : Component Properties

Please specify the target properties of the different components.

Oracle Exadata Storage Server

Cell Name	ILOM IP Address
cm01cel01	172.16.1.17
cm01cel02	172.16.1.18
cm01cel03	172.16.1.19

Ethernet Switch

Ethernet Switch Name	SNMP Timeout (seconds)	SNMP Community String
cm01sw-ip.centroid.com	5	

PDU

PDU Name	PDU Module	SNMP Port	SNMP Timeout (seconds)	SNMP Community String
cm01-pdua.centroid.com	Module1	161	5	
cm01-pdub.centroid.com	Module1	161	5	

Figure 20-12. Component properties

The final discovery wizard screen will summarize your machine configuration, as displayed in Figure 20-13. If everything looks right, click Confirm.

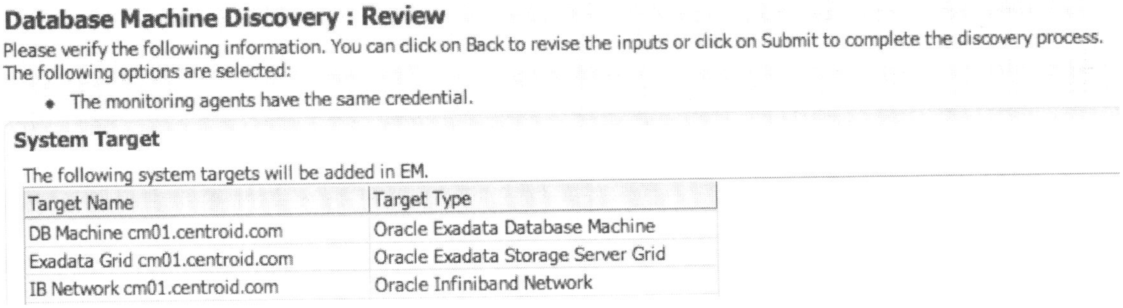

Database Machine Discovery : Review

Please verify the following information. You can click on Back to revise the inputs or click on Submit to complete the discovery process. The following options are selected:

- The monitoring agents have the same credential.

System Target

The following system targets will be added in EM.

Target Name	Target Type
DB Machine cm01.centroid.com	Oracle Exadata Database Machine
Exadata Grid cm01.centroid.com	Oracle Exadata Storage Server Grid
IB Network cm01.centroid.com	Oracle Infiniband Network

Figure 20-13. Discovery review

At this point, Enterprise Manager Cloud Control will discover your Exadata Database Machine and add the necessary targets to the repository. When complete, you should see your Exadata Database Machine targets registered as depicted in Figure 20-14.

Figure 20-14. Exadata EM targets

After your Exadata targets have been added, you can optionally add Grid Infrastructure and Cluster targets to your Cloud Control environment. Navigate to Setup RA Add Targets RA Add Targets Manually and choose to add Oracle Cluster and High Availability Service non-host targets as depicted in Figure 20-15.

Figure 20-15. Add Oracle Cluster and high availability service

Enter the host name of your first compute node on your Exadata Database Machine. (See Figure 20-16.)

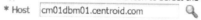

Figure 20-16. Add Cluster target host

The discovery wizard will find the cluster name, Grid Infrastructure home, SCAN name and port, and ONS port as shown in Figure 20-17.

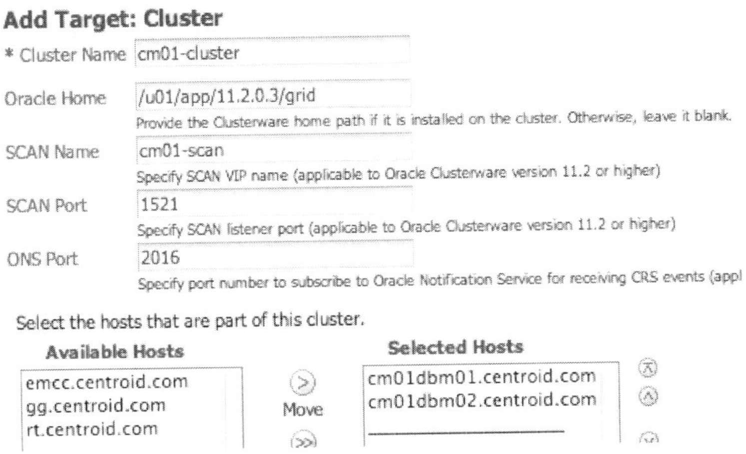

CHAPTER 20 ■ POST-INSTALLATION MONITORING TASKS

Figure 20-17. Add target: Cluster

After submitting the cluster targets, you can add your Oracle RAC services. Navigate to Setup [RA] Add Targets [RA] Add Targets Manually, choose to add non-host targets using the guided discovery process, and select Oracle Database, Listener, and ASM services (Figure 20-18).

Figure 20-18. Adding Oracle RAC services

Choose the host name of your first compute node server as shown in Figure 20-19.

Add Database Instance Target: Specify Host
In order to add targets to be monitored by Enterprise Manager, you must first specify the
Type the host name or click the icon to select the host.
* Host cm01dbm01.centroid.com
☑ TIP If the host you specify is a member of a cluster target,
the process will allow you to add cluster database
targets on the cluster.

Figure 20-19. Specify host

After selecting your host, you will be promoted to specify your source. Choose to add all hosts in the cluster. (See Figure 20-20.)

589

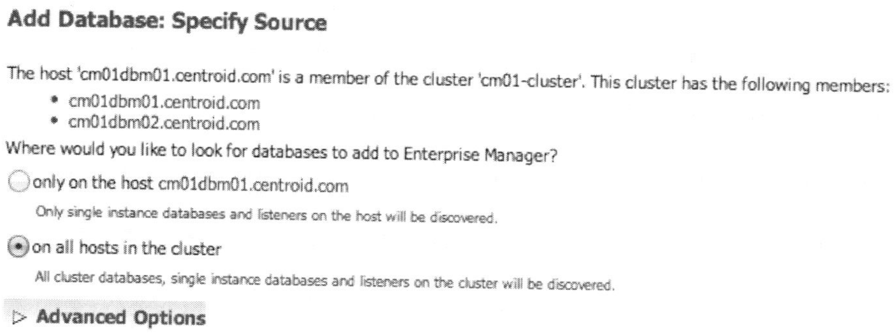

CHAPTER 20 ■ POST-INSTALLATION MONITORING TASKS

Add Database: Specify Source

The host 'cm01dbm01.centroid.com' is a member of the cluster 'cm01-cluster'. This cluster has the following members:

- cm01dbm01.centroid.com
- cm01dbm02.centroid.com

Where would you like to look for databases to add to Enterprise Manager?

○ only on the host cm01dbm01.centroid.com

  Only single instance databases and listeners on the host will be discovered.

◉ on all hosts in the cluster

  All cluster databases, single instance databases and listeners on the cluster will be discovered.

▷ **Advanced Options**

Figure 20-20. *Adding all hosts in the Oracle RAC cluster*

When the guided discovery process completes, your Oracle database, listener, and Oracle ASM targets should be discovered. You should click the Configure button to configure credentials and validate the configuration for each component discovered as displayed in Figure 20-21.

Figure 20-21. *Cluster targets*

When the entire process is complete, you should see your Exadata Database Machine targets discovered and available in Enterprise Manager Cloud Control. Figure 20-22 shows your Exadata schematic.

CHAPTER 20 ■ POST-INSTALLATION MONITORING TASKS

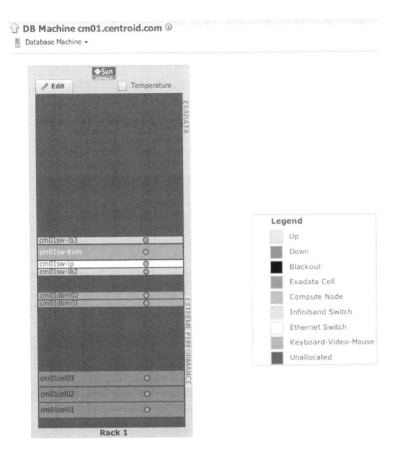

Figure 20-22. *Exadata Database Machine schematic*

Per the Exadata Agent Kit README.txt file, you can optionally install the Exadata Database Machine dashboard. We will skip this step in this recipe; consult the README.txt file for details.

How It Works

Oracle Enterprise Manager Cloud Control is Oracle's complete, cloud-enabled Oracle enterprise management and monitoring software suite designed to provide a comprehensive Oracle systems monitoring solution. Oracle delivers a comprehensive and robust set of monitoring and management capabilities with Enterprise Manager Cloud Control, and while it is not mandatory for an Exadata DMA to monitor their Exadata environments with EM Cloud Control 12c, it is generally considered an operational best practice based on Oracle's comprehensive, Exadata-specific management framework design.

Oracle provides a robust mechanism called the Exadata Agent Kit that allows you to install and configure Cloud Control agents on your Exadata Database Machine. In summary, the process works as follows:

1. Install and validate Oracle Enterprise Manager 12c Cloud Control.

2. Download and unzip the Exadata Agent Kit.

3. Modify and validate the /opt/oracle.SupportTools/onecommand/em.param configuration file.

4. Run the `setupem.sh script` on the first compute node to install Cloud Control agents.

5. Add Oracle Grid Infrastructure targets to EM Cloud Control.

6. Add Oracle RAC targets to EM Cloud Control.

7. Optionally install the Exadata dashboard report.

Note If you wish to install Oracle Enterprise Manager Grid Control agents for a previous version of Enterprise Manager, see MOS note 1308449.1.

20-2. Configuring Enterprise Manager 12c Cloud Control Plug-ins for Exadata

Problem

You wish to install Enterprise Manager 12c Cloud Control plug-ins for Exadata to monitor your Exadata Database Machine components.

Solution

If you have an Enterprise Manager 12c Cloud Control environment, follow the instructions outlined in Recipe 20-1. If you have a pre EM 12c Grid Control environment, please refer to MOS note 1308449.1.

How It Works

Exadata monitoring plug-ins are installed when you use the Exadata Agent Kit for Enterprise Manager 12c Cloud Control. At the time of this writing, MOS note 144095.1 provides information about the Exadata Agent Kit.

On earlier versions of Enterprise Manager, such as Oracle Enterprise Manager Grid Control, Exadata storage cells, InfiniBand switches, and other non-compute node resources will be managed and monitored using Grid Control plug-ins. As stated in the solution of this recipe, My Oracle Support note 1308449.1 is your best reference for installing Exadata plug-ins for previous releases of Enterprise Manager.

20-3. Configuring Automated Service Requests

Problem

You wish to configure Automated Service Requests, or ASRs, on your Exadata Database Machine to enable for automatic Oracle Service Request submission in the event of Exadata hardware faults.

Solution

In this recipe, you will learn how to configure ASRs for your Exadata Database Machine. First, log in to My Oracle Support as the administrator of your Exadata hardware Customer Support Identifier (CSI) and identify your hardware and assets. Figure 20-23 displays where to find this information.

CHAPTER 20 ■ POST-INSTALLATION MONITORING TASKS

Figure 20-23. Exadata hardware assets

Next, you need to identify a server to use as your ASR server. This server should to be outside your Exadata rack; in other words, you should not use one of the Exadata servers, as this choice would defeat the purpose of monitoring in the event the node you installed the ASR server were down. At the time of this writing, the ASR server is supported on either Linux or Solaris. If you choose to install the ASR server on Oracle Linux as we demonstrate in this recipe, it needs to be on Oracle Enterprise Linux 5.5 or higher:

```
[root@ovmsrv01 ~]# uname -a
Linux ovmsrv01.centroid.com 2.6.32-100.26.2.el5 #1 SMP Tue Jan 18 20:11:49 EST 2011 x86_64
    x86_64 x86_64 GNU/Linux
[root@ovmsrv01 ~]# cat /etc./oracle-release
Oracle Linux Server release 5.6
[root@ovmsrv01 ~]#
```

Now read My Oracle Support note 1185493.1 to obtain the latest Auto Service Request and Oracle Automated Service Manager (OASM) patches and download the ASR Manager patch. Figure 20-24 shows that at the time of this writing this patch was provided via 12809941.

Figure 20-24. ASR Manager Patch 1.3.1

593

Next, download the latest Auto Service Request patch as referenced from MOS note 1185493.1, which at the time of this writing and as shown in Figure 20-25 is ASR 3.9, patch 14042885.

Figure 20-25. *ASR Patch 3.9*

After downloading and unzipping the patch, log in to your ASR server and confirm that /opt/SUNWswasr/bin is in your path. Run asr register as root:

```
[root@ovmsrv01 ~]# asr register

1) transport.oracle.com
Select destination transport server or enter full URL for alternate server [1]:

If a proxy server is required for HTTPS communication to the internet,
enter the information below.  If no proxy is needed, enter -
Proxy server name []:

An Oracle Single Sign On (OSSO) account is required for data submission.
If you do not have an account or have forgotten your username or
password, visit http://support.oracle.com
Username [john.clarke@centroid.com]:
Password:
Password again (to verify):

Please wait.  Restarting Oracle Automated Service Manager with new settings.
Contacting transport servers. Please wait...
Registration complete.
Successfully submitted ASR Registration Request.
[root@ovmsrv01 ~]#
```

When complete, you can show your ASR registration status and validate your connection:

```
[root@ovmsrv01 ~]# asr show_reg_status
Registered with ASR backend.
[root@ovmsrv01 ~]# asr test_connection
```

```
Connecting to endpoint @ https://transport.oracle.com/v1/queue/sasm-ping
Sending ping message.
Ping message sent.
test_transport completed successfully.
[root@ovmsrv01 ~]#
```

Next, log in to a compute node as root and run the following command to add ASR SNMP traps for the compute nodes:

```
[root@cm01dbm01 ~]# dcli -g ./dbs_group  -l root \
> "/opt/oracle.cellos/compmon/exadata_mon_hw_asr.pl -set_snmp_subscribers \
> \"(type=asr, host=ovmsrv01.centroid.com, fromip=11.11.1.113, port=162, community=public)\"
cm01dbm01: Try to add ASR destination Host - ovmsrv01.centroid.com IP - 11.11.1.113 Port - 162
    Community - public From IP - 11.11.1.113
cm01dbm02: Try to add ASR destination Host - ovmsrv01.centroid.com IP - 11.11.1.113 Port - 162
    Community - public From IP - 11.11.1.113
[root@cm01dbm01 ~]#
```

After this, add the SNMP traps for your storage server nodes and validate:

```
[oracle@cm01dbm01 ~]$ dcli -g ./cell_group  "cellcli -e alter cell \
snmpSubscriber=\(\(host=\'ovmsrv01.centroid.com\', port=162,community=public, type=ASR\)\)"
cm01cel01: Cell cm01cel01 successfully altered
cm01cel02: Cell cm01cel02 successfully altered
cm01cel03: Cell cm01cel03 successfully altered
[oracle@cm01dbm01 ~]$
[oracle@cm01dbm01 ~]$ dcli -g ./cell_group  cellcli -e list cell attributes name, snmpSubscriber
cm01cel01: cm01cel01    ((host=ovmsrv01.centroid.com,port=162,community=public,type=ASR))
cm01cel02: cm01cel02    ((host=ovmsrv01.centroid.com,port=162,community=public,type=ASR))
cm01cel03: cm01cel03    ((host=ovmsrv01.centroid.com,port=162,community=public,type=ASR))
[oracle@cm01dbm01 ~]$
```

From the ASR server, validate your assets:

```
[root@ovmsrv01 ~]# asr list_asset

IP_ADDRESS    HOST_NAME         SERIAL_NUMBER   ASR       PROTOCOL   SOURCE   PRODUCT_NAME
------------  ----------------  --------------  --------  ---------  -------  ------------------------
172.16.1.18   cm01cel02-ilom    1104FMM0LG      Enabled   SNMP       ILOM     SUN FIRE X4270 M2 SERVER
172.16.1.19   cm01cel03-ilom    1104FMM0M2      Enabled   SNMP       ILOM     SUN FIRE X4270 M2 SERVER
172.16.1.17   cm01cel01-ilom    1104FMM0MG      Enabled   SNMP       ILOM     SUN FIRE X4270 M2 SERVER
172.16.1.15   cm01dbm01-ilom    1105FMM025      Enabled   SNMP       ILOM     SUN FIRE X4170 M2 SERVER
172.16.1.16   cm01dbm02-ilom    1105FMM02N      Enabled   SNMP       ILOM     SUN FIRE X4170 M2 SERVER
[root@ovmsrv01 ~]#
```

Once this is complete, you'll need to activate non-ILOM assets using asr activate_exadata. The example below is for a single compute node; you'll need to perform this on each of your nodes:

```
[root@ovmsrv01 ~]# asr activate_exadata -i 172.16.1.10 -h cm01dbm01 -n cm01dbm01-ilom
Succesfully submitted activation for the asset
Host Name: cm01dbm01
```

```
IP Address: 172.16.1.10
Serial Number: 1105FMM025
The email-address associated with the registration id for this asset's ASR Manager will receive
an e-mail highlighting the asset activation status and any additional instructions for
completing activaton.
Please use My Oracle Support https://support.oracle.com to complete the activation process.
The Oracle Auto Service Request documentation can be accessed on http://oracle.com/asr
```

When complete, log on to My Oracle Support to approve your ASR activations. See Figure 20-26.

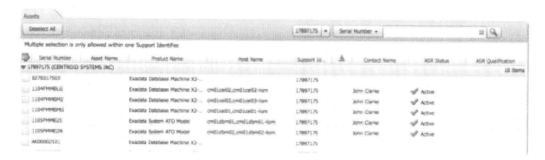

Figure 20-26. *Approve ASR activations*

After approving, list your assets from the ASR server:

```
[root@ovmsrv01 ~]# asr list_asset

IP_ADDRESS      HOST_NAME        SERIAL_NUMBER   ASR       PROTOCOL   SOURCE            PRODUCT_NAME
-----------     -------------    -------------   -------   --------   --------------    --------------
172.16.1.18     cm01cel02-ilom   1104FMM0LG      Enabled   SNMP       ILOM              SUN FIRE X4270 M2
172.16.1.19     cm01cel03-ilom   1104FMM0M2      Enabled   SNMP       ILOM              SUN FIRE X4270 M2
172.16.1.17     cm01cel01-ilom   1104FMM0MG      Enabled   SNMP       ILOM              SUN FIRE X4270 M2
172.16.1.15     cm01dbm01-ilom   1105FMM025      Enabled   SNMP       ILOM              SUN FIRE X4170 M2
172.16.1.16     cm01dbm02-ilom   1105FMM02N      Enabled   SNMP       ILOM              SUN FIRE X4170 M2
172.16.1.13     cm01cel02        1104FMM0LG      Enabled   SNMP,HTTP  EXADATA-SW,ADR    SUN FIRE X4170 M2
172.16.1.14     cm01cel03        1104FMM0M2      Enabled   SNMP,HTTP  EXADATA-SW,ADR    SUN FIRE X4170 M2
172.16.1.12     cm01cel01        1104FMM0MG      Enabled   SNMP,HTTP  EXADATA-SW,ADR    SUN FIRE X4170 M2
172.16.1.10     cm01dbm01        1105FMM025      Enabled   SNMP,HTTP  EXADATA-SW,ADR    SUN FIRE X4170 M2
172.16.1.11     cm01dbm02        1105FMM02N      Enabled   SNMP,HTTP  EXADATA-SW,ADR    SUN FIRE X4170 M2

Please use My Oracle Support 'http://support.oracle.com' to view the activation status.

[root@ovmsrv01 ~]#
```

Next, validate your ASR SNMP traps on both the compute nodes and storage servers:

```
[oracle@cm01dbm01 ~]$ dcli -g ./dbs_group  -l root  -n \
> "/opt/oracle.cellos/compmon/exadata_mon_hw_asr.pl –validate_snmp_subcriber -type asr"
OK: ['cm01dbm01', 'cm01dbm02']
[oracle@cm01dbm01 ~]$
[oracle@cm01dbm01 ~]$ dcli -g ./cell_group "cellcli –e alter cell validate snmp type=asr"
cm01cel01: Cell cm01cel01 successfully altered
cm01cel02: Cell cm01cel02 successfully altered
cm01cel03: Cell cm01cel03 successfully altered
[oracle@cm01dbm01 ~]$
```

After confirming SNMP traps, you will receive an e-mail confirmation to the administrator of your customer support identifier (CSI) as displayed in Figure 20-27.

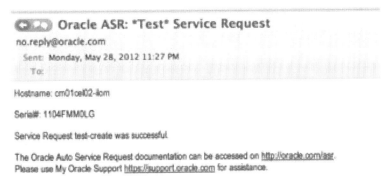

Figure 20-27. *ASR e-mail confirmation*

How It Works

Oracle's ASR functionality is designed to provide a framework to automatically raise Oracle Service Requests (SR) in the event of failure. MOS note 1402646.1 provides information about Oracle's ASR functionality, as well as your Exadata Owner's Guide. You can also refer to MOS note 1450112.1 for information on Oracle's ASREXACHECK utility, which is designed to test your ASR configuration, and MOS note 1110675.1 to learn more about Oracle Database Machine Monitoring.

Once you set up ASR functionality for your Exadata, all hardware and other configured faults will be raised and Oracle SRs will be automatically created and dispatched to an appropriate Oracle support engineer. After the point that the SR is created, the normal support processes will be followed.

On the storage and compute nodes, Exadata uses a Baseboard Management Controller, or BMC, to control and sense components in the server. On the storage servers, the BMC raises IPMI (*Intelligent Platform Management Interface*, integrated ILOM interface) alerts to the alert repository stored in the system area. Both compute and storage cells can be configured to send SNMP traps to an ASR server based on events raised by the BMC, which we have discussed in the Solution section of this recipe. For example, you can check your current sensor information using ipmitool on either the compute or storage servers:

```
[root@cm01dbm01 ~]# ipmitool sdr|grep -v ok
    1e |HOST_ERR        | disabled      | ns
    26 |PCIE0/F20/UP    | disabled      | ns
    28 |PCIE1/F20/UP    | disabled      | ns
    2a |PCIE2/F20/UP    | disabled      | ns
[root@cm01dbm01 ~]#
```

You can confirm your bmcType on the storage servers by running the dcli command below. This should display IPMI for the bmcType:

```
[oracle@cm01dbm01 ~]$ dcli -g ./cell_group cellcli -e list cell \
> attributes name, status, bmcType
cm01cel01: cm01cel01     online   IPMI
cm01cel02: cm01cel02     online   IPMI
cm01cel03: cm01cel03     online   IPMI
[oracle@cm01dbm01 ~]$
```

Note At the time of this writing, Oracle provides Platinum Services Support, which includes setting up Oracle ASR functionality. Please refer to www.oracle.com/us/products/database/exadata-support-ds-071121.pdf for additional details.

CHAPTER 21

Post-Install Database Tasks

In this chapter, we will demonstrate optional post-installation Exadata database tasks that can be performed by the Exadata Database Machine administrator to exploit Exadata functionality, ready the database machine for use, or enable additional administrator activities.

One thing you'll notice about the recipes in this chapter is that they are not specific to Oracle Exadata; they entail administrative tasks that you could perform on non-Exadata Oracle environments as well, depending on your Oracle software version. The reason we include this chapter is because these tasks are often performed on Exadata Database Machines to maximize performance, leverage Exadata hardware and software functionality, and enable your system to meet your business needs.

21-1. Creating a New Oracle RAC Database on Exadata

Problem

You have installed your Exadata Database Machine and wish to build an Oracle RAC database on your compute servers.

Solution

Creating a new Oracle RAC database on Exadata can be done using the Database Configuration Assistant (dbca) or manually via scripts. We recommend using dbca because of its ease of use and its ability to use the Exadata Database Machine template created during your Exadata installation.

Since most Oracle DBAs and Exadata DMAs are familiar with using dbca, we will not cover the Database Configuration Assistant in detail but will instead outline a set of recommendations for creating databases using dbca on Exadata:

- If you wish to create an Oracle RAC database, make sure that you have selected the desired nodes in your compute grid. It is common to select all compute nodes, but this is not a requirement.

- If you have an Enterprise Manager 12c Cloud Control environment installed in your organization, we typically elect *not* to configure new databases with Enterprise Manager with dbca. Rather, we prefer discovering our cluster database using the EM 12c Cloud Control web interface as described in Recipe 20-1.

- For the database storage type, you must select Automated Storage Management (ASM). Choose the appropriate ASM disk group for your database file locations.

- If you wish to configure a Fast Recovery Area or archiving, we recommend using the RECO ASM disk group.

- The dbm template will seed memory settings, character sets, and other options; you can choose to modify these when running dbca based on your database's requirements.

Note If you are unfamiliar with the Database Configuration Assistant, please refer to the Oracle documentation at http://docs.oracle.com/cd/E11882_01/server.112/e25494/create002.htm#ADMIN12479.

When the Database Configuration Assistant completes, you will have an Oracle RAC cluster registered with your cluster registry and all instances on all nodes should be up. Validate this using srvctl as oracle:

```
[oracle@cm01dbm01 ~]$ srvctl status database -d visx
Instance visx1 is running on node cm01dbm01
Instance visx2 is running on node cm01dbm02
[oracle@cm01dbm01 ~]$
```

After you've confirmed your database is available and healthy, depending on the version of your DBM template, you may need to set or modify some of your database settings including cluster-related and recovery-specific database initialization parameters, temporary tablespace files and sizes, audit actions, and block change tracking. The code below demonstrates these activities. Connect to SQL*Plus as SYSDBA and execute the following code based on your needs and Exadata configuration:

```
SYS @ visx1> alter database enable block change tracking using file '+DATA_CM01';
Database altered.
SYS @ visx1> alter system set fast_start_mttr_target=300;
System altered.
SYS @ visx1> audit delete on aud$;
Audit succeeded.
SYS @ visx1> create temporary tablespace temp3 tempfile '+RECO_CM01' size 50m;
Tablespace created.
SYS @ visx1> alter database default temporary tablespace temp3;
Database altered.
SYS @ visx1> drop tablespace temp1 ;
Tablespace dropped.
SYS @ visx1> drop tablespace temp2 ;
Tablespace dropped.
SYS @ visx1> create temporary tablespace temp1 tempfile '+RECO_CM01' size 32767M autoextend on;
Tablespace created.
SYS @ visx1> create temporary tablespace temp2 tempfile '+RECO_CM01' size 32767M autoextend on;
Tablespace created.
SYS @ visx1> alter database default temporary tablespace temp1;
Database altered.
SYS @ visx1> drop tablespace temp3;
Tablespace dropped.
SYS @ visx1> alter system set cluster_interconnects='192.168.10.1' scope=spfile sid='visx1';
System altered.
```

```
SYS @ visx1> alter system set cluster_interconnects='192.168.10.2' scope=spfile sid='visx2';
System altered.
SYS @ visx1> alter tablespace temp1 add tempfile '+RECO_CM01' size 32767M;
Tablespace altered.
SYS @ visx1>
```

How It Works

On Exadata, Oracle RAC databases are created using the Database Configuration Assistant the same way that they are on non-Exadata 11gR2 environments—if you've used dbca in the past, you will find no surprises when running it on Exadata.

There are a few items that you'll need to keep in mind when creating RAC databases on Exadata:

- Make sure you select all of the RAC nodes that you want your Oracle RAC instances to run on. If unsure, you can always add RAC instances at a later date, but we generally recommend to err on the high side and use all available compute node servers, shutting down instances or deploying RAC services appropriately at a later date if necessary.

- Use the Database Machine template to eliminate configuration missteps and to provide consistency.

- Select the appropriate Oracle ASM disk groups for both data files and recovery structures.

- When complete, set your `cluster_interconnects` initialization parameter using the InfiniBand address, make sure your temporary tablespaces are properly sized, and so forth.

21-2. Setting Up a DBFS File System on Exadata

Problem

You wish to implement an Oracle Database File System on Exadata for external files.

Solution

A typical Oracle Exadata installation is built with an interesting set of storage cell grid disks and ASM disk groups prefixed with DBFS. By default, these will be used to store your Oracle Cluster Registry and voting disks, but you can also use these to create an Oracle Database File System (DBFS).

■ **Note** On Exadata you can use any available ASM disk groups for DBFS storage, but in the example below we'll use the DBFS_DG ASM disk group.

1. Log in to your database or Oracle ASM instance and determine the space available for your target ASM disk group by running the script in Listing 21-1:

   Listing 21-1. lst21-01-dbfsspace.sql

   ```
   SQL> select name,total_mb,free_mb
   from v$asm_diskgroup
   where name='DBFS_DG'
   /
   ```

CHAPTER 21 ■ POST-INSTALL DATABASE TASKS

```
NAME                              TOTAL_MB    FREE_MB
------------------------------    --------    --------
DBFS_DG                             894720      892200

SQL>
```

Knowing that in our case we're using ASM normal redundancy, we've got approximately 435 GB of free space to use in this ASM disk group for DBFS storage.

2. Create a BIGFILE tablespace in this ASM disk group for your DBFS storage. In Listing 21-2, we're specifying a size of 100 GB:

Listing 21-2. lst21-02-dbfs-createtbs.sql

```
SQL> create bigfile tablespace dbfs_tbs
  2   datafile '+DBFS_DG' size 100g
  3  /

Tablespace created.

SQL>
```

3. Next, create a database user. In the example in Listing 21-3, we'll call it DBFS:

Listing 21-3. lst21-03-dbfs-creatuser.sql

```
SQL> create user dbfs identified by dbfs
quota unlimited on dbfs_tbs
/
User created.
SQL>
SQL> grant create session, create table, create procedure,
dbfs_role to dbfs
/
Grant succeeded.
SQL>
```

4. You now need to perform some operating system tasks as root, as listed below. You should run these commands on each compute node on which an instance for your database is running:

```
[root@cm01dbm01 ~]# usermod -a -G fuse oracle
[root@cm01dbm01 ~]# echo "user_allow_other" > /etc/fuse.conf
[root@cm01dbm01 ~]# chmod 644 /etc/fuse.conf
[root@cm01dbm01 ~]# mkdir /data_dbfs
[root@cm01dbm01 ~]# chown oracle:dba /data_dbfs
[root@cm01dbm01 ~]#
```

■ **Note** The FUSE Linux package is required to mount DBFS file systems on your Exadata Compute Nodes. This package should be installed by default on your compute servers.

CHAPTER 21 ■ POST-INSTALL DATABASE TASKS

5. Log in to SQL*Plus as your DBFS user and create your DBFS data store using
    $ORACLE_HOME/rdbms/admin/dbfs_create_filesystem.sql as is displayed in Listing 21-4:

    Listing 21-4. lst21-04-dbfs-createstore.sql

    ```
    SQL> conn dbfs/dbfs
    Connected.
    SQL> @$ORACLE_HOME/rdbms/admin/dbfs_create_filesystem.sql DBFS_TBS DATA_DBFS
    ... Script comments omitted
    No errors.
    --------
    CREATE STORE:
    begin dbms_dbfs_sfs.createFilesystem(store_name => 'FS_DATA_DBFS', tbl_name =>
    'T_DATA_DBFS', tbl_tbs => 'DBFS_TBS', lob_tbs => 'DBFS_TBS', do_partition =>
    false, partition_key => 1, do_compress => false, compression => '', do_dedup =>
    false, do_encrypt => false); end;
    --------
    REGISTER STORE:
    begin dbms_dbfs_content.registerStore(store_name=> 'FS_DATA_DBFS', provider_name
    => 'sample1', provider_package => 'dbms_dbfs_sfs'); end;
    --------
    MOUNT STORE:
    begin dbms_dbfs_content.mountStore(store_name=>'FS_DATA_DBFS',
    store_mount=>'DATA_DBFS'); end;
    --------
    CHMOD STORE:
    declare m integer; begin m := dbms_fuse.fs_chmod('/DATA_DBFS', 16895); end;
    No errors.
    SQL>
    ```

6. When this DBFS data store is created using the script above, it will create the file
    system with compression disabled, de-duplication disabled, encryption disabled, and
    partitioning disabled. You can change any of these settings by using $ORACLE_HOME/rdbms/
    admin/dbfs_create_filesystem_advanced.sql. Listing 21-5 shows an example of this:

    Listing 21-5. lst21-05-dbfs-createstore-adv.sql

    ```
    SQL> conn dbfs/dbfs
    Connected.
    SQL> @$ORACLE_HOME/rdbms/admin/dbfs_create_filesystem_advanced.sql DBFS_TBS DATA_DBFS
    nocompress nodeduplicate noencrypt non-partition
    << comments omitted >>
    No errors.
    --------
    CREATE STORE:
    begin dbms_dbfs_sfs.createFilesystem(store_name => 'FS_DATA_DBFS', tbl_name =>
    'T_DATA_DBFS', tbl_tbs => 'DBFS_TBS', lob_tbs => 'DBFS_TBS', do_partition =>
    false, partition_key => 1, do_compress => false, compression => '', do_dedup =>
    false, do_encrypt => false); end;
    --------
    ```

```
REGISTER STORE:
begin dbms_dbfs_content.registerStore(store_name=> 'FS_DATA_DBFS', provider_name
=> 'sample1', provider_package => 'dbms_dbfs_sfs'); end;
--------
MOUNT STORE:
begin dbms_dbfs_content.mountStore(store_name=>'FS_DATA_DBFS',
store_mount=>'DATA_DBFS'); end;
--------
CHMOD STORE:
declare m integer; begin m := dbms_fuse.fs_chmod('/DATA_DBFS', 16895); end;
No errors.
SQL>
```

7. Once your DBFS data store (file system) is created, you need to mount it. The first thing you should need to do is create a text file containing the DBFS password. Below, we've created this password file in /home/oracle/dbfs/passwd.txt on both nodes of our Quarter Rack:

Note This password file is only required when mounting the DBFS file system. Once it is mounted, you do not need the password file.

```
[oracle@cm01dbm01 ~]$ echo "dbfs" > /home/oracle/dbfs/passwd.txt
[oracle@cm01dbm01 ~]$ scp /home/oracle/dbfs/passwd.txt oracle@cm01dbm02:/home/oracle/dbfs
passwd.txt
100%    5     0.0KB/s    00:00
[oracle@cm01dbm01 ~]$
```

8. Next, mount your DBFS file system on each node using the command below:

```
[oracle@cm01dbm01 ~]$ nohup $ORACLE_HOME/bin/dbfs_client dbfs@visx \
> -o allow_other,direct_io /data_dbfs < /home/oracle/dbfs/passwd.txt &
[1] 8060
[oracle@cm01dbm01 ~]$ nohup: appending output to 'nohup.out'

[oracle@cm01dbm01 ~]$ ls /data_dbfs
DATA_DBFS
[oracle@cm01dbm01 ~]$
```

9. Once mounted, list the contents of your file system directory and validate from each compute node:

```
[oracle@cm01dbm01 ~]$ ls /data_dbfs
DATA_DBFS
[oracle@cm01dbm01 ~]$
```

10. After the file system is created and mounted, you're going to need to complete a few more tasks so that you can use it:

   a. Create an Oracle directory pointing to the DBFS file system mount point

   b. Grant permissions on the directory to whatever Oracle user needs to access it

c. Specify quotas as necessary for the Oracle schemas that will need to store data on the DBFS file system

d. Create external tables and specify an appropriate degree of parallelism for segments using this DBFS data store as appropriate

Listing 21-6 will show how to create an Oracle directory on this DBFS file system and grant permissions so that an APPS schema can access the directory with unlimited quotas:

Listing 21-6. lst21-06-dbfs-dir-perm.sql

```
SQL> create directory dbfs_dir
    as '/data_dbfs/DATA_DBFS'
/
Directory created.
SQL> grant all on directory dbfs_dir to apps
/
Grant succeeded.
SQL> alter user apps quota unlimited on dbfs_tbs
/
User altered.
SQL>
```

How It Works

Oracle's Database File System on Exadata functions as it does on non-Exadata 11gR2 Oracle installations. With Oracle Exadata, use of DBFS is widely recognized as a very fast mechanism to load data into your database from external files, and as such, is used in many Oracle migrations to Exadata DBFS for performance reasons.

At its core, DBFS uses storage defined inside the database and externalizes this to operating system file systems. Its roots are with Oracle iFS (Internet File System), but its functionality and capabilities have been extended with Oracle 11gR2. Some of the reasons why DBFS can be an excellent fit in your Exadata environment include the following:

- Operations against DBFS files can be parallelized using parallel query for optimal performance.
- A data load strategy involving external tables on DBFS file systems, with parallel operations, typically yields the fastest way to bulk load data into your database.
- When you store files in DBFS, they can participate in the same RMAN backup strategy and deployment as the rest of your database files.
- DBFS file systems can reside in ASM disks, so you can get the performance and availability features of ASM within your DBFS file system.
- DBFS file systems can be mounted using a number of performance, security, and storage features including compression, de-duplication, encryption, and partitioning. The encryption configuration on DBFS provides the framework for Oracle Secure Files.

■ **Note** To learn more about Oracle DBFS file system mount options, please consult the Oracle 11gR2 Secure Files and Large Objects production documentation at http://docs.oracle.com/cd/E14072_01/appdev.112/e10645/adlob_client.htm. To learn more about Oracle Secure Files and DBFS, please refer to http://www.oracle.com/technetwork/database/features/secure-files/dbfs-benchmark-367122.pdf.

21-3. Configuring HugePages on Exadata

Problem

You wish to configure HugePages on your Oracle Exadata databases to provide a larger page size, eliminate potential for swapping, relieve TLB (Translation Lookaside Buffer) pressure, decrease page table overhead, eliminate page table lookup, and provide faster overall memory performance.

Solution

In this recipe, we will provide an example for configuring HugePages on an Exadata Quarter Rack with three active databases on it. The steps below can be reproduced on any Exadata configuration and with any number of databases.

1. First, configure the memlock setting to unlimited for the Oracle database and Grid Infrastructure (ASM) owner on each compute node. In the example listing below, we have multiple oracle software owners, each with unlimited memlock settings:

   ```
   [root@cm01dbm01 ~]# grep memlock /etc/security/limits.conf
   #         - memlock - max locked-in-memory address space (KB)
   oracle    soft    memlock    unlimited
   oracle    hard    memlock    unlimited
   grid      soft    memlock    unlimited
   grid      hard    memlock    unlimited
   oraprod,  soft memlock unlimited
   oraprod,  hard memlock unlimited
   oratest,  soft memlock unlimited
   oratest,  hard memlock unlimited
   oradev soft memlock unlimited
   oradev hard memlock unlimited
   [root@cm01dbm01 ~]#
   ```

2. Next, log in to your compute nodes as each software owner and validate the memlock settings using ulimit -l:

   ```
   [root@cm01dbm01 ~]# su - oracle
   The Oracle base has been set to /u01/app/oracle
   [oracle@cm01dbm01 ~]$ ulimit -l
   unlimited
   [oracle@cm01dbm01 ~]$
   ```

3. For each database on your machine on which you wish to configure HugePages, disable Automatic Memory Management (AMM) by setting memory_target and max_memory_target to 0:

   ```
   SYS @ visx1> show parameter memory

   NAME                                 TYPE          VALUE
   ------------------------------------ ------------  -------
   hi_shared_memory_address             integer       0
   memory_max_target                    big integer   0
   memory_target                        big integer   0
   shared_memory_address                integer       0
   SYS @ visx1>
   ```

CHAPTER 21 ■ POST-INSTALL DATABASE TASKS

■ **Note** Oracle AMM and `HugePages` are incompatible. Please refer to MOS note 361323.1 for details.

4. Determine your HugePages kernel parameter setting, vm.nr_hugepages, to the appropriate value for your environment. The appropriate value can be determined by running hugepages_settings.sh, which you can download from MOS note 40179.1. Ensure you have all of your databases up when running this command to provide the most accurate setting:

    ```
    [root@cm01dbm01 ~]# ./hugepages_settings.sh

    This script is provided by Doc ID 401749.1 from My Oracle Support
    (http://support.oracle.com) where it is intended to compute values for
    the recommended HugePages/HugeTLB configuration for the current shared
    memory segments. Before proceeding with the execution please make sure
    that:
     * Oracle Database instance(s) are up and running
     * Oracle Database 11g Automatic Memory Management (AMM) is not setup
       (See Doc ID 749851.1)
     * The shared memory segments can be listed by command:
         # ipcs -m

    Press Enter to proceed...

    Recommended setting: vm.nr_hugepages = 25226
    [root@cm01dbm01 ~]#
    ```

5. For the case in the preceding example, the script is recommending a value of 25226 for our vm.nr_hugepages kernel parameter. Check your current setting on each compute node by running the `sysctl` command:

    ```
    [root@cm01dbm01 ~]# sysctl -a|grep huge
    vm.hugetlb_shm_group = 0
    vm.nr_hugepages = 16388
    [root@cm01dbm01 ~]#
    ```

    As you can see from this output, on this Exadata Compute Node we had at some point configured a smaller HugePages setting than what is currently recommended.

6. Once you've confirmed the value for vm.nr_hugepages, change your kernel parameter accordingly. We recommend editing /etc/sysctl.conf and running `sysctl -p` to maintain consistency across reboots:

    ```
    [root@cm01dbm01 ~]# grep nr_hugepages /etc/sysctl.conf
    # bug 8268393 remove vm.nr_hugepages = 2048
    vm.nr_hugepages = 25226
    [root@cm01dbm01 ~]# sysctl -p
    << output omitted >>
    vm.nr_hugepages = 25226
    << output omitted >>
    [root@cm01dbm01 ~]# sysctl -a|grep huge
    ```

607

```
vm.hugetlb_shm_group = 0
vm.nr_hugepages = 25226
[root@cm01dbm01 ~]#
```

7. When complete, set or validate the database initialization parameter use_large_pages. The default is TRUE on Oracle 11gR2, which will suffice in most cases. Here are your options and what they mean:

   - use_large_pages = TRUE will attempt to use HugePages if configured by the operating system;
   - use_large_pages = FALSE indicates to not use HugePages;
   - use_large_pages = ONLY means to not start the instance if your HugePages setting is too small to fit the entire memory footprint of the instance;
   - use_large_pages = AUTO is an 11.2.0.3 feature that will dynamically adjust your operating system HugePages setting based on the instance you're starting. It will not make changes to /etc/sysctl.conf but rather dynamically adjust as instances are started.

■ **Note** Since the compute nodes in an Oracle Exadata Database Machine run on 64-bit Oracle Linux, it is not necessary to set the use_indirect_data_buffers initialization parameter. This is a common misconception that is discussed in MOS note 361312.1.

8. After validation, you will need to shut down your databases and Oracle CRS on each node. After your instances are stopped, check your free HugePages from /proc/meminfo:

```
[root@cm01dbm01 bin]# cat /proc/meminfo|grep Huge
HugePages_Total:   25226
HugePages_Free:    25226
HugePages_Rsvd:    0
Hugepagesize:      2048 kB
[root@cm01dbm01 bin]#
```

9. Next, restart your Oracle CRS resources and database instances using crsctl or srvctl. When complete, again validate /proc/meminfo. When comparing with the output above, after the restart you should see the number of reserved HugePages (HugePages_Rsvd) with a non-zero number:

```
[root@cm01dbm01 ~]# cat /proc/meminfo|grep Huge
HugePages_Total: 25226
HugePages_Free:  19122
HugePages_Rsvd:  19104
Hugepagesize:    2048 kB
[root@cm01dbm01 ~]#
```

10. Check your database instance alert log for information for `Large Pages Information`, as displayed in the next code:

> **Note** The `Large Pages Information` alert log messages are new in Oracle 11.2.0.3. Prior to 11.2.0.2, you will see `HugePages Information` sections in your alert log at startup.

```
****************** Large Pages Information *****************

Total Shared Global Region in Large Pages = 16 GB (100%)

Large Pages used by this instance: 8193 (16 GB)
Large Pages unused system wide = 16404 (32 GB) (alloc incr 32 MB)
Large Pages configured system wide = 25226 (49 GB)
Large Page size = 2048 KB
************************************************************
```

My Oracle Support note 1392497.1 provides a good description of how to correlate the information in the alert log with the /proc/meminfo HugePages output:

- `Large Pages configured system wide` should equal `HugePages_Total` from /proc/meminfo, which is the value you specified when you modified your kernel parameters above.
- `Large Pages used by this instance` = the number of pages locked now, plus pages reserved for future usage.
- `Large Pages unused system wide` = the number of available HugePages, which is `vm.nr_hugepages` minus any allocated or reserved pages at the time the instance started. If you compare each instance's alert log after the startup, you'll see different numbers for each instance, depending on which one was started first, second, third, and so on.
- HugePages reservation was introduced in Linux kernel 2.6.17 to postpone allocating all an instance's required pages at startup for performance reasons. On recent Exadata patch levels, you should have a kernel version that supports this.

How It Works

Using HugePages for Oracle databases running Linux is a way to improve memory management and performance that typically helps with OLTP workloads on databases with large memory requirements. For Oracle Exadata configurations running Oracle Linux, it is a means to increase the memory page size from 4 KB to 2 MB. Some of the benefits of using HugePages include the following:

- HugePages are not swappable, so there is no page-in/page-out overhead.
- Using HugePages relieves pressure on Translation Lookaside Buffer (TLB) functions. A TLB is a buffer on a processor that contains part of the system's page table, used to do virtual memory address translation. With HugePages, fewer translations will be required, TLB entries will cover a larger part of the overall address space, and fewer TLB misses will occur.
- With large page sizes, there is potentially much less page table overhead.
- Page table lookup overhead is reduced since HugePages pages are not subject for replacement.
- Since fewer pages are required with HugePages, bottlenecks for page table access are avoided.

All of these factors contribute to HugePages being able to improve overall performance. On Exadata, with 96 to 144 GB of physical memory and potentially large (or multiple large) SGAs, HugePages can provide a significant benefit over normal memory sharing or Oracle Automatic Memory Management (AMM) features.

21-4. Configuring Automatic Degree of Parallelism

Problem

You intend to use parallel execution features to maximize performance and optimize system resource utilization for the databases deployed on Exadata and you wish to optimize parallel operations by configuring Oracle 11gR2 Automatic Degree of Parallelism, or Auto DOP.

Solution

In this recipe, we will cover the basics for setting up Automatic Degree of Parallelism in your Oracle 11gR2 database.

1. Log in to your Oracle database and seed I/O calibration data, per MOS node 1269321.1. This step is required in order for Auto DOP to function:

    ```
    SYS @ visx1> delete from resource_io_calibrate$;

    1 row deleted.

    SYS @ visx1> insert into resource_io_calibrate$
      2  values(current_timestamp, current_timestamp, 0, 0, 200, 0, 0);

    1 row created.

    SYS @ visx1> commit;

    Commit complete.

    SYS @ visx1>
    ```

2. Set parallel_degree_policy to AUTO.

■ **Note** On Exadata, setting parallel_degree_policy enables parallel statement queuing as well as In-Memory Parallel Execution, the latter of which could yield negative side effects. Please read details in Recipes 21-6 and 21-7 or the discussion in the How It Works section of this recipe for more information.

```
SYS @ visx1> alter system set parallel_degree_policy=AUTO scope=both sid='*';
System altered.

SYS @ visx1> alter system flush shared_pool;
System altered.
SYS @ visx1>
```

3. Color your tables with a DEFAULT degree of parallelism using the logic below:

```
SYS @ visx1> select 'alter table '||owner||'.'||table_name||' parallel (degree default);'
  2  from dba_tables
  3  where owner='INV'
  4  /
alter table INV.MTL_TXNS_HISTORY parallel (degree default);
alter table INV.MTL_MATERIAL_TRANSACTIONS_HCC parallel (degree default);
alter table INV.MTL_LSP_ONHAND_BALANCE_TMP parallel (degree default);
alter table INV.MTL_CLIENT_PARAMETERS parallel (degree default);
... output omitted for brevity
SYS @ visx1> alter table INV.MTL_TXNS_HISTORY parallel (degree default);
Table altered.
SYS @ visx1> alter table INV.MTL_MATERIAL_TRANSACTIONS_HCC parallel (degree default);
Table altered.
SYS @ visx1> alter table INV.MTL_LSP_ONHAND_BALANCE_TMP parallel (degree default);
Table altered.
SYS @ visx1>
... output omitted for brevity
```

How It Works

Parallel query works the same on Exadata as it does on non-Exadata 11gR2. With Exadata, which you've cost-justified based on your database's performance requirements, business criticality, or some other reason, you want to get the most performance out of your investment, so exploiting the benefits of parallel query is important.

Some of the historical challenges with parallel query have included the following questions:

- How many parallel query slaves does my query need?
- How many concurrent parallel operations will saturate my system?
- How can I ensure that parallelism will scale up to the point of saturation but not exceed it?
- How can I ensure that my query will only run if it can establish a minimum amount of parallel query slaves?

Prior to 11gR2, finding this balance has been difficult. With 11gR2, Oracle has introduced Automatic Degree of Darallelism, or Auto DOP. Auto DOP automatically calculates the degree of parallelism on a per SQL statement basis and is implemented using the parallel_degree_policy initialization parameter. When parallel_degree_policy is set to AUTO, Oracle will automatically parallelize SQL statements that the optimizer estimates will take longer than parallel_min_time_pct_threshold seconds, which defaults to ten seconds. This is true regardless of how the table's parallel degree is configured.

Depending on which size rack you have, the Exadata X2-2 compute grid has 24 cores, 48 cores, or 96 CPU cores, and your storage grid has even more. When SQL statements are executed that qualify to be parallelized, Oracle will establish parallel query slaves based on the degree of parallelism capable, specified, or calculated. These parallel query slaves will "divide and conquer" the work (I/O), typically returning results faster.

■ **Note** The X2-8, X3-2, and X3-8 configurations have different numbers of processor cores than the Exadata X2-2 models. Please refer to Chapter 1 or Oracle's documentation for additional information.

In addition to determining the ideal degree of parallelism for a SQL statement, Auto DOP also introduces the concepts of parallel statement queuing and In-Memory Parallel Execution. Parallel statement queuing performs what the name suggests; it causes parallel query operations to be queued when the calculated DOP is higher than the maximum number of parallel processes in the system. Recipe 21-6 provides a deeper discussion on this topic.

In-Memory Parallel Execution is a feature that calculates the working set size of a parallel operation and determines if it will fit in the aggregate Oracle database buffer cache. If so, blocks requested via parallel query will be read into the buffer cache and not satisfied via direct read mechanisms. With potentially large buffer cache sizes, on Exadata this could lead to fewer parallel direct reads and by consequence, prevent Smart Scan and cell offload features. To combat this, you could do the following:

- Set parallel_degree_policy=LIMITED, which will enable Auto DOP to determine the right number of parallel query processes but disable In-Memory Parallel Execution and parallel statement queuing

- Set "_parallel_statement_queuing"=TRUE, which will enable parallel statement queuing

```
SYS @ visx1> alter system set parallel_degree_policy=LIMITED scope=both sid='*';
System altered.
SYS @ visx1> alter system set "_parallel_statement_queuing"=TRUE scope=both sid='*';
System altered.
SYS @ visx1>
```

With an approach like this, you can achieve the best of both worlds with Auto DOP and Exadata.

21-5. Setting I/O Calibration on Exadata
Problem

You wish to use Auto DOP on Exadata and you are required to perform I/O calibration in order for Auto DOP functionality to work.

Solution

In this recipe, we will demonstrate how to identify when I/O calibration is required and how to implement I/O calibration.

First, log in to your Exadata 11gR2 database and configure Automatic Degree of Parallelism:

```
SYS @ dwprd1> alter system set parallel_degree_policy=LIMITED scope=both sid='*';
System altered.
SYS @ dwprd1> alter system set "_parallel_statement_queuing"=TRUE scope=both sid='*';
System altered.
SYS @ dwprd1>
```

Next, color a table or tables with the default degree of parallelism to enable Auto DOP functionality to work:

```
SYS @ dwprd1> alter table myfact.my_fact_detail
  2  parallel (degree default);
Table altered.
SYS @ dwprd1>
```

Then run a full table scan query against your target table with autotrace enabled:

```
SYS @ dwprd1> set autotrace on
SYS @ dwprd1> select count(*) from myfact.my_fact_detail;

  COUNT(*)
----------
1.1098E+10
1 row selected.
Execution Plan
... Execution plan details omitted
Note
-----
   - automatic DOP: skipped because of IO calibrate statistics are missing
```

Under the Note section of the execution plan details, you will see a message indicating that Auto DOP operations are skipped due to I/O calibration statistics missing. To resolve this, you will need to calibrate I/O using the dbms_resource_manager.calibrate_io procedure, as displayed in Listing 21-7:

Listing 21-7. lst21-07-io-calibrate.sql

```
SQL> delete from resource_io_calibrate$;
1 row deleted.
SQL> insert into resource_io_calibrate$
    values(current_timestamp, current_timestamp, 0, 0, 200, 0, 0);
1 row created.
SQL> commit;
Commit complete.
SQL>
```

To confirm that the above operation properly seeded I/O calibration statistics, run the same SQL statement above that performs a full table scan and confirm that Auto DOP is functioning as expected:

```
SYS @ dwprd1> set autotrace on
SYS @ dwprd1> select count(*) from usagefact.search_fact_detail;
  COUNT(*)
----------
1.1098E+10
Execution Plan
... Execution plan details omitted
Note
-----
   - automatic DOP: Computed Degree of Parallelism is 96 because of degree limit
```

As you can see above, with I/O calibration statistics seeded, Auto DOP functionality is able to properly estimate and assign an appropriate degree of parallelism for your query.

How It Works

Auto DOP requires I/O calibration statistics to be present in your database. In 11gR2, this is typically achieved by executing the following DBMS_RESOURCE_MANAGER.CALIBRATE_IO procedure as documented in Oracle's documentation at http://docs.oracle.com/cd/E11882_01/appdev.112/e10577/d_resmgr.htm and in Listing 21-8:

Listing 21-8. lst21-08-io-calibrate-drm.sql

```
SQL> set serveroutput on
declare
 lat  integer;
 iops integer;
 mbps integer;
begin
 dbms_resource_manager.calibrate_io(&&num_disks,10,iops,mbps,lat);
 dbms_output.put_line('Max IOPs = '||iops);
 dbms_output.put_line('Latency  = '||lat);
 dbms_output.put_line('Max MBPS = '||iops);
end;
/
```

In the above script, you would enter the number of disks on your Exadata Storage Servers (36 for a Quarter Rack, 84 for a Half Rack, and 168 for a Full Rack) and a desired I/O latency, which in the script above is set to 10 milliseconds When complete, the resource_io_calibrate$ table is populated with the values calculated by the procedure.

The odd thing about this procedure is the 10-millisecond latency input parameter; after all, how would you know what your maximum disk latency truly is, other than trusting published benchmarks? The answer is that you cannot know this, especially considering potential variations with different workloads. This fact renders dbms_resource_manager.calibrate_io relatively useless, but Auto DOP still requires for I/O calibration to be performed.

Luckily, the only column in resource_io_calibrate$ that Auto DOP requires is max_pmbps. As such, simply inserting a value of 200 into this column and restarting your database will enable Auto DOP to properly and automatically parallelize your queries.

> **Note** You may wonder where the number 200 comes from; this is the number that Oracle uses internally to test Auto DOP on Exadata and is referenced in My Oracle Support Note 1297112.1.

21-6. Measuring Impact of Auto DOP and Parallel Statement Queuing

Problem

You have implemented Auto DOP on your Exadata databases and wish to measure the impact of parallel statement queuing on your database.

Solution

In this recipe, we will show you how to implement Auto DOP with parallel statement queuing and demonstrate how to measure the impact of parallel statement queuing. Specifically, we will present a test case with multiple parallel-enabled, full-scan operations running concurrently, use SQL monitoring to measure the impact of parallel statement queuing, and compare the test case execution times with and without Auto DOP and parallel statement queuing.

First, we will construct a test case that runs a full scan against a table with over 27 billion rows and a parallel degree of DEFAULT:

```
SQL> select degree,num_rows from dba_tables
where owner='D14' and table_name='DWB_RTL_SLS_RETRN_LINE_ITEM';

DEGREE                        NUM_ROWS
------------------            ----------------
    DEFAULT                   27,193,740,703
SQL>
```

For this test, we will start with Auto DOP disabled and our `parallel_degree_limit` initialization parameter set to CPU, which on an Exadata Quarter Rack means that our parallel degree limit will be capped at 96. The test performed was executed using the following shell script and the lst21-09-autodoptest.sql script in Listing 21-9:

```
#!/bin/sh
for i in 1 2 3 4 5
do
nohup sqlplus d14/d14 @lst21-09-autodoptest.sql $i &
done
```

Listing 21-9. lst21-08-autodoptest.sql

```
set serveroutput on size 20000
variable n number
exec :n := dbms_utility.get_time;
spool autodop_&1..lst
select /* queue test 0 */ count(*) from DWB_RTL_SLS_RETRN_LINE_ITEM;
begin
   dbms_output.put_line
   ( (round((dbms_utility.get_time - :n)/100,2)) || ' seconds' );
end;
/
spool off
exit
```

While executing five concurrent executions of our SQL statement, a SQL monitor report will be shown, as depicted in Figure 21-1.

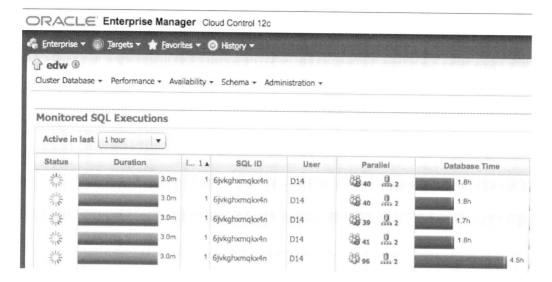

Figure 21-1. SQL monitoring without parallel statement queuing

The SQL monitor screen in Figure 21-1 shows us the following information:

- Each of the five executions of the SQL statement is actively running and not queued.

- The bottom-most session is running with 96 parallel query slaves and without any parallel degree downgrade.

- The first four queries were all downgraded by Oracle; in other words, Oracle determined that there were not enough system-wide parallel query slaves available and adjusted the degree of parallelism accordingly, and then it executed the SQL statements with this lower degree of parallelism.

- The total number of parallel query slaves is 256, which is computed based on (parallel_max_servers)*(parallel_server_instances). On an Exadata Quarter Rack, parallel_max_servers is set to 128 by default.

With the sql_id listed in Figure 21-1, use the script in Listing 21-10 to display the statement's database time per session_state and/or event from Oracle's Active Session History (ASH). The script shows that the queries spent the bulk of their time on cell smart table scan wait events, indicating Exadata Smart Scan was being utilized. Note that there is no indication of parallel statement queuing:

Listing 21-10. lst21-10-ash-bysqlid.sql

```
SQL> select sql_id,evt,count(*) dbt from
    (select sql_id,sample_id,sample_time,session_state,
    decode(session_state,'ON CPU','CPU + CPU Wait',event) evt
    from gv$active_session_history
    where sql_id = '&&sql_id'
    and sample_time > sysdate-&&mins_ago/1440)
    group by sql_id,evt
    order by 3 desc
 /
Enter value for sql_id: 6jvkghxmqkx4n
```

sql_id	CPU or Event	Time (sec)
6jvkghxmqkx4n	cell smart table scan	165126.00
6jvkghxmqkx4n	CPU + CPU Wait	3104.00
6jvkghxmqkx4n	resmgr:cpu quantum	49.00
6jvkghxmqkx4n	DFS lock handle	48.00
6jvkghxmqkx4n	latch free	24.00
6jvkghxmqkx4n	os thread startup	11.00

During the test above, we captured the query completion times using dbms_utility.get_time and spooled the output to a series of text files. If we examine these files, we see the following query completion time ranged from 431 seconds to 873 seconds:

```
[oracle@cm01dbm01 autodop]$ grep seconds *lst
autodop_1.lst:873.03 seconds
autodop_2.lst:853.1 seconds
autodop_3.lst:790.17 seconds
autodop_4.lst:431.05 seconds
autodop_5.lst:863.5 seconds
[oracle@cm01dbm01 autodop]$
```

Now we will implement Auto DOP so we can compare results. To implement Auto DOP, set parallel_degree_policy to LIMITED and "_parallel_statement_queuing"=TRUE to enable both Auto DOP functionality and parallel statement queuing.

■ **Note** Setting parallel_degree_policy=AUTO will implement both of these features but also enable In-Memory Parallel Execution, another 11gR2 parallel query optimization. On Exadata, this feature can potentially disable Smart Scans by bypassing direct read algorithms and performing buffered reads. To learn more about In-Memory Parallel Execution on Exadata, please see Recipe 21-7.

```
SYS @ edw1> alter system set parallel_degree_policy=LIMITED scope=both sid='*';
System altered.
SYS @ edw1> alter system set "_parallel_statement_queuing"=TRUE scope=both sid='*';
System altered.
SYS @ edw1>
```

After launching the same test case as above, Figure 21-2 displays a SQL monitoring window during the test execution.

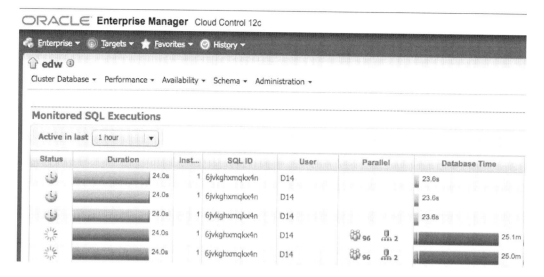

Figure 21-2. SQL monitoring with parallel statement queuing

The SQL monitor screen in Figure 21-2 shows us the following information:

- The left-most column in the top three SQL executions indicates that the parallel operations are being queued by Auto DOP, as indicated by the clock graphic.

- The bottom two SQL statement executions were each allocated 96 parallel query servers.

- None of the SQL executions suffered parallel server downgrade.

Using the script in Listing 21-11 to display the statement's database time per session_state and/or event from ASH, we still see that the queries spent the bulk of their time on cell smart table scan wait events, indicating Exadata Smart Scan was being utilized. In this case, however, we also see 1,372 seconds of database time spent waiting on the resmgr:pq queued wait event, an indication that parallel statement queuing was taking place.

Listing 21-11. lst21-11-ash-bysqlid.sql

```
SQL> select sql_id,evt,count(*) dbt from
    (select sql_id,sample_id,sample_time,session_state,
    decode(session_state,'ON CPU','CPU + CPU Wait',event) evt
    from gv$active_session_history
    where sql_id = '&&sql_id'
    and sample_time > sysdate-&&mins_ago/1440)
    group by sql_id,evt
    order by 3 desc
  /
Enter value for sql_id: 6jvkghxmqkx4n

sql_id              CPU or Event                    Time (sec)
---------------     ---------------------------     ----------
6jvkghxmqkx4n       cell smart table scan           143010.00
6jvkghxmqkx4n       CPU + CPU Wait                    3241.00
6jvkghxmqkx4n       resmgr:pq queued                  1372.00
6jvkghxmqkx4n       resmgr:cpu quantum                 145.00
```

6jvkghxmqkx4n	library cache: mutex X	18.00
6jvkghxmqkx4n	os thread startup	9.00
6jvkghxmqkx4n	DFS lock handle	6.00
6jvkghxmqkx4n	enq: XL - fault extent map	2.00
6jvkghxmqkx4n	PX Nsq: PQ load info query	2.00
6jvkghxmqkx4n	PX Deq: reap credit	1.00

If we examine the test times for the five executions, similar to the previous test without parallel statement queuing, we see that the lower-bound of SQL execution completion times was between 340 and 375 seconds; these were the first two SQL statements that operated with a non-downgraded 96 way degree of parallelism. The remaining three SQL statements took longer to complete due to being queued, but in comparison with the initial test case, the overall elapsed time was 22% less than without parallel statement queuing (2,973 seconds vs. 3,810 seconds):

```
[oracle@cm01dbm01 autodop]$ grep seconds *lst
autodop_1.lst:375.95 seconds
autodop_2.lst:659.27 seconds
autodop_3.lst:736.17 seconds
autodop_4.lst:862.5 seconds
autodop_5.lst:339.59 seconds
[oracle@cm01dbm01 autodop]$
```

This demonstrates that parallel statement queuing with Auto DOP can in some cases improve overall parallel query response times by ensuring that SQL statements do not start until they are guaranteed their ideal degree of parallelism.

How It Works

Understanding parallel query functionality with Auto DOP on Exadata is important for the Exadata DMA and Exadata performance engineer. While Auto DOP functionality is generic to Oracle 11gR2, it often plays a significant role on Exadata systems because many Exadata database workloads are characterized by large parallel full-scan SQL queries. Getting the most mileage from parallel query operations on Exadata is a crucial element to ensuring predictably fast query response time.

Parallel statement queuing was introduced with Auto DOP as a means to prevent parallel-enabled SQL statements from executing unless and until enough parallel query servers are available to satisfy the request. Parallel statement queuing will be enabled under the following conditions:

- When parallel_degree_policy = AUTO, or
- When parallel_degree_policy=LIMITED and "_parallel_statement_queuing"=TRUE, as demonstrated in the solution of this recipe

Under these conditions, when a SQL statement is issued, the following occurs:

- Oracle determines whether the statement qualifies for parallel execution based on its parallel degree setting (see dba_tables.degree).
- Oracle's Auto DOP algorithms calculate the degree of parallelism based on the table or table's block counts; the larger the segment, the higher the automatically calculated DOP.

- The per-SQL statement limit is calculated by the parallel_degree_limit initialization parameter. On Exadata, this typically is set to CPU, which means that the parallel degree limit is calculated based on the number of processors on the Exadata compute grid. In the examples above, we saw a parallel limit of 96; the formula that Oracle uses to set this parallel limit when parallel_degree_limit=CPU is calculated based on the query in Listing 21-12:

Listing 21-12. lst21-12-parallel-limit.sql

```
SQL> select decode(p1.value,'CPU',
            p2.value*p3.value*p4.value,
            p1.value) parallel_limit
    from v$parameter p1, v$parameter p2,
         v$parameter p3, v$parameter p4
    where p1.name='parallel_degree_limit'
    and p2.name='cpu_count'
    and p3.name='parallel_threads_per_cpu'
    and p4.name='parallel_server_instances'
/

Parallel Degree Limit
-----------------------
                    96
```

- If the requested parallel query degree exceeds the setting of parallel_servers_target *minus* the number of active parallel query servers, the statement is queued. On Exadata, parallel_servers_target is typically set to 128.
- If a SQL statement is queued with parallel statement queuing, it will post a wait on Oracle's resmgr:pq queued wait event and be queued until sufficient parallel query servers are available to meet the query's calculated degree of parallelism. Oracle then de-queues these SQL statements in the order in which they were queued.

To measure parallel statement queuing with Auto DOP, use SQL Monitoring to show your queuing behavior and look for resmgr:pq queued wait events from ASH, Oracle AWR, or other wait-interface-related dynamic performance views.

■ **Note** One item worth mentioning is the SQL hint NO_STATEMENT_QUEUING. With this hint, you can disable parallel statement queuing on a per-statement basis, if required, and allow un-hinted SQL statements to operate with parallel statement queuing.

21-7. Measuring Auto DOP and In-Memory Parallel Execution
Problem

You have enabled Auto DOP on Exadata and wish to measure the impact of In-Memory Parallel Execution, or In-Memory PX.

Solution

In this recipe, we will show you how to do the following tasks:

- Configure Auto DOP with In-Memory Parallel Execution enabled
- Identify SQL statements that take advantage of Auto DOP's In-Memory Parallel Query feature using data from Oracle AWR
- Compare query performance of In-Memory PX parallel queries vs. traditional parallel direct reads with Smart Scan
- Perform a simple test to measure the impact of In-Memory PX vs. Exadata Smart Scan with concurrent query executions

First, enable Auto DOP by setting parallel_degree_policy=AUTO:

```
SQL> alter system set parallel_degree_policy=AUTO scope=both sid='*';
System altered.
SQL>
```

Confirm that your database is ready for Auto DOP by checking your parallel query initialization parameters and I/O calibration status using the script in Listing 21-13:

Listing 21-13. lst21-13-autodop-check.sql

```
SQL> select name,value,decode(value,'AUTO','Auto DOP is enabled',
     'LIMITED','Auto DOP is implemented in limited fashion',
     'MANUAL','Auto DOP is not implemented') descr
   from v$parameter
   where name='parallel_degree_policy'
 /

Parameter                    Value           Notes
-----------------------      ------------    -------------------------
parallel_degree_policy       AUTO            Auto DOP is enabled

SQL>
SQL> select    a.ksppinm name, b.ksppstvl value
    from x$ksppi a, x$ksppsv b
    where a.indx = b.indx
    and a.ksppinm in ('_parallel_cluster_cache_pct','_parallel_cluster_cache_policy','_parallel_statement_queuing')
    order by 1,2
 /
Parameter                                Value
---------------------------------        ----------------
_parallel_cluster_cache_pct              80
_parallel_cluster_cache_policy           CACHED
_parallel_statement_queuing              TRUE
SQL>
```

The preceding output shows us that Auto DOP is enabled because parallel_degree_policy=AUTO and In-Memory PX are enabled because the underscore parameter _parallel_cluster_cache_policy is set to CACHED.

Note that the _parallel_cluster_cache_pct parameter determines the percentage of the aggregate buffer cache size that is reserved for In-Memory PX; if segments are larger than 80% the size of the aggregate buffer cache, by default, queries using these tables will not qualify for In-Memory PX.

Once you have enabled Auto DOP and confirmed that In-Memory PX is enabled, use Oracle AWR data to find SQL statements that executed with parallel query option and utilized In-Memory PX by running the script in Listing 21-14:

Listing 21-14. lst21-14-autodop-impx.sql

```
SQL> select    ss.sql_id,
          sum(ss.PX_SERVERS_EXECS_total) px_servers,
          decode(sum(ss.io_offload_elig_bytes_total),0,'No','Yes') offloadelig,
          decode(sum(ss.io_offload_elig_bytes_total),0,'Yes','No') impx,
          sum(ss.io_offload_elig_bytes_total)/1024/1024 offloadbytes,
          sum(ss.elapsed_time_total)/1000000/sum(ss.px_servers_execs_total) elps,
          dbms_lob.substr(st.sql_text,60,1) st
    from dba_hist_sqlstat ss, dba_hist_sqltext st
    where ss.px_servers_execs_total > 0
    and ss.sql_id=st.sql_id
    and upper(st.sql_text) like '%IN-MEMORY PX T1%'
    group by ss.sql_id,dbms_lob.substr(st.sql_text,60,1)
    order by 5
/

                PX Servers            In-Memory  IO Offload  Elps Sec
SQL ID          Per Exec   Offloaded  PX         MB          Per Exec  SQL
--------------  ---------  ---------  ---------  ----------  --------  ------------------------------
5ccq67fmtr7ud          4   No         Yes              .00     15.67   select /* in-memory px t1 */
                                                                       count(1) from RTL.R_DWB_RTL_TRX
2mg9wcry8cwn1          4   No         Yes              .00     16.23   select /* in-memory px t1 */
                                                                       count(1) from RTL.R_DWB_RTL_TN
4a9kcdqxdzvn1         50   Yes        No          101289.44    20.38   select /* in-memory px t1 */
                                                                       count(1) from D14.DWB_RTL_TRX
g0p8nhj3959hs         50   Yes        No          101530.05    21.07   select /* in-memory px t1 */
                                                                       count(1) from D14.DWB_RTL_TNDR_
8tsyw5tnxa521         74   Yes        No          143567.71    27.52   select /* in-memory px t1 */
                                                                       count(1) from RTL.R_DWB_RTL_SLS
6s2qvx403y097         96   Yes        No          903247.23   184.01   select /* in-memory px t1 */
                                                                       count(1) from D14.DWB_RTL_SLS_R

SQL>
```

In the output above, please note the following:

- We are retrieving SQL statistics from AWR for SQL statements that match a specific string, which we have limited based on knowledge of our workload;
- We have limited the output to include only cursors that used parallel execution;
- The second column displays the number of parallel query servers used for the cursor;
- The third column indicates whether the SQL statement was offloaded to the storage cell;
- The fourth column indicates whether the cursor was satisfied using In-Memory PX; if the number of parallel servers is greater than zero but the bytes eligible for predicate offload is zero, it's a good indication that In-Memory PX was in use.

To compare this In-Memory PX behavior with In-Memory PX disabled, set parallel_degree_policy=LIMITED. Below we will show this, along with setting "_parallel_statement_queuing"=TRUE to enable parallel statement queuing as discussed in Recipe 21-6. The rationale for setting these parameters is to allow Auto DOP to still estimate the proper DOP for your queries, continue to implement queuing, and only remove the In-Memory PX functionality:

```
SQL> alter system set parallel_degree_policy=LIMITED scope=both sid='*';
System altered.
SQL> alter system set "_parallel_statement_queuing"=TRUE scope=both sid='*';
System altered.
SQL>
```

After bouncing your database, you will see that _parallel_cluster_cache_policy is set to ADAPTIVE, which indicates that In-Memory PX is disabled:

```
SQL> select    a.ksppinm name, b.ksppstvl value
    from x$ksppi a, x$ksppsv b
    where a.indx = b.indx
    and a.ksppinm in ('_parallel_cluster_cache_pct','_parallel_cluster_cache_policy','_parallel_statement_queuing')
    order by 1,2
  /

Parameter                               Value
-----------------------------------     --------------------
_parallel_cluster_cache_pct             80
_parallel_cluster_cache_policy          ADAPTIVE
_parallel_statement_queuing             TRUE
```

Next, run a sample workload with In-Memory PX disabled and run the script in Listing 21-15 to measure the results:

Listing 21-15. lst21-15-autodop-impx.sql

```
SQL> select    ss.sql_id,
            sum(ss.PX_SERVERS_EXECS_total) px_servers,
            decode(sum(ss.io_offload_elig_bytes_total),0,'No','Yes') offloadelig,
            decode(sum(ss.io_offload_elig_bytes_total),0,'Yes','No') impx,
            sum(ss.io_offload_elig_bytes_total)/1024/1024 offloadbytes,
            sum(ss.elapsed_time_total)/1000000/sum(ss.px_servers_execs_total) elps,
            dbms_lob.substr(st.sql_text,60,1) st
    from dba_hist_sqlstat ss, dba_hist_sqltext st
    where ss.px_servers_execs_total > 0
    and ss.sql_id=st.sql_id
    and upper(st.sql_text) like '%IN-MEMORY PX T1%'
    group by ss.sql_id,dbms_lob.substr(st.sql_text,60,1)
    order by 5
/
              PX Servers            In-Memory   IO Offload  Elps Sec
SQL ID        Per Exec   Offloaded  PX          MB          Per Exec  SQL
-----------   ---------  ---------  ---------   ----------  --------  ----------------------------
5ccq67fmtr7ud         4  No         Yes               .00      15.67  select /* in-memory px t1 */
                                                                      count(1) from RTL.R_DWB_RTL_TRX

2mg9wcry8cwn1         4  No         Yes               .00      16.23  select /* in-memory px t1 */
                                                                      count(1) from RTL.R_DWB_RTL_TND
```

```
gnd3dauwfn0sc          3   Yes        No         6802.22     3.74  select /* in-memory px t2 */
                                                                   count(1) from RTL.R_DWB_RTL_TRX
0ck89ssfcnraw          3   Yes        No         7539.18     4.00  select /* in-memory px t2 */
                                                                   count(1) from RTL.R_DWB_RTL_TND
... Output for similar rows omitted
```

In the output above, the in-memory px t1 SQL comments represent the tests performed with In-Memory PX enabled and the in-memory px t2 comments represent the tests with In-Memory PX disabled. From this AWR data, you can see the following:

- With parallel_degree_policy=LIMITED, Auto DOP calculated a slightly different degree of parallelism on the same queries;
- With In-Memory PX disabled, the query was offloadable and satisfied via Smart Scan;
- With In-Memory PX disabled, Smart Scan enabled the queries to run in significantly less time as compared to buffered reads with In-Memory PX.

This example illustrates a potential shortcoming with In-Memory PX on Exadata; with buffered reads, Smart Scan is disabled and with Smart Scan disabled, queries can run longer.

Both of the test cases conducted so far were done using single SELECT statements against a small number of larger tables, and the results demonstrated that In-Memory PX can have a detrimental impact on query performance by disabling Smart Scan. But how does this behavior hold up under higher levels of concurrency? Let's run 24 concurrent SELECT statements for one of our queries with In-Memory PX enabled and disabled and compare the results. The script in Listing 21-16 shows our SQL statement performance information from DBA_HIST_SQLSTAT:

Listing 21-16. lst21-16-autodop-impx-comp.sql

```
SQL> select    ss.sql_id,
               sum(ss.executions_total) execs,
               sum(ss.PX_SERVERS_EXECS_total)/sum(ss.executions_total) px_servers,
               decode(sum(ss.io_offload_elig_bytes_total),0,'No','Yes') offloadelig,
               decode(sum(ss.io_offload_elig_bytes_total),0,'Yes','No') impx,
               sum(ss.io_offload_elig_bytes_total)/1024/1024 offloadbytes,
sum(ss.elapsed_time_total)/1000000/sum(ss.executions_total)/sum(ss.px_servers_execs_total) elps,
               dbms_lob.substr(st.sql_text,60,1) st
    from dba_hist_sqlstat ss, dba_hist_sqltext st
   where ss.px_servers_execs_total > 0
     and ss.sql_id=st.sql_id
     and upper(st.sql_text) like '%IN-MEM PX%'
   group by ss.sql_id,dbms_lob.substr(st.sql_text,60,1)
   order by 5
  /

                PX Servers              In-Memory IO Offload Elps Sec
SQL ID        Execs Per Exec Offloaded  PX        MB         Per Exec SQL
------------- ----- -------- ---------  --------- ---------- -------- ---------------------
1aqccjsvucnn3  24      3     Yes        No        163253.25      1.74 select /* in-mem px
                                                                      disabled */
                                                                      count(1) from RTL.R_DWB_RTL_
85vtwj08fbm28  24      4     No         Yes             .00       .72 select /* in-mem px
                                                                      enabled */
                                                                      count(1) from RTL.R_DWB_RTL_T
```

The information above shows us that for this test case, the elapsed time per execution for each parallel server process was less than half the time with offload, Smart Scan, and no In-Memory PX. And this is in fact the goal of In-Memory PX; to buffer smaller parallel query results sets in the database buffer cache and provide access times at the speed of memory access. In the How It Works section of this recipe, we will discuss this in more detail.

How It Works

Auto DOP is designed to accomplish three main goals:

- Automatically determine a query's degree of parallelism, or DOP, based on the sizes of the tables being accessed and the system's parallel query processing capabilities. Auto DOP automatically parallelizes a SQL statement on 11gR2 when the optimizer determines that the query will take longer than `parallel_min_time_pct_threshold` seconds, which defaults to ten seconds.

- Queue parallel SQL statements using Auto DOP's parallel statement queuing functionality.

- Provide buffered read capability for suitable statements using In-Memory PX.

To use In-Memory PX, simply set `parallel_degree_policy=AUTO`. To disable In-Memory PX, set `parallel_degree_policy=MANUAL` or `LIMITED`.

When In-Memory PX is enabled, Oracle will perform buffer reads for each parallel server's session when the size of the underlying table or tables is less than `_parallel_cluster_cache_pct` times the aggregate size of the instance's database buffer cache; this defaults to 80%. So, on a two-node RAC cluster on an Exadata Quarter Rack with a 10 GB buffer cache on each instance, tables that are less than 16 GB will qualify for In-Memory PX with Auto DOP.

Prior to Auto DOP and In-Memory PX, parallel queries always performed direct reads; with In-Memory PX, Oracle enables buffered reads as an optimization strategy to cache blocks returned from parallel server operations, providing subsequent block requests to be satisfied in memory.

On Exadata, buffered reads disable Exadata Smart Scan and as you know, Smart Scan is arguably Exadata's top performance feature. For this reason, many Exadata DMAs are taught to disable In-Memory PX by either not using Auto DOP or setting `parallel_degree_policy=LIMITED`. But is this the right answer for your environment? The last test in the solution of this recipe showed a benefit from In-Memory PX for certain queries. The answer, like most Oracle performance questions, is, "It depends."

In-Memory PX will disable smart scans for certain parallel query operations, but *only* for those in which the tables are smaller than 80% the combined sized of each instance's buffer cache and when the optimizer determines to parallelize the statement with Auto DOP based on `parallel_min_time_pct_threshold`. This means that your larger tables will still have a good chance of not being eligible for In-Memory PX and benefiting from smart scans.

This being said, the larger the Exadata configuration, the larger the size of your aggregate buffer cache. With large SGAs on Exadata and eight nodes in a Full Rack, this increases the likelihood of In-Memory PX kicking in, eliminating Smart Scan, and potentially placing a strain on your shared memory resources. With mixed-workload environments, this can be very detrimental.

Our advice is to test In-Memory PX thoroughly using the methods in this recipe before enabling it in production; the last thing you want to do is invest in Exadata and allow a parallel query feature designed for generic Oracle 11gR2 databases to prevent Smart Scans without measuring the benefit and approving based on a holistic workload analysis. For this reason, we typically recommend starting with `parallel_degree_policy=LIMITED` to enable automatic DOP calculations and setting `"_parallel_statement_queuing"=TRUE` to enable parallel statement queuing.

21-8. Gathering Optimizer Statistics on Exadata
Problem
You have deployed a database or databases on Exadata and wish to ensure that your Oracle Cost-Based Optimizer (CBO) statistics are being collected in a comprehensive, efficient manner.

Solution

The topic of Oracle's optimizer and statistics collection is both broad and complex. In this recipe, we will provide guidance on how to validate and configure statistics collection on an Exadata database in a step-by-step process and ideally provide a framework to guarantee that your optimizer statistics are being gathered accurately and efficiently. Specifically, you will learn the following:

- How to identify how your optimizer statistics are currently being gathered for you automatically on Oracle 11gR2

- How to gather object statistics automatically and set statistics collection preferences for automatic sample sizing, parallel degree determination, cascade options, granularity determination, histogram population, and stale statistics thresholds

- How to gather system statistics on Exadata

- How to gather fixed object and data dictionary statistics

Validating Optimizer Statistics Collection with an AutoTask Job

In Oracle 11gR2, optimizer statistics collection is automated by default and will be gathered using an Oracle AutoTask job. To validate that this is the case in your Oracle database, run the query in Listing 21-17:

Listing 21-17. lst21-17-stats-autotask.sql

```
SQL> select ac.client_name,ac.status,
            at.task_name,
            sp.program_action
     from dba_autotask_client ac,
          dba_autotask_task at,
          dba_scheduler_programs sp
    where ac.client_name='auto optimizer stats collection'
      and ac.client_name=at.client_name
      and upper(at.task_name)=upper(sp.program_name)
  /

AutoTask Client                   Status    Task Name           Program
-------------------------------   -------   -----------------   ------------------------------
auto optimizer stats collection   ENABLED   gather_stats_prog   dbms_stats.gather_database_stats
                                                                _job_proc

SQL> select ac.client_name,ac.window_group,wm.window_name,
            to_char(win.next_start_date,'DD-MON-RR HH24:MI:SS') next_start_date
     from dba_autotask_client ac,
          dba_scheduler_wingroup_members wm,
          dba_scheduler_windows win
    where ac.client_name='auto optimizer stats collection'
      and ac.window_group=wm.window_group_name
      and wm.window_name=win.window_name
  /
```

```
AutoTask Client                     Window Group        Window              Next Start
----------------------------------  ------------------  ------------------  -------------------
auto optimizer stats collection     ORA$AT_WGRP_OS      SUNDAY_WINDOW       07-OCT-12 06:00:00
auto optimizer stats collection     ORA$AT_WGRP_OS      SATURDAY_WINDOW     13-OCT-12 06:00:00
auto optimizer stats collection     ORA$AT_WGRP_OS      FRIDAY_WINDOW       12-OCT-12 22:00:00
auto optimizer stats collection     ORA$AT_WGRP_OS      THURSDAY_WINDOW     11-OCT-12 22:00:00
auto optimizer stats collection     ORA$AT_WGRP_OS      WEDNESDAY_WINDOW    10-OCT-12 22:00:00
auto optimizer stats collection     ORA$AT_WGRP_OS      TUESDAY_WINDOW      09-OCT-12 22:00:00
auto optimizer stats collection     ORA$AT_WGRP_OS      MONDAY_WINDOW       08-OCT-12 22:00:00
SQL>
```

The above information shows us the following:

- Automatic statistics collection is enabled using an 11gR2 AutoTask job.
- The job is implemented by a program called gather_stats_prog, which runs the procedure dbms_stats.gather_database_stats_job_proc.
- The automatic statistic collection job is scheduled to run in the ORA$AT_WGRP_OS scheduler window group and inside a scheduling window on each day of the week.

The dbms_stats.gather_database_stats_job_proc is an Oracle internal statistics collection program that gathers statistics for tables with missing or stale optimizer statistics. When executed, the procedure will operate in a similar manner to running dbms_stats.gather_database_stats, dbms_stats.gather_schema_stats, or dbms_stats.gather_table_stats. When the procedure runs, it calls DBMS_STATS to gather statistics using predefined statistics preferences, which is an Oracle 11g feature designed to set statistics collection preferences at the database, schema, or table level.

■ **Note** Prior to Oracle 11g, global statistics collection settings were defined using statistics parameters as set using dbms_stats.set_param and retrieved using dbms_stats.get_param. These statistics parameters are deprecated in 11g and starting with 11g, preferences should be used.

Displaying and Setting Your Optimizer Statistics Preferences

Run the script in Listing 21-18 to see your current statistics preferences:

Listing 21-18. lst21-18-stats-prefs.sql

```
SQL> select dbms_stats.get_prefs('CASCADE') prefs from dual;
DBMS_STATS.AUTO_CASCADE
SQL> select dbms_stats.get_prefs('DEGREE') prefs from dual;
NULL
SQL> select dbms_stats.get_prefs('ESTIMATE_PERCENT') prefs from dual;
DBMS_STATS.AUTO_SAMPLE_SIZE
SQL> select dbms_stats.get_prefs('METHOD_OPT') prefs from dual;
FOR ALL COLUMNS SIZE AUTO
SQL> select dbms_stats.get_prefs('NO_INVALIDATE') prefs from dual;
DBMS_STATS.AUTO_INVALIDATE
SQL> select dbms_stats.get_prefs('GRANULARITY') prefs from dual;
AUTO
```

```
SQL> select dbms_stats.get_prefs('PUBLISH') prefs from dual;
TRUE
SQL> select dbms_stats.get_prefs('INCREMENTAL') prefs from dual;
FALSE
SQL> select dbms_stats.get_prefs('STALE_PERCENT') prefs from dual;
10
SQL>
```

On Exadata databases and all Oracle 11gR2 databases, we recommend automating statistics preferences to the greatest extent possible unless your database or workload justifies changing Oracle's default behavior. Doing so will lead to more accurate optimizer statistics with the least amount of performance overhead. To set your optimizer statistics parameters, run the script in Listing 21-19. (Note that many of these will implement the default behavior; text outlined in bold is not the default behavior and will be discussed after the script output is displayed.)

Listing 21-19. lst21-19-stats-setprefs.sql

```
SQL> exec dbms_stats.set_database_prefs(pname=>'CASCADE',
                pvalue=>'DBMS_STATS.AUTO_CASCADE');
PL/SQL procedure successfully completed.
SQL> exec dbms_stats.set_database_prefs(pname=>'DEGREE',
                pvalue=>'DBMS_STATS.AUTO_DEGREE');
PL/SQL procedure successfully completed.
SQL> exec dbms_stats.set_database_prefs(pname=>'ESTIMATE_PERCENT',
                pvalue=>'DBMS_STATS.AUTO_SAMPLE_SIZE');
PL/SQL procedure successfully completed.
SQL> exec dbms_stats.set_database_prefs(pname=>'GRANULARITY',
                pvalue=>'AUTO');
PL/SQL procedure successfully completed.
SQL> exec dbms_stats.set_database_prefs(pname=>'METHOD_OPT',
                pvalue=>'FOR ALL COLUMNS SIZE AUTO');
PL/SQL procedure successfully completed.
SQL> exec dbms_stats.set_database_prefs(pname=>'STALE_PERCENT',
                pvalue=>'10');
PL/SQL procedure successfully completed.
SQL> exec dbms_stats.set_database_prefs(pname=>'NO_INVALIDATE',
                pvalue=>'DBMS_STATS.AUTO_INVALIDATE');
PL/SQL procedure successfully completed.
SQL> exec dbms_stats.set_database_prefs(pname=>'PUBLISH',
                pvalue=>'TRUE');
PL/SQL procedure successfully completed.
SQL> exec dbms_stats.set_database_prefs(pname=>'INCREMENTAL',
                pvalue=>'TRUE');
PL/SQL procedure successfully completed.
SQL>
```

The following is a summary of these recommended statistics collection preferences:

- For the CASCADE option, DBMS_STATS.AUTO_CASCADE instructs DBMS_STATS to cascade statistics collection for all dependent indexes on a table.

- For the DEGREE option, DBMS_STATS.AUTO_DEGREE samples the number of blocks in the segment and automatically adjusts the degree of parallelism to use when gathering statistics. In general, the larger the segment, the higher degree of parallelism. If Auto DOP is enabled, Oracle will use the Auto DOP algorithms as discussed in Recipe 21-2.

- For the ESTIMATE_PERCENT option, DBMS_STATS.AUTO_SAMPLE_SIZE will determine the appropriate block sample size to use when gathering statistics. With 11gR2, this often will yield a low percentage as compared to previous Oracle versions, but in nearly all cases Oracle will choose an appropriate sample size. In our experience, this is one of the better features of statistics collection in 11g; with smaller estimate percentages, statistics gathering is more efficient, has less overhead, and generally runs faster.

- For the GRANULARITY option, AUTO will gather statistics on all dependent table partitions and sub-partitions based on the partitioning type of the table.

- For the METHOD_OPT option, FOR ALL COLUMNS SIZE AUTO will create histograms on the appropriate columns, with the appropriate bucket sizes, based on the workload of your database. It does so whether the column(s) are indexes or not and uses query predicate information from SYS.COL_USAGE$ to determine which columns to build indexes for.

Note FOR ALL COLUMNS SIZE AUTO assumes your database has had a representative workload run. If not, the first iteration of statistics collection may not build the correct histogram. When migrating to Exadata, it is often considered good practice to create empty tables, run a sample workload, gather statistics to build the proper histograms, and then load data before opening the database to the users. This practice may or may not be practical for a number of reasons, but if you can do it, it will ensure that accurate column statistics and histograms are accurate before users run production queries on your database.

- For the STALE_PERCENT option, the recommended value of 10 means to re-gather statistics when the percentage of block changes for a segment exceeds 10% that of the number of blocks in the segment. DBMS_STATS tracks this by examining information from SYS.MON_MODS$ and DBA_TAB_MODIFICATIONS.

- For the NO_INVALIDATE option, DBMS_STATS.AUTO_INVALIDATE generally instructs DBMS_STATS to invalidate dependent cursors, forcing re-parsing of a depending SQL cursors.

- For the PUBLISH option, TRUE indicates to publish statistics immediately after collection. You can choose to defer statistics publishing if you are sensitive to SQL plan changes by setting PUBLISH to FALSE.

- For the INCREMENTAL option, DBMS_STATS will only gather statistics on partitions that have changed since the last statistics collection on the table or table's partition. Depending on how you maintain your partitions, this can eliminate a great deal of unnecessary work during statistics gathering by bypassing statistics collection for dormant partitions. For incremental statistics functionality to work, you need to set PUBLISH to TRUE, GRANULARITY to AUTO, and ESTIMATE_PERCENT to DBMS_STATS.AUTO_SAMPLE_SIZE.

Gathering Data Dictionary and Fixed Object Statistics

Once your object statistics collection preferences are set using the steps above, gather your data dictionary and fixed object statistics using the two DBMS_STATS procedures listed in Listing 21-20:

Listing 21-20. lst21-20-stats-dictfo.sql

```
SQL> exec dbms_stats.gather_dictionary_stats;
PL/SQL procedure successfully completed.
SQL> exec dbms_stats.gather_fixed_objects_stats;
PL/SQL procedure successfully completed.
SQL>
```

System Statistics and Exadata

Finally, tackle your system statistics. System statistics seed SYS.AUX_STATS$ and are designed, in general, to provide the optimizer with information about your system's CPU speed, single block read times, multi-block read times, multi-block read count, and so forth. Generally speaking, each Exadata Database Machine of the same configuration should have the same capabilities in these areas and as such, system statistics are not required to be collected on Exadata. One interesting optimizer challenge on Exadata, however, is that the optimizer does not take into consideration the reduced cost of full scans; in other words, the optimizer is not "Smart Scan" aware. For queries in which both a full scan and index scan are available options based on query predicates and table structures, this could lead the optimizer to choose an index access path over a full scan based on the optimizer's traditional access path costing calculations. Oracle solved this problem by introducing a new DBMS_STATS.GATHER_SYSTEM_STATS option specifically with this smart-scan-costing alternative in mind. If you are on Exadata patch bundle 8 for 11.2.0.3 or patch bundle 18 for 11.2.0.2, patch 10248538 will allow you to run the following DBMS_STATS.GATHER_SYSTEM_STATS procedure as listed in Listing 21-21:

Listing 21-21. lst21-21-sysstats-exa.sql

```
SQL> exec dbms_stats.gather_system_stats('EXADATA');
PL/SQL procedure successfully completed.
SQL>
```

Using this method, Oracle will seed system statistics indicating a 128-block multi-block read count (instead of the default of 8) and set the I/O transfer speed (IOTFRSPEED) to 200 MB, which better reflects Exadata's I/O capabilities. This will lead the optimizer to generate lower costs for full scans, increasing the likelihood for Smart Scan.

How It Works

As stated in the Solution section of this recipe, Oracle's optimizer and the topic of statistics collection is a very broad and complex topic. The methods outlined in this recipe provide some tips on how to configure your statistics collection processes to be largely automated and with what Oracle considers as "best practices" settings for Oracle 11gR2. The tips in this recipe are largely unrelated to Exadata specifically; they are provided as general guidelines for all 11gR2 databases. There are, however, parts of this recipe that are especially germane to Exadata databases.

Most of the automatic statistics collection settings and preferences will cause DBMS_STATS to do the least amount of work required to generate accurate statistics. Statistics accuracy is of paramount importance for the optimizer; the preferences provided in this recipe all aim to provide high levels of accuracy. In addition, they tend to generate the least amount of work and most efficient use of system resources. On Exadata, databases are generally large in size or consolidated on an Exadata Database Machine so efficiency is very important to your overall statistics collection routines.

Likewise, it is common on Exadata to deploy data warehouses or other databases with large, partitioned tables. Incremental statistics is a means to reduce statistics collection times and system resource utilization for partitioned tables and is a good thing to consider when deploying on Exadata.

One of the exciting optimizer statistics enhancements provided in recent patch levels on Exadata is the "Exadata-aware" system statistics. Prior to this enhancement, it was common for the optimizer to favor index scans over smart-scan capable full scans simply because the optimizer's costing algorithms had no way of quantifying the performance benefit of Smart Scans. With DBMS_STATS.GATHER_SYSTEM_STATS('EXADATA'), Oracle is able to seed meaningful system statistics that the optimizer is able to evaluate in costing alternate access paths. This can lead the optimizer to favor full-scan operations over index range scans and take advantage of the power of Exadata Smart Scans.

Before winding down this recipe, it is worth mentioning that the tips provided above are certainly general in nature; optimizer statistics collection preferences and procedures definitely are not a "one-size-fits-all" solution. We have provided advice for using automatic statistics collection with AutoTasks (the default in 11g) as well as a series of database-wide or system-wide automatic statistics preferences. Depending on your workload, you can override these settings at a table or segment level to provide the statistics you desire. Some common things to consider include the following:

- Disabling automatic statistics collection using the DBMS_AUTO_TASK_ADMIN.DISABLE procedure. This is sometimes required if your application requires a non-standard statistics collection framework, such as Oracle e-Business Suite or other commercial off-the-shelf applications.

- Using extended statistics or multi-column statistics to provide the optimizer with additional statistics information for columns with correlated values.

- Using expression statistics for columns in which a function is applied to a column in query predicates.

- Adjusting statistics preferences on a per-table, per-column, or per-segment basis in situations when you have a better idea of what the statistics should be than DBMS_STATS ever would.

As each of these points and more are truly based on knowledge of your application and workloads, we will not cover any detail on any of the above. Please refer to Oracle's documentation on the optimizer and DBMS_STATS for more information.

Index

A

Administration tasks and utilities
    cell server process, 165
    Cisco Catalyst 4948 switch, 187–188
    Exadata health check
        exachk utility, 173–174
        findings needing attention, 175
        working principle, 176
    ILOM interface
        browser method, 171
        normal snapshot dataset mode, 172
        snapshot utility, 171
        SSH connection, 172
        working principle, 173
    InfiniBand switch, 181
    key configuration files and directories
        exadata compute nodes, 164
        locations and executables, 162
        working principle, 163
    MegaCLI utility, 178–179
    secure shell, 159
    storage cell administration
        CellCLI, 167–168
        dcli utility, 168–170
        ipconf, 179–180
        sundiag.sh utility, 176–177
Administrative network
    client access network
        bondeth0 interface creation, 300
        ifconfig output, 300
        nodes VIP and SCAN address, 300
        Oracle cluster networking, 300
        working principle, 301
    computer node, working principle, 299
    grid Infrastructure network
        cluster HAIP, 306
        components and resources, 306
        Database and SCAN Listeners validation, 308
        oifcfg command, 306
        ora.network.type cluster resource, 306
        SCAN network and listeners checking, 307
        srvctl config network command, 307
        VIP and SCAN address validation, 307
        working principle, 309
    InfiniBand private interconnect
        bondib0 interface, 302
        cluster_interconnects initialization parameter, 302
        core Oracle CRS process, 302
        oifcfg, 302
        Oracle's Cluster HAIP framework, 302
        skgxpinfo, 303
        working principle, 303–304
    IP address changes,
        Cisco Catalyst switch, 317–318
        compute node Ethernet, 321–322, 326
        Exadata Quarter Rack, 312
        InfiniBand switch Ethernet network, 314, 316
        KVM switch, 316
        machine preparation, 313–314
        network changes, 312
        power distribution unit, 318
        Storage Cell Ethernet, 319, 321
    Oracle RAC network resources, 326, 329
        post-change procedures, 330
    Oracle SCAN listener configuration
        checking, 304
        nslookup command, 304
        SCAN IP address changing, 305
        working principle, 305
    storage server ethernet network, 309–311
        cell.conf network, 310
        configuration changing, 311
        eth0 interface, 309
        ifconfig command, 309
        working principle, 311

Administrative network (*cont.*)
    validation
        ifconfig command, 297
        ListenAddress, 298
        NET0/admin interface, 297–298
        NET0 network, 297
        nslookup, 297
        routing rules modification, 298
        service network restarting, 299
ASM disk group redundancy configuration, 149
ASM-scoped security, 362–364
Automated Storage Management (ASM)
        disks, 14, 58
Automatic Degree of Parallelism (DOP)
        configuration, 610
    benefits of, 611
    challenges of, 611
    In-Memory Parallel Execution, 612
    parallel_degree_policy initialization
        parameter, 611
Automatic DOP
    and In-Memory Parallel Execution
        AWR data, 624
        goals, 625
        SQL statement performance
            information, 624
    and parallel statement queuing
        Active Session History, 616
        dbms_utility.get_time, 617
        enabled conditions, 619
        SQL executions, 615
        SQL monitoring, 618
        test case, 615
Automatic Workload Repository (AWR), 78, 451
    Hybrid Columnar Compression, 93
    industry-defined definitions, 80
        Physical Reads, 79
        Segments by, 79
        SQL ordered by, 79
    smart scans
        Exadata simulation, 87
        OFFLOADABLE, 85
        requirements, 85
    software features, 79
    Timed Foreground Events, 78
    workload fit assessment, 79–80

B

Backup and recovery, 189
    CELLBOOT USB flashdrive
        content check, 192
        directory validation, 191
        internal USB drive, 191
        mount and validate, 192
        partition identification, 191
        performance, 192
    cluster registry and voting disks
        ASM disk group, 236
        backups, OCR, 236
        ClusterWare, 235
        crsctl replace votedisk command, 238
        DBFS_DG group, 235
        disk group, 236
        grid infrastructure, 237
        high availabiltiy services, 236
        OCR recovery, 235
        RAC voting, 235
        -restore method, 237
        -showbackup, 237
        SYSASM, 236
        voting disk restore, 237
    database machine administrator (DMA), 189
    enterprise backup software
        agent software, 196
        compute nodes, 195
        design, third party, 196
        ethernet, 196
        tasks, 195
        third party, 196
        working, 196
    external USB drive
        bootable recovery image, 193
        configuration copy, 195
        format the device, 195
        make_cellboot_usb, 194
        volume labeling, 193
        working, 194
    failed storage server patch
        imageinfo command, 223
        solution, 222
        validation framework, 223
    InfiBand switch recovery
        config_backup.xml, 233–234
        configuration, 232
        dialog window, restore, 233
        ilom-admin, 232
        maintanence, 232
        restart OpenSM, 234
        restored files, 234
    InfiniBand switches
        configuration, 203
        failure and replacement, 204
        firmware, 204
        ILOM interface, 203
        OpenSM configuration files, 203
        passphrase warning, 204
        patches, 204
        performance, 204
        transfer method, 203

INDEX

LVM snapshots
    compute node server, 197
    directory mount, 199
    logical volume, 197
    lvcreate, 199
    mkfs.ext3 format, 197
    mount and validate, 198
    point in time copy, 200
    point in time snapsots, 199
    query, volumes, 198
    -S and-L options, 200
    SAS disks, 196
    solutions, 197
    undersizing volumes, 200
    unmount file systems, 200
    vgdisplay, 197
    volume devices, 199
Oracle DB with RMAN
    1 GBe NET3 networks, 202
    automatic storage manager (ASM), 201
    change tracking, 202
    disk parallelism, 202
    on Exadata, 201
    fast recovery area (FRA), 201
    field topics, 201
    functionality and usage, 201
    InfiniBand on servers, 202
    level 0 backup, 201
    optimization on, 202
    RAC instances, 202
    recovery time objectives (RTO), 202
    ZFS storage, 202
recovering compute server
    attaching image to CD-ROM, 225
    boot device change, 226
    boot device to default, 228
    diagnostics image, 224
    diagnostics, splash screen, 226
    ILOM web console, 225
    launch remote console, 225
    LVM based snapshots, 227
    LVM snapshots, 223
    NFS share, 224
    recovery types, 229
    redirection, 224
    snapshot backups, 223
    validate command, 224
    working, 228
reimaging node
    cluvfy, 231
    computeImageMaker file, 229
    directory creation, 231
    documenting, 232
    ILOM tasks, 230
    makeImageMedia.sh, 230

    network validation, 230
    peer compatibility, 231
    performance, 231
    RAC cluster, 229
    replicate Linux groups, 231
    SSH setup, 231
storage cells
    alert logs, 206, 209
    amber LED, 207
    ASM disk status, 208
    ASM redundancy, 210
    automatic disk management, 209
    celladmin, 205
    cell disk status, 206
    critical status, 208
    disk failure, 209
    disk_repair_time, 210
    grid disk status, 206
    lun command, 206
    poor performance, 209
    predictive failure, 208
    root, 205
    service light, 207
    service request, 205
    status change, 209
    status to normal, 208
    sundiag.sh script, 205
    tasks to perform, 205
storage servers
    CELLBOOT USB flashdrive, 189
    OS and cell software, 189
    recovery manager (RMAN), 190
    storage cell software, 190
    system area, 190
    third party backup client, 190
    volume partitions, 190
system volume, CELLBOOT rescue
    additional cell boot, 222
    boot device selection, 216
    cell configuration, 220
    cell rescue option, 213
    CELLSRV, 218
    cell status, 219
    CELL_USB_BOOT_CELLBOOT_usb_in_rescue_
        mode, 212
    data loss risk, 222
    documenting, 222
    failgroup-status.sql, 219
    flash cache, 220
    force command, 219
    ILOM web interface, 217
    importForceRequired, 219
    internal CELLBOOT, 210
    periodical mount, 222
    recover from a damaged system, 214

Backup and recovery (cont.)
    reimage_boot mode, 217
    reinstall, 214
    replace, single disk, 211
    rescue partitioning, 215
    rescue process, 221
    shell login, 216
    solutions, 210
    splash screen, 212
    storage grid, 218
    temporary system volumes, 215
    working, 221
Baseboard Management Controller (BMC), 376

C

Capacity planning exercise, 97
    ASM redundancy requirements
        data storage usable capacity, 119
        failure probabilities, 120
        MTBF, 121
        probability definitions, 121
    backups, 134
    CPU requirements
        Average Active Sessions, 100–101
        calculation, 103
        core multiplier parameter, 105
        database CPU statistics, 100
        DBA_HIST_OSSTAT, 107
        DBA_HIST_SYSSTAT, 107
        DBA_HIST_TIME_MODEL, 107
        input variable descriptions, 104
        I/O vs. non-I/O processor requirements, 103
        number of CPUs, 100
        Oracle CPU, 100
        recommendations, 98, 107
        Snapshot duration, 100
    database growth, 125
    disaster recovery strategy, 133
    forecasting storage
        backup and recovery strategy, 122
        Hybrid Columnar Compression, 123
        performance-based requirements, 124
        working principle, 124
    FRA and RECO disk storage, 136
    I/O bandwidth requirements, 113, 116–118
        &asm_redundancy_data, 117
        &asm_redundancy_redo, 117
        DBA_HIST_SYSSTAT, 118
        margin of error, 116
        working principle, 118
    IOPs requirements
        &asm_redundancy_data, 111
        &asm_redundancy_reco, 111
        counter-based metrics, 113

        DBA_HIST_SYSSTAT, 112
        IOPs metrics from AWR, 110
        LAG analytic function, 112
        &margin_err, 111
        &num_addtl_dbs, 110
        Oracle-published disk, 112
        &pct_resource_load, 110
        read and write requests, 108
        redo log writes, 108
        write and redo writes, 113
CellCLI, 167–168
CellCLI monitoring commands, 371
Cell offload
    cell_offload_plan_display parameter, 448
    dbms_xplan, 447
    direct path reads
        cached block threshold, 465
        dirty block threshold, 466
        for full-scan operations, 465
        parallel direct operations, 468
        serial direct reads, 468
        _small_table_threshold setting, 464
        statistics-driven direct read decisions, 467
    enable/disable
        ASM disk group, 451
        controlling techniques, 451
        for session, 450
        for SQL statement, 450
    fast object checkpoints, 475
        bottlenecks, 475
        description, 475
        KO-fast object checkpoint, 475
        OLTP application, 475
    offload efficiency
        description, 461
        for multiple SQL statements, 458
        for Oracle session, 460
        for SQL statements, 458
    overloaded storage cells, 474
    partial identification
        chained rows, 474
        measure, consistent reads for session, 474
        SQL statement, measure, 474
    Smart Scan behavior
        block counts, 472
        cell_offload_processing parameter, 472
        dbms_states.gather_system_stats, 473
        drop indexes, 469
        full table scan, 469
        invisible indexes, 470
        _optimizer_ignore_hints, 471
        opt_param hint, 472
        _serial_direct_read, 471
        _small_table_threshold parameter, 472
        working, 473

■ INDEX

Smart Scan operation, 10046 Trace files, 461
SQL cursors, 455, 457
  from v$sql, 455
  Real-Time SQL Monitoring feature, 457
  storage cell I/O statistics, 457
STORAGE FULL operation, 448
Cell services process, 165
  staring, 166
    cellcli command, 166
    Linux service, 166
  stopping, 165
    ASM disks, 165
    celladmin, 165
  working principle, 167
CheckSWProfile.sh utility, 181–182
Cisco Catalyst 4948 switch, 187
Cluster Ready Services (CRS) configuration, 38

■ D

DATA and RECO ASM disk groups
  Backup Method, 148
  considerations, 148
  sizing of, 149
  usable storage capacity, 149
Database and Oracle ASM extent sizes, 152
Database Machine configuration worksheet, 154
  Cell Alert Delivery Configuration Worksheet, 155
  Default Oracle Environment Settings, 154
  General Configuration Worksheet section, 155
  Network Configuration Worksheet section, 155
  working principle, 156
Database-scoped security, 364, 366–367
DNS configuration, 143
  host names, 143
  working principle, 144

■ E

Exadata Database Machine, 33
  components, 3
    compute grid, 3
    network grid, 3
    storage grid, 3
  compute and storage servers, 8
  compute servers
    architecture details, 14
    disk storage details, 23
    dmidecode, 15
    function of, 15
    imagehistory execution, 15
    OPatch utilities, 15
    required and optional network, 16
    working principle, 16

features, 9
InfiniBand switches
  administrative tasks, 32
  OpenSMInfiniBand subnet manager, 31
  ILOM web interface, 30
Oracle 11gR2 database(s), 35
Oracle Cluster Registry and voting disks, 42
storage servers
  architecture details, 10
  ASM, 14
  disk storage details, 17
  dmidecode, 10
  flash storage, 27
  grid performance, 12
  imagehistory execution, 11
  imageinfo command, 11
  Oracle Enterprise Linux 5.5, 10
  working principle, 12
storage server software
  administrator or workload characteristic impact, 33
  features, 34
  goals, 35
  working principle, 7
X2-2, 4
X2-2 Full Rack, 7
X2-8, 4
X3-2, 5
X3-8, 5
Exadata network planning, 139
  administration network, 140
  client access network, 140, 142
  compute server additional network, 140
  InfiniBand network, 140, 142
  management network, 142
  working principle, 141
Exadata's pre-delivery survey, 153

■ F, G

Fast Recovery Area (FRA), 136
Flash disks, 61

■ H

HugePages configuration, 606
  benefits of, 609
  memlock setting, 606
Hybrid columnar compression (HCC), 93, 477
  compression units (CU), 477
    conventional inserts, 495
    working, 495
  conventional inserts
    attributes, 494
    comptype.sql, 494

637

Hybrid columnar compression (HCC) (cont.)
    into HCC segments, 494
    query high, 494
  DBA_HIST_SEG_STAT, 93
  database analysis, 95
  decompression
    database servers, 504
    scripts, 504
    smart scans, 504
    smart scan vs traditional block I/O, 503
    uncompressed transmit, 504
    working, 504
  decompression, 502
    database buffer, 502
    decompstats.sql, 503
    multiple test, 503
    Qracle, data, 502
    results gathering, 502
  DELETE and UPDATE DML operations, 95
  disk space savings
    compressed tables, 479
    Compress For Query Low, 479
    DBMS_COMPRESSION.GET_COMPRESSION_RATIO, 479
    output, 478
  disk space savings, 477
    compadv.sql, 478
    estimation, 477
    Oracle products, 477
    ratio, 477
    requirements, 477
  and DML, 495–501
    allcomptypes.sql, 500
    block dump, 497
    compressed block, 498
    compression type of an updated row, 496
    concurrency, 500
    documentation, 495
    dump destination, 498
    extract compression types, 497
    getrowidinfo.sql, 497
    hcclocks.sql, 501
    locking, 500
    migrated row identification, 499
    MYOBJ_DMLTEST, 500
    percentage finding, 500
    query re-run, 496
    qury high, 496
    ROWID, 497
    tbcr.sql, 499
    uncommited transaction, 501
    working principle, 501
  Oracle compression
    archive, 482
    block_row_dump string, 485
    block ump, 486
    DBA_OBJECTS, 482
    HCC vs OLTP, 486
    on HCC table, 484
    LZO compression, 486
    nonlinear, ratios, 483
    OLTP, 482
    performance, 483
    physical storage, 484
    pseudo column, 484
    pstack command, 486
    query high, 484
    uncompressed table, 483
    warehouse, 482
  path inserts into segments, 493
    append, 493
    comptype.sql, 492
    CTAS, 492
    INSERT /*+ APPEND */, 493
    tablespace compression, 493
    working principle, 493
  performance impact for queries, 491
    high compressed table, 491
    performances, 491
    SQL ID, 491
    sqls.sql, 490
    system statistics, 489
    test results, 489
    and uncompressed tables, 490
  query comression, 477
  segment compression, 488
    comptype.sql, 487
    configurations, 487
    DBMS_COMPRESSION.GET_COMPRESSION_TYPE function, 488
    MMT_COMPQUERYHIGH, 487
    MTL_MATERIAL_TRANSACTIONS, 487
    performance, 488
    settings, 487
    type determination, 487
  tables and partitions
    attribute for tablespaces, 481
    clause, level, 480
    compression clauses, 482
    compression types, 482
    compsettings.sql, 481
    create table, 479
    create table as select (CTAS), 480
    for high query, 479
    OLTP, 482
    uncompressed and compressed partitions, 480
    with HCC partitions, 480

I, J, K, L

InfiniBand network, 183
    commands and utilities
        bad link identification, 183
        infinicheck, 185
        infinicheck utility, 185
        interface checking, 186
        relay errors, 184
        root users, 184
    diagnostics utilities and scripts, 187
    Exalogic backups, 147
    topology verification, 182
    validation, 181–182
    working principle, 147
Instance caging, 505
I/O calibration, 612
I/O resource management (IORM), 505
    consumers and DBs, utilization by category
        alter iormplan, 514
        catplan, 513
        CellCLI statements, 517
        cell disk saturtion, 516
        cell services, 516
        dbplan, 513
        dcli, 513
        graphical representation, 515
        IORM architecture, 515
        IORM plan, 513
        IORMPlanningCalculatorV1.xlsx, 516
        key concepts, 516
        percentage for I/O request, 516
        performance, 514
        process flow, 515
    CPU resources with caging, 527
        cpu_count, 527
        database instance, 527
        working principle, 527
    database resource manager (DBRM), 505
    limiting I/O utilization
        dbplan, 508
        DB to configure, 507
        limit clause, 507
        performance, 508
    performance monitoring, IORM enabled
        cell metrics, 517
        important metrics, 520
        list metriccurrent, 518
        list metricdefinition, 519
        list metrichistory, 518
        metric_iorm.pl, 519
        Perl Script, 519
        transfer numbers, 518
        working principle, 520
    plan information
        category plan, 522
        cellsrv, 521
        inter-database plan, 523
        I/O queues, 524
        IORM STATS, 523
        list iormplan, 525
        statedump, 521
        text editor, 521
        working principle, 525
    prioritizing I/O, by database
        alter iormplan, 507
        CellCLI command, 506
        commands process, 506
        interdatabase IORM plan, 505
        performance, 507
    resources management
        dcli to disable, 526
        demonstrate, 508
        on exadata, 510
        performance, 510
        resource plan, 510
        sessions assign, 509
        smart flash control, 526
        solution, 526
        visx_plan, 509
        working principle, 526
    utilization by category
        CAT_MEDIUM, 512
        DBRM assign, 511
        intradatabase IORM plan, 511
        IORM plan, 512
        performance, 512
        resource utilization, 511

M, N

Monitor storage cells, 371
    with activerequests
        consumerGroupName attribute, 381
        dbName attribute, 381
        describe command, 380
        ioReason, 381
        I/O requests, 376
        ioType attribute, 381
        objectNumber attribute, 381
        Predicate Pushing and Predicate Filtering, 377
        requestState attribute, 381
        sessionNumber and sessionSerNumber attribute, 381
        sqlID attribute, 381
    alerts
        alter and drop alerts, 374
        Baseboard Management Controller, 376

Monitor storage cells (*cont.*)
  dcli/cellcli command, 373
  list alertdefinition detail command, 375
  list alerthistory command, 371–372
  Stateful and Stateless alerts, 372
 dcli command
  special characters, 391–393
  grid disk I/O bottlenecks, 404
 host interconnect bottlenecks, 406
 I/O bottlenecks, 400
 I/O load and I/O waits per database measurement, 407
  metrichistory, 393, 399
  using Oracle tables and SQL, 399
  using R script, 393
 small I/O vs. large I/O requests, 402
 with metrics
  alertState attribute, 384–385
  cell disks, 386
  collectionTime, 384
  describe metricdefinition command, 382
  description, 386
  Flash Cache, 388
  Flash Logging, 388
  grid disks, 387
  host interconnect, 387
  IORM category, 388
  IORM consumer group, 387
  IORM_DATABASE, 387
  metriccurrent object, 383
  metrichistory object, 385
  metricObjectName, 384
  metricType, 384
  metricValue, 384
  objectType attribute, 383–384
  thresholds, 389–391

O

Oracle, 53
 ASM disks
  configuration, 58
  data storage, 58
  Exadata database storage, 60
  grid disks, 59
  redundancy, 59
  working principle, 60
 cell services processes
  cellsrv, 63–64
  Management Server, 63–64
  ps-ef command, 62
  Restart Server, 63–64
  flash disks, 61–62
 CellCLI, 62
  Smart Flash Cache, 61
  Smart Flash Logging, 61
  working principle, 62

InfiniBand
 cluster interconnect, 70
 ibdump command, 70
 RAC interconnect validation, 69
 skgxpinfo command, 69
 WireShark display, 70
I/O requests
 cellsrv, 67
 DBWR process, 65
 for non-Exadata systems, 67
 iDB message transmission, 67
 working principle, 65–66
 LUNs, 53
physical disks, mapping
 fdisk, 54
 lsscsi command, 53
 output, 56
 storage entity mapping, 57
 System Area, 54
 using CellCLI, 54
 working principle, 56
tracing cellsrv
 bottlenecks or performance issues, 72
 I/O requests, 73
 process threads, 71
 sendmsg and recvmsg, 72
Oracle 11gR2 database(s), 35
 cluster_inerconnects parameter, 36
 cluster installation and database storage validation
  crsctl query crs activeversion, 45
  login, 44
  resource configuration, 45
  tablespace data file storage, 46
  validation steps, 44
  VISX database, 45
  working principle, 47
 cluster network installation
  client access network, 48
  Cluster HAIP, 48
  InfiniBand network, 48
  oifcfg, 48
  SCAN and SCAN listener configuration, 50
  skgxpinfo command, 49
  srvctl config network, 50
  VIPs, 51
  working principle, 52
 database configuration, 36
  Grid Infrastructure, 38
  CRS configuration, 38
 Grid Infrastructure cluster resource
  crsctl, 39
  diskmon process, 41
  resource management, 38
  shut down command, 40

start and stop command, 40
working principle, 41
xdmg and xdwk, 41
with Oracle RAC and Oracle ASM, 38
software version information, 35
Oracle ASM disk groups
Smart Scan process, 286–287
Oracle ASM disk groups, 239
asmDiskGroupName and asmDiskName
attributes, 241
ASM-scoped and database-scoped security, 242
balancing extents
ASM extents, 254
benefits, 258
disk partnership, 256
cellcli commands, 239
cell disks interleaving, 281
cell disk sizes, 240
cell disks, rebuilding
backup and validate, 261
cluster, health validation, 272
ClusterWare resources, 268
control file backup and file system
copy, 262
creation, 266
DBFS_DG ASM disk group, 269
disk group creation, 271
drop celldisk and create celldisk
commands, 274
dropping, 265
impacts of, 274
ocrconfig-restore command, 270
srvctl stop database, 263
configuration
ALTER DISKGROUP command, 246
au_size attribute, 247
cell.smart_scan_capable attribute, 247
compatible.rdbms and compatible.asm
attributes, 247
Pro-Active Disk Quarantine function, 247
CREATE DISKGROUP statement, 245
creation, 245
DATA_CM01 disk group, 241
disk partnership, 253
Exadata grid disks, 282–285
flash-based grid disks, 292–293, 295–296
goals, 239
grid disks interleaving
high_redundancy, 279
normal_redundancy, 278
planning aspects, 245
redundancy
failure groups, 251–252
high, 250
normal, 249
redundancy options, 243

Smart Scan process, 286, 289–291
storage servers, 244
unassigned grid disk, 248
validation, 240
Oracle Cluster Registry and voting disks, 42
DBFS_DG ASM disk group, 42
ocrconfig-showbackup, 42
storage location, 43
working principle, 43
Oracle Cluster Registry (OCR), 41
Oracle Cost-Based Optimizer (CBO)
statistics, 625
auto task, 626
collection preferences, 628
data dictionary and fixed object statistics, 630
dbms_stats.gather_database_stats_
job_proc, 627
step-by-step process, 626
system statistics, 630
working principle, 630
Oracle Database File System (DBFS), 601
Oracle Exadata X3-2, 3
Oracle RAC database, 599
Oracle's checkip.sh script, 144
Oracle's Cluster High Availability IP
framework, 302

P

Patching, 331
compute nodes and databases
database updates, 349
directory creation, 343
enable repository, 345
OPatch, 342
opatch auto command, 348
opatch prereq CheckSystemSpace
argument, 348
package updates, 345
QDPE patches, 347
RPM key, import, 344
ULN subscriptions, 342
yum repository, 342
definitions, 331
descriptions, 333
Enterprise Manager systems management
software, 352
Exadata Storage Servers, 335, 338, 341
compute nodes, 335
minimal packs, 341
patchmgr utility, 341
prerequisite tasks, 341
-rolling option, 338
using patchmgr, 335
InfiniBand Switches, 349
latest releases, 334

Patching (cont.)
    My Oracle Support, 333, 335
    QFSDP patch, 334
    README files, 335
Performance monitoring, host and DB
    cell I/O, SQL statement, 442
    compute node and stroage statistics, 412
    exadata targets in cloud control, 418
    exadata with wait events, 435–436, 438
    smart scans by DB time and AAS, 432, 434
    SQL monitoring, 422–425
    statistics and counters, exadata, 441
    storage grid, 419–421
    Performance monitoring, host and DB, 411
    cell I/O, SQL statement
        description, 444
        I/O load, 442
        myiostats.sql, 442
        PIVOT statement, 444
    collectl
        download and install, 415
        execute, no command line, 415
        performance analysis, 417
        Perl scripts, 415
        report verbose information, 416
        running on single node, 415
        save output, 417
        sD switch, 416–417
        subsystems, 415
    compute node and storage statistics
        Black Box Analyzer, 414
        bzcat command, 413
        compressed files, 414
        CPU and memory, 411
        exadata node, 413
        exadata targets in cloud control, 418
        locating, 418
        metrics information, 412
        OSWatcher, 411–412
        OSWBB, 414
        pstree listing, 413
        system initialization, 413
    by database time,
        AAS from enterprise manager, 432
        active session history (ASH), 425
        ashcurr-details.sql, 430
        average active sessions (AAS), 425
        bydtl.sql, 428
        bytype.sql, 425
        dba_hist_active, 431
        description, 431
        detailed, monitoring and AAS from ASH, 427
        details.sql, 427
        for SQL statements, 428
        fro wait events, 428
        recent, detailed and AAS metrics, 430

        script, input, 427
        summarized, monitoring and AAS
            from ASH, 425
        time range calculation, 431
    exadata with wait events
        approaches, 439
        from ASH, 436
        from AWR, 438
        awr.sql, 438
        current events, from v$session, 435
        diagnosing, 435
        exawait-ashcurr.sql, 436
        gv$session, 436
        sess.sql, 435
        time_waited, 437
        v$active_session_history, 437
        v$event_name, 439
    monitor, enterprise manager
        12c Cloud Control, 417
        storage grid, 418
    real time node and statistics
        collectl-utils, 416
        colmux utility, 417
        host commands, 414
        monitoring simultaneously, 416
        utilization metrics, 414
    smart scans by DB time and AAS
        ashcurr-details.sql, 432
        ashpast-details.sql, 434
        cell smart scan, 434
        description, 434
        frequency measure, 432
        historical, metrics from ASH, 433
        recent and current, metrics fron ASH, 432
        time consumption, 432
    SQL monitoring
        cell offload efficiency, 425
        dbms_sqltune, 421
        dbms_sqltune.report_sql_monitor, 424
        execution details, 422
        from enterprise manager, 422
        interface and output, 424
        key performance, 424
        list-text.sql, 424
        monitored execution, 423
        plan from monitor, 423
        real time monitoring, 421, 424
        reports with dbms_sqltune, 423
        sqlid-html.sql, 423
        target landing page, 422
        wait activity, 422
    statistics and counters, exadata, 440
        common statistics, 441
        DB performance, 440
        DMA, 441
        framework, 440

methodology, 441
query references, 440
reporting, 440
v$sesstat, 440
storage grid
    database, performance information, 419–421
    exadata grid, 418
    performance, 419
    workload distribution, 419

Post-installation Exadata database tasks, 599
    Oracle RAC database
        cluster related and recovery-specific database initialization parameters, 600
        Database Configuration Assistant (dbca), 599, 601
        using srvctl, validation, 600

Post-installation monitoring, 579
    automated service requests
        activations approval, 596
        asr register, 594
        ASR server, 593
        asset validation, 595
        baseboard management controller (BMC), 597
        bmcType, 598
        configuring, 592
        connection validation, 594
        customer support identifier (CSI), 592
        e-mail confirmation, 597
        functionality, 597
        hardware assets, 593
        ipmitool, 598
        manager patch 1.3.1, 593
        non-ILOM assets, 595
        patch 3.9, 594
        SNMP traps, 595
    cloud control agents for Exadata
        adding targets, 583
        agent monitoring, 585
        agent owner, 582
        cluster target host, 588
        cluster targets, 590
        component properties, 587
        database home and agent selection, 584
        database machine, 583
        database machine schematics, 591
        discovey review, 587
        dixcovery components, 585
        EM targets, 588
        enterprise manager 12c, 579
        Exadata agent kit, 579
        high avilabiltiy services, 588
        host credentials, 586
        host specification, 589
        InfiniBand discovery, 584
        machine components, 585
        monitoring credentials, 586
        node as root, 581
        non-host targets, 583
        OMS details, 580
        ONS port, 589
        options for installing, 579
        Oracle cluster, 588
        Oracle RAC cluster, 590
        parameter settings, 580
        performance, 591
        RAC services, 589
        robust mechanism, 591
        SCAN name, 589
        selecting agent, 584
        setupem.sh, 581
        SNMP subscription, 586
        SSH key, 581
    plug-ins for Exadata, 592

Q, R

Quarterly Database Patch for Exadata (QDPE), 342

S, T

Secure Shell (SSH)
    user equivalency,
        cellcli command, 161
        oracle account, 161
        storage cells, 161
        working principle, 162
    exadata compute and storage node
        domain name validation, 160
        management interface, 159
        terminal emulator, 160
        working principle, 160

Security, 355
    ASM-scoped security, 362–364
    database-scoped security, 364, 366–367
    Oracle RDBMS Homes, 359–361
    Oracle software owners
        compute node, 357
        description, 358
        restrict SSH access, 358
        role-separated authentication, 356, 358
        security policies, 356
        standard OS authentication, 355
        sudo access, 358
        useradd command, 356

Smart Flash, 529
    cache performance measure
        AWR reports, 546
        awrstat.sql, 542
        cache behavior, 541

INDEX

Smart Flash (cont.)
    DMA, 546
    FLASHCACHE, 545
    FLASHLOG, 545
    IORM objectType, 546
    metrichistory, 546
    objectNumber, 544
    query modify, 542
    script report, 542
    seg.sql, 544
    SFC hits per object, 544
    SFC usage for DB, 541
    SFC usage for SQL statements, 543
    sqlawr.sql, 544
    sqls.sql, 543
    statistics, 541
    storage server metrics, 545
    sysstat.sql, 541
  cache storage determining, 534
    available capacity, 534
    free space, 534
    sfcconsumer.pl, 534
    working principle, 536
  database machine, 529
  database objects are cached
    cachedsize, 533
    cache status, 532
    demo, 533
    flashcachecontent, 532
    in SFC, 532
    I/O request, 533
    objectnumber, 532
    PO.RCV_TRANSACTIONS, 533
    working principle, 533
  managing cache and logging
    create flashcache all, 530
    dcli, 530
    memory chunks, 531
    PCI flash, 531
    smart flash cache (SFC), 529
    smart flash logging (SFL), 529
    solution, 530
    SSH keys, 530
    storage server, 531
    working principle, 531
    write request, 531
  Oracle's caching algorithm, 529
  PCI flash, 529
  pinning objects in SFC
    ALTER TABLE MOVE command, 548
    cachedKeepSize, 548
    cache hits, 547
    CellCLI commands, 548
    CELL_FLASH_CACHE, 546
    DATA_OBJECT_ID, 547–548
    hitCount, 548
    I/O request, 547
    segments, 546
    serviced I/O, 548
    SLAs, 549
    working principle, 548
  querying uncached data
    additional blocks, 540
    cell flash cache, 540
    data insertion, 540
    DML operation, 540
    metrics, 538
    output, 539
    RCV_TRANSACTIONS, 538
    read I/O requests, 539
    statistics, 539
    working principle, 540
  querying uncached data
    clean test, 537
    execution plan, 536
    flashcachecontent, 536
    RCV_TRANSACTIONS, 537
    sfc-mysess.sql, 538
  SAS disks, 529
  SFL benefits quantify
    FLASHLOG, 549
    impact measure, 549
    scripts, 549
    undocumented parameter, 551
    with image version, 550
    working principle, 550
Smart Scan, 447, 451
  ASM disk group, 451
  in SQL execution plans and EXPLAIN PLAN output, 447
  statistics measurement
    from AWR, 454
    for specific reason, 452
    for own session, 453
    I/O statistics, 455
    systemwide, 452
Storage indexes, 553
  direct path read operations, 555
  disable storage indexes, 575
  I/O savings, 553
  logical representation, 556
  query predicate conditions
    and BETWEEN predicates, 560
    and bind variables, 560
    with LIKE and Wilcard predicates, 563
    and multiple predicates, 563
    and Null values, 561
    and unbounded range scans, 562
  region index, 556
  storage regions, 556

tracing
    eight columns, 568–569, 571–572
    tables, 573–574
    troubleshoot, 576
well-ordered and randomly ordered data, 557–559

U

Unbreakable Linux Network (ULN), 341

V

Virtual IP Addresses, or VIPs, 51

W, X, Y, Z

Workload qualification, 77
    AWR report
        Physical Reads, Segments by, 79
        Physical Reads, SQL ordered, 78
        smart scans, 81
        Timed Foreground Events, 78
    Exadata Storage Software, 79
    industry-defined definitions, 80
    I/O characteristics, 77
    smart scans, 80

Made in the USA
San Bernardino, CA
22 May 2013